C0-AWX-134

Communication

Communication

Making Connections

TENTH EDITION

William J. Seiler
University of Nebraska–Lincoln

Melissa L. Beall
University of Northern Iowa

Joseph P. Mazer
Clemson University

PEARSON

Boston   Columbus   Indianapolis   New York   San Francisco   Amsterdam
Cape Town   Dubai   London   Madrid   Milan   Munich   Paris   Montreal   Toronto   Delhi
Mexico City   São Paulo   Sydney   Hong Kong   Seoul   Singapore   Taipei   Tokyo

Publisher, Communication: Karon Bowers
Program Manager: Anne Ricigliano
Project Manager: Maria Piper
Editorial Assistant: Nikki Toner
Product Marketing Manager: Becky Rowland
Senior Managing Editor: Melissa Feimer
Procurement Manager: Mary Fischer
Senior Procurement Specialist: Mary Ann Gloriande
Associate Creative Director: Blair Brown

Senior Art Director: Maria Lange
Cover Designer: Maria Lange
Cover Credit: Rawpixel/Fotolia
Digital Media Specialist: Sean Silver
Full-Service Project Management and Composition: Integra Software Services, Pvt. Ltd.
Printer/Binder: Manufactured in the United States by RR Donnelley
Cover Printer: Phoenix Color/Hagerstown

Copyright © 2017, 2014, 2011, by Pearson Education, Inc. or its affiliates. All Rights Reserved. This digital publication is protected by copyright, and permission should be obtained from the publisher prior to any prohibited reproduction, storage in a retrieval system, or transmission in any form or by any means, electronic, mechanical, photocopying, recording, or otherwise except as authorized for use under the product subscription through which this digital application is accessed. For information regarding permissions, request forms, and the appropriate contacts within the Pearson Education Global Rights & Permissions department, please visit www.pearsoned.com/permissions/.

Acknowledgments of third party content appears on page 430 which constitutes an extension of this copyright page.

PEARSON, ALWAYS LEARNING, and REVEL are exclusive trademarks in the U.S. and/or other countries owned by Pearson Education, Inc. or its affiliates.

Unless otherwise indicated herein, any third-party trademarks that may appear in this work are the property of their respective owners and any references to third-party trademarks, logos or other trade dress are for demonstrative or descriptive purposes only. Such references are not intended to imply any sponsorship, endorsement, authorization, or promotion of Pearson's products by the owners of such marks, or any relationship between the owner and Pearson Education, Inc. or its affiliates, authors, licensees or distributors.

Library of Congress Cataloging-in-Publication Data

Seiler, William J.
   Communication : making connections/William J. Seiler, Melissa L. Beall, Joseph P. Mazer.
      pages cm
   Includes bibliographical references and index.
   ISBN 978-0-13-418497-5 (student edition) — ISBN 978-0-13-419996-2 (student value edition)
   1. Communication.   I. Beall, Melissa L.   II. Mazer, Joseph P.   III. Title.
   P90.S3994 2015
   302.2—dc23

                                                                 2015036401

Student Edition
ISBN-10:   0-13-418497-1
ISBN 13: 978-0-13-418497-5

Books á la Carte
ISBN-10:   0-13-419996-0
ISBN 13: 978-0-13-419996-2

Brief Contents

Contents

4   Connecting through Verbal Communication   73

5   Connecting through Nonverbal Communication   96

6   Connecting Listening and Thinking in the Communication Process   119

Preface

Facebook founder Mark Zuckerberg said, *"The thing that we are trying to do at Facebook is just help people connect and communicate more effectively."* This is exactly why we wrote *Communication: Making Connections*—to help students "make connections" in their daily lives, to communicate more effectively, and to strive to be successful and productive citizens. Imagine what life would be like without iPods, iPads, wireless Internet access, GPSs, or the many forms of social media such as Facebook, Twitter, and Snapchat that we use every day. Perhaps we cannot imagine it because these tools are woven into the very fabric of our lives; we take them for granted as they become more and more an extension of who we are. It is clear that Zuckerberg and the founders of Google, Apple Computers, and many other high-tech companies have, in fact, attained their ambitious goal of changing how we live.

Clearly our world, particularly our social world, has changed and will continue to change, perhaps more quickly and dramatically than at any time in our past. Further—and a key point we'll emphasize throughout the text—these changes have important implications for our communication and for the communication field. As in previous editions, we are committed to bringing readers the latest and most up-to-date information regarding communication and its importance to our everyday lives.

We continue to be gratified and grateful that so many instructors have chosen *Communication: Making Connections* for their students. With this new edition, we remain committed to our primary goal of helping students become more competent communicators in a variety of contexts. We also continue to strive for balance between thorough, straightforward explanations of basic communication principles and a solid theoretical foundation supported by the latest research findings.

What's New in the Tenth Edition?

REVEL™

Educational technology designed for the way today's students read, think, and learn

When students are engaged deeply, they learn more effectively and perform better in their courses. This simple fact inspired the creation of REVEL: an immersive learning experience designed for the way today's students read, think, and learn. Built in collaboration with educators and students nationwide, REVEL is the newest, fully digital way to deliver respected Pearson content.

REVEL enlivens course content with media interactives and assessments—integrated directly within the authors' narrative—that provide opportunities for students to read about and practice course material in tandem. This immersive educational technology boosts student engagement, which leads to better understanding of concepts and improved performance throughout the course.

Learn more about REVEL

http://www.pearsonhighered.com/revel/

Rather than simply offering opportunities to read about and study communication, REVEL facilitates deep, engaging interactions with the concepts that matter most. For example, in Chapter 1 while learning about the basics of communication, students will encounter the "Self-Perceived Communication Competence" self-assessment instrument to gauge their comfort in various communication scenarios ranging from presenting a speech to talking with a friend. After completing the survey, the student is shown what his or her responses say about his or her level of self-perceived communication competence. By providing opportunities to read about and practice communication in tandem, REVEL engages students directly and immediately, which leads to a better understanding of course material. A wealth of student and instructor resources and interactive materials can be found within REVEL. Some of our favorites include:

- **Short Speech and Conversation Excerpts** Abundant in-text excerpts from speeches and interpersonal conversations let students listen to audio clips while they read, bringing examples to life in a way that a printed text cannot.

- **Videos and Video Quizzes** Video examples of sample conversations, presentations, and discussions as well as expert advice throughout the narrative boost mastery, and many videos are bundled with correlating self-checks, enabling students to test their knowledge.

- **Interactive Figures** Several interactive figures (such as Chapter 2's "Perceptual Differences" and Chapter 4's "Ladder of Abstraction") give students a hands-on experience, increasing their ability to grasp difficult concepts. For instance, by interacting with the Perceptual Differences figure, students are able to more closely examine specific differences to help provide a complete understanding of the concept. The interactive "Ladder of Abstraction" also serves a unique purpose, allowing students to take a step-by-step walk through the process of refining language use to lessen the chance for misunderstanding.

- **Integrated Writing Opportunities** To help students connect chapter content with personal meaning, each chapter offers two varieties of writing prompts: the Journal prompt, which elicits free-form topic-specific responses, and the Shared Writing prompt, which encourages students to share and respond to each other's responses to high-interest topics in the chapter.

For more information about all the tools and resources in REVEL and access to your own REVEL account for *Communication: Making Connections* Tenth Edition, go to www.pearsonhighered.com/REVEL.

In addition to the immersive learning experience offered by REVEL, we've refined and updated the content in this new edition. The introductory communication course, with a solid foundation of rhetorical tradition, is constantly evolving, but its central premise, that communication remains the number-one skill that leads to success in both our professional and personal lives, remains a constant. We take each revision seriously to ensure we make it fresher, more useful, and more readable. This edition is no exception, and we believe we have met our goal.

- **Increased Emphasis on Technology** We provide updated information in this edition on communication technologies, from texting to online social networking, from blogging to web video. We explore the influence of technologies on our communication, beginning with an expanded discussion of communication and technology in Chapter 1.

- **Particular Focus on the Implication of Communication via Social Media** We emphasize the implications of new communication technologies for the messages we send and receive, such as the use of Facebook, Twitter, Snapchat, Vine, and other social media tools; for how emotions are communicated online; and, ultimately, for our interactions and relationships.

- **Streamlined Coverage** We recognize the increased demands on time, so we have re-evaluated every line, streamlining and editing to ensure that only the most relevant information and research findings are presented in the most useful and concise ways.

- **Numerous new examples** In recognition of the need to continuously update and refresh the book to keep up with both the ever-changing world and the communication discipline, we have replaced, updated, or added examples to be relevant to today's students. All new chapter openings make communication come alive to students as they encounter real-world experiences.

- **New Research Findings** Every chapter is updated with the newest and most recent research findings and theoretical perspectives.

- **New Goal-Oriented Learning Objectives** Learning objectives appear at the start of each chapter, and each one is tied to a specific section of the product (in both REVEL and print). They highlight the specific concepts, principles, and practices students will learn and actions or behaviors they will gain. Chapter summaries highlight each objective and provide a usable way to review the chapter and ensure that objectives have been met.

- **New Pedagogical Aids** This edition, like previous ones, retains our commitment to the "making connections" theme—helping students understand communication as the means of connecting with others. We have added and updated research to support our theme, as well as included several features:

  - **Sample Speech Excerpts** In Chapter 9, a sample informative speech is used to illustrate both the full-sentence and the presentational outlines. In Chapter 10, a sample outline illustrates the effective use of PowerPoint for an informative speech. In Chapter 11, the sample speech from Chapter 9 is repeated, this time to illustrate an analysis and evaluation of informational speaking. Finally, in Chapter 12, a sample outline for a persuasive speech illustrates comprehensive analysis and evaluation of persuasive speaking.

  - **Chapter Summaries and Discussion Starters** Chapter summaries are organized by learning objectives to help students focus on what they were to have learned and understood in each chapter. They help students clarify what should be gained from reading each chapter. Discussion starter questions can be used as a springboard for classroom discussions or used for individual study and review.

  - **Guidelines** Boxed guidelines succinctly summarize key skill-oriented concepts.

In addition, we have made specific changes in every chapter.

- **Part 1, Making Connections through Communication: Chapter 1,** on process and principles, includes a completely revised and updated section on communication and our technological society, an addition on social media in the communication and career development section, a completely rewritten section on communication as transactional, a revised mass communication section, a revised section on communication via social media, and a new section on distinguishing social media from face-to-face communication. Chapter 2, on perception, includes a new and revised section on the perception process and a new section on interpretation based on verbal communication. Chapter 3, on the self, has an expanded section on the personal-social identity continuum that provides insight into intergroup connections that help us form our self-concept. Chapter 4, on verbal communication, features a stronger connection between thinking and language choice. Our language choices reflect our thinking, and thus we need to choose language carefully and be prepared to explain ourselves to others who may not think as we do. Chapter 5, on nonverbal communication, includes a revised and updated section on what nonverbal communication is, expansion of information on cultural emotional cues and nonverbal differences, and a completely rewritten section combining the ability to send and interpret nonverbal communication. Chapter 6, on listening, covers more on the ways we think and how that affects listening. A new model of listening, the Harfield Cognitive Listening Model, shows how different preferred modes of thinking affect the way we listen and respond to others.

- **Part 2, Connecting in the Public Context:** Chapter 7, on topic selection and audience analysis, has a new emphasis on the thought process and discusses the effect of social media as we search for speaking topics. Chapter 8, on gathering and using information, has been reorganized and now includes a new section on the research plan. Chapter 9, on organizing and outlining, places more emphasis on the analysis of organizing and outlining. Chapter 10, on communication anxiety and speech delivery, has major changes, including discussions on the use of social media to enhance presentations and using Prezi and PowerPoint as presentational aids, and additional discussions on the cognitive aspect of managing anxiety. Chapters 11 and 12, on informative and persuasive speaking, show how technology and social media aid speech development. Both include outlines, speeches, greater emphasis on analyzing and applying information in chapters, and strategies for putting it all together for effective finished presentations.

- **Part 3, Connecting in Relational Contexts:** Chapter 13, on interpersonal communication, is updated and now provides a solid understanding of the significant theories (uncertainty management theory, social information processing theory, social exchange theory, interpersonal needs theory, dialectical theory, and social penetration theory) related to interpersonal communication. Chapter 14, on developing and maintaining relationships, includes new sections on interpersonal communication competence and relationship maintenance strategies. Chapter 15, on group and team communication, includes revised sections on defining what makes a group and a new section on using social media to establish group culture. Chapter 16, group and team participation, includes an expanded section on

leadership, a revised section on discussing the problem and its solution (with the addition of functional theory, which outlines three conditions for group success), and a new section on online conflict.

- **Appendix, Career Development: Preparing for Your Future:** The fully updated appendix now includes a revised section on understanding qualities employers seek, a section on conducting the job search, an updated list of suggestions for applying electronically, a section on creating a website or blog, a section on creating a favorable first impression, and a new section on writing a thank you note.

Organization of the Text

As in all previous editions, the chapters are arranged to provide a practical and workable approach to teaching the fundamentals of communication. Part One, "Making Connections through Communication," provides the necessary background and basic principles for all communication. Part Two, "Connecting in the Public Context," helps students develop their speaking skills as they learn to select a topic, analyze an audience, gather and use supporting and clarifying materials, organize and outline speech material, deliver a speech with confidence, and effectively inform and persuade an audience. Part Three, "Connecting in Relational Contexts," describes communication in relationships and small groups and teams.

Foundations are presented first. Then public communication skills are discussed, followed by interpersonal and group communication. We discuss public communication skills early, before interpersonal communication, because we believe the confidence and skills of public speaking are fundamental to all communication. To communicate effectively throughout life—whether socially, on the job, in one-to-one situations, in small groups, or before an audience—a person must be able to communicate with confidence, support and clarify his or her thoughts, organize information, analyze those with whom he or she is communicating, and inform and persuade effectively.

This sequence of concepts is also based on the recognition that, although students in an introductory communication course must master a great deal of information before they give a speech, because of time constraints they need to begin preparing and presenting speeches as early in the term as possible. Introducing public speaking skills first provides a more even balance between speech presentations and other classroom activities, and curbs the tendency to focus exclusively on speech making at the end of the term.

Considerable demands are placed on instructors and students of introductory communication courses and a wide variety of ways to teach them are available. Instructors should feel free to organize the course in whatever way is appropriate and meets the needs of their students.

Special Features of the Text

MAKING EVERYDAY CONNECTIONS In this edition we have strengthened and reinforced our "making connections" theme by bringing in more student and real-life examples illustrating our connections in today's world. Each chapter opens with a **"Making Everyday Connections"** scenario that describes communication situations or issues likely to be part of students' real-life everyday communication encounters, such as what to disclose and not to disclose on Facebook and other social networking sites or how texting is affecting family relationships. Each scenario is followed by thought-provoking questions that ask students to think about the issues and apply them to their own lives.

> ## Making Everyday Connections
>
> Carly slowly walks into her apartment. She looks as if she has just seen a ghost. Tears form as she sits down on the sofa, and she begins to cry openly and uncontrollably.
>
> Her friend Dana puts her arm around her and pats her on the shoulder gently. Carly looks at Dana. Carly's face and demeanor tell Dana something is really wrong, as if Carly's whole world has just come crashing down. Dana doesn't know what to say, so she continues to comfort Carly by holding her hand. Carly is unable to control her emotions or speak. Finally, Carly looks at Dana, and her face shows concern as if to say, "What is going on?"
>
> Neither uttered one word as they held each other tightly at their expressions and touch said everything
>
> ### Questions to Think About
>
> 1. How does nonverbal communication make communication easier? More difficult?
> 2. Why do you think we give so little thought to our nonverbal communication?
> 3. Why do you think nonverbal communication is considered more believable than verbal communication?
> 4. Explain what nonverbal communication is and is not.

> ## Making Connections for Success
>
> ### What You Say Can Hurt You! It's All about Perception
>
> The following quotation was given in an interview and reported in the *New York Times* when a potential candidate for a U.S. Senate seat was asked why she believed she would make a good senator:
>
> So I think in many ways, you know, we want to have all kinds of different voices, you know, representing us, and I think what I bring to it is, you know, my experience as a mother, as a woman, as a lawyer, you know.[2]
>
> 1. Based solely on what the person said in the interview your initial perceptions of wh
>
> 2. In what ways would your initial perceptions of the person change if you learned that in the course of the interview she said "you know" 142 times?
>
> 3. How would your perceptions of the person's communication alter if you found out that she had written seven books, including two on the Constitution and two on American politics; that she had graduated from Harvard University and Columbia Law School; and that her family name was well known in national politics?
>
> 4. ... hange

MAKING CONNECTIONS FOR SUCCESS We live in a connected world. Communication helps us make daily connections with each other and with events around the world as they unfold. Technology allows communication to take many forms and has changed the avenues through which communication occurs and how it occurs on the web.

The ever-changing array of technological options has added to the challenge of presenting and receiving messages—of communicating effectively with others. This tenth edition focuses not only on the different communication channels available but also on the implications of media for our communication, for the quality of the messages we send and receive.

"Making Connections for Success" boxes in each chapter are designed to encourage students to think critically about communication in their lives. Each box contains skill-building activities and stimulating questions to help students reflect on issues and their own communication behavior, and become more competent communicators. Many of these boxes are designed to emphasize the role and importance of technology in our interactions. In addition, we've expanded our discussions of communication via social media within the text and have emphasized technology and its influence in numerous other boxed features and text discussions. This feature allows students to see how technology influences the messages we send and how it can both help and hinder competent communication.

MAKING CONNECTIONS AS YOU STUDY Numerous pedagogical aids help students review, retain, and master important chapter concepts. Boxed features reinforce the "making connections" theme throughout, demonstrating how communication connects us in a variety of contexts: the workplace, family, friends, community, school, public communication settings, the Internet, and across cultures. They will provide students with real-life examples and help them better understand how to send and receive communication more competently. In addition, each chapter contains one, or more, "Guidelines" box. These guidelines clearly and quickly summarize each chapter or section's key skill-oriented concepts.

> ## Guidelines
>
> ### Check Your Perceptions: Competent Communicators Do!
>
> 1. **Separate fact from assumptions.** It is easy to accept assumptions, but we must realize that assumptions are not facts, nor are they always accurate. When we make assumptions we are drawing conclusions with little or no basis of fact. Thus, we should label assumptions so that when we communicate them, they are differentiated from facts.
> 2. **Recognize your personal biases.** We all have biases that can influence our perceptions, and we must be careful that those biases don't inaccurately slant our perceptions. We should always qualify, when recognized, that our biases may have influenced our communication about events, ... and people.
>
> that not everyone sees the world as you do, and this is especially true of people who come from different cultural backgrounds. For example, it is not unusual for someone who lives in Europe or the Middle East to walk with someone of the same sex holding hands or kissing them on the check. How this might be perceived depends on differences in cultural norms or background.
>
> 5. **Remember that perceptions are a function of the perceiver, the perceived, and the situation in which the perception occurs.** To ensure accuracy it is important to understand that perception is in the eye of the beholder, to understand what is perceived and why, and to take into account ...

Instructor and Student Resources

Key instructor resources include an **Instructor's Manual** (ISBN 0-13-419997-9), **Test Bank**, (ISBN 0-13-420000-4), and **PowerPoint Presentation Package** (ISBN 0-13-419998-7). These supplements are available at www.pearsonhighered .com/irc (instructor login required). MyTest online test generating software (ISBN 0-13-420002-0) is available at www.pearsonmytest.com (instructor login required).

For a complete listing of the instructor and student resources available with this product, please visit the *Communication: Making Connections* e-Catalog page at www .pearsonhighered.com/communication.

Pearson MediaShare

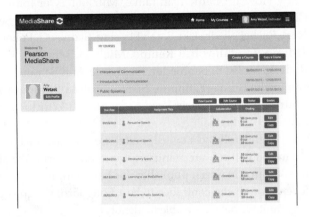

Pearson's comprehensive media upload tool allows students to post video, images, audio, or documents for instructor and peer viewing, time-stamped commenting, and assessment. MediaShare is an easy, mobile way for students and professors to interact and engage with speeches, presentation aids, group projects, and other files. MediaShare gives professors the tools to provide contextual feedback to demonstrate how students can improve their skills.

Structured like a social networking site, MediaShare helps promote a sense of community among students. In face-to-face and online course settings, MediaShare saves instructors valuable time and enriches the student learning experience by providing contextual feedback.

- Use MediaShare to assign or view speeches, outlines, presentation aids, video-based assignments, role plays, group projects, and more in a variety of formats including video, Word, PowerPoint, and Excel.

- Assess students using customizable, Pearson-provided rubrics or create your own around classroom goals, learning outcomes, or department initiatives.

- Set up assignments for students with options for full-class viewing and commenting, private comments between you and the student, peer groups for reviewing, or as collaborative group assignments.

- Record video directly from a tablet, phone, or other webcam (including a batch upload option for instructors) and tag submissions to a specific student or assignment.

- Set up learning objectives tied to specific assignments, rubrics, or quiz questions to track student progress.

- Embed video from YouTube to incorporate current events into the classroom experience.

- Set up quiz questions on video assignments to ensure students master concepts and interact and engage with the media.

- Sync images to media submissions for more robust presentation options.

- Import grades into most learning management systems.

- Ensure a secure learning environment for instructors and students through robust privacy settings.

- Upload videos, comment on submissions, and grade directly from our new MediaShare app, available free from the iTunes store and GooglePlay; search for Pearson MediaShare.

Pearson MediaShare is available as a standalone product, as part of MyCommunicationLab, or in a package with REVEL.

Acknowledgments

Numerous people have contributed to previous editions as well as this current edition. First and foremost are the students who used this text and shared their time and learning experiences with us, the instructors who patiently taught us about communication and life, the colleagues who shared their expertise with us, the many graduate students who worked in our basic communication courses over the years, and the hundreds of undergraduate assistants and assistant supervisory instructors who assisted in the University of Nebraska's Personalized System of Instruction basic communication course for the past 41 years.

A project of large proportion, this edition required the talents and hard work of many people. We extend our appreciation to Kelli Smith, past Assistant Director of Career Planning and Placement, and Chris Timm, Assistant Director of Career Planning and Placement at the University of Nebraska–Lincoln, for her review and guidance in the writing of the Employment Interview appendix. A very special thanks goes to Jeff Child, at Kent State University, for his insightful review and suggestions regarding Chapters 8, 13, and 14. Special thanks go to Marilyn Shaw, instructor of the Introductory Communication course at the University of Northern Iowa, for assisting with the Instructor's Manual. We also thank Tiffany Wang with Brigit Talkington, University of Nebraska, Lincoln, for her help in revising the Test Bank. In addition to Brigit and Tiffany, many other faculty and graduate students helped us by providing ideas and suggestions too numerous to mention here, especially: Jenna Abetz, Elissa Arterburn, Chase Aunspach, Diane Badzinski, Arleen Bejerano, Karla Bergen, Brandon Boatwright, Mary Bort, Dawn Braithwaite, Ann Burnett, John Caughlin, Kane Click, Susan Cusmano, Linda Dickmeyer, Sara Dirks, Josh Ewalt, Gus Friedrich, Marianne Glaser, Getachew Godana, Bobbie Harry, Christina Ivey, Haley Kranstuber Horstman, Adam Jones, Jack Kay, Jody Koenig Kellas, Emily Lamb Normand, Karen Lee, Ronald Lee, Kristen Lucas, Rob Patterson, Drew McGukin, Michelle Maresh-Fuehrer, Carol Morgan, Bill Mullen, Richard Murphy, Damien Pfister, Jack Sargent, Kaitlyn Dernovich, Paul Schrodt, Jordan Soliz, Sara Steimel, Brigit Talkington, Blair Thompson, Shawn Wahl, Tiffany Wang, William (Bill) Wilmot, and Nicole Zumbach.

A very special thank you goes to Sarah Johansen and Michael Schwabe, two University of Nebraska students, for providing us with their informative and persuasive speeches. Sarah's informative speech is in Chapter 11, and Michael's persuasive speech is in Chapter 12. Both of these students not only provided outlines and transcripts of their speeches, but also allowed us to video record their informative and persuasive speeches. Their speeches were rated by other students as the top two speeches in their class.

We thank all the undergraduate and graduate students at University of Nebraska–Lincoln. University of Northern Iowa, and Clemson University who provided resources and examples. We are especially grateful to the following honor students at Wayne State College in Wayne, Nebraska, who provided scenarios and boxed information for this edition: Alyssa Bish, Lindsey Boyum, Spencer J. Bradley, Tabitha Burger, Kelsey Doht, Logan J. Fischer, Kylie Funk, Kjirsten Gedwillo, Amanda E. Gubbels, Alexander Hamilton, Ashley Nicole Hammond, Jessica Henderson, Brittany Hermsen, Cody Howser, Callie Jean Janke, Mitchell Tyler Johnson, Clarissa Kracl, Zachary D. Leitschuck, Cassie Minor, Sean Neal, Rachel Niedbalski, Sarah Plessing, Sydney G. Pokorny, Tiffinie Randall, Elisa Rempe, Michala Remund, Kella Rodiek, Molly B. Schroeder, Stephanie Ann Schumacher, Samantha Siewert, Bonnie Sisco, Chelsea Simmerman, Courtney Wiese, Chris Varney, Stephanie Whitlow, and Zachary J. Zobel.

We gratefully acknowledge all those at Pearson who had a hand in getting our manuscript into book form. We also thank Karon Bowers, publisher, for her continued support (even though she continues to be a Longhorn, which is the only fault we have been able to identify).

The publishing of any book requires people dedicated to high quality, and this edition of our book is no exception. We thank all those who participated in the review process of the first nine editions of the book:

Ritta Abell, Morehead State University
David Allison, Liberty College
Philip M. Backlund, Central Washington University
William Patrick Barlow, Madison Area Technical College
Matt Barton, Southern Utah University
Marty Birkholt, Creighton University
Barbara L. Breaclen, Lane Community College
Scott Britten, Tiffin University
Allan R. Broadhurst, Cape Cod Community College
Michael Bruner, University of North Texas
Diane O. Casagrande, West Chester University
Patricia Comeaux, University of North Carolina at Wilmington
Juanita E. Dailey, University of Rio Grande
Linda Y. Devenish, Ithaca College
Carley H. Dodd, Abilene Christian University
Terrence Doyle, Northern Virginia Community College
Sean M. Dunn, Bridgewater College
Richard C. Emanuel, University of Montevallo
Skip Eno, University of Texas at San Antonio
Jeanine Fassl, University of Wisconsin at Whitewater
Julia Fennell, Community College of Allegheny County, South Campus
Mary C. Forestieri, Lane Community College
Robert E. Frank, Morehead State University

Angela Gibson, Shelton State Community College
Anne Grissom, Mountain View College
Kelby K. Halone, Clemson University
Roxanne Heimann, University of Northern Iowa
Ted Hindermarsh, Brigham Young University
Colleen Hogan-Taylor, University of Washington
David D. Hudson, Golden West College
Mary Lee Hummert, University of Kansas
David A. Humphrey, College of DuPage
Stephen K. Hunt, Illinois State University
Karla Kay Jensen, Nebraska Wesleyan University
Kathryn C. Jones, Northern Virginia Community College, Annandale Campus
Erik Kanter, Virginia Tech University
Alyssa Kauffman, Suffolk County Community College
Thomas J. Knutson, California State University at Sacramento
Charles J. Korn, Northern Virginia Community College
Donald L. Loeffler, Western Carolina University
Louis A. Lucca, La Guardia Community College (CUNY)
Mary Y. Mandeville, Oklahoma State University
Corinne E. Morris, Northeast Community College
William L. Mullen, Liberty University
Kay E. Neal, University of Wisconsin, Oshkosh
Dan O'Rourke, Ashland University
Nan Peck, Northern Virginia Community College
Kelly Petkus, Austin Community College
Sandra E. Presar, West Virginia Wesleyan College
Marlene M. Preston, Virginia Polytechnic Institute and State University
Richard G. Rea, University of Arkansas
Marc E. Routhier, Frostburg State College
Thomas Ruddick, Edison Community College
Jared Saltzman, Bergen Community College
Susan Schuyler, University of Wisconsin, La Crosse
Marilyn M. Shaw, University of Northern Iowa
Donald B. Simmons, Asbury College
Cheri J. Simonds, Illinois State University
Donald Smith, Northern Virginia College

Theresa Tiller, Rose State College
Mary Anne Trasciatti, Hofstra University
Beth Waggenspack, Virginia Polytechnic Institute and State University
Catherine Egley Waggoner, Ohio State University
Gretchen Aggertt Weber, Horry-Georgetown Technical College
Kathie A. Webster, Northwest Missouri State University
Larry A. Weiss, University of Wisconsin at Oshkosh
Cherie C. While, Muskingum Area Technical College
Karen Wolf, Suffolk Community College
David W. Worley, Indiana State University

Finally, thanks to those who provided analysis of the tenth edition and made recommendations and suggestions for this new edition:

Roxanne Heimann, University of Northern Iowa;
Charles J. Korn, Northern Virginia Community College-Manassas
Joseph Ganakos, Lee College
Dr. Cora Ann Williams, Lone Star Kingwood
Amy Lenoce, Naugatuck Valley Community College
Charlotte Toguchi, Kapiolani Community College
Bob Alexander, Bossier Parish Community College

Some Concluding Comments…and a Request for Your Thoughts

It is time to ask for *your* help again. As we have in previous editions, we spared no effort to make this new edition the best ever. Although we are always striving for perfection, we more often than not fall short on some things. There is always room for improvement! We sincerely request your comments. If there's something you feel can be improved, please let us know. Write, call, fax, or email us at one of the contacts below. We will listen and respond to your comments as quickly as possible. Thank you in advance for your help.

William (Bill) J. Seiler
Department of Communication Studies
University of Nebraska
Lincoln, NE 68588-0329
Phone: 402-472-2197
Fax: 402-472-6921
bseiler@unl.edu

Melissa L. Beall
Department of Communication Studies
University of Northern Iowa
Cedar Falls, IA 50613-0139
Phone: 319-273-2992
Fax: 319-273-7356
Melissa.Beall@uni.edu

Joseph (Joe) P. Mazer
Department of Communication Studies
Clemson University
Clemson, SC 29634-0533
Phone: 864-656-5254
Fax: 864-656-0599
jmazer@clemson.edu

About the Authors

Bill Seiler is a professor in the Department of Communication Studies, University of Nebraska–Lincoln, where he has taught since 1972. He was department chair for over 20 years and now teaches and directs the introductory course full-time. The Undergraduate Leadership Award was renamed the William J. Seiler Undergraduate Leadership Award to honor him and his leadership of the department. Other honors include Outstanding Educator of America, Outstanding University and College Teacher by the Nebraska Communication Association, Outstanding Young Alumni and Distinguished Alumni Awards from the University of Wisconsin at Whitewater, and 2002 Boss of the Year Award. Bill received the 2013 National Communication Association's Basic Course Division's "Distinguished Faculty" award and was named to the 2013 Central States Association's "Hall of Fame," and in 2015 he received the National Communication's "Wallace A. Bacon Lifetime Teaching Excellence Award." Bill earned a bachelor's degree in education from the University of Wisconsin at Whitewater, a master of arts from Kansas State University, and a doctorate from Purdue University. He is an experienced educator, consultant, researcher, and author in the area of communication and has an adjunct appointment in the Education & Human Sciences College.

He is an avid golfer who plays every chance he gets, which unfortunately for him is never enough. He loves his Nebraska Huskers. Bill and his wife Kathi's family includes two daughters, Dana and Dionne; two sons-in-law, Lee and Wade; two grandchildren, Grant and Will; and three step-grandchildren, Zach, Stephanie, and Taylor.

Melissa Beall is a professor in the Communication Studies Department and a member of the teacher education faculty at the University of Northern Iowa. Dr. Beall, a proud Husker fan, received all three degrees from the University of Nebraska–Lincoln. Her areas of expertise include listening, intercultural listening, intercultural communication, communication and technology, and communication theory. She teaches oral communication, listening, language and communication, public speaking, critical thinking, college teaching, communication and technology, intercultural communication, interpersonal communication, and communication theory. Dr. Beall currently serves as the chair of the UNI Graduate faculty. Her honors include Iowa Board of Regents Faculty Excellence recipient, 2012 Central States Communication Association Hall of Fame, International Listening Association's Outstanding Listening Educator, Listening Hall of Fame, and numerous teaching awards. She has served on numerous editorial boards; presented over 600 papers, programs, or workshops; is past president of the Iowa Communication Association and the Nebraska Speech Communication and Theatre Association; and is vice president of three organizations: the World Communication Association, the Pacific and Asian Communication Association, and the International Association of Communication Sciences. She is an officer in her local AAUP chapter and is a past president of the Central States Communication Association and of the International Listening Association; she has also served as an officer in many divisions of the National Communication Association.

Joseph Mazer is an associate professor and associate chair of the Department of Communication Studies at Clemson University. At Clemson, he is Director of the Social Media Listening Center, an interdisciplinary research lab and teaching facility that provides a platform to listen, measure, and engage in more than 650 million sources of social media conversations. His research and teaching interests are in instructional communication, social media and interpersonal relationships, quantitative research methods, and the introductory communication course. Joe is listed among the top 1 percent of prolific scholars in the discipline of Communication Studies spanning 2007–2011, according to a study published in *Communication Education*, a journal published by the National Communication Association. He has received international, regional, university-wide, and departmental recognition for outstanding teaching. Joe is a past recipient of the Outstanding New Teacher Award from the Central States Communication Association and the Outstanding Professor of the Year Award from Clemson University's Department of Communication Studies undergraduate student body.

Joe is an active member of the National Communication Association and Central States Communication Association, where he has held several leadership roles; serves on editorial boards for several journals; and is Consulting Editor for Forums for *Communication Education* and an Associate Editor for *Journal of the Scholarship of Teaching and Learning*. Joe received his Ph.D. in communication studies from Ohio University, a master's degree in communication from Illinois State University, and a bachelor's degree in mass communication from Mansfield University. Joe resides in Clemson, South Carolina, with his wife, Chrissy, and their children, Claire and Owen. As of this writing, they are participating in Clemson University's Faculty in Residence program and make their home in a first-year student residence hall on campus. Together, they enjoy spending time with students in their community and cheering for the Clemson Tigers!

Chapter 1
Connecting Process and Principles

 Learning Objectives

This chapter will help you:

1.1 Explain how communication competence allows you to make connections with the outside world.

1.2 Define communication.

1.3 Identify four reasons for studying communication.

1.4 Explain the fundamental principles of communication.

1.5 Define the essential components in the communication process.

1.6 Differentiate the various types of communication: intrapersonal, interpersonal (including group), public, mass, and communication via social media.

1.7 Differentiate social media from face-to-face communication.

1.8 Summarize five common myths about communication.

Making Everyday Connections

Think for a moment about how many social media tools you have at your fingertips: Facebook, Twitter, Vine, Snapchat, Yik Yak, Tinder, LinkedIn, Pinterest, Tumblr, Instagram, Flickr, Meetup—the list could go on and on. Without a doubt, there are many benefits to these tools, but there are some drawbacks as well. Nearly all social media tools allow us to make fast connections with people. However, some social media require us to remain anonymous, which can cause some people to send messages that others may perceive as hurtful and offensive. Apps like Tinder allow for online dating, but the speed with which connections can be made can lead to dangerous encounters with users who have ulterior motives for using the tool.[1]

While drawbacks to using social media do exist, the benefits can far outweigh the consequences. President Barack Obama forever changed the nature of political campaigning as well as communication by and with a president of the United States. Obama's campaign made extensive use of YouTube, blogs, tweets through Twitter, and other tools on the Internet. Pope Francis, head of the Roman Catholic Church, maintains Twitter accounts in several languages to connect with people across the globe. And even the Pope points to the key characteristic of social media—it is "a network not of wires but of people."[2]

A U.S. president, a pope, and most students and professors are highly dependent on social media to communicate and connect in everyday life and remain in touch with family, friends, and others. At the end of September 2014, Facebook reported that it surpassed 1.35 billion monthly active users. Approximately 80 percent of those monthly active users were outside the United States and Canada. Available in more than 70 languages, Facebook also reported that 1.12 billion monthly active users used the social network's mobile applications on their smartphones and other digital devices.[3] The International Association for the Wireless Telecommunications Industry notes that as of June 2013, nearly 90 percent of U.S. households use wireless service while 39 percent of U.S. households are "wireless-only households"—meaning the family abandoned its landline telephone and uses only cell phones. In June 2013, the Association estimated that nearly four out of every 10 American adults and 45 percent of American children live in wireless-only households. Nearly 45 million Americans use mobile phones as their primary Internet device.[4] Furthermore, the Pew Research Center found that 18-24-year-olds will, on average, send and receive approximately 4,000 text messages per month—or about 130 per day.[5] In May 2014, Snapchat users were sending over 700 million photos and videos each day.[6] Where will this communication lead? And how will it affect each of us as communicators?

Questions to Think About

1. How much time do you spend texting, on Twitter, Facebook, Instagram, or with some other form of social media?
2. What different forms of communication do you use on a given day?
3. How much time do you spend listening to others?
4. Can you explain the characteristics of an effective communicator?
5. What public figures are effective communicators? Why?
6. How often do you think about how effectively you communicate with others face-to-face and through social media?

Communication: Making Connections

1.1 **Explain** how communication competence allows you to make connections with the outside world.

We live in a connected world. Everywhere we look we see someone talking on a cell phone or listening to an iPod or MP3 player. At work and for our studies, we are connected to the Internet. The Internet is *the* source of information on every aspect of our lives, from resources for class papers and presentations, to emails that allow us to contact our professors, to Facebook, which allows us to present ourselves in the ways we choose and to connect with our friends and family. In our free time, we are linked to the Internet, TV, cell phones, music, or video games. Life is a series of connections, mediated or face-to-face. Despite these connections, we don't really reflect much on how we make and maintain them. Communication is something we take for granted. We talk—therefore, we communicate. But just because we can talk, can we *really* communicate effectively? What is competent communication? For our purposes, **communication competence** is the ability to take part in effective communication that is characterized by skills and understandings that enable communicators to exchange messages successfully.

communication competence

The ability to take part in effective communication that is characterized by skills and understandings that enable communicators to exchange messages successfully.

Communication helps us *make connections* with each other and with the world. We communicate daily with many people in a variety of situations. We listen to professors, employers, coworkers, family members, friends, and many others every hour. We continually text our friends and family. Facebook allows us to tell the world how we're feeling and connect with others whether close or distant. Twitter provides a way to stay socially linked in 140 characters or less. Whatever your cultural background, learning style, or geographical location, you'll find that your communication proficiency can mean greater academic success, improved relationships, a better job, and greater satisfaction in your life.

When you stop to really think about a typical day in your life, you'll discover that you spend a lot of time *making connections*. And, you'll realize that communication allows you to make those connections. Communication takes many forms and you, as a communicator, must have a wide range of behaviors that will allow you to adapt to the various situations in which you find yourself. In this text, we provide a variety of ideas and approaches to help you learn more about the exciting ways people make connections through communication. This chapter presents the concepts and processes of effective communication in everyday life. We examine the essential components and principles, the types and contexts, and the myths about communication. You will have the opportunity to think about the role of communication in an increasingly multicultural and technological world. We will differentiate face-to-face communication from that occurring via social media. We'll provide hands-on activities and reflective questions to apply to your personal life and to use communication to *make connections* in all areas of your life.

What Is Communication?

1.2 **Define** communication.

What is communication? And what do we mean when we say that communication occurs? How do we know when we have communicated effectively? How do we use communication to *make connections* in our lives? The answers to these questions require an understanding of the principles and process of communication as well as some guidelines for achieving success.

Generally, we can say that communication is a process that allows us to share and create meaning. More formally, we define **communication** as the simultaneous sharing and creating of meaning through human symbolic interaction. It might seem obvious but bears repeating: Communication is complex. If it were simple, people would have few difficulties with it, and we would not need to study it! This complex and challenging process, however, is critical to making connections in all of our relationships, from the professional to the romantic and everything in between.

communication

The simultaneous sharing and creating of meaning through human symbolic interaction.

Communication as a discipline has existed for thousands of years. Scholars in ancient Greece and Rome recognized communication as a powerful means of influence. Classical rhetoricians studied the principles of effectively composing and delivering persuasive speeches. In the Middle Ages in Western Europe, such religious leaders as St. Augustine developed written and spoken communication, including letter writing and preaching, to spread the Christian faith. In the Western world, public speaking, storytelling, and debating have been important means of changing public opinion and persuading others to take political action. African, Eastern, and Middle Eastern cultures, too, have long emphasized the importance of effective communication. According to intercultural communication scholars Samovar and Porter, "the Buddha advised his disciples to avoid 'harsh speech.'"[7] Communication colleagues in Japan, Korea, and Malaysia confirm that the study of communication is an ancient and valued tradition in their cultures. Well-known practitioners of this art include Barack Obama, Condoleezza Rice, Hillary Rodham Clinton, Maya Angelou, Toni Morrison, Abraham Lincoln, Mother Teresa, Eleanor Roosevelt, Oprah

Making Connections for Success

Communication Competence

Communication is central to our ideas of a "good" life. Communication is even identified as a way to make the world a better, safer place. In the United States numerous public figures are identified as competent communicators. Presidents Barack Obama, Ronald Reagan, Bill Clinton, and Franklin Delano Roosevelt have been known as effective communicators. Reagan, on leaving the presidency, reportedly said, "I've been called The Great Communicator. If I am it's because I have great things to communicate." Media figures Oprah Winfrey, Ellen DeGeneres, and Dr. Phil have award-winning talk shows that draw large audiences because each knows how to connect with people. Think about these examples and then answer the following questions:

1. What qualities do you think "great communicators" have?
2. Do the seven people identified above have any communication characteristics in common? What are they?
3. How do you think the ability to communicate effectively made a difference in the lives of these public figures?
4. Which people in your life do you consider to be effective communicators? Why are they effective?

Compare and discuss your answers and reasons with others in your class or in your workplace. How many on your list were on the lists of others? Were their reasons similar to yours?

---

communications

Generally used to denote the delivery systems for mediated and mass communication.

Winfrey, Franklin Delano Roosevelt, Ronald Reagan, Bill Clinton, Winston Churchill, Mohandas Gandhi, Martin Luther King Jr., Mao Tsetung, and Colin Powell.

While *communication* refers to the process by which we create and share meanings, **communications** is the word generally used to denote the delivery systems for mediated and mass communication. People often confuse the two words, but they are quite different. Communication is what you and your friend do when you discuss the next speech assignment. Communications involve ways of disseminating information, as in "The Internet is a vital communications link for humans."

According to the definition used in this text, communication involves a range of behaviors and occurs in a variety of situations: public and private, business and social, home and school, formal and informal. The diverse situations are all linked by one common thread—*human symbolic interaction*, or people using a symbol system (language) to share thoughts, feelings, beliefs, attitudes, customs, and ideas. As you read this text, you will learn about human symbolic interaction as it occurs within and among individuals, groups, organizations, cultures, and co-cultures. You will discover more about the nature of the communication *process*: listening, thinking, speaking in public settings, speaking in small-group settings, and speaking with one, two, or a small number of people in your interpersonal relationships. Your ability to communicate by using speech will be one of the determining factors in your success in the classroom, in the workplace, and in your personal life. Being an effective communicator saves time, makes life more enjoyable, allows people to establish and maintain relationships successfully, and facilitates accomplishing personal goals.

Why Should We Study Communication?

1.3 Identify four reasons for studying communication.

Although you have communicated for many years, you probably have not had the opportunity to learn about communication competence. The ability to communicate might seem natural because, unless disabilities are present, most of us readily develop speaking skills. But the ability to *communicate* (not simply to utter words) is learned; the process of becoming a competent communicator is a difficult, lifelong project. You can make progress quickly, however, if you work hard to learn the principles and concepts and then apply them in everyday situations. These skills will enable you to reap benefits in career development, ethical behavior, and the promotion of positive relationships among people of diverse cultural backgrounds. We live in a time of rapid technological change. Put simply, effective communication is critical to living successfully in today's society.

Communication and Our Technological Society

Can you remember a time when you did not rely on some form of technology to communicate? Your answer to this question is most likely a definite "no." Even if you reflect back to when you were an infant, your parents may have placed a two-way baby monitor by your crib to alert them when you started crying. In many ways, that two-way monitor was probably your first interaction with the rapidly developing world of communication and technology. Today, the baby monitor is gone, but you rely on a host of technological tools to remain connected with the people in your life. We use **social media**—highly accessible technologies that facilitate communication, interaction, and connection with others.

> **social media**
> Highly accessible technologies that facilitate communication, interaction, and connection with others

The way technology has sped the pace of communication adds to the challenge of both presenting and receiving meaningful messages. We use social media to remain connected with others in our **social network**—a group of individuals who are connected by friendship, family, common interests, beliefs, or knowledge. Our social networks are now larger than ever. Take a look at Figure 1.1. The evolution of technology is depicted along this continuum. In the mid-1800s to mid-1900s, people likely had simple social networks made up of close friends and family they saw on a regular basis and others with whom they connected via postal mail or maybe a rare telephone call. When the first telephone call was made in the late 1800s, families and friends were likely quite excited because they were now better able to remain connected with others. Notice the large gaps between important points on the first half of the continuum. Technology was evolving, but at a slow rate. Now, look at the points on the right half of the continuum. Since the first communication satellite (Telstar 1) was launched in 1962 and the first cell phone call was made in 1973, technology has evolved at a rapid rate. In the span of a few short years, the first text message was sent, Google entered the Internet scene, and Facebook, MySpace, YouTube, and Twitter emerged as popular social media outlets.

> **social network**
> A group of individuals who are connected by friendship, family, common interests, beliefs, or knowledge.

Now, our social networks are significantly more complex than those of our ancestors. We rely heavily on Facebook to remain connected with our friends across the country and the world; we text our friends to check in and maybe make plans for later in the day; we access YouTube for those informative and sometimes hilarious videos (we may even post some ourselves); we update the world (our followers) through "tweets" on Twitter; we may get breaking news alerts on our iPhones or other smartphones. Perhaps most fascinating, we can do *all* of these things in a matter of seconds from our desktop computers, our laptops, and even our cell phones. These social media may constitute the bulk of what we use to practice communication. No matter where we are, we are *plugged in* to our social networks and what is happening in the world.

Social media often make it possible for us to experience historic events just moments after they occur, sometimes even *while* they are occurring. Memorable images are frequently repeated courtesy of modern technology. The Islamic State in Iraq and Syria (ISIS) has used social media and the Internet to control the stories told of the conflict in Iraq and Syria. In essence, social media users are able to experience news as it happens anywhere in the world. Natural disasters such as earthquakes and tornadoes on the news bring others' devastation into our homes. We use digital cameras on our computers or cell phones and send images or visit face-to-face with people around the globe. If you happen to be in the right place at the right time, witnessing a news event or simply crossing the path of a reporter in search of a story or a curious individual with a cell phone camera, your image, words, or voice may be instantaneously transmitted to your community, the nation, or the world. Consider Sohaib Athar, who tweeted on May 2, 2011, "Helicopter hovering above Abbottabad

Figure 1.1 The Evolution of Social Media

Notice the large gaps between the important points on the first half of the continuum. Technology was evolving, but at a slow rate. As the points on the right half of the continuum illustrate, technology has rapidly evolved in recent years.

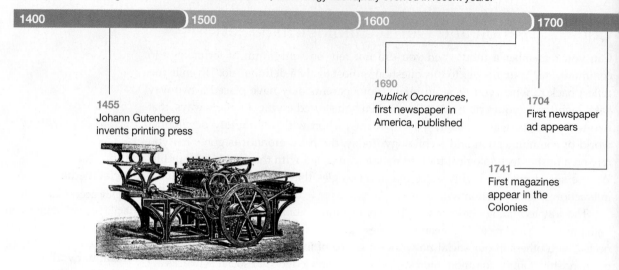

| 1400 | 1500 | 1600 | 1700 |

1455
Johann Gutenberg
invents printing press

1690
Publick Occurences,
first newspaper in
America, published

1704
First newspaper
ad appears

1741
First magazines
appear in the
Colonies

at 1AM (is a rare event)." Little did he know U.S. Navy SEAL Team 6 was preparing to invade the compound of Osama bin Laden, the founder of al-Qaeda, the militant organization that claimed responsibility for the September 11 terrorist attacks on the United States. Athar's tweet was displayed in media across the world.

The sheer volume of communication presented through electronic media can seem overwhelming. How does the competent communicator choose the appropriate channel and materials from among many options? What does technology do to the quality of one's messages? Do social media harm or help the quality of interactions? These questions and answers are some you will need to address, and this text will provide guidelines and ideas to help with that. Developments in social media are exciting because they increase avenues of communication and make the process quick and easy. Those who take time to learn and practice the principles of sound communication will best utilize social media to develop and maintain connections with others.

Communication and Career Development

Most of us aspire to succeed in our chosen careers. We enter college to better ourselves and prepare for satisfying jobs. Communication plays an important role in career success. Leaders in education, business, and industry have identified several life skills critical to success in the workforce, and communication is one of the most valued areas of expertise. For example, several recent studies[9] reinforce what previous research had already shown: Employers want workers at all levels who know how to communicate and relate to others both verbally and in writing. They want workers who work well in groups and teams and exhibit strong analytical, problem-solving, and computer/technical skills. And finally employers want workers who are flexible and able to adapt to new situations on the job, and they demand a strong work ethic and initiative.

In other words, effective workplace communicators can explain ideas clearly and give good directions. Effective communicators are good listeners who work harmoniously with others and represent their companies well in small and large group

Technology allows us to make connections with each other and with the world. At the same time, the many communication tools available sometimes make our messages less personal than they would be in face-to-face communication. Social media are indeed changing our way of communicating and how we connect with and relate to others.

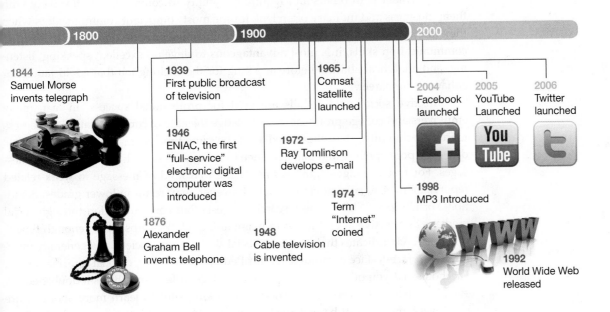

1800

1900

2000

1844
Samuel Morse invents telegraph

1939
First public broadcast of television

1965
Comsat satellite launched

2004
Facebook launched

2005
YouTube Launched

2006
Twitter launched

1946
ENIAC, the first "full-service" electronic digital computer was introduced

1972
Ray Tomlinson develops e-mail

1998
MP3 Introduced

1876
Alexander Graham Bell invents telephone

1948
Cable television is invented

1974
Term "Internet" coined

1992
World Wide Web released

Making Connections for Success

How Do You Remain Connected?

Most of us cannot begin to imagine life without the gadgets and the instant access we have to everyone and everything. It was a tweeted image that first captured the forced miracle landing of US Airways flight 1549 in the Hudson River. Biz Stone and Evan Williams conceived of Twitter as a basic communication tool providing social networking applications. It has grown into one of the "world's most valuable real-time information caches." Twitter has now evolved into a powerful new marketing and communication tool. Regional emergency preparedness organizations are looking at Twitter as a way to reach millions of people during a disaster. NASA is using it to regularly update interested parties about the status of space shuttle flights. A Manhattan bakery tweets when warm cookies come out of the oven.[8] Through our Facebook profiles we present what we want to the world. We use Vine to record and share six-second looping videos of our daily lives. Snapchat lets us take photos and record videos and quickly share our Snaps with people—before our Snaps are automatically deleted forever. LinkedIn allows us to make contacts with people in our profession or those in the profession to which we aspire. It can help us get recommendations as well as networking possibilities. Facebook was initially created for college students but is now populated by people of all ages (including your authors), who use this to maintain connections with friends and colleagues both near and far. With that in mind, answer the following questions and share them with friends/classmates to compare your stories.

1. Do you tweet? When? Why?

2. Have you or a friend ever experienced an online relationship? How did the relationship develop?

3. What rules did you and your friend follow in establishing and maintaining this relationship?

4. What concerns do you have about this kind of relationship? Why?

5. Did anyone ever attempt to monitor or stop your use of the Internet? How? For what reasons?

6. How is communication through social media easier or more difficult than face-to-face communication with family and friends?

7. Do you have a Twitter, Facebook, or LinkedIn account? How and for what do you use each?

settings. Too often, employers believe these skills are lacking in their employees. Introductory courses in communication, such as the one to which this text is geared, focus on these skills.

Personnel directors have described their needs regarding prospective employees as follows: Send me people who know how to speak, listen, and think, and I'll do the rest. I can train people in their specific job responsibilities, as long as they listen attentively, know how to think, and can express themselves well.[10] In fact, most careers involve contact with others and require the ability to communicate effectively with them. Business and industry often look for the most competent communicators when they hire new employees. Although some companies provide on-the-job training in communication skills, it is most advantageous to develop excellent speaking, listening, and analytical abilities before applying for the exciting job that could launch or enhance your career.

Effective social media skills are vital for professional success. In fact, many employers and college professors acknowledge the ease of communication and access to information offered by these media. At the same time, some of those same people decry the poor spelling and damage done to the quality of both written and oral messages. For text messages "gr8" is fine. Using that kind of message in work-related reports, memos, emails, or class papers, however, may result in lower grades, demotions, or job loss. While some research suggests that communication through social media is as effective at building and maintaining relationships, given enough time,[11] other research indicates that it reduces social skills, harms society, and generally interferes with face-to-face communication.[12] Perhaps you share personal information via Facebook that you otherwise might not share face-to-face, but this is a double-edged sword in that employers search social networking sites to learn more about future employees and, on that basis, have been known to rescind interviews and job offers. Facebook page content has cost some employees their jobs. This text will suggest how to effectively use social media in your personal and professional life.

Communication and Ethical Behavior

All societies hold certain ethical standards—ideals about what is right and what is wrong—and unethical behavior often carries a penalty. **Ethics** refers to an individual's system of moral principles. People have been removed from political office, lost their jobs, or been publicly chastised for violating ethical standards and codes. Such behaviors often involve unethical acts related to communication. Consider former New York Congressman Anthony Weiner. In May 2011, Weiner sent via Twitter a sexually suggestive photograph of himself to a 21-year-old woman. For days the congressman denied the allegations, until he admitted to his unethical use of social media during a planned news conference. His credibility as an honorable public servant now tarnished, Weiner resigned from Congress. As an additional example, financiers have received prison terms for participating in insider trading—using illegally obtained information to make money on the stock market. Sharing such information constitutes an illegal act of communication. Another unethical behavior is telling lies, whether done to hurt someone else or to protect or enhance one's own position. Though politicians spring to mind as typical offenders in this category, the problem is more widespread: for instance, enhancing one's résumé to increase the chances of being hired or "borrowing" a friend's old term paper or speech to pass a course.

Sometimes people think they need to find so-called shortcuts to accomplish tasks, whether they involve questionable accounting procedures in business, insider trading to keep more money, or stealing ideas to complete a presentation or paper. **Plagiarism** is the use of another person's information, language, or ideas without citing the originator and making it appear that the user is the originator. Technology allows us to find and use all kinds of information, but it also presents new ethical dilemmas. Technology may tempt us to use someone

ethics

An individual's system of moral principles.

plagiarism

The use of another person's information, language, or ideas without citing the originator and making it appear that the user is the originator.

Employers want workers who can speak effectively, listen carefully and efficiently, and think critically. Strong communication skills are vital to today's global workplace.

Making Connections for Success

Your Communication Effectiveness in the Workplace

In the surveys cited in the text, executives indicated that all employees need to improve their communication skills. The executives also noted that greater flexibility and higher ethical standards should be a focus of career preparation. If a prospective employer asked you the following questions, how would you respond?

1. Are you an effective communicator at work? Why? Why not?

2. What are five of your workplace communication concerns?

3. What anxieties about communication do you have? (James McCroskey and his colleagues developed the Personal Report of Communication Apprehension [PRCA]

to help identify the strength of your communication anxiety. Try a web search on communication apprehension and complete a PRCA found on the web. We discuss communication apprehension more fully in the public speaking section.)

4. What areas of communication do you need to improve at work? How do you know you need to work on these areas?

5. Describe one instance in which you found yourself wishing that you were a better listener at work.

6. What were you doing the last time you found yourself wishing you were a better communicator? What did you mean by the term?

7. In what recent situations did you find yourself wondering how to be more effective in workplace relationships?

else's work or perhaps information that hasn't been carefully screened or evaluated for authenticity or truthfulness. A quick search of the Internet provides numerous sources for A, B, or even C papers for a "minimal cost" and "minimal risks to you." While those papers can save time and effort, they can also cost you a passing grade, or even a diploma from your institution.

The Internet creates more opportunity for plagiarism because of easy access to information. So many sites exist, with so much information, that people often believe they can go to a site, take what they want, and never be caught. Social media can foster plagiarism and also make it more likely that you will get caught. For example, on Twitter, communication is meant to be short and fast. An initial tweet may properly attribute the original source, but as the message is retweeted, somewhere along the way the attribution can be lost. Plagiarism, in whatever form, is still unethical; and just as it has consequences in educational institutions, in the workplace, plagiarism and other unethical behaviors can result in a demotion or even job loss.

Ethical communicators speak responsibly and give credit to any sources that contribute to the message being conveyed. An ethical communicator does not plagiarize and does not lie. Aristotle, a Greek rhetorician (384–322 BC), suggested that communication was most powerful when the speaker's character, or *ethos* (ethical appeal), was engaged in presenting the truth.[13] (Chapter 10 further develops this concept.) Quintilian (ca. AD 35–100), another rhetorician, stated (before the days of inclusive language) that communication needed presentation by "a good man speaking well."[14]

An important distinction to make here is that unethical communication may, in fact, constitute effective communication. If one person persuades another to do something morally wrong, the communication has been effective, but it is not virtuous. Unethical communication should never be condoned, even when it has appeared to succeed. We need a good deal of critical thinking in our attempt to be effective *and* ethical communicators who evaluate others' communication to determine its ethical content.

Today, many colleges and universities offer or require ethics classes to encourage students to take ethical responsibilities seriously and to remind them that the need for responsible, ethical behavior pervades all aspects of life. Throughout this text, examples of ethical dilemmas and perspectives will help you become aware of the need for ethical communication behaviors.

Making Connections for Success

Ethical Perspectives

Every few weeks we hear examples of unethical behavior. In June 2014, we learned that a Facebook emotion study allegedly breached ethical guidelines by failing to obtain informed consent from nearly 700,000 Facebook users. When research participants give informed consent, they formally agree to participate in a research study. Critics claimed that Facebook wrongly manipulated users' news feeds to test whether certain content would affect their emotions. Some said the study was very harmful because it changed users' moods. Others said that researchers should not get a free pass because a user checked a box next to a link to a website's terms-of-use policy. In the end, researchers are held responsible for making sure all participants offer their informed consent. Several years ago, Rod Blagojevich, former Illinois governor, was arrested for political corruption, impeached, and removed from office because he tried to sell Barack Obama's vacant U.S. Senate seat. In 2011, Blagojevich was sentenced to 14 years in federal prison. In what some labeled a mockery of the system, he appointed former Illinois Attorney General Roland Burris to the seat. After being seated in the Senate, Burris admitted he hosted fund-raising activities for the governor and had been asked for money. These examples demonstrate some of the risks created by failing to meet ethical standards.

1. Where do we get our views of ethics?
2. What are your own views of ethical behaviors?
3. What specific behaviors violate your ethical code to the point that you would have to confront someone if he or she acted in a certain way?
4. Would you ever plagiarize? When? Why? Why not?
5. What other examples of ethical violations currently or recently in the news can you identify?
6. What policies does your college or university have in place for plagiarism and/or breaches of ethics?
7. What are the penalties for such behavior?

Communication and Our Multicultural Society

Job transfers, changes in economic and political conditions, and numerous other factors cause people to move from place to place, often leaving their country of birth to put down roots elsewhere. Many countries are experiencing an increase in this trend. In the United States, for example, the population that was once characterized by a white majority with European roots is now a diverse mosaic comprising people of different ethnic and cultural backgrounds. In this environment, we can grow to appreciate the distinctions that make each culture unique as well as the interconnectedness shared by all, sometimes described as the "global village." But a great deal of knowledge, flexibility, and sensitivity is necessary if people of diverse cultural backgrounds are to communicate successfully and live well together.

Current demographic trends and projections in the United States create the necessity to interact successfully with people of all racial, ethnic, cultural, and religious heritages. See Table 1.1 for the 2010 U.S. Census Bureau report about the demographic breakdown by race (all ages).[15]

Table 1.1 U.S. Population by Race (2000 and 2010)

Group	Population Numbers in 2000	Population Numbers in 2010
One Race:	274,595,678	299,736,465
…White	211,460,626	223,553,265
…Black or African American	34,658,190	38,929,319
…American Indian and Alaska Native	2,475,956	2,932,248
…Asian	10,242,998	14,674,252
…Native Hawaiian and Other Pacific Islander	398,835	540,013
…Some Other Race	15,359,073	19,107,368
Two or More Races	6,826,228	9,009,073
Total Population	281,421,906	308,745,538

SOURCE: U.S. Census Bureau.

This translates to roughly the following 2010 percentages: 72 percent of the population is white, 13 percent is black or African American, 5 percent is Asian, and 1 percent is American Indian. Projections from the Census Bureau suggest a significant increase in Hispanic, black, and Asian numbers in the near future, with a decline or stable percentage for whites. The changes in "how we look" are already occurring in elementary schools and high schools, as well as college and university classrooms. Language differences complicate communication within many schools. Some kindergarten-through-twelfth-grade schools on the East and West Coasts, as well as in other populous areas such as Chicago, Cincinnati, Dallas, and St. Louis, have students that represent 50 to 100 or more different native languages. College and university classrooms, too, have increasing numbers of students whose first language is not English, and each one's cultural and ethnic background affects the way these students communicate in the classroom, the residence hall, the supermarket, and the workplace.

Language structure itself influences and is influenced by culture. Nonverbal communication behaviors, such as physical stance, eye contact, and style of speaking, are also largely determined by cultural background. It takes a great deal of patience, understanding, and respect to learn to communicate effectively in situations involving different language backgrounds and different social and conversational customs. Thus, it is important to discover all we can about the backgrounds of the people with whom we relate at school, at work, or in the community; to consider how our own customs might seem unusual to a person of a different heritage; and to cultivate an open mind and a good sense of humor. These attitudes will facilitate communication and enrich our lives.

Principles of Communication

1.4 **Explain** the fundamental principles of communication.

To appreciate the true nature of communication, it is important to understand four fundamental principles:

1. Communication is a process.
2. Communication is a system.
3. Communication is transactional.
4. Communication can be intentional or unintentional.

These principles apply readily to life beyond the classroom (and they improve interactions within the classroom as well). No doubt, situations from your personal life—family relationships, work experiences, or your participation in sports teams, music groups, social clubs, or political or community action organizations—will come to mind as we discuss the dynamics of communication. An understanding of these principles should make a difference in your life, building greater understanding and cooperation into relationships at any level.

Communication Is a Process

Communication is considered a **process** because it involves a series of actions that has no beginning or end and is constantly changing.[16]

Communication also involves variables that can never be duplicated. The interrelationships among people, environments, skills, attitudes, status, experiences, and feelings all determine communication at any given moment. Think about a relationship you developed with someone recently. How did it occur? It may have happened by chance (striking up a conversation with someone you met while walking

process
A series of actions that has no beginning or end and is constantly changing.

to class), or it may have been a prearranged meeting (a business meeting with a prospective client). No two relationships are developed in the same way. And, like the weather, some relationships are warm while others are cool.

Communication is both ever changing and capable of effecting change. Saying something you wish you hadn't said is an excellent example of this principle. No matter how hard you try to take back your comment, you cannot. It made its impact and has, in all likelihood, affected your relationship with another person in some way. The change might not be immediate or significant, but it does happen as a result of your communication.

Furthermore, communication and the changes it produces might not have a clearly identifiable beginning or end. Certain events led up to it, and as we noted, results will follow in its wake. Communication generally is not characterized by abrupt endings and beginnings; rather, it takes place within a flow. If you were to stop mid-conversation and walk away, that conversation would still affect you; it would not end. You would carry away some new information or at least a general impression, whether positive or negative. Understanding that communication is a process will enable you to see how events and relationships constantly change, yet also have continuity.

Communication Is a System

system

Combination of parts interdependently acting to form a whole

Simply stated, a **system** is a combination of parts interdependently acting to form a whole. The human body is an excellent example of a system. All parts of the body are interdependent and work together to form one complex system. If something is not functioning correctly, some response usually occurs either to correct what has gone wrong or to warn that something is going wrong. When you have a headache, it affects not only your head but also the rest of your body. You may find that you have trouble seeing and even walking. You may not wish to eat because your head pain seems to have taken over your body. If your headache is severe, you may experience trouble thinking clearly. You may also have difficulty explaining something to your coworkers or friends. Because all parts of the system are connected, your inability to think clearly, speak lucidly, or listen carefully leads to ineffective communication.

Systems also exist in the workplace, in the family, and in the classroom. If your supervisor had a fight at home, that event may affect his or her relationship with coworkers; the supervisor may be irritable and snap at you and others. Although you don't know what has caused the irritability, it does affect all who must deal with it. In other words, the supervisor's fight at home has an impact not only on the home system but also on the system at work. In a similar sense, the communication process is a system and occurs only when the necessary components interact. If components of communication malfunction or are absent, communication is prevented or ineffective.

Communication Is Transactional

transactional

Exchange of communication in which the communicators act simultaneously; that is, encoding and decoding occur at the same time.

Communication is often viewed as a highly complex and **transactional** process—the simultaneous sending (encoding) and receiving (decoding) of messages. To best understand the transactional nature of communication, it is useful to compare it with the related ideas of *action* and *interaction*. If we view communication as strictly action, we would consider a source who sends a message to a receiver or audience. An action perspective does not consider the reaction from the receiver. Early communication research suggested that communication was as simple as injecting receivers with our messages.[17]

If we think about communication from an interaction perspective, we consider not only the source's message but the receiver's reaction as well. Such a view marked a clear step forward in our concept of communication. The interaction perspective explains that communication is not a simple one-way process. An example of communication as an interaction is a phone conversation between Chris and John. Chris speaks and John listens, then John speaks and Chris listens, and so on. Each message is a separate action. Even though a reaction to each sent message does occur, the reaction and message are not simultaneous.

Most face-to-face communication does not occur as a series of distinctly separate actions. Today, nearly all communication scholars view communication as a transactional process. Much like the interaction view, the transactional perspective considers the listener's reaction to our message, but goes further and explains how people simultaneously act as speaker and listener in communication situations. In any given interaction, people talk, offer feedback, and respond as each person contributes through constant participation. Consider an interaction between a professor and the student she suspects has committed plagiarism. If we view communication as an interaction, we would look first at what the professor says, then consider what the student says, then examine what the professor says, and so on. However, if we view the exchange as a transaction, we would look simultaneously at the professor and the student. The professor may vary the content or tone of the conversation on the basis of the student's nonverbal behaviors. Simultaneously, the student may respond to the professor's communication cues by changing his behavior.

Without simultaneous actions, the communication transaction would be extremely limited, like sending a letter to someone and then having to wait a week or two for a response. In face-to-face communication, each person affects the other and shares in the process simultaneously. When you're emailing or texting someone, unlike in face-to-face communication, you are both sender and receiver, but not simultaneously. The lag time can be frustrating because you have to wait a bit to respond. The advantage is that the written message helps you follow the flow of ideas. The principle of transaction is more fully depicted in Figure 1.2.

The transactional nature of communication also considers the context or the setting in which interaction takes place. Not only do participants constantly influence each other, but the communication context also affects how they interact. For instance, a funny comment made by friends in the school cafeteria can take on a very different meaning in a professional work setting. In many ways, our understanding of the transactional nature of communication highlights the complexity of communication and enhances our competence to effectively interact with others.

Communication Can Be Intentional or Unintentional

When one person communicates with another, he or she intends that specific messages with specific purposes and meanings be received. Communication can occur, however,

---

Figure 1.2 Communication as Transaction

In a transaction, the persons communicate simultaneously. That is, both Chris and John are communicating at the same time. This does not mean they are both speaking at once. Instead, each is aware of and reacting to the other. The sender is also a receiver, and the receiver is also a sender. Each is actively involved in what is happening.

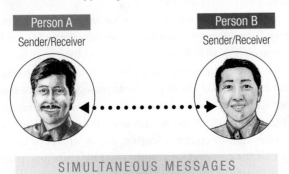

Person A
Sender/Receiver

Person B
Sender/Receiver

SIMULTANEOUS MESSAGES

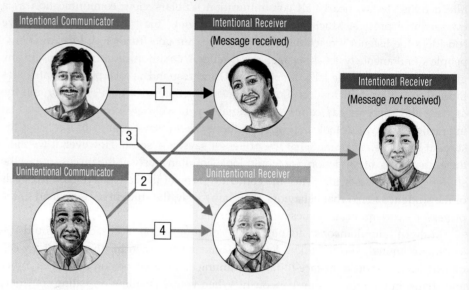

Figure 1.3 Types of Intentional and Unintentional Communication

Communication occurs both intentionally and unintentionally. Thus, we must be aware that even when we do not intend it, communication can occur. Can you recall any instances in which you unintentionally communicated to another person?

intentional communication

A message that is purposely sent to a specific receiver.

unintentional communication

A message that is not intended to be sent or was not intended for the individual who received it.

regardless of whether it is intended. **Intentional communication** is a message that is purposely sent to a specific receiver. **Unintentional communication** is a message that is not intended to be sent or was not intended for the individual who received it. On the basis of intent or lack of intent, four possible communication situations can occur, as illustrated in Figure 1.3. Arrow 1 is generally the way communication takes place. Arrow 2 indicates a situation in which a person unintentionally communicates something to someone who is intentionally trying to receive a message or messages. This situation occurs every time someone reads more into a communication act than was intended by the source. For example, when a work supervisor frowns at everyone and generally speaks abruptly whenever anyone addresses her, the employees immediately begin to attribute meanings to her behavior. One worker may believe that the business has economic problems and his position is at risk. Another might believe that she has done something wrong and is going to face discipline for her behavior. A third person decides that the supervisor had an argument with her husband and is taking it out on everyone at work. In reality, the supervisor actually had a headache and did not intend to communicate anything negative about the job, but others read meaning into her behavior, and she may have to explain her actions.

Arrow 3 illustrates the opposite situation. Here the source intends to send a message, but the person for whom the message is intended is not consciously or intentionally receiving it. Such a situation happens in the classroom when students daydream while the instructor is lecturing.

Arrow 4 shows that communication can be unintentional for both the source and the receiver and can occur without anyone intentionally sending or receiving a message. Communication that is not intended, or that is at least not consciously sent and received, is usually nonverbal. For example, the clothing a person wears might not be worn to communicate any specific message, and persons observing the clothing might not intentionally or consciously receive any message through it, but they do see it. Thus, communication occurs even though neither the person nor the observer has any intention of communicating. Think of a time when you received a message not intended for you and you were upset by your interpretation. Why were you upset?

Making Connections for Success

Communication Principles in the Workplace

Erin is a server at a local restaurant. She receives $4.15 per hour plus her tips. It's important for her to connect with her customers. If she has a bad day and lets it affect her verbal and nonverbal communication, it will likely also affect the amount of tip money she receives. Even when she is tired, she has to smile and act friendly and perhaps even energetic when she's with her customers.

1. How is Erin's physical or emotional state likely to affect her communication? How must she change if she wants good tips?

2. Why should Erin change her behavior? Is it ethical to do so?

3. What principles of communication do you find in this example?

4. Compare some of your own workplace situations with those of others in your class. How did you see communication principles in these examples?

Essential Components of Communication

1.5 **Define** the essential components in the communication process.

Although no exhaustive list of the myriad components of communication has been compiled, eight of the most basic elements are worth examining in detail:

1. Source/Sender

2. Message

3. Interference/Noise

4. Channel

5. Receiver

6. Feedback

7. Environment

8. Context

Figure 1.4 illustrates how these components interact when two people are communicating, yet it depicts each element's movement and interdependence on the other elements only in a limited way. During actual communication, these components are constantly in flux as the communicators react to each other. The model also shows that communication is a process, that the components work together as a system, that interaction and transaction are both possible modes of communication, and that intentional and unintentional communication can occur—thus illustrating the principles of communication we have already discussed.

Now that you can see how these elements relate during communication, we will discuss each one separately.

Source/Sender

The **source** is the creator of the message. Because communication usually involves more than one person, more than one source can exist at one time. In the model in Figure 1.4, both persons function as a source. Likewise, both the teacher and the students in a classroom can function as sources, sending messages simultaneously to one another—teacher to students, students to teacher, and students to students.

source

The creator of the message.

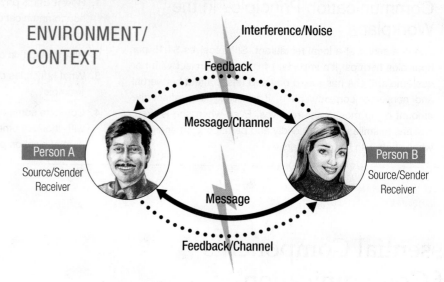

Figure 1.4 Model of the Essential Components of Communication

The essential components of the transactional communication process are constantly changing, ongoing, and dynamic, and they affect one another.

The communication source performs four roles: He or she determines the meaning of what is to be communicated, encodes the meaning into a message, sends the message, and perceives and reacts to a listener's response to the message. James, when acting as source, also brings into play the communicative skills, knowledge, attitudes, and sociocultural background that make him a unique individual. No two communicators are identical in their abilities to communicate, nor do they see others, events, or situations in exactly the same way. The greater the differences between James and Maggie, the more effort and skill it will take for James to effectively communicate with Maggie. Respecting another person's views, even when they differ from one's own, is the first step to communicating well in such situations.

DETERMINING MEANINGS The meaning behind the message determines how you'll create the message. Your word choices and tone of voice, as well as other, nonverbal behaviors, will help convey your meaning to those with whom you communicate and will require careful choices on your part. When you tell your friends you're going to Belize for spring break, you have to choose the ultimate intended meaning. Do you want them to be excited for you? Do you want them to be jealous? Do you want them to ask about going along? Or do you wish to let them know about the good deal on travel and lodging? Or perhaps you just want to express your pleasure about this destination. How do you choose words and behavior to do that?

encoding

Process by which the source translates thoughts or feelings into words, sounds, and physical expressions, which together make up the actual message that is to be sent.

ENCODING Once a source has chosen a meaning, she or he **encodes** it. In other words, a source translates the thoughts or feelings into words, sounds, and physical expressions, which make up the actual message to be sent. According to symbolic interactionism, a theory created by sociologist George Herbert Mead and his students, the most human and humanizing activity people engage in is talking with one another. Our conversations with others—our participation in the communication process in social settings—allow us to construct meaning. For example, the postal carrier rings your doorbell and asks you to sign for a package. Without looking at the return address, you tell her you've been anxiously waiting for your new laptop to arrive. Symbolic interactionism also explains that we talk to ourselves (intrapersonal communication) as we sort through difficult circumstances, solve problems, and make decisions.

SENDING   The source then sends the message, which involves the source's ability to communicate overtly, that is, to use voice and body to express the intended meaning accurately. For example, if your internal meaning is to tell the other person how pleased you are to go to Belize for spring break, you must use words and actions to illustrate what you are feeling and thinking.

REACTING   Finally, a source must interpret the receiver's response to the message. A source's perception of a receiver's response in most communication situations is simultaneous with the response. For example, the person you are telling about your trip to Belize will send you messages (smiles, nods of the head, eye contact) as you speak, in reaction to what you are saying. If you interpret that response as positive, you will probably continue to tell more about your trip.

Message

A **message** is the communication produced by the source. Messages are composed of words, grammar, organization of thoughts, physical appearance, body movement, voice, aspects of the person's personality and self-concept, and personal style. Environment and noise can also shape the message. Any stimulus that affects a receiver is a message from the source, regardless of whether the source intended to send it. Hence, if you ask a frowning friend what is wrong and the friend says, "Oh, nothing," you're sure to believe that there *really is* something wrong. The frown communicates that the words and actions do not fit together, and you're more likely to believe the frown than the words. Your friend may not want to discuss anything with you, but you still attach meaning to all that occurs.

Remember, each message is unique. Even if the same message were to be created over and over again, it would differ in each instance because messages cannot be repeated or received in exactly the same way or in the same context. To illustrate this, imagine reading the headline "The World Has Been Invaded by Small Green People!" in a comic book and then in your local newspaper. Although the words might be the same, the messages conveyed would be quite different.

message
The communication produced by the source.

INTERFERENCE/NOISE   Anything that changes the meaning of an intended message is called **interference**. It is included in our model because it is present, to one degree or another, in every communication environment.

Interference can be external and physical, such as noise caused by the slamming of a door, someone talking on a cell phone, or the blasting of a stereo. Other examples of external interference include an unpleasant environment, such as a smoke-filled room or a room that is too cool or too hot; an odor, such as that of overly strong perfume; or distracting characteristics of the speaker, such as too much makeup, a speech impediment, talk that is too fast or too slow, mumbling pronunciation, or weird clothing.

Interference can also be internal and psychological. For example, thoughts going through a person's mind can interfere with the reception or creation of a message. A person who speaks in a loud voice to get someone's attention may create both physical and psychological interference. If the receiver perceives the loudness as anger, the loud voice creates not only a distraction from attending but also a distortion of interpretation. If the receiver responds accordingly, the sender may be quite surprised. Essentially, interference is anything that reduces or distorts the clarity, accuracy, meaning, understanding, or retention of a message.

interference
Anything that changes the meaning of an intended message.

Channel

A **channel** is the means by which messages flow between sources and receivers. The usual communication channels are light waves and sound waves, which allow

channel
The means by which messages flow between sources and receivers.

us to see and hear one another in face-to-face interactions. However, if a letter is sent from one person to another, the paper itself serves as the means by which the message is conveyed. If you settle in to watch the evening news on television, the television set serves as the channel. Books, films, DVDs, computers, radios, magazines, newspapers, and pictures are channels through which messages may be conveyed.

We also receive communication by smelling, touching, and tasting. We sometimes take these senses for granted, but imagine walking into a bakery and not being able to smell the aroma or taste the flavors. And, all you have to do is hug someone you care about to recognize how important touch is. All five senses, therefore, contribute to communication.

Receiver

receiver

The individual who analyzes and interprets the message.

decoding

The process of translating a message into the thoughts or feelings that were communicated.

Both persons function as receivers in the model depicted in Figure 1.4. A **receiver** analyzes and interprets messages, in effect translating them into meaning. This process is called **decoding**. *You are simultaneously a receiver and a source.* As you listen to another person's message, you react with body movements and facial expressions, and the person sending the message receives the information conveyed by your physical reactions. Like the source, a receiver has several roles: to receive (hear, see, touch, smell, or taste) the message; to attend to the message; to interpret and analyze the message; to store and recall the message; and to respond to the source, message, channel, environment, and noise. In addition, Maggie also has communication skills, knowledge, attitudes, and a sociocultural background that differ from those of James. The greater the differences between James and Maggie, the more effort Maggie must make to be a competent receiver.

Feedback

feedback

The response to a message that a receiver sends back to a source.

Another component in the communication process is **feedback**, the response to a message that a receiver sends back to a source. Feedback enables a sender to determine whether the communication has been received and understood as intended. To share meaning accurately, the sender must correct faulty messages and misconceptions, repeat missed meanings, and correct responses as necessary.

Feedback is a natural extension of effective receiving. Receivers have the responsibility of attending to, decoding, and determining a message's intended meaning. The next logical step is to provide responses (feedback) that let the sender know the message was received and understood. It is then up to the sender to decide whether the feedback provides enough information to judge whether the receiver accurately interpreted the message. Thus, feedback serves as a kind of control mechanism in the communication process. Unfortunately, we too often fail to monitor our own communication and, more important, others' reactions to it, so we are often not heard or are misunderstood. For example, consider the following scenario. Restaurant employees requested a pay raise or bonus because of an especially profitable and successful party. The boss told them they would get a bonus in the next paycheck but failed to tell payroll. The employees wondered what went wrong.

Feedback is an essential component of the communication process because it is both a corrective device and a means by which we learn about ourselves. It helps us adjust to others and assess ourselves. Giving feedback to others is just as important as receiving it, making communication truly a shared process.

Feedback offers other advantages. A classic study found that when feedback is increased, reception of information is enhanced.[18] The experiment required four groups of students to construct geometric patterns that were described by a teacher under conditions that differed for each group: (1) zero feedback—the teacher's back was turned to the students, and they were not allowed to ask questions or make noise; (2) visible audience feedback—the students could see the teacher's face but could not ask questions; (3) limited verbal feedback—the students were allowed to ask the teacher questions, but the teacher could respond only with yes or no; and (4) free feedback—all channels of communication were open, with no limits placed on the type of questions asked of the teacher or the depth of response the teacher could provide. Students provided with no opportunity to receive feedback from the teacher fared poorly, whereas each increasing level of feedback produced better results. This study resulted in two important findings: (1) As the amount of feedback increases, so does the accuracy of communication; and (2) as the amount of feedback increases, so does the recipient's confidence in her or his performance.

Environment

The **environment**, or atmosphere, refers to the psychological and physical surroundings in which communication occurs. The environment encompasses the attitudes, feelings, perceptions, and relationships of the communicators as well as the characteristics of the location in which communication takes place, for example, the size, color, arrangement, decoration, and temperature of the room.

environment
The psychological and physical surroundings in which communication occurs.

The environment affects the nature and quality of the communication. For example, it is much easier to carry on an intimate conversation in a private, quiet, and comfortable setting than in a public, noisy, and uncomfortable setting. Most of us find it easier to communicate with someone we know than with someone we do not know. Some environments appear to foster communication, whereas others seem to inhibit it. Consider these contrasting environments. One office is clean, is painted light blue, and has quiet music playing in the background. The office has a pleasant and inviting smell. Two people, seated in soft, comfortable desk chairs at clean and organized desks, are working alongside each other, smiling, and they take frequent breaks to share funny stories and family updates. They show genuine concern for each other. Their communication is open and caring. Another office is cluttered, is painted dark brown, and has no music playing in the background. The office has a musty odor. Desks are cluttered and set up in small cubicles. Two people sit in uncomfortable chairs in a cubicle, side-by-side. One person blasts his music at high volume on his computer and disrupts the other's work. They show little respect for each other. Their communication is guarded.

How does the appearance of the room ultimately affect the communication? Both effective and ineffective forms of communication are, in part, products of their environments. Effective communication can occur anywhere and under most circumstances, but pleasing, comfortable environments (along with open, trusting relationships) are more likely to produce positive exchanges.

Context

The broad circumstances or situation in which communication occurs is called the **context**. Communication does not take place in a vacuum. It happens in informal and formal settings, such as between two friends; among five colleagues in a business meeting; or between a rabbi, priest, cleric, or minister and a group of worshippers. The number of people, the type of communication, and the situation in which the communication occurs all lend themselves to the context. Each context affects what we say and how we say it. Contexts also help determine the type of communication used.

context
The broad circumstances or situation in which communication occurs.

Guidelines

Understanding Yourself and the Communication Process

1. **Always strive to be a competent communicator.** Competent communicators do everything they can to help their listeners understand the communication in the way it is intended.

2. **Understand that interference can detract from your message.** Interference from both external and internal sources may make the communication act difficult to interpret the way you, the sender, intend it.

3. **Recognize that you often cannot control environmental factors (heat or lack of it, outside noise, dim or too-bright lighting).** But you can control your own speech rate, volume, use of pauses, use of gestures, and correct pronunciations, and these factors can increase your effectiveness.

4. **Carefully choose your words and the way you present your message (encoding).** If you do this, your listeners have a better chance of understanding you.

5. **Observe your listeners (receivers).** If you do this, you will learn how to read their nonverbal feedback and be able to adapt your message to them.

6. **Remember that listening is a critical aspect of the communication process.** Effective listeners communicate that they are active participants in the communication process.

Types of Communication

1.6   **Differentiate** the various types of communication: intrapersonal, interpersonal (including group), public, mass, and communication via social media.

Type of communication is usually distinguished by the number of people involved, by the purpose of the communication, and by the degree of formality with which it occurs. Each type of communication involves appropriate verbal and nonverbal behaviors. Five types of communication are discussed in this text: intrapersonal, interpersonal, small group, team, and public. We also refer to elements of social media and communication here and throughout the text.

Intrapersonal Communication

intrapersonal communication

The process of understanding information within oneself.

To communicate with others, we must first understand how we communicate with ourselves. This process of understanding information within oneself is called **intrapersonal communication**. As we mature, we learn a lot about our surroundings and ourselves. Much of what we learn is gained from our own experiences. Even though we are taught many things by others, we must learn many things through our own experiences and can learn no other way.

Intrapersonal communication also occurs anytime we evaluate or attempt to understand the interaction occurring between us and anything that communicates a message to us. We are involved in intrapersonal communication as we receive, attend to, interpret and analyze, store and recall, or respond in some fashion to any message.

Intrapersonal communication includes diverse internal activities such as thinking, problem solving, conflict resolution, planning, emotion, stress, evaluation, and relationship development. All messages that we create first occur within us. Ultimately, all communication takes place within each of us as we react to communication cues. Intrapersonal communication may occur without the presence of any other type of communication, but all other types of communication cannot occur without it. In fact, intrapersonal communication is almost always happening, yet we don't often think about it as a type of communication.

Interpersonal Communication

interpersonal communication

The creating and sharing of meaning between people who are in a relationship.

Interpersonal communication is creating and sharing meaning between persons who are in a relationship. It is similar to intrapersonal communication in that it helps us share information, solve problems, resolve conflicts, understand our perception of self and of others, and establish relationships with others. (In the chapters on relational contexts, interpersonal relationships and our relationships with friends and family members are discussed in more detail.)

A subcomponent of interpersonal communication is dyadic communication. **Dyadic communication** is simply defined as an exchange of information between two people. It includes informal conversations, such as talks with a parent, spouse, child, friend, acquaintance, or stranger, as well as more formal ones, such as interviews. An **interview** is a carefully planned and executed question-and-answer session designed to exchange desired information between two parties.

Another subcomponent of interpersonal communication is **small-group communication**, an exchange of information among a relatively small number of people, ideally five to seven, who share a common purpose, such as completing a task, solving a problem, making a decision, or sharing information. (The chapters on the small-group context discuss the purposes, characteristics, leadership, participation, decision making, problem solving, and evaluation of communication in small groups.)

dyadic communication
An exchange of information between two people.

interview
A carefully planned and executed question-and-answer session designed to exchange desired information between two parties.

small-group communication
An exchange of information among a relatively small number of people, ideally five to seven, who share a common purpose, such as completing a task, solving a problem, making a decision, or sharing information.

Public Communication

In **public communication**, a message is transmitted from one person who speaks to a number of individuals who listen. The most widely used form of public communication is a public speech. We find ourselves on the listening end of a public speech in lecture classes, political rallies, group meetings, and religious services.

Although many similarities exist between public speaking and other types of communication, some differences can also be noted. Public speaking almost always is more highly structured than the other types. To be done well, it demands much detailed planning and preparation by the speaker. Unlike participants in other forms of communication, listeners do not regularly interrupt the speaker with questions or comments. It is the public speaker's responsibility to anticipate questions that listeners may have and to attempt to answer them.

Public speaking almost always requires a more formal use of language and a more formal delivery style than the other types. The use of jargon, poor grammar, or slang is usually not accepted or tolerated in public speeches. The speaker must use language precisely and must speak clearly in order to be heard throughout the audience. This may require the speaker to eliminate distracting vocal and physical mannerisms that might be tolerated in other types of communication.

Public speeches are often presented for three purposes: to inform, to persuade, and to entertain. They are also presented to introduce, to pay tribute, to accept, and to welcome. (These topics are considered in detail in the section on public speaking.)

public communication
Transmission of a message from one person who speaks to a number of individuals who listen.

Mass Communication

Mass communication generally signifies that professionals are communicating with or to a very large number of people via radio, television, newspapers, magazines, books, or movies. These channels constitute the means by which messages are directed to a large group (mass) of people. In these instances, the professional communicator—news reporter, anchor, or book author—acts as the source. The large audience functions as receivers. In mass communication, opportunities for feedback are often minimal, given the one-way nature of communication. In some situations, though, an individual audience member (receiver) may write a letter to the editor of a newspaper, send an email to a news reporter, or call in to a radio show.

mass communication
Occurs when professionals communicate with or to a large number of people via radio, television, newspapers, magazines, books, or movies.

Communication via Social Media

communication via social media

Any communication transmitted through digital devices or platforms (iPhones, text messaging, Facebook, Twitter, Vine, Snapchat, etc.).

Communication via social media is any communication transmitted through digital devices or platforms (smartphones, text messaging, Facebook, Twitter, Vine, Snapchat and so on). These technologies are often highly accessible and allow us to accomplish multiple objectives. For example, you can use your smartphone to text with a friend review your Facebook and Twitter feeds, tweet to your followers, send and receive emails, snap a picture and post it to Facebook, and record a video and post it to Vine Snapchat, or YouTube.

Technology has advanced so quickly and is so popular that we can purchase relatively inexpensive hardware and software and have global "face-to-face conversations." Digital cameras allow us to share pictures of ourselves, our families, and special events with friends all over the world. Skype and FaceTime allow us to video conference with others in near or faraway places. As technology continues to develop and change, one thing remains consistent: Communication is the process that helps us *make connections*. Communication is a learned tool that enables us to function in our personal and family lives, in our social and work lives, and in our roles as citizens of the world. Many people are concerned that technology will negatively affect the way we interact with each other on a one-to-one basis. Therefore, it becomes increasingly important to search for ways to use it in a positive manner. If you email a campus administrator or an employer, remember to use appropriate grammar, spelling, and punctuation. Do not use emoticons that are common in texting. If you're making a request by mail or phone, be sure you are courteous and clear about who you are and what you seek. You are judged by how well you communicate through whatever means you choose.

Distinguishing Social Media from Face-to-Face Communication

1.7 Differentiate social media from face-to-face communication.

We tend to use social media because we perceive it as quick and convenient. Is one form of social media different from another type of technology? Are social media really that different from face-to-face communication? The simple answer is "yes." The complete answer, though, is much more complex. For many years, communication technology scholar Nancy Baym has examined how humans create personal connections in an age of increasing reliance on social media.[19] She writes that seven concepts help us distinguish different forms of social media from one another and from face-to-face communication.

Interactivity

interactivity

Refers to the ability of a communication tool to facilitate social interaction between groups or individuals.

Interactivity refers to the ability of a communication tool to facilitate social interaction between groups or individuals. Unlike most television shows and, to a certain degree, radio, social media allow us to talk back. Because social media foster interactivity, they also lead to new possibilities to remain connected and engaged with others. Face-to-face communication, like certain forms of social media, is highly interactive. Facebook and text messaging permit us to remain linked with our local and long-distance friends and family. Many businesses use Facebook and other social networking tools to remain connected with and gather feedback from customers.

Temporal Structure

Face-to-face communication is instantaneous—you say something to your friend, and almost immediately he responds with verbal and nonverbal messages. Certain forms of social media may not feature this luxury. A device's **temporal structure** refers to the time it takes to send and receive messages. Face-to-face conversations, phone calls, and online instant messages occur in real time and are **synchronous** forms of communication whereby each person simultaneously serves as sender and receiver. When we use email, send a text message, or post on a friend's Facebook wall, delays often occur and we must alternate being the sender and receiver of a message. These interactions are **asynchronous** methods of communication, but often, they could be just as synchronous as a phone call. How quickly does it take you to respond to a text message? More than likely you feel a strong need to respond and maintain a connection with the person who texts you. In the workplace, colleagues often send and reply to emails so quickly that the exchange could easily be viewed as a synchronous form of communication.

Synchronous social media can make messages feel more personal,[20] and even make you feel more connected with your significant other when you are far apart.[21] Unlike some synchronous social media, the asynchronous types may permit you to more strategically manage your self-presentation. You can spend considerable time crafting an email to your professor that explains your most recent absence from class. If you get into a heated argument with your romantic partner and storm out of the room, you may find it easier to compose a long email that details your frustrations, feelings, and plans for the future. We can place fewer demands on a person's time when we use asynchronous social media, but we will likely wait longer than we would like for a response.

temporal structure
Refers to the time it takes to send and receive messages.

synchronous
Channels of communication that allow participants to simultaneously serve as sender and receiver.

asynchronous
Channels of communication that allow participants to take turns serving as sender and receiver.

Social Cues

Many of the challenges we experience with social media derive from a lack of **social cues**—the verbal and nonverbal features of a message that offer more information about the context, the meaning, and the identities of the involved parties. Face-to-face social cues often include facial expression, vocal tone, eye contact, and hand gestures. The absence of specific social cues with *lean* social media devices can create interpersonal challenges and misinterpretations. *Rich* forms of communication, such as Skype, FaceTime, and face-to-face communication, offer a full range of social cues, while other lean tools, such as a telephone, provide fewer.[22]

Rich social media devices provide more social cues than do lean devices. In calling your friend's cell phone when you are both on campus, what is the first thing you say after your friend answers the phone? You probably say something like, "Hey, where are you?" As is the case with many lean forms of social media, we have no idea of the physical location of our conversational partners. Yet, we seek this information to develop an understood context and make the media appear richer than it really is. In face-to-face conversations, you know for sure whether your friend is busy, preoccupied, and unable to talk. If we are on a cell phone, we are unaware of these social cues unless we ask. Apps like Vine are rich in social cues and allow users to quickly capture and edit six-second-long looping videos of their location and share it with followers on social media.

social cues
The verbal and nonverbal features of a message that offer more information about the context, the meaning, and the identities of the involved parties.

Replicability

Face-to-face conversations are difficult, if not impossible, to replicate. Stated simply, it is extremely difficult to recreate the exact words, nonverbal communication cues, and emotions felt during a particular interaction. You may find it difficult to explain to

replicability

When communication occurs in an environment that makes it easy to record and redistribute past messages.

your mother what was said during a recent fight with your boyfriend. Social media's **replicability** means that communication can occur in an environment that makes it easy to record and redistribute past messages. The posts we make to an online blog or a friend's Facebook page can easily be replicated and shared with others. One thing is for sure—we can never go back in time and change what message we sent; the meaning will always remain.

Storage

In many ways, face-to-face conversations, once they occur, are gone forever. Social media's ability for storage allows messages to be digitally saved and made accessible to other people. Facebook, Twitter, and other tools can log conversations and create a permanent storage space for our messages. Posts to a friend's Facebook page may be there to stay unless the friend deletes them. The harsh and abrasive asynchronous email that you send to a coworker can be easily forwarded along to your supervisor, where it may be stored for future use. After a friend uploads pictures to Facebook following a fun weekend, how long does it take before people are tagged in those photos? Not long. In a matter of minutes, the record of your activities can be stored online. Apps like Snapchat let users take photos and videos (known as "Snaps") and send them to a list of recipients. The user can set a time limit (usually 1-10 seconds) for how long recipients can view their Snaps before they are automatically deleted. Although Snapchat uniquely eliminates the storage feature of social media, now, more than ever, we must remain attuned to the differences between social media and face-to-face communication—especially in light of social media's reach.

Reach

Unlike face-to-face communication, social media have tremendous reach, or the ability to connect with individuals in local and long-distance places. Face-to-face communication is often limited to those individuals who can fit in a particular room. However, in one single keystroke or tap of a smartphone screen, a message can be sent to thousands or perhaps millions of people. Twitter provides a platform for messages to **"go viral"**—or reach enormous audiences by "infecting" viewers and users with the message.

go viral

A phrase used to describe a message that reaches enormous audiences by "infecting" viewers and users with the message.

Feedback is a critical component of the communication process. It allows a sender to determine whether the communication has been received and understood as intended.

In July 2014, media personalities in the United States began participating in what quickly became known as the ALS Ice Bucket Challenge, an activity designed to promote awareness of and donations to the research of amyotrophic lateral sclerosis (or ALS). Within 24 hours of being challenged, participants must record a video in which they announce their acceptance of the challenge, pour a bucket of ice water on their heads, and then nominate more people to take the challenge. Participants then post their videos to social media. Various versions of the challenge exist. In the most popular version, the participant is expected to donate $10 to ALS if they take the challenge or $100 if they do not. After the ALS Ice Bucket Challenge appeared on several popular television shows, it went viral. The viral videos made their way to Facebook and Twitter, where friends and friends of friends posted the video to their pages, accepted the challenge, and then posted their Ice Bucket Challenge video to social media. Public awareness and charitable donations to ALS charities soared. As of October 2014, the activity raised over $34 million to expedite the search for treatments and a cure for ALS.[23] The incredible reach of social media has dramatically changed how we send, receive, and interpret messages. The ability to record a video, snap a picture, and send a message to thousands now rests in the palms of our hands.

Social media's reach has dramatically changed how we send, receive, and interpret messages. Within one day, Ted Williams—"The Man with the Golden Voice"—went from being a disheveled panhandler to a well-groomed voice-over artist who was appearing on several national television shows.

Mobility

The various forms of social media feature varying degrees of mobility, or the extent to which a device is portable or stationary. Unlike social media, face-to-face communication is mobile to the extent that we are able to walk, run, or travel to a particular location to engage in conversation. Clunky desktop computers and landline telephones tie us to a specific spot. Social media users can access applications on a stationary desktop computer, a portable laptop, or a smartphone from any location on earth—as long as cell phone service or wireless Internet access exists. The mobility of certain social media enables us to always be in touch with our friends and family. Facebook and other social networks are not accessed only on a desktop computer; they are readily available on smartphones and other tablet devices.

Because social media keep us connected with others at all times, we are often expected to respond instantly to an email, text message, or tweet. Social media have connected us but essentially made us accountable to others at all times. And new devices like the Apple Watch will further increase our ability to remain connected with others.

Misconceptions About Communication

1.8 **Summarize** five common myths about communication.

Several misconceptions keep many of us from examining *our own* communication more closely. Notice the emphasis on *our own*! Most of us who have problems communicating tend to look for the fault in places other than ourselves. Becoming aware that these misconceptions exist and that many people accept them as truths should help us understand why the study of communication is necessary. Here are some of the most common myths that interfere with the improvement of personal communication skills.

Myth 1: Communication Is a Cure-All

The first misconception is that communication has the magical power to solve all of our problems. The act of communicating with others does not carry any guarantees. Obviously, without communication, we cannot address problems, but sometimes communication can create more of them than it solves.

Here is one example: Our neighbor is a realtor. She created a flyer for distribution in the neighborhood and asked me to read it and tell her what I thought about it. She had obviously spent a great deal of time on the project. When I looked it over, I told her that I thought the message would not reach what she indicated was her intended audience. She became quite agitated and said that I was the only one who had anything negative to say. I had taken her message literally, when she really wanted affirmation that she had done a good job. How might I have avoided angering her?

Communication can help to eliminate or reduce our problems, but it is not a panacea. Communicating itself does not make the difference; the message that is communicated does.

Myth 2: Quantity Means Quality

We often assume that the more we communicate, the better. People who communicate a great deal are often perceived as more friendly, competent, and powerful and as having greater leadership potential than those who do not. However, quantity of communication is not the same as quality. A mother tells her high school son that he cannot wear a certain shirt to his older brother's college graduation ceremony. The younger son likes the shirt and feels that it is appropriate and that everyone else wears similar shirts. Neither mother nor son will change her or his view, and they continue to argue. Each becomes more defensive and louder until another family member steps in to stop the argument. In this case, as in the one described in the first myth section, it isn't the act or the amount of communication, but the content of communication, that makes the difference.

The convenience of social media allows us to send email messages, tweets, and text messages in rapid succession. Have you ever received multiple texts from a friend within seconds? Perhaps the initial text autocorrected to a word your friend did not intend to send and, as a result, your friend fired off a text to correct the error and then a series of others to apologize and add on to the conversation. One carefully composed text message would have been much more effective than a series of short texts with typographical errors.

Myth 3: Meaning Is in the Words We Use

If your sister tells you that she doesn't feel well, what would that mean to you? That she is sick? That she has a cold? That she has an upset stomach? That her feelings have been hurt? It could mean any number of things because without context and more information, the statement is not clear. If she tells you that she has a cold and doesn't feel well, is that message clear? Well, at least it would narrow the choices a little. Confusion may arise because the statement "I don't feel well" is relative; that is, it might not signify the same thing to you as it does to her. Some people use this statement to refer to a minor discomfort, whereas others mean they are more seriously ill. The words themselves could refer to many degrees or types of conditions. Thus, *meanings are in people and not in the words they use.*

The notion that words contain meanings is probably the most serious misconception of all. Words have meaning only when we give them meaning. *No two people share the same meanings for all words because no two people completely share the same background and experiences.* Thus, the meaning of a word cannot be separated from the person using it.

Myth 4: We Have a Natural Ability to Communicate

Many people believe that because we are born with the physical and mental equipment needed for communication, it must be a natural ability. This simply is not true. The capacity to communicate, like almost everything we do, is learned. Most of us possess the physical ability to tie our shoes, but we still have to learn how the strings go together. Similarly, most of us are born with the ability to see, but that does not make us able to read. Reading requires knowledge of the alphabet, the acquisition of vocabulary, and practice. The ability to communicate requires not only capability but also an understanding of how human communication works and an opportunity to use that knowledge. By taking this class, you are working toward improving very important communication skills.

Competent communication is essential in all aspects of our everyday lives. Effective communication enhances our personal, social, and career relationships and allows us to make connections with people from other cultures.

Myth 5: Communication Is Reversible

All of us sometimes make a mistake in communication. We might think that we can take something back, but that is impossible. Once something is said, it is out there; the listener will have to deal with that message, and the speaker will have to try to explain and compensate for what was said. For example, in a moment of anger, we say something that we regret and later ask the other person to "forget I even said that." Although the other person may forgive us for speaking in anger, it is not likely that he or she will forget what was said. When we communicate through writing, we can take things back until we let someone else see what we've written. When we send oral messages, others can hear and will respond to what we say, even if we don't really mean to say things the way they come out.

If you are exchanging email messages with a manager or colleague, it is important to remain aware of your receivers. If you raise a sensitive workplace issue in an email and quickly click "send," you may later notice that your boss was inadvertently copied on the email. If you did not intend to send this email to your supervisor, you may have some explaining to do. Always remember that communication is irreversible. As in face-to-face communication, the moment we send a message through social media, that message is out there for the world to see and react to. It is important, therefore, to carefully organize our thoughts and choose our words before we utter (or type) them to others.

repertoire

Wide range of communication behaviors from which effective communicators make choices.

Guidelines

Improving Communication Competence

1. **Understand the role of communication in your life.** Be aware of the complexity of the communication process and different types of communication, and understand how face-to-face communication is different from communication via social media.

2. **Recognize the many misconceptions about effective communication.** We need to realize that myths about communication may hinder our ability to develop effective communication.

3. **Increase your knowledge of effective communication behaviors.** Good communicators have developed a broad communication **repertoire**, a range of communication behaviors from which to choose.[24]

4. **Competent communicators possess the ability to coordinate several communication tasks simultaneously.** For example, a competent communicator will, at the same time, choose a way of conveying a message, consider what the receiver's various responses might be, and plan a way to restate the message if the first attempt is not effective.

5. **Background knowledge about communication, practical experience, and feedback given in the classroom will help you think on your feet and make better decisions as you communicate.** You will also gain confidence and the ability to evaluate your skills as your work in this course progresses.

Summary

Communication: Making Connections

Objective 1.1 **Explain** how communication competence allows you to make connections with the outside world.

Communication competence is the ability to take part in effective communication that is characterized by skills and understandings that enable communicators to exchange messages successfully.

What Is Communication?

Objective 1.2 **Define** communication.

Communication is the simultaneous sharing and creating of meaning through human symbolic interaction. It involves a range of behaviors and occurs in a variety of situations.

Why Should We Study Communication?

Objective 1.3 **Identify** four reasons for studying communication.

The ability to *communicate* (not simply to utter words) is learned; learning to be a competent communicator is a difficult, lifelong project.

- We live in a technological society and use social media to interact with others in our social network.
- Communication plays a vital role in career success.
- Communication involves a high degree of ethical behavior.
- We live in a multicultural society and interact with people from different cultures.

Principles Of Communication

Objective 1.4 **Explain** the fundamental principles of communication.

To appreciate the true nature of communication, it is important to understand four fundamental principles. These principles are readily applicable to life beyond the classroom.

- Communication is a process because it involves a series of actions that has no beginning or end and is constantly changing.
- Communication is a system, a combination of parts interdependently acting to form a whole.
- Communication is transactional because messages are simultaneously sent and received between people.
- Communication can be intentional or unintentional.

Essential Components Of Communication

Objective 1.5 **Define** the essential components in the communication process.

Several components interact when two people are communicating. These components are constantly in flux as communicators react to each other.

- The source/sender is the creator of the message.
- A message is the communication produced by the source.
- Anything that changes the meaning of an intended message is called interference.
- A channel is the means by which messages flow between sources and receivers.
- A receiver analyzes, interprets, and translates messages into meaning.
- Feedback is the response to a message that a receiver sends back to a source.
- The environment includes the psychological and physical surroundings in which communication occurs.
- The broad circumstances or situation in which communication occurs is referred to as the context.

Types of Communication

Objective 1.6 **Differentiate** the various types of communication: intrapersonal, interpersonal (including group), public, mass, and communication via social media.

The type of communication is usually distinguished by the number of people involved, by the purpose of the message, and by the degree of formality with which it occurs.

- Intrapersonal communication is the process of understanding information within oneself.
- Interpersonal communication is creating and sharing meaning between persons who are in a relationship.
- Public communication occurs when a message is transmitted from one person to a number of individuals who listen.
- Mass communication means that professionals are communicating with or to a very large number of people via radio, television, newspapers, magazines, books, or movies.
- Communication via social media is any communication transmitted through digital devices or platforms such as smartphones, text messaging, Facebook, Twitter, Skype, and so on.

Distinguishing Social Media from Face-to-Face Communication

Objective 1.7 Differentiate social media from face-to-face communication.

Several concepts help us distinguish different forms of social media from one another and from face-to-face communication. These concepts help us understand how we make connections with others in an age in which we rely more and more on social media.

- Interactivity refers to the ability of a communication tool to facilitate social interaction between groups or individuals.
- A social media device's temporal structure refers to the time it takes to send and receive messages.
- Social cues are the verbal and nonverbal features of a message that offer more information about the context, the meaning, and the identities of the involved parties.
- Social media's replicability means that communication can occur in an environment that makes it easy to record and redistribute past messages.
- Unlike face-to-face communication, social media's ability for storage allows messages to be digitally saved and made accessible to other people.

- Unlike face-to-face communication, social media have tremendous reach, or the ability to connect with individuals in local and long-distance places.
- Social media feature varying degrees of mobility, or the extent to which a device is portable or stationary.

Misconceptions About Communication

Objective 1.8 Summarize five common myths about communication.

Several misconceptions keep many of us from examining *our own* communication more closely. Many people who have problems communicating tend to look for the fault in places other than themselves.

- Communication has the magical power to solve all of our problems. It does not.
- We often assume that the more we communicate, the better. However, the quantity of communication is not the same as the quality.
- Meaning is in the words we use. Actually, meanings are in people and not in the words they use.
- We have a natural ability to communicate. That ability, like almost everything we do, is learned.
- Communication is reversible. In truth, once something is said, it is out there. We cannot take it back.

Discussion Starters

1. Why is communication regarded as difficult and complex?

2. Whom do you identify as an effective communicator?

3. What is the role of communication in our lives?

4. Explain what it means when we say that communication is a process.

5. How does a system differ from a process?

6. How can feedback motivate you to be more effective?

7. What can you do to improve your own communication with people from another culture?

8. What are some of the differences between face-to-face communication and communication via social media?

9. What social media devices influence our communication and the quality of the messages we send and receive?

Chapter 2
Connecting Perception and Communication

 Learning Objectives

This chapter will help you:

2.1 **Make** the connection between perception and your communication competence.

2.2 **Understand** the three stages of perception and how they affect your communication.

2.3 **Identify** seven reasons why different people may perceive the same situation in different ways.

2.4 Accurately **interpret and check** your perceptions to improve your communication competence.

Making Everyday Connections

As discussed in the opening of Chapter 1 and throughout that chapter, it is clear that social media plays a predominant role in our everyday lives. We knowingly share information electronically, but many of us don't realize the extent of what is communicated through social media without our knowledge or permission, and how that information may be perceived or used. For example, Jill, a college student, is a relatively conservative person compared to most, especially when it comes to what she posts on her Facebook pages, where she also limits access to her closest friends. Jordan, a friend from the same hometown, and Jill have been writing on each other's wall for several years. Much of what they write is conversational in tone, but it often contains misspellings, incomplete sentences, and some inappropriate language. At a large party in their hometown, Jordan took photos of Jill and others acting a bit crazy and suggestive after they had too much to drink. Jordan tagged the photos to Jill and several others. At the time, Jill laughed when she first saw the photos. However, several weeks later she realized that the photos of her were getting around to too many of her friends and others. She asked Jordan to delete them. He did.

Jill, a graduating senior, finally got an interview with the Gallup Corporation in Omaha, Nebraska, for her dream job. Jill had the interview and thought she did really well and was pretty certain she would get an offer. Joyce, the hiring supervisor at Gallup, knew that Nicole, an employee who works with her, attended the same small liberal arts college as Jill. Joyce asked Nicole if she knew anything about Jill. Nicole said she didn't know Jill well, but knows of Jill. Nicole, a Facebook friend of Jordan's, receives all of his posts and photos. She told Joyce that she has seen several posts and a lot of photos of Jill on Jordan's page. Joyce asked if she could see what was posted. On the basis of the photos, the supervisor decided not to offer Jill the job.

Questions to Think About

1. Was the supervisor justified in her perception of Jill? Why or why not?

2. Was Nicole ethical in sharing the photos of Jill without Jill's knowledge? Why or why not?

3. What influences our perceptions more—what we see or what we hear? Explain.

4. What lessons can we learn from the above scenario about perception and its role in communicating with others?

5. How might a competent communicator respond to the above situation? If you were Jill, what might you say to the supervisor, if anything? To Nicole?

6. Describe a situation or situations in which technology, such as a social networking site, a text, a tweet, Instagram, or even broader media, influenced your perceptions of others or an event.

Perception and Communication

2.1   Make the connection between perception and your communication competence.

Perception involves selecting, organizing, and interpreting information to give meaning to our communication and lives. Our perceptions, based on our experiences, give meaning to our communication and also influence what and how we communicate with others.

Perception is at the heart of our communication. It can also be argued that without communication perceptions could not exist. Thus, equally true is the statement that communication lies at the heart of our perceptions. Robert L. Scott, a communication scholar, writes, "Nothing is clear in and of itself but in some context for some person."[1] A difference between two people's perceptions, for example, does not necessarily make the perception of one person more correct or accurate than that of the other. It does, however, mean that communication between individuals who see things differently may require more understanding, negotiation, persuasion, and tolerance of those differences.

Perception, like communication, is a complex phenomenon. To receive stimuli from our surroundings and to form perceptions require that we use at least one of our five senses: hearing, touching, smelling, seeing, and tasting.

Perception

The process of selecting, organizing, and interpreting information to give personal meaning to the communication we receive.

Our perceptions do influence our reactions and our communication. It is virtually impossible for our feelings about things to be the same as others'. We perceive feelings based on past experiences and communication, sometimes from unreliable sources. Why do you think Tim Tebow, a quarterback in the NFL, is kneeling? Based on rumors circulating in November 2014, Tebow was said to be arrested for soliciting a prostitute. How would that news affect your perceptions? The rumors were published by *Daily Leak*, a website that publishes fake news stories.

Our perceptions—whether complete or incomplete, accurate or inaccurate—influence our communication and decisions, as illustrated in the "Making Everyday Connections" example at the beginning of the chapter. For example, Jordan's Facebook photos showing Jill acting wild or foolish were perceived negatively by the supervisor, even though she had never met Jill and didn't know anything about her. Our perceptions of people, situations, events, and objects and how they communicate represent our reality. However, our perception of reality may not be the same as someone else's. For example, when one person says to another, "I understand how difficult this might be for you," the statement is based on one person's perception of another's reality. It does not mean he or she actually knows what the other person is experiencing. Competent communicators understand the role of perception and its influence on communication and vice versa. Competent communicators also know that their perception of a single communication, event, or situation may be only part of the story, and that they often need more information before drawing final conclusions. They are not afraid to seek out more information or to ask questions before coming to any conclusions.

The Perception Process

2.2 Understand the three stages of perception and how they affect your communication.

Perceiving in and of itself appears simple enough. After all, we do it all the time, and it seems so natural that we hardly give it much thought. But perceiving is a complex thought process that, if not understood, could lead to communication misunderstandings—some quite costly—such as losing an internship, a promotion, or a friend. The first stage of perception is awareness of our surroundings and selecting what we will attend to. Second, we organize the information in a way that makes sense to us. Third, we interpret or assign meaning to the information we receive. Finally, we must be able to communicate our perceptions to others. This process is summarized in Table 2.1.

Selection

Many people imagine the brain to be similar in operation to a video camera; information enters through one of the senses and is stored in the brain. Actually, the

Table 2.1 The Perception Process

Term	Definition	Example
Selection	Sorting one stimulus from another	Selective exposure Selective attention Selective retention
Organization	Sorting, organizing, or categorizing	Closure Proximity Similarity
Interpretation	Assigning meaning to stimuli	Based on past experience Based on new situations Based on opinions of others

environment has far too much information for the brain to absorb at once, so the brain ignores much of it. It accepts a certain amount of information and organizes it into meaningful patterns. All of these connections happen in milliseconds. For example, the first time you walked into a classroom, what did you notice? More than likely your senses were fully or at least partially engaged and you observed who else was in the room. You saw and heard other students, some of whom you may have known from previous classes, and others whom you didn't know. You may have seen a smart board, the teacher, and other aspects of the classroom and those in it. The question is, what did you take away from the experience and why? What did you communicate, if anything, to others you know?

We process and catalog each person, sound, object, or surrounding, especially when new or novel. However, we all are creatures of habit, and when others behave in routine or predictable ways, we are more likely to gloss over or ignore important details, which can lead to misunderstandings, missed communication, or inaccurate communication. Competent communicators are *aware* of what is happening so that they make good choices about what to ignore and what to attend to. Because they know it is impossible to attend to, sense, perceive, retain, and give meaning to every stimulus or message they encounter, they *select* the relevant information and narrow their focus. **Selection** occurs when we mentally sort one thing from another, based on our previous experiences. Selection is of three types: selective exposure, selective attention, and selective retention.

selection
Sorting of one stimulus from another.

SELECTIVE EXPOSURE The deliberate choices we make to experience or to avoid experiencing particular stimuli are referred to as **selective exposure**. For example, when we choose to attend to one thing over another we are using selective exposure. Taking in the sights, sounds, smells, and so on occurs only if we are paying attention to them.

selective exposure
The deliberate choices we make to experience or to avoid particular stimuli.

SELECTIVE ATTENTION Focusing on a specific message while ignoring or downplaying other stimuli is called **selective attention**. That is, you concentrate on something or someone of interest, and you eliminate or reduce the effects of all extraneous messages. For example, you focus on the accent and ignore the message. Attending to something usually requires a decisive effort, but even the best attempts to concentrate can be interrupted by distractions. For example, a cell phone going off in a quiet classroom, a loud sneeze, background talking, a siren, a baby's cry, a call for help, an odor, or a movement easily averts our attention. Continuing to attend to the original task usually requires extra effort. Similarly, when we converse with someone in a crowded lounge with loud music in the background, we focus on each other's words more attentively and ignore the other sounds. This blocking out of all extraneous stimuli to retain concentration is an instance of selective attention. Competent communicators quickly determine what is important to focus on and ignore extraneous stimuli, so that their communication is accurate.

selective attention
Focusing on a specific message while ignoring or downplaying other stimuli.

SELECTIVE RETENTION Because we cannot possibly remember all the information that we encounter, we also are selective in what we retain. **Selective retention** occurs when we choose to process and store specific information we want to eventually retrieve and use again. We are more likely to remember for a longer time any information that agrees with our views and to selectively forget information that does not. In addition, after perceiving and selecting certain stimuli, we may retain only a portion of them. For example, how many times have you listened to an instructor tell how to prepare an assignment and then, several days later, asked a classmate or the instructor about the assignment only to discover that, thinking you had completed it, you had actually finished only a portion? This happened because you selectively retained the pleasant parts and forgot the not-so-pleasant parts. Selection plays an important role in what, why, and how we communicate.

selective retention
The processing, storing, and retrieving of information that we have already selected, organized, and interpreted.

Organization

To help understand how we organize the information we receive and its effect on communication, consider what happens when you enter a room filled with people. When you first walk in, you begin to sort and organize people into groups or categories. Chances are you will initially look for people you know; by doing so, you are categorizing the people in the room according to those you know and those you don't. People you know and who happen to be nearest to you are those with whom you will likely communicate first. You will also probably spend more time with people you perceive to be like you than with those who are not.

The way our minds organize and sort information has a profound effect on how we perceive others, how we talk with them, and how they respond to us. We perceive things, places, and people because of who we are, our backgrounds and experiences, and how we see ourselves. We are also likely to focus on concrete aspects, such as a person's height, attractiveness, age, or race, rather than on abstract psychological aspects, such as sincerity, honesty, and so on.

Cognitive complexity is a term used by psychologists to measure and explain our ability to process, interpret, and store simple to intricate information. The more cognitively complex we are, the more sophisticated our perceptions. For example, as a cognitively complex person, you will notice several attributes about a person at the same time: talks a lot, dresses well, tells good jokes, and is attractive in appearance. A person who is less cognitively complex may only notice one of these characteristics. At an abstract psychological level, you might infer that the behaviors you observe reflect an extroverted, sincere, and self-confident personality. This level of assessment is a sophisticated explanation because it involves perceptions of why the person acts as he or she does, and it is based solely on concrete observations.

People with high levels of cognitive complexity are likely to be flexible in interpreting complicated events and situations and are able to integrate new information into their perceptions. Such people are also likely to use "person-centered" messages and take multiple attributes into account when communicating with others. For example, they are able to incorporate others' values, beliefs, appearance, and emotional needs into their messages. This ability allows those with high levels of cognitive complexity to be effective communicators because they are able to understand and process multiple perspectives at one time.

CLOSURE   One way to organize the stimuli around us is to fill in missing pieces and to extend lines in order to finish or complete a figure. This completion process is called **closure**. In Figure 2.1, we see a figure with what appear to be random, unconnected shapes. Through the process of closure we may transform the random shapes into an image of a cow. This occurs because we are always trying to make meaningless material meaningful. We perceive the image of the cow by mentally connecting the white spaces.

Filling in the blank spaces or missing information helps us categorize, label, and make sense of the things we see and hear. We sometimes do the same thing as we try to understand people. For example, if we met a Muslim student wearing a burka in one of our classes, we may fill in unknown information, such as the person's value system, beliefs, political views, or whether she is well educated or affluent, to help us understand the person. Unfortunately, what we fill in may be based on biases and ignorance.

When supplying missing information, competent communicators remain aware of what they are doing and remember to distinguish between what they know and what they don't. Otherwise they increase their chances of forming a wrong or inaccurate perception of the person. Inaccurate perceptions can adversely affect communication and can cost you a relationship, a job, or a new experience. For example, you decide, without complete information and based on a casual comment, that the person doesn't share your religious or political views, and so you don't listen, lose interest, or disregard the information because you see it as counter to your views. It may be that

cognitive complexity

A measure of our ability to process and store simple to complicated information.

closure

Filling in of details so that a partially perceived entity appears to be complete.

Figure 2.1 Closure: Cow or Incomplete Drawing?

The partial outlines of this shape lead us to fill in the missing lines so that we can make sense of it. This drawing of the visual data allows us to give meaning to the drawing.

you haven't probed enough to really know the person's views, and you may have just lost a possibly rewarding relationship.

Perceptions and their interpretations regarding people and events occur all the time. Differences in how those perceptions are interpreted depend upon the information received, our biases, and experiences. For example, the killing of Michael Brown, an 18-year-old black man who was fatally shot by Darren Wilson, a 28-year-old white Ferguson police officer, in Ferguson, Missouri, has led to both peaceful and violent protests regarding the killing of blacks by white police officers. The circumstances of the shooting and the subsequent decision of the grand jury not to indict Officer Wilson illustrate how perceptions of this tragedy not only influence our communication, but our behaviors as well.

PROXIMITY **Proximity** is the grouping of two or more stimuli that are close to one another based on the assumption that because objects or people appear together, they are similar. It is not unusual for some of us to think that people whose appearance, nationality, race, and origin are similar and who reside in the same community or belong to the same organization (fraternity, sorority, club, church, etc.) perceive others, events, and activities in the same way. For us to assume that they do would not only be inaccurate, but also wrong. Thus, we must be careful not to categorize or to communicate as if those who appear together think, behave, and believe the same way on every issue or situation. Competent communicators verify and do not categorize individuals based on their proximity to one another.

Proximity

The grouping of two or more stimuli that are close to one another.

SIMILARITY Organization based on **similarity** involves the grouping of stimuli that resemble one another in size, shape, color, or other traits. For example, Shelley, a sophomore who likes to party, might believe that others who enjoy partying resemble her in other ways as well. Thus, if Shelley likes both partying and hiking, she might assume that others who like to party will also like hiking. Of course, this may be wishful thinking on her part; just because two people are similar in one attribute doesn't automatically mean they will be similar in another. We sometimes make perceptual assumptions, much as Shelley did, when we see people from different cultures. We tend to assume that because people are similar in appearance, they must behave and think similarly as well. Another example may be the events surrounding the killing of Michael Brown, Eric Garner, and Tamir Rice. The similarities are that

Similarity

The grouping of stimuli that resemble one another in size, shape, color, or other traits.

Making Connections for Success

The Web and Perception

Kevin is a senior whose Facebook page is loaded with pictures of him partying and goofing around. He spends hours making sure his page lets others know of the fun he has, whether it be on spring break or just having a good time with friends. Most every picture he posts or is tagged in show him with a beer or some other drink in his hand. His Instagram photos and messages are extensions of his Facebook page, which show him as less than serious about his education.

In his LinkedIn bio, Kevin indicates he has a 4.00 GPA, and that he is president of the Honors Club in Chemistry, which is his major. He also indicates he plans to go to med school after he graduates next month. He comes from a professional family; his mother and father are surgeons at the local hospital. He has been extremely active in a variety of campus and community organizations and is a member of a debate team.

1. Based only on the description of Kevin in the first paragraph, how would you describe him as a person, a student, or as a colleague if a friend were to show you his Facebook page?
2. You are on LinkedIn and you happen to come upon Kevin's bio. Again, having never met him in person, how would you describe him as a person, as a student, or as a colleague?
3. You meet Kevin at a party and find him to be really quite crazy in terms of his behaviors, but you also have seen his LinkedIn bio. How would you describe him as a person, as a student, or as a colleague?
4. What can we learn about perception and communication from this exercise?

---

all three of these individuals were black and all three were killed by white police officers who were acquitted of any wrongdoing. Based on this limited information and media coverage, we might group the three killings as the same and not perceive the differences. All three incidents are very different, and yet so much of the communication related to the three killings portrays them as similar. When we perceive people, events, or objects as similar it is difficult to see differences, and thus our communication with others often doesn't distinguish them from one another. This, in turn, makes discussion of differing perceptions of such tragedies difficult, if even possible.

Interpretation

interpretation
Assigning of meaning to stimuli.

Interpretation of what we see, hear, taste, touch, and smell is an integral part of who we are and how our perceptions influence our communication. **Interpretation** is the assigning of meaning to stimuli. We use our experiences, both past and present, as well as the opinions of others to help interpret the meaning of stimuli.

INTERPRETATION BASED ON PAST EXPERIENCE   Our interpretations of stimuli depend on our past experiences. For example, when you first arrived on campus, you probably either asked for help or consulted a map to locate various buildings and classrooms. With each passing day, however, you found it easier to get around and even discovered shortcuts from one place to another. As we become familiar with our surroundings, we don't have to think about where we are going; we just go. When we give directions to someone on how to get from one place to another on campus, it seems intuitive because we have done it so many times. We falsely assume that the person we are giving directions to will understand exactly what we are telling them. A distinct relationship exists between our perceptions and communication.

INTERPRETATION BASED ON NEW SITUATIONS   Although past experiences form a basis or foundation for interpreting our environment, we must be careful not to let them keep us from finding fresh meanings in new situations or events. For example, a bad experience with one professor does not automatically mean it will be the same with another. The competent communicator will view the previous experience as a lesson to ask more questions and do more research before he or she reaches a final opinion.

Competent communicators know that information, regardless of its source or form, must always be interpreted in order to have meaning. However, they also know

Perceptual Differences

2.3 Identify seven reasons why different people may perceive the same situation in different ways.

Our past experiences, our physical makeup, our cultural background, and our current psychological state determine what we perceive; how we interpret, evaluate, and organize our perceptions; and our actions in response to them. The following sections discuss how these factors influence our perceptions.

Perceptual Set and Stereotyping

When we ignore new information and instead rely solely on our past experiences—fixed, previously determined views of events, objects, and people—to interpret information, we are using a perceptual set.[3] A **perceptual set** allows our past experiences to control or focus our perceptions so that we ignore information that is different or has changed about an event, object, or person. It is a form of stereotyping. **Stereotyping** refers to the categorizing of events, objects, and people without regard to unique individual characteristics and qualities. Stereotyping, for example, exists in nearly every intercultural situation, usually because of people's unfamiliarity with the other culture. Stereotyping is pervasive because of the human psychological need to categorize and classify information. Through stereotyping, we profile people and their behaviors. This tendency may hamper our communication by causing us to overlook individual characteristics and differences.

perceptual set
A fixed, previously determined view of events, objects, or people.

Stereotyping
The categorizing of events, objects, and people without regard to unique individual characteristics and qualities.

In addition, stereotypes often oversimplify, generalize, or exaggerate traits or qualities and thus are based on half-truths, distortions, and false premises—hardly fertile ground for successful communication. Finally, stereotypes repeat and reinforce beliefs until they come to be taken as the truth. For example, it is not unusual for some of us to assume that student athletes go to college only because they want to participate in their sport. Stereotypes ultimately perpetuate inaccuracies about people and thus may impede or reinforce our communication about those whom we stereotype. Although many stereotypes are negative, positive stereotypes can be found as well. When we stereotype male students as decisive or female students as sensitive, for instance, we project positive images that should apply equally to both genders.

Perceptual set may prevent us from seeing things that differ from what we expect to see and hear or from noticing changes in people and things. Massimo Piattelli-Palmarini, in his book *Inevitable Illusions: How Mistakes of Reason Rule Our Minds,* uses the example of the St. Louis arch to illustrate the point that "the eye sees what it sees, even when we know what we know."[4] He points out that the arch is as wide as it is tall, yet it appears to be taller than it is wide. According to Piattelli-Palmarini, this inability to see the similarity between the arch's height and width demonstrates that our minds are unable to adjust our perceptions even when we know the facts. He says the errors, or illusions, usually occur without our being aware of them. Perceptual set operates in a similar manner. Differences among what we do, what happens to us, and what is innate within us create bias, something that all of us have.[5] Our brains always make sure, or at least try to make sure, that what we see or hear, or both see *and* hear, represents reality rather than assumptions that may be false. A 19th-century humorist, Artemus Ward, put it this way: "It ain't so much the things we don't know that get us in trouble. It's the things we do know that ain't so."[6] We are all, at times, victims of unconsciously making inaccurate assumptions that can seriously affect our communication.

Perceptual sets, like stereotypes, do not always limit or hinder us. Sometimes they help us make decisions more efficiently. They provide us with expectations of how things, events, or people should be, and they enable us to compare our expectations with the reality of the moment and to respond accordingly. For example, when a student from China comes to the United States to attend college, many of us would expect the student to lack fluency in English. However, after talking with the student for just a few minutes, you find that not only is she fluent in English, but she also sounds more American than many of us who were born in the United States. You ask her where she learned to speak English so well, and she tells you that she has studied English most of her life, that she studied in England for five years while growing up, and that she is a translator of Chinese to English for government officials in China. A competent communicator avoids the assumption that perceptual sets or stereotypes will always be complete or accurate. Many communication scholars believe that *the greatest single problem with human communication is the assumption that our perceptions are always correct.*[7]

Attribution Error

Attribution

The complex process through which we attempt to understand the reasons behind others' behaviors.

It is human nature to attribute, or assign, causes to people's behavior. **Attribution** is the complex process through which we attempt to understand the reasons behind others' behaviors. Two factors influence our assumptions about our own and others' behavior: the *situation* (environment) and the *disposition* (traits of the person). We are always trying to explain why people behave the way they do; to seek an explanation, we must make assumptions. For example, imagine that you witness the following scene. A classmate arrives over an hour late for a study session. He walks in and drops his iPad on the floor. While trying to pick it up, his glasses fall out of his coat pocket and break. Reaching for his glasses he spills his Coke all over the floor. How would you explain these events? The chances are good that you would reach conclusions such as, "He is disorganized and clumsy." Are your attributions accurate? Perhaps. But it is also possible that he was late because his car would not start, dropped his iPad because it had a slick cover, and spilled his Coke because he was picking up his glasses. Research shows that we are more likely to overestimate dispositional causes and underestimate situational causes of others' actions. This bias is referred to as the **fundamental attribution error**.[8] Fundamental attribution error occurs when we perceive others acting as they do because they are "that kind of person" rather than because of any external factors that may have influenced their behavior.

Fundamental attribution error

Perceiving others as acting as they do because they are "that kind of person" rather than because of any external factors that may have influenced their behavior.

Suppose you come across a fellow student who is having trouble starting her car. You decide to help by giving her some suggestions on how to start it. She looks at you as though you were an idiot, snaps at you, and ignores you. You get a bit angry and think to yourself, "*she's* the idiot"; she is rude, insensitive, and self-centered, and doesn't value the help you were offering. Is it possible that several others had already offered the same advice and it failed? Or that she has had an extremely rough day, having failed an exam and broke up with her boyfriend, and the car problem was the icing on the cake? This is another example of a fundamental attribution error. The error is often made because we have no other reference point except the observable behavior of the person in question; thus, we are likely to make a judgment about the person to appease ourselves. It also can lead to faulty and inaccurate communication, especially if we communicate without verification of the facts or situation.

In our own case, we know the situation, so we know what accounts for our behavior. It is often easier to "assume" rather than determine what actually causes someone to behave the way he or she does. For example, a student who speaks with an accent and has trouble expressing himself in class might be perceived as not very intelligent. However, after the first exam you learn that the same student scored the highest grade on the exam. This surprises you because of your first impression of the student; but then, in talking with the student, you discover that he is a biological science major with a straight-A GPA. What you didn't know is that the student suffers from communication apprehension. It is not uncommon to make this attribution error and make judgments that are inaccurate based on a person's ability to express hemselves. This is a fundamental attribution error based on the assumption that, because the student does not speak fluently, he lacks intelligence.

Think about the times when a person has communicated something about us without knowing what we have been going through; it probably angered us to some extent. As competent communicators, we need to learn how to avoid making fundamental attribution errors and taking too narrow a perspective. We should stop and think before making judgments about other people's behavior and at least ask ourselves if we are possibly overreacting or misjudging the situation. Through such questioning, we will improve our ability to form accurate perceptions, as well as our communication.

Physical Characteristics

Our weight, height, body shape, health, strength, and ability to use our five senses can account for differences in what we perceive. For example, if you are visually impaired, you likely experience the world in ways that a sighted person may find difficult to comprehend or even imagine. Sighted people might not automatically take such differences into account, thus making communication a bit awkward.

It is not unusual that when we meet someone for the first time, we react to a variety of factors, no matter how superficial, resulting in emotional reactions that lead to a positive or negative image of that person. One such factor is the clothing the person is wearing. Beyond such factors as neatness or perceived cost, clothing color and style appear to have an effect on our perception. It seems that we make an automatic association between brightness and affect; specifically, bright is good, and dark equals bad.[9] Perceptions are also influenced by observable disabilities, the presence of eyeglasses, a person's height and physique, and facial hair on men.[10] Once again, perceptions can lead to assumptions, and those assumptions can influence how and what we communicate with others.

Psychological State

Another factor that influences or alters our perceptions of people, events, and things is our state of mind. All information coming to us passes through various filters and screens that sort and color what we receive and how we perceive it. Obviously, when everything is going well and we are in a positive frame of mind, we view things, events, and people much more positively than when our mind-set is negative. When we are under a great deal of stress or if we have a poor self-image, these conditions will influence how we perceive the world around us. Sometimes this distortion is small and temporary and has no appreciable effect on communication. At other times, our state of mind can actually reverse meaning or alter a message, changing how we select, organize, and interpret it. It is undeniable that psychological disposition can color or alter perceptions and, ultimately, communication. Think about how you feel when you are upset, angry, or frustrated with someone or something and when you are not. How does your disposition affect your communication with others? In the next chapter, the connections between self-concept and perception are discussed in more detail.

Cultural Background

Cultural background can also affect the perception of other people, events, and things. Culture has well over a hundred different definitions, each taking a different perspective. For our purposes, **culture** may be defined as "a set of interpretations about beliefs, values, norms, and social practices, which affect behaviors of a relatively large group of people."[11] A culture evolves through communication, beliefs, artifacts, and a style of living shared among people. A group's culture usually includes similarities in religion, language, thinking, social rules, laws, perceptions,

Culture

A set of interpretations about beliefs, values, norms, and social practices that affect behaviors of a relatively large group of people.

communicative style, and attitudes, all of which contribute to a group's identity as distinct from that of other cultural groups.

Take a moment and reflect on the cultural beliefs you hold that influence how you perceive the world and interact in it. Your views on work, education, freedom, age, competitiveness, personal space, cleanliness and hygiene, gender, loyalty, death and mourning, etiquette, health, status differentiation, bodily adornment, courtship, family, art, music, technology, and the like all play a role in your cultural identity. Your views also affect how you communicate and interact with others.

Cultural identity has little or nothing to do with physical features, such as skin color, shape of eyes, or sex, because these characteristics are passed on genetically and not by communication. Because people of a particular race or country are often taught similar beliefs, values, and attitudes, those similarities have created such labels as "African American," "Hispanic," "Native American," or "European American." Each of these labels, by definition, suggests that cultural differences exist among these groups, but the labels do not suggest that differences may also be found within the groups. Most of us have been conditioned to believe that people who are similar in race or nationality think and behave in the same way. This way of thinking, however, is likely to lead to misunderstandings and perceptual errors. For example, two Hispanic business owners, one in New York City and the other in rural Nebraska, while labeled "Hispanics," could have different values, beliefs, and lifestyles because of where they live. Yet both are labeled Hispanic. Therefore, to assume that they think and act similarly because they both are Hispanic or because of their physical features is an assumption that could prove wrong. The competent communicator does not rely on labels or physical characteristics to make assumptions about people's values, attitudes, beliefs, or behaviors. The competent communicator does, however, learn about others through communication and observations of their behaviors. The competent communicator seeks information and asks questions to ensure the accuracy of what is being perceived and communicated.

Culture is an integral part of each of us and determines many of our individual characteristics. Culture identifies us as members of a particular group and shapes our values and biases. Much cultural influence occurs without our realizing it: Typically, we are not conscious of how much of our behavior is conditioned by culture. The way we greet others, the way we use language, our opinions about what and when to eat, and many of our personal preferences are all culturally conditioned.[12]

The connection between culture and communication is extremely complex. In fact, because of culture we learn to communicate, according to McDaniel, Samovar, and Porter. For example, a Korean, an Egyptian, or an American learns to communicate like other Koreans, Egyptians, or Americans, respectively. Each knows that certain behaviors convey certain meanings because they are learned and shared in their respective cultures.[13] Just as they behave in a certain way, people also perceive and organize their thoughts, observations, and values according to the dictates of their culture. For example, in a purely scientific sense, the moon is a rocky sphere; yet, when they look at the moon, many Americans see the "man in the moon." Some Native Americans view this same image as a rabbit; the Chinese interpret it as

Culture evolves through communication, beliefs, artifacts, and a style of living shared by others. Traditions and customs also play a role in shaping a culture and communicating it to future generations, such as this Indian celebration with special food, dress, and rituals.

Making Connections for Success

Perceptual Differences

Create a list of groups, such as Korean Americans, Midwesterners, Catholics, homosexuals, Muslims, ranchers, Protestants, and so on. You can use these groups if you wish, but you could also create your own list of three to five groups. Now select two groups and list traits that describe each. For example, for athletes, you might list such traits as competitive, aggressive, dedicated, skilled, and so on.

1. What role does perception have, if any, in creating your list of traits?

2. In what ways would the list of traits and characteristics influence how you communicate about or with individuals in these groups?

a lady fleeing her husband; and Samoans see in it the shape of a woman weaving.[14] These particular differences might not seem significant, but they point to the way that people from different cultures can view the same phenomenon quite differently. When cultural differences are apparent, sensitivity, patience, and tolerance are required to avoid or reduce misunderstandings that can create barriers to effective communication and to relationship development.

Being unable to appreciate ideas, customs, or beliefs that differ from those of one's own cultural background and automatically assuming that one's own view is superior to that of any other culture is referred to as ethnocentrism. **Ethnocentrism** is a learned belief that our own culture is superior to all others.[15] Those who lack interaction or contact with other cultures may find it difficult to understand that other cultures and their practices may be as acceptable as our own. Even if we know of weaknesses in our own culture (too competitive, too materialistic, too informal, and so on), we are unlikely to criticize our own culture when comparing it to others.

Ethnocentrism is not necessarily a bad thing, but it does alter our perceptions and often colors how we regard others who are different from us. We learn to behave through culture, and the way we behave, most of us believe, is the way everyone else should behave. We use our culture and our cultural behaviors as a yardstick by which to judge all other cultures and people. The difference between a person's own culture and other cultures is often judged on a superiority–inferiority scale. People often view cultures different from their own as inferior. The greater the differences seen between cultures, the greater the degree of perceived inferiority.

Ethnocentrism

A learned belief that our own culture is superior to all others.

Gender

Another factor that affects the way we perceive our world is gender. Unlike biological sex, **gender** is socially constructed and involves learned behaviors related to masculinity, **androgyny**, and femininity. Some theorists believe that where we fall on the masculine-and-feminine scale determines how we learn to understand the world around us, resulting in the way we perceive and communicate.

It has been shown, in groups containing both females and males, that males in general tend to talk for longer periods of time, take more turns at speaking, exert more control over the topic of conversation, and interrupt females more frequently than females interrupt males. In addition, what males say appears to be taken more seriously than what females say.[16] These communication differences may occur because of how females and males understand their roles and how those roles are defined by culture.

Our view of gender not only communicates who we believe ourselves to be, but also helps us construct a sense of who we want to be. Julia T. Wood has identified feminine and masculine themes in U.S. society. The feminine themes are as follows: appearance still counts; be sensitive and caring; accept negative treatment by others; and be superwoman. Masculine themes are these: don't be female; be successful; be

Gender

A socially constructed concept related to masculine and feminine behaviors that are learned.

Androgyny

A socially constructed concept related to having both masculine and feminine traits.

aggressive; be sexual; and be self-reliant.[17] Our understanding of masculinity and femininity changes continually.

An interesting study on voice pitch and perceived affection in initial interactions by Kory Floyd and George B. Bay, two communication scholars, found that men whose voices were higher pitched were seen as weak or effeminate and would therefore not be regarded by women as a good relational fit.[18] However, with women, the opposite was found to be true. Women with higher-pitched voices were perceived to be more affectionate than women with lower-pitched voices. The researchers' conclusion is that men's voices are perceived to be friendlier and less dominant or aggressive when they are lower in pitch, whereas women's voices are perceived to be friendlier and less dominant when they are higher in pitch.[19]

A great deal of uncertainty remains about what causes the differences in the roles of men and women in our society. We are told about "the gender gap" and about how men and women don't understand each other or speak the same language. Some social scientists believe that when men and women communicate they are using a form of cross-cultural communication in which the sexes are not speaking from different cultures or dialects, but rather "genderlects."[20] The argument that is used is that women and men interact in ways that are powerful but often not perceived. Men are often confused when women want to continue talking about something they think has been settled; women often find themselves frustrated when men don't seem to listen or respond to what they say. The perceptions that men and women have of each other and of themselves are not always clear, especially in this time of transition, in which the roles of men and women are constantly changing. Most of us today believe that both men and women can pursue careers or can be involved in homemaking and child care. Americans, as a group, have to some extent enlarged their perspectives on the roles and abilities of both men and women.

Media

Sometimes other people influence our perceptions deliberately. Advertisers, government leaders, political advocates, and many others attempt to shape our views. Advertisers have mastered techniques to encourage us to think and behave in ways that will benefit their clients.

Have you ever wondered how much the media influences our perceptions? In recent elections, candidates have hired people often referred to as "handlers" or "spin doctors." Their job is to create a positive image of their candidates and to protect them from any exposure that might create a negative image. Besides trying to create favorable impressions by using positive messages related to their candidates, they also try to create negative messages and images of their candidates' opponents. It is often said that while negative ads are seen as unfavorable by most, they do have more of a persuasive effect than positive ads.

What about the shows we watch on television? Do they create or alter our perceptions? Although family sitcoms, for example, present families who are generally atypical, regardless of race or ethnic background, they still influence our image of families. Network news shows select events from all the reports they receive and present them to us in a half-hour broadcast which, when the commercials are removed, amounts to approximately 24 minutes of actual news. The information we see is not only limited but also selected and edited for our consumption, affecting our perceptions of the world.

The influence of the media on our perceptions was no more evident than in the coverage of the events surrounding the shooting of Michael Brown, an unarmed black teenager, by Darren Wilson, a white police officer, in Ferguson, Missouri, on August 9, 2014. November 25, 2014, a grand jury decided, based on the evidence and witness reports they received, not to indict Officer Wilson. Protests had been occurring since the shooting but were generally peaceful, until the grand jury's verdict. Many blamed the protests on the media and the various people who spoke about this tragedy in the media in support of the Brown family.

According to reports by the *New York Times,* the events that led to Brown's tragic death were as follows: At 11:54 a.m., Michael Brown and a friend left a convenience store, where a surveillance video shows Brown stealing cigarillos and shoving the store owner to get out the door. At 12:01 p.m., Officer Wilson, by himself, told two men to get off the street and onto the sidewalk. He noticed that one of the men appeared to fit the description of one of the suspects in the convenience-store theft. At 12:02 p.m., Officer Wilson called the dispatcher about the two men. He then moved his patrol car to block them from going further. The events that followed led to significant speculation as to what really took place. Many media outlets reported the following:

> On the afternoon of Aug. 9, a police officer fatally shot an unarmed, black teenager, Michael Brown, in Ferguson, Missouri. Details remain in dispute. Eyewitnesses have said that Brown was compliant with police and was shot while he had his hands up. Police maintain that the 18-year-old had assaulted an officer and was reaching for the officer's gun. One thing is clear, however, is that Brown's death follows a disturbingly common trend of black men being killed, often while unarmed and at the hands of police officers, security guards and vigilantes. (*The Huffington Post,* by Nick Wing, posted August 14, 2014.)

It is important to recognize that our selection of Internet sites may be based on our biases and our desire to reinforce our own beliefs and convictions. Competent communicators always attempt to evaluate the information they are receiving, even if it does not reinforce their views. They might look at the reviews of others who have gotten information from the site, or they themselves may research other sites to determine the accuracy of information they are seeing.

Many of us who use social media believe that our messages do not create perceptions or that, if they do, the perceptions cannot be interpreted. However, as with anything we communicate, our use of emails, Facebook posts, or tweets does create perceptions and can be interpreted in ways we might not intend. As senders of emails or users of Facebook, for example, we should always be aware that the messages we send or post are open to inferences and interpretations by those who receive them. Therefore, we need to be careful in what and how we write and what we show or don't show. Those who receive our emails or view our Facebook page form impressions and make inferences based on the language we use, spelling accuracy, the tone in which we write our messages, or the photos we post.

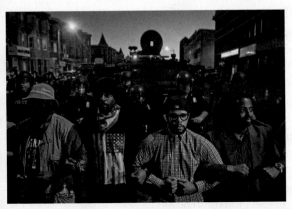 

During the 2015 Baltimore riots that occurred in the wake of the death of Freddie Gray, a number of striking images were used in media reports. The image on the right shows a Baltimore CVS being guarded by the police as it burns. The image on the left shows a line of Baltimore citizens linking arms to protect the police officers. The media's choice of which photo to use would likely affect our perception of the riots and the events that led up to them.

Making Connections for Success

Perceptions and Ethics

Bob, a photographer, is hired by your college to take pictures to make the college appear as attractive as possible for its Internet web page. When he gets to campus, Bob notices right away that it is located in an undesirable part of the city, parking is difficult, and the campus is in need of lots of maintenance. Therefore, he does not take any photos that show the surroundings. He does, however, photograph a student dressed to look like a successful businessperson approaching the newly remodeled entrance of the administration building. He takes close-up photos of a diverse group of students to show the diversity on campus. He takes a shot of a small pond in front of one of the campus buildings, using a wide-angle lens to give the illusion of a lake. Bob has created the impression on the Internet that the college attracts a variety of students, has a modern campus, and has a lake.

1. What do you think of what Bob has done regarding the perceptions he has created through the photos he took?

2. Because the area around the campus is blighted and a poor neighborhood, Bob decides to take photos of attractions and homes in another part of the city and use them, giving the impression that they are close to the campus. Is this ethical? Why or why not?

3. How can you be sure that the Internet sites you view are presenting images and messages in a truthful way?

We must also keep in mind that the information we receive via the Internet and social media is only as good or reliable as the sources. What we see, hear, or read on the Internet, in emails, on Facebook pages, or in tweets does affect our perceptions and ultimately our view of the world. The Internet and social media are powerful tools and, as with other media, cannot be assumed to always contain reliable information.

The example of the media's influence on the public perception of the killing of blacks by white police officers shows how the media can mold and reinforce perceptions in powerful ways. You might believe there is nothing wrong with this, but think about how we depend on the media for information and how people often accept what is presented to them by the media without question. The gap between reality and what is presented to us can be huge. Competent communicators check the information they receive—especially when the source is unknown to them—to determine its truthfulness and accuracy.

Improving Perception Competencies and Perception Checking

2.4 Accurately **interpret and check** your perceptions to improve your communication competence.

To be competent communicators, we must understand the impact that perceptions have on us, how we communicate with others, and what we accept as reality through the communication we receive. We tend to take the validity of our perceptions for granted and fail to look beneath the surface. For example, you and Stephanie are taking the same biology class. You have heard from another student that Stephanie goes out a lot and really likes to party. Her Facebook page is loaded with sexy photos, and she is holding a beer in many of them. You see her as a party girl and assume her only motivation to be in college is to have a good time. She seldom is on time for class, misses class more than most, and doesn't say much in class unless she is called on; but she does always seem to know the correct answer. The midterm exam is coming up and you have heard from her roommate that, not only does she go out a lot, but she hardly has cracked a book, let alone study. You see Stephanie shortly after the exam and ask her how she did? She tells you she aced it and that it was pretty easy. You say "really?" and that you thought the exam was pretty hard. Later you find that Stephanie received the second-highest grade in the class. You could infer that Stephanie cheated, because there is no way, from what you know, that she could have done that well on the exam. No matter what reason you choose, you are making an inference, and if you communicate that inference without labeling it as such, you may be communicating false—or at the very least misleading—information about Stephanie to others. To become a more competent communicator, you must realize that your perceptions are partial and subjective and could be wrong.[21] To avoid misperceptions, you must be an active perceiver, recognize that you may not perceive the same as others, be aware that fact differs from inference, learn about the role of perception in communication, keep an open mind, and, when possible, always perception check.

Become an Active Perceiver

First, we must be active as perceivers. We must be willing to seek out as much information as possible about a given person, subject, event, or situation. The more information we obtain, the deeper our understanding, and the more accurate our perceptions will be. We must question our perceptions to determine how accurate they are. By acknowledging that we may misinterpret information, we prompt ourselves to confirm facts and impressions before we draw conclusions. Taking time to gather more information and recheck the accuracy of our perceptions is well worth the effort. For example, is Stephanie late for class because she is lazy or because she has another class across campus right before biology? Does she miss class because she is not interested or because the bus sometimes doesn't run? An active perceiver will ask Stephanie why she is often late or misses class and will not make attribution errors.

Recognize That Each Person's Frame of Reference Is Unique

Second, we must recognize the uniqueness of our own frame of reference. We must remember that our view of things may be only one of many views. Each of us has a unique window to the world, as well as a unique system of understanding and storing data. Some of us make judgments about people based on appearance, whereas others base their judgments on ability, income, education, gender, ethnicity, or other factors. This variety of approaches shows that all of us operate according to different perceptual systems, and it is wrong to assume that one system is better than another.

Distinguish Facts from Inferences

A third way to improve our perceptions and interpretations is to distinguish facts from inferences or assumptions. A fact is a statement put forth as objectively real that can be verified. For example, it is a known fact which science building on campus is the tallest, that Gina has been late to class five times this semester, and that the volleyball team has won its last six games. An inference is an interpretation that goes beyond what we know to be factual. For example, Stephanie is almost always late to class, received a 96 on the midterm exam, and generally does not say much while in class. These events or behaviors are what you have observed and are verifiable and therefore are facts. However, when you say Stephanie is lazy, unprepared, disorganized, and unmotivated to learn, you are making inferences that may or may not be accurate.

Because facts and inferences are often extremely difficult to distinguish, it is easy to confuse them. We sometimes treat inferences as if they are facts. A statement such as "Stephanie is lazy" sounds factual, and we tend to accept those types of statements as truth rather than communicating to find out what is fact and what is inference. We need to label our statements as inferences when we communicate

Making Connections for Success

Just the Facts and Nothing but the Facts

Competent communicators can distinguish facts from inferences—can you?

1. College students who party are less likely to do well on exams—fact or inference?

2. There are more women than men going to college today—fact or inference?

3. Chapter 2 discusses perception and communication—fact or inference?

4. College graduates, on average, make more money than non–college graduates—fact or inference?

5. Students who use social media during their classes have low motivation to learn—fact or inference?

6. Athletes who use special equipment to enhance their performance are unethical—fact or inference?

For answers see page 51.

Competent communicators qualify inferences by labeling them as such. How would you qualify the above statements that are not factual?

---

them. For example, saying "Stephanie seems to be lazy" is much more tentative and is not stated as a fact or with certainty. A next step might be to learn more about Stephanie; try to draw her out, and find out if anything is affecting her life or discover more about her background before making a judgment about her.

Become Aware of the Role of Perceptions in Communication

A fourth way to improve our perceptions and interpretations is to be aware of the role of perceptions in communication, to take others' perceptions into account, and to avoid the tendency to assume too much about what we perceive. To make the most of the information we receive, we must first evaluate it. We should check the source of the information and the context in which it was acquired. We should make sure we are not reading too much into the information. To help ensure the accuracy of our perceptions, we should ask questions and obtain feedback whenever possible. We cannot determine whether our perceptions are accurate without testing them.

Keep an Open Mind

A fifth way to improve our perceptions and interpretations is to keep an open mind and remind ourselves that our perceptions may not be complete or accurate. Thus, we must continue to make observations, seek out additional information, be willing to describe what we observe both mentally and out loud, state what a given observation means to us, and put our perceptions into words to test their logic and soundness. For example, is it possible that Stephanie doesn't communicate much in class because she is shy, or is it because she hasn't come prepared, or is some other reason at work? If she didn't cheat, then either she is very smart or she studies a lot. We need to perception check to ensure the accuracy of what we are thinking and communicating.

Perception Checking: Being a Competent Communicator

Finally, to improve the accuracy of our perceptions and interpretations, we must learn to check perceptions. When it comes to interpreting perceptions, the variables and possibilities for misunderstanding are abundant; therefore, the potential for jumping to conclusions without fully knowing all of the information is large. For example,

Making Connections for Success

Competent Communicators Check Their Perceptions for Accuracy

In this chapter, we have discussed perception, its relationship to communication, and our competence as communicators. To check our perceptions, we should (1) try to state what we observed as best we can, (2) recognize that what we observe is a possible explanation, (3) consider other possible explanations, and (4) ask or check on the accuracy of the possible explanation(s).

Example: You saw Jason, an athlete friend, walking out of a clinic known for its distribution of steroids; Jason has shown a significant improvement in his athleticism over the past several months.

Perception-checking steps: I saw Jason, a good friend and athlete, coming out of a clinic that has been rumored to sell steroids. [(1) This is what was observed—describe, don't infer.] Jason was there to buy steroids. [(2) This is one possible explanation.] Jason was at the clinic to get his sprained ankle checked out, to check on a friend who was hurt, or to get painkillers for his ankle sprain. [(3) These are other possible explanations.] Which explanation is the correct one, if any? [(4) Check on the accuracy or qualify the observation by stating that you don't know the reason Jason was coming out of the clinic.]

Example for you to create your own perception-checking statements: Debra, a friend of yours who has been struggling in her speech class with Cs on her speeches, borrows an outline of a speech for which you received an A grade last semester. You overhear her bragging to another friend that she received an A on her last speech.

1. How would you use perception-checking steps in the above example?
2. What did you learn from the use of perception-checking steps?

a friend of mine and I exchange emails periodically, but if I don't respond within a day or so of receiving his email, he assumes that I am upset with him. Of course, I am not upset with him, but that is what he perceives when he does not receive an instant response from me. Think about this example and of how many times others have jumped to inaccurate conclusions about your thoughts, feelings, or motives.

Developing the skill of perception checking should help prevent jumping to the wrong conclusions about others' thoughts, feelings, or motives. For example, when a favorite teacher walks by, you say "Hi" and smile, but the teacher does not even acknowledge your presence, although you believe she looked directly at you. It would be very easy to assume that the teacher ignored you because she doesn't think much of you or that you are simply unimportant to her. A competent communicator would employ perception-checking skills, which would include the following:

1. Describe the observed behavior—a fact: Your roommate ignores your presence.
2. Think of at least two interpretations of the friend's behavior—inferences: (1) She was ignoring you because she doesn't think much of you, or (2) she was ignoring you because her mind was preoccupied and she didn't hear or see you.
3. Finally, verify your interpretation: You might ask the friend, "What's going on, is there something wrong?" This would immediately clarify any possible misunderstandings.

By using such checking as a means of verifying your perceptions, you are less likely to assume that your first interpretation is the only one or the correct one. To prevent misunderstandings or misinterpretation of perceptions requires cooperation and willingness to communicate, as well as being open minded about the communication received.

Guidelines

Check Your Perceptions: Competent Communicators Do!

1. **Separate fact from assumptions.** It is easy to accept assumptions, but we must realize that assumptions are not facts, nor are they always accurate. When we make assumptions we are drawing conclusions with little or no basis of fact. Thus, we should label assumptions so that when we communicate them, they are differentiated from facts.

2. **Recognize your personal biases.** We all have biases that can influence our perceptions, and we must be careful that those biases don't inaccurately slant our perceptions. We should always qualify, when recognized, that our biases may have influenced our communication about events, objects, and people.

3. **Remember that perceptions, especially first impressions, are not always accurate.** This is important because when we make judgments based on limited information or our first impression, we may cling to that impression or perception as if that is all there is to know.

4. **Recognize that people from different cultural backgrounds do not always attach the same meanings to events, objects, and people.** It is important to recognize that not everyone sees the world as you do, and this is especially true of people who come from different cultural backgrounds. For example, it is not unusual for someone who lives in Europe or the Middle East to walk with someone of the same sex holding hands or kissing them on the check. How this might be perceived depends on differences in cultural norms or background.

5. **Remember that perceptions are a function of the perceiver, the perceived, and the situation in which the perception occurs.** To ensure accuracy it is important to understand that perception is in the eye of the beholder, to understand what is perceived and why, and to take into account the situation or context of the perception.

6. **Don't be afraid to communicate to verify your perceptions.** It is important that you ask questions and seek additional information to ensure the accuracy of your perceptions. You do not want to leave yourself open to interpretations or misunderstandings that could be avoided.

7. **Be willing to admit misperceptions and to change them when necessary.** It is important to correct misperceptions and admit when perceptions are not accurate. It is also the responsibility of the perceiver to make changes when errors or misunderstanding occur.

Summary

Perception and Communication

Objective 2.1 Make the connection between perception and your communication competence.

Perception is the process of selecting, organizing, and interpreting information to give it personal meaning. It lies at the heart of the communication process and is a part of everything we do.

The Perception Process

Objective 2.2 Understand the stages of perception and how they affect your communication.

Perception involves selecting, organizing, and interpreting.

- Selection is the process of mentally sorting one thing from another.
- Organization is the categorizing of stimuli so that we can make sense of them.
- Interpretation is the assigning of meaning to stimuli.

Perceptual Differences

Objective 2.3 Identify seven reasons why people may perceive the same situation in different ways.

Because everyone is different, their perceptions of an identical situation may vary.

- The perceptual set—a fixed, previously determined view of people, things, or events—can distort our perception of reality. Stereotyping, a form of perceptual set, can also lead to inaccuracies in our perception and, ultimately, our communication.
- Attribution error can occur when people perceive others as they do because of the kind of people they are rather than through external factors that may have influenced their behavior.
- Physical characteristics can account for differences in perception.
- Psychological state or our state of mind can alter our perceptions of people, events, and things.
- Cultural backgrounds can affect the way people perceive others, as well as events and things.
- Gender is socially constructed and can affect the way we perceive the world around us.
- Media, including newspapers, magazines, television, and all forms of social media, can and do influence our perceptions of people, places, events, and things.

Improving Perception Competencies and Perception Checking

Objective 2.4 Accurately interpret and check your perceptions to improve your communication competence.
To be competent communicators, we must recognize the effect of differences in perception.

- An active perceiver seeks out information.
- Perceptions are not always the same for everyone.
- Facts are objective; inferences are subjective.
- Perception plays a role in communication.
- It is possible that another perception may be valid.
- It is always wise to check your perceptions.

Discussion Starters

1. Why does perception play such a huge role in our communication with others?

2. Explain the connection between perception and communication competence.

3. Given what you have read, what is the influence of social networking sites on perception? What advice would you give regarding communication on these sites?

4. Describe a personal experience that illustrates attribution error. How did the error affect communication?

5. How has technology affected our perceptions and how we communicate with others?

6. Explain the role of Hollywood media in shaping our perceptions and, ultimately, how we perceive the world around us.

Answers

Making Connections for Success: Just the Facts and Nothing but the Facts (p. 48)

Numbers 2, 3, and 4 are facts; and 1, 5, and 6 are inferences.

Chapter 3
Connecting Self and Communication

 Learning Objectives

This chapter will help you

3.1 **Differentiate** among self-concept, self-image, and self-esteem.

3.2 **Identify** social media factors that influence self-concept.

3.3 **Characterize** the role of culture in determining self-concept.

3.4 **Characterize** the role of gender in determining self-concept.

3.5 **Explain** the roles of self-fulfilling prophecy and impression management as they relate to self-concept.

3.6 **Identify** six ways to improve self-concept.

Making Everyday Connections

The greatest fear today for some of us is that no matter how hard we try or how successful we think we are—no matter how highly we rate ourselves as a student, friend, coworker, teammate, person, lover, etc.,—it may not be good enough. We may see others as smarter, more attractive, thinner, more muscular, faster, or more powerful than we see ourselves. High self-esteem usually requires us to feel special and above average. For some of us to be considered average is an insult and seen as a failure. One way to deal with this is to constantly make social comparisons in which we continually try to inflate our image at the expense of others; another is accepting that we just aren't as good as others. Neither of these approaches seems to satisfy our view of self in a positive way.

We have often been told, more or less, to believe that what others say about us, either in person or on social media, influences our self-esteem—especially if what is communicated is from those whom we hold in high esteem and admire. For example, imagine if a close friend, a romantic partner, a parent, a professor, a music instructor, a coworker, or a coach whom you admire says one of the following to you:

"You're talented. You are amazing—you are doing great."

"You don't know what you are talking about. You simply don't get it."

"You are really smart. You always have the right answer."

"You're really not very good and that's why I don't expect much from you."

"You're a lot of fun; you make me laugh."

"I don't know why I even try to help you; you don't listen and that's why you're failing."

"I am so glad you are on my team; you are the best player."

"Wow, you're not very bright. How you ever got this far, I'll never know."

"You sure have gained a lot of weight."

These comments or actions, whether they are posted on social media or said in person, influence temporarily, and sometimes permanently, how we see or think of ourselves and how we communicate about ourselves to others.

Questions to Think About

1. Why do you think our self-concept is so affected by what others say and/or how they behave toward us?

2. Describe how your view of self can affect your communication with others. Discuss both positive and negative effects.

3. How can the understanding of self help you to become a more competent communicator?

4. What does it mean to be average and why is average not good enough?

5. How does our ability to control what others learn about us through social networking sites and other Internet venues affect how we see ourselves and, importantly, how others see us?

A question that most of us have asked or at least thought about asking at one time or another is, "Who is the real me?" When college students are asked, "Who are you?" or "How do you describe yourself?" their answers typically consist of references to relationships (e.g., Melissa's boyfriend, son of Bill and Frances); social identities (e.g., a sophomore at Clemson; a major in communication studies; a member of the swim team; part of the Christian Student Fellowship; Nebraskans for Peace member; member of Nebraska Young Democrats, member of Sigma Lambda Chi; from Charleston, South Carolina; graduate from Central High School in Chicago); or personal traits (e.g., good student, hard worker, organized, athletic, kind, friendly, sincere, trustworthy). But do these descriptions really tell who we are or describe the real you? We know from Chapter 2 that our perceptions of others, events, and things are subjective. We also learned in Chapter 2 that the accuracy of our perceptions is often questionable because what we perceive may not be the same as what others perceive or what actually is real or true. So, who is the real you?

Barbara Corcoran, real-estate mogul, wrote, "The best mistake I ever made was believing that I was stupid." Corcoran tells the story of a teacher who changed her life. The teacher saw her inattentiveness and pulled her right out of her chair. The teacher looked directly into her eye and said, "If you don't learn to pay attention, you will always be stupid." As an 8-year-old, Corcoran was affected by the incident in two ways: She hid her true self, and she became the quietest kid in class. Corcoran says her insecurity made her a meticulous preparer; it made her work twice as hard, and she was constantly trying to prove she wasn't stupid. She knew she could succeed, but still she doubted herself. In 2001, she sold her business, which employed 1,000 people and was worth $66 million. In 2008, she became a real-estate expert for the *Today Show* and in 2012 she began counseling entrepreneurs on ABC's reality show *Shark Tank*. So who is the real Barbara Corcoran?[1] On her website (www.barbaracorcoran.com), you will learn more about her and why she says "taking chances almost always makes for happy endings."

Each of us is extremely complex. Early in life we begin to learn who we are—or at least, who we think we are. We develop a social identity, or self-definition, that includes how we see and evaluate ourselves. Most of us manage to maintain a coherent image of our self, yet recognize that we define ourselves and behave differently in different situations. For example, when you are at home with your parents, your self image as a responsible adult might at times come into question. You might not pick up after yourself, or you might even expect that someone else will do your laundry. However, when you are away at college, you perform these tasks competently and see yourself as a responsible adult. Despite such readily admitted pockets of irresponsibility, do you see yourself as irresponsible? No, of course not! Our self-concept and our communication with others depend on the context, the situation, and the other person or people involved; how we evaluate ourselves in that context or situation; and how we compare ourselves to the other person or people. Do we see ourselves as superior, inferior, or average?

The way others act toward us and communicate with us, and how we believe they will act toward and communicate with us in the future, have important implications as to how we see ourselves. When it comes to self-perception, no person is an island. When we suspect that others might reject us because of some flaw or inadequacy we believe they see in us, we could choose to change only that particular flaw or inadequacy that we believe might lead to rejection. In other words, people can attempt to hide some aspects of the self from others who disapprove. To become competent communicators, we must understand that our image of self has a significant role in how we communicate and how others communicate with us. We must, therefore, try to understand the idea of self-concept and its connection to our communication.

Understanding Self-Concept

3.1 Differentiate among self-concept, self-image, and self-esteem.

self-concept

A person's perceived self, which consists of an organized collection of beliefs and attitudes about self.

self-image

A person's mental picture of him- or herself.

self-esteem

A person's feelings and attitudes toward him- or herself.

Our **self-concept**, or self-identity, is our perceived self, which consists of an organized collection of beliefs and attitudes about self. Our perceived self is determined by our experiences and communication with others, the roles and values we have selected for ourselves, and how we believe others see us. Self-concept consists of two subcomponents: **self-image**, how we see ourselves or our mental picture of self (for example, I see myself as not very attractive, an athlete, a student, a worker, a female, a daughter, and a first-year student); and **self-esteem**, our feelings and attitudes toward ourselves or how we evaluate ourselves (for example, I feel that I am OK, liked, lonely, confident, successful, unappreciated, alone, respected) (see Figure 3.1). Both self-image and self-esteem determine our self-concept.

Self-concept and perception are closely related, so it is difficult to separate them. They constantly interact. For example, what you think about yourself shapes, and in many ways determines, what you do and say. Your opinion of yourself is influenced by the information you receive from others and how you see and feel about yourself, which creates an image of who you are. If you regard yourself as a good speaker, you would take positive comments made about your communication as affirmation of your ability. If someone made a disparaging comment, however, you probably would dismiss it as not a reflection of your perception of your ability to communicate. In fact, you might interpret the comment as a sign of jealousy or humor, or you

Figure 3.1 The Self-Concept

Self-concept is determined by our experiences and communication with others, the roles and values we have selected for ourselves, our perception of how we think others see us, and how we evaluate ourselves.

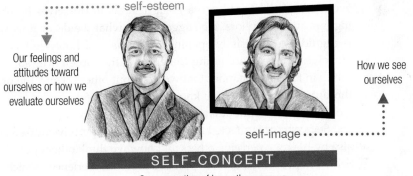

might simply feel that the person who made the comment isn't very knowledgeable about communication or you.

Why is it important for us to understand the connection between communication and self-concept? Think about this question and read on to find an answer.

Development of Self-Concept

When we were children, our first communication involved sensing our environment—all the sights, sounds, tastes, and smells that surrounded us. We learned about ourselves as others touched us and spoke to us. Their responses helped to determine how we view ourselves. Parental communication, both verbal and nonverbal, generally has an extremely strong impact on the initial development of self-concept. For example, the clothes and toys they provided and what and how they communicated to us affected who we have become in some way. As we age and expand our environment and relationships, the communication of others may reinforce or alter our perceptions of self. In her book *Old Is Not a Four-Letter Word: A Midlife Guide,* Anne Gerike writes that aging has its advantages. For example, she says that aging brings increased self-confidence, a more reliable inner voice or "gut feeling," an acceptance that we are not perfect, a sense of perspective that difficult situations get worked out, an acceptance that life isn't fair, and a willingness to take responsibility instead of directing the blame elsewhere.[2]

Making Connections for Success

Who, Then, Are You?

Do an Internet search using the words "self-esteem test." This will take you to several sites with a number of choices related to self-assessment and self-understanding. Choose an inventory that measures both your self-esteem and your communication skills, and that provides you with results and a brief interpretation of those results.

1. Now that you completed the inventory, what did you learn about yourself that you didn't know before?

2. What do you think about self-inventories or self-assessment tests? Is there value in doing them? Explain.

3. How can understanding "who you are" help you to improve your communication competencies?

4. If you were asked on an online job questionnaire to describe yourself, what would you say? How would you describe your strengths? Your weaknesses?

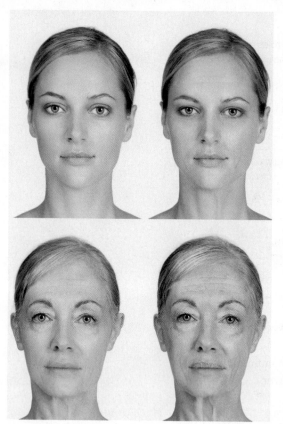

We develop our self-concept early in life, and it is based on how others react to us and how we perceive their reactions.

values

A person's perceived self, which consists of an organized collection of beliefs and attitudes about self.

attitude

An evaluative feeling, or way of thinking about oneself, others, events, ideas, or objects.

belief

A conviction or confidence in the truth of something that is not based on absolute proof.

Assuming that Gerike's observations are correct, why do you think such developments occur with age?

Social psychologist Daryl J. Bem believes that sometimes we don't know our own attitudes, feelings, or emotions directly. We therefore focus on others to obtain such information.[3] Bem does, however, indicate that we learn a great deal about ourselves by observing our own behaviors. He suggests that what we do or how we act is a guide to what is happening inside us and how we feel about ourselves. Further, according to Bem, we draw inferences about ourselves in the same manner that we do about others. Thus, the process through which we come to know ourselves is very similar to the one we use to learn about others.

Self-concept is affected not only by how we perceive ourselves, but also by how we perceive others and how we think others perceive us. Self-concept is based on both past and present experiences, which affect how we will perceive ourselves in the future. Our self-concept is further determined by the values, attitudes, and beliefs we possess; how we attribute these qualities to others; and how they connect them to us.

VALUES   Relatively long-lasting principles or standards that guide our behavior or judgment of what is important in our lives are called **values**. Values can be classified into broad categories, such as aesthetic, religious, humanitarian, intellectual, and material. Each category determines our behavior as well as our communication, and is often reflected in who we are as a person. For example, if material possessions and financial success are more important to us than helping others, then these values express who we are as a person and what we value. A desire to have nice things is not unusual, at least in our society, but the strength of the desire can greatly affect our behavior toward ourselves and others, and how we communicate. Possessions can become such an important reflection of how we see ourselves, for example, that we might think that the clothes we wear are going to make us more likeable, more respected, and more appreciated. But do they? We may have and wear expensive clothes, but that doesn't always translate into personal satisfaction, better relationships with others, or a more positive self-image. Thus, values can have both positive and negative influences on how we behave, communicate, and see ourselves.

ATTITUDES   An evaluative judgment in terms of likes and dislikes about oneself, others, events, ideas, or objects is called an **attitude**. Attitudes help determine self-concept; but, unlike values, they are more narrowly defined. The relationship between values and attitudes is close because values are reflected in our attitudes. For example, if you don't see yourself participating in competitive college sports, your attitude might be that college sports wastes a lot of money at the expense of getting a good education. Your attitude says something about your value system; in other words, you value academics over athletics. What this says about you is that you see college sports as a waste of money that could be better spent on educating students.

BELIEFS   Closely related to attitudes are beliefs. A **belief** is a conviction or confidence in the truth of something that is not based on absolute proof. We have, for example, beliefs about history, religion, schools, events, people, and ourselves. We say, "Space exploration is helpful to humanity," "God is good to us," "Communication class is important for getting a good job," "Going to college is a good thing," or "I am going to get a high grade on my next speech." These statements and hundreds of similar statements made daily could begin with "I believe…."

Our beliefs, like our attitudes and values, have a hierarchy of importance. That is, some are much more important than others. Our most important beliefs, such as those

Making Connections for Success

Values, Attitudes, and Beliefs about People with Disabilities

Be honest: Have you ever felt uneasy in the presence of a person with a physical disability? Words and phrases such as "handicapped person confined to a wheelchair" or "young woman stricken with cerebral palsy" can shape incorrect perceptions of people with disabilities. Stigma and negative attitudes are often the greatest barriers those with disabilities must overcome. People with disabilities are more similar to people without them than most of us think. Most people with disabilities don't see their disability as a liability or limitation but, rather, view it as who they are. The problem for most of us is that we are strongly influenced by the visible characteristics and appearance of others. We might not be conscious of these reactions until they are pointed out. However, our actions, whether conscious or not, communicate our values and attitudes, and ultimately affect our beliefs as well.

1. Why do phrases like the previous examples form our values, attitudes, and beliefs about people with disabilities?

2. What are some values, attitudes, and beliefs held by many people that make them see the disability, rather than the person, first?

3. How might you use what you have learned here to help you communicate with sensitivity? Develop your own suggestions first and then search the Internet, using the key words "interacting with people with disabilities" to find suggestions you haven't thought of.

4. Provide a written example of a value, attitude, or belief of your own to share with your classmates.

An excellent resource on communicating with people with disabilities is the *Handbook of Communication and People with Disabilities: Research and Application,* edited by Dawn O. Braithwaite and Teresa L. Thompson (Mahwah, NJ: Lawrence Erlbaum Associates). For a fascinating perspective regarding self-esteem, listen to an interview with Lucy Grealy, author of *Autobiography of a Face* (to access the interview, conduct an Internet search for "Charlie Rose: A Conversation with Lucy Grealy").

about religion, education, and family life, do not change easily; but the less important ones, such as those about today's weather, the outcome of a sports event, or a grade, are only temporary or until the outcome is known.

Making clear and absolute distinctions among values, attitudes, and beliefs is difficult because they are interrelated. Consider, for example, how closely related the following three statements are:

Value (ideal): A college education will be beneficial to our society's success.
Attitude (feeling or position): A college education is good for our society.
Belief (conviction): A college education will make our society better.

Attitudes differ from beliefs in that attitudes include an evaluation of whether someone or something is good or bad. Beliefs, in turn, reflect the perception of whether something is true or false. Your attitudes and beliefs about college may change as a result of your experiences, but the value you place on education endures. Table 3.1 provides definitions and examples of values, attitudes, and beliefs, with space for you to add your own examples.

Table 3.1 Values, Attitudes, and Beliefs

Term	Definition	Example	Your Examples
Values	Broad-based ideals that are relatively long-lasting	Social media have made our lives more convenient.	
Attitudes	Evaluative dispositions, feelings, or positions about ourselves, other persons, events, ideas, or objects	Social media users are more tech savvy than nonusers.	
Beliefs	Convictions or confidence in the truth of something that lacks absolute proof	Social media are the only way to communicate effectively with others.	

Communication and Self-Concept

Self-concept and the way we communicate have a direct connection: Communication affects our self-concept, and our self-concept influences how and what we communicate. A model developed by social psychologist John W. Kinch[4] illustrates this relationship (see Figure 3.2). Our perceptions of how others respond to us (P) affect our self-concept (S). Our self-concept affects how we behave (B). Our behavior is directly related to how others react to our behavior (A). The actual responses of others relate to our perceptions of others' responses (P), and so we have come full circle.

According to Kinch, our conception of self emerges from our social interaction and, in turn, guides or influences our behavior.[5] His theory postulates that the way others react to us and how we perceive those reactions function to direct or alter our behavior. To test whether or not the Kinch theory is correct, four male students in one of his classes decided to see if they could actually change someone's self-concept. One woman in class was rather plain looking but not unattractive. The four students selected her to run their experiment. The four guys, one at a time over a period of a few weeks, began interacting with the female student as if she were one of the most beautiful women on campus. They agreed to do this as naturally as possible so that she would not be aware of what they were doing. One after the other asked her for a date. Whenever they were with her, they behaved and interacted with her as if she were extremely attractive. After a few weeks, the results of their efforts began to show. She dressed more neatly, wore her nicest clothes, had her hair styled, and was more outgoing in her interactions with those around her. In fact, by the time the fourth male asked her out, she informed him that she would not be available for some time because of other dates she had.

According to Kinch, because of how the student perceived the behavior and responses of these male students, she changed her self-concept, which in turn changed her behavior. The interesting aspect of the experiment is that male students also changed how they viewed the female student. They no longer regarded her as "plain Jane," but now as a more desirable and beautiful young woman, thus confirming Kinch's theory as circular.[6] In other words, how others behave and interact with us affects how we see ourselves, and our behaviors and interactions with others influence how they see themselves.

Figure 3.2 Kinch's Model of the Connection between Self-Concept and Communication

Kinch illustrates the relationship between self-concept and communication. Our self-concept is based on our communication with others.

SOURCE: J. Kinch, "A Formalized Theory of the Self-Concept," *American Journal of Sociology* 68 (January 1963): 481–486. University of Chicago Press. Reprinted by permission.

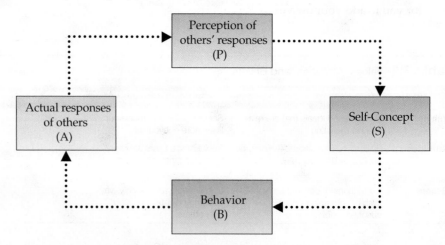

Making Connections for Success

The Excuse?

Suppose that you are meeting a good friend for dinner, and she is late. You receive the following text message: "@ party, good time, leaving soon." However, after an hour, you begin to suspect that your friend will not arrive. Finally, she appears on the scene and says, "Sorry, I just got so involved with some friends at the party that I completely lost track of time!" What is your friend's message saying about you?

Now imagine that she instead texts you, "OMG car accident, HUGE backup, CUL8R." Now what is her message saying about you?

If this is the first time your friend has been late for a meeting, and this type of excuse has never surfaced before, you may accept the explanation as true.

Now suppose that your friend is always late when it comes to meeting you and has used similar excuses all the time, but when she meets others she is the first to arrive. In addition, this time she doesn't call or send you any message—she just doesn't show up.

1. What is your friend telling you?
2. How will her behavior affect your self-concept? Or will it?
3. Is it easier to "get away with" excuses by texting, Facebooking, or email than if you had to explain a situation in person?
4. Has technology changed how we make excuses for our inconsiderate behavior?

Personality theorists, such as the late Carl Rogers, believe that self-concept is the single most important aspect of our personalities. Our image of self forms our personality, which in turn determines our communication style and how we do or don't communicate with others. For example, Simon Cowell—music mogul, television personality, and producer of many TV shows, including *American Idol*—is known for his blunt and often controversial criticisms, insults, and wisecracks about contestants and their abilities. He thinks of himself as competent and important, the ultimate judge of talent, who doesn't care much what others think of him; as a result, he regards himself as better than others and therefore believes he can say what he wants, even if it's self-serving or offensive to others. Furthermore, because he perceives that others don't know what he knows about talent, his perception of himself influences how and what he communicates to others. When interactions are considered with respect to self, it becomes necessary to take into account the context and the person or people with whom you are communicating. It is generally agreed that people with high social self-concepts function better in most interpersonal situations than do those with low social self-concepts. The question here is not so much, "Who are you?" but rather, "Who are you when you are with your best friend, your mother, your father, both your mother and father, people you don't know, and so on?" In other words, our image of self determines our communication style as seen by others and as internalized by us, which in turn affects how we communicate with others. Kinch's experiment, described above, illustrates this notion quite clearly when the female student began to internalize the men's communication with and behavior toward her, which, in turn, affected how she communicated and behaved with others.

A fundamental principle of the self, the social identity perspective,[7] says that individuals perceive themselves differently depending on where they are at a particular moment in time. This principle is illustrated by the **personal-social identity continuum**. The personal identity end of this continuum refers to when we think of ourselves primarily as *individuals*. The social identity end refers to when we think of ourselves as members of specific *social groups.* Because it is impossible to experience all aspects of our self-concept simultaneously, the specific aspect of our identity that is prominent at any given moment will influence how we think about ourselves, and this, in turn, has consequences for our behavior. This idea is evident when we think of ourselves as unique individuals. Our personal identities are prominent, and this

personal-social identity continuum

The two ways the self can be categorized: at a personal level, in which the uniqueness of the individual is emphasized; and at the social identity level, in which the self is thought of as a member of a group.

is likely to result in self-descriptions that emphasize how we are different from others. For example, you might describe yourself as a fun-loving person when thinking of yourself at the personal identity level—you are emphasizing your self-perception as a person who has more fun than those individuals with whom you compare yourself.

Personal identity self-description can be seen as an intragroup comparison, which involves comparisons with other individuals with whom you share a group membership. For this reason, our description of ourselves depends upon which group we are using for the comparison.[8] For example, how might you see yourself if you were asked to describe how you differ from others? You could label yourself as liberal when comparing yourself to your parents, but if you were indicating how you differ from other college students, you might say that you are more conservative. The point is that when we characterize ourselves we depend upon comparisons to others. According to Kristen Neff, Education Psychologist, the need to continually positively evaluate ourselves often comes at a high price. High self-esteem generally requires feeling special and above average. Being thought of as *average* is considered by most to be an insult. For example: "How did you like my speech yesterday?" "It was okay." "Just okay, ouch." Why is it that we all have to feel that we are better than average? According to Neff it is impossible for every one of us to be above average at the same time.[9]

At the other end of the personal-social identity continuum, we can perceive ourselves as members of a group, which means we emphasize the ways we are similar to other group members. At the social identity level, we describe ourselves in terms of the attributes shared by members of our group as well as what differentiates "our group" from other groups. That is, descriptions of the self at the social identity level are intergroup in nature and usually involve contrasts between groups. For example, you may see yourself in terms of your social identity as a member of the school band and describe yourself as musically talented and extroverted, attributes you perceive to be shared with other members of the band and as simultaneously differentiating the band group from other groups, such as members of the debate team, whom you see as studious and scholarly.

On other occasions, you might think of yourself in terms of your gender group. For example, if you are a female, you might emphasize what attributes you share with other females (e.g., being warm and caring) and what you perceive as differentiating women from males. What's noteworthy is that when you think of yourself as an *individual*, the *content* of your self-description is likely to differ from when you regard yourself as a member of a *category* that you share with others.

Of course, most of us belong to a variety of groups (e.g., groups defined by age, religion, nationality, ethnicity, sexual orientation, occupation, sports, artistic ability), but all of these will not be prominent at the same time. When any particular social identity is prominent, people are likely to communicate in ways reflecting that aspect of their self-concept. Can we say that one of these "selves" is the "true" self—either the personal self or any one of a person's potential social identities? No, not really. Each view of self contributes to a larger general image of self, which is in essence who we are and what identifies us.

So, in any given context or time we can describe ourselves differently, thus creating many different "selves." Which of these descriptions can we say is the "true" self? We can't. All of the descriptions potentially reveal the true self, but they depend on the context and comparison dimension.[10] So, how we think of ourselves from one context to another could result in opposite self-descriptions (e.g., fun vs. reserved; open vs. closed; liberal vs. conservative).

Making Connections for Success

Social Media and Your Real Identity?

Jot down what you believe your Facebook page communicates about you. Then show your page to a classmate who knows very little, if anything, about you and ask this classmate to describe your social identity or image on the basis of what he or she sees on your page. Ask the following questions:

1. How would you describe me? For example, am I a good student, a professional, a party animal, a family person, disorganized, an airhead, a typical Greek member?

2. What did my Facebook page specifically communicate to you that brought you to that conclusion?

Now reflect on the other person's description. How does it compare to how you want to be seen by others? What, if anything, surprised you about how this person saw you? What changes, if any, will you now make in your Facebook page?

Social Media and Self-Concept

3.2 **Identify social media factors that influence self-concept.**

Our attitude toward online communication is another important factor that influences our self-concept. Attitude shapes how we interact with other people and how we present ourselves through social media. This orientation toward social media has been called **online communication attitude** and it influences our media choices. Researchers have identified five attitudes toward online communication that shape how we approach or avoid opportunities to communicate through social media: online self-disclosure, online social connection, convenience, online apprehension, and miscommunication.[11] As you read about these attitudes, consider how they relate to your own experience.

online communication attitude

Attitudes that shape how we interact with other people and how we present ourselves through social media.

Online Self-Disclosure

Online self-disclosure is the degree to which an individual self-regulates what they reveal about themselves using social media. People using social media vary widely in this regard. The range of these tendencies can be seen easily by just looking at the Facebook pages of your friends. Some people reveal nothing more than their name and location. Others use Facebook to display their personal philosophy, gender preferences, interests, and other private details. Still others go further by posting photos of everything from pets to the latest party they attended. All of these examples represent a different comfort level with online self-disclosure. Interestingly, research has found that many people who share a great deal of personal information through social media are less likely to do so in face-to-face interactions with their friends. In some cases, these individuals come to depend on social media as an important outlet for sharing important details in their life. As a result, their communication through social media can affect their self-concept.

online self-disclosure

The degree to which an individual self-regulates what they reveal about themselves using social media.

Online Social Connection

Those who use social media generally assume that this is an effective means of connecting with one's social network. The belief that online communication enables social contact is known as **online social connection**. By comparison, older generations relied on other means, such as the mail and telephone, to stay in touch with friends and family. Research indicates that a person's communication competence is positively associated with his or her attitude toward online social connection.[12] This means that users

online social connection

The belief that online communication enables social contact.

can be motivated to more competently use online communication to socially connect with others. In turn, their online communication and tendency to connect with others through social media can influence their self-concept.

Convenience

convenience

The ease with which people connect with others through social media.

Another dimension of online communication attitude is the ease with which people connect with others through social media. We call this **convenience**, and it encompasses the level of appreciation and enjoyment a user associates with social media. As you might expect, one's sense of ease with social media is governed by how long a person has been an active user of communication technology. Newcomers naturally feel more apprehensive and less competent than those with longtime usage experience. The convenient nature of social media can carry implications for how you present yourself to others. You can easily snap a picture or video with your smartphone at a party, and within seconds, post it to your Facebook page or Snapchat account and tag your friends. Within seconds, you not only alter your online image, but also that of your friends. Although the use of social media is quite convenient, it can quickly affect how others perceive your interpersonal communication competence, which can impact your self-concept.

Online Apprehension

online communication apprehension

Anxiety and nervousness associated with communicating through social media.

Anxiety and nervousness associated with communicating through social media is known as **online communication apprehension**. Individuals who are nervous about the opportunities and challenges associated with social media often develop negative attitudes toward online communication in general. One's reluctance to use online media may stem from a general lack of familiarity with social media or it may be limited to certain communication contexts. For example, some people feel little anxiety in using social media for communicating with friends but totally avoid using it in the context of their work environment. Many people avoid social media in the workplace because how they present themselves online can have implications for their careers. Your supervisor seeing your photos from a friend's bachelorette weekend can influence whether or not you are promoted, disciplined, or even fired.

Miscommunication

miscommunication

The understanding that social media may naturally inhibit the clarity of communication.

Another attitude related to online communication is the understanding that social media may naturally inhibit the clarity of communication. This belief is called **miscommunication**, and it could apply to many inherent aspects of social media, from sending messages with misspellings or unintended emotional inferences to wondering why a friend didn't get back to you as quickly as you got back to them. Experienced users learn to anticipate miscommunication and manage ways to prevent it. You can improve your communication competence by assuming that online communication can often inhibit understanding of a message's meaning.

Culture and Self-Concept

3.3   **Characterize the role of culture in determining self-concept.**

The development of self-concept varies from one culture to another and is determined by a specific combination of cultural norms and behaviors. Because our self-concept forms in a cultural context, one would expect differences across cultures. Specific cultural factors can influence the development of self-concept. For example, researchers have found that young Palestinians living in Jordanian refugee camps often have a low positive self-concept because they are raised in an autocratic setting of traditional

Arab families and schools, and have little independence and responsibility.[13] However, among Chinese secondary school students, a cohesive, "achiever" family environment is found to be associated with a more positive self-concept and less depression.[14]

Aging is a certainty for most all of us, and how it is viewed, and how it affects our self-concept as well as communication, is something not often discussed as it relates to culture. Howard Giles, Shardé Davis, Jessica Gasiorek, and Jane Giles in their book *Successful Aging: A Communication Guide to Empowerment* write that aging is not only a biological inevitability, but it also can be a social construct. People look at the aging process, according to Giles et al., differently, for example, depending on the country in which they live. They point out that when "young adulthood" begins and ends depends upon the country: for example, in the United States it begins at 17 and ends at 28, while in Bulgaria it begins at 16 and ends at 32. Middle age in the United States begins at 33 and ends at 59, while in Mongolia it begins at 29 and ends at 45. Elderly age begins in the United States at 61 and Ghana at 50.[15]

In Western societies it is not uncommon to hold negative attitudes about older people. This seemingly unfavorable view often translates for some into stereotypes that can be harmful, as they shape our expectations of aging as well as how younger people behave and treat older people. For example, some stereotypes imply older people are less competent, slow-thinking, hopeless, naïve, selfish, lonely, depressed, and so on thus, potentially affecting elderly people's self-concept and ultimately how they communicate and see themselves.[16]

Much research related to cultural differences has focused on the effects of individualism versus collectivism on the self-concept. An **individualistic orientation** stresses self or personal goals and achievements over group goals, an "I" consciousness, and a tendency to focus on individual accomplishments. Somewhat unique to the Western World are cultures that stress individualism and prescribe self-interest as a central determinant of one's behavior.[17]

individualistic orientation
Tendency to stress self or personal goals and achievements over group goals and achievements.

A **collectivistic orientation** tends to put aside individual goals for the wellbeing of the group. Researchers have examined the influence of specific situational arrangements of Japanese and American students in which the students were asked to describe themselves as: in a group, with a faculty member, with a peer, and alone.[18] They found self-concept variations as a function of culture, of the situation, and of the interaction between the two. For example, Japanese students were not only more self-critical but also more affected by the situation than were American students. While American students were more likely than Japanese students to provide self-descriptions in terms of abstract, internal attributes, as well as to refer to friends and family with statements such as, "I love my family." Japanese students tended to describe themselves more in terms of physical attributes and appearance, activities, the immediate situation, and possessions, saying, for example, "I am the youngest child in my family." Americans overall tended to generate more positive self-descriptions than did the Japanese. Why do you think Americans are more likely to express positive self-descriptions?[19]

collectivistic orientation
Tendency to put aside individual goals for the well-being of the group.

Our ability to communicate with individuals from different cultural backgrounds requires an understanding both of their culture and of their culture's influence on self-concept and the skill to adapt communication to accommodate differences. One African American woman stated one reason such communication is difficult: "If people don't share the same life experiences, they can't be expected to understand each other. If whites haven't been exposed to blacks, there will be a 'fear of the unknown.'"[20] This same fear or potential for misunderstanding can arise whenever people from different backgrounds or experiences come together. Interestingly, in today's global society, our self-concept is in part established through social interaction

Self-concept variations are a function of culture. Those in collectivistic-oriented societies usually put individual goals aside for the well-being of the group or whole of society.

with others both inside and outside our culture. Contact with other cultures in the early development of self-concept might help us to avoid some of the communication problems between people of different backgrounds.

Gender and Self-Concept

3.4   Characterize the role of gender in determining self-concept.

Gender is a crucial element in our personal and social identity. That is, you might or might not pay much attention to your social class or ethnic identity, but it would be extremely rare for you to be unaware and unconcerned about being male or being female. In hundreds of ways we are reminded each day of our gender by how we dress, how we act, and how others respond to us.

Sex and Gender

The terms sex and gender are often used interchangeably. We defined gender in Chapter 2 as socially constructed masculine and feminine behaviors that are learned. **Sex** is defined in biological terms as the anatomical and physiological differences between males and females that are genetically determined.[21]

Sex

The anatomical and physiological differences between males and females that are genetically determined.

The origin of gender differences is sometimes a matter of dispute, but most researchers agree that gender attributes are based entirely on what one learns (such as an association between hairstyle and femininity), whereas other attributes may be based entirely on biological determinants (such as the presence of facial hair). Each of us has a gender identity: A key part of our self-concept is the label *male* or *female*. According to Julia Wood, a communication scholar, for the vast majority of people, biological sex and gender identity coincide, though for a relatively small proportion of the population, gender identity differs from biological sex, such as for a female who has always thought of herself as male.[22]

Some male and female differences may be explained by biological differences in brain structure and development. Research—not conclusive, however—indicates that although both men and women use both hemispheres of the brain, each tends to specialize in one. Men generally exhibit greater development of the left hemisphere of the brain (the locus of mathematical abilities, analytical thought, and sequential information processing), whereas women manifest greater development of the right hemisphere (the locus of intuitive thought, imaginative and artistic activity, and some visual and spatial tasks).[23] Research reported suggests that women are more likely to use both sides of the brain to do language tasks, whereas men are more likely to depend on the left side. Women's brains don't seem, according to the research, to work as hard as men's to understand emotions.[24]

From the moment of birth, our biological sex slants the treatment we receive, such as wrapping a baby in a blue or pink blanket or dressing a child in "feminine" or "masculine" clothing. The type of toys children are given or the type of games they are encouraged to play can shape their behavior. It appears that these initial influences lead to gender stereotyping and expectations that strongly influence a person's self-concept.

Gender identity thus occurs when gender becomes part of one's self-concept. We develop a sense of self that includes maleness and femaleness,[25] and somewhere between the ages of 4 and 7, the concept of gender consistency (the sense that one is permanently male or female) develops. We become aware of our bodies and of the differences between us and the "other" sex. We may even view the other sex, for a short time at least, as "icky" and choose to play only with all girls or all boys. We may communicate in different ways as well; for example, boys use communication to assert themselves and their ideas or to achieve something. Girls use collaborative, cooperative talk to create relationships and generally try to avoid criticism or put downs.[26] We begin to accept the principle that gender is a basic attribute of ourselves. As soon as these attributes become known to us and are firmly in place, our perceptions of self are affected by what we believe about our gender as well as how we communicate with others.

Gender Stereotypes

A research study found that when children (ages 5 to 9) and adolescents (age 15 to college age) were shown videos of four 9-month-old infants, both age groups agreed that the babies identified as female (named Karen or Sue) appeared to be smaller, more beautiful, nicer, and softer than those identified as male (named William or Matthew).[27] Actually, the experimenters had assigned a male or female name to infants of both sexes. For example, each male baby was identified correctly as a boy for half the participants and incorrectly as a girl for the other half; similarly, each female baby was identified for half the participants as a girl and as a boy for the other half. The findings illustrate that gender stereotypes determined how the infants were perceived.

Even though societies have made great strides to reduce stereotypical thinking about males and females, stereotypes and narrowly defined role expectations are still accepted by many in Western culture and even more so in certain other cultures. These stereotypes affect communication behavior. Many similarities can be found in the communication behaviors of men and women. For example, there are soft-spoken men and verbally aggressive women; many men discuss their families and friends, and many women discuss sports and investments. It is, however, commonly accepted in the U.S. that men and women communicate differently and prefer to discuss certain subjects over others.

Females have often been the objects of stronger and more persistent stereotypes than males. Female stereotypes are often more negative in content than those applied to males. The positive stereotypes of feminine behaviors include characteristics such as nurturance, sensitivity, and personal warmth. These traits are believed by some to be less desirable and less suited for the valued roles of leadership and authority than are the gender stereotypes for males.[28] This issue is complex because such gender differences, even if observed, may be more a reflection of our stereotyping and their self-confirming nature than of actual differences between females and males.[29]

Research and evidence, however, point to the following: Some differences between males and females do exist with respect to some aspects of behavior and aging; but, in general, the magnitude of these differences is much smaller than past and prevailing gender stereotypes might suggest.[30]

Gender Expectations

An overwhelming body of evidence demonstrates that sex differences in communication result from gender expectations. According to psycholinguist Deborah Tannen, men and women do see themselves as different, and, as a result, they communicate differently. She says, "In this world [the man's] conversations are negotiations in which people try to achieve and maintain the upper hand if they can and protect themselves from others' attempts to put them down and push them around. Life, then, is a contest, a struggle to preserve independence and avoid failure." The man's world is a hierarchical social order in which people are either one-up or one-down. In the woman's world, according to Tannen, "conversations are negotiations for closeness in which people try to seek and give confirmation and support and to reach consensus. They try to protect themselves from others' attempts to push them away. Life, then, is a community, a struggle to preserve intimacy and avoid isolation." The woman's world is also hierarchical, but the order is related more to friendship than to power and accomplishment.[31]

Making Connections for Success

Public and Private Selves: Our Image

A headline in the *Lincoln Journal Star* read, "DYING TO BE THIN." The newspaper ran a three-day series on the pressures of being thin in American culture. It is clear that we focus on weight and body image. The image of thinness is portrayed on television, in movies, on the Internet, in magazines, and in store catalogs. Probably the most famous such representations are the Victoria's Secret swim summer catalog and the *Sports Illustrated* swimsuit issue.

1. How do the media affect our self-image? Has too much emphasis been placed on physical appearance by the media?

2. How does technology influence how we communicate about ourselves?

3. Are we more likely to share information via seemingly "impersonal" channels such as email or the Internet?

4. How does this type of information sharing differ from more traditional face-to-face communication?

5. What are the implications of the media, the Internet, advertising, social networking sites, and other technology for self-image?

In Western culture, the media create and reinforce expectations about ideal weight and body image, particularly for women.

Are we really different?

According to sociologist Dr. Cynthia Fuchs Epstein, "the two sexes are essentially similar and … the differences linked to sexual functions are not related to psychological traits or social roles."[32] She further believes that most gender differences are relatively superficial and that perceived differences are socially constructed in one's cultural upbringing. The differences between males and females, therefore, are more or less learned and reinforced by culture.

When asked to describe themselves, males and females differ in their descriptions. Males tend to mention qualities such as ambition, energy, power, initiative, and control. They are likely to discuss their success in sports and with females. Females, however, typically list attributes such as generosity, sensitivity, consideration, and concern for others.[33] Males, it seems, are expected to be powerful and authoritative, whereas females are expected to be concerned with relationships and expressiveness.

Despite some strides toward equality of the sexes, many cultures still have a cultural bias toward masculinity. But because communication behaviors are learned and are culturally defined, they can be unlearned and changed over time. To some extent, this has happened. For a long time in Western society, women expected, and were expected by others, to stay home and rear children, whereas men were regarded as the breadwinners. According to U.S. Bureau of Labor statistics, from 2012 to 2022 the women's civilian labor force is projected to increase by 5.4 percent, compared to a 5.6 percent increase for men.[34] Women's participation in the labor force in 2013 accounted for 57.2 percent of women of working age, while 69.7 percent of men of working age participated in the labor force.[35] Women make up 46.8 percent of the civilian labor force, while men represented 53.2 percent in 2013.[36]

Women outnumber men in such occupations as financial managers; human resource managers; education administrators; medical and health services managers; accountants and auditors; budget analysts; property, real estate, and social and community association managers; preschool, kindergarten, elementary, middle, and secondary school teachers; physical therapists; and registered nurses. The report notes that when women hit the proverbial "glass ceiling" or encounter situations that make it difficult for them to balance work with home life, they often venture out on their own.[37] These data illustrate not only that, increasingly, women have changed the expectations of what women can do and are doing, but also that women around the world embrace this change. The expectations and accomplishments of women in the business world, as well as in areas such as education, athletics, and many other careers, have influenced how women see themselves and what they believe they can accomplish.

If men and women are to break the stereotypes and expectations applied to them, we must avoid categorizing behaviors as exclusively male or female. Psychologists indicate that women and men who are androgynous—have both male and female traits—are more likely to be successful in their interactions and careers than are those who are totally masculine or feminine in their behaviors. For example, as you move from interactions with coworkers to those with your family, you might move from more "masculine" behaviors to more "feminine" behaviors. If you are a supervisor or owner of a business, you are expected to be assertive and task oriented; but when you spend time taking care of your children, you are expected, instead, to be patient and caring.

Self-Fulfilling Prophecy and Impression Management

3.5 **Explain the roles of self-fulfilling prophecy and impression management as they relate to self-concept.**

In addition to values, attitudes, and beliefs, expectations determine how we behave, who we eventually become, and what we communicate to others and ourselves. Our own expectations and those of others influence our perceptions and behavior. Thus, our self-concept is affected by our past experiences, our interactions with others, the expectations others have of us, and how we present ourselves to create an image.

Self-Fulfilling Prophecy

Our own and others' expectations lead us to act in predictable ways. The expectation becomes a **self-fulfilling prophecy**.[38] It can be a powerful force for shaping our self-concept. A research study asked college students who were either characteristically optimistic or generally pessimistic to describe their future selves.[39] According to the research, both types of students could imagine a positive future, but the optimistic students had higher expectations about actually attaining a positive self than did those who were pessimistic. Thus, we are more likely to succeed if we have positive expectations and believe that we have the potential to be successful. By the same token, we are more likely to fail if we believe ourselves to be failures.

Self-esteem can affect the predictions people make about themselves. It is a matter of attribution: People with positive, high self-esteem confidently attribute their success to past successes; therefore they expect to succeed in the future. People with low self-esteem, however, attribute any success they might have had to luck and so predict they will not necessarily succeed again unless they are lucky. How we describe ourselves is a powerful influence on our expectations. Our expectations therefore are a potent force for shaping our self-concept.

Most of us set positive expectations for ourselves, and most of us manage to see ourselves favorably much of the time. The fact that the majority of us show the *above-average effect*—which is thinking we are better than the average person on almost every dimension imaginable—is strong evidence of our desire to see the self in a relatively positive light.[40] Even when others communicate negative social feedback that contradicts our rosy view of ourselves, we often forget such instances and instead communicate information that supports our positive self-perceptions.[41]

self-fulfilling prophecy

Expectations we have of ourselves or that others have of us that help to create the conditions that lead us to act in predictable ways.

An *American Idol* contestant's image and self-esteem are influenced by the self-expectations he or she has. These expectations become a self-fulfilling prophecy, leading to success or, sometimes, disappointment.

We easily accept communication that suggests we are responsible for our successes. This acceptance is especially true for those with high self-esteem.[42] Culture-based limits on our willingness to "grab the credit" do exist, however. For the Chinese, for example, modesty is an important basis of their self-esteem.[43] Accordingly, Chinese students attribute their success in school to their teachers, whereas American students credit it to their own skills and intelligence. Conversely, when it comes to failure, Chinese students are more likely to explain their failure as stemming from their own flaws, while Americans tend to think of them as someone else's fault.

You can probably think of many times when the expectations you had for a certain outcome didn't come to pass. Thus, the more we understand about the role of expectations in our lives and recognize their influences on our self-concept, the better we will be able to set realistic expectations not only for others but for ourselves as well.

The self-fulfilling prophecy is a communicative force that influences self-concept; however, it cannot explain all outcomes. It is important to communicate high expectations for others rather than place unnecessary limitations on them, but the expectations we communicate should be realistic and obtainable.

Impression Management

Do you care if you make a good first impression on others? You should, according to the research findings, because such impressions seem to exert strong and lasting effects on others' perceptions of us. A recent study of 10,526 participants in HurryDate sessions—in which men and women interact with each other for very short periods, usually less than three minutes, and then indicate whether they are interested in future interaction—found that individuals know almost instantly if a person appeals to them when they see them. Men and women in the study assessed potential compatibility within moments of meeting. They based their compatibility on physically observable attributes such as age, height, attractiveness, and physique, instead of harder-to-observe attributes such as education, religion, and income, which seemed to have little effect on their choices.[44] It is clear that the way others first perceive us strongly influences their behavior toward us and whether they want to interact with us.

So what, exactly, are first impressions? How are they formed? And what steps can we take to make sure that we make good first impressions on others? The desire to make a favorable impression on others is strong, so most of us do our best to "look good" to others when we meet them for the first time. The creation of a positive image of oneself to influence the perceptions of others is referred to as **impression management** (or self-presentation).

impression management

Creating a positive image of oneself to influence the perceptions of others.

As your own experiences have probably suggested, impression management can take many forms. Most fall into two major categories: self-enhancement (efforts to boost your own image) and other-enhancement (efforts to make a target person feel good in your presence).

To better understand impression management, we have to know more about "self." Our *perceived self* is a reflection of our self-concept. This self is the person we believe ourselves to be at any given moment of self-examination. We keep many aspects of our perceived self private because we don't wish to tell others; for example, we might see ourselves as too fat even though everyone else tells us we are too thin, as inept in social settings with people we don't know well, or as smarter than everyone else.

Our *presenting self* is the public image, or the way we want to appear to others. Most of us seek to create an image that is socially acceptable: nice person, good student, articulate, hardworking, friendly, wild, ambitious, truthful, loyal friend, funny, competent, highly motivated, likeable, and so on. A research study asked college students to self-select 15 adjectives from a list of 108 possible adjectives describing their perceived self and presenting selves. Men and women described themselves similarly n 12 of 15 choices, differing in only 3. Both men and women were most likely to select active, attractive, busy, capable, curious, faithful, friendly, generous, happy, independent, polite, and responsible. Men also selected able, funny, and smart, whereas women also selected careful, sensible, and special.[45] When describing their most commonly presented characteristics, men and women were similar in the following characteristics: able, active, proud, and responsible. Men listed wild, strong, smart, brave, capable, and rough, whereas women more commonly presented the qualities of bright, funny, independent, sensible, and warm.[46] How would you describe your presenting self?

A question some researchers have asked is, "Does the use of social media enhance or diminish our self-esteem?" Social networking sites are, according to communication scholars Amy Gonzales and Jeffrey Hancock, designed to share information about ourselves with others, including likes/dislikes, activities we participate in, personal musings described on "wall posts," and "status updates."[47] They discovered that when participants in their study became self-aware of their Facebook profile, their self-esteem was enhanced. Gonzales and Hancock concluded from their findings that when participants in their study viewed their Facebook profiles, their self-esteem was enhanced, and when participants updated their profiles and viewed them during the experiment, self-esteem was reported to be greater.[48] Remember that self-esteem comprises our feelings and attitudes toward ourselves, which function to determine our self-concept. So what you communicate about yourself on social networking sites can influence your self-esteem. Is this due to the selective nature of the information we provide on our social networking site and how we impression manage it? Probably. According to Gonzales and Hancock's research, self-esteem may rise because the selectivity afforded by the site gives us the opportunity to present more positive information about ourselves while eliminating or not including any negative information.[49]

Specific tactics used when presenting the self to others are referred to as facework. **Facework** is a term first used by sociologist Erving Goffman to describe the verbal and nonverbal ways we act to maintain our own presenting image.[50] Goffman says that each of us creates various roles or characters that we want others to believe represent us. He also suggests that we maintain face by putting on a front when we desire to impress others. The front consists of our choice of behaviors and what we communicate when we are around others whom we want to impress. Think about the notion of facework for a moment and what you do differently when you are by yourself versus when you are with others. How do you behave and communicate when at school, at

"On the Internet, nobody knows you're a dog."

How we portray ourselves to each other on the Internet may be very different from who we really are. In presenting ourselves this way, what risks do we take and how might our Internet portrayal affect how we communicate with others, and others with us?© The New Yorker Collection 1993 Peter Steiner from cartoonbank.com. All rights reserved.

Facework

A term that is used to describe the verbal and nonverbal ways we act to maintain our own presenting image.

Making Connections for Success

Self-Respect, Ethics, and Self-Image

We express our values and image in a thousand ways— when we hold the door open for a stranger, when we give up our seat to an elderly person or pregnant woman, when we return money to the clerk who has made a mistake or a wallet to the stranger who lost it on the street, when we teach our children, and when we help our friends and families. Most of us try to "do the right thing" because we care about how others perceive us. This is especially true when it comes to our family, friends, fellow students, teachers, and coworkers.

1. Describe what it means to have personal integrity.
2. What does it mean to be ethical?
3. How might social media influence or affect our integrity?
4. Provide examples of how social media might be used to raise or lower a person's integrity.
5. What can you do, if anything, to ensure that others see you as a person of integrity?

home, at the library, at work, on a first date, or at a job interview when you want to make a favorable impression on someone? How do facework behaviors reflect a person's self-concept?

Do impression management tactics work? Do they really boost one's self-concept? In other words, do they succeed in creating a positive feeling and reaction in the people toward whom they are directed? The answer provided by an overwhelming body of research indicates yes, provided the tactics are used correctly. For example, a 2009 review of research studies related to impression management found that the tactics do work in job interview situations.[51] It seems, according to the study, that those who used impression management effectively were quite successful in obtaining high ratings from the interviewers and thus were more likely to be hired.

Many other studies achieved similar results with impression management tactics, but it must be noted that if they are overused, or used incorrectly, they can backfire and elicit negative rather than positive reactions from intended targets. For example, one study reported that overuse of different tactics of impression management (especially too much flattery of others) can lead to suspicion and mistrust rather than an increase in liking or higher evaluation.[52] It is clear from these findings that while impression management usually succeeds, this is not always the case, and sometimes it may have the opposite effect.

Enhancing Self-Concept

3.6   Identify six ways to improve self-concept.

Throughout this chapter, we discussed what self-concept is, how it's developed, and how it connects to communication. Most of us already have a pretty good image of ourselves, but most of us also have areas we would like to improve or change. Most of us have aspects of ourselves that could be improved or altered, but improvement and change require effort and a willingness to accept that something needs to be done. Almost everyone wants a positive self-image and wishes to be viewed by others as positively as possible. Building on these ideas of self-concept, we now explore possible ways to enhance or change self-concept and to grow as a communicator. The "Improving Self" guidelines help you begin the process.

Guidelines

Improving Self

1. **Decide what you would like to change or improve about yourself.** For change to occur, you must know or state what needs to be changed. Describe, as accurately, specifically, and completely as you can, what you would like to change or improve about yourself. If you are unhappy about something or don't like something about yourself, identify it and make a statement about it—for example, "I don't want to be afraid when I speak in public," "I want to be taken seriously by my friends," or "I want to be better organized."

2. **Describe why you feel the way you do about yourself.** Is your problem or shortcoming brought on by you or by others? Many students, for example, do not want to be in college or in a certain major. They go to college or take a major because that is what their parents or friends

expect or pressure them to do. Although many of these students would rather do something else, they are afraid to take a stand or do what they really want to do. Before you can begin to feel better about yourself, you must recognize why you are unhappy and who contributes to your problem. You might think that you can't change majors, that you are not capable of earning good grades in a particular subject, or that you are too shy to make new friends. If you want to change something about yourself, you must first ask yourself why you feel that way. For example, are you living out a self-fulfilling prophecy?

3. **Make a commitment to improve or change.** Changing our self-concept or aspects of ourselves is not easy, especially if what we want changed has been with us for a long period. However, nothing ever changes by itself; thus, to make a change, we must begin with a concentrated effort, a strong commitment, and a belief that changes can

occur. For example, on the TV show the *The Biggest Loser*, which involves a competition to lose the most weight, the people on the show, in spite of external rewards, will not reach their goal unless they have made a personal commitment to do so. Wishing or thinking something should change may be the first step, but only wishing or thinking won't make it happen—you have to commit to the change before it can occur. The process requires that you state what you want changed and decide you are going to make the change.

4. **Set reasonable goals for yourself.** You must be reasonable in setting your goals. You may be able to change some things overnight, but others may require long-term effort. For example, you might decide that you are going to improve your grades by studying for several hours every night. You can begin your new study schedule immediately, but actually raising your grades could take much longer.

5. **Decide on the specific actions you are going to take.** Determine an action plan that will lead to the outcome you want. Of course, anytime you act, you run the risk of failure, but successful people learn that, without risk, nothing can be accomplished. When you understand your shortcomings, learn how to deal with them, believe and commit yourself to making changes, and then take the appropriate actions, you will accomplish your goals. It is important to realize that changing your self-concept not only requires commitment and action but also almost always takes time.

If you feel unsure about, or lack confidence in, communicating with others, you might overcome or manage these feelings by approaching them in small steps. For example, you might feel hesitant to visit your professor in his or her office. Why not start by speaking briefly with your professor before or after class? You might begin by asking a question about your progress. Once you begin to feel more comfortable, ask for an appointment or stop in to visit during office hours. To start the conversation, you might have a few questions prepared. If you continue such visits, you will gradually gain more confidence.

6. **Associate with positive people whenever possible.** Try to surround yourself with people you like and trust. This will make it much easier to discuss any problems you have and to ask for support. When others know what you are trying to do, they can provide support to help you make the changes you desire.

Summary

Understanding Self-Concept

Objective 3.1 Differentiate among self-concept, self-image, and self-esteem.
Self-concept (or self-identity) is how we perceive ourselves, which consists of our beliefs and attitudes about self. Self-image is how we see ourselves—our mental picture of self. Self-esteem is our feelings and attitudes toward ourselves or how we evaluate ourselves.

- Self-concept is based on our values (long-lasting ideals that guide our behavior), attitudes (evaluative dispositions, feelings, or positions about oneself), and beliefs (convictions that we hold or confidence in the truth of something that is not based on absolute proof).
- Our self-concept determines our behavior and the related communication.

Social Media and Self-Concept

Objective 3.2 Identify social media factors that influence self-concept.

- Online self-disclosure is the degree to which an individual self-regulates what they reveal about themselves using social media.
- The belief that online communication enables social contact is known as online social connection.

- Convenience is the ease with which people connect with others through social media.
- Anxiety and nervousness associated with communicating through social media is known as online communication apprehension.
- Miscommunication is the understanding that social media may naturally inhibit the clarity of communication.

Culture and Self-Concept

Objective 3.3 Characterize the role of culture in determining self-concept.
Competent communicators know that communicating with people from different cultural backgrounds requires an understanding of other cultures as well as an ability to adapt to each.

Gender and Self-Concept

Objective 3.4 Characterize the role of gender in determining self-concept.
Those who understand gender roles are more likely to be successful in their interactions and careers than are those who do not.

- Gender identity, not the biological sex, becomes part of a person's self-concept.
- Gender stereotyping can affect communication behaviors of both males and females.

Self-Fulfilling Prophecy and Impression Management

Objective 3.5 **Explain** the roles of self-fulfilling prophecy and impression management as they relate to self-concept. Our own and others' expectations determine how we behave.

- Self-fulfilling prophecy is a communicative force that influences self-concept.
- Behaviors intended to create a positive self-image of us to influence others is referred to as impression management.

Enhancing Self-Concept

Objective 3.6 **Identify** six ways to improve self-concept.

- Decide what you would like to change or improve about yourself.
- Describe why you feel the way you do about yourself.
- Make a commitment to improve or change yourself.
- Set reasonable goals for yourself.
- Decide on the specific actions you will take.
- Associate with positive people whenever possible.

Discussion Starters

1. What steps can you take to help others improve their self-concept?

2. How does understanding the influence of self-concept improve communication competency?

3. What does your use of social networking sites—profile, photos, and wall posts—communicate to others about how you view yourself and about the image you wish to convey?

4. Discuss the influence of culture on self-concept.

5. In what ways does gender affect self-concept?

6. Discuss how we use impression management techniques to create a positive image of ourselves.

7. What information in this chapter was most useful in helping you become a more competent communicator?

Chapter 4
Connecting through Verbal Communication

 ## Learning Objectives

This chapter will help you

4.1 **Assess** the importance of language in communication events.

4.2 **Demonstrate** how the elements of language (sounds, words, grammar, and meaning) affect communication.

4.3 **Explain** how language can create barriers to effective communication.

4.4 **Illustrate** the impact of technology on language usage.

4.5 **Describe** how accurate, vivid, immediate, appropriate, and metaphorical language can help you be a more effective communicator.

Making Everyday Connections

All media is full of positive and negative examples of language use. There are dozens of examples from politicians, celebrities, news anchors, and talk show hosts, as well as students and professors. Because of the prevalence of social media, and the need to exploit the sensational, the examples quickly go viral. TV news anchor Brian Williams is known as a good storyteller who uses words well. His storytelling created problems in 2014 when he claimed, on air, that he had been in a helicopter that was shot down in Afghanistan. The "truth" was the helicopter ahead of his went down under enemy fire. Because Williams essentially lied to his viewers, he was suspended without pay for six months and then demoted to a less prestigious news anchor role at NBC. In February 2012, talk show host Rush Limbaugh made highly personal attacks on Georgetown law student Sandra Fluke. Limbaugh called Fluke a "slut" and a "prostitute" and further equated her plea for coverage for contraception with getting paid to have sex: "She wants you and me and the taxpayers to pay her to have sex. What does that make us? We're the pimps."[1] The next day he again brought Ms. Fluke into his talk show, saying, "Here's the deal: If we are going to pay for your contraceptives and thus pay for you to have sex, we want something for it. And I'll tell you what it is. We want you to post the videos online so we can all watch."[2] As a result, Limbaugh lost advertisers and 50 stations dropped his show.

In 2015, Limbaugh's remarks went viral when he made up negative songs about AIDS victims. Social media constantly monitor Limbaugh and others' inappropriate use of language, and report it so that millions hear the hateful, inflammatory words. Those protesting this kind of "hate speech" believe in freedom of speech, but they also believe that such nastiness can lead to bullying, hate crimes, violence, and even murder, and needs to be brought to people's attention so Limbaugh and others who use their media platform for hate speech and bullying can be boycotted or otherwise held accountable.[3]

Questions to Think About

1. Why do you think media personalities "embellish" their behaviors or lash out at specific groups?
2. What makes these situations a violation of our expectations?
3. What can we learn about "an unfortunate choice of words" from these examples?
4. Can you identify specific instances where social media and other electronic mediated communication affected the spread of distortions of the truth?

Language is a powerful tool we use to share meaning. Every culture has one or more languages that help them share meaning with others. In fact, some linguists estimate that there are more than 6,000 languages in the world today; there were only an estimated 60 languages 70–80 years ago. Social media has created many new words: "Selfies" are prevalent in many cultures, and those photos often end up on Twitter, Facebook, or LinkedIn.

Research provides information on the specialization of different areas of the brain. One component of our specialized brain is language, and each part of the brain has its own language. People are attracted to other people speaking the same language. Have you ever heard someone say, "It's like we speak the same language"? Chances are, that is *exactly* what is happening—the persons in dialogue are speaking from the same thinking preference. How we give information, how we listen, and our perspective on the information we give and receive are, in good part, shaped by our thinking preferences.[4]

The Importance of Language

4.1 **Assess the importance of language in communication events**

language

A structured system of signs, sounds, gestures, or marks used and understood to express ideas and feelings among people within a community, nation, geographic area, or cultural tradition.

Language is a structured system of signs, sounds, gestures, or marks used and understood to express ideas and feelings among people within a community, nation, geographic area, or cultural tradition. Language has the power to influence our perceptions of others (and theirs of us) as we use language to share who we are. It affects our emotions and allows us to make connections with others. Language helps us gain and maintain relationships with loved ones, family, friends, and others. Without language, little or no human communication as we now know it would exist. Language allows us to encounter our world in significant ways because it enables us to share meaning with others. Can you imagine what it would be like to be unable to tell someone what you know or think or feel? Language is a powerful tool. But it is only as effective and efficient as the people using it. Although we often believe that language is neutral, in actuality it communicates much about what we are and what we think; therefore, language is subjective, must be carefully used, and should be chosen according to the context. Furthermore, language for writing differs from language for the ear.

A short YouTube clip called "The Power of Words" shows a blind man sitting on the sidewalk with a sign that reads, "I'M BLIND. PLEASE HELP."[6] He received few donations until a young woman changed the sign to read: "IT'S A BEAUTIFUL DAY AND I CAN'T SEE IT," and most passing people threw money into his container. This example demonstrates the power of words.

Words create images in our minds. We attribute meaning to what we hear, and can accept or reject a speaker's message just because we don't attribute the same meaning to the message. Social theorists raise issues about perspectives on language because they want an inclusive world. In her book *Fighting Words*, Patricia Hill Collins, black feminist and author, investigates how effectively black feminist thought confronts the injustices African American women currently face. Her book examines poverty, mothering, white supremacy and Afrocentrism, the resegregation of American society by race and class, and the ideas of Sojourner Truth and how they can serve as a springboard for more liberating social theory.[7]

Language has the power to create biases for everyone. For instance, when you hear the word *doctor*, what image comes to mind? What about a *strong leader*? When you hear *nurse*, what is the image? Many people think of leaders and medical doctors as men and nurses as women, but increasingly that's not the case. In his poem "New Kid on the Block," Jack Prelutsky shows us how wrong our images based on language can be. The narrator of "The New Kid" describes the kid as "tough, angry, and strong." The last line of the poem surprises us when Prelutsky says, "I don't care for *her* at all." Effective language ensures that people perceive inclusiveness but also clear knowledge of intent.

Conversations are a vital part of our everyday lives. Language allows us to share our thoughts and feelings with others in meaningful ways.

Making Connections for Success

What Did I Say?

Have you ever heard someone describe a situation that you also witnessed and wondered how their impression was so different from yours? Why do three people who witness the same event see and describe it in various ways? People have vastly different perspectives and attach different meanings to the words they use to describe those perspectives. In fact, differences in thinking preferences can be so great that they create separate and distinct "languages"; thus, we can understand the explosion of the number of languages in the world. While superficially using the same vocabulary, these preferences allow us to assign different meanings to the same words, thereby describing worlds seen from vastly different perspectives.[5]

1. How or why do some communication interactions work better than others?

2. What kinds of problems do you encounter when communicating with others?

3. What do you do to get around those problems or reach understanding?

4. What unique circumstances are created when the conversation partners come from different cultures?

5. Identify a time when you used the same language for a written exchange as for an oral one with negative results. Why did this happen?

muted group theory

Suggests that under-represented groups (women, poor, people with disabilities, seniors, gays, blacks, Hispanics, etc.) often are not as free or as able to say what they mean, when and where they wish.

style-switch

A term that identifies when people from co-cultures speak the language of their own culture but switch to that of the dominant culture when needed and appropriate.

Communication scholar Cheris Kramerae suggests that people who do not have the power of "correct or appropriate" language have little voice in their worlds. Her **muted group theory** suggests that status and power are clearly linked.[8] Kramerae says that muted groups are often women and ethnic minorities or out-groups (people with disabilities, the elderly, and the poor). Another communication scholar, Marsha Houston, reports that African American women and other out-groups **style-switch**, or move between "dominant culture" language and the language of their own co-culture, to successfully operate in both the dominant society and their own co-culture.[9] First Lady Michelle Obama is a role model and a popular speaker both in the United States and around the world and clearly demonstrates her ability to function effectively in both cultures.

Language allows us to share our thoughts and ideas with others. We can name things and converse with others to learn what we have in common. Words can cause us to take up specific causes or create a better environment. Sometimes, however, we don't have the words to fully explain our thoughts, but we can usually reach the point where we understand each other fairly well. For these and other reasons, communicators need to make careful choices in the language we use to communicate.

The Elements of Language

4.2 **Demonstrate** how the elements of language (sounds, words, grammar, and meaning) affect communication.

Language, talk, speech, and communication are four different but related phenomena. *Language*, as noted earlier, is a shared structured system of signs, sounds, gestures, or marks (in other words, *symbols*) that allows people to express ideas and feelings to others; *talk* is what we do every day; *speech* is one vehicle used to transmit language; and *communication* involves the exchange of meanings. Language is one means by which we communicate, and speech is one way we use language. The fact that we process language does not automatically mean that we communicate well, but we cannot verbally communicate without some language, and all language would be useless if it did not help us convey meanings. Of course, nonverbal communication also allows us to express ourselves.

The goal is to coordinate language and speech to produce effective communication, or transfer the meaning intended. You can learn more about language by examining four of its key elements: sounds, words, grammar, and meaning.

Sounds

Most of us learn to speak language before we learn to write it, and most of us are born with the physical mechanisms that enable us to make speech sounds. However, we do not all learn to produce sounds in exactly the same way. Though using the same language, people of certain geographic regions or cultural groups may speak quite differently. Dialects and other speech patterns can complicate communication between people who speak the same language.

Words

words

A symbol that stands for the object or concept that it names.

Words are symbols that stand for objects and concepts. A word can represent an object or an abstract concept: The word *desk* represents an actual piece of furniture, an object, while the word *anger* represents a whole range of emotions associated with our feelings when we are extremely upset and unhappy.

Words have meanings because communities and cultures give them meaning. People agree that certain sound combinations signify certain things. One of the

Making Connections for Success

The Power of Language

Arabs have a great appreciation of the power of language. An ancient Arab proverb clearly illustrates this power: "A man's tongue is his sword." In the Arab culture, words used to describe events can become more significant than the events themselves. Communication scholars Samovar and Porter suggest that, in Arabic, "Words are used more for their own sake than for what they are understood to mean. Whereas North Americans can adequately express an idea in ten words, the Arabic speaker may use one hundred."[10]

People in the Arab culture know language is powerful. But, other cultures, too, share that view. African cultures often use the spoken word over the written word, and use proverbs to demonstrate issues. African Americans also place a high value on talk, conversation, and the oral storytelling tradition. An example from Kenya is: "Having a good discussion is like riches." This proverb demonstrates that both history and news are shared in the oral tradition.[11] People in El Salvador, for example, have at least five specific forms of the English word "you." *Usted* is used when speaking to an elder or a superior, while *tu* is used for informal situations, but not with elders or superiors.

1. Identify an instance where you learned about the power of language.
2. If you speak another language in addition to your first language, what have you learned about using your second language among people for whom that language is the first language?
3. How have social media affected language?

---

intriguing aspects of languages is the **idioms**, or words whose meanings cannot be understood according to ordinary usage. If you hear someone say "that happens once in a blue moon," you may realize that something is a rare event, but someone from another culture who uses English as a second language may be totally lost because the phrase cannot be literally translated. All parties in the communication event must agree on meanings if we wish to understand each other.

idioms
Words whose meanings cannot be understood according to ordinary usage.

Grammar

Just as language has rules that govern how sounds may be joined into words, it also has rules that govern how words may be joined into phrases and sentences. This set of rules is called **grammar**. For example, the English grammar system requires that singular nouns take singular verb forms and plural nouns take plural verb forms (*friend is; friends are*).

grammar
Rules that govern how words are put together to form phrases and sentences.

As we join sounds together to form words and join words together to form phrases, sentences, and paragraphs, we use language's sound and grammar systems simultaneously. The ability to use sounds and grammar correctly is crucial to competent communication. Grammar enables us to make complete sentences and to understand sentences made by others.

Despite the many rules that govern language, the number of different messages that can be created is virtually limitless. It has been estimated that in the English language, it is possible to create ten quintillion 20-word sentences.[12] This does not include sentences either shorter or longer than 20 words. Thus, the number of possible sentences and messages is nearly infinite.

Meaning

The study of meaning, or the association of words with ideas, feelings, and contexts, is called **semantics**. If language did not have meaning, it would serve little or no purpose. Because words and word patterns can be used to exchange meanings between people, language is a useful tool for communication.

semantics
The study of meaning, or the association of words with ideas, feelings, and contexts.

DO WORDS CONTAIN MEANING? We tend to associate language symbols (words) with specific meanings and to take that relationship for granted. But it is important to understand that, in fact, language by itself has no meaning.

Look at this photo and think about how mediated communication has changed the way we communicate, especially in shortcuts with language.

This notion might seem to contradict our entire discussion so far. You might wonder how language can be a system involving rules and meanings, yet still has no meaning itself. Actually, it is entirely arbitrary, for instance, that the word *skunk* represents those four-legged mammals that are stinky if you get too close to them. Nothing about the letters s, k, u, n, and k is essentially related to the being of a skunk. When we see or hear the symbol, we fill in the meaning.

Words are symbols that represent people, objects, concepts, and events; the word is not actually the person, object, concept, or event. For example, *freedom, chaos, love, car,* and *poverty* are only words, not the entities they symbolize. It is easy to miss this distinction. Even though words are symbols, try screaming, "I'm bleeding!" in front of someone who gets nauseous at the sight of blood, and you will quickly see how words cause reactions—as if the words were actually the thing they were depicting.

The belief that words hold meaning in themselves is widespread. During the past several years, we have asked students in communication classes whether words have meaning. The data, though not scientifically collected, suggest that more than 75 percent of the students believe words do have meaning. But the simple fact is that words do *not* contain meanings by themselves. Words acquire meaning only through the context in which they are used and by the fact that those who use them give them meaning. Figure 4.1 shows how two different people attach different meanings to the word *house*.

The following dialogue from Lewis Carroll's *Through the Looking Glass* illustrates this idea. Humpty Dumpty and Alice become involved in an argument about language and meaning:

> "I don't know what you mean by 'glory,'" Alice said.
>   Humpty Dumpty smiled contemptuously. "Of course you don't—till I tell you.
> I meant there's a nice knock-down argument for you!"

Figure 4.1 Meanings Are Not in Words but in People

We cannot assume that using words we consider appropriate and adequate to convey a particular message will succeed with every listener. As this figure illustrates, different people associate different meanings with even the simplest words because words are symbols only—people fill in the meaning.

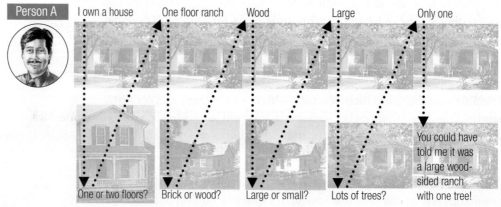

"But 'glory' doesn't mean 'a nice knock-down argument,'" Alice objected.

"When I use a word," Humpty Dumpty said, in a rather scornful tone, "it means just what I choose it to mean—neither more nor less."

"The question is," said Alice, "whether you can make words mean so many different things."

"The question is," said Humpty Dumpty, "which is to be master—that's all."[13]

Who determines meaning? *You.* You control which words you use, the meaning you wish to give them, and, if you have mastered the art of communication, how people react to them. Although everyone has the ability to impart meaning to words, not everyone does so in the same way. Thus, a sender might intend one meaning for a message, but the receiver might either intentionally or unintentionally give the message a different meaning. Disparity between the meaning sent and the meaning received can be a greater problem when the sender and receiver have different cultural backgrounds or even different experiences and knowledge. For example, people who keep up with computers and technology often use specialized language unfamiliar to someone who doesn't have much knowledge about computers. Care in choosing words is especially important in such situations.

WORDS HAVE DENOTATIVE AND CONNOTATIVE MEANINGS   Denotation is the common meaning associated with a word—its standard dictionary definition. Denotative meanings are usually readily understood. Many people use words as if they had only a denotative or specific meaning, but this is not the case. Although commonly understood dictionary definitions (denotative meanings) exist, when we communicate we usually use words connotatively.

Connotation is the subjective meaning of a word; what a word suggests because of feelings or associations it evokes. The connotative meaning is based on the context in which the word is used, how the meaning is expressed nonverbally (tone of voice, facial expression of the speaker, and so on), and the understanding of the person who is receiving it. The competent communicator can differentiate between denotative and connotative meanings and understands which is being used in a given situation. Connotative meanings may be generally accepted by most people who use the language, by people within a particular group, or by an individual. To someone who lives on either coast or throughout much of the South, the Midwest *farm* evokes connotative images of farms as large fields of corn and farmsteads with chickens, pigs, and cows. To a Midwesterner, on the other hand, a *farm* represents a different connotative image of a "home," or a place to live and work, and may have nothing to do with farming. Although not all farms have livestock, they still retain the denotative meaning, but not necessarily the connotative meaning held by those unfamiliar with farms.

WORDS CAN BE CONCRETE OR ABSTRACT   **Concrete words** are symbols for specific things that can be pointed to or physically experienced (seen, tasted, smelled, heard, or touched). For example, words such as *flag, house, food,* and *soda (pop)* are concrete words. They represent specific, tangible objects, and therefore their meanings are usually quite clear. We can be even more specific with *Buick Enclave, ranch-style home, pizza,* and *Dr. Pepper.* Consequently, communication based on concrete words leaves little room for misunderstanding, and any disagreement can typically be resolved by referring to the objects themselves.

Abstract words, however, are symbols for ideas, qualities, and relationships. Abstract words represent intangible things, or things that cannot be experienced through the senses; thus, their meanings depend on the experiences and intentions of the persons using them. For instance, words such as *beauty, love, ethics, music,* and *determination* stand for ideas or symbols that signify different things to different people.

---

denotation

The objective meaning of a word; the standard dictionary definition.

connotation

The subjective meaning of a word; what a word suggests because of feelings or associations it evokes.

concrete word

A symbol for a specific thing that can be pointed to or physically experienced.

abstract word

The symbol for an idea, quality, or relationship.

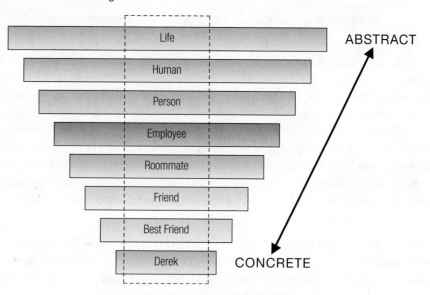

Figure 4.2 The Ladder of Abstraction

Word meanings become more concrete when they refer to a specific person, place, or thing. Concrete language helps to reduce the number of possible interpretations of messages, leaving less chance for misunderstanding.

The "ladder of abstraction" (Figure 4.2), first described by Alfred Korzybski in 1933 and expanded on by S. I. Hayakawa in 1964,[14] remains a useful way to explain concrete and abstract words and meanings. Figure 4.2 illustrates the varying degrees of concreteness among related words. *Derek* is the most tangible word because it refers to a specific individual named Derek. You can see that as words move from concrete to abstract, they refer to more general and more intangible ideas that are open to differing views.

WORDS CAN BE SPECIFIC OR VAGUE Just as abstract words provide little in the way of tangible things, specific and vague words can interfere with the meaning you intend. Someone who says, "Call me later" when she leaves the meeting at 5 p.m. gives an open time frame. So if you call after 9 p.m. and are confronted with a grumpy person who answers the phone, "You're calling too late—it's my child's bedtime," the lack of specificity makes for hurt feelings. You can see that misinterpretations can easily occur. The use of vague words confuses the issue and sends unclear messages. Specific words allow the listener to share in the meaning you intend. Vague language can easily lead to misunderstandings and result in ineffective communication, as illustrated by the following conversation:

SASHA:	Enrique, you said I could choose the movie and you would choose the restaurant for Friday's evening. Have you made reservations?
ENRIQUE:	Nah, we don't need reservations.
SASHA:	Why not?
ENRIQUE:	I don't know when we'll get there.
SASHA:	Why not?
ENRIQUE:	Yesterday, I told the boss I'd stay late for a meeting, and I don't know how long it will last.
SASHA:	And when were you going to tell me?
ENRIQUE:	I just did.

This conversation is problematic because Enrique is vague and has not kept Sasha informed about his meeting and how it might affect their plans. Sasha expects to go to a movie and dinner and suddenly learns that neither one may be possible. The result is likely to be, at the very least, a disagreement about their plans. Enrique's responses

Making Connections for Success

What Do Words Really Mean?

The conversation between Sasha and Enrique illustrates much more than the use of vague or specific words. Culture, educational background, social status, age, the nature of the relationship, and gender are only a few of the factors that influence language choice and word meanings. Numerous communication scholars have discussed gender and cultural differences in the way people use language to communicate. Psychologist Deborah Tannen became a pop culture phenomenon for her books and assertions that men and women are different in their communication styles and language choices. Think about language choice in the following situations:

1. Identify two specific instances in which you and a person of the opposite sex had different views of language. What was the result of each?

2. What language differences between generations have you noticed? Would you talk or write to your grandmother the same way you would to your best friend? Why or why not?

3. List the characteristics of language appropriate to writing a class paper or work report. Then, list the characteristics of language appropriate for making an oral presentation in class or at work.

4. Together with your classmates, compare and contrast the two lists. What are the similarities and differences?

5. How would making a presentation to a group of high school students versus a group of retired professionals affect your language choices?

---

were vague, and the lack of specificity and clarity led to unfulfilled expectations on Sasha's part. It's always a good idea to explain, define, or illustrate any vague words that may be misunderstood.

MEANING DEPENDS ON COMMONALITIES   The more communicators have in common in terms of background, experience, and attitudes, the more likely they are to hold similar meanings for the words they exchange. However, competent communicators do not assume too much about how others will interpret their messages; they continuously refine messages based on the feedback they receive. Consider the following situation:

> Taylor and Danica are roommates. They have trouble budgeting for household expenses. Taylor wants to buy the economy sizes of dish and laundry soap because they can save money over the semester. Danica becomes upset because she doesn't want to spend her entire budget the first week of the month. *Economy, budget*, and *careful spending* mean different things to the two, and stating those words usually causes a major conflict.

Instead of talking things through, each person goes her own way and spends the joint budget in ways she thinks best. The problem is that the roommates have never taken the time to try to understand the other's position. Their own backgrounds and experiences make a big difference in the way they choose and use language and meaning, and unless they can talk about it, they will not achieve a common understanding.

LANGUAGE CAN OBSCURE MEANINGS   Words mean different things to different people, based on each person's experiences and the direct relationship of those experiences to particular words. *Unfamiliar words*, such as technical medical terms, can negatively influence a listener's views. When you have no frame of reference for certain words, you're lost in a conversation when they are used and not explained. When you choose more understandable words, you will help listeners comprehend the nature of the issue, and reduce some of the frustration about lack of knowledge and information.

In addition, the *meanings of words*, like words themselves, change from time to time and from place to place. It is easy to

Language, or jargon, used by a particular group or discipline may be too specialized or technical to be understood by the general public. In such a situation, one would need specific knowledge about the subject to understand what is being said.

forget that the meaning we have for a word might not match one held by others. For example, ask a person over age 80 the meanings of these words: *twerking, rofl, phablet, jorts, hashtag, viral, tech-head, digital detox, girl crush,* or *bromance*; and see what response you get. We constantly add words to our language, especially technology-related words. How many new words have been added to the language because of these advances? *Blogging, texting, Googling, Facebook, LinkedIn, Twitter* and *tweet, Wi-Fi, TiVo, spamming, catfishing, emoji,* and *phishing* are some fairly recent examples.

Regional differences also exist. Word meanings vary from region to region. For example, in some regions of the United States, if you ask for *pop* at a store, the clerk will not understand you until you rephrase your question and ask for *soda* or a Coke. In Nebraska and Iowa, people get a drink of water from the drinking fountain, but in Wisconsin, people use a bubbler. Regional word use can lead to misunderstandings, and we must be sensitive to such potential differences. Further, cultures and co-cultures hold differing meanings for certain words. For example, for most Americans *very dear* means something that is highly valued or loved, whereas in Ireland *very dear* means very expensive and has nothing to do with personal value or love.

Co-cultures within a language community sometimes use words or phrases in ways that are unique to their group. Scientists, engineers, and health care providers use language that might be too specialized to be understood by the general public. This unique language use is referred to as **jargon**. Other co-cultures, such as students, might use **slang** or words used to communicate only with those who know the words, and the words and meanings change quickly. Sometimes those words become so known and accepted they end up in the dictionary. Twerking was a relatively unknown word until Miley Cyrus twerked on a stage, and then the word and the image went viral. In newspapers and house-for-sale advertising, a real estate agent might use the term *handyperson's special* to refer to a house in need of repair.[15]

Numerous colleges have created slang projects they regularly update. You might want to go to your browser and key in "slang terms" to see if other schools have slang terms similar to those in your school. This search provides an opportunity to add new slang terms as well as indicate whether one uses specific terms in his or her geographical location. Slang words are constantly discarded and new ones invented or refined—sometimes just to make sure that people outside a particular group will not catch on to their meanings. All kinds of groups, including members of a given profession, college students, ethnic groups, and gangs, develop and use slang terms.[16]

Language is used to share meaning, but it also can be used to obscure, distort, or hide meaning. One way to obscure meaning is to use a euphemism. A **euphemism** is an inoffensive or mild expression given in place of one that may offend, cause embarrassment, or suggest something unpleasant. Our society also uses euphemisms to avoid taboo subjects or words that can trigger negative reactions. Euphemisms can defuse the emotional charge associated with controversial or difficult concepts. For example, when a person dies, we often use a euphemism such as "passed away" instead of the blunter word. The phrase "passed away" seems to make a difficult, complex situation more approachable.

Euphemisms can also be used to enhance something, to make it seem a little more glamorous than it actually is. In our society, we have become so concerned with labels that we have renamed many things to give them a more positive connotation. For example, we rarely use the term *salesman* because, apart from being sexist, it also conjures up a negative image not exactly characterized by scrupulous business ethics. This unfavorable connotation is fostered by the media and sometimes by personal experience. Thus, referring to a person who sells merchandise as a sales associate, sales consultant, or sales representative sounds more positive. Sometimes the terms *trash* or *garbage collector* are recast as *sanitation engineer*, which makes the job seem more attractive.

Language can also be used to create **doublespeak**, or deliberately ambiguous messages. William Lutz, a professor at Rutgers University who wrote a book,

---

jargon

Language used by certain groups or specific disciplines that may be technical or too specialized to be understood by the general population.

slang

Language used by groups to keep the meaning of the communication within the group. Slang words change frequently and are specific to specific regions or groups.

euphemism

The use of an inoffensive or mild expression in place of one that might offend, cause embarrassment, or suggest something unpleasant.

doublespeak

The deliberate misuse of language to distort meaning.

Doublespeak, denounces the use of words to conceal meaning. He says he can live with ordinary euphemisms, but his teeth are set on edge when a worker is told he has been "dehired" because the firm is experiencing "negative employee retention." Actually, the employee has been fired in a layoff. But no one is willing to say so, laments Lutz.[17] SourceWatch is an online project of the Center for Media and Democracy and provides a list of doublespeak terms and their meanings. Examples are "shock and awe" for the massive bombing in Iraq and "security contractors" for mercenary troops or agencies that provide them.[18] Lutz thinks the practice is "disgraceful, dangerous to democracy, perverse, and pervasive." It's hard work, too. Doublespeak isn't just the natural work product of the bureaucratic mind, painstakingly invented by committees to cloak meaning. Doublespeak is not a slip of the tongue or language used improperly because of ignorance. It is a tool that the powerful use to achieve their ends without clearly communicating with those who may be affected by their actions or who may foot the bill for them. According to Lutz and other scholars, doublespeak is particularly harmful when it makes something inappropriate or negative appear appropriate or positive.

As you can see, language and meaning are inseparable parts of communication. They mesh smoothly in successful communication. Unfortunately, a type of communication also occurs when a message is misunderstood.

Language-Based Barriers to Communication

4.3 **Explain** how language can create barriers to effective communication.

Although it takes little physical effort to say something to someone, it does take mental effort to ensure that what we say conveys our intended meaning. Even if we create what we *think* is the perfect message, the possibility always exists that the receiver will misinterpret the message or find it ambiguous. Therefore, the receiver must also make an effort to understand the intended message.

"There are over 300 different languages in everyday use in the United States. This number includes more than 160 Native American languages, the languages of the colonizers (English, French, and Spanish), languages of immigrants—both old and new—and a variety of dialects spoken in various regions of the country."[19] We must recognize that communication is a symbolic interaction rich in subtlety. It will never be strictly concrete or objective and thus always carries the potential for misunderstanding. Misunderstandings occur for numerous physical, mental, and cultural reasons. Ineffective use of language is one reason. Among the most common language-based barriers to effective communication are bypassing, indiscrimination, and polarization.[20]

Meanings Can Be Misunderstood

What a speaker means and what is *heard* and *understood* by the listener often differ. Such misunderstanding between a sender and a receiver is called **bypassing**. How many times have you said to someone, "But that's not what I meant"? Here is an illustration of bypassing:

> Your supervisor says, "Get the figures on how much space there is in the new office complex and give me a report as soon as you can." You find the information, make the calculations, make comparisons, identify advantages and disadvantages, and three days later take the supervisor your report. You're dismayed when you're told, "What took you so long? I wanted that

bypassing

A misunderstanding that occurs between a sender and a receiver because of the symbolic nature of language.

information two days ago. It's too late now." The supervisor never said the information was needed or wanted the next day, and you worked hard to get a polished report. Who's at fault? Was the supervisor not clear? Did you ask any questions?

Bypassing occurs in similar situations every day.

Bypassing usually results from the false belief that each word has only one meaning and that words hold meaning. But a glimpse at our everyday language quickly illustrates that most words have multiple uses and meanings. Words acquire many meanings because they change over time, are used and understood differently in various cultures and regions, and often reflect the knowledge and situation of the user. It is therefore crucial that all of us as communicators, both senders and receivers, stay alert to the fact that different people can interpret words differently.

The interpretation of words becomes even more complex when people from different cultures exchange everyday communication. The problem is magnified when someone uses common phrases unfamiliar to nonnative speakers of English. For example, consider this sentence: "Won't you have some tea?" The nonnative speaker of English listens to the literal meaning of the question and would answer no if he or she did in fact want tea. Because they use this wording so frequently, native English speakers forget it contains a negative. But a nonnative speaker might not know that, in practice, "Won't you have some tea?" and "Will you have some tea?" mean the same thing. In this situation, bypassing occurred because of cultural differences between the two speakers

Some speakers deliberately invite bypassing and use euphemisms or double-speak to soften or distort meanings. It is important to be aware of this. Politicians and advertisers sometimes say one thing to get people to believe or accept something else. President Obama was surprisingly candid in the early weeks of his presidency when he admitted, "I screwed up." Listeners should critically examine what is being said. Both speaking and listening involve ethical considerations. Issues of conscience—what is right or wrong and what is beneficial or harmful—are everyone's responsibility.

Guidelines
Reducing Bypassing[21]

1. **Be person-minded, not word-minded.** Think about words and their meanings but also consider the persons using the words and the meanings they might give to them. Constantly question your own interpretation: "This is what the word means to me, but what does it mean to the others?"

2. **Query and paraphrase.** Ask questions and paraphrase your message or the meaning you've derived from others' messages whenever there is potential for misunderstanding. Differences in background, age, gender, occupation, culture, attitudes, knowledge, and perceptions may affect communication. If you are uncertain, ask others to explain. Restating a message in your own words gives you and the sender a chance to check that you received a message similar to what was sent. As the importance and complexity of a message increase, so does the need to ask questions and paraphrase.

3. **Be approachable.** Encourage open and free communication. The most frequent barrier to effective communication is an unwillingness to listen to others. Allow others to question and paraphrase your messages and show respect for what they say. It is not always easy to listen for specific meaning but the effort will ensure a clear exchange of information.

4. **Be sensitive to contexts.** Consider the verbal and situational contexts of your communication interactions. The meaning of a word can be more precisely interpreted when you consider the words, sentences, and paragraphs that precede and follow it and the setting in which communication takes place.

5. **Consider the impact of social media.** Your generation is the digital generation, while your parents and grandparents may have no clue as to your meaning when you use words or phrases associated with mediated forms of communication.

Language Can Shape Our Attitudes

Indiscrimination is the neglect of individual differences and the overemphasis of similarities. Indiscrimination is a form of perceptual set in which a person chooses to ignore differences and changes in events, things, and people. Language plays a significant role in our tendency to see similarities between things, even when they don't exist. Nouns that categorize people *(teenager, divorcé, student, professor, African American, conservative, Southerner, friend, government official, politician, athlete, salesperson)* encourage us to focus on similarities. Statements such as "Professors are unfair" and "People in my parents' generation and older know very little about computers and social media" may be interpreted to include all people over 50, instead of some parents and some grandparents. They fail to distinguish among individuals. Such categorization often results in stereotyping.

When we stereotype, we categorize events, objects, and people without regard to unique individual characteristics and qualities. Stereotypes are often negative, but they may also be positive—for example, "All liberals are hardworking," "All conservatives want peace," "All teachers are dedicated professionals," and "All environmentalists are concerned citizens." Whether the stereotype is negative or positive, the problem is the same: Individual qualities are ignored. It is quick and easy to stereotype because it does not require analysis, investigation, or thought. When we preclude distinctions, stereotypes give us neat, oversimplified categories that facilitate but also distort our evaluation of people, situations, and events.

There are ways to reduce indiscrimination in our communication. **Indexing** is one way to point out differences that distinguish various members of a group and thus reduce indiscrimination. Indexing identifies the specific person, idea, event, or object to which a statement refers. When you hear someone say something that lumps people, ideas, events, or objects into a single category, such as, "All professional athletes are egotistical," "All professors are liberal," "Feminists don't care about family values," or "All Republicans are Tea-Party thinkers," you need to think and ask, "Which people are you talking about?" Everyone is unique. None of us is all one thing or another, and none of us is exactly like anyone else. Even though the media play up politicians who are greedy, sell their votes, or are otherwise influenced by lobbyists, each politician is different. The same is true of professional athletes, professors, and Republicans. They may belong to a class or group with an identity and whose members have similarities, but the group is composed of unique individuals.

Dating, another technique for reducing indiscrimination, is a form of indexing that sorts people, ideas, events, and objects according to time. By telling when something occurred, we acknowledge that things change over time and add specificity to a statement. As an example of how important dating is, indicate the year in which you think each of the following news bulletins was probably made:

Pope Condemns Use of New "Horror" Weapons

Vatican City—Prompted by widespread fears that new weapons of mass destruction might wipe out Western civilization, the Pope today issued a bulletin forbidding the use of these weapons by any Christian state against another, whatever the provocation.

Moral Rot Endangers Land, Warns General

Boston—The head of the country's armed forces declared here today that if he had known the depth of America's moral decay, he would never have accepted his command. "Such a dearth of public spirit," he asserted, "and want of virtue, and fertility in all the low arts to obtain advantages of one kind or another, I never saw before and hope I may never be witness to again."[22]

indiscrimination
The neglect of individual differences and overemphasis of similarities.

indexing
A technique to reduce indiscrimination by identifying the specific persons, ideas, events, or objects a statement refers to.

dating
A form of indexing that sorts people, events, ideas, and objects according to time.

The thoughts expressed in these two paragraphs could easily apply to today's events, but, in fact, the first paragraph pertains to a statement made by Pope Innocent II in 1139, and the second is a comment made by George Washington in 1775.

Did you think that these news bulletins referred to recent events? If so, you fell victim to indiscrimination. Why do such errors occur? How can we avoid or prevent them? The contexts of the statements in these news bulletins could be greatly clarified merely by adding dates: Vatican City, 1139, and Boston, 1775. Dating gives listeners valuable information that can increase their understanding of the intended message.

Language Can Cause Polarization

polarization

The tendency to view things in terms of extremes.

Polarization is the tendency to view things in terms of extremes—rich or poor, beautiful or ugly, large or small, high or low, good or bad, intelligent or stupid—even though most things exist somewhere in between. This either–or, black-or-white way of thinking is aggravated by aspects of language.

pendulum effect

Escalating conflict between two individuals or groups that results from their use of polar terms to describe and defend their perceptions of reality.

Polarization can be destructive, escalating conflict to the point at which two parties simply cannot communicate. This escalation is referred to as the **pendulum effect**. The pendulum represents a person's perception of reality, which includes feelings, attitudes, opinions, and value judgments about the world. When the pendulum hangs in the center, a person's perception is considered realistic, virtuous, intelligent, sane, honest, and honorable. Of course, most of us believe that our pendulums are at or near the center most of the time. When two individuals disagree in their perceptions of reality, their pendulums begin to move in opposite directions. The distance the pendulum swings represents their differences in opinion or conviction. As the conversation intensifies, each remark provokes a stronger reaction from the party to whom it is directed until both parties are driven to positions at opposite extremes. For example, when two roommates argue over whose turn it is to clean, one might begin by saying, "It's your turn. I did it last time." The other is likely to respond, "No, I did it last time. Now it's your turn." If the disagreement continues and no solution is found, both will become more entrenched in their positions, and their comments may turn into personal attacks: "You're always so messy and lazy." "And you're always so picky and critical." The situation can degenerate to such a degree that one or the other threatens to move out. Such an extreme outcome is typical of a discussion driven by the pendulum effect. Emotions can eventually run so high that differences between the parties seem insurmountable and a mutually agreeable settlement seems unattainable.

If you view this picture of a Brazilian city and think only of the extremes between rich and poor, you may need to think about the bigger picture. What else can this image tell us?

Speakers can avoid the dangers of polarization if they recognize the potential for misunderstanding and avoid statements that represent general extremes. For example, a noncontroversial statement such as "Iowa is hot in the summer" is not as meaningful as it could be because the word *hot* represents a generalized extreme. Further information will prevent misunderstanding: What is the basis of comparison (Arizona or Manitoba)? Are Iowa summers all the same, or do they vary from year to year? Is an Iowa summer the same in all parts of the state, or does it vary from north to south? What is the average summer temperature? The problem of an incorrectly over-generalized and extreme statement is avoided here: "Iowa summers can be hot. The average temperature is 85 degrees Fahrenheit, with lows around 74 degrees and highs around 105 degrees." Such clarification is especially important when the topic at hand is likely to provoke emotional, defensive, or unpredictable reactions.

Language Can Be Sexist or Homophobic

Men and women show a difference in how they use language and converse with one another. Psychologist Deborah Tannen, for example, suggests that men tend to use language to assert status, whereas women use language to establish and maintain social relationships.[23] Tannen says that, rather than language used to dominate another, women tend to establish closeness and support with it. Men, by contrast, dominate or compete via language. The result, according to Tannen, is that the game of communication for men and women is the same, but the rules are different. When men and women communicate with each other, the potential for clash and conflict arises because of different language use. The problem is magnified when sexist language is used either consciously or unconsciously. Our goal should be to use **gender-inclusive language**—language that does not discriminate against males or females.

Unfortunately, the English language was structured with an inherent bias in favor of men. For example, English has no singular gender-neutral pronouns. Therefore, traditionally, the masculine pronouns (*he, him, his*) have been used to refer to people in general, even if the referent could be a male or female. Use of the masculine pronoun is not incorrect grammatically, but its use in generic situations is a social issue. Language sets expectations that at times discriminate against and stereotype people. According to traditional usage, the omnipresence of *he* and *him* and the general absence of *she* and *her* subtly but powerfully give the impression that men hold important roles but women do not. Thus, our language creates the expectation that males are active and have important roles, while females are inactive and do not hold important roles. Furthermore, sexist language can be misleading. When a speaker constantly uses only female or only male pronouns such as "she can expect this," or "it is in his best interests," members of the excluded sex will believe the message has little or no relevance to them. When that happens, about 50 percent of listeners may not pay attention to information that could be vital to them. If it's a medical situation, those who think that it doesn't affect them might not heed the precautions and may expose themselves to greater danger because "it doesn't apply."

Sexual stereotypes and the assumption that one gender is superior characterize **sexist language**.[24] In our society, sexist language involves an attitude as much as the use of specific words. Words with a positive connotation are often used to describe males—*independent, logical, strong, confident*, and *aggressive*; females are often associated with words having negative connotations—*dependent, illogical, weak, gullible*, and *timid*. Sexist language suggests that one gender is more important than, and superior to, the other. Language used to discriminate can be quite subtle. We barely register the comment, "He's president of the company." Consider, however, these statements: "She is president of the company, and she's a woman"; "Susan got that position because she's a woman." They describe women who have risen to high authority positions, but they also imply that women do not typically hold these positions or that the only reason Susan got the position was because she's a woman. In other words, they imply that women are less qualified than men.

Stereotypes do not occur in a social vacuum. On the contrary, they often exert powerful influence on the lives of those who are stereotyped. Gender stereotypes influence perceptions and behaviors of both men and women. Stereotypes affect both how people are treated in society and how they think of themselves. Language is one significant means of perpetuating these stereotypes. You make positive steps to rid your language of stereotypes when you avoid sexist language and substitute gender-inclusive terms.

Other stereotypes are reinforced when we use homophobic language. When someone asks another to "tell me what to look for so I can recognize gays or lesbians and then avoid them," the speaker demonstrates both insensitivity to individuals and

gender-inclusive language

Language that does not discriminate against males or females.

sexist language

Language that creates sexual stereotypes or implies that one gender is superior to another.

Guidelines

Using Gender-Inclusive Language

1. **Remove sexism from your communication. Use they and their instead of he or she when referring to others.**

2. **Practice and reinforce nonsexist communication patterns.** The ultimate goals are to use nonsexist language effortlessly in private conversation and to think in nonsexist terms.

3. **Use familiar language whenever possible.** When you must choose between sexist language and an unfamiliar phrase, choose the unfamiliar phrase and practice it until it becomes familiar.

4. **Do not arouse negative reactions in listeners by using awkward, cumbersome, highly repetitious, or unnecessary words.** There are so many graceful and controlled ways to state your message inclusively that you need not use bland or offensive constructions.

5. **Not all words need to be changed.** Be sure to carefully analyze whether meanings of words need to be changed before doing so.

6. **Check every outgoing message** —written, oral, nonverbal, and email—for sexism before sending it.[28] Refer to the person and not the gender whenever you can.

7. **Honor the wishes of those who do not use "he" or "she" to describe themselves.** Ask questions to determine what they prefer or simply refer to them by name.

a general negative categorization of a group of people, each of whom is unique. Some in the gay, lesbian, bisexual, and transgender community do not want to be identified by gender terms; because they don't identify with any gender labels, use of such terms would not be appropriate. Honor a person's wishes when they tell you they don't accept the pronouns "he" or "she" to identify them.

Competent communicators use inclusive language and avoid demeaning others. Language influences how we see others around us. Inappropriate language causes perceptual and social problems that should not be tolerated in our society.

Culture Affects Language Use

Just as gender differences characterize language use, so, too, do cultural differences. Each language has its own grammatical rules, and some seem very strange to new speakers of a language. Anthropologist Edward T. Hall asserted "all people are captives of the language they speak."[26] Intercultural communication scholars and linguists look at how different cultures use words. The multiple meanings of words and the use of slang that may or may not sound like dictionary words are confusing. Add to that mixture a different culture and a different set of language rules as well as numerous new experiences, and it's easy to see why nonnative speakers of U.S. English have concerns about their language use. Linguist Guy Deutscher suggests that while we reject the view that language determines our thoughts and our perception of reality, we do need to recognize that "when we learn our mother tongue, we do…acquire certain habits of thought that shape our experiences in significant and often surprising ways."[27] Deutscher further suggests that since habits of speech are cultivated from the earliest age, it is only natural that they can settle into habits of mind that go beyond language itself, affecting your experiences, perceptions, associations, feelings, memories, and orientation in the world.[28] Spanish, French, German, and Russian languages assign a male or female gender to a whole range of inanimate objects, and an object that is male to a speaker of Spanish may be female to a German language speaker. Deutscher provides examples of a remote Australian aboriginal tongue, Guugu Yimithirr, where directions determine space. They always describe where cardinal directions locate things: north, east, south, west. They might warn you to "look out for that big ant just north of your foot."[29]

Contemporary linguists suggest that the habits of mind our culture instills in us from infancy shape our orientations to the world and our emotional responses to the objects we encounter. Thus, our first step to understand others is to remember that not everyone thinks or speaks the same.[30]

When we communicate, we first form thoughts and then decide how we're going to express them. Competent communicators begin with clear thinking, and make careful language choices that reflect an understanding of what language is, how it is used, and what effects it might have on listeners.

James Neuliep, a communication scholar, connects language and culture in this way:

> Our ability to put thoughts into a code in order to communicate with someone else empowers us beyond imagination....If how we think is a reflection of the language we speak, then the speakers of two very different languages must think very differently. This could render effective and successful intercultural communication extremely difficult, if not insurmountable.[31]

Further, anthropologist Edward T. Hall suggests that for some cultures the situation in which a particular communication occurs tells us a great deal about its meaning.[32] In a **high-context culture**, the meaning of the communication act is often inferred from the situation or location. In Japan (a high-context culture), for example, businesspeople do not conduct business in a social setting, although they might refer to their business interests. If one visits Japan on business and is invited to dinner, there is no hidden agenda—the objective for the evening is to eat a meal together, not to conduct business. Business is saved for the office or the meeting place. A dinner is a social event at which business is not conducted. Also, in a high-context culture, language is indirect, nonspecific, and not assertive. In a **low-context culture**, the meaning of the communication act is inferred from the messages being sent and not the location where the communication occurs. According to Hall, the United States is a low-context culture in which businesspeople are as likely to conduct business on the golf course, in a restaurant, or at a reception as they are in the workplace. People in a low-context culture typically are more assertive and more direct. They get to the point immediately. Because understanding such distinctions is essential to sending and receiving messages successfully, the competent communicator will learn as much about language and cultural differences as possible.

high-context culture

A culture in which the meaning of the communication act is inferred from the situation or location.

low-context culture

A culture in which the meaning of the communication act is inferred from the messages being sent and not the location where the communication occurs.

Making Connections for Success

Understanding High- and Low-Context Cultures

One aspect of culture and language that global travelers or those who interact with people from other cultures—whether face-to-face or through social media—need to know is how time is identified. People in high-context Central and South America tend to be polychronic and have views of time and its importance that differ from what most people in the monochronic and low-context nations of Western Europe, the United States, and Canada have. In Canada and the United States, students expect to receive a detailed syllabus for their classes and assignments. In a polychronic country such as Peru, students may never get complete explanations

directly. They expect to discover the rules and expectations for each class.

A staff lounge in a low-context country may have signs on the microwave or refrigerator reminding users to clean up before they leave. People from high-context cultures do not need to be reminded. They know what is expected of them.

1. Now that you know the differences between high- and low-context cultures, identify possible sources of conflict between people from two different context cultures.

2. What is the difference between the two cultures in language use?

3. How would you be able to tell if listeners understand your message?

You should also be aware that some cultures have greater or lesser expectations for an individual's involvement in communication events. Students in China, Finland, France, Japan, Korea, Mexico, most of South America, Indonesia, and Thailand are expected to listen to their professors and not ask questions during class unless the professor gives them permission. These cultures seem to prefer low involvement on the part of students. In Russia, Denmark, Canada, and the United States, however, students are expected to have high involvement in the learning process and are encouraged to ask questions and otherwise participate.

Language and Technology

4.4 **Illustrate** the impact of technology on language usage.

Media communication scholar Neil Postman once wrote that use of technology creates "a bargain with the devil."[33] In *Technopoly*, he says that technology redefines culture through its control over and elevation of information and claims that for every good thing technology provides, it also gives us negatives or disadvantages. Postman is concerned that technology will take over the world and remove too many of the face-to-face interactions that make us interacting social beings as we "amuse ourselves to death."[34] Given the rapid growth of technology, it is likely that some changes will occur simply because of technological advances. Facebook, Hulu, YouTube, Twitter, and other social media outlets already enhance awareness of war, famine, dictatorships, and inhumane treatment. Social media can be credited for toppling dictatorships and exposing the inhumanity of people such as Joseph Kony and his rebel army. Language and the visualization of people's inhumanity toward others influences thought and will bring even more changes in the future. Jeff Child, a communication scholar, researches how social media affect both the language choices we make and the lack of privacy that result from our social media use.

Making Connections for Success

Invisible Children: Internet Activism

Invisible Children is an international campaign to end the use of child soldiers in Joseph Kony's rebel war. It uses film, creativity, and social action in an attempt to restore peace and prosperity to communities in Central Africa affected by the LRA (Joseph Kony's "Lord's Resisting Army"). In March 2012, Invisible Children created a YouTube video to create awareness of Kony, whose rebel warriors kidnapped hundreds of children and created warriors of the young men and sex slaves of the women. The organization lobbied to bring in international troops (including U.S. soldiers) to expel Kony and his troops during 2012, the video went viral and had over 9 million hits in 24 hours. The YouTube clip with appealing language and video was promoted on Facebook, Twitter, and other social media, and did more to raise awareness in 24 hours than anyone or anything else had done in the past decade. Donations came pouring in to the Invisible Children headquarters. U.S. president Barack

Obama promised military help to combat Kony's terrorists. Some believe that social media ensured no more "Rwandas." Others denounce Invisible Children and their crew because only one-third of the donations support African children and the other two-thirds pays for offices, workers, public relations, and media. One thing is certain: Invisible Children raised the awareness of atrocities committed against children and their families.

1. Go online to learn more about the mission of Invisible Children and its work on the Kony campaign.

2. What aspects of effective language use do you find?

3. Does the organization address critics' views?

4. Invisible Children says its work has been greatly enhanced by social media. How did the originators use language to create a solution to the problem of children who lose their childhood?

5. What other socially mediated events have made international headlines and helped focus attention on specific global acts?

How to Use Language Effectively

4.5 **Describe** how accurate, vivid, immediate, appropriate, and metaphorical language can help you be a more effective communicator.

People of all ages, cultures, and educational levels use language every day. Nevertheless, the ability to use language efficiently and successfully requires years of practice and study. Although many variables influence the effectiveness of language, five aspects merit special attention. They are accuracy, vividness, immediacy, appropriateness, and metaphor.

Use Accurate Language

Use of accurate language is as critical to a speaker as accurate navigational directions are to an air traffic controller. A wrong word can distort your intended message, misguide your receiver, and undermine your credibility. When you speak, your goal should be precision. Don't leave room for misinterpretation. You should constantly ask, "What do I want to say?" and "What do I mean?" When necessary, consult a dictionary to be sure you choose the correct word to express your message.

The more words you can use accurately, the greater the likelihood you will find the one you need to make your meaning clear. You must expand your vocabulary. Two of the best ways to do this are through listening to others and reading. Pay attention to words you don't understand. Whenever you come across an unfamiliar word, determine the context in which it is used and consult a dictionary to find its meaning. Once you have learned a new word, try to put it to use. Unused words are typically forgotten. A larger vocabulary takes effort and time, but, with practice, it can become part of your daily routine.

One word of warning: As you continue to develop your vocabulary, avoid the temptation to use long or little-known words when short or common words serve the purpose. Be sure, also, that you know the shades of meaning and connotations of new words before you use them, and remember that words may have different meanings for different people.

Sometimes a message is unclear because it was not constructed effectively. Poor sentence structure and word usage can wreak havoc on a statement's clarity. For example, classified ads in newspapers frequently are so condensed that their intended meaning becomes distorted or obscured. The result might be "TV ads boost eating of obese children" and "Baby born 10 months premature." We hope these headline writers knew what they wished to communicate, but their failure to accurately phrase their messages interfered with their intended meaning.

When we converse, we can usually clear up misunderstandings caused by scrambled sentence structure or poor word choice. But to do so, we must first be aware of listeners' reactions to what we are saying. If they appear confused or ask a question, we should rephrase the message more clearly.

Effective speakers do not assume what is clear to them will necessarily be clear to listeners. They are especially aware of this potential problem in situations such as public speeches, during which listeners might not be able to ask questions. To ensure comprehension, such speakers strive to make their meaning clear by, among other tactics, using familiar and concrete, rather than abstract, language and by being aware of the connotations associated with particular words.

Use Vivid Language

To communicate effectively, make your message animated and interesting. Direct, fresh language conveyed in the active voice can bring a sense of excitement, urgency, and forcefulness to what you say. Such **vividness** tells your audience that they had better listen because what you have to say is important.

vividness

Active, direct, and fresh language that brings a sense of excitement, urgency, and forcefulness to a message.

Making Connections for Success

Using Vivid Language

Compare the following two messages. President Franklin D. Roosevelt said the first. The second expresses a similar thought, though in a different way.

> I see one-third of a nation ill housed, ill clad, ill nourished.

> It is evident that a substantial number of persons within the continental boundaries of the United States have inadequate financial resources with which to purchase the products of agricultural communities and industrial establishments. It would appear that, for a considerable segment of the population, perhaps as much as 33.333 percent of the total, there are inadequate housing facilities, and an equally significant proportion is deprived of the proper types of clothing and nourishment.

1. How would you describe the word choice in each message?
2. How does each message affect your emotions?
3. What impression do you have of each speaker?

Communicators would do well to create vivid messages through the imagery of language. Vivid images are apparent to the viewer in the vibrant, attention-grabbing decorations in this photo.

For example, suppose an organization is trying to raise money for homeless people. It could take one of two approaches in seeking a donation from you: (1) Present statistics to illustrate the number of people who are believed to be homeless; or (2) present cases of actual individuals who are homeless, including children and their families. The first approach is rational, informative, abstract, and emotionally distant. The second approach is emotional, urgent, concrete, and forceful. The vividness of the second approach is at least likely to get your attention and perhaps influence you to contribute.

According to social psychologists, vivid language affects us in several ways. It is more persuasive than a flat, pallid presentation of information, because it is more memorable and has an emotional impact. Vivid messages are more likely to create readily retained and recalled mental images. Finally, people tend to listen more attentively to vivid messages than to uninspiring or uninteresting messages.[35]

Effective communicators use vivid language in all their interactions, whether it's one-to-one with friends or family, in small groups, or in the public arena. Use interesting words, try to include active verbs, and provide variety in the length of your sentences. Whenever possible, avoid clichés and use slang appropriately and with the appropriate audience. You are more likely to keep your listeners interested in what you have to say if you use fresh language to present your ideas in new and exciting ways.

Use Immediate Language

verbal immediacy

Identifies and projects the speaker's feelings and makes the message more relevant to the listener.

Verbal immediacy identifies and projects the speaker's feelings and makes the message more relevant to the listener. Verbal immediacy draws listeners in and involves them in the subject at hand. The following statements illustrate different levels of verbal immediacy. The first sentence displays a high immediacy level, and the last displays a low immediacy level:

1. We will have a great time at the baseball game.
2. You and I will enjoy the baseball game.
3. I think you and I may enjoy baseball.
4. People often enjoy baseball games.

The first statement is directly related to the speaker, the listener, and the situation. It is assertive, and the speaker makes a connection with the listener by using the word *we.* In each successive statement, the speaker decreases the intensity of this association with the listener and the event. The language becomes less immediate, more distant in tone.

Verbal immediacy also makes the speaker appear relaxed, confident, competent, and effective. In addition, receivers tend to more readily view messages characterized by immediacy as similar to their own beliefs than those cast in language unrelated to the speaker, topic, or receiver.

Use Appropriate Language

Each time you speak, your listeners have specific expectations about the kind of language you use. Different kinds of language are appropriate to different situations. For example, the language you would use in addressing the president of your college or university would be much more formal than the language you would use when chatting with friends. You would be unlikely to call the president by a nickname, and you would be equally unlikely to call a friend Dr. or Mr. or Ms., except in professional settings or in jest.

Use of inappropriate language for a given situation damages your credibility, and your message might be misinterpreted or disregarded as disrespectful. It is therefore crucial to assess each communicative situation and adjust your language accordingly. In public situations, profanity, improper grammar, and slang are always inappropriate.

Use Metaphorical Language

According to some language scholars, our way of looking at the world around us is fundamentally metaphorical. A **metaphor** is a figure of speech that associates two things or ideas, not commonly linked, as a means of description. Metaphors help us to structure what we think, how we perceive the world, and what we do. Metaphorical language pervades our everyday language and our thoughts.

metaphor
A figure of speech that associates two things or ideas, not commonly linked, as a means of description.

Metaphorical language is culture bound, and most metaphors have meaning only within a specific language community. If your receivers cannot identify with a particular metaphor you use, it will be meaningless to them. Also, as we pointed out earlier in the chapter, avoid metaphors that negatively or unfairly categorize a specific person or group of people.

As a student, you probably can think of many metaphors to describe your college experiences. For example, some students have said college life is like a roller-coaster ride: There are many ups and downs, as well as turns. What are some other metaphors that vividly express your college experiences?

The misuse of language involves more than misuse of words. Misused language affects our ability to think. Thought and language are inseparable. Most scholars agree that words help us form thoughts. How many times have you found yourself struggling to find *the* right word and, without it, a frustrating inability to express what you really meant? When you take the time to think for a minute, however, the word usually appears. It is important to carefully consider language choices before we speak. We cannot erase what we said. We can correct or retract a statement and apologize for it, but we cannot eliminate the fact that we said it.

Those whose career success is profoundly affected by the ability to communicate expend great effort in evaluating the potential effects of using certain words. Many songwriters have examples of songs that just didn't quite come together for years until they were inspired and found the words that previously eluded them. President Obama, normally a fluent speaker, has made verbal gaffes. When in Austria in March 2009, he said "I don't know what your Austrian word is, but...." This was considered a blunder because in Austria, Austrian German is the official language. Leaders are supposed to think things through very carefully, and this example might be attributed to a failure to think. Such a mistake has the potential to affect a politician's political life, especially on the world stage. And, language also has the potential to create positive or negative impressions. Lord Chesterfield, 18th-century British statesman and "man of letters," once said, "Words, which are the dress of thoughts, deserve surely more care than clothes, which are only the dress of the person."[36]

Summary

The Importance of Language

Objective 4.1 **Assess** the importance of language in communication events.

- Language is the way we create and share meaning with others.
- Language is powerful.
- Language allows us to make connections with others.
- Language has the power to influence our perceptions of others and theirs of us.
- Language affects our emotions.
- Language affects our relationships

The Elements of Language

Objective 4.2 **Demonstrate** how the elements of language (sounds, words, grammar, and meaning) affect communication.

- The four elements of language are sounds, words, grammar, and meaning.
- Most of us are born with the ability to make speech sounds, but people do not all learn to produce the sounds in the same ways.
- Words represent objects and concepts.
- Grammar is the set of rules we use to join words into phrases and sentences.
- Meaning allows us to use words and patterns to exchange messages between people.

Language-Based Barriers to Communication

Objective 4.3 **Explain** how language can create barriers to effective communication.

- Language can be misunderstood because meanings depend on commonalities.
- Language can be misunderstood because people believe words have meanings in themselves.
- Language can shape our attitudes.
- Indiscrimination occurs when we neglect individual differences and lump things together.
- When we fail to identify people, objects, ideas, and events by time, we are open to misunderstanding.
- Language can cause polarization when we view and use extremes. This either-or language leads to failure to communicate.

- We should avoid sexist or homophobic language if we wish to avoid stereotypes and use language to help us make connections with others.

Language and Technology

Objective 4.4 **Illustrate** the impact of technology on language usage.

- Advances in technology have created a faster, global means of communicating.
- New words come into the language rapidly.
- Social media outlets have a tremendous impact on our lives and our communication with others.

How to Use Language Effectively

Objective 4.5 **Describe** how accurate, vivid, immediate, appropriate, and metaphorical language can help you be a more effective communicator.

- Accurate language allows you to be precise and to eliminate misinterpretations.
- Vivid language allows you to be animated and interesting.
- Immediate language identifies the speaker's feelings and allows the message to be more relevant to the listener.
- Language is used differently in varying situations. You should choose language that is appropriate for the listener and the context. Remember, too, language for the ear is different from language for the eye. Writing and speaking require different choices.
- Metaphorical language can help you create shared meanings when you compare the known and the unknown. Metaphors allow us to structure and describe what we think, how we perceive the world, and what we do.
- Technology has created new words and affected the ways we connect with others on a global level, but, again, we need to make effective choices in order to share meaning with others.
- Language is culture bound, so we need to be especially aware of effective language in order to communicate clearly.

Discussion Starters

1. Provide two personal examples of the power of language.
2. Explain the relationship between language and thought.
3. Why are language, communication, talk, and speech defined separately and not considered synonymous?
4. We say that language has rules, but we also say that language is arbitrary. Why might this be a contradiction in terms?
5. How and why should we defend against the use of inappropriate language?
6. Why is "meanings are in people" an important concept?
7. Which of the language barriers discussed is most likely to occur in your interactions?
8. How do competent communicators use indexing and dating in their communication efforts?
9. List words resulting from advances in technology that are commonly used in conversations.
10. In what ways has technology affected our use of language?
11. Identify four differences between spoken and written language.
12. How does language help us both identify ourselves and others, and also connect with others?

Chapter 5
Connecting through Nonverbal Communication

Learning Objectives

This chapter will help you

5.1 **Differentiate** nonverbal communication from verbal communication.

5.2 **Explain** the six key characteristics of nonverbal communication.

5.3 **Identify** the five common functions of nonverbal communication.

5.4 **Compare and contrast** different types of nonverbal communication and the ways competent communicators are aware of their nonverbal communication.

5.5 **Explain** why it is difficult to interpret and understand nonverbal communication and how to ensure that the message received is accurate.

Making Everyday Connections

Carly slowly walks into her apartment. She looks as if she has just seen a ghost. Tears form as she sits down on the sofa, and she begins to cry openly and uncontrollably.

Her friend Dana puts her arm around her and pats her on the shoulder gently. Carly looks at Dana. Carly's face and demeanor tell Dana something is really wrong, as if Carly's whole world has just come crashing down. Dana doesn't know what to say, so she continues to comfort Carly by holding her hand. Carly is unable to control her emotions or speak. Finally, Carly looks at Dana, and her face shows concern as if to say, "What is going on?"

Neither uttered one word as they held each other tightly, yet their expressions and touch said everything.

Questions to Think About

1. How does nonverbal communication make communication easier? More difficult?

2. Why do we give little or no thought to our nonverbal communication?

3. Why do you think nonverbal communication is considered more believable than verbal communication?

4. Explain what nonverbal communication is and is not.

5. What are the challenges of communicating emotions online or via text message? Are there risks?

What Is Nonverbal Communication?

5.1   **Differentiate** nonverbal communication from verbal communication.

Nonverbal communication includes all behaviors, symbols, attributes, or objects—whether intended or not—that communicate messages with social meaning. Nonverbal communication includes tone of voice, facial expressions, posture, gestures, and appearance, all of which communicate messages. Nonverbal communication can enhance or change the meaning of words, such as when tone of voice, volume, or facial expression adds emphasis to meaning. According to communication scholar Mark Knapp and social psychologist Judith Hall, it is important to understand that the division of "verbal and nonverbal behavior into two separate and distinct categories is virtually impossible."[1] Unfortunately, nonverbal communication can also change the intended meaning of a message or make it confusing and unclear.

We tend to take nonverbal communication for granted because it is so basic, but its importance is unmistakable, and its connection to communication is undeniable. In most communication situations, we spend more of our time communicating nonverbally than verbally, and our nonverbal messages can carry more meaning than our verbal messages.

A review of nonverbal communication research by Knapp and Hall concluded that some people depend more heavily on verbal messages, whereas others seem to rely more on nonverbal messages.[2] Another research study found that nonverbal behaviors were 12 to 13 times more powerful in impact than the accompanying verbal message.[3] These findings indicate the importance and impact of nonverbal behaviors.

Without realizing it, we often base many daily decisions on nonverbal communication. When are others more likely to do favors for you—when they are in a good mood or a bad one? Can you think of recent decisions you made on the basis of another's nonverbal communication? For example, your professor's facial expression suggests that she is in a really good mood, so you decide that now is a good time to ask her whether you can miss next week's class to attend a friend's wedding. In situations like this, as well as ones where we can't ask others how they feel, we are more likely to pay careful attention to nonverbal cues, such as changes in facial expressions, eye contact, posture, body movements, and other expressive actions to determine mood. According to psychologists, such behavior is extremely difficult to repress or control, so even when others try to conceal their inner feelings from us, they express those feelings through their nonverbal cues.[4]

nonverbal communication

Behaviors, symbols, attributes, or objects—whether intended or not—that communicate messages with social meaning.

Characteristics of Nonverbal Communication

5.2 **Explain** the six key characteristics of nonverbal communication.

Students often ask, "Why study nonverbal communication?" Of the many reasons for such study, the primary one is the pervasive effect of nonverbal communication on what and how we communicate; we always communicate something nonverbally. In addition, nonverbal communication depends on context, is more believable than verbal communication, is a primary means of expression, is related to culture, and is at times ambiguous or easily misunderstood.

Nonverbal Communication Occurs Constantly

When another person is aware of you, or you of them, communication occurs whether something is said or not. If you make eye contact, smile, frown, or totally ignore the other person, you are communicating. Sometimes what is said is less important than what is not said. For example, if you did not attend a meeting when you were expected, you came late to an employment interview, you wore jeans when you were expected to dress formally, you wore a suit when jeans were expected, you talked about a sad situation with a smirk on your face, or you spoke to someone but never looked him or her in the eye all convey strong messages. Facial expression, appearance (sex, race, physique), clothing, willingness to make eye contact, body movements, and posture all communicate.

To illustrate that we always communicate, whether intentionally or unintentionally, consider the two students pictured: Sam dresses as a perfectly groomed professional and smells of expensive cologne. Oliver wears a hat to cover his hair and an old T-shirt. If we only look at them, we cannot tell what these two actually intend to communicate. Sam might simply be neat and use cologne because it gives him confidence, or he might really want to communicate that designer clothes and expensive cologne are important to him, or he wants to let everyone know he's got money. Oliver might simply like to show that he will not conform to everyone else, alternatively, he may communicate that he disdains society's obsession with outward appearances. Ultimately, it's not so much what Sam and Oliver intend to "say" as what others perceive. Both indicate something about themselves through their appearance whether intentional or not.

The messages you send via your appearance, facial expressions, clothing, eye contact, body movements, and posture may not always be clear or what you intended. What is perceived, however, is what is communicated, whether it's intended or not.

Nonverbal Communication Depends on Context

The context in which nonverbal communication occurs plays a crucial role in its interpretation. Pounding on a table to make a point during a meeting means something entirely different from pounding on the table in response to being called a liar. Direct eye contact with a stranger can mean something entirely different from such contact with a close friend.

When you communicate, nonverbal and verbal cues usually supplement and support each other. Your appearance, tone of voice, eye movement, posture, and facial expression provide cues about the communication relationship. For example, when you talk to a friend, your relaxed tone of voice, eye contact, and posture reveal much about your friendship. Your nonverbal cues can tell your friends how much you value them, how comfortable you feel, or how intimate your relationship is. Such nonverbal communication is interpreted within the context of your friendships and is complemented by casual and personal conversations.

Nonverbal Communication Is More Believable Than Verbal Communication

Most of us tend to believe nonverbal communication, even when it contradicts the accompanying verbal message. Consider this conversation between a mother and her daughter regarding the daughter's husband:

JESS'S MOTHER:	"What's wrong? Are you upset with Chad?"
JESS (STARING AND FROWNING):	"Whatever. I'm not upset, why should I be?"
JESS'S MOTHER:	"You seem to be in a funk, and you are avoiding talking to me. So what's wrong? Did you and Chad have a fight?"
JESS (SHOUTING ANGRILY):	*"I said nothing is wrong! Please leave me alone! Everything is fine!"*

Throughout the conversation, Jess seems upset and is snappy in tone; she sends a signal to her mother that there's more to the story. It seems clear from the interaction and the mother's intuition that Jess is hiding something—hence, the second inquiry. Indeed, the real story is that Jess and her husband have problems. They fight over money, and the mother senses that something is on Jess's mind. Nonverbal messages are much more difficult to control than verbal messages because nonverbal cues are more representative of our emotions, which are also more challenging to control.

Is nonverbal or verbal communication more likely to be true or more accurate? Verbal communication is more conscious; it involves more processing of thoughts and impulses into words. Although nonverbal messages can be conscious and deliberate, they often, as we have suggested, are unintentional and subconsciously generated. It is almost always easier to determine what you are going to say, but it is very difficult for most of us to control our voices, facial expressions, and other body movements when we are upset, hurt, or angry. Jess's mother interpreted her daughter's nonverbal communication as a more accurate reflection of Jess's feelings than her verbal communication.

Nonverbal Communication Is a Primary Means of Expression

We can often detect other people's feelings of frustration, anger, sadness, resentment, or anxiety even when they actually say nothing. We can detect others' emotions because nonverbal communication is powerful. Almost all of our feelings and attitudes are expressed through our nonverbal behaviors. For example, at a graduation party attended by many young children, a little girl entered with her parents and spotted a neighbor. She turned up her nose and walked away. Her mother, running after her, asked why she had suddenly left, to which the girl replied, "I don't like that girl over there." The nonverbal communication really didn't need much explanation; it was obvious what the little girl was saying through her actions.

Nonverbal Communication Is Related to Culture

Culture contributes significantly to differences in nonverbal behavior. Norms and rules that govern the management of behavior differ from culture to culture. Yet because human beings around the world share common biological and social functions, it should not be too surprising to also find areas of similarity in nonverbal communication. For example, studies comparing facial expressions have found that certain universal expressions, such as those indicating sadness and fear, are easily understood across various cultures. Although much outward behavior is innate (such as smiling, touching, eye contact, moving), we are not born knowing what meanings such nonverbal messages communicate.[5]

Most scholars agree that cultures formulate rules that dictate when, how, and with what consequences nonverbal expressions are exhibited. For instance, the way people sit can communicate different and important messages across cultures. In the United States, being casual and open is valued; thus, people, consciously or unconsciously, convey this quality by the way they sit. Males in the United States often sit in a slumping and leaning-back position, as well as sprawled out, so they occupy a lot of space.[6] However, in other countries, such as Germany and Sweden, where more formality prevails, slouching is considered a sign of rudeness and poor manners. The way your legs are positioned also has cultural meaning. For example, the innocent act of ankle-to-knee leg crossing, typical of the way many American males sit, could be interpreted as an insult in Saudi Arabia, Singapore, Thailand, or Egypt.[7] Many sexual connotations for gestures are tied to culture as well. In the United States, the middle finger is used to send an insulting, obscene message. This gesture, however, is not universal. In some cultures, the gesture used to represent the same insult is the forming of an O with the thumb and index finger, which means "A-OK" in American culture. The same gesture in France means "zero" or "worthless," in parts of Latin America and the Middle East it indicates "a__hole," and in Japan it signifies "money."

People from different cultures also infer emotions in somewhat different ways.[8] For example, Americans typically look at facial expressions, body posture, and other nonverbal cues. Japanese, in contrast, might consider not only those same cues but also the relationship the person has with other people. In other words, in the Japanese culture a smiling person can't really be happy unless other important people in that person's life also experience positive reactions.[9] Although nonverbal cues provide important information about others' emotions in all cultures, the extent to which they are used to infer others' feelings can and does vary across cultures. In the United States, because we are an individualistic culture, facial expressions, body movements, eye contact, and other nonverbal cues are a primary source of such information. In contrast, in collectivist cultures, relationships and status between people are significant. So where does emotion reside, inside people or between them? The answer appears to depend on your culture.

Nonverbal Communication Is Ambiguous

Although nonverbal channels are absent, many people prefer text messaging to talking on the phone or face-to-face-communication. A focus-group study[10] revealed that people might feel a greater level of control in asynchronous communication (such as texting) than in synchronous communication (responding to others immediately). The reasons people favor the asynchronous type include greater control and the opportunity to think through their responses, thus they can better control how they will be perceived.

Although using forms of asynchronous communication, such as email and texting, may seem advantageous, these can actually lead to miscommunication and misunderstandings. Research shows that email receivers often fail to understand the

Making Connections for Success

Body Language and Facial Expressions: It's All about Culture and Meaning

Examine the photos below and interpret what the gestures mean. Each gesture has a specific meaning in the United States and most other Western cultures.

1. What are the gestures/behaviors communicating to you?
2. Show the photos to people from other cultures (especially non-Western cultures) to determine whether they interpret the gestures as you do.
3. What advice would you give to someone about nonverbal communication and traveling to different cultures?

Canopy/Corbis & Image Source/Stockbyte/Getty Images

sender's expressions of sarcasm or humor (even with emojis). For example, nonverbal expressions (such as tone of voice) used to detect sarcasm are absent in texts, social media, and email, thus messages may be misunderstood and possibly offensive. At the same time, email creators, according to the research, believe that every email they send will be fully understood regardless of the method of communication.[11]

Unless we understand the context of the communication, it is almost impossible to tell what a specific nonverbal behavior may mean. In fact, misunderstandings can occur even when the context is fully understood. That is why we must think twice about our interpretation of others' nonverbal behavior and their possible interpretations of ours. When you see and hear nonverbal communication without a complete understanding of the context, you might not receive the intended message. When you assume too much about a nonverbal message, further miscommunication and misunderstanding can result.

Because nonverbal messages are always present, we must recognize their importance or impact and also exercise care when interpreting them. Like verbal communication, nonverbal behavior can be ambiguous, abstract, and arbitrary. We cannot assume that nonverbal messages have only one meaning. For example, does crying always signify grief or sadness, or does it also express joy or pain? If we effectively interpret nonverbal behavior we need to understand the context in which it takes place and the cultural norms governing it. But even when a person understands these dynamics, it is still easy to misinterpret nonverbal behaviors. For example, does a fellow student's yawn signal boredom or fatigue? Does a speaker tremble because of nervousness or excitement? Most nonverbal behaviors have a multitude of possible meanings, and to automatically assume that you have grasped the *only* possible meaning could lead to a serious misunderstanding. No consistent rules are in place for using or interpreting nonverbal communication.

Why Should You Know about Nonverbal Communication? An Overview

You should understand nonverbal communication for many reasons. The following are some of the more important ones. Nonverbal communication:

- carries most of the meaning of a message, particularly feelings and attitudes toward others.
- is a frequent source of misunderstandings.
- is not governed by a set of universal rules.
- is multichanneled, complicated, and ever-changing.
- is bound to context and culture.
- is more likely than verbal communication to be spontaneous and unintentional.
- is powerful and more believable than verbal communication.
- is learned (not always consciously).
- is critical in relationship initiation, development, and termination.

Functions of Nonverbal Communication

5.3   Identify the five common functions of nonverbal communication.

Nonverbal communication adds life to our exchanges by complementing, repeating, regulating, and substituting for our words. Sometimes we even use it to deceive others (see Table 5.1).

Complementing Verbal Behavior

The use of nonverbal cues to complete, describe, or accent verbal cues is called **complementing**. For example, after shooting a chip shot from about 75 yards, a golfer tells her partner that she missed the cup by inches and uses her thumb and index finger to show the distance. When you say hello to a friend, you show your genuine interest with a warm smile, steady eye contact, and holding the friend's hand.

We use complementary nonverbal cues to accent verbal behavior by emphasizing or punctuating our spoken words. For example, a mother tries to get her children to be quieter and softly asks, "Will you please keep it down?" If that doesn't work and the noise really bothers her, she might raise her voice to indicate that she wants quiet immediately.

People who are excited or enthusiastic are more likely to use nonverbal cues to accent their messages than are people who are restrained, have a difficult time expressing themselves, do not pay attention, or do not understand others' meanings.

complementing

The use of nonverbal cues to complete, describe, or accent verbal cues.

Table 5.1 Functions of Nonverbal Communication

Category	Characteristic	Example
Complementing	Completes, describes, or accents a verbal message	A person needs help immediately, so he yells as loudly as possible.
Repeating	Expresses a message identical to the verbal one	A person says "yes" and nods her head up and down.
Regulating	Controls flow of communication	A person nods his head as a way of communicating, "I am interested in what you are saying," implying "tell me more."
Substituting	Replaces a verbal message with nonverbal signals to exchange thoughts	Two people use hand signals to communicate, because the environment is too loud to hear each other's voices.
Deceiving	Nonverbal cues that purposely disguise or mislead to create a false impression	A doctor examining a patient discovers a serious problem, but the doctor's facial expressions remain neutral so as not to alarm the patient.

Repeating Verbal Behavior

Repeating behavior expresses a message identical to the verbal one. For example, a father attempts to keep his child quiet at an adult gathering places his index finger to his lips and says, "Shhhh!" A speaker states she has two points to make and holds up two fingers. The actions of the father and the speaker are called **repeating** because they convey the same meaning as the verbal message.

Such repetition is especially common in sports. For instance, a referee on a basketball court shouts, "Traveling!" while rolling her arms in a circular motion, or a baseball umpire cries "Strike!" while raising his right arm. These repeating nonverbal signals are deliberately planned so that all players and spectators will know the official's call.

repeating

The use of nonverbal cues to convey the same meaning as the verbal message.

Regulating Verbal Behavior

As illustrated in the introductory "Making Everyday Connections," nonverbal cues can also be used to control the flow of communication, a behavior known as **regulating**. For example, we frequently use nonverbal signals to indicate that we want to talk, to stop another person from interrupting us when we are talking, or to show that we are finished and that the other person may take a turn. When we truly listen, we might nod our heads rapidly to suggest that the speaker hurry up and finish, or we might nod slowly to show that we want to hear more.

Senders might not even realize when they send regulating cues, but receivers are usually aware of such signals. In class, for example, a professor receives a clear message when students put on their coats or close their notebooks to indicate class is over. The students may demonstrate their recognition of the clock–it's time to leave, but the professor may receive an entirely different message. If your friend interrupts you during a conversation, you might extend your hand with an outward palm to indicate to your friend that she should stop cutting you off in mid-sentence.

regulating

The use of nonverbal cues to control the flow of communication.

substituting

The use of nonverbal cues in place of oral messages when speaking is impossible, undesirable, or inappropriate.

deceiving

Purposely misleading others by using nonverbal cues to create false impressions or to convey incorrect information.

Substituting for Verbal Behavior

When we use nonverbal messages in place of oral messages, we are **substituting**. It is common when speaking is impossible, undesirable, or inappropriate. For example, ramp controllers at airports use hand signals to guide planes to their unloading positions because the noise level is too high for spoken communication; friends often exchange knowing looks when they want to communicate something behind another person's back; some people with hearing impairments use a sophisticated formal sign language in place of the spoken word. When we include symbols, emojis, or emoticons in our communication, they serve as substitutes for oral messages—for example, ☺ # @ ♥. You may use hashtags in social media to stand in the place of oral messages and convey emotion. Consider the following tweet: "Just got to my 8am class only to learn the professor canceled class! #annoyed #8amclassessuck."

President Obama and Arizona Republican governor Jan Brewer's greeting of each other appears to be less than cordial. By pointing her finger at him, she communicates her anger and frustration toward him.

Deceiving

When we purposely mislead others with nonverbal cues to create false impressions or to convey incorrect information, we are **deceiving**. Among the most common of such *deceiving* nonverbal behaviors is the "poker face" that some use when playing cards. By masking their facial expressions, they try not to let the other players know what they have in their hand. Masking is a form of deceiving. We might try to appear calm when we are really nervous or upset, and we often act surprised, alert, or happy when, in fact, we are feeling quite the opposite.

Detection of deception usually results from nonverbal cues such as facial expressions, eye contact, and body language that can help us decide whether a person is lying.

Research suggests that most people lie at least once a day[12] and use deception about 20 percent of the time in their social interactions. Deception occurs for many reasons, such as to avoid hurting someone's feelings, to conceal our real feelings or reactions, or to avoid being caught for some misdeed. This apparent fact raises a couple of questions: (1) How good are we at recognizing when someone deceives us? (2) How can we do a better job at detecting when someone is deceives us? The answer to the first question is not very promising. The research seems to suggest that we do slightly better than 50/50 in determining if someone deceives us.[1] Many reasons account for our inability to detect deception, the least of which is that we want to believe that people tell the truth; another is our lack of attention to nonverbal cues that might reveal that someone is deceiving us.[14] One more reason has come to light—most of us assume that if people are truthful in one situation or context, they are likely to be truthful in all others, and this may prevent us from recognizing they might lie on some occasions.[15] One study found that people who lie make fewer hand movements and tend to look away from a person when they tell untruths. The research further found that liars' voices could also be a telling sign; there is a tendency to hesitate and to shift pitch more often than when telling the truth.[16] Another study found that liars often try to control their voices, which often leads to sounding over-controlled or under-controlled, indicating anxiety or deception.[17]

Recent research indicates that when people find themselves on the receiving end of lies, they react with mistrust of, and dislike toward, the liar.[18] In fact, the more lies a stranger tells, the more that person is disliked and the less he or she is trusted. Interestingly, once exposed to someone who has lied, most people are more willing to engage in such behaviors themselves.[19] The researchers told participants in their study that a person in the video they were about to watch was lying. Some lies involved exaggerations (e.g., the liar said that he had been an honor student in high school when this was not true), and others involved minimizations (e.g., the liar indicated that her academic record was worse than it really was). The researchers also varied the number of lies so that the liars engaged in deception only once in four times. When participants rated the liars, they gave lower scores for likeability and trustworthiness to the frequent liars and to the liars who had exaggerated rather than minimized their own achievements. This finding seems to suggest that some lies are worse than others.

In spite of what we know about people's nonverbal behaviors when they do not tell the truth, very few of us are able to detect or interpret these behaviors as signs of

Making Connections for Success

Telling the Truth: It May Not Be What You Say; It's How You Behave

If deception is an all-too-common aspect of social life, what are its effects? As you might guess, they are largely negative. Often, we make assumptions about people's truthfulness based on the inconsistencies of their nonverbal and verbal messages. A student's eyes wander during a test—he claims he's not looking at his neighbor's test; a student smiles as she looks at her laptop screen, and, when asked what she is looking at, claims she is taking notes; or a student has his head down, peering at his cell phone, but, when asked about texting, he claims he was just checking the time.

1. What nonverbal cues can signal that a person is not being truthful?

2. On a scale of one to ten (with ten being extremely confident), how confident are you to conclude, on the basis of nonverbal cues, that a person is not being truthful? Explain your rating.

3. When is it appropriate to be deceptive, if ever?

deception. People who can detect untruthfulness usually consider more than one nonverbal cue to determine whether someone tells the truth. A very fine line divides the nonverbal behaviors of someone who is legitimately anxious from those of someone who is not being truthful. Therefore, lying cannot be confirmed on the basis of nonverbal behaviors alone.

Are men really clueless about nonverbal cues? The answer, as revealed by research on gender differences, is somewhat mixed. Overall, there is no clear evidence that women are better than men at all aspects of nonverbal perception. But they do seem to be superior in performing several important tasks, such as judging another's specific personality characteristics,[20] recognizing their current moods, and both sending and interpreting nonverbal cues.[21]

Women are clearly superior in their ability to read facial expressions; they also have the edge in interpreting body movements and gestures.[22] However, they have a lesser ability for interpreting voice tone and for noticing discrepancies between nonverbal cues—for instance, inconsistencies between facial expressions and body cues.

While the research is not completely conclusive, it does suggest that women are better than men at both sending and interpreting nonverbal cues, and better at remembering details. This gives women an important advantage in many situations and may account for the widespread belief in women's intuition and their ability to recognize when someone's nonverbal communication is consistent with what that person is saying.

Types of Nonverbal Communication

5.4 **Compare and contrast** different types of nonverbal communication and the ways competent communicators are aware of their nonverbal communication.

When you dress in a suit for a meeting, smile at someone, sit in a specific seat in class, use hand gestures as you talk, play with a pen or pencil as you listen, dim the lights to create a romantic atmosphere, play music loudly, look someone directly in the eyes, or burn incense to create a pleasant odor, you are communicating nonverbally. We perform a wide range of nonverbal behaviors every day without even thinking about them. Because nonverbal communication is so diverse, complex, common, and informative, we need to be sensitive to its many manifestations. In the following pages, we examine some of the more significant forms of nonverbal communication, such as kinesics (body movements, including gestures, facial expressions, and eye behavior), physical characteristics, haptics (touch), proxemics (space), chronemics (time), vocalics or paralanguage (use of voice), silence, artifacts, and environment.

Facial Expressions and Body Movements

We use body movements—gestures, facial expressions, and eye behavior—to create an infinite number of nonverbal messages. **Kinesics**, sometimes referred to as *body language*, is any movement of the face or body that communicates a message. Two particularly significant categories of kinesics are eye behavior and facial expressions. **Eye behavior** is a subcategory of facial expressions that includes any movement or behavior of the eyes; it is also referred to as **oculesics**, the study of eye movement or eye behavior. The eyes, through eye contact with others, have the primary function of establishing relationships. **Facial expressions** include configurations of the face that can reflect, augment, contradict, or appear unrelated to a speaker's message.

EYE BEHAVIOR OR OCULESICS   According to some researchers, eye behavior is the first and primary characteristic we notice about others. Researchers found that, during

kinesics

Sometimes referred to as "body language"; any movement of the face or body that communicates a message.

eye behavior

A category of kinesics and a subcategory of facial expressions that includes any movement or behavior of the eyes.

oculesics

Study of eye movement or eye behavior

facial expressions

Configuration of the face that can reflect, augment, contradict, or appear unrelated to a speaker's vocal delivery.

interactions, people spend about 45 percent of the time looking at each other's eyes.[2] Through eye behavior, we establish relationships. Eye behavior also conveys a variety of other important messages. For example, we notice a speaker's eye contact, share mutual glances with friends, and feel uncomfortable when others stare at us. Eye behavior, according to communication scholar Dale Leathers, can serve one of six important communicative functions: (1) influence attitude change and persuasion; (2) indicate degree of attentiveness, interest, and arousal; (3) express emotions; (4) regulate interaction; (5) indicate power and status; and (6) form impressions in others.[24]

Eye gaze at the interpersonal level communicates sincerity, trustworthiness, and friendliness. Romantic partners are more likely to gaze into each other's eyes for prolonged periods when they express their affection for one another.[25] Members of groups or teams use eye contact to build their relationships and to show unity or a sense of belonging to the group or team. In Chapter 10, we discuss the importance of eye contact between a speaker and an audience. In general, effective speakers use more frequent eye contact with their audiences than do less effective speakers. Eye contact is also important for listeners, because looking at the speaker indicates interest in what is said and is a sign of respect for the speaker.

Have you ever had a conversation with someone wearing dark glasses? If you have, you know that it is a bit uncomfortable because you can't completely see how the other person reacts to you. We learn much about others' feelings and emotions from their eyes. For example, we associate a high level of gaze or direct eye contact from another as a sign of liking or friendliness.[26] In contrast, if others avoid eye contact with us, we are likely to conclude that they are unfriendly, don't like us, or are simply shy.[27] Although a high level of eye contact can be interpreted as positive, some exceptions to this rule occur. If people look at us continuously and maintain eye contact regardless of actions we take, they are said to be staring. When confronted by unwanted staring, most of us tend to withdraw from the situation.[28] Generally, people find being stared at an unpleasant experience; it makes most of us nervous and tense.[29] This is especially true of what is referred to as a "cold stare" because it is a form of intimidation, and unwanted stares are often interpreted in our society as a sign of hostility and anger.[30] This is one reason experts on road rage—highly aggressive driving by motorists, sometimes followed by actual assaults—recommend that drivers avoid eye contact with people who disobey traffic laws and rules of the road.

FACIAL EXPRESSIONS   Facial expressions are windows to our emotions. They provide clues about our and others' emotional states, which at times can be very complex and difficult to interpret accurately.

More than 2,000 years ago, the Roman orator Cicero stated, "The face is the image of the soul." By this, he meant that human feelings and emotions are often reflected in our faces. Modern research suggests that Cicero and others who observed human behavior were correct: It is possible to learn much about others' current moods and feelings from their facial expressions. Researchers have found that from a rather early age our faces clearly depict six different basic emotions: anger, fear, happiness, sadness, surprise, and disgust.[31] Other research suggests that contempt may also be a basic emotion.[32] However, agreement on what specific facial expression represents contempt is less consistent than is the case for the other six emotions.

It is important to realize that the relatively small number of basic facial expressions in no way implies that human beings are limited to them. The human face is said to produce more than a thousand different expressions. Emotions often occur in many combinations (for example, joy tinged with sorrow, surprise combined with fear), and each of these reactions can vary greatly in emphasis. Thus, while facial expressions may have only a small number of basic themes, the range of variations on these themes is immense.

Facial expressions play an extremely powerful role in communication and relationships. Of all body motions, facial expressions convey the most information.

Our facial expressions typically display our emotions, but because of their complexity, these emotions can be difficult to interpret. Researchers have identified more than 1,000 different expressions made by the human face.

In examining the judgments we make about another's facial expressions, researchers found that we judge not only emotions but also personality—such as the tendency to be friendly or unfriendly, harsh or kind—on the basis of facial expressions.[33] We perceive people with relaxed facial expressions as people with more power who are more controlled than those whose facial expressions seem nervous.[34]

Overall, then, it seems safe to conclude that although facial expressions are not completely universal—cultural and contextual differences exist about precise meaning—they generally need very little translation, compared to spoken language. However, despite cultural rules, our faces often communicate feelings and emotions spontaneously in reaction to a situation. For example, if you open the door to your house and a group of your friends hiding in the dark turn on the lights and yell, "Surprise!" your face will probably automatically and unconsciously express shock and surprise. If you open the door and they yell, "Boo!" your face will probably show fear or anxiety.

Although many facial expressions are unconscious and involuntary reactions to certain stimuli, researchers found that facial cues may be only partially reliable in terms of what they express. In a study of facial expressions in everyday conversations, communication researcher Michael Motley found they are extremely difficult to interpret and may be relevant only as they relate to specific conversations or situations in which they occur.[35] This is in part because most of us have learned to conceal our real feelings from others.[36] Most of us have learned how to control our facial muscles in order to hide inappropriate or unacceptable responses. Such controlling behaviors regarding our facial expressions are referred to as **facial management techniques**. Facial management techniques may be used to intensify, deintensify, neutralize, or mask a felt emotion[37] (see Table 5.2).

facial management techniques
Control of facial muscles to conceal inappropriate or unacceptable responses.

Table 5.2 Facial Management Techniques

Technique	Definition	Example
Intensifying	Exaggeration of reactions to meet others' expectations	You receive a gift and try to look completely surprised, excited, and delighted.
Deintensifying	Understatement of reactions to meet others' expectations	You receive an A on a speech; a friend receives a C. You tone down your elation, just in case your friend feels bad about receiving a lower grade.
Neutralizing	Avoidance of any emotional expression in a situation; "poker face" shows no emotion	You show no fear or sadness when, although fear or sadness may be justified, you don't want to show your emotions.
Masking	Replacement of one expression with another considered more appropriate for the situation	You smile when a friend wins a scholarship and you don't, even though you think you deserve it.

Table 5.3 Categories of Body Movements and Facial Expressions

Category	Characteristics	Examples
Emblems	These translate directly into words and are used for specific words or phrases. Meanings of emblems are like those of words—arbitrary, changeable with time, learned, and culturally determined.	A hitchhiker's extended thumb, the thumb and circle sign for "OK," the peace sign
Illustrators	These accent, reinforce, or emphasize a verbal message.	A child holding up his hands to indicate how tall he is while saying, "I'm a big boy"; an instructor underlining a word on a PowerPoint slide to emphasize it
Regulators	These control, monitor, or maintain interaction between or among speakers and listeners. These are cues that tell us when to stop, continue, hurry, elaborate, make things more interesting, or let someone else speak. The dialogue at the beginning of the chapter is a good example of the need for regulators.	Eye contact, shift in posture, nod of the head, looking at a clock or wristwatch
Affect displays	These are body movements that express emotions. Though your face is the primary means of displaying affect, your body may also be used.	Sad face, slouching, jumping up and down
Adaptors	These help one feel at ease in communication situations. They are difficult to interpret and require the most speculation.	Scratching, smoothing hair, playing with coins, putting hands in front of the face, moving closer to someone

BODY MOVEMENTS To make sense of thousands of different body movements, psychologists Paul Ekman and Wallace Friesen devised a classification system based on the origins, functions, and coding of nonverbal behavior.[38] Their system divides body motions into five categories: emblems, illustrators, regulators, affect displays, and adaptors (see Table 5.3). Because there are so many body motions, and many are interdependent, it is important to understand that categories are not mutually exclusive. Some body motions may fall into more than one category.

Finally, body movements and posture can reveal much about our physical states (vigor, age) and perhaps the extent to which we possess certain traits.[39] Evidence from several research studies supports these conclusions. For example, one study investigating males and females in four age groups (5 to 7, 13 to 14, 26 to 28, and 75 to 80 years old) asked participants to walk back and forth at a pace they felt was comfortable.[40] The walkers were recorded, and then the video was shown to others, who rated the walkers on various dimensions, such as gait, traits, age, and sex. By using adjustments and lighting techniques, the researchers were able to disguise the walkers so that the subjects saw only their gait.

The subjects made judgments about the walkers two different times. The first time, they rated the walkers' gait in terms of revealing certain traits (submissive or dominating, physically weak or physically strong, timid or bold, sad or happy, unsexy or sexy). The second time, they rated the walkers' gait in terms of several other characteristics (amount of hip sway, knee bending, forward or backward lean, slow or fast pace, stiff- or loose-jointed gait, short or long strides). In addition, the subjects were asked to estimate each walker's age and guess whether each was female or male.

The results were interesting and clearly indicate that people's gaits provide important nonverbal cues. For example, as predicted, ratings of traits and gaits did vary according to age. Ratings of sexiness increased from children to adolescents and young adults but decreased for older adults. Further analysis revealed that possession of a youthful gait (one characterized by hip sway, knee bending, arm swing, loose-jointedness, and more steps per second) was strongly related to ratings of the walkers' happiness and power. Thus, persons with a youthful gait—regardless of their actual age—were rated more positively along several dimensions than persons with an older gait. Can you think of a situation or time when the way a person walked influenced what you thought of him or her? In what ways did the style of walking affect your perception?

Physical Characteristics

Whereas body movements and facial expressions change quickly and can be controlled to some extent, physical characteristics, such as body type, attractiveness, height, weight, and skin tone, are fairly constant and more difficult to control, especially in the course of a single interaction. In our culture, physical appearance plays a significant role in communication and relationships. Segments of our society have become obsessed with physical appearance and general health, and spend billions of dollars each year to modify, preserve, and decorate their bodies. We might say "beauty is only skin deep," but we are likely to respond positively to those who are attractive and negatively to those who are unattractive.[41]

Physical attractiveness is an extremely powerful influence on everyday communication. It appears that both males and females are strongly influenced by attractiveness, though males seem to be more responsive to appearance than are females.[42] Overall, though, an appealing physical appearance is perceived as a positive characteristic that influences interpersonal attraction (see Chapter 14 for more on interpersonal attraction) and interpersonal preferences. Numerous stereotypes are consistently associated with physical appearance, and it would not be surprising if you hold some of them. Consider how you respond to the photos of the young woman before and after a makeover, on page 110.

Numerous research studies have indicated that attractive people are perceived to be more popular, successful, sociable, persuasive, sensual, and happy than unattractive ones. Attractiveness affects credibility and a person's ability to persuade others, to get a job, and to gain a higher salary. Handsome men are likely to be viewed as more masculine, and beautiful women as more feminine, in comparison with those perceived as less attractive.[43]

Touch

Touch is referred to as either tactile communication or **haptics**. Haptics is one of the most basic forms of communication. You talk with someone, and he or she touches you. How would you react? What does the person's touch communicate? The answer to both questions most likely depends on several factors relating to *who* touches you (a friend, a stranger, a member of your own or the other gender); the nature of contact (brief or prolonged, gentle or rough, what part of the body is touched); and the context in which the touch took place (at school, work, a social setting, a doctor's office). Depending on the person and context, touch can suggest caring, affection, sexual interest, dominance, or aggression. Despite such complexities regarding what touch communicates, existing evidence suggests that when touch is appropriate, it is likely to produce positive reactions in recipients.[44] To be seen as positive, however, it must be viewed as appropriate.

As one of our most primitive and yet sensitive ways of relating to others, touch is a critical aspect of communication. It plays a significant role in giving encouragement, expressing tenderness, and showing emotional support, and it can be more powerful than words. For example, when you receive some bad news, a pat on the shoulder from a friend can be far more reassuring than any number of understanding words.

The kind and amount of appropriate touch varies according to the individuals, their relationship, and the situation. Researchers identified categories to describe variations of touch as it relates to the dominant culture of the United States. The categories are functional–professional, social–polite, friendship–warmth, love–intimacy, and sexual arousal.[45] Definitions and examples are given in Table 5.4.

haptics

Tactile, or touch, communication; one of the most basic forms of communication.

Making Connections for Success

You Can't Judge People by Their Appearance, or Can You?

Look at the young woman in the photographs that follow and think about what she might be like. Look at the "before" photo and respond to number 1 below; then look at the "after" photo, taken after she had a makeover, and respond to number 1 below; then respond to 2, 3, and 4.

1. Make a list of the physical characteristics that describe this person. Then, on the basis of those characteristics, describe the person in terms of her sociability, intelligence, poise, independence, masculinity or femininity, popularity, vanity, potential for success, integrity, concern for others, temperament, sexuality, and other features.

2. How do you think your or others' interactions with the person shown in the "before" photo might differ from those with the person shown in the "after" photo?

3. Do you think men and women differ in their responses to the above questions? Why or why not?

4. Given the two photos, do any stereotypes emerge? If so, describe them.

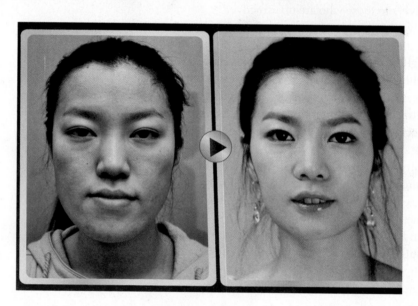

Table 5.4 Touch/Haptics

Category of Touch	Definition/Explanation	Example
Functional–professional	Unsympathetic, impersonal, cold, or businesslike touch	A doctor touches a patient during a physical examination or a tailor touches a customer while measuring.
Social–polite	Acknowledges another person according to the norms or rules of a society	Two people shake hands in American culture or kiss in other cultures to greet one another.
Friendship–warmth	Expresses an appreciation of the special attributes of another or warm feelings for another; the most misinterpreted type of touching behavior	Two men or two women meet in an airport, hug, and walk off with their arms around each other. Athletes touch a shoulder or pat each other on their buttocks.
Love–intimacy	Occurs in romantic relationships between lovers and spouses; highly communicative and usually requires consent between both parties, even though one party might not reciprocate	Two people hug, caress, embrace, and kiss.
Sexual arousal	The most intimate level of personal contact with another; expresses physical attraction between consenting individuals	Sexual touch behavior includes foreplay and intercourse.

The meaning of a particular touch depends on the type of touch, the situation in which the touch occurs, who is doing the touching, and the cultural background of those involved. Some cultures are more prone to touching behavior than others. Research states that people in the United States are less touch oriented than persons in other cultures. For example, a classic study of touching behavior during a one-hour period in a coffee shop found that people in San Juan, Puerto Rico, touched 180 times in an hour; those in Paris, France, touched 110 times; and those in Gainesville, Florida, touched only twice.[46]

Gender differences in touching behavior are also noteworthy. Men tend to touch more than women do, women tend to be touched more often than men, and women seem to value touch more than men do. Little research exists regarding sex differences in touching behavior. One study found that a light, comforting pat on the arm can create feelings of security among both men and women—but only if women do the touching.[47] Another study investigated sex differences in amounts, types, and factors influencing same-sex touch in a sports context. The study found that females performed more touch behaviors than males overall, but that males performed more touch behaviors at away games than home games, while females performed more touch behaviors than males after negative game events.[48] Gender differences in touch behavior may be partially attributed to men's sexual aggressiveness in U.S. culture and their expression of power and dominance.

Space

Statements such as "Give me some room to operate," signs that say "Keep Out," and the bumper sticker that reads "Keep Off My" followed by a picture of a donkey are all attempts to regulate the distance between people. Such behaviors are of special interest to researchers in **proxemics**, the study of how we use space and the distance we place between ourselves and others when we communicate. Edward T. Hall, anthropologist and author of two classic books, *The Silent Language* and *The Hidden Dimension*, coined the term *proxemics*.[49] Hall was a pioneer who explained how space is used in North American culture. In his study of proxemics, Hall identified four zones. *Intimate space* is defined as the distance from no space between two individuals to one-and-a-half feet between two individuals. This zone is the most personal, and it is usually open only to those with whom we are well acquainted, unless such closeness is physically forced on us, such as in a crowded train or elevator.

The second zone is referred to as *personal space* and ranges from distances of one-and-a-half feet to four feet between people. It is not unusual for us to carry on conversations or other activities with close friends and relatives in this zone. If someone we don't know enters this zone, we are likely to feel uncomfortable or violated. The

proxemics
The study of the use of space and of distance between individuals when they are communicating.

Making Connections for Success

When Doing International Business, What Should You Know about Nonverbal Communication?

American culture doesn't often give as much weight to nonverbal communication as other cultures. Thus differences in cultural interpretations can lead to misunderstanding and lost business. Search the Internet using such key words as "cultural differences in nonverbal communication" or "nonverbal communication in international business."

1. What did you learn about the various ways different cultures communicate nonverbally in the business environment?

2. What nonverbal communication advice would you give to someone doing business internationally?

3. What are some of the common nonverbal mistakes Americans make in international business situations?

third zone is called *social space*. It ranges from four to twelve feet and is where mos professional conversations occur, as well as group interactions, such as meetings *Public space*, the fourth zone, is twelve feet or more. This distance is common for publi speaking situations or other formal presentations.

The need to identify certain amounts of space as our own is an aspect of prox emics called **territoriality**. We often position markers such as books, coats, pencils papers, and other objects to define our space. Some students become upset when someone else sits in a seat they usually occupy, even when seating is not assigned This uneasiness stems from a strong desire to stake out and protect territory. Simila reactions occur when someone enters a room without knocking or tailgates when driving; it seems like an invasion of our territory.

We usually give little conscious attention to the role of space in our communica tion, yet the way others use space gives strong clues to their thoughts and reaction to us. Many variables influence our use of space when we communicate; status, sex culture, and context are but a few.

Status affects the distance maintained between communicators. Research show that people of different status levels tend to stay farther apart than do individuals o equal status. Furthermore, people of higher status tend to close the distance between them and people of lower status, but seldom do people of lower status move to close the distance between them and a person of higher status.

Men and women tend to differ in their proxemic patterns, but the differences in par hinge on whether the interaction is with someone of the same or opposite sex. In same sex situations, men prefer, expect, and usually establish greater conversational distance than women do. Opposite-sex distancing depends on how intimate the relationship is.

Culture creates a wealth of differences in the way individuals use distance for communication. For example, people from the U. S. tend to stand farther apart during conversations than do those from many European and Middle Eastern countries. Arab males, for example, consider it polite to stand close to other males with whom they are communicating. There are as many culture-based differences as there are cultures, and it is not unusual for one group to be perceived as cold and unfriendly and another as pushy and forward because of their use of space. Competent communicators recog nize that not all cultures or people view distance in the same way.

Context also influences the amount of space maintained between individuals. For example, people in line at an automated teller machine usually stand back far enough to give the person using the machine the feeling that a transaction is relatively private But passengers waiting to board a bus ordinarily stand close together to avoid losing their places.

Time

Chronemics is the study of how people perceive, structure, and use time as commu nication.[50] People in most Western cultures are preoccupied with time. Everything seems to have a starting and an ending time. For example, they worry about how long they have to wait for something and how long it takes to do something. They even go so far as to say that time is money. Because they place such a high value on time, it plays a significant role in nonverbal communication. They are particularly sensitive to people and events that waste their time or make exceptional demands on it. Consider your reaction, for instance, when your date keeps you waiting, when an instructor continues to lecture after the bell has signaled the end of class, or when your super visor gives you only one day to complete a major project. Your feelings might range from confusion to indignation to outrage, but you will almost certainly not be neu tral. To some extent, your reaction depends on the identity of the other person. You will probably be more tolerant if the offending party is a friend or someone who has authority, such as your boss. For example, if a blind date keeps you waiting too long

---

territoriality

The need to identify certain areas of space as one's own.

Chronemics

The study of how people perceive, structure, and use time as communication.

you might decide to leave; but if your professor is late for an office appointment, you will probably suffer in silence and continue to wait for his or her arrival.

We tend to have many expectations about how time should be used, and we often judge others by their use of time. For example, workers are expected to be on time for work. Therefore, punctual workers are more likely to create a positive impression, whereas consistently late ones may be perceived as irresponsible, lazy, or uninterested. We must constantly be aware of the messages we send through our use (and misuse) of time.

Individuals can differ in their approaches to time. For example, some people always look to the future; others long for the past, and still others live for the moment. Each approach communicates something about people and the ways they use time to communicate who they are. Each culture teaches its members about time expectations, and these expectations vary. In some cultures, punctuality is expected; in others, it is not important, and, in fact, people are expected to be late. In U.S. culture, for example, you are expected to be on time for a dinner party, but being up to 20 minutes late is socially accepted and still considered "on time." In some foreign countries, such as Japan, arriving late for a dinner party is considered an insult.[51] Our use of time communicates messages about us, so it is important to adhere to the time-related norms of the culture in which we communicate.

Men in Western cultures generally tend to keep a conversational distance between each other, but in certain circumstances, such as teammates at athletic events, standing close to each other, or even touching, is not unusual.

Paralanguage/Vocalics

Do you remember the first time you heard a recording of your own voice? If you are like most of us, you likely were a bit surprised because the voice you heard didn't sound like you. **Paralanguage or vocalics** is the way we vocalize, or say, the words we speak. Paralanguage includes speech sounds but also speech rate, accents, articulation, pronunciation, and silence. Sounds such as groans, yawns, coughs, laughter, crying, and yelping, which are nonsymbolic but can communicate very specific messages, are also included. Expressions such as "um," "uh-huh," "ya know," "like," and "OK" are referred to as vocal fillers and are considered paralanguage. Vocal fillers are often sprinkled throughout conversations without forethought or a set order. They might reflect nervousness, speech patterns of a particular subculture, or a personal habit. In any case, the use of vocal fillers can influence our image positively or damage and degrade us and others.

Paralanguage or vocalics
The way we vocalize, or say, the words we speak.

Paralanguage includes pitch (how high or low the voice is), vocal force (intensity or loudness of the voice), rate (speed), quality (overall impression of the voice), and pauses or silence. The way we vary our voices conveys different meanings to receivers. For example, a person who speaks quickly may communicate a different message than a person who speaks slowly. Even when the words are the same, if the rate, force, pitch, and quality differ, the receiver's interpretations will differ. Researchers estimate that approximately 38 percent of the meaning of oral communication is affected by the use of voice, by *the way* something is said rather than by *what* is said.[52]

On the basis of paralanguage, we make many judgments about words, the person saying them, the speaking and listening roles, and the credibility of the message. Of course, judgments about people based on paralanguage can be just as unreliable as those based on body type. We must therefore recognize the effect of paralanguage on communication and adjust accordingly.

Silence

The sound of silence is a contradiction in terms; as hard as you try, it is almost impossible to have complete and absolute silence. Silence or vocal pauses are communicative, powerful messages that often speak volumes, whether intended or not. **Vocal pauses** or hesitations are usually short in duration, whereas **silence** generally refers to extended periods of time without sound. Vocal pauses can be used to emphasize a word or thought or to make a point to get others' attention. For example, a speaker stands in front of an audience and gazes at the audience in the hope of gaining the audience's attention so they will listen. A teacher pauses during a lecture to get students' attention. Sometimes, people use vocal pauses to gather their thoughts or to allow others time to think. Vocal pauses or prolonged periods of silence can also create the perception that you are unsure of yourself, unprepared, or nervous. Regardless of why vocal pauses occur, they do send messages.

Silence sometimes seems very awkward in a conversation, especially when you are talking to someone whom you do not know well and who might be of higher status than you. Most of us in this situation feel or sense the pressure to say something to get the conversation restarted. Have you ever said "hello" to someone you admire or respect and he or she didn't reply or acknowledge you? You likely felt slighted or less than important. It is not unusual to use silence to prevent communication with others. Silence can prevent certain topics from surfacing or stop someone from saying something he or she might later regret.

Silence is expected in certain contexts, for example, during a funeral or while listening to a speech or presentation, or it can be self-imposed as a way of thinking or doing nothing at all. Silence has many possible meanings, none of which is easily interpreted. The next time a good friend says, "hi," try pausing for five to ten seconds before reacting. You will quickly learn the effect silence can have as a message.

Cultural differences are also related to silence. What are some negative perceptions conveyed in U.S. culture by silence at a business meeting or social gathering? In many cultures, silence is seen more positively. In Japan, for example, silence is considered more appropriate than speech in many situations.[53] Silence in Japan is also associated with credibility. In Japan, someone who is silent is more likely perceived as one of high credibility than someone who talks a lot. The Japanese also use silence to avoid both conflict and embarrassment.[54] For example, "a typical practice among many Asian peoples is to refuse to speak any further in conversation if they cannot personally accept the speaker's attitude, opinion, or way of thinking about particular issues or subjects."[55] The intercultural implications of silence are as diverse as those of other nonverbal cues. Competent communicators know they must be careful not to assume that others communicate *only* when they are talking.

Vocal pauses

A hesitation, usually short in duration.

silence

An extended period of time without sound.

Making Connections for Success

It's Not What You Say, but How You Say It!

"My job is really difficult."

Read the preceding statement aloud in four different ways: (1) with no expression at all, (2) as if your job is extremely difficult, (3) as if your job is anything but difficult, and (4) as if you are trying to convince someone that your job is difficult. Note how you can change the meaning without changing the words.

1. What did you do to your voice to change the meaning of the sentence?

2. Did you notice anything else about your other nonverbal behavior while using your voice to change the meaning of the sentence?

3. What did you learn about vocal expression from this exercise?

4. How can vocal expression help you to become a more competent communicator?

Artifacts

Artifacts are personal adornments or possessions that communicate information about us. Such things as automobiles, eyeglasses, briefcases, grooming, clothing, hair color, body piercings, tattoos, and makeup communicate information about our age, gender, status, role, class, importance, group membership, personality, and relationship to others. For example, what do you tell people by the type and color of vehicle you drive? A black SUV with tinted windows conveys a different message from a green sedan, as do a sports car versus a minivan and a Hummer versus a Chevy Volt.[56]

How do you react to people who have body piercings and tattoos? Effective communicators learn to adapt their use of artifacts to a specific situation and not to judge others by appearance alone. If you want people to view you as a nonconformist, you will likely use different artifacts than those used by someone who wishes to be viewed as a conformist. For example, if you wear a suit to a job interview, you send a different message than if you wear a sweatshirt and jeans.

Artifacts

A personal ornament or possession that communicates information about a person.

Environment

Environment, as discussed in Chapter 1, is the psychological and physical surroundings in which communication occurs, including the furniture, architectural design, lighting conditions, temperature, smells, colors, and sounds of the location, as well as the attitudes, feelings, perceptions, and relationships of the participants. The environment has an impact on the individuals, their backgrounds, and their perception of what is important to them at the time of interaction. The best environment allows a speaker's intended message to be delivered accurately. Thus, soft background music, dim lights, a log burning in a fireplace, a tray of hors d'oeuvres, and two candles would create the perfect environment for a romantic encounter but would not work for a pregame pep rally.

Improving Our Ability to Send and Interpret Nonverbal Communication

5 **Explain** why it is difficult to interpret and understand nonverbal communication and how to ensure that the message received is accurate.

We must be continuously aware of our nonverbal messages and how others receive them. Competent communicators constantly monitor their communicative behaviors to ensure they are not misunderstood and that the intended message is received. When you act to show you care how others perceive your behavior, you engage in self-monitoring. **Self-monitoring** involves the willingness to change behavior to fit a given situation, an awareness of how we affect others, and the ability to regulate nonverbal cues and other factors to influence others' impressions. It entails concern with both projecting the desired image and the ability to assess the effects of the image communicated to others.

Our nonverbal messages greatly influence how others perceive our communication and us. For example, an extremely bright and talented student was constantly turned down for jobs for which he was well qualified. When asked why he thought this was happening, he replied that he had no idea. To find out, friends filmed a mock interview in which another student interviewed him. Upon review of the tape, he immediately noticed that he never looked at the interviewer. Instead, his gaze wandered about the room. The student's lack of direct eye contact gave the impression he lacked confidence and he might not be completely candid in his

Self-monitoring

The willingness to change behavior to fit situations, the awareness of effects on others, and the ability to regulate nonverbal cues and other factors to influence others' impressions.

communication. Once he knew why he was being rejected, he could work to change his behavior. To help him practice, his friends made a video of another interview session. This time, he was reminded to look at the interviewer each time his gaze wandered. After several such sessions, he learned to feel more comfortable with direct eye contact and consequently appeared more confident and truthful in his communication.

Although change of nonverbal behavior is not simple, it can be done with a little effort and desire. The key is to conscientiously examine how nonverbal cues may undermine your intended message. If you realize that you have distracting mannerisms, such as smirking, playing with coins, twisting your hair, shuffling your feet, or saying "you know," "like," or "OK" too much, ask others to call your attention to these behaviors. You can then make a conscious effort to change.

Nonverbal communication is complex, but you can do some things to improve your interpretation. First, be observant of and sensitive to the nonverbal messages you receive. Second, verify unclear or inconsistent nonverbal messages. For example, think about a friend who used to visit regularly who hasn't come over in several weeks. It might seem logical to conclude that she doesn't want to see you anymore; but, then again, she might have become wrapped up in her studies, taken a part-time job, or fallen ill. To accurately interpret her behavior, consider all the possibilities and don't jump to conclusions. Because it is so tempting to make inferences based on nonverbal behavior, it is important to remember not to go beyond actual observations.

At least three reasons for misinterpreting nonverbal communication are possible:

1. *Nonverbal cues have multiple meanings.* Nonverbal communication is difficult to understand because a single behavior can have many potential meanings. A frown might indicate unhappiness, sadness, anger, pain, thought, aggressiveness, disapproval, dejection, fear, fatigue, discouragement, disapproval, or a combination of these. Unlike words, nonverbal cues lack dictionary definitions.

   Interpretations are unreliable because they depend so heavily on perceptions. Suppose, for example, you just walked out of a sad movie and see a friend with tears in her eyes, talking to her sister. Her tears may reflect her reactions to the movie—or to a breakup with her boyfriend; she may be injured, or she may have just heard about a death in the family. Her tears could even result from laughing hard at something that occurred after the movie. Of course, some nonverbal behaviors, such as nodding the head for "yes" and shaking it for "no" (in U.S. society) are consistent in both their meaning and their interpretation. Unfortunately, such consistency is the exception rather than the rule.

2. *Nonverbal cues are interdependent.* The meaning of one nonverbal cue often depends on the correct interpretation of several other simultaneously occurring cues. For example, when we see someone enter a room, we begin to select certain cues about that person, such as gender, physical traits, facial expressions, voice characteristics, and clothing. Each cue intermeshes with the others and adds to the total picture. This interdependence of nonverbal behaviors and our inability to perceive all aspects of any one nonverbal communication make interpretation risky.

   When we look for meaning of more than one nonverbal message at a time we use the **functional approach**. This approach examines nonverbal behavior not by isolated nonverbal cues, but by seeing how each cue interacts and works with the others to perform various communicative functions.

3. *Nonverbal cues are subtle.* Many nonverbal behaviors are subtle and difficult to observe. One person might overlook a cue that another person notices immediately.

functional approach

Using more than one nonverbal message at a time to look for meaning.

Making Connections for Success

Texting Is All Thumbs, Isn't It?

We may believe nonverbal communication such as facial expressions and tone of voice express more meaning in a spoken message than emojis in a text message or email. But is this really true?

If you were to communicate the phrase "thts gr8t" (that's great) to a friend and you wanted to express this in a positive tone rather than a sarcastic one:

1. What would you do to ensure that the message you sent was received as intended?

2. Are there other options for sending the same message without increasing its length? If so, what are they?

3. Why do you think texts and emails are often misunderstood? What are the advantages over face-to-face or phone communication?

You send an email to your instructor with your term paper project attached, and you send it early. However, the reply from your instructor says only "received."

1. You know the instructor received your paper, how else could you interpret the instructor's message? *Should* you read anything else into his or her message? How do we learn to interpret email or text messages that lack nonverbal communication cues such as tone of voice or facial expressions? How do greetings such as "hi," "wassup?" or "dear," or closings such as "take care" or "best wishes," influence the overall message?

2. Without using more words, how might the instructor have communicated "nice going" or "good job"?

---

thus, multiple interpretations may be made in the same situation. For example, a friend tells you that a person in whom you have an interest has been looking at you, but you haven't noticed the glances or you see the eye contact as more accidental than a deliberate message of interest in you.

One method to help verify the meaning of a nonverbal message, if you are not certain of the sender's intention, is to use **descriptive feedback**. Descriptive feedback is not always necessary, but when a message seems inconsistent with the situation or other behaviors or when you're not sure you accurately interpreted an important message, you should verify your perceptions with the other person. When you use descriptive feedback, do not express agreement or disagreement or draw conclusions; simply describe the message you believe was communicated. For example, if you think someone's behavior indicates that he is uncomfortable around you, but you're not sure, don't ask, "Why are you so nervous when I'm around?" Rather, describe the situation nonjudgmentally: "Jim, I get the impression that you may not be comfortable around me. Is that the case?" This allows the other person to explain without feeling defensive, and it enables you to avoid inaccurate interpretations.

descriptive feedback

Describing to the sender what you perceived the message to mean.

Guidelines

Sending and Interpreting Nonverbal Communication

Sending

1. Be aware of how people react to you.
2. Ask friends or colleagues for their help.
3. Create and view a video to see how you appear to others.
4. Adapt to the context or situation in which you find yourself.

Interpreting

1. Nonverbal cues have multiple meanings.
2. Nonverbal cues are interdependent.
3. Nonverbal cues are subtle.
4. Use descriptive feedback to reduce misunderstandings.

Summary

What Is Nonverbal Communication?

Objective 5.1 **Differentiate** nonverbal communication from verbal communication.

Nonverbal communication includes all behaviors, symbols, attributes, or objects, whether intended or not, that communicate messages with social meaning. It is not only what we say, but also how we say it with our tone of voice, body movements, appearance, and use of space, touch, and time.

Characteristics of Nonverbal Communication

Objective 5.2 **Explain** the six key characteristics of nonverbal communication.

There are many reasons to study nonverbal communication, the primary one is its pervasive effects on what we communicate to others.

- Nonverbal communication occurs constantly.
- Nonverbal communication depends on context.
- Nonverbal communication is more believable than verbal communication.
- Nonverbal communication is a primary means of expression.
- Nonverbal communication is related to culture
- Nonverbal communication is ambiguous.

Functions of Nonverbal Communication

Objective 5.3 **Identify** the five common functions of nonverbal communication.

Nonverbal communication adds life to our interaction because it

- complements what is being said;
- repeats verbal behavior;
- regulates verbal behavior;

- substitutes for verbal behavior; and
- deceives.

Types of Nonverbal Communication

Objective 5.4 **Compare and contrast** different types of nonverbal communication and the ways competent communicators are aware of their nonverbal communication.

Every day we perform a wide range of nonverbal behaviors without thinking about them:

- Facial expressions and body movements
  - Eye behavior, or oculesics
  - Facial expressions
  - Body movements
- Physical characteristics
- Touch
- Space
- Time
- Paralanguage/vocalics
- Silence
- Artifacts
- Environment

Improving Our Ability to Send and Interpret Nonverbal Communication

Objective 5.5 **Explain** why it is difficult to interpret and understand nonverbal communication and how to ensure that the message received is accurate.

To avoid misinterpretation, competent communicators are observant of, and sensitive to, the nonverbal messages they receive; consider all their possible meanings; and avoid jumping to conclusions.

Discussion Starters

1. In what way or ways have texting, emailing, and other communication technologies affected nonverbal communication?
2. In developing relationships with others, what role does nonverbal communication play?
3. "You cannot not communicate." Describe situations in which you thought you weren't communicating anything but later found out that you were.

4. Explain why paralanguage is important to effective communication.
5. Explain why you think nonverbal communication is more believable than verbal communication.
6. What is the most important lesson you learned from this chapter?

Chapter 6
Connecting Listening and Thinking in the Communication Process

 ## Learning Objectives

This chapter will help you:

6.1 **Describe** how listening helps you make connections with others in all aspects of your life.

6.2 **Explain** the complex nature of listening as a cognitive process.

6.3 **Differentiate** among three functions of listening behavior.

6.4 **Select** specific attitudes and behaviors to help you overcome your barriers to listening.

6.5 **Identify** instances in which you must be a critical listener/thinker.

6.6 **Characterize** the speech and actions of a competent listener.

6.7 **Use** technology to take better notes and organize your work.

6.8 **Identify** the similarities and differences in listening behavior in different cultures.

Making Everyday Connections

How often do you find yourself attempting to do many different things at the same time? Everyone seems to require us to multitask. We talk on the phone while finishing a report for a manager as we text with a friend. We text friends as we walk down the hall, wait in the elevator, or sit in class. Although multitasking *seemingly* occurs all the time and in many situations, listening and cognitive psychology researchers have found that multitasking is a *myth*; we cannot truly multitask. Instead, researchers say, electroencephalographic (EEG) test results show that our brains can focus on only one thing at a time. We concentrate on one thing and then quickly shift so that it may seem as if we're doing things simultaneously, when it's actually one quick thing at a time before we move on to the next activity as our focus switches to something else, and then back again.[1] Neuroscientists have found that attempting to multitask results in 50% more mistakes, 50% of the time. Skilled listening requires time, attention, and practice. The ability to devote time requires both focus and attention.[2]

Questions to Think About

1. How much time do you attempt to spend in multitasking?

2. When is it important to listen and not make use of the technological networking available to you?

3. Think of a job task or class assignment in which your failure to listen resulted in more work, embarrassment, or even a lower grade. What factors led you *not* to listen as well as you could have? What did you learn from that negative experience?

4. When is it appropriate to incorporate technology into your everyday communication?

5. Think of a situation in which your good listening made a difference. How did that make you feel? Why were you a better listener in that situation?

This chapter will help you become an effective listener and, as a result, an effective respondent. To enhance your listening competence, you need to understand the importance of effective listening, the elements of listening, the functions of listening, and the most common barriers to listening. You should analyze and evaluate what you listen to and make the connection between listening and thinking, which are separate but related cognitive processes, as well as learn the difference between listening and hearing.

Because most of us take listening for granted, we tend to think of it as a simple task. However, listening is actually quite complex. Scholars agree that listening, like communication in general, is closely linked to the thinking process. Listening scholars, including Harfield, Brownell, Janusik, Wolvin, and Coakley, state that listening is a distinct behavior, separate from other intellectual activities.[3] Listening scholars and teachers agree that hearing and listening are not the same. **Listening** is a continuous cognitive activity and is defined as the active process of receiving, constructing meaning from, and responding to spoken or nonverbal messages. **Hearing** is the passive physiological process in which sound is received by the ear. It is impossible to listen to sounds without first hearing them, but it is possible to hear sounds without listening to them. What distinguishes listening from hearing?

Communication scholars agree that the major difference between listening and hearing is that listening is cognitive while hearing is physical. In addition, depending on the situation, listening should always be an active process. Hearing is a physical process. Either you receive the sounds or you don't. If you have normal hearing, your ears receive sounds.[4] You don't have to work at hearing; it just happens. People can have excellent hearing and be terrible listeners. Listening, on the other hand, is cognitive, is *active*, and requires energy, desire, focus, and attention.

People bring a variety of learning styles into the classroom: auditory, kinesthetic, and visual are among the most common. Some of us are visual learners. We need to be able to see what is discussed. Whiteboard text and drawings or PowerPoint or Prezi presentations help the visual learner. The kinesthetic learner experiences things. She or he needs to move around, touch things, watch things work, and take things apart or put them back together. The auditory learner, by contrast, listens to messages and processes information. This kind of learner doesn't need models or hands-on experiences

listening

A cognitive activity that is defined as the active process of receiving, constructing meaning from, and responding to spoken or nonverbal messages.

hearing

The passive physiological process in which sound is received by the ear.

much as he or she needs to listen to and process information. What kind of learner are you? What is the role of listening in your learning? How do you know? What kinds of activities help you learn? What kinds of activities help you listen?

Skills in listening, analyzing, processing, and recording information are often neglected during formal education. Have you ever had any formal training in listening? If you are a typical college student, you will complete course work in reading, writing, and speaking, but few students ever enroll in a listening course. Not only are there few opportunities for formal listening instruction, but also informal listening training is also not generally provided. Yet as students, you are expected to listen approximately 50 percent of the time—listening is proportionately the most used language skill.[5] University of Northern Iowa graduate student Sarah Baker completed research to identify the basic communication skills employers seek in recent hires from among recent Kirkwood Community College graduates. Of the employers she surveyed, 100 percent identified listening as the number one skill.[6] In Chapter 1, we discussed surveys from business executives who suggested that graduates need more work on communication skills; *listening* is consistently high on all lists.[7] Listening has been identified in numerous other surveys and research projects as one of the top communication skills employers seek in entry-level hires as well as in those being promoted. Even though the research suggests that listening skills are critical, according to listening scholars Robert Bohlken, Laura Janusik, Carolyn Coakley, and Andrew Wolvin, listening receives the least instruction in school.[8] Even in the course where this book is used it is likely that only 7 percent of class and text time is spent on listening.[9] Inefficient listening is a prevalent (and expensive) problem in our lives, in terms of time wasted, poor customer relations, and the need to redo many tasks. The International Listening Association (ILA) is a professional organization of members dedicated to the study, application, and improvement of listening in all contexts. Check out their website at listen.org to learn more facts about listening.

The Importance of Effective Listening

.1   Describe how listening helps you make connections with others in all aspects of your life.

Most misunderstandings in our daily lives occur because of poor listening habits. Poor listening skills can create serious personal, professional, and financial problems. For students, poor listening can result in missed appointments, misunderstood directions, incorrect or incomplete assignments, lower grades, and lost opportunities. In relationships, poor listening can cause misunderstandings, arguments, and loss of friendships.

It might surprise you to realize how much of your waking day you spend listening: When you are not talking or reading, you are probably listening to something or someone. Many listening scholars have discovered that college students spend 50 percent or more of their time listening, almost one-fifth in speaking, and less than one-fifth in reading and writing combined (see Figure 6.1).[10] In a German study, Imhof and Weinhard found that German primary school children are expected to listen for about two-thirds of classroom time.[11] Given these figures, it is easy to appreciate the importance of listening. U.S. studies have similar results stating that listening is the most common activity in the classroom.[12]

From the time we get up in the morning until we end the day, we constantly listen to something. Yet most of us give little thought to the part that listening plays in our everyday experiences. Parents and children both complain, "They don't listen to me." A similar refrain may be heard from relational partners, workers and bosses, and teachers and students. You might even have heard a friend say to you, "You really

Figure 6.1 Proportional Time Spent by College Students in Communication Activities

The graph indicates how typical college students spend their waking time. The proportions given in this graph are averages and, of course, can vary dramatically from person to person and situation to situation.

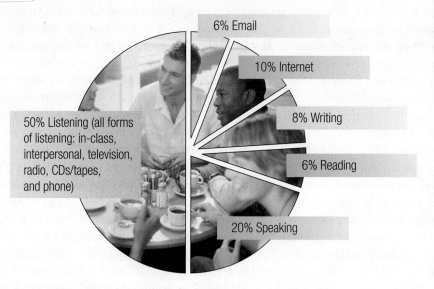

ought to listen to yourself." As simple as listening *appears* to be, many of us are not efficient listeners.

There can be little doubt that communication, and listening in particular, assumes a significant role in society. Because we spend so much time as *consumers* of communication, we need to learn as much as we can about effective listening. We live and work in a global world. Careful listening to the messages of people from other cultures and backgrounds is a successful life skill. The prevalence of all our technology and devices (iPods, iPads, and smartphones) cause interruptions and distractions and create barriers to listening. In addition, we are surrounded by electronic messages clamoring for our attention. It is hard to shut out these distractions simply because of their almost overpowering presence. A YouTube clip, "Did You Know? 2014," discusses this paradigm shift and provides interesting ideas about the impact of technology on the world. The clip reports that in 2013 over 6 billion Google searches were conducted every month (or 59 billion searches each day), 24 hours of videos were uploaded on YouTube every minute, and 175+ million users were connected on Facebook every minute. It further suggests that if Facebook were a country, it would be the third most populated country in the world. In addition, 87 percent of all teenagers text, and they send an average of 3,339 texts per month. Over 2.4 billion people of all ages are now connected to the Internet, and the number of text messages sent every day is double the population of the planet.[13] (Several versions of this information can be found on YouTube; search for "Did You Know? 2014" or "Shift Happens" to view a recent version.) As a point of comparison, when Google was founded in September 1998, it served ten thousand queries each day. By the end of 2006 that same number was served in a single second. In early July 2015, Google processed an average of 40,000 search queries every second. This translates to over 3.5 billion searches per day and 1.2 trillion searches per year worldwide.

Listening scholars believe we can learn to reduce mediated as well as internal and other external distractions through cognitive, affective, and behavioral strategies.

Listening scholar Andrew D. Wolvin, author of *Listening in the Quality Organization*, indicates that the individuals who make up organizations must be effective listeners. His book identifies the role of listening in the communication process and provides

Making Connections for Success

Your View of Effective Listening

Think about someone you believe is a good listener.

1. What behaviors exhibited by this person make you think she or he is a good listener?

2. What does this person do and say that make you aware of their effective listening?

3. How can you tell they are cognitively aware of messages?

4. How do you compare your own listening behaviors with those of the person you identified as a good listener?

5. How do you think your friends would rate you as a listener?

6. What three things can you do to improve your own listening and thinking?

---

suggestions for people to become more effective listeners. He concludes, "Quality listening then, is a benchmark for the quality organization of the twenty-first century. Some organizations have gotten there, while others are yet to develop a listening culture.... The challenge to get there is significant, but the rewards are tremendous. Indeed, our very economic, technological, political, and social lives depend on quality listening."[14]

Effective Listening

6.2 **Explain** the complex nature of listening as a cognitive process.

Listening is a complex behavior. Many people have tried to determine what happens when people listen. What is involved? What happens from the time someone makes sounds to the point at which you make meaning from those words and the accompanying nonverbals?

Sensing

Hearing, as we learned earlier, is the physiological process in which sound is received by the ear. Accurate reception of sounds requires the listener to focus attention on the speaker, discriminate among sounds, and concentrate.[15] Given the difference between hearing and listening, answer this question: When you play music while you study, do you simply *hear* the music, or do you really *listen* to it? The sounds provide background that you hear; your hearing becomes listening only when you also carry out the remaining stages of the listening process. Please note that listening is a cognitive activity. It begins in the brain and is processed in the brain, and the brain tells us how to respond. Newer[16] research shows that listening is also affected by all of the senses: hearing, smell, taste, touch, and vision. The listening process starts in the brain and all information, taken in through the senses, is processed in the brain. Thus the listener takes in information through all the senses and the brain processes the information to make sense of it, use it, and store it for future reference.

Information Processing (Evaluation, Interpretation, and Understanding):

Information processing uses **evaluation**, interpretation, and understanding to address comprehension when listening. In the fast pace of today's world, a premium is put on our time, energy, and attention. Each time we enter into a listening situation we have to evaluate the message and information. *Is the information critical? Is the information credible?* We then **interpret** the information based on tools such as our thinking preferences, the degree that we focused on the information, our existing knowledge, and **paralanguage**, or *how* we say things. Paralanguage—nonverbal components like

evaluation
Occurs when we assess the meaning of infermation.

interpret
Explaining the meaning of information.

paralanguage
The sound of words including silence.

intonation—and gestures or body language can also be significant factors in how we interpret a message. Upon interpreting the stimuli, we then give it meaning so we may have understanding. Understanding allows us to know something in our own minds, that is, in our own thoughts and language. A question at this point arises: Does the understanding we have mesh with the information the sender is transmitting?[17]

Information processing

Assigning meaning to the stimuli that have been selected and attended to.

Information processing means that you weigh information and assign meaning to the stimuli you sense (hear, see, smell, taste, or touch). The ability to accurately follow directions is one of the ways we can measure whether we listen to what we sense. Each of us is frequently in situations where we must process the information and find shared meaning. Past experience plays an important role in information processing; you relate and compare new sounds and ideas to those you have previously heard or otherwise sensed. To learn statistics, for example, you must first learn algebra and other mathematical principles. If you are unprepared and do not have this knowledge, you can still attend to what your statistics teacher says; but because you are unable to interpret what she is saying, you will not understand what she has presented. This inability to understand reduces your listening effectiveness. These concepts will be further discussed as we explain the Harfield Cognitive Listening Model.

Remembering

remembering

Recalling something from stored memory; thinking of something again.

As a student, you are aware of the importance of **remembering**, or recalling something from stored memory. Most of your professors and employers expect you to recall and apply what you have heard in class or in meetings. Researchers say working memory and long-term memory are both essential processes and different aspects are required for different situations. Listening scholar Laura Janusik found that when people were presented with a series of unrelated sentences and asked to remember the last word of each sentence, they could remember, on average, 2.805 items out of 7. In a dynamic conversational listening task in which people were asked to remember a series of related questions and respond to them, people could remember and respond to 2.946 items.[18] This finding suggests that if the topic seems more relevant, people will remember slightly more than they do if it seems irrelevant. As you'll recall from Chapter 2, the process of perception (selective perception and selective attention) can also account for the loss of information. We tend to remember only information that supports our own views. Other information is forgotten. Remembering helps you complete assignments. Memory will also be important in your work responsibilities when an employer expects you to acquire and apply knowledge, as well as in family and friendship situations.

Effective listening is important to success in all aspects of our lives. It may surprise you to realize how much of your waking day you spend listening, but when you are not talking or reading, you are probably listening to something or someone.

Thinking

Many scholars view listening as a cognitive construct. That is, the brain is the center of the listening process; listening is how we receive all kinds of information to process, store, and/or use immediately or in the future. Also, memory or "remembering" is a critical component of the listening process. Neuro-scientific research opened new avenues of understanding on both the sites of specific memories and the ways learning, listening, and memory can be enhanced. The brain has more plasticity or flexibility than previously believed. Nobel Prize winning scientist Eric Kandel has spent his entire professional life determining how the brain works and how people can better remember the things they need to remember. Thus, the most current research

n listening indicates we need to teach people how to remember as well as to listen
ffectively.

Dwight Harfield developed the Harfield Cognitive Listening Model to expand
nd increase the emphasis on cognitive processes and listening. Harfield's model
dds thinking preferences, focus and attention, information processing, and remem-
ering to the listening model as they occur throughout listening experiences.[19] The
vay we think affects both what and how we think. The Harfield Cognitive Listening
Model identifies five aspects of information processing: sensing or taking in infor-
nation (and please note all five senses—hearing, seeing, tasting, touching, and
melling—are involved in this intake process), understanding, interpretation, evalua-
ion, and responding. Harfield also identifies the three cognitive processes of thinking
preferences, focus and attention, and remembering. The model also identifies internal
ilters that may interfere with how well and when we listen. Those filters include but
ire not limited to education, culture, attitudes, values, biases, previous experiences,
ind our roles in the communication event. We briefly discuss each of these aspects in
his section.

Harfield also depicts two models to represent the functions of the brain seen in
Figure 6.2 and 6.3. The idea of thinking preferences was assembled and popularized
oy researcher Ned Herrmann, who at the time was responsible for executive train-
ng at General Electric. Herrmann experimented with questionnaires and surveys
ind developed an assessment tool to measure the strength of thinking and language
preferences in four distinct thinking styles. He suggested the brain could be meta-
ohorically divided into specialized quadrants—the rational self, the safekeeping self,
he feeling self, and the experimental self—each with its own characteristics and
anguage.

Figure 6.2 Whole Brain Model

This figure depicts the four quadrants of the brain and identifies the type of thinking that occurs in
each quadrant. Ned Herrmann created the concept of brain dominance as a way to demonstrate
how different parts of the brain work.

SOURCE: Depicted by Dwight R. Harfield, and used with permission.

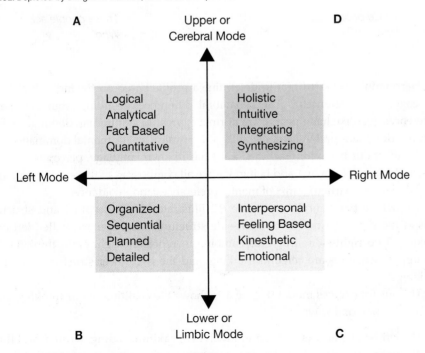

Figure 6.3 Our Four Different Selves

This figure identifies the specific thinking skills of each of the four quadrants of the brain. Herrmann suggests that each quadrant engages the thinker in different behaviors.

SOURCE: Depicted by Dwight R. Harfield, and used with permission.

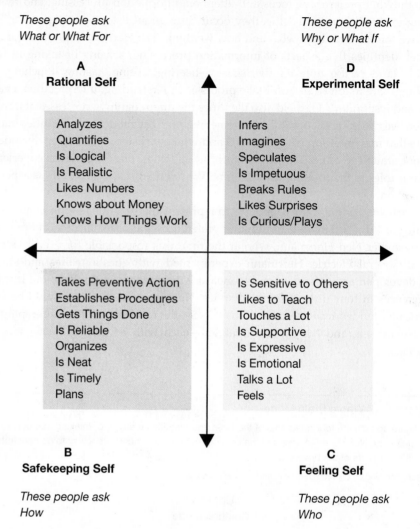

These people ask What or What For

A
Rational Self

> Analyzes
> Quantifies
> Is Logical
> Is Realistic
> Likes Numbers
> Knows about Money
> Knows How Things Work

These people ask Why or What If

D
Experimental Self

> Infers
> Imagines
> Speculates
> Is Impetuous
> Breaks Rules
> Likes Surprises
> Is Curious/Plays

> Takes Preventive Action
> Establishes Procedures
> Gets Things Done
> Is Reliable
> Organizes
> Is Neat
> Is Timely
> Plans

> Is Sensitive to Others
> Likes to Teach
> Touches a Lot
> Is Supportive
> Is Expressive
> Is Emotional
> Talks a Lot
> Feels

B
Safekeeping Self

These people ask How

C
Feeling Self

These people ask Who

Herrmann's work led him to determine a profile based on the individuals' opti-mal cognitive preferences.[20] The behavioral differences resulting from our mental preferences, just like handedness, are normal expressions of human dominance. Each of us has dominant preferences, mentally and physically; our mental dominances ulti-mately affect our behavior. Each quadrant has its own language, perception, values, gifts, and ways of knowing and being. We are all composites of those differing modes according to our particular mix of mental preferences and avoidances.

The whole brain model in Figure 6.2 illustrates the conceptual and structural basis of the profile grid. The two left-side structures are popularly called left-brain thinking. Two right-side structures combine to represent right-brain thinking. The two upper structures are cerebral thinking, and the two lower structures are limbic thinking.[21]

The our four selves model (Figure 6.3) shows the coalition of our thinking selves in a more behavioral way:

- The left hemisphere is *verbal*, and involves speaking, reading, writing, and think-ing with numbers. Analytic and sequential processing of information is car-ried out mostly in the left hemisphere for most people. A *left-brain* approach to problem solving is fact-based, analytic, and step-by-step, favoring words, numbers, and facts presented in a logical sequence.

- The right hemisphere is *visuospatial and emotional*, and involves simultaneous processing, pattern recognition, creative and holistic thinking, spatial perception, and geometry. Mental map making and our ability to rotate shapes in our mind are predominantly performed in the right hemisphere. A *right-brain* strategy seeks out insight, images, concepts, patterns, sounds, and movement, all to be built into an intuitive sense of the whole.

Each hemisphere has functions of its own, ordered processing of information, and unique "modes of knowing." The mind is composed of complementary parts, each enriching the other, and crucial to our successful functioning as human beings. Brain dominance is expressed in terms of how we prefer to learn, understand, and express or communicate something. These are called *thinking or cognitive preferences*, or *preferred modes of knowing (PMK)*.

Our thinking preference, or preferred mode of knowing, compares strongly with *what* we prefer to learn or do and *how* we go about it. It is the part of the brain we are most likely to use when we need to solve a problem, perhaps even in spite of or in addition to, our training. For example, a left-brained person may prefer to learn about engineering or law. A right-brained person, in contrast, may prefer to study psychology or music. If both people were to study dance, for example, the left-brained person may learn about productions, history, facts regarding names, and so on. The right-brained person, though, would likely learn about dancing by watching and doing it.

FOCUS AND ATTENTION Our culture currently works against people's ability to develop the skills of focus and attention in a number of ways:

- Movies and TV shows with large volumes of information are directed at us in short, stimulating, or shocking snappy scenes.
- Our society and education system are dumbed down.
- People are given information that lacks intellectual stimulation.
- We are fed an increasing amount of propaganda that asks us to believe what we are told rather than what we assemble and believe in our own minds.
- We believe we can multitask: People have so many things to do and are on the go so much that they try to do more than one thing at a time.
- Increasingly complex electronic technology in everyday living throws large masses of small bits of information at us.
- We have the growing ability to communicate with others, even when we don't want to, without ever directly seeing or hearing those people.

All these things contribute to our lack of ability to practice focus and attention. How we focus is crucial to how we learn (that is, how we acquire knowledge and skills) and remember (how we store and retrieve information). If you want to master and retain certain information, it is critical to pay close attention to it in the first place.[22]

Interpreting

When we interpret, we simply try to make sense of the information received. The **interpreting** process has two parts: "[Y]ou take into account the total communication context so that you are better able to understand the meaning of what is said from the speaker's point of view,"[23] and you let the speaker know that you understand the message. In this stage, the specific situation and nonverbal aspects of communication come into play. An effective listener knows that facial expressions,

interpreting
The process of understanding the meaning of the message from the speaker's point of view and letting the speaker know that you understand.

The main difference between hearing and listening is understanding. Once we have heard, selected, and attended to sounds, we must assign meaning to them for listening to be complete. We can enhance our listening by being open and receptive to what the speaker has to say.

posture, eye contact (or the lack of it), silence, and even paralanguage (the way thing sound) affect messages. Good listeners will work to develop greater sensitivity to these dimensions of communication.

Evaluating

evaluating

The listener analyzes evidence, sorts fact from opinion, determines the intent of the speaker, judges the accuracy of the speaker's statements and conclusions, and judges the accuracy of his or her own decisions.

In **evaluating**, the listener analyzes evidence, sorts fact from opinion, determines th intent of the speaker, judges the accuracy of the speaker's statements and conclu sions, and judges the accuracy of personal conclusions. Once we begin to assess th message we received and understood, we might no longer hear and attend to othe incoming messages. Later in the chapter, we further discuss analyzing and evaluating messages.

Responding and Sending Feedback

Responding

Overt verbal and nonverbal behavior by the listener, indicating to the speaker what has and has not been received.

A receiver who has listened to a message can connect with the sender by verbally or nonverbally verifying the message's reception or indicating a lack of recep tion. This verification is referred to as responding or feedback. **Responding** is the listener's overt behavior that indicates to the speaker what has and has not beer received. Examples of such behaviors are total silence (didn't hear the message ignored the message, or was angry about what the message said), smiling or frown ing (agreeing or disagreeing with the message), and asking for clarification of wha was received.

Feedback is an important part of being an effective listener. Feedback was definec in Chapter 1 as the response to a message sent by a receiver back to a source. Feedback helps to ensure understanding and helps speakers determine communication success Feedback should be appropriate to the situation, deliberate, thoughtful, and clear When it is important that you grasp every detail of a message, you should paraphrase or repeat the information for the sender to verify your reception, understanding, anc recall of it. This also indicates to the sender that you are actively listening and are committed to receiving the intended message.

Making Connections for Success

Listening and Thinking

Andrew Wolvin, listening scholar, says listening is probably one of the most complex of all human behaviors.[24] So far in this chapter, we have talked about how much listening skills are valued and used and what's involved in the listening process, as well as references to thinking. This chapter is titled "Connecting Listening and Thinking in the Communication Process." It's time to think about those connections. Margarete Imhof, a German listening scholar, found students were able to improve their listening comprehension in difficult classes when they used active thinking prior to listening and as they listened to difficult or new material. Students were asked to use precognitive strategies, that is, create questions to help them determine meaning in the hardest lecture course they had, prior to attending class. Imhof suggests that students ask questions of themselves prior to the communication event, and then,

during the communication, work to find areas of interest and possible application. Try the following:

1. Pick a talk show or news broadcast on a television channel you don't normally watch.
2. Watch the show for 30 minutes without interruptions from other sources (shut off your cell phone, put the computer to sleep, and stay in a room without other people).
3. Create a list of questions you want to have answered before you watch the program.
4. Tell yourself that you need to focus on the programming content.
5. At the end of the 30 minute period, check to see if your questions were answered.
6. Did a focus on the relevance of the material make a difference?
7. Could you see how the person(s) had reasonable views, even if you did not share the views?

Students provide their instructors with feedback, both consciously and unconsciously. Some students, however, might not always be completely honest in their responses. They might be totally confused but still indicate through verbal and nonverbal cues that they are listening to, understanding, and agreeing with everything being said—even if the communication has made little sense to them. This behavior, unfortunately, can lead to more unclear messages and further confusion. When those who are confused admit their bewilderment, instructors are more likely to improve their presentations. Active listeners always try to get the most from the message and make sure they received it accurately and completely. And, since there's a strong connection between listening and thinking, we need to think about how to use "working memory" to better facilitate effectiveness.

If you want to keep information in your working memory for future use, you have to find strategies to process and put it into long-term memory. Listening scholar Judi Brownell suggests five techniques for storing items in memory so they can be used later.

- The first strategy is *association*. You probably already use this in some ways to connect something new to something you already know. Situations often provide the stimulus for associations. If you remember that Tom is a tattoo artist whom you met in Toronto and use his name, these cues can help you remember Tom, where he is, and what he does.

- *Categorization* is a second strategy. When you organize information into categories, you can often remember better and longer. Plan your grocery shopping according to the aisles where the products are located. Remembering the categories helps you study for exams and determine what divisions to include in reports and what tasks you need to accomplish. Categorization can increase your work efficiency because the logical order facilitates retrievable memory from storage.

- Meaningful information is much easier to retrieve. Unrelated pieces of data are harder to remember. *Mediation* works in the following ways. (1) Form a meaningful word out of foreign words or meaningless syllables. This author went to Denmark to find relatives. The street name, we were told, meant "church on the hill" in Danish, so we looked for a church on a hill before we looked for Danish street signs and found the right place. (2) Words can be made out of the initial letters of the items presented. For example, *ALS* or *Lou Gehrig's disease* is much easier to remember than *amyotrophic lateral sclerosis*. Create "words" to enhance your ability to recall information. (3) Another mediation technique is to create a word that links two or more words and ideas. If you need to remember *cat, ball,* and *pillow,* you might link them with the word *soft*. This can help you connect the seemingly unrelated items.

- Most information is processed into your memory through two sensory channels: the visual or the auditory. To tap into this, you can use *imagery*, by creating visual or mental images from the information presented. If you want to remember something, you create vivid mental images of that information in order to later recall and apply it.

- *Mnemonics* is the fifth technique. You create ways to make sense of the information presented and use visual imagery to make the impression vivid. When you combine meaningful words and vivid images, you can recall information more quickly and accurately.

Memory is only one aspect of the thinking process. The more we are able to remember, the more effectively we can analyze, evaluate, and apply concepts to the information we gain. We can use memory and thinking to be better listeners and consumers of information.

Guidelines

Working Memory

Many listening scholars suggest approaches to enhance your working memory. The following strategies from Judi Brownell will help you retain information long enough to use it.

1. **Repetition.** With this strategy, you repeat things to keep them in mind. When you have to go to the bookstore to get school supplies without a written list, you might constantly repeat your needs as you walk over: "Stapler, staples, index cards, special pen for art class, laptop case, book for listening class." Any kind of interference, however, can make you forget some or most of your list.

2. **Chunking.** When you have many things to remember, you might group them into categories so you have fewer details to remember. Have you ever thought about why telephone numbers are created as they are? Researchers suggest we can remember up to seven individual pieces of information. If you use chunking, keep your groupings in seven or fewer categories to retain information long enough to use it immediately or help move it to long-term memory.

3. **Identification of logical patterns.** If you can identify patterns or themes in the information you hear, it is usually easier to remember, at least for a short time. Numbers in a sequence, acronyms, or mnemonics ("gee, I'm a tree" to remember how to spell geometry or "every good boy does fine" and "face" to remember the notes on the treble clef musical scale), are logical patterns that some of your earlier teachers may have used to help you remember their subjects.

Adapted from Judi Brownell, *Listening: Attitudes, Principles, and Skills,* 4e. Published by Allyn and Bacon, Boston, MA, pp. 151–52. Copyright © 2010 by Pearson Education. Reprinted by permission of the publisher.

The Functions of Listening

6.3 **Differentiate** among three functions of listening behavior.

You wake in the morning to the sound of an alarm clock, the noise your roommate makes moving around in the next room, or the ring of a telephone. While you dress, students talk outside your door, and a fire engine wails in the street. You turn on your radio. At breakfast, you join in a heated discussion about the proposed destruction of a historic building on your campus. Then you rush off to the last lecture before an upcoming exam. In the evening, you go to a concert. After the concert, you meet a good friend who is upset because he received a low grade on a test.

Throughout the day, you listened to many different people and things for a variety of purposes. You listened to the alarm clock to get up at the right time; you listened to your friends' opinions on the proposed removal of the oldest building on campus; you listened to your professor to acquire information about a subject; you listened to the concert for enjoyment; you listened to your troubled friend to understand his feelings. In each case, listening served a different function and involved different skills. Let's look at each of these functions in greater detail and the listening skills that each requires.

Listening to Obtain Information

listening for information

Listening to gain comprehension.

You probably spend great amounts of time **listening for information**, that is, listening to gain comprehension. You listen as your teacher discusses process, perception, nonverbal and verbal communication, famous speakers, and similar topics to learn about speech skills. Each day, you listen for information such as news, weather forecasts, sports scores, directions, orders, assignments, names, numbers, and locations.

Listening to Evaluate

evaluative listening

Listening to judge or analyze information.

Evaluative listening is listening to judge or to analyze information. A car owner who hears a squeak coming from the front end rolls down the window and does some evaluative listening. The owner tries to pinpoint the exact location and cause of the othersome noise. A teacher listens to students' speeches to discrimi-nate between presentations and to assign grades. In most situations we should all listen critically: constantly judge evidence, arguments, facts, and values. We need to ask questions to be effective listeners. We are bombarded by messages asking us to believe, accept, or buy things. While we sometimes want to hear sounds in the background, when we do listen, we should evaluate everything.

Listening with Empathy

Empathy is an important skill or characteristic in all relationships and is especially important when listening because it allows you to connect with others and become both a better listener and a better friend. We define **empathy** as follows: the intellectual identification with or vicarious experiencing of the feelings, thoughts, or attitudes of another—in other words, when we have the capacity to recognize and, to some extent, share feelings (e.g., happiness or sadness) that are experienced by another.[25] **Empathic listening** occurs when you listen to what someone else is experiencing and seek to understand that person's thoughts and feelings. It is not sympathy, which means that you feel sorry for the other person. Empathy means that you try to put yourself in another person's place to understand what is happening to that person. We might find it difficult to avoid making judgments when we listen to someone else's problems, but that is exactly what we must do to listen with empathy. Listening empathically can be a healing and soothing process. Empathic listening indicates that we are aware, appreciative, and understanding of another person's feelings. Empathic listeners create a supportive climate by expressing understanding of what the speaker says and means. They also reflect and clarify feelings by **perception checking** with the speaker and ask questions in order to be sure to correctly understand the points made. And, empathic listeners are always genuine—they suspend judgment and let speakers share as fully as they wish.[26] Caring about someone requires a great deal of sensitivity as well as the ability to communicate that sensitivity. It is not easy to listen; it is even more difficult to listen with empathy. If we fail to empathize with others, however, we also fail to understand them.

Empathic listening occurs when we listen to what someone else is experiencing and seek to understand that person's thoughts and feelings. When we empathize, we try to put ourselves in the other person's place to understand what is happening to him or her.

empathy
The intellectual identification with or vicarious experiencing of the feelings, thoughts, or attitudes of another.

empathic listening
Listening to understand what another person is thinking and feeling.

perception checking
Asking questions in order to see if your interpretation is correct.

Listening for Enjoyment

When we listen purely for pleasure, personal satisfaction, and appreciation, we **listen for enjoyment**. We usually listen to music, for example, simply because we enjoy it. The same is true for most of us when we combine listening and viewing as we watch television or a movie.

listen for enjoyment
Listening for pleasure, personal satisfaction, or appreciation.

Making Connections for Success

Listening Behaviors

A simple experiment illustrates what people tend to remember and for how long. For three minutes, read a newspaper or magazine article to a friend and then ask the friend to repeat the key information. Do the same with several other friends. Most people will be able to report only about 50 percent of what they've heard. Then wait 24 hours and ask each person to repeat the information again.

1. Discuss with your friends what you learned from the exercise.

2. Did some people do better than others? If so, why do you think they did?

3. Tell someone what you learned about listening from doing this exercise.

Listening for enjoyment involves more than merely sitting back and letting sounds enter our ears. It also engages the thinking process. We evaluate what we sense to understand something or to learn more about it. As we listen to music, we try to find some personal value or relevance in the lyrics and instrumentation. Even if we attend an opera for the first time and do not understand the language, we can enjoy the performance as we seek to understand it. In other words, listening for enjoyment consists of the same process as other kinds of listening: We select, attend, understand, evaluate, and remember. We construct meaning from what we hear and respond to it in some way.

Barriers to Effective Listening

6.4 **Select** specific attitudes and behaviors to help you overcome your barriers to listening.

Why are most people poor listeners? The answer is surprisingly complex. The quality of our listening changes from time to time and from situation to situation. We've already mentioned the impact of technology on listening—sensory overload and distractions from all forms of technology and media compete with messages from others and make it difficult to listen. A number of other barriers contribute to our ineffectiveness as listeners. The context of each communication will affect how important each barrier actually is, and some of the barriers that reduce our listening effectiveness are under our control, whereas others are not. Ralph Nichols, the "father of listening research," identified barriers to effective listening.[27] Nichols and other researchers have replicated his research in subsequent studies and found similar results. Although these barriers may not be the only ones, they are the most common. And remember, listening, like communication, is a learned behavior, so we *can learn* to overcome the obstacles that interfere with our listening effectiveness.

Consider the Topic or Speaker Uninteresting

The level of interest and the amount of importance we place on a subject or a speaker usually govern how much effort we put into listening. Deciding that a subject or person is uninteresting or boring often leads us to conclude that the information being presented is not important. However, this is not necessarily true. What appears to be dull or insignificant might very well be vital for passing an exam, doing an assignment correctly, learning something, following your supervisor's instructions, making a sale, or learning a new way of doing something on the job. In other words, a competent listener keeps an open mind.

Criticize the Speaker Instead of the Message

How many times have you judged a speech by the number of "ahs" and "ums" the speaker used? How many times has a speaker's volume, mispronunciations, or accent influenced your opinion? Have you ever missed a message because you were focusing on a mismatched shirt and tie, bizarre earrings, or the speaker's facial expressions or nervous behaviors?

Of course, when possible, speakers should do everything in their power to eliminate personal quirks that may distract attention from their message, but listeners must also share responsibility for receiving the message. An effective listener must be able to overlook the superficial elements of a person's delivery style or appearance to concentrate on the substance of the presentation. In short, the listener must stay involved in the message, and not be distracted by the speaker or the speaker's attire or behaviors.

Concentrate on Details, Not Main Ideas

Many of us listen for specific facts, such as dates, names, definitions, figures, and locations, assuming they are the important things to know. But are they? Specific facts are needed in some situations, but we often focus too much on details. As a result, we walk away with disjointed details and no idea how they relate to each other and to the total picture.

Competent listeners focus on the main or most important ideas, not on every single word. All stages of the listening process are affected adversely when we forget that general ideas can be more significant than the details that surround them. For example, note when your communication professor says, "Be sure to write this in your notes," what follows is more important than when the information is only briefly mentioned. Or, if your supervisor asks you to be sure to notify her when a specific person calls for an appointment, be sure to keep that name in mind, with perhaps a note on your desk as a reminder.

Avoiding Difficult Listening Situations

Most of us find it difficult to keep up with the vast amount and increasing technical complexity of the information that confronts us each day. Text messages, chatting online, or checking Facebook, Twitter, or your email are activities that compete for your time. Add media messages about global warming, human atrocities around the world, failed financial institutions, the unemployment rate, and a global economy rocked by a series of factors, and you become distracted, trying to make sense of the impact and significance of these issues while attending to the business of life. There are times, we might deal with complex listening situations by giving up and ignoring what is presented.

Concentration and energy are needed to overcome the temptation to ignore or avoid what might seem difficult and confusing. When you are faced with a difficult listening situation, the best approach is usually to ask questions. For example, physicians often use complex medical terminology when talking to patients, but patients can take the responsibility for gaining understanding. They can ask the physician to explain terms, to review procedures, and to supply missing information. The same principles apply to the classroom or to the workplace. You should never hesitate to ask about something when you don't understand it, because without understanding, you cannot learn.

Sometimes, you might not listen to new and difficult information because you lack motivation, but once again, the responsibility falls on you to make the effort to listen. Try consciously and continually to listen to such communication. Each time you are successful at staying tuned in, you will acquire not only some information but also improved confidence and ability.

Tolerate or Fail to Adjust to Distractions

Distractions constantly disrupt our concentration. As listeners, we have the responsibility to adjust to, compensate for, or eliminate distractions and to focus on speakers and their messages despite the competing factors from technology and the media.

We can control some distractions. If noise from another room competes with a speaker, for example, the listener can close the door, ask the person who is creating the noise to be quiet, move closer to the speaker, or ask the speaker to talk louder.

Some distractions must be overcome through mental rather than physical effort. A noise in the background can become a major distraction, or we can reduce it to a minor nuisance by forcing ourselves to listen more intently to the speaker. When distractions occur, we must consciously focus on selecting the appropriate messages and attending to them. We must filter out extraneous noise and distractions, such as people walking by, a cell phone's vibration, or the sound of a lawn mower outside and concentrate on the sounds important to us. We need to forget about tomorrow's work and concentrate on what's going on at the moment. If we cannot modify internal and external noise, we must alter our internal listening behavior to understand the speaker's message.

Technology often creates distractions just because it's so readily available. It's easy to check our phones when the professor or supervisor seems to be droning on about something that doesn't seem valuable (and certainly is not interesting). We need to remember that multitasking is impossible. When you're in class or in a meeting, resist the urge to text your friends or play games on your phones. Remember why you're there and don't let technology create even more sensory overload.

Fake Attention

At one time or another, everyone pretends to pay attention to something or someone. You appear to listen intently, but your mind is elsewhere. You might even smile in agreement when all you are really doing is maintaining eye contact. In class, you might pretend to take notes, although your mind might not follow what is said.

Pretending to pay attention can become a habit. Without even realizing what you are doing, you might automatically tune out a speaker and let your mind wander. If after a speech, you cannot recall the main purpose or essential points presented by the speaker, you were probably faking attention. Although it might seem harmless, such deceptive behavior can lead to misunderstandings and cause people to question your credibility and sincerity.

Table 6.1 summarizes the differences between ineffective and effective listening habits.

Competent listeners need to ask themselves, "Am I *really* paying attention?" When listeners realize they are distracted, they should make an effort to pay attention. Good listeners recognize when they are not listening well and do whatever it takes to return their attention to the speaker. While you may think, "What's in it for me?" when someone shares something that seems irrelevant to you, if you make use of your critical thinking and critical listening skills, you'll try to determine how it may be helpful at some point, even if it's not right now. Competent listeners demonstrate attitudes, behaviors, and thinking that allow them to focus on others. They know that listening is an active process and requires energy and effort.

Bias and Prejudice

Self-perceptions, prejudices, and personal biases can include anything that is *a barrier or that gets in the way of understanding a speaker's message*. Some typical examples include egocentrism, personal interests, biases/dogmatism, defensiveness and apprehension, or a know-it-all attitude.[28] Biases and prejudices often create barriers. We have

Table 6.1 Ineffective and Effective Listening Habits

Bad Listener	Good Listener
Thinks the topic or speaker is of no interest	Finds areas of interest—keeps an open mind
Focuses on the speaker's appearance and delivery	Concentrates on the content of the presentation and overlooks speaker characteristics—stays involved
Listens only for details	Listens for ideas
Avoids difficult material	Exercises the mind—prepares to listen
Is easily distracted	Resists distractions
Fakes attention	Pays attention

trouble listening to others when we are biased against the message or the speaker. If the speaker's views are different from our own, it is easy to tune out and think about other things; we may even decide not to listen at all. Although it takes extra effort to listen when our minds are closed, it is ultimately worthwhile to learn the views of others. If we give in to our biases, we limit ourselves in what we know and can do.

Preferred Thinking

Our preferred thinking can create barriers in the listening process from the perspective of giving or receiving information. As each quadrant has its own language, an individual whose primary thinking is in one quadrant can grossly misinterpret an individual whose primary thinking is in the opposite quadrant. The result can be exacerbated if the listener has a very low preference in the quadrant from which the speaker is delivering the information. For example, think of an organizational (B quadrant) thinker, a safe-keeper of information, telling a coworker how a process works. The creative (D quadrant) coworker is listening to a "this is the way we do it because this is the way we have always done it" message, while simultaneously thinking and listening in "if we do it this way we can do it in a fraction of the time with better quality" language.[29]

Critical Listening and Critical Thinking: Analyzing and Evaluating Messages

6.5   Identify instances when you must be a critical listener/thinker.

As listeners, our goal is more than simply understanding a message; we also try to become critical listeners. **Critical listening** involves analyzing and assessing the accuracy of the information presented, determining the reasonableness of its conclusions, and evaluating its presenter. In other words, we must ask ourselves questions about the message: Is the message true? Is it based on solid evidence? Is it complete? Is it logical? What motivates the speaker to present the message?

We are constantly confronted with choices and decisions. For example, we are exposed to numerous commercial messages each day in addition to the interpersonal messages we receive at school, at home, at work, and in recreational situations. We also live in an increasingly technological world. Web searches to find information for our college papers and presentations, to enhance a presentation at work, or even to learn more about a city, country, or company provide an infinite number of resources very quickly. (We discuss web searches for speeches in greater detail in Chapter 8.) Because we are limited in the amount of experience we can acquire on our own, we must depend on others to provide information and advice. Thus we must evaluate and assess that information to judge its value and utility. We do this through critical thinking. Critical thinking is integrally linked to critical listening, because they are both part of the process of gaining an understanding of our world. Critical thinking has many definitions. One definition of **critical thinking** suggests that critical thinkers ask and answer the right questions to determine the appropriate responses to problems and issues.[30] In an earlier work, critical thinking scholar Robert Ennis defined it as the ability to analyze and assess information.[31] From these two definitions alone, you should be able to make the connection between listening and thinking. You must listen carefully and construct meaning from ideas, messages, and so forth if you are to make sense of the world around you. Critical thinking has become so important to academic institutions and to employers that more and more colleges and universities include courses or units in critical thinking in their curricula; some even provide a web page devoted to the characteristics of the critical thinker. Bellevue Community

critical listening

Listening that judges the accuracy of the information presented, determines the reasonableness of its conclusions, and evaluates its presenter.

critical thinking

The ability to analyze and assess information.

College's web page identifies nine characteristics of a critical thinker and two implica-tions and six aspects of critical thinking.[32] Basically, you need to remember that the link between critical thinking and critical listening is that critical thinkers have specific attitudes and mental habits. They are intellectually curious, flexible, objective, persis-tent, systematic, honest, and decisive. They use their critical listening abilities to assess information and choose the best options from among those available. Critical thinkers are aware of the ways they learn best and capitalize on opportunities to expand their learning abilities. One goal of a liberal arts education is to encourage students to think critically, to develop "habits of mind" to enable them to become effective thinkers, listeners, and communicators.

Critical thinking and critical listening are closely linked. The critical thinker knows how to analyze and assess information. The critical listener knows how to make connections between messages and issues. The critical listener also uses the ability to analyze and evaluate messages to determine whether ideas are logically pre-sented and whether the speaker is well informed and exhibits clear thinking. Critical thinking and critical listening are closely related parts of a complex process. Listening with a critical ear involves two phases: (1) assessing the speaker's values and intent and (2) judging the accuracy of the speaker's conclusions.[33]

Assess the Speaker's Motivation

Assessing a speaker's motivation generally involves three stages of information pro-cessing: (1) make a judgment about the speaker's beliefs, (2) compare our standards with those of the speaker, and (3) evaluate the worth of the message being presented.

Values are strongly held beliefs central to the communication process and to each individual's perceptual system. They affect perception and interpretation of both the messages we send and the messages we receive. The first consideration in listening, therefore, is to determine the speaker's values by examining the message: We criti-cally think about what the speaker is saying and how it compares to our own value system. Of course, we should not automatically dismiss a message merely because the speaker's values conflict with our own. However, anytime we are confronted with a message that differs from our own views—one that asks us to do something, buy something, or behave in a certain way—we should be aware of the purpose behind it.

The second consideration is to determine whether the message urges us to con-form to or go against our principles or standards. Finally, we consider how to evaluate and respond to the messages. Critical thinking skills help us recognize and under-stand the motivation behind the messages we receive.

Making Connections for Success

Listening Self-Assessment

Now that you've read and thought about listening in general, take a few minutes of reflection time to determine how well you listen in a variety of situations. Answer the following questions and follow up with a specific plan to capitalize on what you already do well and correct those areas where you are not as efficient as a listener.

1. When do you listen well?
2. What specific speaker or situation characteristics are operating when you listen well?
3. What makes you listen poorly?
4. What specific speaker or situation characteristics are operating when you do not listen well?
5. In what behaviors do you engage to help you stay focused on the speaker/speech?
6. How do you motivate yourself to listen at work or in the classroom when you know you'll need the information later?
7. What will you do to improve your listening attitudes and behaviors?

Guidelines

Competent Listeners

1. **Be prepared to listen.** Learn to control internal and external distractions.

2. **Behave like a good listener.** Stop talking and let others have their say. Do not interrupt. Concentrate on what is being said, not on who is saying it or what the speaker is doing. Good listeners maintain eye contact with speakers, ask questions at appropriate times, and maintain flexibility as they carefully listen to the speaker's views.

3. **Take good notes.** Listen for main ideas and write down the most significant points; don't attempt to write down every word. Good note taking helps listeners remember better and longer, and provides a written indication of ideas to remember. Brevity is usually best so you can carefully listen to the speaker and analyze the speaker's intent. Write legibly and review your notes as soon after the event as possible to help you recall them later. Finally, reorganize your notes, if necessary, for clarity, before filing them for future reference. Do not get so involved in note taking that effective listening is lost. Note taking is an aid to listening, not a replacement for it. In effective listening, all six stages of the process are brought into play. Never concentrate so hard on writing everything down that you fail to think about what is said.

4. **Ask questions to clarify information.** Make sure you know what your supervisor or teacher requires.

Judge the Accuracy of the Speaker's Conclusions

To make accurate judgments and to think critically about important messages, ask the following questions:

- Is the speaker qualified to draw the conclusion?
- Has the speaker actually observed the concept or issue about which he or she is talking?
- Does the speaker have a vested interest in the message?
- Does the speaker present adequate evidence to support the conclusion?
- Is the evidence relevant to the conclusion?
- Is there contrary evidence that refutes the information presented?
- Does the message contain invalid or inadequate reasoning?

Improve Listening Competence

6.6 **Characterize the speech and actions of** a competent listener.

With appropriate knowledge and practice, we can become better listeners. First, we must recognize the importance of effective listening. Second, we must think of listening as an *active* behavior that requires conscious participation. Third, we must recognize that a willingness to work and a desire to improve are essential to increased listening effectiveness.

In some situations, we need not listen with full attention. For example, if we listen to a CD while conversing with a friend, we're not likely to create problems by attending closely to the friend and partially to the music. However, each listener must be able to identify when total energy and involvement in the listening process are crucial. Effective listening often requires both energy and concentration; listeners need to constantly remind themselves that listening is vital to communication. People call on different listening skills, depending on whether their goal is to comprehend information, critique and evaluate messages, show empathy for others, or appreciate a performance. According to the National Communication Association, competent listeners demonstrate (1) knowledge and understanding of the listening process, (2) the ability to use appropriate and effective listening skills for a given communication situation

Making Connections for Success

Listening and the Job Interview

Most of us spend a great deal of time on the Internet. Can we listen on the Internet? If we can, how do we do it? In today's job market, many early aspects of matching applicants and jobs are completed via some technological venue. Programs such as Skype or GoToMeeting allow employers and potential employees to see and hear each other during the interview. Email allows both to ask and answer questions prior to or after the online interview so that everyone can see if the candidate will fit the position. Listening becomes even more critical because the technology can distract. Callie Angove, a graduate student at the University of Northern Iowa, conducted a study to determine if Skype interviews created positive or negative impressions of job candidates.

The results show there were more negative impressions of a candidate interviewed via Skype than in face-to-face settings.[34] Think about these questions and share your answers with a classmate.

1. How do you adapt to online interviews where you can see and hear each other versus the old way of listening to and observing responses in person?

2. How do you think an employer adapts to Skype or GoToMeeting interview information, versus the traditional face-to-face interview?

3. Can you listen to what is not being said when you communicate online?

4. Does the Internet keep us from stereotyping people, or does it make us more likely to stereotype? Why do you think as you do?

and setting, and (3) the ability to identify and manage barriers to listening (all are covered in this chapter).

Competent listeners work at listening. They are prepared to listen and know what they wish to gain from their listening experiences. Competent listeners also engage in appropriate listening behaviors. They realize that being a good listener is an active and complex process. They know that they must pay attention. They do not interrupt others, they look at the speaker, they listen to ideas, and they concentrate on what is being said.

Listening and Technology

6.7 **Use** technology to take better notes and organize your work.

Just as some people fear computers and technology will destroy families and relationships, some believe smartphones, computers, email, social networking, and the Internet will harm listening in all areas of our lives. What we and other communication scholars have found in our communication classrooms, however, is that technology can be used to students' advantage if it is used as a tool. Taking notes helps us become better listeners, and appropriate technology as a delivery tool can also serve that function. Recent studies reported at professional conventions indicate that an increasing use of computer-enhanced presentations (such as PowerPoint and Prezi) and an expanding ability to take better notes help students perform better on exams when technology and note-taking instruction are provided early and reinforced throughout the semester.[35] Some suggest the act of actual writing helps listeners remember better simply because the writing process is slower and you accelerate learning as you signal the brain "this information is important."[36] Some businesses and organizations require PowerPoint or Prezi, while others believe a return to fewer visuals will better hold the listeners' attention. Others fear that computer-enhanced presentations result in audience members who sleep or become noninvolved nonlisteners.[37]

Avoid Overdependence on Media

Listeners must remember to think independently. The words on the screen cannot eliminate individual choices. It is too easy to let screen images take priority. But, as we

Making Connections for Success

Impact of Technology on Listening

Think about the things that distract you. Do you text your friends while at work or in class? Do you check email on your iPhone while you're in class? Do you check Facebook as you talk to a friend on the phone? How does this affect your listening? Has it ever negatively affected you? What other distractions are created by technology? Can you really listen well to the professor, the friend, or your boss when you're texting or checking Facebook and email? How can you rid yourself of these distracting behaviors when listening would be more advantageous?

---

have pointed out in this chapter, listeners must listen with their minds, their bodies, their hearts, *and* all their senses with undivided attention. In the classroom, students must listen with care to determine where the instructor's and speakers' emphases are and take notes accordingly. Effective listeners devote extra effort to understanding and interpreting content with and without media. In the section above discussion of critical listening and critical thinking, there are specific guidelines to help you be an effective consumer of information. Because mediated communication is so prevalent, particular attention to the guidelines might improve your listening competence.

Digital Literacy

Digital literacy is the set of attitudes, understanding, and skills needed to handle and communicate information and knowledge effectively, in a variety of media and formats.[38] Building communication skills should be emphasized so we can share and develop ideas online.[39] When we use social media as a platform for critical reflection to share our ideas, we should remember to use them judiciously. There are times and places for social media, and a discerning speaker and listener will know when and when not to use them. Historic events around the world have spotlighted the role of social media in our lives. Citizen uprisings against dictators in Africa and the Middle East were attributed to Facebook messages from people angry about oppression. Warlord Joseph Kony and his rebel army kidnapped dozens of young children in east and central Africa. The Kony 2012 Facebook video attracted more than 50 million views in its first week on the web and the 2015 version still attracts viewers and volunteers. "Occupy Wall Street" on Facebook made many other groups take up a cause in a public way after it had gone viral. While these events have instantaneously spread around the world via social media, we need to use critical listening and thinking skills to determine what is missing. Asian listeners are taught to "listen between the lines," and social media users should also learn to do so. It's easy to take things we see and hear as valid when they spread so quickly on Facebook or some other form of social media, when, in fact, even more distortions can occur with social media messages because the creator doesn't always stand in front of us to present messages. As a cautionary measure, think deeply about the message and do what you can to ascertain the truth and relevance of the message as well as be sensitive to what else may be going on. "We must operate the Web as dynamic thinkers no longer content to have information and entertainment merely presented to us.... The Web is about interactivity, the ability of the user to choose information pathways and explore them with newfound ease."[40] The bottom line is: Use critical listening and critical thinking skills; do not rely too heavily on social media or any other mediated form of communication, at least until you've analyzed and verified the source and information given. Finally, don't let mediated communication keep you from being a good listener.

Digital literacy

The set of attitudes, understanding, and skills needed to handle and communicate information and knowledge effectively, in a variety of media and formats.

Technology can both enhance and detract from effective listening; it sometimes creates sensory overload and multiple distractions. We need to focus on the ways technology can help us be effective listeners.

Intercultural Listening

6.8 **Identify** the similarities and differences in listening behavior in different cultures.

Research in intercultural listening is relatively new, thus information is always being added to our knowledge base. Chen and Starosta (2005) provide a working definition of listening between cultures as a "reciprocal attending to verbal and nonverbal messages of someone of different history, linguisticality, and socialization in an attempt to create a ground of mutual understanding.[41] We know that people in all cultures are required to listen. We also know that some cultures value listening much more than we do in the United States. Interviews with international students suggest that people in Asia, Mexico, and South America especially value listening. In contrast, Northern European students report that listening is "just something we do" and "something that is expected of us. We aren't really taught to listen." Interviews with teachers in Europe indicate that they would like to know how to get their students to be better listeners.[42]

When asked how listening is taught in Eastern cultures, interviewees state that children are taught to listen to others in a respectful way. Much of the teaching in schools is done through examples and specific statements of expectations to be courteous and to attend to what others are saying. Students in Asia and in Mexico are taught to listen first and ask questions later. Students in Malaysia and Indonesia, on the other hand, are still taught to be respectful, but they are also encouraged to ask questions during or soon after the communication event. The Chinese symbol for the phrase *to listen* is made up of symbols for eyes, ears, heart, and undivided attention, and corresponds with the Chinese view that people must listen with their entire beings: their eyes, their ears, their senses, and, most especially, their hearts. And they must focus and attend to speakers and messages with undivided attention.[43] (see Figure 6.4). People in many of the world's cultures believe that listening is essential: when one listens, nothing else should occur, because listening should take one's entire attention

---

Figure 6.4 Listening with Undivided Attention

The elements of this Chinese character for the phrase "to listen" incorporate a person's entire being: the eyes (the left character), the ears (the upper-right character), and most especially the heart (the lower-right character); and, the line separating the ears and heart represents undivided attention.

and energy.[44] Cocultures within the United States also believe listening encompasses the whole being. Native Americans believe a good listener will reflect on what is said before responding. A quick response is a faux pas and should be avoided. A thoughtful response demonstrates the listener's thoughts about the previous speaker's message.

Although we don't know all similarities and differences in listening in every culture of the world, we do know that communicators need to be aware of and sensitive to both. In the United States, we think nothing of interrupting a speaker in conversation. According to interview responses, in places such as China, Colombia, Costa Rica, Hong Kong, Japan, Korea, Mexico, Peru, and Venezuela, if you interrupt, you will be branded a discourteous person, and the local residents will avoid you. The best advice for communicating with people from other cultures is to (1) respectfully ask questions and (2) be aware of cultural differences.[45] The guidelines for competent listeners apply equally to intercultural listening and domestic listening experiences. Listening requires energy and commitment in every communication situation.

Summary

The Importance of Effective Listening

Objective 6.1 **Describe how listening helps you make connections with others in all aspects of your life.**
Listening is relational; that is, it depends on two or more people interacting with each other and simultaneously being a sender and receiver. Effective listening is required in all aspects of our lives.

Effective Listening

Objective 6.2 **Explain the complex nature of listening as a cognitive process.**
The listening process is composed of five interrelated aspects, plus remembering, attention and focus, and thinking preferences; there is a listening-thinking connection that incorporates thinking and information processing.

- Accurate reception of sounds requires the listener to focus attention on the speaker, discriminate among sounds, and concentrate.
- We know that past experience plays an important role and that you relate and compare new sounds and ideas to those you have previously heard.
- If the topic seems more relevant, people will remember slightly more than if it seems irrelevant.
- Memory or "remembering" is a more critical component of the listening process than previous research suggests.
- In the interpreting stage, the listener simply tries to make sense of the information received.
- In the evaluating stage, the listener analyzes evidence, sorts fact from opinion, determines the intent of the speaker, judges the accuracy of the speaker's statements and conclusions, and judges the accuracy of personal conclusions.

- Responding is the listener's overt behavior that indicates to the speaker what has and has not been received.

The Functions of Listening

Objective 6.3 **Differentiate among three functions of listening behavior.**
We listen to obtain information, to evaluate, to be entertained, and to be empathic with others.

Barriers to Effective Listening

Objective 6.4 **Select specific attitudes and behaviors to help you overcome your barriers to listening.**
We can use cognitive, affective, and behavioral strategies to help us be better listeners. We need to learn ways to overcome both internal and external interference to listening.

- The listener must stay involved in the message and not be distracted by the speaker or the speaker's attire or behaviors.
- Competent listeners focus on the main or most important ideas, not on every single word.
- We need concentration and energy to overcome the temptation to ignore or avoid what seems difficult and confusing.
- As listeners, we have the responsibility to adjust to, compensate for, or eliminate distractions and to focus on speakers and their messages, despite the competing factors from technology and the media.
- Competent listeners need to ask themselves, "Am I *really* paying attention?"
- If we give in to our biases, we limit ourselves in what we know and can do.

- Our preferred thinking can create barriers in the listening process from the perspective of giving or receiving information.

Critical Listening and Critical Thinking: Analyzing and Evaluating Messages

Objective 6.5 **Identify** instances in which you must be a critical listener/thinker.
We should always listen and think about what we hear.

- We need to be good consumers of information.
- We need to differentiate between fact and opinion.

Improve Listening Competence

Objective 6.6 **Characterize the speech and actions of a competent listener.**
All of us can become better listeners. We must recognize the importance of listening effectively, think of listening as an active behavior, and be willing to work and want to improve.

Listening and Technology

Objective 6.7 **Use technology to take better notes and organize your work.**
Technology as a tool can be used to students' advantage.

- Listeners must remember to think independently. The words on the screen cannot eliminate individual choices.
- The emphasis should be on building communication skills so we can share and develop ideas online.

Intercultural Listening

Objective 6.8 **Identify the similarities and differences in listening behavior in different cultures.**
The best advice for communicating with people from other cultures is to (1) respectfully ask questions and (2) be aware of cultural differences.

Discussion Starters

1. Why do we take listening for granted?
2. How important is effective listening?
3. What are the characteristics of effective listening?
4. How would you describe the listening-thinking connection?
5. Explain the role of memory in the listening process.
6. Why is listening identified as a continuous cognitive activity?
7. What can you do to improve your memory?
8. Why is it important to understand the different functions of listening?
9. Explain what it means to listen with empathy.
10. What effects has technology had on listening, both good and bad?
11. In what ways can you use technology to help you listen more effectively?
12. Provide three guidelines to help you listen to people from other cultures.

Chapter 7
Selecting a Topic and Connecting to the Audience

 ## Learning Objectives

CHAPTER OUTLINE

This chapter will help you:

7.1 Apply the requirements to choose topics for your speeches and presentations.

Select a Speech Topic

7.2 Create general and specific purpose statements.

Determine the General Purpose, Specific Purpose, and Thesis of a Speech

7.3 Evaluate the suitability and relevance of the topics to make better connections with the audience.

Audience Analysis: Connecting with the Listeners

Making Everyday Connections

The one skill most sought after by employers, according to the Upper Rio Grande Workforce, and others, is "the ability to listen, write, and speak effectively." Successful communication is critical in all work areas.[1] A late 2014 survey discovered that "employers want new hires with technical knowledge related to the job," but indicated that's not nearly as important as good teamwork and decision-making and communication skills.[2]

Communication skills are as critical in the workplace as in the classroom. People make many presentations in their lives. Here are some examples some alums have shared:

- Lacey presented new job request formatting in her area for her coworkers in the John Deere plant.
- Kelly gave a presentation to the patients in the medical clinic where she works, on the new reporting procedures that affect them.
- Zach provided information about new stocking procedures with the new technology Kohl's implemented to save time and allow staff to spend more time with customers.
- Josh, a Boy Scout troop leader, shared information about the new standards for badges.

These students prepare for public communication events, even though each event is labeled as work. The ability to give effective presentations in classes, organizations, residence hall meetings, sports team meetings, government campaigns, political demonstrations, or other events on and off campus is critical. In such instances, the speaker is the central focus of a listener's attention. The ability to communicate is one of the most important skills a person can possess. Public speaking and listening are two vital forms of communication. Beginning public communicators frequently express two concerns: fear of nothing worthwhile to say and fear of speaking in front of others. Both of these concerns will be discussed in detail in this part of the text.

What you learn about and apply toward making effective presentations will help for the rest of your life. The speech-making process will help you develop researching, organizing, listening, and thinking skills for both oral and written communication. In addition, these skills will help you gain self-confidence.

Questions to Think About

1. When do *you* make formal presentations? Informal presentations?
2. What topics do you enjoy sharing?
3. When you have a choice about presentations or papers, where do you begin?
4. What do you know about your listeners in this class that will help you select a topic you like and that's relevant to them?
5. How do you feel about making presentations?
6. What concerns do you have about choosing a topic?

Students often complain that they have to "give speeches" in class when they "know" they will never give a one outside the classroom. Just because we've all been talking for a number of years doesn't mean we know how to effectively communicate. What some of these complaining students fail to consider is that public communication involves more than "giving speeches" and more than just talking. We frequently make all types of presentations. As you read in the Making Everyday Connections feature, employers seek hires who are effective communicators. This section of the text is designed to help you become a more effective and competent public communicator.

Topic selection is important in communication and English classes (and in situations at work or in the community, as well). Dr. Jesse Swan, a University of Northern Iowa professor of language and literature, talks with students about how to choose a topic for their class papers, he always "firmly tells them the topic comes from a very personal perspective."[3] In other words, whether you pick a topic for a speech or a paper in your classes, it must be something personal and yet important, as well as relevant to the assignment and the situation.

It is never too early to start thinking about the speech situation, the topic, and how it serves the needs of your listeners. Your task is to choose a topic of personal interest, one your listeners can connect with as well as one you'll enjoy learning more about and sharing.

Although we don't want people to make cookie-cutter speeches, established principles and guidelines of public communication help people prepare for the numerous times they *will* give speeches. Although you might never be a public speaker, you can expect to give speeches on the job, in social organizations, in your place of worship, in the courtroom, or in the classroom. At some time, almost all of us are called on to "give a presentation or a speech." We may even be called upon to create a webinar, give an online training session, or both present and evaluate online speeches.

Select a Speech Topic

7.1 **Apply** the requirements to choose a topic for your speeches and presentations.

Public speaking is the art of effective oral communication with an audience.[4] Topic selection is the first step in speech preparation. In these chapters on public communication, you will read about topics presented in a variety of classroom, business, and professional situations. The choice of topics is often prompted by the situation itself, the needs of others, and the position and qualifications of the speaker. Careful selection of a topic appropriate to the situation and suitable for you requires thought and a systematic approach.

public speaking

The art of effective oral communication with an audience.

Select an Appropriate Topic

Many factors contribute to an effective speech presentation, including research, organization, wording, and delivery, but none is more important than selecting an appropriate topic. The topic and your interest and motivation as you develop and move through the process to the presentation are vital to your success as a speaker. The best topic for you, your audience, and the assignment isn't always easy to determine.

Some beginning speakers are concerned they won't be able to think of a good topic. If you read Internet sources, newspapers, magazines, get news and weather updates on your phone, receive Google Alerts, or watch television, you are exposed to a variety of stimulating and interesting topics from a broad range of issues. When a topic isn't assigned by the instructor, the trick is to identify a topic that matches *your* interests and qualifications, the interests and existing knowledge of your audience, and the requirements of the speech assignment. If you are vitally concerned about the topic and enthusiastic to share it with others, your concerns can be drastically reduced.

Techniques for Finding a Topic

If you have difficulty thinking of interesting subjects, some of the following techniques might help you: self-inventory; brainstorming; reviewing current media; and

Making Connections for Success

Reflections on Memorable Presentations

Many of your classes require papers, and speeches or presentations. In most beginning communication classes, you are likely to make three or more formal presentations and several informal presentations. For each, you'll need to choose a topic, complete research, organize the information, and prepare, practice, and present speeches in front of your classmates and instructor. While this may seem frightening, it's a common experience for all of us, and this textbook and course are designed to help you through the process. Take a few minutes to reflect on public communication in your life. If the opportunity presents itself, share your reflections with others.

1. Identify memorable speeches or presentations you've heard.
2. Was it the *content* or the *presentation* that made the presentation memorable? Why?
3. What specific ideas do you remember?
4. What makes a topic enjoyable to you as a listener?
5. How do you respond when the speaker does something special to involve you?
6. Describe previous experiences that involved either a formal or an informal presentation. Explain how you chose your topic and then prepared for your presentation.

Many factors contribute to an effective speech presentation, including research, organization, wording, and delivery, but none is more important than selecting an appropriate topic. The topic and your interest and motivation in developing and presenting it are vital to your success as a speaker.

conducting an Internet search. All four techniques will generate a wide range of possible topics from which you can then select the most appropriate.

self-inventory

A list of subjects that you know about and find interesting.

SELF-INVENTORY   A **self-inventory** is a list of subjects you know about and find interesting. The list might include books and newspaper articles you've read; television shows you watch; hobbies you enjoy; sports you participate in; and community, state, regional, national, or international issues of concern. Here are some sample topics for how to prepare your own self-inventory:

Books, Articles, Music, Web Sources, Movies You Should See

> *Barnes and Noble's Top 100 Books of 2015*
> *Web games—are they addictive?*
> The Latest Health Issue

Technology/Media

> iTouch, Nook, Kindle, eReaders, the iPad—What's next?
> Social Issues and YouTube
> Social media: Facebook, LinkedIn, Twitter—Where do we go from here?

Campus/Community Issues

> Why tuition rates are rising
> Student organizations you should know
> Liberal Arts core classes prepare one for the workforce

Regional, National, International

> Global Poverty
> Financial crises and their effect on the world
> The power of nature

Hobbies/Personal

> Computer Games
> Fantasy Sports
> Is reading dead?

Sports/Recreation

> Newest Fitness Craze
> What is the most effective fitness strategy?
> Meditating to de-stress

Health Issues

> Medical issues affecting college students
> Does your pharmacist talk with you about prescriptions?
> Eating for Good Health

Another self-inventory technique involves listing broad categories and then narrowing them down to specific examples. Here are some possibilities:

ENVIRONMENTAL ISSUES

Climate change
Dwindling water supplies
Water consumption
Water economy and you
How you can economize on water use to save a precious resource

The category of Environmental Issues was narrowed to a specific area, how you can economize on water use to save a precious resource.

Making Connections for Success
Your Own Self-Inventory

We previously suggested a self-inventory as a place to start thinking about the kinds of topics you might choose for your speeches. Supply as many items as you can for each of the categories in this self-inventory. Then, examine each item to determine whether it could be an appropriate speech for you, the audience, and the situation.

Media Sources

_____

_____

Hobbies/Interests

_____

_____

Books/Music/Movies/Internet Sources

_____

_____

Events

_____

_____

Pet Peeves/Personal Causes

_____

_____

Sports/Recreation

_____

_____

People

_____

_____

Activities

_____

_____

Objects

_____

_____

Reflection

1. Which of the categories most interests you? Why?
2. Which specific topics would you avoid?
3. What other categories would you like to pursue?

Share in class what you learned about personal topics from this exercise.

brainstorming

A technique used to generate as many ideas as possible within a limited amount of time, which can be used to produce topics, information, or solutions to problems.

BRAINSTORMING   Another useful way to select a topic is through brainstorming. **Brainstorming** is a technique used to generate as many ideas as possible within a limited amount of time. Set aside a short period of time (5 minutes) for intensive concentration and list all the ideas that come to mind as topics. To keep things simple, write key words or phrases only. Don't stop to think about whether the ideas are good or bad. The goal of brainstorming is to generate many ideas, so every word or phrase is appropriate.

After listing as many ideas as you can, select those that appeal to you. Then have another brainstorming session to list more ideas related to them. For example, the term *education* could serve as the springboard for an entirely new list:

- Distance learning
- Online classes
- Online classes for nontraditional, special needs, or home-schooled students
- Online degrees
- Rising rates of tuition and fees
- Mandatory community service for K–12 or college classes

With a little effort, brainstorming will help you generate a number of potential topics in a short time. And the process can be repeated over and over until you find a suitable topic.

reviewing the current media

A technique for developing a list of possible topics by looking at current publications, television, movies, and other forms of public communication.

REVIEW THE CURRENT MEDIA   A third way to generate topic ideas involves the popular media. While Google made a world of information available to us, and YouTube gives us both information and entertainment, there are other sources that help you find topics. We'll look at web sources later. Older, but helpful, media sources include: newspapers, books, magazines, television, and movies. **Reviewing the current media** is an effective way to develop a list of potential topics. Consider such sources as documentaries, news specials, cable channel programs, and even regular programming. *The Readers' Guide to Periodical Literature* is a source of hundreds of up-to-date topics. For example, you can find listings of articles on technology, education, finance, government, marketing, terrorism, crime, air safety, health, television violence, technology, and entertainment.

ENGAGE LISTENERS WITH SOCIAL MEDIA   Most of us are familiar with the popularity of Instagram, Pinterest, Yik Yak, Snapchat, Facebook, Twitter, and blogs where users create online communities to share information, ideas, personal messages, and other content and thus turn written communication into interactive dialogue among individuals and organizations.[5] Any of the social media outlets just listed can provide possible topics and sources of information. One special website that creates talks and

Making Connections for Success

Brainstorming

Brainstorming can be an effective tool to help you find an appropriate topic for your speeches.

Use brainstorming to generate topics you might use for your next informative speech. Take 5 minutes and write down whatever ideas come to mind; do not stop to evaluate them. Then look over your list and select terms that appeal to you. Next, brainstorm for another 5 minutes, and list topics related to your shorter list. Look at the list and follow these steps:

1. Determine the criteria to choose the *best* topic for your presentation.
2. Apply those criteria to the topics you've generated.
3. Use the criteria you established to determine the topic you will use.

Compare and contrast the criteria you listed for selecting the best topic with the criteria provided in the chapter.

invites people to discuss current talks and respond to those on the site is TED (www.ted.com/talks). TED is an excellent idea-generator, as well as a source for current speakers' expertise on newsworthy topics. TED is a nonprofit devoted to Ideas Worth Spreading. It started in 1984 as a conference bringing together people from three worlds: Technology, Entertainment, and Design. The group holds two annual conferences in Long Beach and Palm Springs, California, each spring and the TED Global conference in Edinburgh, United Kingdom, each summer. Currently, nearly 2,000 talks are available, ranging from language to deep ocean organisms. Browsing through the available talks might give you both a topic and a source. It is reported that it takes three days to prepare the TED Talks. Is it a surprise, then, that your instructors recommend a careful research and preparation process?

A caution should be noted about using any media to generate speech topics. Some beginning speakers have a tendency to rely on one media source for the entire speech. A summary of an interesting article or movie is not acceptable for most classroom speaking assignments. Though an excellent source for potential topics, media are only a *starting point* from which to build.[6] The content must be adapted to suit you and your specific audience, and most classroom assignments require a variety of sources. You should always bring something new to your topic—a fresh insight or an application suitable to the speaking situation.

SURF THE WEB The rapid development of technology, the ever-increasing number of websites, and the amount of new information on the web provide unique opportunities for students in a speech communication class.[6] Use of one or more of the many available search engines provides unique topics and sources of information on the topic. Because information is often not reviewed and accepted by experts or authorities on the subject before it is placed on a web page, and because anyone who knows how to put a web page together can put data online, students need to carefully evaluate both the information presented and its source. Internet research is further

Making Connections for Success

Social Media Research

Most of us use social media. MapQuest helps you plan trips, and your GPS makes sure you get there. Want to fly somewhere for spring break? Travelocity, Orbitz, CheapFares, or individual airline websites allow you to find the least expensive fares. Businesses use Facebook posts to generate sales, but Facebook can also be a source of ideas for speeches. If you're interested in food recipes and preparation there are thousands of sites to provide anything you want or need to know. If you want to find movie clips, try Hulu. YouTube clips provide an infinite range of possibilities, from entertainment to politics and everything in between.

We use the web not only to find information but also to help us choose topics for our presentations. Try the following exercise.

1. Take a minute to brainstorm 10 topics in which you have some interest, already know something about, or about which you want to learn something more.

2. Choose five of the most interesting.

3. Access a search engine you have not used before or one that is relatively unfamiliar (e.g., Dogpile,

http://www.dogpile.com; or Good Search, http://www.GoodSearch.com).

4. Click on the help area or the icon that informs your effective search.

5. Key in the words of your first topic.

6. How many hits did you get? What does this number tell you?

7. Check the first 10 hits: scroll through the list and read those responses.

8. Pick the most interesting one. Carefully read and evaluate that site. You want current, objective information from credible sources. How do you know the source you picked is trustworthy?

9. Does this topic seem like a good one? If so, pursue it further. If not, go back to the next most interesting topic and repeat the process.

This combination of personal brainstorming and web surfing helps you find topics with adequate information. This process uses the web to help you choose a topic that your web research reveals has adequate information.

discussed in the chapter on gathering and using information. For now, remember to look at who put the information on the website: What are their credentials? Are they trustworthy? When was it posted? Is the information objective rather than subjective? How current is it? How do you know?

How you find your topic is not the critical issue. What *is* important is that you begin your search as soon as possible. Over the years we've asked successful students about their topic search and one common factor emerges: They start looking for a topic as soon as they receive the assignment. Students who delay always have more difficulty finding an appropriate topic. Whenever you find something you think might be a good idea, write it down. The more ideas you accumulate, the easier your job of selecting a good topic will be. In addition, the earlier you choose your topic, the more time you will have to research, prepare, and practice your speech.

Assess the Appropriateness of a Topic

Once you have identified a possible topic, the next step is to determine whether it is appropriate for you, your assignment, and your audience. Ask yourself these questions:

1. Does the topic merit the audience's attention?
2. Will the audience see a connection between you and the topic and a personal connection to the topic?
3. Will the topic meet the objectives of the assignment?
4. Does the audience have sufficient knowledge and background to understand the topic?

Guidelines

Select an Appropriate Topic

1. **Choose a meaningful topic.** The more meaningful a topic, the more likely you are to put the necessary time and effort to research and develop your speech. The stronger your commitment to a topic, the more enthusiastically you will present it. A speaker's commitment to a topic usually transfers to the audience members and gets them involved. Audience involvement in a topic can be an effective gauge of your success as a speaker. The reason for giving a speech, besides completing the assignment, is to gain your listeners' attention; this is more easily accomplished if *you* consider the topic important.

2. **Choose a topic that allows you to convey an important or relevant thought to your audience.** The thought does not have to be a matter of extreme urgency, but it should at least be relevant to your audience's interests, have some direct effect on them, or be something that you believe the audience should know. Ask yourself the following questions:
   - Will the audience want to learn more about the topic?
   - Will the audience believe the topic is relevant?
   - Will the audience be affected in some way by the topic, either now or in the future?
   - Will the audience benefit from listening to a presentation on the topic?

   - Will the audience believe you are a credible speaker on the topic?

   If you can answer "yes" to each of these questions, you are on your way to selecting an appropriate topic.

3. **Choose a familiar and/or interesting topic.** This will make the development and delivery of your speech easier and more enjoyable. Some knowledge of taking effective photos with your smartphone or other device might lead to a speech on how to take better photos with a camera or a smartphone. You may enjoy selecting a topic in which you are interested but about which you know little. For example, you are intrigued by the idea of meditation as stress relief but do not know the exact procedures involved or the issues surrounding it, so your research allows you to learn and share that kind of information. Choosing an interesting topic increases the likelihood of audience attentiveness and speaker credibility. (We discuss speaker credibility in the chapter on persuasive speeches.)

4. **Think like a listener.** Evaluate your topic as though you were the listener. Focus your attention on what the audience likes and wants to hear about this topic you know and enjoy, and you are well on your way to choosing an interesting, informative, relevant, and potentially useful topic. What will the listener gain from your presentation?

5. Can you make the topic understandable to everyone in the audience?

6. Is the topic of sufficient interest to you that you will be motivated to present it effectively?

7. Do you have adequate knowledge of the topic?

8. If you are not already familiar with the topic, will you be able to learn enough about it to give an informed speech?

9. Is the topic appropriate for the class assignment and situation?

If you've answered "no" to any of these questions, return to the techniques to find a topic.

Narrow the Topic

Once you determine an appropriate topic, the next step is to decide whether it is narrow enough to fit the time limit and accomplish the goal of the assignment. This step can save you much time and trouble because a well-focused topic is much easier to research than one that is too general. For example, you could work for months on a speech titled "How to Create an Effective Portfolio" and still not exhaustively cover all the information. If you restrict the scope to the most important points to cover, materials to include, and the language to effectively present strengths in a succinct manner, you have more time to develop ideas in the speech. You could narrow the topic even further by choosing how to include examples of work that demonstrates strengths for specific jobs. When you narrow your topic, you increase its potential depth, but make sure you have enough developed information to meet the requirements for your presentations.

The more abstract the topic, the more important it is to narrow it to meet the constraints of the speech situation. Let's say you have an assignment for a 10-minute speech on a concept about which you wish to gain more information for yourself and your listeners. You think holidays would be a good topic. Obviously, you cannot address all holidays in 10 minutes. So you narrow the topic to "cultural holidays." There is still an abundance of information, far too much to cover. You decide to focus on the "cultural holidays of my hometown." This is still too broad, so you narrow to one specific holiday, "St. Patrick's Day in O'Neill, Nebraska."

This continual narrowing allows you to focus your research and content development on a more clearly defined area of the topic. This will be helpful to the speaker, as well as the listeners, because you will present more substance on an important concept. Speakers can narrow the scope of a subject according to the time limits, function, goals, location, and requirements of a specific topic. Narrowing the topic is a skill critical to your success as a communicator not only in the classroom, but also in the workplace and in any organizations where you may make presentations.

Determine the General Purpose, Specific Purpose, and Thesis of a Speech

7.2 Create general and specific purpose statements.

Once you have chosen and narrowed your topic, you need to start thinking about how the final presentation will be structured. Speakers should begin their preparation with a clear idea of the general purpose, the specific purpose, and a specific thesis statement. In this section, we briefly discuss each of these concepts. Chapter 11 provides in-depth coverage of informative speaking, and Chapter 12 is devoted to persuasive speaking.

The General Purpose

general purpose

The overall goal of a speech, usually one of three overlapping functions: to inform, to persuade, or to entertain.

The **general purpose**, or overall goal, of a speech is usually to perform one of three overlapping functions: to inform, to persuade, or to entertain. A speech rarely serves only one function. Even though most classroom speech assignments are intended to emphasize a single function, the speeches themselves may contain aspects of all three functions. For example, a speech about duct tape art is meant to inform, but the speech may contain some persuasive and entertaining elements as well. If you are assigned an informative or expository speech, however, you need to think carefully about how to organize and present ideas to your listeners. If the general purpose is to inform your audience, you should emphasize presentation of information about a new, interesting, and potentially useful and relevant topic.

For classroom speaking assignments, your general purpose is usually specified by the instructor, but for speeches outside the classroom, the occasion, what the audience knows or doesn't know about your topic, and how you want the audience to respond will determine whether you speak primarily to inform, to persuade, or to entertain.

The speaking goal is usually designed to affect the listeners in some purposeful way. The reaction of the listeners determines whether your speech has accomplished its purpose successfully.

informative speech

A speech that enhances an audience's knowledge and understanding by explaining what something means, how something works, or how something is done.

INFORMATIVE SPEECHES When the general purpose of your speech is to inform, you are expected to convey your knowledge of a particular subject. An **informative speech** enhances an audience's knowledge and understanding by explaining what something means, how something works, or how something is done. According to the Writing Guide: Informative Speaking at Colorado State University, "The purpose of the informative speech is to provide interesting, useful, and unique information to your audience."[7] The goal is to clearly and accurately share information and make the learning experience as enjoyable as possible for the audience.

Whether you describe how to protect yourself during an assault, discuss a proposed regulation to restrict the number of people allowed in rental houses, explain the differences among social networking sites, or report the university's proposal to honor diversity on campus, you should assume that most of your audience does not already know *all* the information you plan to present. The content of the speech depends heavily on what you think the audience knows and on how much you know or are able to learn about the topic. Your task as a speaker is to provide more information than the audience would normally get from reading an article, reading a web source, or listening to the news.

When a topic is controversial—for example, "embryonic stem cell research"—speakers whose general purpose is to inform should not take sides; instead, they might choose to provide background on what is involved in stem cell research, how it is used, and for what purpose. The informative speaker might identify the pros and cons but will not take a stand. The speaker presents the information and lets the listeners draw their own conclusions.

persuasive speech

A speech that attempts to change listeners' attitudes or behaviors by advocating or trying to gain acceptance of the speaker's point of view.

PERSUASIVE SPEECHES A **persuasive speech** attempts to change listeners' beliefs, attitudes, or behaviors by advocating or trying to gain acceptance of an idea or point of view. When speakers try to convince audience members to endorse a program to limit the damage caused by Yik Yak posts denigrating cultural diversity on campus, or ask citizens to petition for traffic roundabouts in high-traffic zones, or to accept that ethical behavior in the United States is on the decline, they are attempting to persuade. Speakers must present evidence and arguments to justify their positions and to win the audience over to their point of view.

The difference between informing and persuading is not always clear-cut. Your goal is persuasive when you try to convince your parents to loan you money for the latest iPhone. However, your message contains both informative and persuasive elements: informing them about the circumstances and your need for the latest iPhone and convincing them that they should loan you the money to purchase it. They may accept your reasons and agree that you need it but still might not loan you the money. In this example, the persuasive purpose is not only to inform and convince your parents that you need the latest iPhone and the money to buy it, but also for them to take action—to actually loan you the money you need. Information is a necessary part of a persuasive speech, but the ultimate goal is action. Once your parents loan you the money, you have achieved your purpose.

While the focus of an informative speech is to convey information and understanding by explaining, reporting, or demonstrating your point of view, the purpose of a persuasive speech is to change beliefs or attitudes or motivate listeners to act in a specific manner. The action might be to think, to respond, or to behave in a certain way. The purpose might be to eat organic foods for better health, to place greater societal emphasis on ethics, to volunteer at the local food bank, or to support greater campus entertainment opportunities.

The important and necessary ingredient that makes persuasion different from information is the action (to think, to respond, to behave) the speaker wants the listener to take as a result of the message presented. The informative speech provides knowledge about a topic, whereas the persuasive speech provides information *and* a direction or course of action.

Entertainment is often the general purpose of special occasion speeches, including toasts given at weddings and other special events. A speech to entertain should be light, use humor, and meet the guidelines of etiquette and good sense. Wedding toasts are examples of brief speeches to entertain.

entertainment speech

A speech that provides enjoyment and amusement.

ENTERTAINMENT SPEECHES An **entertainment speech** provides enjoyment an amusement. Speeches to entertain may be dramatic or humorous in nature an often occur on special occasions, such as weddings, retirements, after a dinner, or a "roast." A speech to entertain generally has three key qualities: It is light, origina and appropriate to the situation. An appropriate speech does not offend the sensibil ties of the audience. The speaker may use humor but not at the expense of the audi ence's sense of values or ethics. Effective speakers do not use offensive language o potentially offensive jokes or situations. Audience members, unlike television or we viewers, are a captive audience and cannot click the mouse or remote to switch o offensive words or ideas. The speaker must use tasteful examples and stories that wi not hurt anyone's feelings or violate their ethical principles.

In using humor, the speaker may create imaginative illustrations and figures c speech, twist meanings, tell amusing stories, create amusing character sketches, o tell jokes—all with the willing participation of the audience and in the spirit of th occasion. This does not mean, however, that an entertaining speech cannot be bot informative and persuasive or that informative and persuasive speeches cannot b entertaining. What distinguishes these three kinds of speeches is the function (inform ing, persuading, or entertaining) on which the speaker places the most emphasis. Th entertaining speech should, therefore, leave the audience members feeling amused o entertained.

The Specific Purpose

specific purpose

A single phrase that defines precisely what is to be accomplished in a speech.

The general purpose of a speech (to inform, to persuade, or to entertain) provide direction for its content. Once you have determined your general purpose, you ar ready to determine your specific purpose. A **specific purpose** is a single phrase tha defines precisely what you intend to accomplish in your speech. Jenna chose *ethnocen trism in Iowa* for her topic. Her specific purpose was "to inform my classmates of thre major ways ethnocentrism is prevalent in Iowa." The clear and concise statement tell exactly what the speaker intends to do and what she wants her audience to know.

An effective specific purpose identifies (1) the general purpose of the speech, (2 the audience, and (3) the exact topic to be covered. These three pieces of significan information help the speaker develop and deliver the speech. The specific purpos

When speakers know the general and specific purposes of the speech, the thesis, and information about the audience to tailor the content to them, they will more likely be perceived as effective speakers and the audience will be actively involved in the speech.

so identifies the audience, which is important, because different audiences may require different information. For example, if a speech is to be presented to children only, to adults only, or to both children and adults, the content will have to be adjusted to fit the particular group. Thus, even though the general and specific purposes are the same, the content of the speech will vary, depending on the listeners' backgrounds, knowledge, and attitudes toward the topic.

The careful writing of a specific purpose is important to all aspects of planning and developing a successful speech. The Guidelines box, Specific Purpose, should help you write an effective specific purpose.

Formulating effective general and specific purposes makes it easier to develop your speech. They will guide your thinking and planning. You should be ready to reconsider your specific purpose, however, throughout the development stages of the speech. As you research a topic, you might find information that leads you to revise your thinking. Or you might learn something about your audience members that will convince you to adjust your specific purpose to their needs.

The Thesis

The specific purpose of your speech states what you wish to accomplish or what effect you wish to have on your audience. It also serves as the foundation for the thesis of the speech. The **thesis** is a sentence that states specifically what is going to be discussed in a speech. For example, the specific purpose, "to explain to my audience the three advantages of using Prezi as a presentational aid," tells what the speaker wants to do but does not describe the content of the speech. A thesis concisely states the content: "Prezi is easier, it saves time, and it is enjoyable for both presenters and audience members." This clearly worded statement precisely identifies the three advantages of Prezi as a presentational aid.

If the specific purpose is "to persuade the audience to petition the College Hill Neighborhood Association to resist the reduction of rental houses in the neighborhood because it harms students," the thesis might be written as follows: "The suggested restrictions for house rentals will significantly harm UNI students and their ability to find housing near the university, it will make traffic more congested, and there will be fewer open parking spots on campus due to the greater distances traveled to campus." The thesis gives the three main ideas the speaker will discuss: (1) the restrictions limit students' ability to find housing near the university, (2) it will increase traffic congestion on campus, and (3) there will be even fewer parking spots on campus. In summary, the thesis should be expressed as a full sentence, should not be in the form of a question, and should be clearly and concisely worded.

Here are two examples showing the relationship of a topic to the general purpose, specific purpose, and thesis:

thesis

A sentence that states specifically what is going to be discussed in a speech.

TOPIC:	Inexpensive, renewable energy
GENERAL PURPOSE:	To inform
SPECIFIC PURPOSE:	To inform my audience about wind as an energy source
THESIS:	Wind is an inexpensive, easily accessible, renewable energy source.

TOPIC:	Stress Reduction through Meditation
GENERAL PURPOSE:	To persuade
SPECIFIC PURPOSE:	To persuade my audience that meditation should be taught to help students deal with stress.
THESIS:	I will demonstrate the need to incorporate teaching meditation in wellness classes and in residence halls as a way for students to de-stress.

You can easily see in these examples how a broad topic area is narrowed as the speaker moves from the specific purpose to the thesis. This procedure is a crucial step in preparing a speech to meet requirements.

Guidelines

Specific Purpose

1. **The specific purpose should include a verb form that describes the general purpose of the speech.** The inclusion of the verb form clarifies the action the speaker hopes to accomplish.

   Ineffective: To inform my audience about meditation.

   Effective: To inform my audience of the three effects of meditation in reducing stress.

2. **The specific purpose should be limited to one distinct thought or idea.** The following ineffective statement is too long and contains more than one subject. An entire speech could be developed around either area. It is best to select only one idea and refine it as the purpose for the speech.

   Ineffective: To persuade my audience about the three effects of alcohol and the four ways to prevent binge drinking by college students.

   Effective: To persuade my audience to promote four wa[y] to prevent binge drinking by college students

3. **The specific purpose should not be a question.** Althou[gh] a question may indicate the topic, it fails to specify t[he] general purpose of the speech.

   Ineffective: What historical events have become bloc[k] buster movies?

   Effective: To inform my audience about three blockbust[er] movies based on historical events.

4. **The specific purpose should be concise and careful[ly] worded.** The ineffective statement given here tries [to] cover too much material, is too general, and does not sta[te] clearly what is to be achieved by the speech.

   Ineffective: Technology has enhanced every aspect of o[ur] lives.

   Effective: To inform the audience that technologies hav[e] enhanced the ability to connect with frien[ds] and family anywhere at any time.

Audience Analysis: Connecting with the Listeners

7.3 **Evaluate** the suitability and relevance of the topics to make better connections with the audience.

Selecting a topic, narrowing it, choosing a specific purpose, and creating a clea[r] thesis statement so that you can connect your speech to the specific listeners in you[r] audience require careful thinking as well as knowledge and understanding of you[r] audience. The development of ideas requires similar understanding and knowledg[e] Therefore, the speaker needs specific information about the listeners. You hav[e] now probably spent several weeks with the people in your communication class It is likely that each of you responded to the activities and class discussions. Wha[t] people say, how they act, and their nonverbal communication have helped you for[m] impressions of your classmates. Those impressions are important, but you migh[t] need additional information to do a good job of connecting with your audience Because this is so critical to a speaker's success, the remainder of this chapter exam ines the audience's point of view, kinds of audience members, key information t[o] gain about audiences, methods for researching audiences, and adapting your speec[h] to an audience.

audience analysis

The collection and interpretation of data about characteristics, attitudes, values, and beliefs of an audience.

Audience analysis is the collection and interpretation of data about character istics, attitudes, values, and beliefs of an audience. Analyzing the audience is a[n] essential step in developing and delivering a speech. An audience becomes activel[y] involved in a speech and reacts to the speaker, to the subject, to what is said, to how it is said, to other audience members, and to the situation. The more speakers know about the audience, the better they can adapt their speeches accordingly.

audience

The collection of individuals who have come together to watch or listen to someone or something, such as to listen to a speech.

Understand the Listeners' Point of View

For our purposes, the **audience** refers to the collection of individuals who com[e] together to watch or listen to a speech. The individuals may become part of th[e] audience for a variety of reasons. Each individual may have several motives, and the audience members may come from many different backgrounds. Members of the hosting organization may attend only because they are loyal to and wish to support the group.

The reason individuals come together to form an audience is an important point for the speaker to consider. If people join an audience because they wish to listen to a speech, it is reasonable to assume that they also want to hear something meaningful. Most individuals ask the same basic questions about their involvement in an audience: "What's in this for me?"

This question suggests that your audience will judge what they hear on the basis of their past experiences and the relevance of the information presented. The more you know about your audience (past experiences, knowledge of the subject, relationship to the subject, and reason for being there), the easier it will be to develop a meaningful speech. For example, imagine that you are an expert on sustainability and prairie plants in agriculture and are asked to give a speech. You decide to title the speech "Assessing the Wildlife Habitat Value of Diverse Prairie Plantings." You have spent many hours getting ready for the speech and are now prepared to present it. Are you really prepared? Have you thought about the members of your audience? Who are they? What do they know about fund-raising? What is their attitude toward sustainability issues? Would you present the same information to biologists, to a group of Sierra Club members, to students in a public relations class at your college, or to a mixed group of citizens in the community? What results would you expect if you used the same approach for all four audiences? What results would you expect if you varied your approaches? The questions and answers are essential for an effective presentation.

An audience is the collection of individuals who come together to watch or listen to a speech. The more you know about your audience's past experiences, knowledge of the subject, relation to the subject, and reason for being there, the easier it will be for you to develop a meaningful speech. What audience considerations might have influenced Oprah's speech about Rosa Parks?

Captive versus Voluntary Participants

Many kinds of people listen to speeches for various reasons, but all are either captive or voluntary participants. Audience members required to listen to a particular speech are called **captive participants**. They may happen to want to hear the speech, but they have no choice but to attend. Some people may resist participation more than others.

Even though few circumstances force a person to be part of an audience, some situations demand attendance to avoid a penalty. For example, your teacher requires attendance during speech presentations, an employer requires employees to attend new product demonstrations, or a military leader orders troops to attend lectures on military maneuvers. In such situations, audience members cannot be absent and cannot leave without being noticed or penalized for doing so. To be effective, a speaker must recognize when he or she is dealing with captive participants.

In contrast to captive participants, **voluntary participants** choose to hear a particular speech because of interest or need. True volunteers attend because of the speaker, the occasion, the topic, or what they expect to hear. There is no other motivation or force behind their presence.

captive participant

A person who is required to hear a particular speech.

voluntary participant

A person who chooses to listen to a particular speech.

Key Audience Information

You should gather two kinds of information about your prospective audience: demographic and psychological. The more you know about your audience members, the better you will adjust to them and relate your topic to them.

demographic analysis

The collection and interpretation of characteristics (age, gender, religion, occupation, and so on) of individuals, excluding values, attitudes, and beliefs.

DEMOGRAPHIC ANALYSIS Demographic analysis is the collection and interpretation of basic information, such as age, gender, cultural or ethnic background, education, occupation, religion, socioeconomic status, geographical location, political affiliation, voting habits, family relationships, marital and parental status, and group memberships. The more similar the demographic characteristics of audience members, the easier it is for a speaker to adapt to listeners' needs and interests.

Age You can select a range of appropriate examples and evidence when your audience members differ in age. An age difference between the speaker and the audience can also alter what messages are presented and how they are expressed. For example, if an audience consists of only 18- to 22-year-olds, the speaker has only one age group with which to deal. If audience members range from 15 to 65 years of age, the speaker will have to take into account several age groups and make language and content choices on the basis of that wide range.

Gender Gender, an important demographic characteristic, presents challenges. Speakers should consider the attitudes of each gender toward the other as well as the same gender attitudes. As we indicated in several places in this text, gender-based biases should be avoided. Speakers should be sensitive to potential gender-based biases—for example, referring to women as "passive" or providing examples of women only in certain careers, such as nursing or teaching. Although some topics may still be more appropriate for one gender than the other, clear-cut distinctions are becoming increasingly rare.

Cultural or Ethnic Background Cultural or ethnic background is often not considered as thoroughly as it should be, even though a tremendous diversity of backgrounds exist in our society. Speakers should be sensitive to the different groups that may be present. The following communication variables are culturally determined and influence the interactions of members from different ethnic and racial backgrounds:

Good of the group	Individual needs
Language usage	Rituals
Polychronic or monochronic time	Appropriate eye contact
Dealing with uncertainties	Appropriate handshakes or touch
High-context versus low-context	Traditions, cultural expectations
Use of silence	Cultural norms
Differing views of age, class, and status	

Each of these variables determines and regulates how an individual creates and interprets messages. Although the list is not exhaustive, it points out some of the important cultural and ethnic factors to consider as you plan a speech. Culture is dynamic and extremely important; culture helps define individuals in relation to the world around them. Speakers who do not take culture into account may embarrass and insult an audience and, ultimately, embarrass themselves. Speech content should not offend the values, customs, or beliefs of audience members.

Education Although it may be impossible to find out exactly what an audience knows and understands about a specific topic, it is often possible to ascertain their general education level. Knowing whether most listeners have completed high school, college, or graduate school can help you to gauge their intellectual level and experience and to adapt your speech accordingly.

Occupation Knowledge of audience members' occupations also tells you something about possible interest in and familiarity with some subjects. For example, professors have one view while students have another. Anyone interested in a specific topic will try to find links to her or his own interests and profession, but the speaker's knowledge of who will be listening can be helpful.

Religion   Speakers must be as sensitive to religion as they are to ethnicity. That is, they must recognize issues that touch on religious beliefs and treat them carefully. If you plan to speak on an issue that may have religious ramifications, you should evaluate how your message will affect audience members. Otherwise, you run a risk of offending or losing the attention of some or all of your audience. For example, a quotation to support your viewpoint might be more appropriately taken from the Koran than from the Bible (or, better yet, from both the Koran and the Bible) if your audience is of the Islamic faith.

Geographical Origins   Knowing your audience's geographical origins can help you adapt your speech to them. For example, people from rural communities are more likely to know and care more about agricultural topics than are those from large urban areas. People from the South might not be interested in information related to heating their homes in winter; but, if they live in an oil-producing state, they might be interested in the price of a barrel of oil.

Group Membership   A group is a collection of individuals who have joined together for some common cause or purpose that may be social, professional, recreational, or charitable. When you know the special interests of individuals in your audience you can relate your speech directly to their needs and concerns. Of course, it isn't always possible to reach every group in your audience; but, by appealing to the largest group, you can create strong attention and interest. For example, a student who belonged to a sorority decided to inform her audience about sorority and fraternity functions other than social activities. Three-quarters of her student audience were not affiliated with a Greek group. Knowing this, she began her speech by talking about her thoughts on Greek organizations before she became a member. By first pointing out her reservations about such groups, she created a common understanding with her listeners. That kind of introduction would be unnecessary with the opposite percentages.

Other Demographic Factors   We earlier identified marital status, family makeup, and socioeconomic status as other possible elements of demographic analysis. This analysis provides information on listeners' priorities and interests. An awareness of socioeconomic status will also supply information about the interests of audience members and their abilities to grasp the ideas presented. All in all, more information about

Making Connections for Success

How Culture Affects the Public Speaker

Dan and Shiho discuss their upcoming assignment: a 10-minute informative speech on a topic demonstrating ethical principles. Shiho says she wants to talk about the concept of "saving face," but Dan does not understand what this expression means and how it is appropriate for the assignment. Shiho explains, "Saving face is a concept that means a person does not purposely do anything to make another lose credibility or status." Shiho says she often does not ask questions of the other students because she is aware the questions could cause them to lose face in their own minds or in the minds of others. According to Japanese beliefs, ethical speakers and ethical listeners will not willingly cause another to lose face, nor will they willingly lose face by

making a mistake. Dan is fascinated and asks more questions to learn about Shiho's culture.

Each of us should be aware of cultural perspectives and how they may affect speakers and listeners in a speaking situation. Think about the cultures (or cocultures) represented in your communication class, and then answer these questions:

1. What values do these other cultures promote? How do you know?

2. How do the cultural values affect the way a person might respond to certain topics? Provide examples.

3. How can you increase your sensitivity and awareness of cultural perspectives?

4. What can you, as a speaker, do to adjust to different cultural values in your communication class?

your listeners and what characteristics they share with you and with others promote a better understanding of how to prepare the speech.

PSYCHOLOGICAL ANALYSIS   **Psychological analysis** is the collection of data on audience members' values, attitudes, and beliefs. A psychological analysis seeks to determine how the audience will react to the speaker, the speaker's topic, and the surroundings in which the speech is presented. In addition to the items related to demographic analysis, a psychological analysis helps the speaker be aware of what motivates listeners to attend to the message of a particular speech. The size of the audience, the physical setting for the presentation, the knowledge level of the audience, and the attitude of the audience toward the speaker, the topic, and the situation all play vital roles in the planning, development, and delivery of a speech.

psychological analysis

The collection and interpretation of data about audience members' values, attitudes, and beliefs.

Size of Audience   The number of audience members has a considerable psychological effect on a speaking situation and strongly influences how a speech should be delivered. The larger the audience, the more difficult it is to use an informal, conversational speaking style. Size also affects the speaker's use of language, gestures, and visual aids. Speaking to 10 to 30 people, as in a typical classroom speech assignment, is quite different from speaking to several hundred people in an auditorium.

The size of an audience can also affect the psychological disposition of the audience members and their relationship to each other and the speaker. For example, each member of a small audience is aware of him- or herself as a unique member of the audience, and each feels a close, intimate relationship to the speaker. As the size of the audience increases, members lose their sense of identity as unique individuals and feel more distanced from the speaker. Effective speakers know this and plan their presentations to meet the requirements of each situation.

Physical Setting   In evaluating the physical setting, consider factors such as room size, ventilation, seating arrangement, lighting, speaker's platform, and potential for using visual aids. Some professional speakers require specific settings and refuse to give presentations if their conditions can't be met. Unfortunately, you do not have that choice in a classroom assignment. You can, however, assess the physical setting and take full advantage of what is available.

The seating arrangement of your audience is often predetermined, as it is in classroom settings, but sometimes a slight modification can make your presentation more effective. For example, a speech communication professor was asked to address a group of 100 administrative law judges. She purposely arrived early so she could see the room and assess the speaking conditions. The seats were arranged in an immovable classroom style: The chairs were placed in uniform rows directly in front of a raised speaker's podium, on which stood a large wooden lectern with a microphone. The professor believed the setting was too formal and would inhibit her presentation, so she quickly rearranged the area in front of the podium so she could move closer to her listeners and make eye contact with everyone. These simple changes gave her presentation a more casual feeling and encouraged audience involvement.

The physical setting can also affect audience members' psychological disposition toward one another as well as toward the speaker. The more relaxed the physical setting, for example, the more open and comfortable audience members will feel in relation to one another and to the speaker. The proximity of audience members to one another can also have an effect. If the audience members are scattered throughout a large meeting room, they will not have the sense of inclusion that occurs in a physical setting where the members are densely packed together. The physical closeness of other people may create a feeling of belonging to the group and help the speaker reach the audience.

Knowledge Level   The extent of an audience's knowledge about a topic has a tremendous effect on the outcome of a speech. If an audience has little or no background

Sometimes the speaker cannot alter the physical setting, but can change body position, or move away from the lectern, or find other ways to better reach out to the audience, as this speaker is doing. He cannot change the seats, but he can avoid the lectern and move closer to the audience.

on a topic and the speaker does not realize this, both the audience and the speaker can become frustrated. When an audience isn't ready to receive information or when the information is too technical for them to recognize, the speaker must present the material in terms everyone can understand.

A speaker must also adjust a presentation to reach a knowledgeable audience. A physician addressing a medical conference would not explain familiar medical terms. If, however, that physician speaks to patients and caregivers, definition of the medical terms is needed.

Making Connections for Success

Connecting with the Listeners

The listeners' knowledge of the speaker strongly influences how a speech should be developed and delivered. Even people well known in their own fields or famous media personalities know they have to connect with their specific audiences. You've probably spent several weeks in this class; your instructor has provided numerous opportunities for all students to share ideas with each other, so from participation and observation, everyone in class already knows a great deal about each other. At the same time, your classmates probably do not know you extremely well. Here's how one student's first sentences helped her connect with her listeners and make a lasting impact on all who heard the speech.

"Two years ago I was riding home from the prom with my three best friends. None of us had been drinking, and we all enjoyed a wonderful, memorable night. Little did I know how memorable that night would be. A drunk driver, traveling at excessive speed, slammed into our car as we were turning,

with the light, to go into Perkins. My friend Lisa died upon impact. The rest of us were injured and taken by ambulance to the hospital but, luckily, had few injuries. The pain of losing Lisa will never leave me. As a result of that prom night accident, I have a new mission in life. Today, I want to share with you the reasons for the slogan, 'If you drink, don't drive.'"

The listeners were very quiet and attentive throughout the speech. As this example illustrates, sharing a personal experience helped the speaker connect with her listeners and, in turn, held their attention. Listeners will always formulate some attitude toward a speaker. Help them form one that keeps them tuned in to your presentation.

1. Identify ways other speakers have effectively connected with their listeners.

2. In what circumstances do listeners not need knowledge about the speaker as a person?

3. Create an example of an event or circumstance in your life you could use to let listeners gain more knowledge of you.

Even though people are apt to be more interested in subjects they know something about, an audience does not want a rehash of familiar information; they want to hear a new twist and add to their existing knowledge. For example, a student decided to present a 5-minute informative speech about the lead pencil. After interviewing his classmates, the speaker noted that they all had a similar response: "What can you say about a lead pencil other than it is made of lead and wood and is used for writing?" On the basis of his analysis, the student developed a creative, fascinating speech. Using a casual and entertaining style, he provided detailed information about the history of the lead pencil and its effect on society. The speech was a great success.

Attitudes and Values Related to the Topic   The audience's attitude and values as they relate to the topic are as significant as their knowledge of the speaker. If audience members do not relate to a topic, the speaker will have a difficult time getting them to listen. For instance, a student chose to speak on individual retirement accounts for his persuasive speech. He researched the subject thoroughly, practiced his delivery, and presented the speech in an enthusiastic manner. His audience remained cool and uninvolved. The speaker failed to consider the value the audience placed on the topic; the age of its members should have tipped him off. Saving for retirement is *not* a high priority for most college students—they're just trying to pay the bills. The speaker could have made the speech more relevant by discussing young people's indifference to retirement saving, and by convincing them to be concerned now.

Attitudes Related to the Situation   The speaker should also examine the audience's relationship to the overall situation in which the speech is presented. Why has the audience gathered? Audience members' expectations influence their attitude toward the situation, which in turn reflects on the speaker and the topic. A speaker who talks about the need to further fund Social Security to a group of 17- to 24-year-old students has chosen the wrong topic for an audience who cares little about retirement and Social Security, which is decades away for them. Listeners who believe a topic is not relevant to their own situations are less likely to listen to the speaker.

Ways to Learn about the Audience

The easiest way to find out about your audience is through observation. Your success with this method depends on the amount of experience you have with your audience and your ability to make accurate inferences. In most classroom situations, observation will yield adequate information to plan a speech, but if you seek more specific data, you may want to use a survey. A survey interview takes planning and time and is not very efficient, but it does provide an opportunity to obtain information in person and to probe for more data when necessary. If you have a large group of people, you may decide to gather information with a questionnaire. Although good questionnaires take time to write, they can be anonymous and can be administered more quickly than survey interviews and often yield more candid responses, especially to sensitive topics.

OBSERVATION   Probably the easiest method of audience analysis is through observation. The speaker draws on accumulated experience with a particular audience and with similar groups. Through **observation**, the speaker watches audience members and notes their behaviors and characteristics. Although this approach relies strictly on the speaker's subjective impression, it can be useful.

No doubt you have already learned a great deal about your audience from classroom assignments. You already know the number of students, the number of males and females, and their approximate ages. Through introductions, general conversations, and other interactions, you have learned about their majors, group memberships, jobs, whether they commute or live on campus, and their interests. You have learned about your classmates' attitudes, interests, values, and knowledge. You know your instructor's views and expectations for your classroom performance. You also

observation

A method of collecting information about an audience in which the speaker watches audience members and notes their behaviors and characteristics.

how the size of the classroom, the location of the lectern (if there is one), the seating arrangement, the availability of audiovisual equipment, and other physical features of the environment. You have obtained all of this information by observation.

SURVEY INTERVIEWS A **survey interview** is a carefully planned and executed person-to-person, question-and-answer session during which the speaker tries to discover specific information that will help in the preparation of a speech. Such interviews can be done in person or over the phone. The purpose of the survey is to establish a solid base of fact from which to draw conclusions, make interpretations, and determine future courses of action. This method of audience research can be highly productive. To be most useful, however, surveys require a great deal of planning and organization, which takes time and energy.

QUESTIONNAIRES A **questionnaire** is a set of written questions distributed to respondents with the aim of gathering desired information. The same questioning techniques used in survey interviews are also used in questionnaires. In some cases, questionnaires are more practical and take less time than interviews. They can be administered to relatively large groups of people at the same time. One advantage is that the respondents can remain anonymous, which often leads to greater honesty and openness in answering questions. Although learning to develop good questionnaires takes time and practice, here are some simple guidelines to help you get started:

- Decide exactly what information you want to gather.
- Decide on the best method for making multiple copies of your questionnaire.
- Decide when, where, and how to distribute the questionnaire.
- Plan the introduction to the questionnaire. Will the respondent need specific instructions on how to answer it?
- Make sure your questions are clear and understandable.
- Limit the number of possible responses to each question.
- Keep the questionnaire as brief as possible.

Figure 7.1 shows a typical questionnaire. Note that it provides simple instructions, is brief, the questions are clear, and the number of possible responses is limited.

Use Information to Connect with Listeners

Your goal in all these types of data collection activities is to gather information so that you can relate and adapt your speech to those who make up your audience. Can you discern any patterns in the information you have gathered? What conclusions can you draw? How certain of them can you be? How can you use what you have learned to improve your speech? Let's say you want to know how students at your school feel about same-sex marriage even though the 2015 Supreme Court of the United States decision covers the legality of the issue. You survey 50 female and 50 male students on your campus, using the questionnaire in Figure 7.1. When you tally the results, you find 79 percent of the women and only 25 percent of the men believe that same-sex marriages should be legal. How will that information help you prepare a speech to convince your listeners that same-sex marriage ought to be supported?

To give the best results, a questionnaire must be completed by a group of people who represent a sample of the entire population. You also need to make sure you have enough responses to make reliable generalizations about the group you are surveying. If your analysis is thorough and correct, you should have a fairly good picture of your audience—their relevant demographics, interests, knowledge levels, and attitudes toward the topic, the speaker, and the general situation. While your findings will rarely be uniform, you should be able to reach some general conclusions. For example, you may find that 60 percent of your audience members strongly disagree with

survey interview

A carefully planned and executed person-to-person question-and-answer session during which the speaker tries to discover specific information that will help in the preparation of a speech.

questionnaire

A set of written questions that is distributed to respondents to gather desired information.

Figure 7.1 Sample Questionnaire

Questionnaires contain a set of written questions and are an excellent way to quickly gather information from large groups of people. If done effectively, they can be practical, take less time than interviews, and provide for the anonymity of the respondent.

Check one: ____ Female____ Male

Directions: Check the response that best indicates the strength of your agreement or disagreement with each statement.

1. Same-sex couples should be allowed to marry.
   ____ Strongly Agree
   ____ Agree
   ____ Undecided
   ____ Disagree
   ____ Strongly Disagree

2. Our society actively punishes gays, lesbians, and same-sex couples.
   ____ Strongly Agree
   ____ Agree
   ____ Undecided
   ____ Disagree
   ____ Strongly Disagree

3. Social support should be provided for same-sex couples who wish to adopt a child.
   ____ Strongly Agree
   ____ Agree
   ____ Undecided
   ____ Disagree
   ____ Strongly Disagree

4. The entire community should show more support for same-sex couples who have a child.
   ____ Strongly Agree
   ____ Agree
   ____ Undecided
   ____ Disagree
   ____ Strongly Disagree

government restrictions on health care, 15 percent have no opinion, and 25 percent strongly agree with government health care options. If your purpose is to persuade them that government health care packages will provide health care for everyone, you must adjust your speech to this audience. How will you encourage those who oppose you to listen to what you have to say? What can you say to draw in those who have no opinion or who already strongly agree with you?

Although it is never easy to win over people who oppose your views, you can try to do so by discussing their views first and then discussing yours. You should also make use of credible, unbiased sources—people are more likely to accept information from them. In addition, you should acknowledge that your listeners' views have as much merit as yours but assert that your views will lead to a better outcome.

If your research indicates that your audience has little or no opinion about the information you are presenting, you need to *provoke their interest*. Tell them why they should listen to what you are saying and show them how the topic relates to them personally. Focus on helping them recognize the benefits and importance of your topic and remember that clearly communicating your own enthusiasm can help generate interest. Tell your listeners a memorable story, using the information you gained.

Finally, when you are dealing with an audience that concurs with your viewpoint or knows a lot about your topic, you need to acknowledge what you share with them

For example, if you and your audience agree that a new auditorium should be built, note that shared agreement and then go on to talk about what can be done to get the new facility built. In the process, you might try to strengthen their beliefs about the need for the auditorium.

No matter what may be the audience's position on your topic, your research will enable you to identify it in advance. You can use this information to pursue your specific purpose and to adjust your presentation. Of course, the more information you have, the better your ability to adapt your speech to your audience.

A Note about Digital Public Communication

People today seem to always be connected to something and/or someone. Technology plays such an important role in our lives that we sometimes cannot disconnect from it, even when we should. Digital public communication is also on the rise. Some of you may be taking this class as an "online" or distance learning class and will present your speeches to audiences you find or create in your communities, and record and upload them on the web so that your classmates may review and offer comments. At some point you may design a webinar for someone at a distance in your employer's company, or you may provide online training sessions so people can get the information on their own time and in the comfort of their homes or offices. Your professors may put their classes online through a platform such as BlackBoard or D2L, and they probably also take staff development training on a variety of issues their schools want them to understand. Most of what we talked about in this chapter (and will talk about in succeeding chapters) applies to digital public communication as well as to other forms. The difference is the kind of interactivity that can be included in online presentations. The need to know your listeners is just as essential in the digital event as in face-to-face speaking. You can be more creative, and more interactive, online, and that gives you more freedom and more creativity in presentation. It also allows you to find more digital sources to enhance the presentation. In fact, you can probably be more interactive in that format than in the regular face-to-face presentations in the classroom. You can use video to bring in examples, as well as to make the presentation. You can actively engage your audience through interactive features, much as we have in this textbook. Many of you are "digital natives" who know more about technology than many of the professors who write about or teach communication classes. You can use that knowledge to your benefit when you're making digital presentations. We'll talk more about this aspect in succeeding chapters. For now, just realize that topic selection is every bit as important for digital speaking as it is in other venues.

Stephen J. Lind suggests that "Digital Oratory" is "thesis-driven, vocal, embodied public address that is housed within (online) new media platforms (and that ideally takes advantage of the developing/flux-laden conventions that the online video context provides). This new form of public address lies somewhere between traditional speech-giving and media production, but it is decidedly oratorical. The public speaking component is highly valuable to a student's all-around development, in its teaching of critical thinking, meaning making, argument development, persuasion theory, general nuance and so on."[8]

Summary

Select a Speech Topic

Objective 7.1   Apply the requirements to choose topics for your speeches and presentations.

When you choose a topic, you should begin with you and then think about the listeners, the setting, and the requirements for the speech; some basic strategies can help you find a topic.

- Self-inventory allows you to think of topics for which you have a special passion for sharing.
- Brainstorming allows your brain to cover numerous potential topics in a short time. Deep thinking comes later.

- Review the current media—this gives you an opportunity to see which print and nonprint sources can provide helpful information and ideas.
- Social media is increasingly more valuable and can help you find a topic and engage your listeners.
- Research can also take you to various places on the web, with an infinite number of possibilities for topics.
- Once you've found a topic, you need to assess its appropriateness for you, your listeners, the situation, and the requirements.
- Before you begin your research, you'll want to narrow the topic to fit the time limit and other guidelines.

Determine the General Purpose, Specific Purpose, and Thesis of a Speech

Objective 7.2 **Create** general and specific purpose statements.

Purpose and thesis statements allow the listeners to know what to expect and the perspective you have on the topic.

- General purpose statements cover the type of speech you will present, including informative, persuasive, and entertainment speeches.
- Special occasion speeches fit within the definitions of these three main types of speeches.
- Specific purpose statements identify which of the three types of speeches will be presented and add further information about the specific topic.
- The thesis statement tells the listeners what you expect them to know or do as a result of listening to your speech.

Audience Analysis: Connecting with the Listeners

Objective 7.3 **Evaluate** the suitability and relevance of the topics to make better connections with the audience..

The more you know about the audience, the more likely you are to gain and maintain their attention with your speech.

- Effective speakers will work to gain knowledge of the listeners and their points of view.
- Captive audience members are required to attend a presentation, while voluntary participants choose to attend the event, listen to a specific speaker, or take the opportunity to gain a perspective on the speaker's ideas.
- Demographic analysis can help you make better connections with your audience as you adapt the topic and delivery to their age, gender, culture or ethnic background, education, occupation, religion, geographical origin, or group memberships.
- Psychological analysis helps you adapt to the audience by considering the size of the audience, the physical setting, their knowledge level, and their attitudes and values toward the topic and situation.
- Common techniques to learn about the audience include observation, survey interviews, and questionnaires.
- Digital presentations require the same kind of thorough research and preparation as other forms of public communication, especially in terms of topic selection, but they allow for more creativity and interactivity in making the content come to life for the audience.

Discussion Starters

1. Why is public communication important in today's media-saturated society?

2. In what ways can effective public communication help you connect with listeners?

3. Identify three criteria you would use to determine whether a topic is appropriate for your class and other public presentations.

4. What is the value of both a general purpose statement and a specific purpose statement?

5. How does a thesis statement help you connect with your listeners?

6. What does demographic analysis provide to help you develop and deliver presentations?

7. Why is it important for the speaker to connect with a captive audience? How can these connections be made?

8. Why do your audience's attitudes toward you and your topic make or break a presentation?

9. What web and social media sources have you previously found useful in choosing topics?

Chapter 8
Research: Gathering and Using Information

 ## Learning Objectives

CHAPTER OUTLINE

This chapter will help you:

8.1 **Develop** a research plan to gather information and find supporting materials for your speeches.

Develop a Research Plan

8.2 **Identify** five principal sources of information for your speech topic.

Research: Gathering Information

8.3 **Differentiate** among the four types of materials to support and clarify your ideas.

Use Research to Support and Clarify Ideas

Making Everyday Connections

Most people use one or more forms of social media to understand the world, find information, and relate to others. Social media such as Facebook, Twitter, LinkedIn, Pinterest, Instagram, and Snapchat give us personal information about people, while YouTube provides video examples of various items of interest and IMD and Bing provide movies, clips, and information. It is estimated that 2.4 billion people of all ages use the Internet; in addition, there are 100 billion Google searches every month. And, if Facebook, with more than 175 million users, were a country, it would be the third largest, behind China and India.[1]

People create YouTube clips as a way to promote themselves, their views, or their companies, or to share whatever they wish to share with a large number of people. YouTube in 2014 was the second largest search engine.[2] Social media such as Facebook and YouTube can be used for good or ill, and they certainly provide ways for people to disseminate the estimated 3.5 zetabytes of unique new information created in 2014.[3] In the fall semester of 2014, a group of students at the University of Northern Iowa, through anonymous parties on YikYak, created racist, sexist, and homophobic posts. The UNI Provost and others responded immediately that the posts were not indicative of UNI's inclusivity and diversity, and "We Can Do Better" events happened across campus for the next several weeks. Social media created negativity; the UNI community turned it into an opportunity to communicate about the issues and create a safe environment for all. The amount of new technical information doubles every year. "Did You Know 2014?" suggests that one week's worth of *New York Times* contains more information than existed in the 18th century. Social media certainly add greater dimensions to information gathering than we could find even 10 years ago.

Questions to Think About

1. What kinds of information do you usually seek from the various forms of social media?

2. Where do you usually start your search for information when you have an assignment for a paper or a presentation? Why?

3. What do you do to determine that the information you find is credible, relevant, timely, and significant?

4. Recall issues or situations in which people went to great effort to get information to share with others—what was the situation and what resulted?

What impresses listeners? Most will respond in a similar manner: Listeners are impressed with worthwhile, current information that is carefully constructed to tell a story in all types of speeches. If you find adequate, credible, relevant, up-to-date information, you can create an impressive speech. Gathering information can be exciting and fun—have you ever become so caught up in seeking out specific information on the web that time flew by far too quickly? The information you gather becomes the backbone of the speech and is only as good as the significance and value of that information. In this chapter, we focus on the research process and how to use the information you gather to support and clarify your message.

Develop a Research Plan

8.1 **Develop** a research plan to gather information and find supporting materials for your speeches.

You are now ready to gather information for speeches. The work and thinking you've done for the previous chapters provides the foundation for your task as you gather and develop the information you've researched to create your speeches. You've already practiced topic generation through self-inventory, brainstorming, and mediated communication searches. You analyzed general information for your presentations. Now you need to think about how to research and what you wish to accomplish: You must strengthen your own previous knowledge about the topic, find evidence to support your ideas, and make your ideas clear and relevant to your listeners. You need to consider how much background reading to do and what sources will be best to achieve this goal. You'll have to think about the types of supporting materials necessary and where you can find those materials. You must also determine how much evidence is required to make your point and convince listeners to accept your views as worthy of consideration. *In other words, you now need to think carefully about what you want to accomplish.* This is not a task for the night before your presentation is due.

Thus, you've already begun the first part of your research plan: *Start early* and *gather more information than you think you'll need*, because more material may be helpful; it's always better to have more than enough information. Do not procrastinate. The longer you wait to begin your research, the more problems you're likely to have.

It takes time to create speeches. You need to find the right supporting materials, and think about what you have so you can refine, add, or delete before the presentation. Think carefully about your topic. *Where should you go to find the best information to create your speech?*

We tell our students they should *prepare a preliminary list of references* to narrow their search to the sources most likely to help them create the speech. Once the list of references is created, determine which materials to find first to provide a background and help set a direction for the speech.

You cannot read all material on the topic, so you *must be selective about materials that will enhance your own knowledge and clarify information for your listeners.* Once you have the background materials read, and complete notes, *look for the best information you can find to support your own views.*

As you read and take notes, be sure you understand your *instructor's specifications for the number and types of supporting materials required.* It's important to use a variety of types of sources, but it's also critical to have different kinds of supporting material to make your points. Variety in the mix of examples, testimony, statistics, mediated sources, and social media will help your listeners remain attentive.

Take good notes and keep complete information on the sources so you don't have to start over. In addition, be sure to identify direct quotes as well as paraphrased materials and include them with sources in the speech to avoid even a hint of plagiarism.

At some point you have to say "enough is enough." There's so much information available that you cannot cover everything, and you do have time limits for classroom speeches. Once you feel you have more than enough to create the speech, stop and analyze how things fit together to make the best presentation for your listeners.

The whole point of developing and carrying out a research plan is to *think critically* about your topic and the information you will use to support the topic and grab your listeners' attention. Your task from this point on is to apply what you learned, choose good information, and use your time efficiently as you move toward speech presentations.

Research: Gathering Information

8.2   Identify five principal sources of information for your speech topic.

While you need to start with yourself and your own interests, most of us then begin our research on the web. Once you've looked at what you've already practiced, choose a topic you really like and begin with the web, move to social media, and then look at library and print sources to round out your research information. You'll need a variety of sources, and not all of your information can come from mediated sources. (Despite our heavy reliance on the Internet and social media, not all information *can or should* derive from those sources.) Check with your instructor or the syllabus to see specific requirements for your class. A word of caution: while few recommend *Wikipedia* as a source, you can often find good lists of resources on topics there, and thus can begin to get ideas about where to go to get reliable information on a topic.

The Internet as an Information Source

Searching the web can be addicting, educational, entertaining, frustrating, interesting, and time-consuming. The web facilitates access to a wealth of information in a relatively short period of time. Web information comes from a variety of sources. Some are reliable and credible, and others are not useful, credible, relevant, *or reliable*. Websites are not subject to the same evaluation and review as most print sources, so it is important that you assess not only the information on a website but also the people or organizations responsible for the site. It is no accident that when you key in the words "critical thinking," many responses will be suggested for evaluating web sources. Several of the scores of critical thinking websites are actually titled "Thinking Critically about Web Sources." Here are the basic questions you should ask and answer about your web-based information:

1. **Author.** Who wrote the material? What qualifications does the writer have? Are they appropriate qualifications for the topic? Can you contact the author if you have questions?

2. **Publishing body.** Who "publishes" or sponsors the website? When you look at the web page, do you see a header or footer that shows a connection to a larger website? Is there a link on the page that takes you to the home page? Some websites promote an organization or product; thus, the information may be biased. You can determine the credibility and objectivity of the material by checking further into the site. In addition, you can learn much from the Internet address (the URL). Check the letters just to the left of the first backslash (/). Look beyond the backslash. If you see a tilde (˜) or if the URL includes terms such as "/users/" or "/people/," you may be looking at an individual's personal page within the official pages of a larger website. If it is a personal page, you have no way of knowing whether the information on the page represents the organization. However, if you know the author's identity and qualifications (say, a librarian at an educational site), you will be able to ascertain the credibility of the personal page.

3. **Currency.** How recently was the website published, created, or updated? This information should be at the bottom of the web page or the home page. Does the document contain data recent enough to be useful? Is there a date connected to that information? (When the population of Hispanics in the United States is given with a

Web searches can provide a wealth of information quickly and easily from a variety of sources. Some sources are reliable and credible; others are not useful, credible, or reliable. It is important to check out sources to ensure they are reliable and accurate.

1990 date, for example, the information is not current.) Does the website have links to other sites that no longer work? (This is usually a hint that the site is not current.)

Purpose. Can you determine why the information is on the web? Does the site provide information, give explanations, persuade, publicize, sell products, or entertain? Sometimes the URL will give you a clue. Part of the URL contains a function indicator, such as .*gov* or .*com*, which indicates the purpose of a website:

.edu or .gov	Provides factual information and explanations
.com	Promotes and sells products, or provides current news and information
.org	Influences public opinion and advocates for particular organizations or issues
.net or .com	Entertains or provides personal information
.info	Especially used to provide truly global general information; most current registrations are in the United States
.biz	Specifically for businesses
.name	Indicates the site is for individuals
.pro	Indicates professionals; attorneys, dentists, or medical doctors, for example, register their sites for easy access (For example, Janedoe.law.pro identifies a site belonging to attorney Jane Doe.)
.museums	Accredited museums worldwide
.aero	Globally recognized suffix for airlines, airports, computer reservation systems, and related industries
.coop	Identifies business cooperatives, such as credit unions and rural electric coops worldwide

5. **Comparison.** How does web information compare with other available resources? If discrepancies exist among sources, check further to find the best possible sources of information. Remember, too, that websites change quickly. You might search a specific topic and find a large number of hits and then return an hour later to find that the number has quadrupled or even been reduced significantly. Information and websites are added rapidly and changed often. In addition, a search engine may sample more or fewer individual sites at different times. Many choices are available. Pick one search engine and look for materials on your topic, and locate specific information; then, check another search engine and/or another site and determine if each has basically the same information. If so, you can probably presume that they are comparable. Then, choose the site that seems to work best for you. When you search, you will sometimes automatically be redirected to another site. At other times, you will need to search further or find another source. This is another good reason for writing down URLs and bookmarking websites: You can go back to the exact site to get further information or direct others to a specific site.

Social Media as an Information Source

Social media dominates much of our lives both in relationships and in the ways we gain and share art, ideas, and information. It also engages all learners. As a student you are likely active on social networks; use blogs, Facebook, Hulu, Instagram, LinkedIn, Pinterest, Tumblr, Twitter, or YouTube. You likely share aspects of your life and your ideas with your friends or classmates. You are able to find video clips, art, and graphics to help enhance your speeches. Google, as you know, is more than a search engine. You find documents, maps, artwork, videos, calendars, and information on every topic, ranging from finance to translations of books. It even catalogs endangered languages (and they own YouTube), leaving some of us to question what we did before Google. Be sure to check your source and think about the credibility of the information. Most forms of social media can provide information, references, and examples of the material used in speeches because they are creative and innovative and thus gain and maintain listeners' attention. Wiki and Google Docs make it easier to take messages beyond the classroom walls. If you don't already use these social

media tools, tutorials can help everyone use social media for his or her own benefi
Social media can provide powerful images and help listeners respond to your speech
Technology's influence on education is both challenging and rewarding. Be sure t
take time to think carefully about what you want to share with your listeners and
make judicious choices of information and images from social media.

George Couros, on the Connected Principals website, identifies five impacts o
social media on education. These impacts also address the use of social media in find
ing appropriate resources for your speeches:

1. It's free. (For speakers, this means unique, accessible, free information is yours a
   the click of your mouse or a touch on a trackpad.)

2. It cuts down the isolation.

3. It builds tolerance and understanding of cultural diversity.

4. It can amplify passion.

5. The world of education is (and needs to be) more open.[5]

Oral communication teachers at the University of Northern Iowa and professiona
speakers suggest that every 10 minutes of speaking time requires at least 10 hours o
research and preparation time. Each topic and speaking occasion will need a differen
amount of information, but there is no question that the more information you have
the better equipped you will be to design and develop your presentation and adapt i
to your audience. Of course, *quality* of information matters more than quantity, espe
cially when your time is limited. That's why it is important to develop your research
skills. When you become skilled at research, you will make better use of your time.

You as an Information Source

Most communication begins with you. You are one of the most valuable sources of
available information.

Your own experiences and knowledge can contribute to the content of your speech
and give you authority to speak on a subject. Abdullah is an international student
from Saudi Arabia. He is active in the Saudi student organization as well as a member
of the International Students Organization. When Abdullah was asked to speak to an
intercultural communication class about his country and culture, he naturally thought
first of his own personal experiences. He knew he had lots of good information to share
with his audience, and he also knew that sources of information that would enhance his
own knowledge were available. Moreover, he wanted to relate aspects of his country to
what his listeners could understand. Think about the effect of Abdullah's comparisons:

> Saudi Arabia is slightly more than one-fifth the size of the United States. We
> have a population of 27 million, of which 8.8 million are registered as foreign
> expatriates and an estimated 1.5 million are illegal immigrants. Unlike Iowa
> with its vast fields of grain crops and pastures, Saudi Arabia has only 1.67%
> arable land. There is some irrigation, but not nearly as much as in Iowa. Because
> our underground water resources are mostly depleted and there are no rivers,
> or lakes, my country has developed extensive seawater desalination facilities.
> As a result, Saudi Arabia has been a party to various international biodiversity,
> climate, and pollution reduction agreements.
>
> Both men and women serve in the military, and like Iowa, we have a
> National Guard as well as Air, Land, Marine, Naval, and Special military forces.
> We are not required to serve in the defense forces, but if we do, we must be
> between the ages of 18 and 49.
>
> Saudi Arabia is known as the birthplace of Islam and home to Islam's two
> holiest shrines in Mecca and Medina. The king's official title is the "Custodian
> of the Two Holy Mosques." One of the king's male descendants will always
> rule the country, as required by the country's 1992 Basic Law. Islam is the

national religion. King Abdallah has continued reform programs in the country and instituted interfaith dialogue initiatives to encourage religious tolerance on a global level.[6] He appointed moderates to various positions and appointed the first female to the cabinet. To promote increased political participation, the government held nationwide elections in September 2011 and announced that women will have the right to vote in future elections. A series of benefits to Saudi citizens was also instituted in 2011, so there are now funds to build affordable housing for all citizens; salary increases for government workers, and unemployment benefits. We also share the problem of illegal immigrants.[7]

From this, I hope you can see that Saudis have some of the same problems and concerns as citizens of the U.S.A. and, that as people, we are more similar than different.

Did Abdullah provide you with a new perspective of Saudi Arabia? While he talked about religion, he emphasized aspects of the geography, politics, and population, noting both similarities and differences. As a result, his classmates regarded the country a bit differently. He welcomed questions and answered them in order to help people learn more about his country and its similarities to the United States.

Probe your own knowledge of a subject to organize your thoughts and develop a research plan and eventually move more quickly through the research process.

The Interview as an Information Source

Of course, for most topics, your firsthand experience and knowledge will not be sufficient. The interview can be a valuable tool for gathering **expert opinion** (ideas, testimony, conclusions, or judgments of witnesses or recognized authorities) and the most up-to-date information to support your own ideas. A good interviewer can often discover information that could never be obtained through any other sources.

An interview is a carefully planned, person-to-person, question-and-answer session aimed at gathering information. An interview requires a constant exchange of questions and answers between two individuals. Both people speak and listen, as in a social conversation. In fact, social conversations constitute the most frequent interview situation because they are frequently a series of questions and answers. Let's look at the steps involved and some questions you need to ask in the interview process.

expert opinion

Ideas, testimony, conclusions, or judgments of witnesses or recognized authorities.

1. **Establish the purpose of the interview.** What do you want to know? What information will be most helpful? How can you learn what you need to know about the topic?

2. **Choose the interviewee.** From whom will you receive the best, most up-to-date information? What are that person's credentials? Is the interviewee willing to openly and honestly provide that information? Is the interviewee accessible? Should other people be interviewed? How many people should be interviewed to obtain complete and accurate information?

3. **Conduct research prior to the interview.** You need to learn as much as you can before the interview, on both the interviewee and your topic, so that you can ask intelligent questions to gain the best, most important information.

4. **Record the interview.** You should either take notes or record the interview to be able to accurately retrieve information later. Be sure to ask for permission before you record someone. Choose the method that allows the best interaction. Use the guidelines on recording interviews, below.

5. **Prepare questions.** Carefully prepare questions in advance. Be flexible during the interview to ask additional questions, to probe further, or to follow an unexpected opportunity the interviewee might provide.

6. **Organize the interview.** An interview, like a speech, usually has three identifiable segments: an opening, a body, and a closing. Organize your interview and provide a template to record the interviewee's responses.

Guidelines

Record Interviews

1. **Ask permission to take notes or to record the interview.** Also let interviewees know they will have the opportunity to check the notes or that you will send a copy of the transcribed notes.

2. **If you are recording, be sure the recording device is in good working order and test it prior to the interview.** Make sure you know how much time you have. Record as inconspicuously as you can during the interview.

3. **Maintain eye contact as much as possible.** The interviewee gives you a gift of time and information; honor that by attending as much as possible. (That's another reason for recording the interview.)

4. **Take notes throughout the interview.** Jot down those ideas that will help you remember and use the recorded information.

5. **Agree to follow any ground rules the interviewee establishes.** Be sure to offer the interviewee the opportunity to review the outline and at least his or her portion of quotations prior to presentation.

6. **Review your notes and recording as soon after the interview as possible.** You'll remember more within a short time after the interview, thus making the transcribing more beneficial.

7. **Remember to be courteous throughout the interview.** Thank the interviewee for taking time to speak with you and let the interviewee know how to contact you and when you'll be back in contact to cover your questions or theirs.

---

7. **Other considerations.** Appropriate dress, punctuality, and attentive listening contribute to a successful interview. Always give the interviewee your complete, undivided attention. If anything is unclear after you check your notes or listen to the recording, contact the interviewee for clarification as soon as possible after the interview.

8. **Use interview clips in your speech.** If your classroom is so equipped, you could either include a (short) recorded interview segment, or even a live comment from your interviewee through Adobe Connect, Skype, or your phone. Check with your instructor to determine whether this is appropriate for your classroom, and if the technology is there.

The Library as an Information Source

Not all information is digitized, and some communication professors require a variety of sources, only some of which can come from the web. Library research requires some effort, but once you understand how the system works—and most libraries use essentially the same system—you will find that the library is a beneficial resource for

Making Connections for Success

Think about the Interview

The most up-to-date information available is gained when you interview an expert or someone with firsthand knowledge of your topic. For the topics listed on the left, identify a person whom you could interview to obtain information about that topic. For each topic, identify at least two individuals who might give you unbiased information. Identify the person you would interview first and explain why. One example will get you started.

Topic	Interviewee
Memory and Your Brain	Psychology professor, especially cognitive psychology, or one whose research deals with memory; Educational psychology person who deals with memory and learning in the classroom.
Social media and their impact on global politics	
Geonomics and the future of personal health	
Sustainability and a Global Society	
Break the Poverty Cycle	

speech preparation. Libraries are user friendly, and most libraries have invested great sums of money for computerized systems that help researchers find materials quickly and easily. Each year these systems improve and become easier to use.

If you do not know how to locate material, there's no time like the present to learn. A little time invested now will save a great deal later; you will find the library is a convenient and pleasant place to locate information. (Some academic libraries have a special area where you can sip coffee or a soda and peruse sources.) Attend one of the tours or orientation sessions many libraries offer. Some provide educational packages or web-based tours with instructions on how to use the library. Principal sources of information in the library include the reference librarian, library computer-assisted search programs, and electronic catalogs.

THE LIBRARY COMPUTER SEARCH   The library provides ample sources for your supporting materials. Many universities and colleges have network systems that allow you to enter the library indexes through home or campus computers. Once you learn the appropriate log-on procedures for access to the library computer, menus guide you through the steps to find what you want. You will learn where the materials are located and whether they are available at your library.

Mediated Information Sources   College libraries have access to an online database of current periodicals: newspapers, magazines, newsletters, transcripts, and wire information. Your library may also subscribe to LexisNexis, an online newspaper service that provides the most current information available. In many cases, you can access LexisNexis and read the next morning's news from another part of the world. Most libraries have an ERIC (Educational Research Information Clearinghouse) database as well. ERIC is called the world's largest digital library of education literature and provides access to reviewed convention papers and a source of the most up-to-date research findings, as well as opinion pieces by experts in their fields. Electronic databases for government documents and a variety of other information sources are also included. Check your library website to see what's available. The *refereed* electronic database material is a credible source for supporting material. When searching an electronic database, you need to determine key words and phrases for your search before you begin so you can maximize your time and effort. Check the options for each; but, generally, the word *and* is used as a connector between key words. This allows the database to search the available materials for the information you need. Complete directions for searches are provided by your library or may be found on the screen where your search begins.

The most common Internet search is the topic-based search. When you identify a general topic (e.g., computers, health issues, or communication), you can access information about all aspects of that topic. You may, however, receive too many responses to your query and may need to narrow your topic to find responses you can easily peruse. Each search engine has a tutorial to help you get started.

When you find information on the web, be sure to write down the specific bibliographic information (the URL, or uniform resource locator, or address; date accessed; page number; and author or producer), print the information, save it on a disk or drive, or bookmark it. If you create a bookmark, you also need to save it on the hard drive or on a disk. Many campus computer labs do not allow users to save information, or it may be saved only for a short period of time. In many cases, you will not be able to save the URL, so be sure to print at least the first page with the URL or write it down so you can find it later, as Internet sites change frequently. You're more likely to retrieve exact pages if you have specific information. As always, evaluate the value and credibility of all sources and information.

The Reference Department   Most library research begins in the reference department. Here you will find sources for specific subject areas such as dictionaries, almanacs, biographical aids, encyclopedias, yearbooks, atlases, bibliographies, indexes, and guides to periodical literature. Many are available online. If you are uncertain about what to use or how to use these materials, ask a librarian.

Specialized indexes are available for particular subjects, such as agriculture and natural resources, business and economics, statistics, biology and life sciences, computers, education, and history. A popular index is the *Readers' Guide to Periodical Literature.* This source provides information from popular periodicals. Issues of the guide, published semimonthly or monthly, are available in both print copy and as an electronic database.

Because magazines, research journals, and newspapers have the most recently available information on a subject, they are the most often used print resources for speech writing. If you want to know the latest opinions and trends on almost any social, political, or economic issue, weekly magazines and newspapers will probably be your best resources.

When you seek current research or classic studies, journals published by professional organizations (e.g., National Communication Association, American Psychological Association) will provide the best information.

If you do not know what your library has to offer, take time to learn about it. The search for knowledge is never easy, but thought and preparation will help you find ample information about almost any speech topic.

Suggestions for Research

Good research has no shortcuts, but the process can be more enjoyable and easier no matter what sources you use. Here are several suggestions:

1. **State a clear purpose before you start the research.** Your search is easier when you know what you want to find. If your speech is to persuade your audience that breakfast is the most important meal of the day, the key word is *breakfast.* Begin your search with that term but also look at *health, nutrition,* or *healthy lifestyles.* Consider all possible areas of research in advance to keep your research productive and efficient.

2. **Begin your research early.** It takes time to find appropriate materials, therefore, start your research as soon as possible. If you wait until the last minute, you might discover that needed materials are unavailable or it takes longer to find them than you anticipated.

3. **Use computer searches when possible.** The computer is one of the simplest means of obtaining the largest number of sources on any topic. If you are unfamiliar with your library's computer system, ask for help. Librarians gladly help find what you need.

4. **Maintain a bibliography of sources.** As you find sources on the computer, in electronic catalogs, in electronic databases, and in periodical guides, copy them in the same form into a computer file or onto a sheet of paper or index cards (3 x 5 inch or 4 x 6 inch). Index cards are an advantage because you can sort them quickly, either alphabetically or by importance to the speech (your computer files also categorize information). List each item separately and note its importance to the presentation. This may seem tedious and time consuming, but if you fail to record something and need it later, it's much easier than starting all over because you cannot find the original. Keying and saving this information into computer files also helps you stay organized and saves time in the long run. If you cannot save your files on the library computers, type the information into an email and send it to yourself.

5. **Add to your information base with appropriate mediated sources.** Refereed material examined by experts in the field is always best to have. There are many mediated sources that can add immeasurably to your data collection. We often recommend viewing TED Talks, archived news programs, and documentaries

Figure 8.1 Sample Note Cards

Note taking, if done accurately and completely, can save you a great deal of time and effort. It is always best to take plenty of notes and to record the sources of the notes correctly.

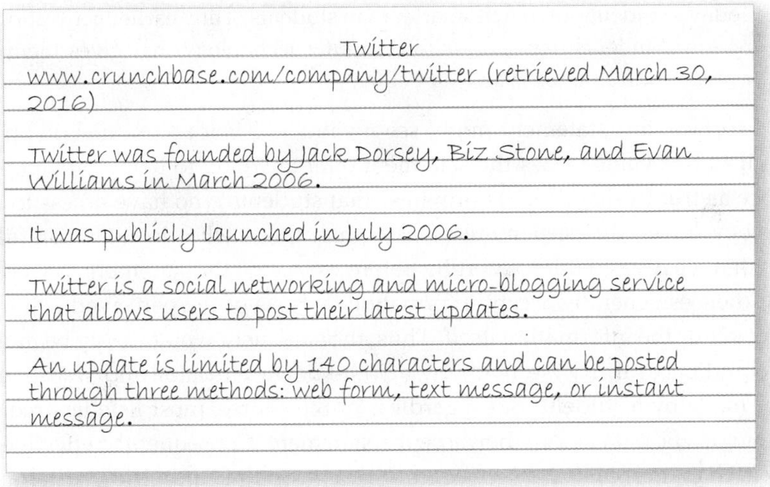

Twitter
www.crunchbase.com/company/twitter (retrieved March 30, 2016)

Twitter was founded by Jack Dorsey, Biz Stone, and Evan Williams in March 2006.

It was publicly launched in July 2006.

Twitter is a social networking and micro-blogging service that allows users to post their latest updates.

An update is limited by 140 characters and can be posted through three methods: web form, text message, or instant message.

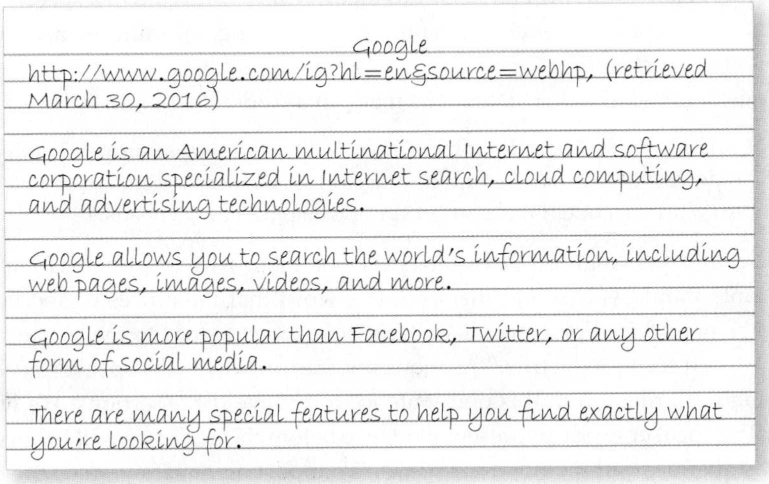

Google
http://www.google.com/ig?hl=en&source=webhp, (retrieved March 30, 2016)

Google is an American multinational Internet and software corporation specialized in Internet search, cloud computing, and advertising technologies.

Google allows you to search the world's information, including web pages, images, videos, and more.

Google is more popular than Facebook, Twitter, or any other form of social media.

There are many special features to help you find exactly what you're looking for.

as sources to at least begin to get a sense of the information available. Mediated sources often provide unique perspectives.

6. **Take notes.** Efficient and accurate note taking is a must. Once you locate information, either record it by hand or photocopy it for later use. Whether you quote a statement verbatim, summarize it, or paraphrase it, record the original information accurately and completely. Take ample notes and always make sure the source is fully and accurately indicated, as in the sample note cards in Figure 8.1. Nothing is more frustrating than information you cannot use because you don't know the source and cannot return to it for additional information. The more information you record, the better. You should always have more than you need to write your speech.

Use Research to Support and Clarify Ideas

8.3   **Differentiate** among the four types of materials to support and clarify your ideas.

More than 2,000 years ago, the famous Greek scholar Aristotle wrote that every speech has essentially two parts: a statement and its proof. Aristotle's description is still valid today, even in presentations and informal speaking situations, if we wish to be competent communicators. How a speaker clarifies and supports ideas determines the quality of the speech. The supporting material provides the *evidence* speakers need to back up or confirm their ideas. Consider the following statement:

> Today's students are much smarter than students of any earlier generation. The reason? Students have access to computer technology that gives them more available information than ever before.

On the surface, this statement might seem valid, but is it accurate? Will an audience accept it at face value? Does the statement offer any data to help you accept the first sentence as true? What proof is provided that students who have access to computer technology have advanced more quickly than those who do not? Careful analysis shows that we need to think carefully before we accept the statement as credible.

Audiences generally accept information because of the perceived believability of the speaker or the information itself. Thus, the statement would likely be more acceptable to audiences if it were made by a well-known educator and researcher than if it were made by a student. But regardless of the source, most listeners require some proof or specific data before they accept a statement. Consequently, effective speakers justify each main idea in their speeches with a variety of supporting materials.

Evidence offers support and clarifies ideas; it also brings life to a speech. Evidence makes the content of a speech appealing, vivid, exciting, meaningful, acceptable, and more useful to listeners.

Consider the following statements made in a student's speech:

> Colleges and Universities offer numerous free or low-cost support services for students with disabilities and the offices of special services should be one of the first places a student looks to get specific help for special needs.

Is this reliable information? Does the speaker explain why this information might be important? Would you accept the speaker's word that the offices of special services should be one of the first places a student looks to get help? On the surface, one may say, "Yes, that seems to be true." As they now read, however, the speaker does not give us enough information in this one sentence to believe the assertions. We want more proof. The speaker needs to present evidence before the audience will believe this.

The quantity and quality of a speaker's supporting materials, plus the speaker's ability to use them correctly, make the difference between a mediocre speech and a

Making Connections for Success

Find Web Information Sources

Through her part-time job in the campus student disabilities office, Sloan has learned a great deal about the services provided but felt that many of her classmates were unaware of what her office does to help others. She chose to talk about the available services for her informative speech.

She found helpful support information in the pamphlets in her office, and interviewed her supervisors to get additional information, but she wanted to provide something that applied to people with disabilities everywhere in the United States. Her first step was searching the web for federal laws governing requirements in educational institutions. A Google search gave her nearly 87 million results in seconds. The first listing was the Disability Support Services of the Virginia Commonwealth University; much later in the list was the

U.S. Department of Education Office for Civil Rights. Here Sloan obtained information about the laws and services, and subsequent results gave her insights into other colleges and universities. She was quickly certain she could find enough information for her 5- to 7-minute speech based on a variety of sources, including accurate web information.

1. How has Sloan's approach to her topic followed the suggestions made in this chapter?

2. How reliable are her sources so far?

3. Do her sources seem to meet the criteria for good sources?

4. What other questions might Sloan ask in a Google search to get additional information?

5. What other sources might Sloan consult?

good one. In this section, we focus on the basic kinds of supporting and clarifying materials used in speeches: testimony, examples, definitions, and statistics.

Testimony

The opinions or conclusions of witnesses or recognized authorities are referred to as **testimony**. Speakers use testimony to support or reinforce points they want their audiences to accept. The value of the testimony is related both to the listeners' opinion of its acceptability and to the speaker who presents it.

The use of testimony usually adds trustworthiness to what a speaker says—a necessity for all speakers who are not yet established as experts on their chosen speech topic. The speaker's own experience can be an excellent form of testimony, as in the previous example. When the speaker's reputation and experience are insufficient, however, the use of a recognized and trusted authority can be invaluable in gaining listeners' acceptance.

Testimony can either support or clarify material or both. Here is an example of testimony that does both:

> Are there issues in your community about which you have strong feelings? In what activities do you participate to address those issues? I've always admired people who give of their time as well as other resources to help those less fortunate, so I reflected on issues in my community. This year, Habitat for Humanity was building a house for a family of four who lost everything in a fire that demolished their home, garage, and vehicles. The family was helped by the Red Cross and the Salvation Army, but the biggest donors were those who helped them with cleanup of their destroyed property and the building of a new house on that lot. I stopped at the house-in-progress and found the supervisor of the project and volunteered my services.
>
> The family members were all on site doing their share, too. I found the experience to be truly inspirational. I'm glad I chose to work on this particular project. We never know when we might be in a position to need the kind of help this family did. It helped me feel that I had "paid it forward" and actually learned a few things about myself as well as some useful construction practices.

The speaker uses testimony and personal experience to help make a point about the importance of civic engagement.

Testimony can be either quoted directly or paraphrased. Paraphrasing is an effective method of condensing a long text or clarifying a technical passage. Sometimes audience members tune out speakers who use long and complex quotations. Restating long quotations in your own words helps to make the words of the source fit the tone of your speech. If you paraphrase, though, do not violate the meaning of the original statement.

Certain statements are so well phrased they cannot be stated any better. An example is the forceful and unforgettable statement made by John F. Kennedy in his 1961 presidential inaugural address: "Ask not what your country can do for you; ask what you can do for your country." Always quote such statements word for word. Misquoting someone can be embarrassing, but even worse, it can destroy your credibility. Double-check every quotation for accuracy and source and never use a quotation out of context.

Testimony should meet two essential tests: The person whose words are cited must be qualified by virtue of skills, training, expertise, recognition, and reputation; and the expert's opinion must be acceptable and believable to your listeners.

The person you quote should be a qualified authority on the subject. For example, an athlete's endorsement of tennis shoes and a movie star's endorsement of cosmetics are fairly believable because they use

testimony
Opinions or conclusions of witnesses or recognized authorities.

The value of testimony is related both to the listener's opinion of the acceptability of the message and to the credibility of the speaker who presents it. Tennis star Venus Williams is a credible spokesperson for Reebok, but she might not be a qualified authority on other subjects.

Making Connections for Success

The Last Lecture

Colleges and universities often hold a "last lecture" series in which professors are invited to present the lecture they would give if it were their last one. Randy Pausch, a popular 47-year-old computer science professor at Carnegie Mellon Institute in Pittsburgh, did, indeed give his last lecture. Pausch was diagnosed with pancreatic cancer and given only a few months to live. He had three children less than 8 years of age and wanted to leave them and his academic family something to remember. His final farewell, "Really Achieving Your Childhood Dreams," may be found on YouTube and across the web.

Go to the YouTube site and listen to at least a portion of Dr. Pausch's speech (the full speech runs about 76 minutes).

1. What, if anything, makes the speech compelling (beyond the obvious emotional appeal of listening to someone who knows he's dying)?
2. Why did Pausch eliminate certain topics?
3. Why did he choose the topics he did?
4. How does he support his ideas?
5. What did you learn about making a speech from this speech?

Randy Pausch's "Last Lecture" was a compelling speech that went viral very quickly after the presentation (and later became a book). He used personal experience, examples, and testimony to make compelling points.

such products in their work. But when celebrities advertise products completely unrelated to their area of expertise, their opinions become less believable. Avoid using names solely because someone is well known. The best testimony comes from a person whose knowledge and experience are related to the topic and who is recognized by your listeners.

For maximum credibility, testimony should also come from objective sources. The objectivity and neutrality of authorities are particularly important when your subject is controversial. For example, in trying to persuade an audience that today's automobiles are more fuel-efficient than those of a decade ago, it is more convincing to quote the American Automobile Association than the president of an automotive company. Listeners tend to be suspicious of opinions from a biased or self-interested source.

Examples

example

A simple, representative incident or model that clarifies a point.

An **example** is a simple, representative incident or model that clarifies a point. Examples are useful when you present complex information to listeners who are unfamiliar with a topic and when your purpose is to inform or instruct. Brief examples, illustrations, and analogies are three kinds of examples that help clarify information for an audience.

brief example

A specific instance that is used to introduce a topic, drive home a point, or create a desired response.

BRIEF EXAMPLES   A **brief example** is a specific instance used to introduce a topic, drive home a point, or create a desired impression.

A series of brief examples can also be used to create a desired impression:

> "Program change" is the label given to academic and departmental changes at many colleges and universities. In our university, these program changes usually only happen when a department hosting the program determines the program is no longer viable. However, an administrator determined program cuts based on the numbers of graduating majors in the programs and ignored

the other factors such as liberal arts core requirements certain programs met, and the number of other majors that depend on those programs so students complete their degrees in a timely fashion. The administrator then looked at only one aspect of the programs, the bottom line—the small number of majors graduating each year—used a budget crisis as the reason to close down programs and lay off faculty. Administrators used these guidelines to identify nearly 80 programs to be dropped, and approximately 50 faculty members were given notice of their "early separation" from the university because of the "budget crisis," for which no factual data was presented except that these programs "had low numbers of graduates each year."

ILLUSTRATIONS   An **illustration**, or extended example, is a narrative, case history, or anecdote that is striking and memorable. Illustrations often exemplify concepts, conditions, or circumstances, or they demonstrate findings. If an example refers to a single item or event, it is an illustration. Because illustrations offer more detail than brief examples, they are useful in establishing proof.

> **illustration**
>
> An extended example, narrative, case history, or anecdote that is striking and memorable.

An illustration lends depth to and explains the point a speaker is trying to make. It also gives the information more meaning. An illustration may be either factual or hypothetical. A **factual illustration** tells what actually happened; a **hypothetical illustration** tells what *could* happen, given a specific set of circumstances.

> **factual illustration**
>
> A report of something that exists or actually happened.

> **hypothetical illustration**
>
> A report of something that could happen, given a specific set of circumstances.

A hypothetical illustration, because it is speculative, asks listeners to use their imaginations. Such examples are often short stories that relate to a general principle or concept. The following hypothetical example helped students envision how to use their voices to express anger, concern, and sadness when delivering an emotional speech:

> What if a "budget crisis" occurs, and your college decides to cut costs and save money by eliminating programs and reducing faculty? When administrators announce program cuts and department closings, you and other students are concerned about how you'll complete all requirements and graduate. Let's say your major is "leadership studies" and the offering for majors and minors will no longer be in place after June 30. Administrators on your campus don't seem to be concerned about your future, so you organize a campaign to make them aware of the importance of the program for many students, not just majors. Your goal is to raise awareness of the dilemma of cutting courses and programs when people need those classes to graduate. Among the actions your group plans are sit-ins, sleep-ins, press releases, press conferences, and a daily rally with speakers providing factual data for a week.

This hypothetical illustration demonstrates that people involved in serious situations must use their voices to make their points. The speech to everyone attending the sit-ins, sleep-ins, and daily rallies must have vivid, forceful, convincing, and highly emotional facts and supporting materials.

The use of a hypothetical illustration can be particularly effective when it involves the listeners. The illustration should create a vivid picture in listeners' minds. The more realistic the situation, the more likely it is that the listeners will become involved. A speaker should always specify whether an illustration is factual or hypothetical.

ANALOGIES   An **analogy** is a comparison of two things that are similar in certain essential characteristics. Analogies explain or prove the unknown by comparing it to the known.

> **analogy**
>
> A comparison of two things that are similar in certain essential characteristics.

Analogies are of two kinds. A **figurative analogy** draws comparisons between things in different categories. For example, in her description of the immigration experience in Postville, Iowa, a student said that in the past, Postville was a "melting pot," an immigration pattern in which new cultures blend with the dominant culture. The immigration experience was a "tossed salad," in which newcomers keep their own cultural practices and do not try to blend in.[8]

> **figurative analogy**
>
> A comparison of things in different categories.

Guidelines
Use Examples

1. **Use factual examples to add authenticity to your presentation.** Factual examples build on the basic information presented and add credibility to both you and your speech.

2. **Use realistic examples that relate directly to you~~r~~ discussion.** If you try to generalize from unusual or ra~~re~~ situations, you risk undermining credibility.

3. **Use authentic, accurate, and verifiable examples.** Alway~~s~~ give credit to the source so your listeners can verify it.

literal analogy

A comparison of members of the same category.

A **literal analogy** is a comparison of members of the same category and make~~s~~ a simple comparison—for example, two majors (communication and English), tw~~o~~ search engines (GoodSearch and Google), or two genres of music (classical an~~d~~ country).

Most topics offer opportunities to use analogies. Figurative analogies make idea~~s~~ vivid and clear, whereas literal analogies supply evidence to support points. Analogie~~s~~ are effective, efficient, and creative means of supporting and clarifying information.

Definitions

You must define all unfamiliar words and concepts, especially technical terms, if yo~~u~~ want listeners to understand and accept your speech. Nothing is more frustrating t~~o~~ listeners than a speaker who uses terminology they do not understand. In most cases~~,~~ it is better to offer too much explanation than too little. Do not, however, patronize your audience by explaining the obvious. You can use several different kinds of definitions to keep the attention of your audience. For example, "Axiology is defined as a~~ ~~branch of philosophical study dealing with values and value orientations. Theorists cite axiology when they want to make sure readers understand that their own personal values influence the way they conduct research to build theories."[9] This information explains what axiology is and what it does.

logical definition

A definition consisting of a term's dictionary definition and the characteristics that distinguish the term from other members of the same category.

A **logical definition**, the most common form, usually contains two parts, a term's dictionary definition and the characteristics that distinguish the term from other items in the same category.

operational definition

A definition that explains how an object or concept works or lists the steps that make up a process.

An **operational definition** explains how an object or concept works, gives the steps that make up a process, or states how conceptual terms are measured. Here's an example:

> A student who has 30 or more hours of credit with a grade point average of 2.80 (on a 4.0 scale) in the major prerequisites will be admitted as a student in good standing in most campus majors.

definition by example

Clarifying a term, not by describing it or giving its meaning but by mentioning or showing an example of it.

A **definition by example** clarifies a term not by describing it or giving its meaning but by mentioning or showing an example of it.

> Business people talk about "lean strategies" in the workplace. By this, they mean anything we can do to make the workplace a better place for everyone without making it a worse place for anyone.

Statistics

statistics

Numerical data that show relationships or summarize or interpret many instances.

Numerical data that show relationships or summarize or interpret many instances are known as **statistics**. Every day we are confronted with numerical analyses. "UNICEF reports there are more than 210 million orphans in the world today with 86 million in India, 44 million in Africa, 10 million in Mexico. Further, UNICEF says 35,000 children die every day from hunger and malnutrition."[10] Although statistics can be interesting or even compelling, they can also be confusing and difficult to interpret.

Guidelines

Use Definitions

1. **Define a term or concept whenever you suspect that your audience might not understand what you mean.** You should also define terms or concepts when multiple interpretations are possible.

2. **Keep definitions short and to the point.** Do not make your explanation more complex than necessary.

3. **Use clear and concise language your audience can easily understand.** Make your definitions come alive for your audience by providing examples.

Statistics enable speakers to summarize a large number of data rapidly, to analyze specific occurrences or instances, to isolate trends, and to calculate probabilities of future events. They are used to clarify and support a speaker's position. For example, consider these two statements:

> Many children around the world will be orphaned by AIDS.[11]

> UNICEF estimates that a child is orphaned by AIDS at the rate of one every 14 seconds. This disease weakens whole nations. We risk losing the next generation.[12]

The first statement is broad and possibly misleading. The second cites a specific cause and numbers and gives listeners a clearer view of the effect of AIDS on children and on nations. The second statement also refers to a current source to add credence to the data. Statistics can be used to emphasize the magnitude of a problem, as seen in the following example:

> By the year 2000, the HIV/AIDS crisis created more than 13 million orphans worldwide. More than 90 percent live in sub-Saharan Africa.[13]

Statistics can also be informative:

> AIDS also impacts the economic progress of developing countries as it claims teachers, doctors, and other specialist human resources. In 1999 alone, an estimated 860,000 children lost their teachers to AIDS in sub-Saharan Africa.[14]

Four guidelines will help make the most of the statistics you've gathered:

1. **Make sure the statistics you present in your speech are from reliable and neutral, credible sources.** The motives of the source of any statistics must be carefully assessed. For example, if you heard two sets of data on fuel economy per gallon of gasoline—one prepared by Ford Motor Company and the other by the Environmental Protection Agency—which would you expect to be more reliable? Although Ford's data may be accurate, listeners would tend to believe the data are biased. It is to a speaker's advantage, therefore, to use the more neutral source: the Environmental Protection Agency.

   It can be difficult to identify the *most* neutral source. For example, whose statistics would you use if you wished to inform your audience about the number of orphans in Africa? Mission One Million is a faith-based organization established in October 2003 to meet the needs of orphaned and abandoned children; to expand Christianity by supporting and raising up missions; and to plan churches in the least evangelized, most populated, and poorest third world countries.[15]

   UNICEF estimates there are over 132 million orphans in sub-Saharan Africa, Asia, Latin America, and the Caribbean. (UNICEF is the driving force that helps build a world in which the rights of every child are realized. This organization has the global authority to influence decision makers and a variety of partners at the grassroots level to turn most innovations into reality to help children.)[16]

Movie and theatre celebrity Hugh Jackman uses his name and fame for various causes and charities. He is a spokesperson for World Vision and World Wide Orphans and regularly makes speeches and travels to specific locations to draw attention to the world's problems. You can hear him speak about adoption, global poverty, hunger, saving the planet, or promoting fair trade.

Numbers may differ, but the goals are similar; thus, the choice is debatable unless you intend to take a position on the issue. Remember, statistics can be used in many different ways and can thus influence interpretations and outcomes.

2. **Take time to explain the statistics you use.** Interpret and relate your statistics to your listeners. Numbers, by themselves, have little meaning until you explain them. Consider the following use of statistics:

> It is estimated that more than 20 million children under the age of 15 living in the sub-Saharan African desert have been robbed of one or both parents by HIV/AIDS. The number of orphans will grow exponentially due to the large number of HIV/AIDS cases already diagnosed. Nearly one-fourth (25%) of the population of children under 15 in 11 sub-Saharan African countries will be orphaned by HIV/AIDS.[17]

This explanation provides meaningful statistics by clearly identifying specific numbers and percentages.

When using data that listeners may have difficulty understanding or visualizing, try to provide appropriate comparisons to make the data more meaningful.

3. **Use statistics sparingly.** Statistics are difficult to comprehend. If you use too many, you run the risk of boring or confusing your audience. Use statistics only when necessary and make sure they are easy to understand. The following example would be difficult for even the most attentive listener to comprehend:

> The most immediate needs households with orphans cannot meet in the Mwanza region of the United Republic of Tanzania include the following: school materials, 41%; health care expenses, 23%; food, 21%; clothes, 11%; and other, 4%.

It would be much easier to understand if the data were presented in pie charts, or verbally, as follows:

> Of the most immediate needs that households with orphans cannot meet in the Mwanza region of the United Republic of Tanzania are three major needs: More than 40 percent cannot supply school materials, almost one-quarter of the homes cannot provide health care expenses, and just over one-fifth of the homes cannot provide adequate food for these orphans.[18]

4. **Round off large numbers when possible.** Listeners more readily understand and remember uncomplicated figures. It's easier to recall that Warren Buffett pledged approximately 10 million Berkshire Hathaway shares, spread over multiple years with annual contributions, to the Bill and Melinda Gates Foundation. The Gates Foundation received 5 percent of the shares, worth about $500,000 in 2006, and comparable amounts in succeeding years. The minute details are difficult to remember, but it's easy to remember the rounded number of shares and their approximate worth.[19]

Guidelines

Tips for Using Statistics

1. **Make sure your statistics come from reliable, neutral sources.** Avoid biased sources such as those selling a product or promoting their own services.

2. **Use statistics sparingly.** Numbers can be compelling but they can also create a loss of interest unless used well.

3. **Take the time to explain the statistics to your listeners.** What do the numbers mean? Numbers or statistics in and of themselves have no meaning until you give them meaning in the context of your speech.

4. **Display statistics visually whenever possible.** This saves explanation time. And, it helps you remember specifics.

Figure 8.2 Visualizing Statistical Data

A chart with statistics can help summarize complex data and make ideas interesting to your audience.

SOURCE: Based on *Africa's Orphaned Generations*, Ch 2, UNICEF, http://www.unicef.org/sowc06/pdfs/africas_orphans.pdf,retrieved March 31, 2012.

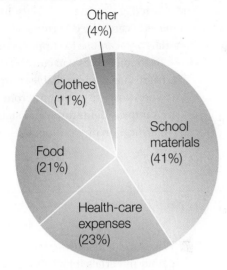

The Most Immediate Needs That Households with Orphans Cannot Meet

UNICEF and other care-giving organizations provide food, water, clothing, school materials, and other necessary supplies to the world's most needy children. According to UNICEF, in the Mwanza region of the Republic of Tanzania alone, the most immediate needs that households with orphans cannot meet include the following: 41 percent cannot provide school materials; 23 percent cannot provide health care expenses, thus causing greater numbers of children to be ill; 21 percent cannot provide adequate food; 11 percent cannot provide clothing; and 4 percent cannot provide other needs.[20]

Figure 8.2 shows how complex data can be summarized and presented in an interesting way. Note how the graphics make it easier to understand the statistics presented.

Summary

Develop a Research Plan

Objective 8.1 **Develop** a research plan to gather information and find supporting materials for your speeches.

You now will be able to build on the knowledge gained in the previous chapters when you practiced topic generation and the creation of general and specific purpose statements and a thesis for speeches.

- Begin early.
- Gather more information than you'll need.
- Think carefully about your topic: where should you go to find the best information to help you create the speech?
- Prepare a preliminary list of references.

- Be selective in choosing materials to enhance your knowledge.
- Meet your instructor's requirements for numbers and types of supporting materials.
- Take good notes and keep complete information on the sources.
- Know when to say, "Enough is enough."

Research: Gathering Information

Objective 8.2 **Identify** five principal sources of information for your speech topic.

Many excellent sources of information for developing your speeches can be found.

- The Internet provides good information, but be sure to carefully evaluate what you find on the web.

- Social media can be a good source of information, as it provides a starting point and possible examples.
- You should be your first source of information. Choose topics you like and/or that are important to you.
- The interview gives you up-to-date information about a topic from an expert on the topic.
- Mediated information databases can help you find current, relevant topics.
- The library provides great amounts of information both in hard copies and through electronic databases.
- All sources should give you reliable, current, consistent information from believable, credible persons.

Use Research to Support and Clarify Ideas

Objective 8.3 **Differentiate among the four types of materials to support and clarify your ideas.**

Once you've selected a topic, developed a research plan, and started gathering materials to support your ideas, you need to carefully determine which of the four types of materials you can use to support your main points.

- Testimony gives you current, relevant information from an expert or reliable source. You gain credibility when you use testimony from trusted sources.
- Examples, definitions, and statistics provide tangible clarification of your topic.

Discussion Starters

1. Why is it important to have a research plan? What is yours?
2. What do you need to know about a topic before you begin your research?
3. Provide three social media sources you might consult to clarify and enhance speeches.
4. What unique perspectives can electronic sources provide?
5. When is an interview a particularly appropriate method?
6. Your speech topic is "date rape." When you go to the library to do research, where should you begin?
7. When and why is the reference section a good place to gather materials for a speech?
8. Identify three good supporting and clarifying materials you've heard others use.
9. On what basis should you judge the effectiveness of a source of information to support a particular point of view?
10. As a listener, how do you feel when you hear someone using statistics in a speech?
11. Why should you evaluate a web source?

Chapter 9
Organizing and Outlining Your Speech

 ## Learning Objectives

This chapter will help you:

9.1 **Identify** ways to organize the body of your speeches.

9.2 **Organize** the introduction of your speech.

9.3 **Compose** an effective conclusion to your speech.

9.4 **Construct** outlines to help you stay organized in your presentations.

CHAPTER OUTLINE

Organize the Body of Your Speech

Organize the Introduction of Your Speech

Organize the Conclusion of Your Speech

Outline Your Speech

Making Everyday Connections

Jeffre was concerned that speeches in the classroom did not match the preparation and organization required for speeches in his workplace. He approached Dr. Johnson before class about the possibility of using other forms of organizing and outlining required for speech assignments. Dr. Johnson said, "That's a great issue, Jeffre. Let's talk about it with the whole class." When class began, she noted Jeffre's concerns and asked if others found similar situations in their workplaces. A show of hands indicated more than half the students had similar experiences. Dr. Johnson then asked students to share their experiences in speech organization in both academic and workplace situations. That discussion produced a list of characteristics of speech organizational patterns for each situation. She briefly noted the types of organizational patterns covered in class (topical, spatial, chronological, problem–solution, cause–effect, and motivated sequence), explained the importance of organization, and asked students if they saw significant differences between the workplace and academic situations in the use of any specific patterns. She also asked students to explain how different organizational methods affected the final produc[t] Dr. Johnson noted "practice in organizing and outlining for clas[s] presentation allows you to learn *how to use* patterns; onc[e] you've learned and used a variety of patterns, you can easil[y] adapt what you know to different venues. Learning and usin[g] specific organizational patterns in class provides a foundatio[n] for using other forms outside the class."

Questions to Think About

1. What do you think makes speakers appear to be organized?
2. How do you feel when you're listening to a speaker who seems disorganized?
3. What helps you *really* listen to a speaker?
4. When you speak, what do you do to help *your* listeners follow your thoughts?
5. Do you think a speaker needs to state *exactly* where she or he is going in the speech? Why or why not?

You now have two of the toughest of the speaker's jobs completed: You've chosen a topic and gathered information. The next task is to organize the information into a sequence or pattern of organization. Organization is a skill and one of the best ways to learn and apply organizational skills is in speech preparation. Although there are no *prescriptions* for success, established organizational patterns can help you learn to present material in understandable ways. The point in using specific organizational patterns for class assignments is that once you have successfully used one these organizational patterns, you can move on to other ways to construct speeches, as Jeffre and his classmates discussed in Dr. Johnson's class in the Everyday Connections feature at the beginning of the chapter.

organizing

Arranging ideas and elements into a systematic and meaningful whole.

Organizing your speech involves arranging its parts into a systematic and meaningful whole. Speeches are usually organized into three main parts: introduction, body, and conclusion. By this point, you have determined general and specific purposes and formulated a draft of your thesis statement. This work should help guide you to organize your speech. Because the body is the main part of any speech, and contains most of its content, we recommend that students begin by working on it first and then prepare the introduction and conclusion; thus, we examine the body first. Note some instructors may want you to take each part of the speech in order, so be sure to follow her/his advice.

Organize the Body of Your Speech

9.1   Identify ways to organize the body of your speeches.

body

The main content of a speech that develops the speaker's general and specific purposes.

The **body** of a speech presents the main content, and organizing the speech will help you formulate your thesis statement. To ensure a well-organized body of your speech, your content must be divided into a limited number of thoughtfully selected, connected, ordered, supported, and stated main points.

Develop the Main Points

Well-developed **main points**, the principal subdivisions of a speech, are critical to an effective thesis statement (and speech). Let's assume your purpose is to inform your audience about social media and you want to discuss its uses and effects. Your research guided you to choose a specific perspective on the topic. To determine your specific purpose and main points and to finalize the thesis for your informative speech on social media, you decide to ask and answer three questions:

main points
The principal subdivisions of a speech.

1. What are social media?
2. How have social media changed the world?
3. What do I need to know to use social media effectively?

Since you have thoroughly researched your subject, you can easily determine the main points. The following is an example of an organization with three main points:

I. Social media include web-based and mobile-based technologies that create user-generated content and interactive communication between individuals, organizations, or businesses.
II. Social media have changed every aspect of our lives, including business, education, relationships, political campaigns, and a degree of awareness of global issues.
III. Social media need to be monitored so we can be effective creators and consumers.

The body of the speech will take shape around these three main points. These points are derived from communication, media studies, sociology, and educational research. While communication professors usually recommend no more than three main points in a 5- to 7-minute speech, some topics lend themselves to four or five main points and some to only two, depending on the topic and time restraints to give your speech.

Not every piece of information you gathered constitutes a main point. Main points are broad, overarching statements that help to organize the many particulars you found through your research. In this example, "Facebook" or "Pinterest" may well be two of the subpoints of the first point, but neither probably would be a complete main point in a short speech.

RELATE MAIN POINTS, SPECIFIC PURPOSE, AND THESIS   The main points serve as the basis for the thesis statement. Together, the specific purpose and the thesis will determine the direction of the speech. Here is a persuasive thesis structured from the main points noted earlier:

SPECIFIC PURPOSE:	To persuade my audience about the impact of social media on our lives, both as creators and consumers.
THESIS:	Social media significantly affect our lives; thus, we need to be effective creators and consumers.

Here is another example of developing purpose, thesis, and main points. Let's say your purpose is to inform your listeners about cyber bullying. Your thesis statement might then be something such as:

We need to understand that social media has a downside; in fact, we need to understand cyber bullying and recognize its strong link to suicide in young people.

This thesis statement establishes three main points: the downside of social media, an explanation of cyber bullying, and the links of social media to youth suicides. Or perhaps you are assigned to present a speech that will persuade your audience to act in some specific way. From your research on social media, you know that both costs and benefits can be found, and you want your listeners to monitor children's use of Facebook and other forms of social media.

You can take numerous approaches, but remember that you ultimately want your listeners to know the benefits as well as the dangers of various forms of social media. In this speech, you are not just reporting facts; you want your listeners to *do* something. You must make a compelling argument to make them listen *and* act.

As you begin to apply your research, think about the general purpose: to persuade my listeners to understand social media. Then ask yourself, "What should my listeners know about social media?" As you generate answers, the main points of your speech will emerge. Eventually, you might determine that blogs, chat rooms, Facebook, LinkedIn, Twitter, and YouTube provide communication and connection, but there are also disadvantages. You are now ready to refine your specific purpose and state your thesis and main points:

SPECIFIC PURPOSE: To persuade my audience that Facebook, LinkedIn, Twitter, and other social media need to be monitored when children and adolescents are connected.

THESIS: Facebook, LinkedIn, Twitter, and other forms of social media keep us connected with others, but they can be used negatively and must be carefully monitored to ensure safe use.

Main Points:

  I. Facebook, LinkedIn, and Twitter are three popular forms of social media used by youths and adolescents.
 II. Social media can create harmful situations for any of us, but especially for young people.
III. Social media should be monitored for content and connections for young people.

PRESENT THE MAIN POINTS   Main points, like the specific purpose and thesis, should be carefully developed and written. They should also be specific, vivid, relevant, and parallel in structure. (We use Roman numerals to designate main points because, as you will see later, they eventually become the main elements in the speech outline.)

Be Specific   The more specific your main points, the less confusion they will create and the more meaning they will have for your audience. It can be easy to misunderstand a speaker who makes vague, over generalized statements. Each main point in a speech should be independent of the others and simple to understand. Compare the following:

Ineffective Main Point:

 I. Widespread use of social media has changed the world, is always available, and is used differently by different generations of users.

Effective Main Points:

  I. Social media have changed communication in every facet of life.
 II. Generational differences exist in the use of social media.
III. Social media, with their "always available" features, create risks of distraction and anxiety.

As you can see, the first example contains three ideas in one point, which makes it too complicated. The second example divides the three ideas into three separate points, thus making each one easier to understand.

Use Vivid Language   We cannot overemphasize the importance of language choice. When you listen to or present speeches, you become aware of words and their effects. You're already aware that the language we use for conversation and speeches (oral language) is more interesting and vital than written language. Now you need to consider how to make the best choices to help you reach your listeners. The more vivid your

Making Connections for Success

Creating Purpose and Thesis Statements

Your assignment is to create and present an 8- to 10-minute informative speech. Your instructor says the topic should be one you find important and relevant. He also suggests you choose a topic on something that has had an effect on your family and friends. As a practice activity, choose one of the following topics and write a general purpose, a specific purpose, and a thesis statement. Be prepared to share and justify your statements with your instructor and classmates.

1. Education majors are in demand
2. Create YouTube clips to promote business services
3. Distance learning provides opportunities
4. The most influential musicians
5. A topic of your own choice

---

main points, the more likely they are to create interest. Main points should be thought-provoking, attention-grabbing ideas that stand out from the supporting materials.

VIVID LANGUAGE: Apple's iBeacon may cause you to spend more on impulse purchases as retailers tempt you with digital coupons and special offers.

LESS VIVID LANGUAGE: Apps already on your phone such as Apple's iBeacon can determine where you are in a store and provide you with special offers and digital coupons just as you approach specific products and tempt you to buy things not on your list.

Vivid phrasing may be shorter or longer than less vivid language, but should not be exaggerated, because anything less than vivid, natural words may hurt the speaker's credibility. The limits of good taste and ethical considerations should be observed.

Show Relevance Main points relevant to the audience's immediate interests encourage greater involvement and empathy. For instance, instead of saying, "Air pollution has reached high levels," say, "Air pollution in our city has reached dangerously high levels." Using direct references to the audience, whenever possible increases the connections between you, what you are saying, and your audience. Audience members like to know how the speaker's subject relates to them and why they should listen.

Create Parallel Structure Main points should be expressed in parallel structure—that is, using similar grammatical patterns and wording—when possible.

Not Parallel:

I. The world's number one health risk is hunger.
II. Tuberculosis, malaria, and AIDS combined do not match the number of deaths by hunger.
III. Over 15,000 men, women, and children will die of hunger today.

Parallel:

I. Hunger is the world's number one health risk.
II. Hunger results in more deaths than tuberculosis, malaria, and AIDS combined.
III. Hunger causes the deaths of 15,000 men, women, and children each day.[1]

Parallel structure of the main points makes material easier to develop and remember. Listeners usually have only one opportunity to hear a speech; therefore, anything you can do to make the main points stand out from the rest of the content works to your benefit. In the above example, the speaker strengthens the bond with the audience by consistently focusing on the effects of hunger and beginning each main point with the word hunger.

LIMIT THE NUMBER OF MAIN POINTS   The number of main points in your speech will depend on at least three considerations.

First, the time available for most classroom speeches is limited by practical considerations. As a result, most classroom speeches have two or three points and no more than five points.

Second, the content to be covered in the speech, especially the amount and complexity of the supporting materials required for each point, affects the number of points. Try to balance the amount of time you devote to each main point. For example, if you are assigned a 5- to 7-minute speech, plan to allow no more than 2 minutes for the introduction and conclusion, distributing the remaining time equally among the main points. Of course, this is a *guideline*. It isn't always possible to exactly balance the main points and you don't want to do so. The nature of some speech topics requires that some main points be emphasized more than others, or that the introduction or conclusion be longer.

Third, an audience should be able to sort out and recall each main point. This recall is impossible if too many points are presented. Common sense tells us three points are easier to remember than five. Therefore, as a speaker, you must set reasonable expectations for both you and your listeners. If you have too many main points and a limited amount of time, you will be unable to develop each point thoroughly enough to make it clear, convincing, and memorable.

ORDER THE MAIN POINTS   Once you identify your main points, you must decide presentation order. This decision takes serious analysis, because the order determines the structure and strategy of your speech. The most effective order of presentation depends on the topic, purpose, and audience. Several basic patterns of presentation have been recommended and used over the years: time sequence (chronological), spatial, topical, problem–solution, cause–effect (or effect–cause), and motivated sequence.

time-sequence (or chronological) pattern

An order of presentation that begins at a particular point in time and continues either forward or backward.

THE TIME-SEQUENCE PATTERN   In the **time-sequence** or **chronological pattern**, the presentation begins at a particular point in time and continues either forward or backward. The key is to follow a natural time sequence and avoid jumping haphazardly from one time period to another. This pattern is especially useful for tracing the steps in a process, the relationships within a series of events, or the development of ideas. Certain topics lend themselves to the time sequence, such as: how to create a readable blog; how to reduce, reuse, and recycle; ways to create an indoor garden in your residence hall room; tips to create an effective website. Here is an example of a time sequence that moves forward from a specific time point.

Main Points:

   I. The first step in establishing an effective website is to acquire a domain name.
  II. The second step is to choose a web host.
 III. The third step is to create an attractive website.

A reverse-order sequence begins at a specific time period and works chronologically backward. For example, a speech discussing citizens' concerns about world hunger, organized in reverse-order time sequence, could be as follows:

   I. The number of the world's hungry people continues to rise.
  II. During the first decade of the 21st century humanitarians and activists began serious efforts to eliminate world hunger.
 III. Hunger and malnutrition were recognized as a major global issue from the 1930s forward.[2]
 IV. U.S. president Herbert Hoover and Norman Borlaug began massive efforts to find solutions to provide food for the world's hungry people in the 1930s.

The time-sequence or chronological pattern can also be used to explain a process as well as move forward or backward to explain how historically significant issues are addressed.

The Spatial Pattern   In a **spatial pattern** of presentation, the content of a speech is organized according to relationships in space—where we can find things. This method is especially appropriate for presentations describing distances, directions, or physical surroundings. For example, a spatial pattern might be used to explain how to create a wildflower space in your yard, strategies to improve your recall of information, or how to make your dorm room more comfortable. A spatial pattern connects the relationships among all the main points. Here is an example of main points organized according to a spatial pattern:

spatial pattern
An order of presentation in which the content of a speech is organized according to relationships in space.

Main Points:

I. The Smithsonian has so many attractions you won't be able to see everything in one trip, therefore you must pick and choose the best areas for you.
II. Make your first stop the Smithsonian Castle, which houses the Smithsonian Visitors Center, for an orientation and free guides and maps.
III. To make the best use of the day, make your way from the Castle via public transportation to the National Mall in downtown DC, where 10 of its 19 museums are found.[3]
IV. Choose your favorites, consult the map, and create a route that allows you to move from one museum choice to the next in a minimum amount of time.

The Topical Pattern   According to the **topical pattern**, the main topic is divided into a series of related subtopics. Each subtopic becomes a main point in the speech, and all main points are joined to form a coherent whole. In this way, the topical pattern is a unifying structure.

topical pattern
An order of presentation in which the main topic is divided into a series of related subtopics.

We use the topical pattern when no other patterns of organization apply to the topic or purpose of a speech. The topical pattern works well for topics such as the health benefits of marijuana, what you gain from a study skills class, or the differences between language usage in papers and speeches. Here's how the topical pattern could be used to organize the main points of a speech on Earth Day:

Main Points:

I. Earth Day was created on April 22, 1970, by Wisconsin senator Gaylord Nelson to bring attention to environmental issues.
II. Earth Day has always capitalized on placing environmental concerns in the forefront of political and public consciousness.
III. Earth Day 2015 events were attended by billions of people from around the globe who spoke out on fighting climate change, planted trees, and cleaned up parks and streams.[4]

Listeners generally find a speaker easier to follow when a strong organizational pattern is provided in the speech. A coherent speech is more interesting and easier to understand.

When the topical pattern is used correctly, each main point is parallel in structure and related to the others. Because the topical pattern is versatile, it can be adapted to most speech purposes and effectively present material on a variety of topics.

Four other patterns (problem–solution, cause–effect, effect–cause, and Monroe's motivated sequence) are primarily used in persuasive speaking and will be discussed in the chapter on persuasion.

CHOOSING THE BEST PATTERN   We emphasized the importance of matching the pattern of organization to your topic, specific purpose, and thesis. You must also consider another key factor: your listeners. The savvy speaker anticipates audience

Making Connections for Success

Learn More about Organizing

Your instructor gives a homework assignment: learn more about patterns of organizing and outlining, using web information.

1. Open your browser and type in "weight loss plans," "what is Yik Yak," "medical marijuana," or a topic of your choice and determine what issues might work as main ideas for a speech.

2. You might watch the YouTube video of mind mapping's creator, Tony Buzan, explaining mind mapping[5] to see if this organizational pattern would work for you and your topic.

3. Search "Monroe's motivated sequence" to learn more about this organizational method.

4. Do a Google (or other search engine) search on "organizational speech patterns." Read one or more of the options, find a pattern you like, and create an outline of a speech for one of the three options.

5. Be prepared to discuss your outline and the strengths and weaknesses of the pattern with your classmates.

responses. Therefore, if your audience analysis indicates that important questions or objections are likely to be raised, you should arrange your main points to meet those objections. For example, if you advocate mandatory community service and are certain someone in your audience will object to mandates of any kind, you might structure your presentation as follows:

Main Points:

I. Community service allows us to create a more caring world.
II. Community service gives us a feeling of satisfaction.
III. Community service today helps establish a pattern for paying it forward.

Culture may influence the way you prefer to organize a speech. Some cultures and cocultures use alternative, but effective, organizational patterns. Many Native Americans, Africans, African Americans, Hispanics, and women, for example, use mind mapping and narratives or storytelling as a way of organizing their presentations. Some speakers effectively use a combination of one or more organizational patterns in a given speech. *Until you're confident* in your ability to organize your thoughts, you may wish to use one primary organizational pattern in any given speech and then branch out to other patterns once you are comfortable about speaking.

Whatever organizational pattern you choose, you can make that pattern work for you when you make the speech compelling. For example, **mind mapping**[6] is an organizational strategy where you visually "map out" how various ideas connect. In a mind map, one starts in the center with a word or symbol and then writes down all the things that come to mind about that word or topic (see Figure 9.1). If you were mind mapping a social media speech, you might begin with a circle labeled "social media" and then identify the aspects of social media that should be considered all around that circle. Another strategy identified above is **narrative** or **storytelling**. A story in a speech doesn't have to be long and involved and need not follow the guidelines for traditional stories. Instead, it is an account that brings more enthusiasm, realism, or even passion to the topic. Think about a speech or class lecture you found enjoyable. What did the speaker do? Why was it enjoyable? For example, one of the authors remembers a class on the religions of the world where note taking was easy, the content was memorable, and the professor's presentations were spellbinding. His lectures may have been written on yellowed paper, but the content was anything but dry and boring. (The professor opened the notebook at the beginning of class and never looked at it again until he picked up the notebook to leave the room.)

mind mapping

A visual organizational strategy that uses words or symbols to identify the concepts and their connections to each other.

narrative or storytelling

An organizational strategy using a reporting of ideas and situations, as in a "story," but without the traditional components of a story.

Figure 9.1 Mind Mapping

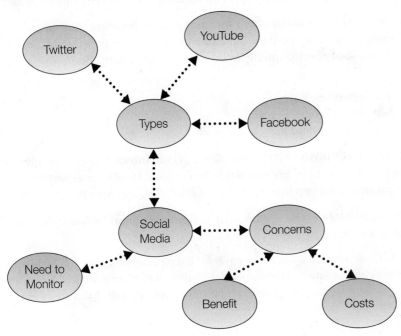

Connect the Main Points

A conversation can move from one unrelated topic to another without losing meaning or impact; but, for a speaker to communicate effectively with an audience who hears the message only once and who is not able to stop the speaker to ask questions, the thoughts in the speech must be systematically connected. The four most common connecting devices speakers use, singly or in combination, are transitions, signposts, internal previews, and internal summaries.

TRANSITIONS   Phrases and words used to link ideas are called **transitions**. They form a bridge between what has already been presented and what will be presented next. Transitions are typically used between the introduction and the body of a speech, between main ideas, between supporting materials and visual aids, and between the body and the conclusion. A transition can review previous information, preview information to come, or summarize key thoughts. Here are some typical transition statements one could make:

> Moving from Facebook to Twitter, …
> Now that I have discussed the history of the Internet, I will talk about its uses.
> Turning now to …
> The final point is …
> Another example is …
> Keep these four items I discussed in mind, as we move to this conclusion.

transition

A phrase or word used to link ideas.

SIGNPOSTS   Just as a traffic sign informs drivers about travel conditions, **signposts** are words, phrases, and short statements intended to let the audience know what is ahead. Here are some typical signposts:

> First, let me explain …
> As you look at this figure …
> My second point is …
> The next point …
> To recap …
> Finally …

signpost

A word, phrase, or short statement that indicates to an audience the direction a speaker will take next.

Questions can also be used as signposts:

> Why are there so many people on the reduced lunch fee program?
> How many people are affected by a minimum wage increase?

What are differences between spoken and written language?
How can we responsibly respond to the large number of orphans in the world?

Such questions draw the audience's attention to a forthcoming answer.

A signpost not only prepares an audience for what to expect next but also aler
the audience that the upcoming information is important. Some examples are a
follows:

The bottom line is …
Solutions we could try are …
One thing you need to recognize is …

internal preview

Short statements that give advance warning, or a preview, of the point(s) to be covered.

internal summary

A short review statement given at the end of a main point.

INTERNAL PREVIEWS Short statements called **internal previews** give advanc
warning, or a preview, of the point(s) to be covered. Here is an example: "Next we'l
look at possible solutions to the problem of flawed budget priorities."

INTERNAL SUMMARIES An **internal summary** is a short review statement given a
the end of a main point. Here is an example:

Let's summarize what we've covered. Eating disorders have the highest mortality rate of any mental illness. Eating disorders affect 8 million Americans—
7 million women and 1 million men. Furthermore, eating disorders are often
untreated.[7]

Support the Main Points

Main points by themselves are nothing more than assertions. It is crucial that each
main point be supported and the support be relevant and logically organized. The
body of a speech expands to outline form, where the main points are followed by subpoints, which in turn may be broken into further supporting points:

I. There are more than 1 billion orphans in the world.
   A. Children over the age of 10 are *unlikely* to be adopted.
      1. Prospective parents want babies or toddlers.
      2. Children with disabilities are viewed as high-risk, high-maintenance
         children.
   B. All children need a loving home.
II. The total number of orphans in sub-Saharan Africa is greater than the total num-
    ber of children in Denmark, Ireland, Norway, Canada, and Sweden.
    A. There are currently an estimated 53.1 million orphans in sub-Saharan Africa.
    B. An estimated 12 percent of all children in sub-Saharan Africa are orphans.[8]

Supporting materials should be clearly related to the specific purpose, thesis, and
main points of the speech.

Organize the Introduction of Your Speech

9.2 Organize the introduction of your speech.

introduction

Opening statements that orient the audience to the subject and motivate them to listen.

Experienced speakers often develop their introductions after, not before, they finish the
body of the speech (because they now know exactly what will be covered). An **introduction** includes opening statements that serve two important functions: motivating the
audience to listen and orienting them to the subject. Therefore, your introduction should
prepare the audience for the main ideas of your speech by setting the stage for the topic.

Your introduction should be based on the information you gathered in your audience analysis. If your analysis was accurate and thorough, you should have a pretty

good understanding of your audience's frame of reference and how it might differ from your own. Your introduction should meet three goals: orient the audience to the topic, motivate the audience to listen, and forecast (preview) the main points.

Orient the Audience to the Topic

Decide how much background information to provide on the basis of what your audience knows or does not know about your subject. This is the appropriate time to gain attention, state your specific purpose and thesis statement, and define terms that are essential to understanding the speech.

Several approaches can be used to gain attention and arouse the interest of your audience, such as referring to the subject or occasion, using personal references or narratives, asking rhetorical questions, presenting a startling statement, using humor, or incorporating quotations. You should choose these devices carefully to fit the audience, occasion, and context. None is *always* effective, and each has limitations. For example, using humor to focus your listeners' attention on a serious topic such as disease would not be effective. Consider the overall speech as you choose your approach because all parts of the speech must fit together well to achieve your desired purpose.

REFER TO THE SUBJECT OR OCCASION You may be asked to speak on a special occasion, such as a holiday, founders' day, graduation, or an anniversary. Here is a sample attention-getter related to an occasion:

> Dr. Galvin has always been my role model for her teaching, research, and service. When asked for information, she readily gives it. When someone needs a helping hand, she's one of the first volunteers. When you look in a dictionary for "service to the discipline of communication," you'll see her picture. It gives me great pleasure to present this distinguished service award to Dr. Kathleen Galvin.

USE PERSONAL REFERENCES OR NARRATIVES Whenever you can relate your own experience to a speech, do so. Personal experiences make your speech more meaningful to your audience and show them that you know your subject. Here's how a speaker used a personal experience to introduce a speech on why she didn't eat chocolate.

> I never wanted to eat chocolate. My friends would always ask for chocolate and offer to share with me, but I wasn't interested. I was taught to eat what was put before me, so when I went to a birthday party and was served chocolate cake with chocolate ice cream I ate it and immediately became violently ill. I was allergic to chocolate. No wonder it never held any appeal for me.

ASK RHETORICAL QUESTIONS A rhetorical question is a question for which no answer is expected. Asking rhetorical questions in an introduction usually encourages an audience to become intellectually involved. (Asking real questions is also an effective way to get your audience interested and involved in the speech, but it is important to let the audience know that you expect answers from them when asking this type of question.) Such questions can also be used to create suspense. Here's one example of a rhetorical question used to involve the audience:

> Have you ever wished you could just eat anything you like, whenever you like? If so, you're in the majority of citizens in the United States.

PRESENT A STARTLING STATEMENT A startling statement can be used when you want to shock or surprise your audience. Startling statements are extremely effective at getting attention,

Nobel Prize–winning author Toni Morrison is a world-renowned novelist who has many resources she can call on to arouse the interest of an audience. She might refer to the subject or occasion, tell stories, use personal and biographical information, present a startling statement, use humor, read passages from her work, or ask rhetorical questions to get her audience's attention.

The New York Public Library

as shown by this example: "The harsh reality is this: Party time is over!" Startling stories can also be used to grab your audience's attention:

> There may be a time bomb within your body. Really. It may be ticking away unmercifully, and unless you recognize the symptoms and change your lifestyle, that time bomb may cause you to have serious health problems and even affect the length of your life. The time bomb within is stress. "We're all under stress," according to Drs. Bruce McEwen and George Chrousos. And, when we're stressed, our bodies react with a "fight-or-flight" response. The body pumps out adrenaline, increasing heart rate and blood pressure (and readying us to fight), and sending more blood to our muscles (so we can flee).[9]

USE HUMOR A funny story, a relevant joke, or a humorous approach not only gains the attention of your audience but also relaxes them. Stories and jokes must be tied to the content of the speech and not offered simply for the sake of humor. One speaker began her talk as follows:

> An airline pilot wrote that on this particular flight he had hammered his plane into the runway really hard. The airline had a policy that required the first officer to stand at the door while the passengers exited, give a smile, and a "Thanks for flying XYZ airline."
>
> He said that in light of his bad landing, he had a hard time looking the passengers in the eye, thinking that someone would have a smart comment, but no one seemed annoyed.
>
> Finally, everyone had gotten off except for one [elderly] woman walking with a cane. She approached and asked, conspiratorially, "Sonny, mind if I ask you a question?"
>
> "Why no Ma'am, what is it?"
>
> "Did we land or were we shot down?"[10]
>
> You may wonder why I'm beginning my speech with a joke, but the answer is easy. My mother and grandmother always told me, "Laughter is the best medicine. It will cure whatever ails you." And, the longer I live, the wiser those words seem to be. Laughter is strong medicine for the mind and body. Research shows that laughter is a powerful antidote to stress, pain, and conflict. Nothing works faster or more dependably to bring your mind and body back into balance than a good laugh.
>
> Let me share four reasons why laughter is good for your health.
>
> 1. Laughter relaxes the whole body.
> 2. Laughter boosts the immune system.
> 3. Laughter triggers the release of endorphins.
> 4. Laughter protects the heart.[11]

Ellen DeGeneres uses her fame to support causes. Her use of quotations, personal experiences, and humor gets her listeners involved and helps them pay attention to the message.

INCORPORATE QUOTATIONS Sometimes a quotation can grab your audience's attention, and if cited accurately, also adds to the credibility of your speech. A student talking about language started her speech as follows:

Lee Iacocca once said, "It's important to talk to people in their own language. If you do it well, they'll say, 'God, he said exactly what I was thinking.' And when they begin to respect you, they'll follow you to the death."[12] Today I want to talk with you about the power of language and how you can use it to help you be a competent communicator.

Whatever you choose to gain attention and maintain interest in your introduction, it should be relevant and should orient the audience to the topic.

STATE THE SPECIFIC PURPOSE AND THESIS Once you have your audience's attention, you need to state the specific purpose and thesis statement of your speech. Both the specific purpose and thesis statement were discussed in detail earlier in this chapter. Sometimes the specific purpose and thesis statement are best stated together; sometimes it is appropriate to state the specific purpose at the beginning and the thesis toward the end of the introduction, where it serves as a preview of the speech. When you state the specific purpose and thesis, you orient the audience to your topic and give them a clear indication of where you are headed with your speech. This preview is also essential in helping your audience recall what you said, because they have only one opportunity to hear your message.

Motivate the Audience to Listen

Design your introductory comments to "hook" your audience. You must hold their interest and attention throughout the entire presentation, but that task will be easier if you can capture them by making the topic significant to them and by establishing your credibility.

A standard way of making your topic relevant is simply to point out the reasons for presenting your speech. The audience must find a reason to listen as early in the speech as possible. You should also consider whether it is necessary to establish your credibility in speaking on the topic you have selected.

Credibility refers to a speaker's believability based on the audience's evaluation of the speaker's competence, experience, and character. For example, if Lady Gaga, singer and entertainer, were to speak on immigration policies or climate change needs, she would have to establish her credibility on the subject by relating to the subject and indicating how she became an expert on the topic.

credibility

A speaker's believability, based on the audience's evaluation of the speaker's competence, experience, character, and charisma.

Forecast the Main Points

Before you finish introducing your speech, let the audience know what you will cover in the speech itself. This is known as *forecasting,* and it affords listeners a "road map" so they know where you will take them in the remainder of your speech. Forecasting helps your audience be better listeners.

Let's look at some sample introductions. The following examples show how to orient and motivate your listeners and forecast the main points of your speech:

> Laughter is a powerful antidote to stress, pain, and conflict. Nothing works faster or more dependably to bring your mind and body back into balance than a good laugh. Humor lightens your burdens, inspires hopes, connects you to others, and keeps you grounded, focused, and alert.
>
> With so much power to heal and renew, the ability to laugh easily and frequently is a tremendous resource for surmounting problems, enhancing your relationships, and supporting both physical and emotional health. Laughter relaxes you, it boosts your immune system, it triggers the release of endorphins that promote an overall sense of wellbeing, *and* it protects your heart.[13]

Can you label the specific parts of the previous introduction? Now look at the following example to see if you can identify the specific parts.

> Grandma used to tell me, "The day is wasted if I have not laughed." She was a wise woman who was able to laugh every day, despite extenuating circumstances and poor health. And, she made sure all of her grandchildren knew how to laugh and laugh frequently. Laughing with others is more powerful than laughing alone. Furthermore, shared laughter is one of the most effective tools for keeping relationships exciting. Humor improves the quality of your connections with coworkers, family members, and friends. Humor allows you to be more spontaneous, let go of defensiveness, release inhibitions, and express your true feeling.[14]

This introduction accomplishes several functions at one time: It gets attention, it relates the topic directly to the audience and to the speaker, it establishes the speaker's credibility on the topic, and it also notes the main points of the speech.

The following sample introduction incorporates background and an attention-getter; it provides listeners with a reason to listen, points out the significance of the topic, lets the listener know "what's in it for me," and states the specific purpose and thesis:

> Three years ago my sister and brother-in-law decided to add to their family by adopting. Since there are so many orphans worldwide, they decided to adopt an international child who might not otherwise be adopted because of age or disabilities. They started their information search on the Internet and found so much information they had to quickly think about what they wanted to know. They learned that the things they should first consider were age, gender, race, and medical needs. My whole family was involved in their decision-making process, so it made sense for us to do our own research, too.
>
> The things we discovered might be helpful to you now or sometime in the future, since the number of orphans waiting to be adopted has risen sharply in the last few years, and you, or someone you know, may find international adoption a possibility. At the very least, you can be knowledgeable about the process if it ever comes up for discussion. I'll share some ideas about where to start, finding your child, and legal considerations when you, family members, and friends are adopting.[15]

Making Connections for Success

Introducing Your Speech

First impressions are very important. Think back to your first day of this class. You made some instantaneous judgments about the class, the professor, and your classmates. Have those first impressions changed? Researchers and business people tell us that speakers, interviewees, and salespersons must get the listener's attention in the first 15 seconds or risk losing them. Communication scholar David Zarefsky says, "The introduction to a speech powerfully affects the audience's first impressions of a speaker."[16]

Analyze this introduction and answer the following questions:

> Men aboard Captain Cook's ship first used the surfboard in March 1779. Surfing is a difficult sport to learn. Today I'd like to share my experience in surfing, the history of surfing, and how to surf.

1. Which of the guidelines for the introduction are not covered?
2. What could be done to make this introduction lively and attention-getting?

Guidelines

Develop Your Introduction

1. **Keep the introduction relatively brief**, making up only 5 to 10 percent of the total content (30 to 50 seconds).
2. **Allow plenty of time to prepare the introduction carefully.** Because it is critical to the success of your speech, it should not be rushed or written at the last minute.
3. **Make the introduction creative and interesting.** To accomplish this, think of several possible introductions, and choose the most effective one.
4. **As you research your speech, watch for material to use in the introduction.** Keep a notebook or file of interesting quotations, stories, humorous statements, and other items that might give your opening some dazzle. But

remember: A successful introduction *must* be relevant to the speech topic.

5. **Develop the introduction after you have completed the main part of your speech.** Relevant introductions are easier to create after you determine the content and direction of the body.
6. **Write out the introduction, word for word.** This section of the speech is too important to improvise or leave to chance. In addition, knowing exactly what you will say at the beginning of your speech gives you confidence and helps you get off to a strong start. Then, practice delivering the introduction until you can present it conversationally, but flawlessly.

Organize the Conclusion of Your Speech

9.3 **Compose** an effective conclusion to your speech.

Your **conclusion** should focus your audience's thoughts on the specific purpose of your speech and bring your most important points together in a condensed and uniform way. Your conclusion should relate to your introduction and help your audience make the connections between the various parts and points of the message. In persuasive speeches, you may also use your conclusion to spell out the action or policies you recommend to solve a problem. In every case, your conclusion should reinforce what you want your listeners to remember.

Because your conclusion is as important as any other part of your presentation, you should give it the same amount of attention. Be especially careful to avoid adding new information in this part of the speech. In addition, remember that you, as a speaker, have only one chance to get your message across to your audience. Repetition is an important strategy to help listeners recall the important information you presented.

conclusion
Closing statements that focus the audience's thoughts on the specific purpose of a speech and bring the most important points together in a condensed and uniform way.

Show That You Are Finishing the Speech

You need to prepare your listeners for the end of your speech; otherwise, they are left hanging and uncomfortable, sensing that something is missing. Do not bluntly state that you are finishing or even say, "In conclusion …" and especially do *not* say, "That's it." Instead, you should carefully and creatively indicate that the speech is winding down. An example might be, "As we've discussed, there are five ways we can become better listeners."

Make Your Thesis Clear

Repetition is important when you have only one chance for the listeners to hear your message. Be sure you creatively remind your listeners of your central idea: "You've already heard me tell you early in my speech that effective listening is a highly valued skill you can learn."

Review the Main Points

Repeating the main points of a speech is particularly helpful anytime you want your audience to remember them. For example, the speaker who informed her audience about barriers to effective listening concluded her speech as follows:

> Let me review the barriers that have the most impact on our listening. They are factual, mental, language, and physical distractions. If you remember these and how they affect listening, you will be a more effective listener.

In addition to helping the audience remember your content, reviewing the speech reinforces both your purpose and the thesis statement.

End with a Memorable Thought

A memorable thought may include referring back to an attention-getting device, citing a quotation, or issuing a challenge or appeal. A memorable quotation is a good way to leave a lasting impression on your audience. When it is relevant and reinforces your thesis statement, a quotation can give your speech additional authority and help increase your credibility. It is crucial that you always cite the source of all quoted information or any information that is not your own. Ethical communicators understand the importance of citing sources as part of the responsibilities of the speaker.

President John F. Kennedy's memorable inaugural address concludes: "And so, my fellow Americans, ask not what your country can do for you; ask what you can do for your country." Obama concluded his inaugural speech in a similar way: "My fellow citizens of the world, ask not what America will do for you, but what together we can do for the freedom of man." Compare the two conclusions: Which do you find more memorable? Why?

If your purpose is to persuade, the conclusion may also include a challenge or appeal to action. The following conclusion recaps the main points and asks the listeners to take action

Sleep researchers are just beginning to understand what we have lost when we lose sleep. Our bodies change drastically when we're sleep deprived and there are many health risks. Hormone levels change to the point that our energy levels are very low when we awaken and are actually comparable to the low morning levels usually associated with the elderly. Furthermore, sleep deprivation may lead to obesity, a decline in immune function, fuzzy thinking, and even to cancer risks. You need to change your schedules! You need at least 8 hours of sleep. Plan your work so that you can always get a good night's rest. If you do get behind, take a nap! A short nap works best—about 45 minutes can improve your health, your attitude, and your thinking. I urge you to take charge of your life. Get some sleep![17]

Signal the audience that your speech is nearing its end by using phrases such as, "Today, we have examined …," "In the past minutes, we have considered …," or "Finally, let me share…." Each prepares the audience for your concluding remarks. The following conclusion lets listeners know the speech is nearly finished, and it summarizes and synthesizes the major points covered. An appeal for action is made, and listeners are left with a memorable thought.

Eating disorders are pervasive in our society. Yet many insurance firms don't offer coverage for treatment. They filter out what they believe to be "legitimate" mental illness—and many don't believe eating disorders fall into that category. This means that countless eating disorder sufferers who are not employed by

Making Connections for Success

Effective Conclusions

One of this writer's colleagues was laughing as she came into the office. "I swear, the next time a student says, 'That's about it' or, 'That's all' I'm going to do a Porky Pig imitation—buhdee, buhdee, buhdee!" Communication professors are not the only ones who get frustrated with speakers who just stop and don't really conclude their speeches. A conclusion should provide a summary and a synthesis and, metaphorically speaking, should "put a bow on the package."

Jeremy Rifkin, author, consultant, economist, and technology guru, gave a speech titled "The BioTech Century" in May 1998 at the City Club in Cleveland, Ohio. Here's his conclusion:

So I am hoping the public can come up into this debate. We are very far behind…. I work with business leaders and CEOs all over the world, and I can tell you the developments going on in the Life Science industries are so fast; they're moving so quick; they're so far advanced from what the public understands that we have a great gap here. The public needs to be informed in discussions like the one we're having today, and then you and I need to be engaged.

We cannot leave these decisions only up to the scientists in the laboratory or the executives in the corporate boardrooms of the Life Science industry, because these technologies should not just be arbitrated in the marketplace. They affect all future generations. If this isn't the technology revolution that we discussed broadly and intimately, which one will we ever? So my hope is that beginning in the next few years, we can begin to engage this great question about the future of our evolution. How do we move into this century of genetic commerce and how do we begin to engage this daunting new science in a way that'll benefit our children and create a renaissance rather than great upheaval for future generations?[18] (You can hear and see the entire speech on the American Rhetoric website.)

1. We say that effective conclusions leave the listener with something to think about and remember. Did Mr. Rifkin do that?

2. What is his final message?

3. What is the effect of the way the words are arranged?

4. Does the conclusion seem to fit the title "The BioTech Century"?

Guidelines

Develop Your Conclusion

1. **The conclusion should be brief and should end with a definite summarizing statement.** The conclusion should account for between 5 and 15 percent of the content of the speech (30 to 60 seconds).

2. **The conclusion should contain no new information.** If it was not mentioned in either the introduction or the body of your speech, it should not be in the conclusion.

3. **The preparation of the conclusion should not be rushed.** Allow plenty of time to develop it, and craft it carefully, but deliver it extemporaneously.

4. **Leave your audience with something memorable.** Think of several possible endings and choose the best one (i.e., the one that best serves the purpose of your speech).

5. **Write out the conclusion word for word.** Then learn it so well you can end your speech smoothly, conversationally, and confidently.

large companies with a group health plan may not be able to receive adequate psychological attention.

Mental health coverage is necessary for treating these diseases, as the cost of eating disorder therapy can reach hundreds of thousands of dollars. Remember the example of the 65-pound young woman I earlier cited who spent five weeks in the intensive care unit.

Please talk with your employers and legislators to change policies for all members—not just those who are part of large corporations—so everyone can receive the psychological care he or she needs.[19]

Synthesize and Summarize

Your conclusion should let the listeners know you are about to finish the speech. It should also clearly remind them of your thesis and the main points you've covered. Essentially, your conclusion leaves your listeners with a summary and synthesis— something memorable that ties your ideas together.

Outline Your Speech

9.4   Construct outlines to help you stay organized in your presentations.

Outlining is one of the most difficult steps in preparing a speech. The outline demonstrates the organization of your speech. **Outlining** involves arranging the entire contents of a speech in a logical sequence and writing that sequence in a standardized form. The outline is often referred to as the blueprint or skeleton of a speech. Organizing is arranging ideas or elements in a systematic and meaningful way. To organize your speech, select one of the patterns of organization discussed earlier in the chapter. Both organizing and outlining involve arranging information to form a meaningful sequence, but outlining is a more rigorous written process. David Zarefsky, communication scholar and public speaking textbook author, says, "Speakers depend on outlines at two stages: when they put the speech together and when they deliver it. Each stage requires a different kind of outline."[20]

Outlining is more detailed than organizing and helps to unify and clarify thinking, to make relationships clear, and to provide the proper balance and emphasis for each point as it relates to the specific purpose of a speech or written paper. Outlining also helps ensure that information is both accurate and relevant.

As you prepare your outline, you gain an overview of your entire presentation. Developing an outline should help you gauge the amount of support you have for each of your main points and identify any points that need further development.

outlining

Arranging materials in a logical sequence, often referred to as the blueprint or skeleton of a speech, and writing out that sequence in a standardized form.

The actual process of outlining usually requires three steps: creating a preliminary outline that identifies the topic and the main points to be covered in the speech, expanding the preliminary outline into a full-sentence outline that clearly and fully develops the speech content, and condensing the full-sentence outline into a presentational outline to aid delivery.

Principles of Outlining

You should keep in mind three principles as you prepare your outlines: subordination, coordination, and parallelism. **Subordination** clearly identifies the hierarchy of ideas. The most important ideas are main points and are supported by subpoints (that is, they are subordinate to the main points), and the outline uses specific rules for format. **Coordination** suggests that ideas with the same level of importance use the same kinds of numbers (Roman and Arabic) and letters (capitalized and not capitalized) to visually indicate the relationships between ideas. **Parallelism** is the term for using similar grammatical forms and language patterns for all ideas, main points, subpoints, and sub-subpoints. If you have a I, you must have a II; if you have a 1, you must have a 2; if you have an A, you must have a B; and each entry must be key words, a complete sentence, or a phrase. You should not mix phrases and complete sentences. Furthermore, your language should be parallel, as demonstrated in earlier examples. The format looks something like this:

subordination

Clearly identifies the hierarchy of ideas: The most important points are main points and are supported by subpoints (that is, they are subordinate to the main points); the outline uses specific rules for format.

coordination

Suggests that ideas with the same level of importance use the same kind of numbers (Roman and Arabic) and letters (capitalized and noncapitalized) to visually indicate the relationships between ideas.

parallelism

Style in which all ideas, main points, subpoints, and sub-subpoints use similar grammatical forms and language patterns.

   I. Listening is learned [main point].
      A. Listening can be taught [subpoint].
      B. Listening skills must be developed [subpoint].
         1. You can change your listening behaviors [evidence].
         2. You can change your attitude about listening [evidence].
      C. Effective listeners learn to avoid common barriers [subpoint].
         1. Ralph Nichols identified ways to overcome barriers to effective listening [evidence].
            a. Find areas of interest [backing for the evidence].
            b. Listen for main ideas, not details.
         2. Listening is an active process; it doesn't just happen [evidence].
      D. Listening is connected with thinking [supporting idea, or subpoint].
  II. Listening is a cognitive construct [main point].

The following sections on preliminary outlines, full-sentence outlines, and presentation outlines follow these rules of outlining and can serve as examples as you prepare your own outlines.

The Preliminary Outline

preliminary outline

A list of all the main points that may be used in a speech.

A **preliminary outline** is a list of all the points that *may* be used in a speech. Suppose you are preparing an 8- to 10-minute persuasive speech on bullying. Because of the limited amount of time, you know you cannot possibly cover everything related to the topic. And because your general purpose is to persuade, you need to focus the content of your speech on that goal. Thus, you recall what you have already read about topic selection, audience analysis, gathering information, and using supporting and clarifying materials. Then, you determine your specific purpose: to persuade my audience to take action against all forms of bullying. On the basis of this specific purpose, you can prepare a preliminary outline of possible main points, as shown in the following sample. Once your possible main points are arranged in this way, you will find it easier to analyze your thoughts. You can then decide exactly which main thoughts to include in your speech and choose the best order for presenting them. Here is what your preliminary outline might look like:

SAMPLE PRELIMINARY OUTLINE FOR A PERSUASIVE SPEECH

TITLE: Take Action against Bullying

GENERAL PURPOSE: To persuade

SPECIFIC PURPOSE: To persuade my audience to take actions against all forms of bullying

POSSIBLE MAIN POINTS

I. What is bullying?
   A. Definition of "bullying"
   B. The forms of bullying

II. Reasons for bullying
   A. Being the "new kid" in the school
   B. Being different from other students

III. The solutions to bullying
   A. Adults look for signs and educate young people about bullying.
   B. Help kids take action against bullying.
   C. What each of us can do to stop bullying.

The Full-Sentence Outline

A **full-sentence outline** expands on the preliminary outline and includes all the ideas you have decided to include in your speech. The full-sentence outline identifies the main points and subpoints you will cover, written as full sentences. Although a full-sentence outline will not include every single word you'll utter, you will have a detailed view of the speech. Some professors require a full-sentence outline as a final outline, turned in with an evaluation sheet prior to speaking. (Other teachers want only a preliminary outline prior to presentation and a presentational outline turned in

full-sentence outline

An outline that expands on the ideas you have decided to include in your speech. It identifies the main points and subpoints you will cover, written as full sentences.

Making Connections for Success

Ordering Ideas in an Outline

For a speech titled "Make Reading Your Hobby," rearrange the following sentences in proper outline form for the body. Think about the principles of outlining as you look over the entries. Make sure to arrange the content in a logical sequence. Place the number of each sentence in the proper place in the outline. (See page 211 to verify your answers.)

1. Low-cost rental libraries are numerous.

2. Reading is enjoyable.

3. It may lead to advancement in one's job.

4. Books contain exciting tales of love and adventure.

5. Many paperback books range in cost from $7.95 to $19.95.

6. People who read books are most successful socially.

7. Reading is profitable.

8. One meets many interesting characters in books.

9. Reading is inexpensive.

I. _____
   A. _____
   B. _____

II. _____
   A. _____
   B. _____

III. _____
   A. _____
   B. _____

Guidelines

Outlining

1. **The preliminary outline should include a list** of the topics that you might cover in the speech.
2. **A good outline should identify the importance of the ideas you will present;** and the consistent format, with subordination, coordination, and parallelism, provides a visual of the hierarchy of ideas.
3. **The outline should provide** an overview of your content.
4. **The outline should help you clarify your thinking;** it gives the ordering of ideas and the amount of supporting material you have for those ideas.

5. **It is sometimes helpful to write out the entire introduction and conclusion in your outline so that you can make sure you have included everything you need.** Check with your instructor to see if that is what he or she requires. Some instructors do not want the introduction and conclusion written out because this may make the speaker dependent on the written word and, consequently, less conversational. Other instructors require both introduction and conclusion to be outlined so speakers can remember what they want to say.

with the evaluation sheet and list of references.) Be sure to ask or listen for any specifics required by your instructor. The full-sentence outline should conclude with a bibliography or list of references identifying all sources you used in your speech; it helps you create a presentational outline, which we'll discuss in succeeding pages.

SAMPLE FULL-SENTENCE INFORMATIVE SPEECH OUTLINE

Sarah Johansen, University of Nebraska–Lincoln (modified slightly; used with permission)

Topic	**TOPIC:** Helen Keller International
Title	**TITLE:** A Charity with Vision: Helen Keller International
General Purpose	**GENERAL PURPOSE:** To inform
Specific Purpose	**SPECIFIC PURPOSE:** To inform my audience about the charity organization Helen Keller International and raise awareness for its cause
Thesis	**THESIS:** To inform my audience about the mission and history of Helen Keller International, how it acts to prevent blindness, and its actions to reduce malnutrition worldwide

INTRODUCTION

Attention-getter—relates topic to the listeners	I. Close your eyes for just a moment. Without sight, you must depend on other senses to remain aware of everything going on around you. Now imagine losing your sense of hearing as well. How would you communicate with others and stay aware of your surroundings?
Orientation	A. Helen Keller was both blind and deaf and still managed to have an incredibly successful and inspirational life and was known for her intelligence and ambition.
Forecasts a main point of the speech	B. One of her many accomplishments was cofounding the organization Helen Keller International (HKI) in 1915 with George Kessler.
Forecasts a main point	C. The organization is a legacy Helen Keller left for us to continue, with her spirit and enthusiasm at its heart, in order to better the world.

BODY

	II. Helen Keller International's Mission and History
Background	A. Helen Keller was blinded at the age of 2 after a terrible fever and soon after lost her sense of hearing.
Supporting material	B. George Kessler was a New Yorker who survived the sinking of the *Lusitania* in 1915 and committed his life to helping soldiers who had lost vision in combat.

C. George and his wife asked Helen Keller for her support and formed the Permanent Blind Relief War Fund for Soldiers & Sailors of the Allies in 1915, which helped blinded veterans learn how to read Braille, make chairs, and knit.

Supporting material

1. The Fund expanded and incorporated civilians as well as veterans, and by 1970 the focus shifted to preventing blindness by distributing vitamin A capsules in Central America and in the Asia-Pacific region.

2. The name Helen Keller International was adopted in 1977 and serves not only the blind but also those who are underprivileged and at risk for blindness.

Further evidence to support the first main point

D. According to www.hki.org, the mission statement is "to save the sight and lives of the most vulnerable and disadvantaged. We combat the causes and consequences of blindness and malnutrition by establishing programs based on evidence and research in vision, health and nutrition."

E. HKI now serves in 22 countries across the globe in Africa, the Asia-Pacific region, and the Americas.

III. Helen Keller International and Preventing Blindness

Second main point: the work of the organization

A. The number one treatable cause of blindness in the world is cataracts.

1. According to the book *Principles of Human Anatomy,* a cataract is the loss of transparency of the lens of the eye, which has a number of causes, including age and sun exposure.

2. HKI trains nurses and surgeons and provides medical equipment in underdeveloped countries so cataract surgeries can be performed for as little as $12 a patient.

B. Vitamin A deficiency is the leading cause of childhood blindness.

1. According to *Africa News,* "an estimated 250,000 to 500,000 vitamin A-deficient children become blind every year, and half of them die within 12 months of losing their sight."

2. HKI provides vitamin A supplementation to children twice a year in order to prevent blindness.

3. Gary Heiting states that vitamin A helps keep the cornea of the eye healthy and helps prevent macular degeneration.

C. In the United States, a program called ChildSight, a branch of HKI, has been instated that screens the eyesight of, and delivers glasses to, underprivileged children.

Second main point is supported by specific evidence on the utility of HKI.

IV. Helen Keller International and Reducing Malnutrition

Third main point: other benefits of the work of the organization

A. Vitamin A supplementation, according to www.HKI.org, "not only can prevent a lifetime of darkness, but can also result in a 25% reduction in child mortality."

B. HKI provides low-cost vitamin and mineral supplements to severely malnourished populations.

C. The Homestead Food Production program created self-sufficient gardens in Cambodia, the Philippines, Bangladesh, and Nepal.

D. Food fortification program provides more nutritious foods for families and communities around the world.

Four subpoints to support the additional features and work of HKI

CONCLUSION

V. Helen Keller International is an exceptional charity that is solely focused on the betterment of lives all around the world

Summary and synthesis of the speech—leave the listeners with something to remember

A. The treatment of blindness in both children and adults has improved the quality of life for many individuals in underprivileged countries.

B. Food production and sustainability provided by HKI will drastically affect the world's hunger and malnutrition problems.

C. Helen Keller's legacy lives on through this organization and will continue to help people all over the world.

Subpoints reinforce the important work of the organization.

REFERENCES

Heiting, Gary. "Vitamin A and Beta Carotene: Eye Benefits." *All About Vision.* N.p., June 2011 (web). Retrieved May 19, 2012, from www.allaboutvision.com/nutrition/vitamin_a.htm.

(continued)

Helen Keller International 2012 (web). Retrieved May 19, 2012, from www.hki.org.

"Nutrition; A Sweet Potato a Day." *Africa News,* Nov. 29, 2011. LexisNexis. (web). Retrieved May 19, 2012, from https://www.lexisnexis.com.

Tortora, Gerard J., and Mark T. Nielsen. *Principles of Human Anatomy*, 12th ed. New York: John Wiley & Sons, Inc., 2012. 728 (print).

The Presentational Outline

presentational outline

A concise, condensed outline with notations, usually a combination of full sentences and key words and phrases.

A **presentational outline** is a concise, condensed outline with notations, usually a combination of full sentences and key words and phrases. This is the outline you will work from when you present your speech. The advantages of the presentational outline as a delivery aid are that it is concise, requires little space, and is comprehensible at a glance.

Your presentational outline should include your main points and sufficient clarifying and supporting material to aid you in the presentation. The outline *may* also include your complete introduction and conclusion, although the choice is up to you (and your instructor). Key words and phrases are important in a presentational outline because they remind you of the points you want to make. Some speakers use codes, symbols, or even colors to remind them of key points, vocal pauses, changes in speaking rate, and so on. But remember, if your presentational outline is too long, complex, or detailed, you can easily get too involved in your notes and lose contact with your audience. The following example of the informative speech on the charity Helen Keller International shows a concise, condensed outline with notations to help the speaker deliver the speech.

The presentational outline can be easily transferred onto note cards. Some speakers prefer to use note cards, and in some classroom situations students are *required* to use them. The number of note cards and their use should be kept to a minimum. Classroom assignments sometimes specify that you use only one side of two or three cards. When this is the case, you need to adjust the amount and type of information you include to aid you in remembering key information. Note cards are easier to handle than a full sheet of paper, and usually require only one hand, so you can gesture. The presentational outline below meets requirements for our classes.

Making Connections for Success

Citing Sources

The web has excellent sources to help you create reference pages. (Some instructors will ask for a bibliography; others, a notes page; and some may want a "sources cited" page. All are acceptable, but be sure to ask your instructor for her or his preference.) The *Modern Language Association Handbook for Writers of Research Papers*, 7th edition, the *Publication Manual of the American Psychological Association*, 6th edition, and the *Chicago Manual of Style*, 16th edition, are all excellent sources to help you put your reference page together. Most can be found online through your own institution's library website. Several universities have complete websites for guidelines to citation. One such website is that of the Duke University libraries.

Complete the following activity to help prepare you for the specific outline and reference page required by your instructor.

1. Go online to find guidelines for citing sources.
2. Determine how to cite two different kinds of print sources.
3. Next, determine how to cite web sources.
4. Look again to see whether you can find examples of how to cite an email interview. If that site does not include personal or email interviews or conversations, search for another site to determine how to cite interviews.
5. Bookmark or print these sites so you have a handy reference for citing sources. (This will be useful when you create the reference page to turn in.)

Guidelines

Using Presentational Note Cards

1. Use only a few note cards (they are a help but cannot capture the whole speech). The object is to serve as an aid or guide.

2. Always number the note cards so that, if they get out of order, you can reorder them quickly. Numbers in the upper left-hand corner will help you stay organized.

3. Write on only one side of the card. Remember, the cards are to help you and should not have complete details.

4. Use abbreviations as much as possible. Just be sure you remember how you use abbreviations.

5. Do not write out your speech—use an outline format. Outlining helps you remain conversational, thus more interesting.

6. If you prefer, write out the introduction and conclusion in their entirety. That does not mean you should read either one word-for-word, but writing them out helps you remember better.

7. List only the main points and subpoints on the cards. Too much information is distracting and may mean you spend too much time looking at the card.

8. If necessary, write out quotations, statistical data, and other information that must be cited accurately. When you want to be totally accurate, this kind of data should be exact when you discuss it in the speech.

SAMPLE PRESENTATIONAL OUTLINE FOR AN INFORMATIVE SPEECH

Sarah Johansen, University of Nebraska–Lincoln (modified slightly; used with permission)

TOPIC: Helen Keller International

TITLE: A Charity with Vision: Helen Keller International

GENERAL PURPOSE: To inform

SPECIFIC PURPOSE: To inform my audience about the charity organization Helen Keller International and raise awareness for its cause

THESIS: To inform my audience about the mission and history of Helen Keller International, how it is acting to prevent blindness, and its actions to reduce malnutrition worldwide.

Topic

Title

General Purpose

Specific Purpose

Thesis

INTRODUCTION

Look at audience.

I. Close your eyes for just a moment. Without sight, you must depend on other senses to remain aware of everything going on around you.

   A. Helen Keller was both blind and deaf and still managed to have an incredibly successful and inspirational life.

   B. One of her many accomplishments was cofounding the organization Helen Keller International (HKI) in 1915 with George Kessler.

Sarah might annotate her presentational outline in this way to help her remember to cover everything in her speech.

Show the website.

   C. The organization is a legacy Helen Keller left for us to continue.

Pause briefly, move, look at audience.

BODY

II. Helen Keller International's Mission and History

   A. Helen Keller was blinded at the age of 2 after a terrible fever and then lost her hearing.

First Main Point

Present picture of Helen Keller as a child.

   B. George Kessler, a New Yorker, committed his life to helping soldiers who had lost vision in combat.

      1. George and his wife asked Helen Keller for her support and formed the Permanent Blind Relief War Fund for Soldiers & Sailors of the Allies.

(continued)

2. The Fund expanded and incorporated civilians as well as veterans; by 1970 the focus shifted to preventing blindness.

3. The name Helen Keller International was adopted in 1977.

C. According to www.hki.org, the mission statement is "to save the sight and lives of the most vulnerable and disadvantaged. We combat the causes and consequences of blindness and malnutrition by establishing programs based on evidence and research in vision, health and nutrition."

D. HKI now serves in 22 countries across the globe.

Show world map, pointing out general areas and specific locations.

Second Main Point

III. HKI and Blindness Prevention

A. Cataracts are the number one treatable cause of blindness.

1. *The Principles of Human Anatomy* identifies a cataract as the loss of transparenc of the lens of the eye.

Project picture of eyes.

2. HKI trains medical teams and provides medical equipment in underdeveloped countries.

B. Vitamin A deficiency is the leading cause of childhood blindness.

1. According to *Africa News,* "an estimated one-quarter to one-half of the vitamin A-deficient children become blind every year, and half of them die within 12 months of losing their sight."

2. HKI provides vitamin A supplementation twice a year.

3. Gary Heiting states that vitamin A helps keep the eye healthy.

C. In the United States, ChildSight, a branch of HKI, screens the eyesight of, and delivers glasses to, underprivileged children.

Show PowerPoint slide of workers delivering glasses.

Pause.

Third Main Point

IV. HKI Reduces Malnutrition

A. Vitamin A supplementation "not only can prevent a lifetime of darkness, but can also result in a 25 percent reduction in child mortality."

B. HKI provides supplements to severely malnourished populations.

C. The Homestead Food Production program created self-sufficient gardens in impoverished areas.

D. Food fortification programs provide more nutritious foods around the world.

Show additional scenes of the work of HKI.

Pause.

CONCLUSION

V. HKI is an exceptional charity solely focused on the betterment of lives.

VI. A. The treatment of blindness has improved the quality of life for many in underprivileged countries.

B. HKI drastically affects the world's hunger and malnutrition problems.

C. Helen Keller's legacy will continue to help people all over the world.

Pause, smile, gather notes, remove visuals, move to sit down (or wait to answer questions if appropriate).

Summary

Organize the Body of Your Speech

Objective 9.1   Identify ways to organize the body of your speeches.

- You can now use your research to develop main points that help you present the most important aspects of your topic. Your general and specific purpose statements guide your listeners so they can recognize what you expect of them.
- Order the main points of a speech to help your listeners interpret your content.
- Assess the organizational patterns described and choose the best for your own speeches.
- Use transitions, signposts, internal previews, and internal summaries in your own speeches.

Organize the Introduction of Your Speech

Objective 9.2   Organize the introduction of your speech.

Introductions should orient the audience to the topic, motivate them to listen, and provide the direction of your speech. You should be able to complete preliminary and presentational outlines for your speeches.

Organize the Conclusion of Your Speech

Objective 9.3   Compose an effective conclusion to your speech.

The conclusion lets your listeners know you are finishing the speech and provides a summary and synthesis of the ideas presented so they leave knowing why you made the speech and what you hoped they would gain from it. The conclusion reinforces your thesis.

Outline Your Speech

Objective 9.4   Construct outlines to help you stay organized in your presentations.

- Outlines are created to help you remain organized. They also help your listeners tune in to your messages.
- To make sure that listeners know your intent, outlines should follow three principles: subordination, coordination, and parallelism.
- Preliminary outlines are often words or phrases you create to help determine how things fit together.
- Full-sentence outlines provide a clear overview, but not the entire speech, to ensure that you stay on track and help your audience listen.
- Presentational outlines help you remember to look at your audience, smile, use your visuals, cover up your visuals, and move in a way that emphasizes the important aspects of your content.

Discussion Starters

1. How does organization help a speaker?
2. Discuss a time when you heard a speaker and had no idea where they were going or why they chose the topic they did. How did you respond to the speech? To the speaker?
3. Identify three specific ideas or strategies you will consider as you work on your own speeches for this class.
4. If you will use different organizational strategies outside the classroom, why do your authors and instructors require the organizational patterns identified in this chapter?
5. What does the introduction accomplish?
6. Why should we *not* end the speech with, "That's it"?

Answers and Explanations

Making Connections: Ordering Ideas in an Outline (page 205)

One set of possible answers: I. (2), A. (4), B. (8), II. (9), A. (1), B. (5), III. (7), A. (3), B. (6).

Chapter 10
Managing Anxiety and Apprehension When Delivering Your Speech

CHAPTER OUTLINE

 Learning Objectives

This chapter will help you:

Managing Speech Anxiety

10.1 Identify ways you can manage your speech anxiety/communication apprehension.

Methods of Delivery

10.2 Demonstrate appropriate use of the four methods of delivery.

Vocal and Physical Aspects of Delivery

10.3 Analyze your own vocal and physical aspects of delivery and find ways to improve both.

Presentational Aids

10.4 Construct presentational aids that enhance your speeches and help your listeners attend to the presentation.

Presentation Software

10.5 Explore how integrating software programs can aid your presentation

Practice Your Delivery

10.6 Perform your speech delivery in practice sessions to help you gain confidence and practice.

Making Everyday Connections

DeRod told his professor he was quite anxious about giving his speech in class. The professor told him that almost everyone has some anxiety when preparing and delivering a speech. He also said that some degree of anxiety is helpful, as long as speakers see and use it in a positive way instead of allowing it to be a debilitating problem. He then suggested that DeRod rethink anxiety as a behavior he could manage. He further explained that preparation and practice would go a long way toward reducing any anxiety he might have.

If you're a typical student, no matter what your age or geographical area, the thought of giving a speech sends a chill down your spine. The fear of public speaking tops most people's list of phobias. Anxiety is a normal response to public speaking, and most of us have some degree of anxiety; others have communication apprehension, that is, more

anxiety that causes greater problems. Both can *usually* be managed with preparation, practice, and strategies to reduce their effects. Before you read the chapter to find suggestions that will help you **manage** your apprehension and deliver effective speeches, take a few minutes to think about and answer the following questions:

Questions to Think About

1. How do you feel about giving speeches and making presentations?
2. When you experienced anxiety before or during a presentation, what specific reactions did you have?
3. What do you normally do to manage your anxiety?
4. What effective strategies worked in the past for you or others?

resenting speeches can be fun. You might not believe that now, but if you have care-
ully completed all your work up to this point, you, too, may enjoy sharing your
houghts with the class. You have researched, organized, and arranged your ideas.
Now you can focus on the delivery.

You should carefully prepare for your speech presentations. If you can, rehearse
n the classroom. If not, find a room comparable to the one where you'll give your
peech and practice out loud. If possible, get someone to listen to you and provide
eedback about both content and delivery. Why? First, it allows you to know how the
peech sounds. The written word and the spoken word are not the same and do not
ave the same effect. Practice helps you hear the difference. Second, practicing in front
f someone provides you with listener response; you need that to help you make the
ight choices and to feel more confident about your speech. Do you still feel anxious
bout your presentation? The following information may help you find ways to alter
our thinking and view anxiety as beneficial. You may also find behavioral strategies
o help you manage your anxiety.

Managing Speech Anxiety

0.1   Identify ways you can manage your speech anxiety/communication
apprehension.

Communication researchers differentiate between **speech anxiety**, a multisystem
esponse that creates a combination of biochemical changes in the body in a commu-
ication situation,[1] and **communication apprehension**, the most severe form, defined
s an anxiety syndrome associated with either real or anticipated communication with
nother person or persons.[2] It is commonly accepted that the more we know about
stage fright and communication apprehension and how to cope with either, the better
ble we are to *manage* the resulting behaviors.

Communication apprehension and speech anxiety are two of the most researched
areas in communication. One of the reasons is that speaking in front of others is identified as people's greatest fear.[3] Most of us have some degree of anxiety when we
speak in front of others. Your authors based on their experiences find that anxiety and

speech anxiety
Fear of speaking before an audience.

communication apprehension
The most severe form of speech anxiety; an anxiety syndrome associated with either real or anticipated communication with another person or persons.

apprehension can give speakers the motivation to do well. Anxiety is a problem only when we cannot manage it or when we choose *not to* communicate because of it.

Communication Apprehension

Communication apprehension can be seen in individuals who either consciously or subconsciously decide to remain silent. They perceive their silence offers them greater advantages than speaking out or that the disadvantages of communicating outweigh any potential gains. Among the fears of those with communication apprehension is that of speaking before a group. However, not everyone who fears speaking before a group necessarily suffers from communication apprehension. That term refers to the much deeper problem of virtually cutting oneself off from most, if not all, communication with others. Communication apprehension often begins at an early age as a result of negative feedback. Children who are not encouraged to communicate or who are punished for doing so are likely to learn that communicating is undesirable and that silence is beneficial. As these children avoid communicating, others may unknowingly contribute further to their fear by asking questions such as "Cat got your tongue?" or "Are you afraid to talk?" Such words can make already anxious people feel inadequate and thus perpetuate the fear and anxiety associated with communicating. Communication-apprehensive individuals fear speaking (or even thinking about speaking) in all contexts, including one-on-one communication and small-group discussions. Because many of us have either some anxiety or communication apprehension, the focus of this chapter is to help you learn to manage those anxieties that keep you from being an effective communicator.

Symptoms of Speech Anxiety

Speech anxiety refers more specifically to the fear of speaking before an audience or group. Anxiety is a chemical reactive condition during which our bodies secrete hormones and adrenaline that eventually overload our physical and emotional responses. These chemical reactions are the same as those you might experience when you are waiting to see a friend you haven't seen in years or going to your first job interview. Your heart begins to beat faster, and your blood pressure starts to rise. More sugar is pumped into your system, and your stomach churns. When you experience these reactions, you may feel as if your body is operating in high gear and that little or nothing can be done about it. You should realize that some of these feelings are normal and, for most us, will not interfere with our speech performance.

Speakers often experience the behavioral signs of speech anxiety listed in Table 10.1. These behaviors can occur separately or in any combination, depending on the degree of apprehension experienced by the speaker. Speakers who feel apprehension may also make telling statements. For example, they may offer self-critical excuses or apologies such as, "I'm not any good at this anyway," "I didn't really

Table 10.1 Behaviors Associated with Speech Anxiety

Voice	Quivering, too soft, monotonous, too fast, nonemphatic
Fluency	Stammering, halting, awkward pauses, hunting for words, speech blocks
Mouth and throat	Breathing heavily, clearing throat often, swallowing repeatedly
Facial expressions	No eye contact, rolling eyes, tense facial muscles, grimaces, twitches
Arms and hands	Rigid and tense, fidgeting, waving hands
Body movement	Swaying, pacing, shuffling feet, weight shifts
Nonvisible symptoms	Feeling too warm, too much saliva, dry mouth, butterflies in the stomach

Many communication professors have lists of behaviors such as the ones here. One of the first lists was published more than 40 years ago but is still viable. [See A. Mulac and A. R. Sherman, "Behavior Assessment of Speech Anxiety," *Quarterly Journal of Speech* 60, 2 (April 1974): 138.]

prepare for this because I didn't have enough time," or "I never was able to say this correctly." These comments tend to draw more attention to speakers' nervousness and thus magnify the problem and usually do not improve the situation.

Speakers who have speech anxiety often overestimate how much the audience notices their behavior, and the audience often tends to underestimate a speaker's anxiety. For example, audiences cannot detect a speaker who is experiencing butterflies unless the butterflies cause an observable reaction or the speaker's voice sounds nervous.

Causes of Speech Anxiety

Just as physicians can better treat an illness if they know its cause, people can better control apprehension or anxiety if they can determine the underlying problem. Many people treat only the symptoms and tend to ignore the causes; when you try to remove the symptoms without understanding the causes it is usually a losing battle.

People may develop speech anxiety if they constantly hear that speaking in front of others can be a terrible experience. When someone says, "Don't worry about it—you'll do fine," only serves to reinforce the notion that something can go wrong. If speakers believe something can go wrong and that they might make fools of themselves, they are apt to lose confidence and develop speech anxiety.

In our society, success, winning, and "being number one" are too often considered all-important. When we can't be the most successful, we sometimes consider ourselves failures. No one likes to fail; therefore, we are likely to believe that success brings rewards and failure brings punishment. If you are a winner, you are praised; if you are a loser, you are ridiculed. Consequently, we place tremendous pressure on ourselves and others to be successful.

When we haven't been successful at something, we are often told to try again. But if the consequences of the failure are dramatic and the payoff for success doesn't seem worth the effort, we may prefer to avoid the situation. Avoidance may result in punishment, but we may perceive that as better than failure. Sometimes society is more lenient. For example, in a competition we assume that there will be a winner and a loser. No one likes to lose, but playing your best and losing is usually acceptable. When someone makes a mistake in a speech, however, we may be more critical. Rather than acknowledge that the person is making an honest effort, we might perceive him or her as inadequate or unskilled. Consequently, the stress created by fear of making mistakes in front of others can be so great that it produces high anxiety and sometimes complete avoidance of speaking situations. We learn to respond in specific ways when facing something that creates anxiety because we have become conditioned to do so. Our reactions to a speech-making situation are *learned*. Because speech anxiety is a learned behavior, the only solution for its sufferers is to examine potential reasons for the anxiety and then use this knowledge to learn how to manage it.

Communication Apprehension, Anxiety, and Cultural Concerns

Increasing numbers of international students and Americans whose first language is not English enter our classrooms each year. Because of language and cultural differences, these students have some anxieties that go beyond those of native speakers. In interviews with international students and their professors, Xiaofan Liao learned that most international students were concerned about talking in class: "I don't know your language as well as I should. I'm nervous about responding in class." They were afraid they would not fully understand the assignment, that others would not understand them, and that they would "lose face" with their American professors and classmates.[4]

Making Connections for Success

How Technology Can Help Manage Anxiety and Apprehension

What happens when you get anxious about speaking? Does your mouth feel as if it were filled with cotton? Or do you have too much saliva? Some people get cold and have clammy hands, while others flush, and every bit of visible skin, especially the neck and face, gets bright red. Communication scholar James McCroskey and his colleagues extensively researched communication apprehension, and while it may be of some comfort to know that most of us experience some degree of anxiety or fear when faced with real or imagined public speaking situations, apprehension causes some of us major problems. There are, however, some strategies to help us work through those states.

We can use technology to help manage communication apprehension or speech anxiety. Those who teach special anxiety sections suggest the first step in learning to manage your anxiety is to *recognize* it. And, you can use various forms of technology to help you manage your fears. Here are some specific steps to help you:

1. List the physical symptoms of your anxiety when you think about giving a speech, or when you're actually making a presentation (e.g., dry mouth, getting red in the face, and the like).
2. Compare your symptoms with the list in Table 10.1.
3. Once you have your speech in good presentational order (and well before the assigned due date), complete the following:
   a. Record yourself as you extemporaneously deliver the speech.
   b. Play back your recording and reflect on what you did well, where you had problems, and how you can improve the presentation.
   c. Adjust your speech and make any refinements or changes you think will help you reduce the difficulties.
   d. Record yourself again and follow the same procedure as above, and record a second or third time.
   e. View the recording and once again and reflect on any changes needed. Practice the new version of your speech.
   f. Create a YouTube presentation and send the link out to five of your family and/or friends; ask them to send their feedback. (If you don't have the necessary equipment or knowledge to create a YouTube presentation, just record your presentation and share that with others.)
   g. Use their feedback to reflect on how you can improve your presentation.
   h. Make any changes in your presentation and create a new YouTube or video recording of your presentation and share it with one of the initial viewers and with one new viewer (e.g., a roommate, coworker, or classmate) and ask for their feedback.
   i. Use their feedback to improve your speech and delivery.
   j. At this point, you will have made the presentation at least five times and reflected on your presentation, and you will have feedback from several other people well in advance of your class presentation.
4. This preparation and practice should help you manage at least some anxiety because you received feedback from others and refined your speech and presentation.

Some international students were concerned about translating from English to their own language and back again and worried that the translation process would be slow and perhaps inaccurate. They also felt that they didn't really fit in; their foreign status often precluded their U.S. classmates from interacting with them. Some of them stated the classroom situation was so different from what they were accustomed to that it made them even more nervous. In each case, they felt that their differences translated to being perceived as in some way inferior to the native-speaking students and called undue negative attention to them. Giving a speech in front of a group is difficult for most of us. Those from different language and cultural backgrounds have additional stresses.

Native Americans represent another group who, because of cultural differences, experience more anxiety when speaking. In the Native American culture, eye contact is limited, and response time or wait time is expected. In speaking situations in the dominant culture, eye contact is expected. Native American students explain they feel even more uncomfortable when told that eye contact is required. In Native American cultures, eye contact with everyone is rarely accepted, and then, only after one has

roved oneself to the elders. Those from different cultural and language backgrounds
eed others to understand their unique situations.

reating Speech Anxiety and Apprehension

lthough speaking before a group can produce stress and anxiety, few people allow
heir nervousness to prevent them from trying and succeeding. In fact, even well
nown speakers and performers feel some nervousness before giving a speech, but
hey have learned to *control* it. Hugh Jackman, internationally acclaimed actor, hosted
he 2009 Academy Awards; in a prebroadcast session, he acknowledged he was ner-
ous because of the number of people in the profession and in the television audience
ho would judge him for a long time if he didn't "do well."[5]

Many classroom teachers admit to some degree of anxiety prior to meeting their
lasses for the first time. Even elected officials and those seeking elected offices admit
hey experience some nervousness prior to giving a speech, but they learn to manage
hat anxiety. In fact, the key to managing anxiety is the desire to do so. To cope with
peech anxiety, we must realize the potential for failure always exists, but we can't
et it stop us from trying. If we allowed the possibility of failure to overwhelm us,
ve probably would never do or learn anything. A child beginning to walk is a prime
xample of how most of our learning occurs. At first, the child wobbles, takes a small
tep, and falls. But when the child falls, someone is usually there to offer help, sup-
ort, and encouragement to continue. In addition, the child usually is determined
o walk regardless of the difficulties. Speech making, like learning to walk, involves
nany of the same processes. Help, support, and encouragement are important, but the
ssential ingredient is determination to succeed.

Most successful people will tell you that before they were successful, they had
ome failures and moments of embarrassment. Their drive and self-confidence
ushed them to try again. Some of our first speeches were not very good, and we
were quite nervous about speaking in front of our classmates. However, it didn't take
us long to realize even the best speakers in the class felt the same way. The only dif-
erence was they weren't afraid to make a mistake. Many of us expect perfection
nd we are often too hard on ourselves. Some students, after giving a speech, said
hey were extremely nervous, although the audience detected no signs of their
nervousness.

Speech anxiety has no cures—only ways to reduce, manage, or control it so it
does not interfere with your presentation.

Giving a speech and completing a pass play in a football game are not the same,
but both require similar preparation. The successful pass play requires research,
organization, learning, observation, practice, willingness to work hard, ability to
perform, confidence, knowing your opponent's defense (or knowing your audience), and timing. A successful speech presentation requires all of the aforemen-
tioned factors in addition to selecting an appropriate topic.

If none of the strategies in the Guidelines feature helps to reduce your anxiety,
you should probably seek professional help. Individuals who suffer from abnormal levels of speech anxiety should know that the negative feelings associated
with speaking in front of others do not simply occur; they develop over a long
time. Therefore, these negative feelings do not always disappear easily. With help,
though, we can do something about apprehension and anxiety. Most colleges and
universities have psychologists or counselors who are trained to reduce the fear of
speaking in public. Some offer special sections of the beginning communication
course for those who are anxious about speaking in front of others. If your fears
cause problems, check with your instructor for strategies or referral to a specialist.

Systematic desensitization is a relaxation technique designed to reduce the
tenseness associated with anxiety.[6] The goal is to help develop a new, relaxed

systematic desensitization
A relaxation technique designed
to reduce the tenseness associated
with anxiety.

Competitive swimmers know that
doing well requires the same kind of
behavior recommended for reducing
your speech anxiety: preparation;
positive thinking; visualizing success;
and practice, practice, practice.

response to the anxiety-provoking event. Try this: Imagine yourself standing in front of this class, ready to give your speech. Visualize the wonderful speech you will give. You confidently place your notes on the lectern, look at the audience, smile, take a deep breath, and begin speaking. Your audience smiles and nods throughout the speech, and you become more and more relaxed as you speak. When you finish, they applaud loudly. Someone says, "That was a wonderful speech!" Remember how it felt to be so relaxed. Go through this visualization process and think about how relaxed you are. This kind of mental rehearsal helps you change negative thoughts to positive ones.

Meditation is another practice used by many to help them relax and focus on the tasks at hand. Meditation is defined as the process of spending time in quiet thought. Meditation is popular, activists, actors, athletes, listeners, politicians, speakers, and people in the public as well as in everyday life have learned the benefits of meditation. Neuroscientists have found meditation is a helpful way to reduce all stress. A number of studies found that the brain and the body both work better and more efficiently in those who use mediation to center themselves and put their concerns to rest. Try this: Find a quiet spot. Stand tall. Close your eyes. Take a deep breath from the abdomen and hold it for a count of 10. Concentrate on holding your breath and counting. Then, slowly release the air by blowing through pursed lips, as if you were blowing a bubble, to the count of five. Wait quietly with your eyes closed for a count of 10 and repeat the process. Repeat 10 times with your eyes closed. The 10 repetitions will slow your breathing, your heart rate, and the brain activity. Next, sit down in a comfortable position and repeat the process another 10 times. Use a modified version of this every time you feel anxious or apprehensive about speaking. On the day of your scheduled presentation, try two or more repetitions before you go to class, and just prior to your turn to speak, use a modified meditation routine to help you calm yourself.

Meditation may be done sitting in the usual fashion, or sitting "lotus style" on your legs. Whatever you try, remember that it's the deep breathing and cleansing of one's thoughts that provides the benefits.[8]

Overcoming anxiety in public speaking situations is not easy, but you must remember that some anxiety can be helpful and is a normal reaction to speaking in public. When we asked students for specific ways they dealt with their anxieties, they suggested the following:

1. Practice and have your introduction, main points, and conclusion clear in your mind. Students believe that once they know their introductions, main points, and conclusions, it is a lot easier to remember the details.

2. Walk confidently to the speaking area. Students believe this helps create confidence. If you're confident, it is likely you will feel relaxed. In other words, positive behavior results in positive outcomes.

3. Do not start your speech until you are ready. Students and instructors suggest that having everything under control before starting to speak makes it easier to relax and concentrate on the speech, rather than on you.

4. Look at your audience and focus most of the time on friendly faces. Students believe that concentrating on those who are likely to give positive feedback will help promote a good feeling about speaking.

These suggestions are probably not new, or surprising, but they will help in your quest to become a successful speaker. The best thing you can do is continue to give speeches in class and take more classes that will afford opportunities to speak under the supervision of a trained instructor. You can reduce and control your fear of speaking, but you need to continue to work at doing so, as well as follow the guidelines and suggestions offered here.

Guidelines

Managing Speech Anxiety

1. **You are not alone.** Almost everyone has some anxiety about giving a speech or making a presentation.
2. **Be prepared.** The more knowledge of and passion for the topic you have, the easier it is to concentrate on what you want to share rather than the fact that you are speaking.
3. **Be informed.** Know your audience and the surroundings in which your presentation will take place.
4. **Think positively.** Prepare yourself mentally for success. Believe you are going to be successful, and you probably will be.
5. **Practice,** practice, and then practice more.
6. **Be informed.** Ask your instructor for additional advice and other possible available treatment programs.
7. **Don't give up.** Others want you to succeed, and you can if you want to do so.

Methods of Delivery

10.2   **Demonstrate** appropriate use of the four methods of delivery.

Effective delivery conveys the speaker's purpose and ideas in a clear and interesting manner so the audience attends to and retains what was said as the speaker intended it. The effectiveness of a speech therefore depends both on what is said and on how it is conveyed. No two speakers are alike. For example, it is unlikely anyone could deliver the "I Have a Dream" speech as effectively as did Martin Luther King Jr. This speech, widely regarded as a masterpiece, was delivered on August 28, 1963, to more than 200,000 people gathered in Washington, DC, to participate in a peaceful demonstration furthering the cause of equal rights for African Americans. If you have heard a recording of this speech, you know how King's delivery affected his audience. He had a rich baritone voice modulated by the cadences of a Southern Baptist preacher and the fervor of a crusader. Although the words of the speech can be repeated and King's style can be imitated, the setting, timing, and circumstances cannot be reconstructed. Therefore, the effect King had on that day can never be repeated. You can view/hear the speech at the American Rhetoric website (www.americanrhetoric.com).

A poorly developed speech can be improved by effective delivery, and a well-written speech can be ruined by ineffective delivery. No set of rules will guarantee an effective delivery in every situation. The only consistent rule is that you must be yourself! Of course, as a beginning speaker, you probably have many questions about how to deliver a speech: How many notes should I use? Will I need a microphone? Where and how should I stand? Where or at whom should I look? How many and what kinds of gestures should I use? How and when should I use my visual aids? How loudly should I speak? How fast or slow should my speaking be?

Such questions are valid, but the answers will vary from person to person and from situation to situation. In the end, effective delivery is achieved by practice under the direction of a competent instructor. An awareness of self and knowledge of effective delivery also help to improve delivery. Although a speech may be delivered in many different ways, the four most common methods of delivery are impromptu, manuscript, memorized, and extemporaneous (see Table 10.2 on page 220).

Impromptu Delivery

The delivery of a speech with little or no formal planning or preparation (no research, no organization) is called **impromptu delivery**. You have used this method many times, perhaps without even realizing it. Whenever you speak without prior preparation, whether in response to a question in class, to a sudden request at a business

impromptu delivery

A delivery style in which a speaker delivers a speech with little or no planning or preparation.

Table 10.2 Methods of Delivery: Advantages and Disadvantages

	Advantages	Disadvantages
Impromptu	Spontaneous; flexible; conversational	No time for preparation; can be inaccurate; difficult to organize; can be stressful
Manuscript	Good for material that is technical or detailed or that requires complete preciseness; high accuracy; can be timed to the second; prepared	No flexibility; great amount of preparation time; difficult to adapt to audience response; may sound mechanical; lack of eye contact
Memorized	Good for short speeches; speaker can concentrate on delivery; easier to maintain eye contact; prepared	Inflexible; requires practice and repetition; speaker can forget or lose place; difficult to adapt to audience response
Extemporaneous	Organized; conversational; prepared	May sound mechanical; may be intimidating to inexperienced speakers; great amount of eye contact required

meeting, or to a comment made by a friend, you use the impromptu method of delivery. The more formal or demanding the situation, the more most speakers prefer to avoid this approach. At times, however, you have no choice. In such cases, muster your self-control, relax, and concentrate on what you wish to say. The lack of preparation time distinguishes the impromptu method from other methods of delivery and forces speakers to depend solely on their ability to think on their feet.

Manuscript Delivery

Reading the speech word for word is known as **manuscript delivery**. Speakers who use this method are never at a loss for words. A speaker should use a manuscript for situations in which every word, phrase, and sentence must be stated precisely. Using a manuscript is not uncommon for politicians, clergy, teachers, and others who need to present information completely and accurately or who are likely to be quoted after their presentations. But for beginners, manuscript delivery is often discouraged because it invites the speaker to concentrate more on the script than the audience and reduces eye contact with the audience. Furthermore, speakers who work from manuscripts are less able to adapt to the reactions of the audience and thus may sound mechanical. They are so busy concentrating on reading the speech they may be unable to respond to their listeners.

Memorized Delivery

Memorized delivery requires you to memorize your speech in its entirety, usually from a word-for-word script. This kind of delivery is suited to short presentations, such as toasts, acceptance speeches, and introductions, and is also commonly used by speakers in contests and on lecture circuits. Speakers frequently memorize certain parts of their speeches, including examples, short stories, statistics, quotations, and other materials they can call up at the appropriate time. Politicians, salespeople, tour guides, and others often have a memorized pitch, or speech, to fit their needs.

Memorization has one advantage: You can concentrate less on what you have to say and focus more on your delivery. Of course, this is true only if you are extremely confident and have memorized your speech so completely you don't need to think about each word. One disadvantage of memorized delivery is its lack of flexibility; it doesn't allow for much, if any, adaptation to your audience. Beginning speakers face another disadvantage: They might forget what they want to say and become embarrassed. In addition, it is difficult to deliver a memorized speech without

---

manuscript delivery

A delivery style in which a speaker writes the speech in its entirety and then reads it word for word.

memorized delivery

A delivery style in which a speaker memorizes a speech in its entirety from a word-for-word script.

Extemporaneous delivery allows this young woman to appear relaxed and conversational. Her smile and natural gestures along with her eye contact help her appear confident and allow her to personally address her listeners.

ounding mechanical. Effective presentation of a memorized address requires a great deal of practice and confidence.

Extemporaneous Delivery

In **extemporaneous delivery**, the speaker uses a carefully prepared and researched speech but delivers it from notes, with a high degree of spontaneity. Extemporaneous delivery is the method most commonly used in speech classrooms and in other public communication situations. When you give a report at work, for example, you will probably be expected to present your remarks extemporaneously. If you are a member of a problem-solving group at your place of worship and you have been selected to present the group's deliberations, you will also be expected to deliver your remarks in an extemporaneous manner. Instructors often require extemporaneous delivery in the communication classroom because it is the best style for most instances of public speaking.

Extemporaneous delivery is situated somewhere between memorized or manuscript delivery and impromptu delivery. Speakers depend on a brief presentational outline or notes and choose the actual wording of the speech at the time of delivery. They sometimes prefer to use a key word outline, which simply outlines the points and subpoints of the speech, using key words. This helps keep the speaker organized and on track but does not allow the speaker to become too reliant on the outline or notes.

An extemporaneous speech might at first seem as difficult as an impromptu speech; in fact it is much easier, because it eliminates memorization and manuscript writing, and leaves more time for preparation and practice. Thus once you have prepared your outline, you can practice your delivery. The goal of the extemporaneous method is a conversational and spontaneous quality. Conversationality and spontaneity are two hallmarks of speech delivery listeners find appealing. It is much easier to listen to and attend to conversational, lively, and spontaneous speakers. Each time you practice your speech, the wording may be somewhat different, although the content remains the same. Your objective should always be to use delivery to help you share meaningful ideas with your audience.

The advantages of extemporaneous delivery are: It gives you better control of your presentation than the impromptu method, it allows more spontaneity and directness than the memorized and manuscript methods of delivery, and it is more adaptable to a variety of speaking situations than the other methods. Most teachers, as well as professional speakers, prefer to use the extemporaneous method because it allows them to adjust to the situation moment by moment—listeners seem puzzled, so the supervisor stops to ask questions; listeners seem to be losing attention, so the teacher skips ahead. Extemporaneous delivery also allows audience members to become more involved in listening to the message.

extemporaneous delivery
A delivery style in which the speaker carefully prepares the speech in advance but delivers it using only a few notes and with a high degree of spontaneity.

Vocal and Physical Aspects of Delivery

10.3 **Analyze** your own vocal and physical aspects of delivery and find ways to improve both.

Without solid content and valid sources, nothing is worth communicating; but without effective delivery, even the most compelling information cannot be clearly and vividly presented. Because the audience is the ultimate judge of effectiveness, you must deliver your speech well to involve them in it. Audience members like to feel as if they are being personally addressed. Try to think of your presentation as a conversation and your audience as your partners in dialogue. Then use your voice and body to create this impression.

Vocal Aspects

Many beginning speakers overlook the important role of voice in delivery. Your voice should be pleasant to listen to, relate easily and clearly to your thoughts, and express a range of emotions. Your voice should convey the meaning you intend. The more natural, spontaneous, and effortless you appear to be, regardless of how hard you work, the more your listener can focus on what you say rather than how you say it. Three aspects of voice that determine the effectiveness of delivery are vocal quality, intelligibility, and vocal variety.

vocal quality

The overall impression a speaker's voice makes on his or her listeners.

VOCAL QUALITY   The overall impression a speaker's voice makes on listeners is referred to as **vocal quality**. Voices may be harsh, nasal, thin, mellow, resonant, or full bodied. Attitude can affect the quality of the voice and reveal to listeners whether the speaker is happy, confident, angry, fearful, or sad. Think about those times when you were extremely tired: How did your voice sound? Did you hide your tiredness from people listening to you? Probably not. Think about times when you were really excited about a topic. How do you think you sounded to your listeners? Generally, when we're really involved and interested in something, the voice carries energy and excitement and draws others into the conversation. Vocal quality is a highly accurate indicator of the presenter's sincerity. In addition, listeners tend to believe that speakers whose vocal delivery is interesting and easy to listen to are more credible and will probably be more willing to listen to those who use their voices effectively.

intelligibility

Speaker's vocal volume, distinctiveness of sound, clarity of pronunciation, articulation, and stress placed on syllables, words, and phrases.

INTELLIGIBILITY   A speaker's **intelligibility**, the degree to which an audience can hear and understand words, is determined by vocal volume; distinctiveness of sound; accuracy of pronunciation; articulation; and stress placed on syllables, words, and phrases. The keys to high intelligibility are self-awareness and consideration for listeners.

- **Volume.** To determine the proper volume, consider the size of the room and observe listeners' reactions. Do listeners look as if they're straining to hear you? Or is your voice too loud or booming for the size of the room?

- **Pronunciation.** We have all been known to mispronounce words. For example, a common word like *February* is often mispronounced as *Feb-u-ary instead of Feb-ru-ary*. Sometimes we mispronounce words out of habit, incorrect learning, or a regionalism. When we mispronounce words, we lower our intelligibility and also run the risk of lowering our credibility. Speakers often drop off word endings, which makes it difficult to understand what is being said: The dropping of the *g* from words ending in *-ing*, for example, makes it difficult for persons from other cultures to understand the words. Saying, "I'm askin' ya …" instead of "I'm asking you …" also may result in a loss of credibility. Effective speakers need to make sure the words they use are clearly spoken, correctly used, and understandable. Always check a pronunciation dictionary for the most accurate pronunciations.

- **Grammar.** Grammatical correctness is an important consideration. Not only is the classroom teacher bothered by incorrect grammar and inappropriate use of words, but we are also judged in the world outside the classroom by the way we present our ideas. This suggests that, before we present a speech, we should practice it before others who might detect our errors, dropped sounds, grammatically incorrect words, and mispronunciations.

  Mispronounced words are different from regional and ethnic dialects that affect pronunciation. The effect of dialect on an audience depends a great deal on the makeup of the audience and whether or not they understand the difference between dialect usage and standard pronunciation of words. Speakers should always strive to learn similarities and differences between their own dialects and those of others and adapt their messages to the situation. An African American student who uses Ebonics when speaking with friends, for example, needs to adjust language in the classroom and the workplace so listeners can easily understand.

- **Articulation.** Good articulation involves producing and saying words clearly and distinctly. Physical problems, such as cleft palate, difficulty in controlling the tongue, or a misaligned jaw, can create articulation problems that require specialized help, but most articulation problems result from laziness. We sometimes chop, slur, or mumble words because we do not take the time to learn the words correctly. People say "gonna" instead of "going to," "didja" instead of "did you," or "dunno" instead of "don't know." These articulation errors can lead your listeners to believe you are less credible and can reduce clarity. Unfortunately, many people don't realize their articulation is sloppy or incorrect unless someone tells them. Listen to what you say and how you sound. Concentrate on identifying and eliminating your most common articulation errors. Correcting articulation errors can be well worth the effort; you will sound more intelligent and more professional, and you will further establish your credibility as an educated person.

- **Vocal fillers.** Fillers such as "um," "uh," "ah," "and uh," "like," and, "you know" can become both distracting and irritating to your listeners. Most communication instructors will note (and probably reduce your grade) when your speech has too many vocal fillers.

VOCAL VARIETY The combination of rate, force, and pitch variations that add to a speaker's overall vocal quality is called **vocal variety**. Such variety gives feeling to your delivery and adds emphasis to what you say. Your voice allows listeners to perceive subtle differences in the intent of your messages by altering rate, force, and pitch, promoting a genuine understanding between you and your audience.

vocal variety
Variations in rate, force, and pitch.

- **Rate.** The speed at which a speaker speaks—usually between 120 and 175 words per minute—is known as **rate**. Speaking at the appropriate rate requires self-awareness. If your rate is too fast or too slow or never changes, it can detract from the impact of your message. Sometimes when we're nervous, our speaking rate increases so much we are practically unintelligible to our listeners. We must learn to control this rapid rate by breathing deeply before we begin speaking and by purposely using pauses to help us slow down and concentrate on the message.

rate
Speed at which a speaker speaks, normally between 120 and 175 words per minute.

- **Pauses.** A **pause** can be an effective means of gaining attention, adding emphasis to an important point, and enabling listeners to follow shifts in ideas. Pauses punctuate and emphasize thoughts. Beginning speakers need to realize the important

pause
A brief stop in speaking to gain attention, add emphasis, separate, or otherwise punctuate ideas.

Making Connections for Success

Effective Use of Your Voice

Have you ever really stopped to listen to broadcast journalists? Take a few minutes to watch the local newscast and also one of the national or international broadcasts (e.g., ABC, BBC, CBC, CBS, CNN, FOX, ESPN, NBC, Al-Jazeera). Television personalities and nationally syndicated radio announcers often have very clear vocal delivery. They don't drop word endings, they have naturally animated vocal patterns, and they rarely use fillers and vocalized pauses such as "um," "uh," "and uh," or "like."

1. Now, listen to your instructors and classmates. How many have "easy-to-listen-to" voices? What is the big difference between those who use their voices effectively and those who do not?

2. What effect do fillers, such as those identified here, have on you?

3. What other vocal characteristics distract you?

4. What vocal characteristics help you stay "tuned in" to the speaker?

Making Connections for Success

Use of Pauses

Read the following (aloud) without a pause.

Aidan said that he had a fear of public speaking and he said getting up in front of people is much more frightening than the thought of death or even taxes and he hoped he would be able to avoid giving speeches even though he had to take an oral communication class.

Now read the same sentence and pause appropriately with periods and commas.

Aidan said that he had a fear of public speaking. He said, "Getting up in front of people is much more frightening than the thought of death or even taxes." He hoped he would be able to avoid giving speeches, even though he had to take an oral communication class.

1. What difference do the pauses make in what you hear?
2. How did the use of verbal punctuation—your pauses— help convey the meaning?

---

contribution of both rate and pauses to the overall effect of their presentations. Listen carefully to accomplished speakers. Notice how an effective speaker varies rate and uses pauses to set off ideas, to prepare for the next point, and to provide silent emphasis for ideas. Again, accomplished speakers tend to do this within the context of a conversational style.

force

The intensity and volume level of the voice.

- **Force.** The intensity and volume of the voice is called **force**. You must choose a volume level that is comfortable for your audience. However, you can use force to communicate your ideas with confidence and vigor, to emphasize an important point, and to regain lagging interest. When you learn how to use force, you can greatly increase your effectiveness as a speaker.

pitch

How low or high the voice is on a tonal scale.

- **Pitch. Pitch** refers to how low or high the voice is on a tonal scale. Variety in pitch can eliminate monotony and add emphasis to keywords. Variety in pitch contributes to greater conversationality and thus makes it easy for the listener to maintain interest in and attention to the speaker and message.

Obviously, any change in rate, force, or pitch makes a word, phrase, or sentence stand out. The greater the amount of change or the more sudden the change, the more emphatic the word or statement. You can use such contrasts to make selected ideas seem more important than material delivered without such variations.

Physical Aspects

An awareness of effective nonverbal communication is essential when you present a speech. Among the physical factors that can affect delivery are personal appearance, body movement, gestures, facial expressions, and eye contact. Each of these must be well coordinated and relevant to the purpose of your speech.

PERSONAL APPEARANCE Personal appearance—what a speaker looks like and the way a speaker dresses, grooms, and presents him- or herself to others—is an extremely important consideration. Typical "student attire" is not always acceptable. As a general rule, you should use common sense in dressing for the occasion. For example, caps, large dangly earrings, and "busy" printed T-shirts may distract your audience from what you are saying (and have a negative effect on the people evaluating your presentation). Most instructors frown on the wearing of caps for a variety of other reasons as well: It is in questionable taste, and caps hide your facial expressions. Exceptions to this include head coverings worn for religious reasons. First impressions are based mainly on appearance. Your audience may form instant, hard-to-change opinions about your attitude toward them and yourself. In this way, appearance can affect your credibility.

When presenting your speech you should be very cognizant of your personal appearance as it can effect your credibility and how the audience perceives you.

Research in nonverbal and relational communication suggests that personal appearance has a function in communication. Appearance can have an impact on a speaker's self-image and thus can affect how the speaker communicates with others.[9] You should dress for a special occasion when you present your speech. When you look good, you feel good, and that positively affects your performance.

BODY MOVEMENT Body movement is closely related to personal appearance. It includes posture, which should be relaxed and natural; avoid slouching. Because an audience's attention instinctively follows moving objects, your motions should be easy and purposeful. The use of movement—stepping to the side, forward, or backward—can hold attention and help to communicate ideas. Movement can also serve as a nonverbal transition between points. Purposeful movement, along with posture, can indicate confidence and convey a positive self-image. Too much movement or unmotivated, nervous movement, however, can distract your audience, make them think you are not poised and confident, and detract from your credibility.

GESTURES You can use **gestures**—movements of the head, arms, and hands—to help illustrate, emphasize, or clarify a point. Gestures should be spontaneous, not forced. For example, when you talk to acquaintances about something you have strong feelings about, your gestures come naturally. If you are sad, angry, or happy, you automatically make gestures that express your emotions. To obtain equally natural gestures when giving a speech, you need to be equally involved in what you are saying. If you concentrate on getting your message across rather than on your gestures, you will find your move more freely and naturally.

When you first learn how to give a speech, gestures might seem a bit uncomfortable, but no gestures might also seem awkward. To overcome this problem, practice the use of gestures in front of others who are willing to offer positive suggestions for improvement. Be assured that, as you give more and more speeches, you will find gestures become more natural and easier. Soon, without even thinking, you'll use strong and smooth-flowing gestures that help to hold your audience's attention and add meaning to your message.

FACIAL EXPRESSIONS Facial expressions are configurations of the face that can reflect, augment, contradict, or be unrelated to a speaker's vocal delivery. They account for much of the emotional impact of a speaker's message. Your face is a highly

gesture
A movement of the head, arms, or hands that helps to illustrate, emphasize, or clarify an idea.

Making Connections for Success

Nonverbal Behavior and Effective Presentation of Information

Physical and vocal factors can play an important part in the effect of your presentation on listeners. Your messages and delivery can be enhanced or damaged by the way you present ideas. In an effort to analyze the behaviors of others in presenting information, take the next few days to observe professors, classmates, and others as they present information. Consider the messages (words, ideas) and the manner of presentation (physical and vocal factors of delivery). Take notes about the presenter and the presentation and then answer these questions:

1. How did speakers use their voices to communicate ideas?
2. How did speakers vary their rates? What was the effect?
3. What positive factors of physical and vocal delivery did you observe? What effect did these positive aspects have on you, the listener?
4. What negative factors of physical and vocal delivery did you observe? What effect did these negatives have on you as the listener?
5. What aspects of delivery made a particularly positive impression on you?
6. What will you remember about presentations from this activity?

This speaker appears confident and natural as she speaks to her audience. Her gestures are expressive and she has moved closer to the audience to help communicate her interest in them and in the topic.

eye contact

The extent to which a speaker looks directly at audience members.

expressive part of your body. Facial expressions quickly and accurately tell your audience a lot about you. For example, whether you are serious, happy, worried, or angry, the audience will be able to "read" your face. Because your audience will infer a great deal from your facial expression, it is important to look warm and friendly. Such an expression will inform your listeners that you are interested in them and in what you are saying. Of course, your topic, your purpose, the situation, and your audience will all determine exactly what facial expressions are appropriate as you progress through your speech.

EYE CONTACT   The extent to which a speaker looks *directly* at audience members, making **eye contact**, is associated with facial expression. Facial expressions indicate a speaker's feelings about the message, while eye contact seems more related to a speaker's feelings about the listeners. Eye contact is the most important physical aspect of delivery, as it indicates interest and concern for others and implies self-confidence. Most speech communication teachers recommend that you look at your audience while you are speaking, not over their heads or at a spot on the wall.

When you look at members of your audience, you establish a communicative bond between them and you. Speakers who ignore their audiences are often perceived as tentative, ill at ease, insincere, or dishonest.

Eye contact with your audience should be pleasant and personal. Give your listeners the feeling you are talking to them as individuals in a casual conversation. When speaking to a small audience (5 to 30 people), try to look at each individual for a few seconds at a time. To avoid looking shifty, move your eyes gradually and smoothly from one person to another. For larger groups, it is best to scan the audience and occasionally talk to a specific member or members. Do not look over people's heads and avoid staring, which can give the impression that you're angry or hostile. Try not to make your listeners uncomfortable. We have students serve as peer listeners and evaluate speakers. They often comment on the failure to establish eye contact and note when a speaker looks at a few listeners and not the entire audience. If you look at only one or two people, others will feel left out, and those whom you "stared at" will feel uncomfortable.

Your eyes should convey that you are confident, sincere, and speaking with conviction. The message the audience should receive from your eye contact is that you care about them and about what you are saying. At first, establishing eye contact with an audience may make you uncomfortable; but, as you gain experience, you will feel more at ease. You will soon find that eye contact puts you in control of the situation and helps you to answer these questions: Can they hear me? Do they understand? Are they listening?

Making Connections for Success

Speech Delivery

Technology has influenced every aspect of our lives, including the way teachers teach, students learn, candidates campaign for office and win support for their priorities, and businesspeople make presentations.

1. Access your web browser.
2. Go to My Communication Lab and access the library of sample speeches.

3. Choose one of the speeches; view it and analyze it as you watch.
4. What do you notice about eye contact, gestures, and body movement? How effective was the physical delivery?
5. View the clip for vocal delivery. What do you notice about vocal variety, rate, pitch, force, and volume?
6. Evaluate the overall delivery of the speech. What worked? What needed improvement?

Table 10.3 Distracting Speaker Behaviors

General Delivery	Eyes	Body
Rapid speech	Rolling eyes	Tense, rigid
Speaking too slowly	Looking at the floor or ceiling	Sloppy posture
Sighing	Staring	Swaying
Nervous laughter or smiles	Lack of sustained eye contact	Dancing
Choppiness	**Voice**	Hunched shoulders
Awkward pauses	Monotone	Leaning on lectern
Face	Singsong patterns	**Feet/Legs**
Scowls	Nasal voice	Shuffling
Listless look	Mumbling	Weight shifts
Hands	Too soft	Crossing legs
Waving	Too loud	Leg or foot shakes
Playing with hair or object (such as note cards or a pen)		
Hands in pocket		

When you work to strengthen your use of positive vocal and physical behaviors and to reduce negative ones you will greatly improve your delivery. Table 10.3 lists several behaviors that can detract from a speech's effectiveness. Observe yourself in front of a mirror or ask a supportive friend for feedback during a practice session to avoid these problems.

Presentational Aids

10.4 **Construct** presentational aids that enhance your speeches and help your listeners attend to the presentation.

Speakers face multiple challenges. Among them are determining how to grab an audience's attention and making information clear to them. Your topic and your delivery (including verbal and nonverbal communication) are extremely important in gaining and keeping an audience's attention. Of course, your audience's need to know or desire to listen is also important in gaining and maintaining attention and interest. Some speeches, because of the complexity of their content, require presentational aids. Presentational aids should be used only when they reinforce, engage, support, and clarify a speaker's message.

Benefits of Presentational Aids

The question you should ask before using presentational aids is: Will a presentational aid enhance, improve, and make my presentation more interesting as well as more understandable to my audience? If the answer is yes, then using a presentational aid makes sense. If, however, a presentational aid is included for no other reason than to use one, it can become a distraction as well as interfere with the message conveyed. Many instructors require students to use presentational aids in at least one of their speeches because of the benefit gained from experience. **Presentational aids**, also referred to as visual aids or audiovisual aids, are materials and equipment—such as diagrams, models, real objects, photographs, tables, charts, graphs, and computer-generated materials—that speakers may use to enhance content as well as delivery. All presentational aids must serve a meaningful purpose to enhance the speech. In

presentational aids

Materials and equipment, such as diagrams, models, real objects, photographs, tables, charts, and graphs, that speakers may use to enhance the speech's content and delivery.

today's media-saturated society, so much of what is communicated has a sound o. visual component to help get a message across to an audience. Thus, when a presen tational aid can be used, it can be quite effective in helping speakers drive home thei point.

Every speaker should consider five conditions before using presentational aids:

1. Will they help make your speech more understandable to the audience?
2. Will they help accomplish your purpose?
3. Will the audience regard you as unprepared if you don't use them?
4. Will they hold the audience's attention?
5. Will they enhance your credibility?

If any of these conditions are not met, then using presentational aids will likely not benefit your presentation.

The use of presentational aids has several advantages, examined in the following paragraphs.

MAKE A SPEECH UNDERSTANDABLE AND MEMORABLE Presentational aids can make it easier for audience members to understand and remember the content of a speech.[10] Of course, a great deal depends on the aids themselves and how they are used. Words, as we all know, are abstract, and listeners have to translate them into mental images. The problem arises when different listeners and especially a cultur-ally diverse audience conjure up different mental images for the same word or words speakers use. Presentational aids, however, can produce a more concrete image or at the very least provide a connection with the messages that speakers wish to convey.

Speakers can better control the images audience members receive when they use both verbal and visual components in their speech. In general, people remember information better when they both hear and see something. Researchers have found that presentations using visuals improve retention of speech content. Audience mem-bers who heard a presentation that included visuals remembered approximately 85 percent of what they heard and saw after 3 hours and 65 percent after 3 days.[11] Audience members who heard the same presentation without visuals recalled approximately 70 percent after 3 hours and only 10 percent of the information after 3 days. It's clear from the research that visuals, if appropriate and used correctly, have a significant impact on retention of information.

ENHANCE SPEAKER CREDIBILITY A well-done visual presentation tells your audience you put additional effort into preparing your speech. Audiences see speak-ers who use presentational aids, according to the research, as more professional, better prepared, more interesting, more persuasive, and more concrete. In some situations, especially business and professional settings, visuals are the norm and are expected. If they are not used, an audience may have the impression that you did not prepare and that you weren't taking the audience seriously. We recommend you know your audience's expectations and the context of the presentation to ensure that you make a successful connection with your audience.

When you use appropriate presentational aids, you show your audience you are believable and thus trustworthy. You let them see for themselves what you are talking about and show them you want them to understand rather than rely solely on words. When you show presentational aids from reliable and credible sources, you tell your audience you are open to their scrutiny and are determined to be truthful and fair minded, which ultimately enhances your credibility.

CREATE AUDIENCE ATTENTION AND INTEREST Gaining and keeping an audi-ence's attention and interest is not an easy process and usually requires a lot of prepa-ration and effort on the speaker's part. We have already indicated that a speech is often more successful when speakers use variety in their voices, gestures, and movements.

It is also true that presentational aids enhance a speech by adding variety and interest. When speakers use pictures, charts, graphs, video clips, slides, or objects, they alter their presentation and thus increase an audience's attention, even if only momentarily. If the presentational aid is done well and is meaningful to the audience, it likely will not only gain the attention of the audience but will also make the speech more interesting, which should be the goal of every speaker. Thus, if presentational aids are carefully developed and add to an understanding of the speech content, they not only will gain the attention of your audience but also will actually enhance the audience's interest.

PROVIDE SUPPORT Presentational aids can serve as an excellent form of evidence, and help bolster speakers' points of view. Suppose you claim that today's television shows have become more violent than just two years ago. You could support this claim by providing a graph that clearly illustrates the increase in violent episodes and you could show some short video clips on how the violence has escalated over the years.

Presentational aids provide another form of support, especially when the aids are from reputable sources: You will, in effect, improve your credibility. For example, when you show a picture of a homeless family living in a car, you illustrate how poverty affects people and provide evidence to support your words. Presentational aids allow your audience to literally see for themselves the real-world representations of concepts in your speech. This makes your message more immediate and believable.

HELP WITH DELIVERY Often, speakers have trouble with their delivery or with remembering part of what they want to say. Thus, many speakers tend to become overly reliant on notes; this reduces their eye contact with the audience and can make them sound mechanical. When overused, notes can give the impression the speaker is unprepared and unrehearsed. The perception of being unprepared reduces credibility or at the very least makes the audience less desirous of listening to the speaker.

There is, of course, no substitute for practicing your delivery, but the use of presentational aids can also help guide your delivery. Correctly used presentational aids can become an outline for parts of your speech. Each year your authors facilitate many workshops for a variety of audiences, and all use technology to project ideas or key words. These visual presentational aids not only help the participants' comprehension, but also function as an outline, reminding speakers and listeners of what is to be addressed and what is coming next. Many beginning speakers have also found that the prompts of presentational aids do help to alleviate speaking anxiety.

Even more than reducing speaking anxiety, presentational aids can actually help make you seem more dynamic. When used correctly, presentational aids allow speakers to move more easily from point to point, and to become more physically active during their presentations. Clearly, presentational aids can increase speakers' confidence.

Research has shown that audiences remember information longer when it is accompanied by audio, visual, or presentational aids.[12] Many businesses require employees to make presentations and to use the computer in enhancing their presentations. Some company managers believe that unless the presenter uses the computer for audio, visual, or audiovisual aids, the speaker is not really performing well. Although classroom teachers do not always require the use of computer-generated or computer-assisted presentational materials, it is important to know they are common in the workplace. More and more, organizations require computer-aided presentations. Medical doctors and dentists, for instance, create multimedia presentational aids to help explain procedures, illnesses, and treatments to their patients. We'll next look at types of presentational aids and the methods of presenting them in speeches.

Choosing and Using Presentational Aids

When planning to use presentational aids, keep the following guidelines in mind:

1. **Presentational aids should serve a need.** They should never be used just for the sake of using them. In some cases, visual aids are not appropriate, but in others they can get a point across better than words alone. For example, it is easier to show an audience how to create PowerPoint slides than it is to tell them. Furthermore, it is easier yet to tell *and* to show them.

2. **Presentational aids should be planned and adapted to the audience and the situation.** The size of the visual aid and the distance between you and your audience should be considered. The visual material should be kept simple and free from too much detail.

3. **Presentational aids should not dominate or take over a speaker's job.** They should supplement, but never replace, the speaker. Do not rely too heavily on visual aids; instead, use them to help elaborate or explain a point or idea or to create interest. In a speech, visual aids *always* require explanation by the speaker in order to make them meaningful.

4. **Presentational aids should look as professionally prepared as possible.** Accurate and neat materials will create a positive impression on the audience and reflect favorably on the competence of the speaker. Aids should be free from factual and spelling errors. They should also be bright, attractive, and easy to read from any spot in the audience. Audience members ought to be able to see, read, and understand the presentational aid once the speaker has carefully explained it.

5. **Presentational aids should be practical—easy to prepare, use, and transport.** Aids should not interfere with the speaker and presentation and should not call undue attention to themselves.

6. **Presentational aids that are not original or that contain information that is not the speaker's require documentation.** Cite the source either directly on the aid where the audience can see it or in the context of the speech.

7. **Visuals should contain only one idea—one graph per poster, and so on.** Remember presentational aids are meant to clarify and strengthen the speaker's message. Limit yourself to one idea per poster, slide, chart, graph, or computer-generated screen so listeners can focus on one idea at the time you are talking about the corresponding point or concept. Too much information distracts listeners.

Using aids during a presentation requires planning and coordination. They should not distract the audience or interrupt the flow of the speech. See the Guidelines feature near the end of the chapter for ideas on using these aids.

Types of Presentational Aids

A variety of different presentational aids and the methods for presenting them to audiences are available. The most frequently used types of presentational aids are computer-generated images, video and digitized video clips, and, when these images and video or video clips are not available or practical, then real objects, models, photographs and prints, diagrams, tables, and graphs.

COMPUTER-GENERATED IMAGES Millions of images that could be used as presentational aids are found on the Internet. All you must do is search for a specific type of visual image, and you are likely to find what you are looking for in just a few seconds. For example, you are interested in "college sports mascots" and want to show some pictures and talk about their meaning, history, or impact. Enter the key words "college sports mascots," and you will find not only pictures of each mascot but its history as well. Almost any image, graph, or chart you want is accessible on the

Internet. If you know how to do a search on a computer, there is no limit to the images you can find on any subject. Of course, it is always prudent to check out the source of the visual aid and to cite its source to ensure yours and its credibility.

VIDEO AND DIGITIZED VIDEO CLIPS   The Internet is a rich source for video clips on thousands of subject areas, and you can also create and place your own digitized video clips for your presentations. When using video in your presentation, it is important for it to have relevance to your presentation. In addition, it should not dominate or distract; an appropriate short video clip can enhance your presentation. For example, a student used a 30-second video clip in her informative speech to illustrate how personal information on the Internet can affect getting into college or getting a job. The clip clearly demonstrated what is reasonable and what may be inappropriate to place on a website.

You can also use short video clips to demonstrate a process or to show part of a famous political speech to make a point more realistic. However, it is important to still maintain eye contact with your audience while the clip is playing. And the video clip should occupy only a very brief portion of your speech; for example, in a 5- to 7-minute speech a video clip should be no more than 30 seconds. For longer speeches (10 or more minutes) a video clip could last up to a minute or more. Remember that the video clip is used to illustrate an idea or point you make. It does not replace the speech itself. Video can be extremely interesting, and a powerful way to express an idea, but can also create problems if not well rehearsed. For example, when equipment malfunctions, or the clip cannot be located, it is difficult for most speakers to recover from such events and achieve their purpose. If at all possible, download clips you will use and have them ready to access at the appropriate time or include a link in your PowerPoint or Prezi slides so you can easily access the clip. We next discuss those presentational aids that could be used in a speech when computer-generated images or video clips are either not available or not practical.

REAL OBJECTS   A real object is any three-dimensional representation that illustrates or brings to life an idea, concept, or activity you wish to communicate to your audience. Objects can make excellent presentational aids if they are (1) large enough to be seen by everyone in the audience and (2) small enough to be effectively used in a speech. To make sure the object is beneficial to your speech, prepare and practice in advance with your object. For example, a musical instrument, a piece of sporting equipment, or a kind of food might be appropriate objects to use in a speech. Using a real object can make your topic come alive, but it can also create problems if the object is too large, too small, or too difficult to show.

Use of any object or prop should help your audience focus on your speech purpose, not serve as a distraction. Pets, for example, are often unpredictable and can be distracting before, during, and after a speech. Thus, we recommend not using anything that you cannot control or that risks becoming a distraction.

MODELS   You should consider a model when it is not practical to display the actual object because of size or cost. A model—or representation of a real object—allows a speaker to enlarge or shrink an object to a convenient size for use in a speech. For example, it may be impractical to show the actual circuitry of a computer microchip, which is no larger than a pinhead, or the inside of a bio-fuel engine, which is too large (not to mention too expensive). Models of these would be appropriate and accomplish the same purpose as the actual objects. Some of these items and some of the models, as well, can be displayed on a digital display presenter (ELMO).

Models can be life size. For example, a premed student who wants to inform classmates about the parts of the brain affected when a football player or boxer takes serious blows to the head can do so by showing one or more models of the brain to illustrate the point. Constructing a three-dimensional model requires skill and effort, and can be expensive. When students used models in our classes, they were often able to borrow them from other academic departments or private businesses or organizations.

PHOTOGRAPHS, DRAWINGS, AND DIAGRAMS When models, objects, or computer-generated images are not available or practical, a photograph, drawing, or diagram might be the solution. Deciding which to use depends on what you wish to illustrate and what is available. A photograph is an excellent tool for explaining details and surroundings. One student, speaking on artistic style, brought in several prints to illustrate the differences. Another student who spoke on poverty in third-world countries brought in a powerful set of photos showing people living in extremely poor conditions. Finally, a student who spoke about the effects of global warming on Alaska's glaciers brought in two enlarged photos from two different personal trips to Alaska. The photos were of the same glacier and clearly illustrated how much the glacier had shrunk in just a 5-year period. Thus, the photos helped reinforce her point.

When photographs or prints are unavailable, are too small, or lack adequate detail, a drawing or diagram may be used. Most of us are not very artistic, but that should not be a concern, since most drawings or diagrams used in the classroom not computer generated or created by a professional artist can be relatively simple. Figure 10.1 illustrates a simple line drawing showing the location of work areas in a workroom-remodeling project.

A speaker could use an architect's blueprint, a table or graph illustrating statistics, a chart illustrating a company's organizational hierarchy, a drawing of basic football plays, or a map of various regions within a country. Virtually anything can be diagramed and drawn. For example, a table is an orderly arrangement of data in columns to highlight similarities and differences, as shown in Figure 10.2.

Figure 10.1 Example of a Simple Line Drawing

Line drawings need not be complex or elaborate, and can, in fact, be rather simple.

Work Table

Supply Table

Completed Projects

Figure 10.2 Example of Data Presented as a Table

Tables display large amounts of data in a relatively small space. The more complex the data, the more explanation is required to make the table meaningful to your listeners. Be sure the table accurately reflects content and keep it simple and brief.

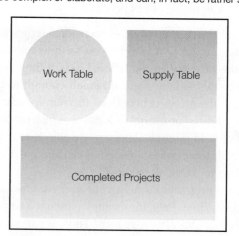

Popular Pharmaceuticals, Uses, Costs, and Effects			
Drug	**Uses**	**Cost**	**Effects**
Tylenol™ Over-the-counter	Aches, pains	$19.95 per 200 tabs	General pain relief; some side effects (minor)
Omeprazole™ Prescription only	Heartburn, stomach ulcers	$145.29 per 90 tabs, 40 mg	Used for treating acid-induced inflammation and ulcer; few side effects
Celebrex™ Prescription only	Joint pain	$124.17 per 180 tabs, 100 mg	Acute pain relief; some side effects, some major side effects

Tables conveniently display large amounts of information or data in a relatively small space, but they can be too complex or lengthy (and perhaps boring) and may even require complex and lengthy explanations. As with any presentational aid, a table must be concise, simple, and clear so that the important information is easy to comprehend by your audience.

Graphs are sometimes better because they can help make statistical data more vivid and illustrate relationships in ways that are easy for an audience to grasp. A line graph, as illustrated in Figure 10.3, can be particularly helpful for clarifying comparative data over time. Graphs can help show trends over a span of days, months, or years.

Bar graphs are another simple way to illustrate comparisons. Figure 10.4 demonstrates how a bar graph clearly illustrates the comparison of popular literary genres and the number of men and women who prefer each type.

Pie graphs illustrate proportional divisions of a whole set of data. Each wedge of the pie represents a percentage of the whole. Pie graphs are often used to show distribution patterns and financial distributions. The pie graph in Figure 10.5 clearly illustrates the percentages of those with and without health insurance. Notice, too, the pie graph starts with a radius drawn vertically from the center to the 12 o'clock position. Each segment is then drawn in clockwise, from the largest down to the smallest.

Figure 10.3   Example of a Simple Line Graph

Line graphs provide all kinds of data. This example illustrates the comparison of population and automobile registrations over a 90-year period.

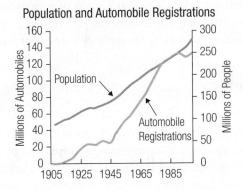

Figure 10.4   Example of a Simple Bar Graph

This bar graph demonstrates favorite book types for men and women. Comparisons are helpful ways to illustrate various kinds of information.

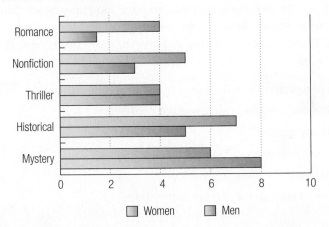

Figure 10.5 Example of a Simple Pie Graph

This pie graph shows how many people have and do not have insurance. It begins with the larger number at the top in the 12 o'clock position and moves clockwise to the smaller.

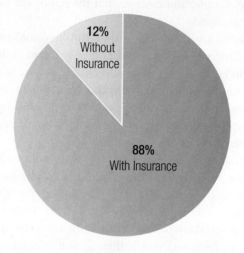

12%
Without
Insurance

88%
With Insurance

Presentation Software

10.5 Understand how integrating software programs can aid your presentation

PowerPoint and Prezi can be either an effective tool or something your intended listeners just tune out. We've all seen some really good and some really bad uses of these formats. What's the difference? As you know, good presentations emphasize content, not technology. An effective speaker knows that all presentational aids are supposed to *enhance* the presentation, not *become* (or replace) the presentation.

Deciding When to Use PowerPoint or Prezi in Your Presentations

Contrary to popular practice, neither PowerPoint nor Prezi is *always* the best presentational aid. When was the last time you were impressed by a PowerPoint/Prezi presentation? Most public speaking instructors place some limitations on its use for classroom presentations. And, when instructors allow or require PowerPoint/Prezi, they have specific criteria for its use. While we should all be prepared to take advantage of whatever presentational technology is available to us, we also should make careful choices about its use. You don't have to use this software just because it's available, unless it is *required* in your job or in a classroom assignment. Whatever you decide, be sure the presentational aid enhances the speech. If you have more than four slides in a 7- to 10-minute speech, you have too many. Many Internet sources from the business sector suggest a maximum of 10 slides in a 20-minute business presentation. If you decide to, or are required to, use PowerPoint/Prezi, keep the following in mind:

1. Your own perspective—what are you trying to accomplish?
2. Does the PowerPoint/Prezi augment your speech?
3. Is the topic appropriate?
4. Does the room/environment support its use?
5. Will it help you make your points?
6. Have you used enough but not too many slides?

Creating Effective PowerPoint or Prezi Presentations

It's important to make the right choices. The use of color, the type and size of the font, and the use of graphics and pictures are all important factors in effective PowerPoint/ Prezi presentations.

COLOR If you want your presentations to connect with your audience and make your content memorable, choose background colors and designs that are clear, clean, and not too busy. For the classroom, we encourage students to select blue or green backgrounds with little or no movement or sound. Blues and greens are calming, but also readable. Keep the material uncluttered. Use contrasting colors. Text colors should be black or white, and can sometimes be yellow in order to connect with the viewers. Red text may pixilate (dance and waver) and is very hard to read. Yellow is an attention-getting color, but too much can make words and images dance on the screen. In classrooms where one cannot adjust the lighting, it's often preferable to have a neutral (beige, gray, or plain white) background with dark bold headings and subheads. Some color can be used in bulleted points or graphics. Be sure to check out the slides in the classroom prior to your presentation to make sure that the size is appropriate and the colors work.

TYPE AND SIZE OF FONT Times New Roman, Times, Helvetica, and Courier are good fonts for your computer-generated presentations. These fonts are in the serif family style of fonts and are clean and easy to read. (Serif typeface letters have "feet" or small flourish strokes at the upper and lower end of the letter.) Avoid fonts with too many curves and extras, which distract and are hard to read. You can create an interest factor by using a sans serif font such as Helvetica for headings and Times New Roman (serif) for bulleted points. Since you want everyone to see and read this part of your presentation, keep these elements big enough for easy readability.

DISPLAYING THE SLIDE SHOW Display your presentation only when you are referring to it. In the slide show view of PowerPoint, by pressing the "B" key on the keyboard, you can blank the screen when you don't need the image or when there's nothing for the audience to view. Press the "B" key again, and the image is restored. In some classrooms, you can draw on the screen with your fingers, or you can use the Ctrl-P key combination to display a pen on the screen. You can then use the mouse to draw on the slide. Erase by pressing the E key, and get rid of the pen and drawing function by pressing the A key or the Ctrl-L key combination. You can also include blank slides for those times when the material might distract or isn't being talked about. Practice these special effects in advance if you plan to use them.

USE OF GRAPHICS AND PICTURES Graphics and pictures help create and maintain interest. They should be used sparingly, however, to keep your listeners connected to your topic. A good rule of thumb is that no more than 25 percent of your slides should have pictures or graphics on them. If you don't know how to import pictures or graphics, use the help function of your computer's program, or check with the technology department or division of your college. Many schools offer both free and course credit workshops in PowerPoint, Word, Excel, and other software packages. If you don't feel comfortable using the computer, one of these free workshops would be beneficial.

Visual presentational aids can greatly enhance a speech if properly used. The visual should enhance but not *become* the speech. Carefully used presentational aids can help the listener stay involved in the speech.

The Internet is filled with good examples of video clips, movie clips, illustrations, and examples. Carefully search and make judicious use of materials readily available to anyone who has computer and Internet access. Make sure your clips are in good taste and truly illustrate what you want them to do.

Check the credibility of these sources, as well. If there's a question on some of the material, either don't use it or explain why or how it's applicable. Of course, you can create your own YouTube clips as well as take your own pictures, or create computer-generated aids. Just remember to make sure that the aids don't take the place of the presentation itself.

The presentational outline with PowerPoint slides for a presentation on typefaces and fonts provides an example for your analysis.

SAMPLE SPEECH WITH POWERPOINT

This presentational outline is for a speech given in a class on message design and delivery. It emphasizes how PowerPoint should *enhance*, not *become*, the presentation.

TITLE: Using Typeface and Fonts in Your PowerPoint Presentations

PURPOSE: To inform the audience about the requirements of typeface, fonts, designs, and colors in PowerPoint in your speeches.

THESIS: Use of PowerPoint requires careful choice in font type, size, amount of text, and background design and colors.

Get the PowerPoint presentation up on the computer.

Do not display slides until needed.

Look at audience and smile.

Notes the speaker makes to himself/herself are in **red**.

INTRODUCTION I want you to think about presentations in and out of the classroom. Briefly jot down your answers to these questions. How many times have you seen a PowerPoint presentation this semester? When was the last time you were impressed by such a presentation?

Pause.

We are often required to create a PowerPoint, and we sometimes think that's the *best* way to get our ideas across. Today we'll look at some of the choices we can make for font size and types as well as background design and colors to create more compelling PowerPoints that actually augment the speech.

(slide 1)

BODY

I. What are typefaces and font size and what do they have to do with making a PowerPoint presentation?

Show title slide (slide 1) while talking and move to slide 2, which explains typeface differences.

a. Typeface refers to a family of type (examples)

    I. Serif

    II. Sans serif

    III. In between

    IV. Where used and why?

(slide 2)

Only ten slides were used in the 12-minute presentation: six slides with text (including the title slide) and four blank slides. Note that the amount of information on each slide is minimal. A blue background was used because the color works and because the classroom lights could be adjusted.

Pause; move to slide 3, which deals with font size.

   b. Font size

      I. Guidelines

      II. 44 points for headings

      III. 36 or 40 points text

      IV. 28 smallest

      V. Auditorium requires larger

Switch to blank screen, slide 4.

II. How much text do I use on slides?

Show slide 5.

   a. How should text be used?

   b. How much is enough?

Switch to blank screen, slide 6.

III. Background design display

Slide 7

   a. Choice of background color or no color?

   b. Best colors

   c. How much design on background?

Switch to blank screen, slide 8.

   d. Should I import graphics?

IV. General guidelines

Show final slide, slide 9 with general guidelines, then show final blank slide, slide 10.

CONCLUSION Now that we've covered some of the basics of design for PowerPoint presentations, I hope you will know what typefaces might work best and what font sizes to use in specific situations. The decision to use a background color or one of the available templates in PowerPoint and whether or not to include graphics depends on you, your topic, and especially the conditions in the room where you present. Good luck! May your next PowerPoint presentation be impressive!

Smile, ask for questions, answer, remove jump drive, and move to sit down.

The slides reinforce the points made in the speech, as well as illustrate the font sizes and types.

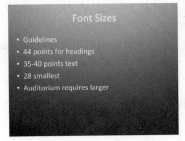

(slide 3)

Blank slides draw the listeners' attention to the speaker and not the slide.

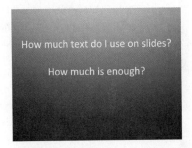

(slide 5)

(slide 7)

(slide 9)

Using Presentational Aids: Who's Really in Control?

Remember that any technology is a tool and should not be allowed to replace the speaker or the message. William Germano, in an article in *The Chronicle of Higher Education,* reminds us that,"… A tool is not a friend and is often a rival."[13] We must learn to use technology and, indeed, any other presentational aids so they serve us, not

Making Connections for Success

The Gettysburg Address

Imagine what President Lincoln might have done with PowerPoint when he delivered the Gettysburg Address. Peter Norvig created a six-slide parody of Lincoln's Gettysburg Address to demonstrate how PowerPoint can become hopelessly irrelevant and boring. Search the Internet to view Norvig's PowerPoint Gettysburg. Compare those six slides to the actual speech:

Fourscore and seven years ago our fathers brought forth on this continent a new nation, conceived in liberty and dedicated to the proposition that all men are created equal.

Now we are engaged in a great civil war, testing whether that nation or any nation so conceived and so dedicated can long endure. We are met on a great battlefield of that war. We have come to dedicate a portion of that field as a final resting-place for those who here gave their lives that that nation might live. It is altogether fitting and proper that we should do this.

But, in a larger sense, we cannot dedicate, we cannot consecrate, we cannot hallow this ground. The brave men, living and dead, who struggled here have consecrated it far above our poor power to add or detract. The world will little note nor long remember what we say here, but it can never forget what they did here. It is for us the living rather to be dedicated here to the unfinished work which they who fought here have thus far so nobly advanced. It is rather for us to be here dedicated to the great task remaining before us—that from these honored dead we take increased devotion to that cause for which they gave the last full measure of devotion—that we here highly resolve that these dead shall not have died in vain, that this nation under God shall have a new birth of freedom, and that government of the people, by the people, for the people shall not perish from the earth.

Now compare the PowerPoint version and Lincoln's original version and answer the following:

1. Which version is the most effective?
2. What distractions does the PowerPoint create?
3. How does PowerPoint take away the meaning?
4. What nonessential items become parts of the presentation?
5. How does the comparison of these two versions affect your thinking about PowerPoint in your own presentations?

The implications seem obvious. Keep this example in mind as you decide whether to use a PowerPoint presentation or some other presentational aid.

take our place as speakers or become the message. Too often the presentation becomes the content, not the means to enhance or illustrate the content. Remember that you are in control, and need to be so. Your audience should remember your points because *you* made the points and your aids reinforced those points.

Murphy's law tells us we can expect the worst to happen. But, well-prepared speeches with carefully constructed presentational aids need not fail. The speaker should be prepared for any eventuality. If you have done your research, organized your materials, made careful choices about the aids you use, and have practiced faithfully, you can overcome whatever difficulties may arise. Your authors always have a plan B or even a plan C when they make presentations in the classroom and in the workforce. We generally have a flash drive or CD with our PowerPoint presentations on them. However, in case the files are not readable, we also bring hard copies of the PowerPoint (generally, we print the four slides per handout in color and bring them along) so we can use the projector function in the room, even if the computer won't read the files. That way, even if we don't have a visual, we can explain what's on the PowerPoint slides and use a chalkboard or white board to illustrate. If the lamp on the projector burns out, you won't be able to project your aids. That means you have to find another way to show your audience what you want. If it's a small enough group and we know how many will be there, we bring hard copies of the most important slides (figures, charts, guidelines).

The important thing to remember is that none of us is perfect and an equipment failure is not the end of the world. Prepare for the best and the worst, and you'll be able to effectively pull off your presentation.

POISE If you've done all that we've recommended in this text, you will be prepared and should feel poised and confident. It's far easier to feel good about a presentation when you're thoroughly prepared for any eventuality.

Guidelines

Using Presentational Aids

1. **Display visual materials only while you are using them.** Do not distract your audience by showing your aids too early or by leaving them on display after you've finished talking about them. Even with a PowerPoint/Prezi presentation, you can create a black, blank, or white screen so as not to distract your listeners.

2. **Keep your presentational aids on display long enough to give everyone ample opportunity to absorb the information.** Find the happy medium between "too long" and "not long enough."

3. **Ensure that everyone can see your aids by making them neat, simple, large, bright, and readable.** If you use computer-generated text, the same guidelines apply. Depending on the size of the room, however, your font size should rarely be less than 36 points. For larger rooms, a 48-point or up to a 60-point font is desirable. The same thing applies to the television screen if you're in a distance-learning classroom. Size, background, and color of text all become critical issues. For televised presentations, a blue background with either a white or yellow text color is preferable. The opposite is true for yellow or white on paper displayed on an ELMO or other projection device, and many posters, charts, or graphs. Light colors fade and are virtually invisible on paper products. Red and black text work better for non-computer presentational aids.

4. **Practice in the room with the equipment you'll use.** This should be done well ahead of time.

5. **Do not talk to your displayed objects or to the chalkboard.** Discuss the content while maintaining eye contact with your audience.

6. **Do not stand in front of your presentational aids.** Determine where you will place or show your aids and use a pointer or a laser to avoid blocking your audience's view.

7. **Practice using your presentational aids until you feel comfortable with them.** It becomes quite obvious to your listeners if you're uncomfortable and unfamiliar with the aids you've selected.

RECOVERY Everyone makes mistakes, and sometimes Murphy's law works its way into our presentations. The only thing you can do is to be ready for anything. If you know your topic, have prepared well, and practiced carefully, your chances of recovering from the little mishaps increases significantly. Don't make a big deal of things you cannot help. One of our colleagues teaches a distance learning class with 25 students in the classroom in the United States, and 10 students in St. Petersburg and 10 in Moscow in Russia, all are connected by two-way interactive technology. The classroom is a "smart classroom" with current technology and the ability to simultaneously see students and teachers in all three classrooms. Our colleague says she always worries about the technical aspects and how they interfere with presentations. One day her students told her, "Hey, don't worry about the technical stuff! We know it, we recognize it's no one's fault. Just go with it and don't call undue attention to it and don't apologize for something you cannot help."[14] We echo their advice: Don't worry about what you have no control over. Know that things happen and be prepared to deal with whatever comes up in the situation.

Practice Your Delivery

10.6 **Perform** your speech delivery in practice sessions to help you gain confidence and practice.

The best way to ensure effective delivery is to practice, practice, and practice. Practice early and often until you feel comfortable with your speech content. Exactly how much practice you will need depends on a number of considerations, including how much experience you have had speaking before audiences, how familiar you are with your subject, and how long your speech is. There is no magic amount of time that will make your delivery perfect.

If your speech is not to be memorized, make sure to use slightly different wording in each run-through. When you memorize a speech, it is possible to master the words

without mastering the content. Your goal should be to learn your content, which wi
mean you have mastered its ideas.

In practicing your delivery, it is important to start with small segments. For exam
ple, practice the introduction, then one main point at a time, and then the conclusio
After you have rehearsed each small segment several times in isolation, practice th
entire speech until you have mastered the content and the ideas flow smoothly.

If possible, practice in the same room where you will speak or, at least, unde
similar conditions. This helps you see how things look from the front of the class an
plan where you should place your visual aids. Your last practice session should leav
you with a sense of confidence and a desire to present your speech.

Finally, concentrate on what you are saying and to whom you are saying it. Abov
all, be yourself.

Summary

Managing Speech Anxiety

Objective 10.1 Identify ways you can manage your speech anxiety.

- Anxiety can be managed through behavioral and cognitive means.
- Communication apprehension is a more serious form of speech anxiety, but it, too, can usually be managed through work and practice, as well as adopting a positive attitude toward change.
- The symptoms of speech anxiety can also be controlled through behavioral and cognitive strategies.
- Speech anxiety has many causes, but through analysis and practice, you can reduce the impact of past experiences.
- Not all cultures can deal with speech anxiety in the same ways. For some, trying to adapt to the majority culture is, in itself, stressful. In such cases, students and instructor should work out some kind of compromise about specific actions.
- Speech anxiety can generally be controlled. This chapter provides specific strategies to help you do so.

Methods of Delivery

Objective 10.2 Demonstrate appropriate use of the four methods of delivery.

- Impromptu delivery is used when it's okay to "wing it" but should usually not be used for formal classroom presentations. Times will arise in the workplace or in community groups when you're called upon to make a speech without prior notice, and practice in this method of delivery can help prepare you for these occasions.
- Manuscript delivery is often mechanical but is also necessary in certain situations in which the exact wording can influence policies or put the speaker in a better light.

- Memorized delivery allows the speaker to move around and get away from the lectern but may cause an uncomfortable situation if memory fails.
- Extemporaneous delivery is usually recommended for most situations and allows speakers to be fully prepared yet conversational in their delivery.

Vocal and Physical Aspects of Delivery

Objective 10.3 Analyze your own vocal and physical aspects of delivery and find ways to improve both.

- Speakers need to use vocal variety—changes in pitch, volume, force, and rate—to make their voices interesting and compelling for the listeners.
- The physical aspects of delivery can greatly increase your listeners' ability to be interested in your ideas. Facial expressions, eye contact, movement, and gestures also help focus the listeners' attention on specific ideas or let them know when you are moving from one topic to another.

Presentational Aids

Objective 10.4 Construct presentational aids that will enhance your speeches and help your listeners stay tuned in to the presentation.

- Presentational aids provide many benefits. They give you the opportunity to make ideas memorable and provide some variety for listeners. Research shows that speeches with presentational aids are better remembered than those without them.
- Speakers should always remember their purpose for speaking and what they hope the listeners will walk away knowing about the topic. Presentational aids can help them focus on the ideas and use the information later.
- While we often think of PowerPoint or Prezi as our best presentational aids, others are equally effective

in certain situations. In fact, some of the more "traditional" aids can add variety and interest as well
as explanations that can get lost in the PowerPoint/
Prezi presentations.

resentation Software

bjective 10.5 **Presentation Software** Explore how
tegrating software programs can aid your presentation.

- If you use PowerPoint/Prezi, make good choices:
  Don't put too much information on any one slide;
  don't have too many slides; find ways to cover the
  slides when they are not in use; and note color, font,
  and size, and what's most effective for the room in
  which you are presenting.
- Assess your presentational aids to ensure they
  clarify and support your speeches.

- Produce effective presentational software aids for
  your speeches.

Practice Your Delivery

Objective 10.6 **Perform** your speech delivery in practice sessions to help you gain confidence and practice.

- If at all possible, practice in the room where you'll
  present, with the equipment you'll be using.
- Ask a friend to listen and observe and then offer
  comments about your speech and delivery.
- Practice helps you find the areas that need improvement or in which you don't seem as confident.
- Practice sessions help you see what might go wrong
  and find alternatives or allow you to adjust to
  things that might go wrong.

Discussion Starters

1. Why do some of us have speech anxiety?
2. What is the difference between speech anxiety or communication apprehension? What are your physical
   and cognitive behaviors associated with each?
3. How can listeners help speakers overcome their
   nervousness?
4. What kinds of delivery methods work best for you?
   When would you use one of the other methods?
5. Why do communication instructors recommend or
   require extemporaneous delivery?
6. What factors of physical delivery have made a positive
   impact on you as an audience member?

7. Think about an effective presentation. What vocal
   and physical factors helped make the presentation
   effective?
8. When and why would you use presentational aids in
   your speeches?
9. When should you use PowerPoint or Prezi in a speech?
10. How does one use presentational aids without letting
    them overpower the content?
11. Why should speakers be listener oriented?

Chapter 11
Informative Speaking

∨ Learning Objectives

This chapter will help you:

11.1 Recognize that information is powerful.

11.2 Explain the distinctions between informative and persuasive speeches.

11.3 Choose appropriate topics for your informative speeches.

11.4 Prepare and develop an informative speech to meet your professor's specific criteria.

11.5 Evaluate and assess your own speeches prior to classroom presentation and apply evaluation criteria to the speeches of others.

Making Everyday Connections

"Professor Lee, how do I present an interesting informative speech? I don't want to sound like a college instructor. I want my listeners to really listen to me. What should I do?" Each semester, students tell their instructors they're unable to think of interesting topics. Some seem to believe that an informative speech is boring. Nothing could be further from the truth. The goal of the informative speech is to provide potentially useful information that may offer a different perspective from what one normally thinks.

Hundreds of informative presentations are made every day. Often, potential speakers have specific knowledge they want to share with others. Sometimes speakers are assigned a topic; at other times, they are free to choose their own topics. Speakers need to carefully analyze their listeners to determine what kinds of informative speeches might appeal to them, and then use language and examples to create interest.

Questions to Think About

1. Explain why you think the concerns described here are or are not accurate?

2. What other concerns do you have about *your* speeches?

3. What differences lie in the types of information you receive and share in the classroom as opposed to other areas of your life?

4. How many times a day do you receive information you need to use immediately or at some time in the future?

We've talked about the preparation process. Now it's time to focus on the informative speech. Is there a reason the informative speech is among the first formal speeches assigned in most communication classes? YES, there is! Much of what we do in our lives involves information—someone asks for information and you provide it, or you ask another person for information and then use what you learned. **Information** is: **1)** Knowledge communicated or received concerning a particular fact or circumstance; news. **2)** Knowledge gained through study, communication, research, instruction, etc.; factual data.[1]

Even if this sounds simple, think about explaining how to create a Facebook page to a friend when you're speaking by phone, about giving someone directions to create an Instagram account when you're not sitting next to each other and neither is at the computer, or describing how to automatically scan a new TV for available channels when you're not side-by-side to show the questioner. If you've ever tried to explain something detailed and relatively complex to one who knows little about it, you know it takes time and careful choice of language, as well as organization, to accomplish your goal.

Teachers inform on a daily basis. People in many jobs are required to present vast amounts of information. If you lack the skills to carefully explain, both you and your listeners may be frustrated. To help with this process, this chapter discusses all aspects of the informative speech, from choosing a topic to delivering the speech. Learning what you need to know and do in informative speaking will help you in your personal and professional life. The informative speech provides the foundation for every speaking situation you face; if you learn the fundamentals of this type of speech, you will be able to apply those concepts to other types of presentations.

information

1. Knowledge communicated or received concerning a particular fact or circumstance; news.
2. Knowledge gained through study, communication, research, instruction, etc.; factual data.

Information and Power

11.1   **Recognize** that information is powerful

Information is beneficial in all aspects of our lives. In preceding centuries, people who had information or knowledge ruled the world. Religious leaders in the church and members of royalty were the only ones who knew how to read. For them information was power, and for us it is, too. When we need information, what do we do? We go to someone who has the information, the web, social media, a book, a newspaper, or a magazine. The greater one's desire to gain important information, the more valuable

Making Connections for Success

Freedom Forum and Newseum.org

The Washington, DC–based Freedom Forum is a nonpartisan, international foundation dedicated to free press, free speech, and free spirit for all people. The foundation focuses on three priorities: the Newseum, the First Amendment, and newsroom diversity. It also provides online resources. Newseum. org features more than 450 newspaper front pages from around the world. Stories are grouped by subject: Newseum, First Amendment, free speech, podcasts, free press, and professional journalism; the top story in each section is featured on the main page.

1. Search the web for "Freedom Forum."
2. Click on one of the top stories on the main page and read it all the way through.
3. Compare that story with one in your hometown or home geographical area. Are the top stories you read also on the front page of your local newspaper?
4. Be prepared to share what you read with others and determine what they learned. Compare similarities and differences.

that information. Thus, people who have information you desire, in a sense, have power over you because they have what you seek. Social media has made information easily available to all who quickly seek it out. Information can spread rapidly online; it is up to the receivers to critically evaluate information that appears in their Twitter feeds and on other platforms. You may read on Twitter that your favorite celebrity died, but how can you be sure that information is true? Knowing how to evaluate information transmitted through social media adds to the power that goes along with possessing information.

The ability to communicate information is essential in our society and has an increasingly important role not only now but in the future. Over the years, we have moved from an economy based on agriculture and heavy industries, such as steel, machinery, and automobile manufacturing, to an economy based on knowledge industries, such as research, health services, banking, training, and communications. Only about 17 percent of our labor force held information-related jobs in the 1950s. This figure has now increased to more than 75 percent. This demand places even more emphasis on workers' needs for greater skills in producing, storing, and delivering information. Some of the information we send and receive is written, but most is spoken. For example, broadcast journalists, teachers, trainers, consultants, media specialists, salespeople, technicians, mechanics, artists, doctors, nurses, lawyers, elected officials, police officers, and managers all depend on oral communication to succeed in their work.

Distinctions Between Informative and Persuasive Speaking

11.2 **Explain** the distinctions between informative and persuasive speeches

The general goal of informative speakers is to increase their listeners' knowledge. The distinction between informing and persuading is very small. The informative speech is meant to increase knowledge, whereas the persuasive speech is meant to alter attitudes and behavior. Information can be presented without any attempt at persuasion, but persuasion cannot be accomplished without attempting to inform.

Two examples will illustrate the difference between information and persuasion. You go into an Apple store to look at the latest MacBook. The salesperson wants to sell one, so she will do her best to persuade you to buy a MacBook. She will share all kinds of information about the computer: its speed, its memory, its flexibility, the ease of maintenance, its security, an explanation of all features, the warranty, and the available technical support. She will provide you with ample information and then make comparisons with other computers or, at the very least, give you compelling reasons to buy that MacBook from her. She may give you knowledge and understanding (information) about the computer, and she tries to persuade you, but you do not purchase the MacBook. She still made a persuasive speech, even though you did not buy, because her goal was persuasive: She wanted you to buy the computer.

Your boss explains how a piece of equipment must be safely used. He wants you to understand how it operates and what safety mechanisms are in place. He does not intend to persuade you on how things should be done; instead, he wishes to help you gain knowledge and understanding so you can solve the problem on your own. He moves to persuasion only if he tries to convince you one method is better than another for solving problems.

The key to understanding the difference between information and persuasion lies in recognizing that *although information may contain some elements of persuasion, all persuasion must provide information.* What separates an informative speech from a persuasive one is the goal of the speaker. Persuasion is discussed in more detail in the next chapter.

We send and receive vast amounts of information every day, in every kind of situation. It's no wonder, then, the informative speech is often one of the first assigned in communication classes such as this one.

Topics for Informative Speeches

11.3   **Choose** appropriate topics for your informative speeches

Are you concerned that you don't know what informative speeches would be interesting to your listeners? Most of us have a wealth of information and a vast list of potential topics based on what we have learned from classes, readings, and other experiences. Think about topics mentioned or covered in other classes, such as social media in the workplace, the Internet, biological discoveries to create better and healthier lives, computers and agriculture, computers and mechanics, computers and art, changes in education, medical advances, alternative health care, global terrorism, gender issues in the 21st century, the impact of an elderly population on our governmental agencies, civic engagement, spirituality and religion, and multiculturalism. The list is endless, and the potential for informative topics is almost limitless.

Connecting with others through communication is easier when they see the value in and uses for the information you share with them. Most of us want the information we receive to be important and useful. We often think, "What's in it for me?" (WIIFM?) You first select a topic you like and know something about, then you need to think about your audience: Is the topic potentially useful to my listeners? Some topics are givens—"preparing for the job interview," "classes to help in the job search," or "getting along with others." These are topics most college students might find useful, if not right now, at least at some point in the future. Topics with less evident personal value, such as "environmental awareness" or "the best cities to visit while on vacation," might seem less interesting, so you will have to clearly answer the question, WIIFM? If you are passionately interested in something, your passion alone can likely help generate interest. Although you may doubt your topic is worthwhile, if you think about your particular interests, past experiences, and special knowledge, you will no doubt discover that you, too, have a great deal to share.

Successful speakers next consider their audiences. They communicate information accurately and clearly, but most important, they make the information meaningful and interesting to their audience by providing new information or correcting misinformation.

Informative speech topics can be classified in many ways. One scheme divides topics into objects, processes, events, and concepts.

Objects

Speeches about *objects* examine concrete subjects: people, animals, things, structures, and places. Here are some possibilities:

Carson Daly
The "Sage of Omaha"—Warren Buffett
First ladies and their accomplishments
The Duggar Family from *19 Kids and Counting*
One World Trade Center
The influence of social media on civil strife around the world
Michael Brown and Darren Wilson
The world's #1 problem: poverty
3-D movies
Benefits of vitamins
Learning, memory, and the human brain
Gay–straight student alliance groups

These topics are general and must be narrowed to meet the guidelines of most classroom speaking situations.

Here are some specific purpose statements for informative speeches about concrete subjects, following the guidelines suggested earlier:

- To inform my audience how vitamins make us healthier
- To inform my audience about the area of the human brain that helps us communicate
- To inform my audience that the teen brain is a work in progress
- To share with my listeners the laws concerning airline travel around the world

Each of these purpose statements is appropriate for an informative speech.

Making Connections for Success

Use the Web to Find Topics

Topics for speeches really are virtually limitless. The Internet can be an excellent *beginning* source of ideas and information. Find additional information from a variety of sources, however, and be sure to meet your instructor's specific criteria and requirements. Here are some possible sources:

1. Use your preferred search engine to look for topics. Search "topics for informative speeches." (Many of the results are companies from which you may buy a list of topics and/or lists of guidelines or even speeches. Do not buy your speech! It's not ethical, and the speeches usually don't suit you or your audience anyway.)

2. Click on a link for an educational institution and then search "topic selection helper for informative speeches." Many include scores of topics ranging from "general subjects" to "personalities" and include a list of "topics based on students' own lives." These lists are good *starting points* to help you think about possible informative topics.

3. The Public Broadcasting System (PBS) has a website highlighting various up-to-date programs. This is a good site to bookmark so you can come back to get more ideas or find additional information. On the main page, go to "Explore" and click on and choose the topic you think might yield good results (Arts & Drama, History, Home & Hobbies, Life & Culture, News & Views, Science & Nature). Once there, scroll through the list and read one of your choice. For example, News & Views offers Business & Finance, Health, Military, Opinion & Analysis, World, Government & Politics, Law & Order, Newsmakers, and Social Issues.

4. Bartleby is a source for free online literature, verse, and reference works. Electronic versions of 35 works are available, including: *The Columbia Encyclopedia, the American Heritage Dictionary, Roget's II: The New Thesaurus, Simpson's Contemporary Quotations, World Orations, The New-Dictionary of Cultural Literacy,* and the *American Heritage Book of English Usage.*

rocesses

process topic usually focuses on a demonstration in which the speaker explains how
nething is done or how it takes place. Here are a few sample specific purpose state-
nts for informative speeches about processes:

To inform my audience about the areas of the brain that correspond to language
activities

To explain how sugar causes the number-one health crisis in North America today

To inform my listeners about how an ordinary citizen can affect the legislative
process

eeches about processes generally serve two purposes: to increase understanding
d to teach someone *how to do something*. This could involve anything from knowing
PR and its life saving effects to how to buy the right car.

Process speeches are usually organized in time-sequence (chronological) order,
eaning that they proceed step by step from the beginning of the process to its end.
r example, let's say your speech is on saving lives through an automated external
efibrillator. You would walk your listeners through all the necessary steps and proce-
ires so they would know exactly what to do if the occasion were to arise.

Description of a process usually benefits from the use of a visual aid. Some pro-
esses may require an actual demonstration to be fully understood. For example, to
form listeners about how to fold fancy napkin shapes, you might have to do the
lding during the speech and ask your audience to follow along.

vents

iformative speeches about events discuss happenings or occasions. The many pos-
ible topics include the following:

The college football playoff

The first private space shuttle

The removal of the confederate flag from the South Carolina statehouse grounds

Robin Williams's death and suicide awareness

Global financial chaos and reform

The Pope Francis Effect

Mardi Gras

The popularity of NASCAR events

Student protests about tuition

Student protests against administrative actions

Same-sex marriage and religious freedom

Darren Wilson trial

Making Connections for Success

Experimenting with Informative Speech Topics

The speech process entails time and effort as you plan, research,
organize, create, and practice the speech. This exercise will give
you some practical application for the actual speech.

1. Select one of the purpose statements from each category
on the previous pages.

2. Indicate the organizational pattern you think will work for
each statement.

3. Identify two useful presentational aids and be prepared
to provide a rationale for why you think they would be
beneficial.

4. Identify three forms of support to help your listeners
attend to and remember this information.

The Dalai Lama is the spiritual leader of the Tibetan people, a world religious figure, and a possible topic for your informative speech. He says he's guided by three major commitments: the promotion of basic human values in the interest of human happiness; the fostering of inter-religious harmony; and the welfare of the Tibetan people, focusing on the survival of their identity, culture, and religion.

Appropriate specific purposes for some of these top might include the following:

- To share the effects of grand jury decisions on race re tions in the United States
- To inform the audience about congressional bipartisan forts to increase funding for embryonic stem cell resea
- To explain how the experiment of the European Uni has failed

Concepts

Speeches about concepts deal with abstract topics such beliefs, theories, ideas, and principles. The challenge is make the subject matter concrete so the audience can easi understand it. Concept-based topics include the following:

Immigration controversies
Increase in all forms of bullying
Social media addiction
Law enforcement and racial profiling
Intercultural communication
Mediated communication
Global warming or climate change?
Communication apprehension
Suicide

These topics are too vague or broad to be meaningful. If you were to ask a doze people what each term or phrase means, you would probably receive a dozen differ ent answers. The speaker is responsible for narrowing and focusing the subject so th audience understands the intended meaning. Here are specific purpose statement based on some of the general, abstract topics:

- To inform my audience about teens' vulnerability to cyber bullying
- To share ways we can improve our intercultural competence
- To share the effects of excessive social media use on depression and loneliness

Speeches about concepts take extra time and effort to develop because of thei abstract nature. These topics require the use of concrete examples, definitions, and clear language.

Whether a speech is about an object, a process, an event, or a concept is not always clear because a subject may overlap these categories. Often, the specific pur-pose the speaker chooses to emphasize determines the category. It is important to decide on your approach to the subject and then develop your speech accordingly.

Guidelines

Choosing a Topic for an Informative Speech

1. **When you prepare an informative speech, you should begin with yourself.** What are your interests? About what topics are you passionately concerned?

2. **Informative speeches should appeal to the audience and provide knowledge of something potentially useful or beneficial.** What are some examples of potentially useful informative speech topics?

3. **Your audience will listen to you if you make the speech compelling.** What can a speaker do to make a speech resonate with you?

eview previous information and class discussion and handouts for more specific
information about topic selection and how to determine which topics may be best
suited for you and your audience (see the appendix at the end of this chapter for
more topics).

Preparing and Developing an Informative Speech

11.4 Prepare and develop an informative speech to meet your professor's specific criteria

The previous chapters on public communication relate directly to the principles and
skills of informative speaking. All aspects of topic selection, audience analysis, information gathering, preparation of supporting and clarifying materials, and organizing,
outlining, and delivering a speech are crucial to the effectiveness and eventual success
of your informative presentation. In addition, you should be familiar with strategies
for competing with distractions and noises, such as students arriving late, a maintenance crew working in the next classroom, a lawn mower outside the window, and
whispering in the audience. Such interferences cannot be ignored if you want to be
successful in transmitting information to others. To achieve your main goal to enhance
the audience's knowledge, you must attain two subgoals: to gain their attention and to
increase their understanding.

Gain and Maintain Audience Attention

Motivating the audience to pay attention is critical to the success of any speech. (See
the chapter on listening for more on motivating your audience to listen.) To accomplish this, you should follow a strategy that will work well for your audience. Gaining
and maintaining the attention of the audience is extremely important when you present information. Audience members must believe they will benefit from the information, perceive it as relevant to their lives, and find it interesting enough to want to
listen. Although this task is quite challenging to the beginning speaker, if you make
your audience the central focus of the speech and use a little creativity, you can easily
gain and hold their attention.

GENERATE A NEED FOR THE INFORMATION A student gave a speech on the
benefits of seat belt use. After reading his peer evaluations and reflecting on the
video of his speech, he emailed to ask why no one liked the speech. When he was
asked whether he had determined how many in his class do not use seat belts, he did
not have an answer. When asked if he knew the average seat belt use in his state, he
did not have those statistics either. When we told him that the latest statistics from
the highway patrol and the department of transportation suggest that 82 percent of
people in his state use seat belts, he was surprised. This should give you two reasons
his listeners did not seem to like his speech: Most of them already knew the benefits
of seat belt use and use them regularly, and he had not done enough research to go beyond what his listeners already knew. As a result, his audience did not feel motivated
to listen. How could he have avoided choosing a topic his audience wasn't interested
in? He might have done a survey to find out what they knew, or he might have looked
carefully at statistics. Or he could have found a way to make the speech more relevant
to his listeners in this way:

> I realize most of you already wear seat belts when you drive or ride in a
> vehicle, but did you know that even in Iowa, where seat belt usage is said to
> be at 82 percent, injuries resulting because a seat belt was not in use account

for more than 25 percent of all traffic deaths? That means that six of us in this class could have life-threatening injuries if we were involved in an automobile accident and were not wearing a seat belt.

This opening acknowledges the high percentage of people in the state who use seat belts, and it also piques interest because it asks a rhetorical question to make the listener aware of the consequences of failure to wear a seat belt. Notice that the speaker also makes the percentages memorable by identifying the number of class members who could be affected.

Let's look at other examples of rhetorical questions used to begin a speech:

- Some medical doctors believe that the high blood sugar epidemic is North America's number one health crisis. Are you aware that around 29 million American adults have diabetes and, of that 29 million, over 8 million are undiagnosed?[2]
- Here in North America we have many blessings, but all countries do not have even the basic necessities, such as food, clean water, and education. For instance, did you know a child dies of hunger every 15 seconds?[3]
- Eating disorders are pervasive in our society. Would you be surprised to learn that eating disorders have the highest mortality rate of any mental illness in the Western world?[4]

Speakers can also use questions meant to generate responses from the audience as a strategy to gain and maintain audience interest and attention.

CREATE INFORMATION RELEVANCE   People are much more likely to pay attention when they believe a speech relates directly to them. A speaker who gives an audience a reason to listen by relating the topic to their needs and interests creates **information relevance**. Ask yourself whether the information you intend to present is relevant to your listeners. If it is not, think about how you might make it so. In one of our classes, a student wanted to talk about "American culture" because we always forget about our own cultures and concentrate on international countries and cultures. Since she lived in an area with Amish populations, she chose to learn more about and share the Amish culture with the class. Her speech was well received because she used facts the students already knew and then added new information.

Another student spent his spring break volunteering for Habitat for Humanity. The group built a home for those who might not otherwise have a stable, safe residence. He talked about the work involved but also gave fascinating information about how many houses have been built and families provided for in this way, and he touched on the good feeling he had because he had done something for someone else. He also discussed the value of volunteering, as well.

information relevance

Making information relevant to an audience to give them a reason to listen.

Melinda and Bill Gates, and Bill Gates Sr., oversee the Gates Foundation, a philanthropy benefitting scores of institutions and individuals around the world. Melinda Gates is also in demand as a speaker because of her unique global perspective.

PROVIDE A FRESH PERSPECTIVE   Information perceived as *new* also attracts the attention of an audience. But whenever this statement is mentioned in class, someone responds, "But there isn't anything new to present." Actually, discussing something new does not necessarily mean you have to present something the audience has never heard. It does mean you need to devise a *new view or angle*. AIDS, safe sex, pollution, use of seat belts, smoking, drugs, and recycling are subjects that communication professors and other listeners have heard discussed too many times. A speaker who provides a fresh perspective on a familiar topic makes it more interesting and thus increases the chances of holding the audience's attention. One speaker informed the audience about illegal drugs that

e medically helpful in treating certain diseases. She began her speech in the fol-
wing manner:

> You have read and heard so much about cocaine, crack, heroin, and other illegal
> drugs you are probably sick of the subject, but these drugs are not all bad. You
> might at first think that I am too liberal, but my mother is on drugs, and I am
> glad. You see, my mother is suffering from cancer, and the only relief she can get
> is from the small doses of heroin she receives each day to ease the pain. Today, I
> am going to inform you about illegal drugs that actually aid our sick and dying.

This approach is not new, but it is *different*. Rather than taking a stand either for
r against illegal drugs, the speaker focused on certain instances in which the use of
legal drugs can be beneficial. This also helped her to stay within the guidelines of the
nformative speech.

OCUS ON THE UNUSUAL   Sometimes a focus on an unusual aspect of a topic helps
 speaker maintain the attention of the audience. A speaker might begin the speech
ke this:

> In an age when equality between the sexes seems closer to reality, there are
> some occupations in which there are still more men than women. One occu-
> pational area is pilots and flight instructors. It may surprise you to know that
> the flight instructor who has the world record for training the most pilots is
> Evelyn Johnson of Morristown, Tennessee. Ms. Johnson logged nearly 58,000
> flight hours, trained more than 5,000 pilots, and covered 5.5 million miles. The
> woman known as "Mama Bird" quit flying in 2006 only after a car accident
> led to an amputation of her leg. Even then she managed the local airport until
> shortly before her death on May 10, 2012.[5]

Increase Understanding of the Topic

Once you have gained your listeners' attention, you've created the opportunity to
increase their understanding. Understanding is the ability to interpret, grasp, or
assign meaning to an idea. You can enhance your audience's understanding by organizing your presentation systematically, choosing appropriate language, and providing clear definitions.

ORGANIZE YOUR PRESENTATION   In a well-organized speech, ideas are managed
in a clear and orderly sequence that makes the material easy to follow and understand.
The most commonly used organizational patterns in informative speeches are chronological or time-sequence, topical, and spatial. Effective organization helps increase
the speaker's credibility and improves the listeners' comprehension and retention of
information. Two organizational techniques that aid understanding in both informative and persuasive speeches are planned repetition and advance organizers.

Making Connections for Success

Make It Lively, Please!

Words can be dry and uninteresting, or they can grab our
attention and compel us to listen to someone. Read the six
sentences or phrases below and see how you can bring them
to life.

- Wall Street caused the economic mess.
- Foreign automobile manufacturers produce better cars.
- iPhones are useful.
- Sugar causes many health problems.
- Community volunteerism is important.
- What kinds of jobs will I find when I graduate?

1. Use definitions, concrete words, or descriptors to make
   the phrases livelier.
2. Compare your words with the original. What are the
   differences?
3. Was it easy to change the phrases so they were lively?
4. Compare your changes with those of your classmates.
   What were the similarities and differences?

planned repetition

The deliberate restating of a thought to increase the likelihood the audience will understand and remember it.

Plan for Repetition   **Planned repetition** is the deliberate restatement of a thought increase the likelihood the audience will understand and remember it. The repetiti of information generally helps us remember things more completely. For example you ask someone for another's cell phone number and have nothing to write the nu ber on until you call, you probably say the number over and over so you can rememb it long enough to add it to your contact list or dial the number.

The guiding principle behind most television commercials is repetition. Althou; we might find it bothersome, constant repetition of the same commercial reminds of the product and thus increases the chances we will purchase it. You can use th same principle in an informative speech to help your audience remember key idea For example, you might say:

> Medical doctors have successfully developed a "smart bomb" on breast cancer that delivers the treatment to tumor cells but leaves healthy cells alone. This experimental "smart bomb" treatment successfully extended the time women lived without progression of their cancers. The treatment appears to improve survival: 65 percent of women who received the "smart bomb" treatment were still alive after 2 years, while only 47 percent of those medicated with standard drugs were still alive after 2 years.[6]

You could also put critical information in a computer slide presentation or o a poster. Or you could write it on the board for additional repetition and emphasi: Internal summaries and previews may also include repetition of the points made an help the audience focus on what is yet to come in the speech.

advance organizer

A statement that warns the listener that significant information is coming.

Use Advance Organizers   **Advance organizers** are similar to signposts in that the signal what is coming, but they also warn that what is about to be said is significant They signal the listener to pay attention.

> It's important for all of us to be a part of this movement. If you understand this next step in the process, you will also understand the need to act quickly.

These warnings grab the attention of your audience and emphasize that forth coming information is both necessary and important. Teachers use advance organizers to make sure students know what is essential. Examples include the following:

> Here's a big hint. What I next tell you will form the background for your involvement in the group projects.
> The following concepts will be critical for you to understand to complete the project.

Advance organizers also serve as previews of main points. Use of advance organizers in introductions helps your audience concentrate on what is coming in the speech. For example, one speaker used the following statements in her introduction to alert her audience and to indicate what was important to meet her specific purpose:

> Anorexia, bulimia, and binge eating disorders often surface during adolescence or the early years of college, but both men and women may show signs of trouble much earlier. There are six signs that can alert you to an eating disorder in another person. Knowing these signs can help you spot potential problems early.[7]

CHOOSE LANGUAGE CAREFULLY   It is extremely important to match your level of language to the knowledge your audience already has about your topic. If you are speaking with experts or with people who are familiar with your topic, feel free to use technical terms without explaining them, but if your audience is unfamiliar with your subject, you will need to choose your words carefully and define any special terms. In some cases, you should avoid technical terms altogether. This may be necessary when such terms would confuse your listeners or when your audience lacks the ability or background to understand them. Sometimes a speaker's use of too many technical terms will turn an audience off or even create hostility. Choose language carefully to avoid creating unnecessary problems. When possible, select concrete rather than abstract words and use descriptions to make your points clearer.

Use Concrete Words To increase understanding, try to use as many concrete words as possible. Concrete words are symbols for specific things one can experience through the senses. In addition, concrete words stand for specific people, places, things, or acts; for instance, Winnipeg, Manitoba, Canada, is more concrete than a Canadian city. Familiar, concrete language allows your listeners to form mental images similar to yours. If you say something is comparable in size to a grapefruit, your listeners should form a fairly accurate picture of what you have in mind. Concrete words leave less room for misinterpretation and misunderstanding.

Abstract words refer to ideas, qualities, or relationships: justice, equality, joy, freedom, or classmates. The meaning of these words relies on the experiences and intentions of the people who express them. If a speaker says, "The travel security system is good," we don't know whether he means air traffic, highway traffic, rail traffic, or bus traffic. We also don't know what is *good*. Abstract language is imprecise and often leaves listeners confused about the speaker's intent.

USE DESCRIPTION To make something more concrete, a speaker might describe its size, quantity, shape, weight, composition, texture, color, age, strength, or fit. These descriptive words are called **descriptors**. The more descriptors a speaker uses that relate to the listeners' experiences, the greater is the likelihood the message will be understood. One speaker used these descriptors in talking about the threat of cyber war:

descriptors
Words used to describe something.

> According to PBS, "Eligible Receiver" is the code name of a government simulation where a team of hackers was organized to infiltrate Pentagon systems. The team was allowed to use only publicly available computer equipment and hacking software. While the information is still classified, we know the hackers were able to infiltrate and take control of the Pacific command center computers as well as power grids and 911 systems in nine major U.S. cities. This simulation demonstrated the real lack of consciousness about cyber warfare. During the first three days of the exercise, nobody believed we were under cyber attack. This whole exercise underscores America's reliance on information technology systems and their vulnerabilities to attack.[8]

The speaker's explanations provide one specific example of what the team was able to accomplish with information technology at the Pentagon, without raising concerns. The descriptors are a chilling reminder that, in modern warfare, the things we take for granted can be used against us.

USE DEFINITIONS One way to ensure your audience's understanding is to define all potentially unfamiliar and complex words. The most common form of definition used by speakers, the logical definition, usually contains two parts: the dictionary definition and the characteristics that distinguish the term from other members of the same category. An operational definition explains how an object or concept works, and a definition by example explains a term or a concept by using examples, either verbal or actual, to illustrate a point. In addition, four other methods can clearly define a term for your listeners: using contrast, synonyms, antonyms, and etymologies.

Making Connections for Success

Specific Word Choice

Concrete words are more easily understandable. If our words are too abstract, we might confuse the listeners or make them tune out. Rewrite the following sentences to make them more concrete:

1. Street violence has increased.
2. The flu is dangerous.
3. Lots of food service programs promote healthier eating.
4. Cyber bullying is a real problem in our schools.
5. Be prepared to share your changes with the class.

contrast definition

A definition that shows or emphasizes differences.

Show Contrasts A **contrast definition** is used to show or emphasize differences. This type of definition is helpful when you want to distinguish between similar terms. For example, a speaker discussing communication apprehension and speech anxiety differentiated one term from the other by stating that communication apprehension is a trait or global anxiety, whereas speech anxiety is a state or situational anxiety. A person suffering from communication apprehension might also have speech anxiety, but a person with speech anxiety will not necessarily have communication apprehension. A contrast definition might also point out differences in causes and effects. Thus, the speaker might point out that people with communication apprehension actively avoid all interaction with others, whereas people with speech anxiety merely feel a bit of controllable discomfort when addressing an audience.

synonym

A word, term, or concept that is the same or nearly the same in meaning as another word, term, or concept.

Use Synonyms The use of synonyms can also help clarify the meaning of a word. A **synonym** is a word, phrase, or concept with exactly the same or nearly the same meaning as another word, term, or concept. In describing a communicative extrovert, a speaker used the phrases "willingness to talk openly" and "ability to speak in any situation without reservation." Each phrase describes the behavior exhibited by a person who is a communicative extrovert.

antonym

A word, phrase, or concept that is opposite in meaning to another word, phrase, or concept.

Use Antonyms In contrast, an **antonym** is a word, phrase, or concept that has the opposite meaning of another word, phrase, or concept. For example, a communicative extrovert is the opposite of someone with communication apprehension. Such a person is not shy, reserved, unwilling to talk, or afraid to speak. The person greatly enjoys talking with others. Using an antonym helps the audience to compare differences and leaves the listener with a memorable definition of an unfamiliar term.

etymology

A form of definition that traces the origin and development of a word.

Use Etymologies An **etymology** is a form of definition that traces the origin and development of a word. One student used etymology to explain how the Olympic Games got their name. In the Greek system of telling time, an Olympiad was the period of four years that elapsed between two successive celebrations of the Olympian. This method of figuring time became common in about 300 BC, and all events were dated from 776 BC, the beginning of the first known Olympic games. Such a definition provides the audience with a novel way to remember key information. Excellent sources of word etymologies are the *Oxford English Dictionary* and the *Etymological Dictionary of Modern English*.

Whenever any possibility exists that your audience may not understand a term or concept, select the kind of definition that provides the clearest explanation. In some instances, more than one kind might be necessary. To err by overdefining is better than an inadequate definition so your audience wonders what you're talking about.

Hints for Effective Informative Speaking

Adhering to the following two additional guidelines should be particularly helpful to ensure success: Avoid assumptions and personalize information.

AVOID ASSUMPTIONS A student began speaking about CPR by emphasizing its importance in saving lives. However, she failed to explain that the acronym CPR stands for *cardiovascular pulmonary resuscitation*; she assumed that everyone already knew what it meant. Most of the audience did understand, but a number of people did not. In addition, some knew what the acronym meant but did not know how the technique worked. Because at least half of her classmates were unfamiliar with the technique, they found the speaker's presentation confusing and frustrating. One mistaken assumption undercut all the work she had put into her speech. Follow these guidelines to avoid assumptions:

1. Ask yourself whether your listeners already know what you are talking about. Audience analysis may be appropriate. If you are addressing your class, randomly

select some of your classmates and ask them what they know about your topic and its related terminology.

2. If you believe that even one audience member might not understand, take the time to briefly define and explain your topic.

3. If you believe a majority of your listeners already know what you mean, say something such as, "Many of you probably know what euthanasia is, but for those who don't...." In this way, you acknowledge those who already know and help those who do not.

4. Do not assume your audience knows the introductory information, especially if you have any doubts about what they know. You can always move through your basic definitions and explanations quickly if your audience seems to understand, but it is difficult to regain their interest and attention once you start talking over their heads.

PERSONALIZE INFORMATION   When you relate your topic to your listeners so they can see its relevance, you are personalizing information. Callie presented a speech about the dreaded "Freshman 15" and the changed eating and activity habits of first-year college students.

> I am one of those students who gained weight and realized I didn't feel good about myself. I'm going to share with you my own ways of moving back to a healthier lifestyle.

Personalized information not only holds attention but also attracts interest. For example, think of your most effective instructors. Chances are they take ordinary material and personalize it into meaningful, interesting knowledge. Listening to a string of facts can be frustrating, but a speech comes to life when it contains personal illustrations.

Most of us are interested in others. If we were not, there would be no *People* magazine, no *National Enquirer*, no *Late Show with Stephen Colbert*, no *Survivor*, no *Oprah*, and no *Dr. Phil*. Stories are much more likely to affect listeners than are statistics. Whenever possible, personalize your information and dramatize it in human terms.

One student began an informative speech about the Heimlich maneuver, a technique used to clear the throat of someone who is choking, by relating the story of a 4-year-old boy who saved his 3-year-old friend. The boy had watched a television show in which the maneuver was used to save the life of one of

Teaching others the fine art of surfboarding requires an understanding of the listeners, careful organization, and planning. When the instructor shares personal stories, the listeners are likely to remember more.

Guidelines

Personalize Information in Your Speeches

1. **Use examples and information that specifically relate to your audience.** This will help you make a stronger connection with your listeners.

2. **Draw conclusions that your audience members can identify with and explain what those conclusions may mean for them.** This will go a long way in building strong rapport with them.

3. **Refer to people who are similar to your audience members**—for example, single parents, nontraditional students, minority students, international students, computer science majors, commuters who must drive to campus.

4. **Refer to topics and events that affect your listeners,** such as campus activities, elections, state and local laws, social events, tax cuts or increases, cultural programs, and career decisions.

the main characters, and simply reenacted what he saw. The use of this dramatic, real-life episode grabbed the listeners' attention and prepared them for his discussion of who developed the technique, how it works, and how many lives it has saved.

Evaluate the Informative Speech

11.5 **Evaluate and assess** your own speeches prior to classroom presentation and apply evaluation criteria to the speeches of others

Every instructor uses specific criteria to evaluate a speaker's competence in content and delivery of a speech. The following are some common criteria used by instructors across the world. Keep them in mind as you prepare your speech.

We include samples of a speaker's self-evaluation form and a listener's evaluation form (Figures 11.1 and 11.2) so both speakers and audience members will be aware of their responsibilities to each other.

Figure 11.1 Speaker's Self-Evaluation Form

After you have completed an informative speech, take a few moments to think about your preparation and presentation. Complete the phrases on this form by stating what you would do similarly or differently, and why, if you were to give this same speech again.

Title of speech: _____.

Date and place given: _____.

My topic was _____.

I liked the topic because _____.

My research could be improved by _____.

The organizational pattern I chose was _____.

The introduction was _____.

The body of the speech needed _____.

My conclusion seemed to be _____.

My explanation of ideas should _____.

The support I provided for my ideas was _____.

My use of language might _____.

My visual delivery was _____.

My vocal delivery needed _____.

The ways I adapted my topic, ideas, and language to this audience were _____
_____.

Things I would change are _____,

because _____.

Things I would retain are _____,

because _____.

If I were to grade myself, the grade would be _____ , because _____
_____.

Figure 11.2 Listener's Evaluation Form

This form can be used to evaluate speeches given by your classmates. Follow your instructor's directions for providing such feedback.

Speaker _____   Topic _____

Date _____ Listener _____

The speaker considered this topic for this class, assignment, and context by
_____.

A new or different perspective I gained was _____.

The organization of the speech was _____.

The reasons for my comments on organization are _____.

Four things the speaker did to keep me listening were:

The speaker's purpose was _____.

The types of supporting materials used included _____.

Presentational aids, if used, enhanced/did not enhance the speech because
_____.

The speaker's language helped/hindered me in the following ways: _____
_____.

The speaker could improve the physical aspects of delivery by _____.

The one comment I wish to make about vocal delivery is _____.

The speaker needed to explain _____.

One aspect I especially liked was _____.

One area that needs improvement in the future is _____.

Topic

The selection of a topic should meet the following criteria:

- The topic should merit your audience's attention.
- The focus of the topic should take into account the audience's level of knowledge.
- The audience should be able to see the relationship between the topic and the speaker and between the topic and themselves.
- The topic of the speech should be adequately covered in the time available. The topic should be narrow enough to be fully developed.

General Requirements

These general requirements hold for all informative speech presentations:

- The purpose of the speech should be clearly to inform and should be stated as such.
- The speech should meet the time requirements set by the assignment.
- The speaker should cite sources of information other than the speaker's own knowledge.

- The speech purpose should be relevant to the assignment and relate to the audience.
- The speech should show evidence of careful preparation.

Audience Analysis

The speaker must shape the speech to suit the audience, which often requires research (for example, determining the listeners' past experiences, beliefs, attitudes, values). The choices made by the speaker regarding content and the development of ideas should be customized for the listeners' benefit.

- The speech should reflect appropriate audience analysis.
- The speech should show the audience why the topic is important to them.
- At several points the speaker should connect with the listeners through familiar examples or identify listeners' preferences or experiences.

Supporting Materials

Supporting materials supply documented evidence that the information conveyed in the speech is accurate and credible.

- The speech should be well documented.
- The sources should be cited completely and accurately.
- The research should be up to date as much as possible.
- The speaker should use adequate and sufficient clarifying materials.
- Visual aids, if used, should be appropriate, add to the audience's understanding of the speech content, and follow the guidelines established by the assignment.

Organization

When judging the speech organization, the evaluator looks for a carefully planned, well-developed informative speech that takes a unified approach to the material being presented.

- The introduction should be properly developed.
  - It should orient the audience to the topic, gain attention and arouse interest.
  - It should include a specific purpose and thesis statement.
  - It should define terms (if necessary).
  - It should be relevant.
  - It should establish credibility.
- The organization of the body should be clear and easy to follow.
  - The main points should be clear and parallel in structure.
  - The main points should relate to the purpose of the speech.
  - Transitions should provide appropriate links between ideas.
  - The organizational pattern should be appropriate.
- The conclusion should be properly developed.

  - It should reinforce the purpose by reviewing the main points.
  - It should end with a memorable thought.

Delivery

Delivery techniques provide evidence the speaker is aware of audience interests, is involved in and enthusiastic about the topic, and truly wants to share the material with the listeners.

- The speaker's stance and posture should be suitable.
- The speaker's eye contact with the audience should be appropriate.
- The speaker should follow the assignment in method of delivery (use of notes and number of note cards).
- The speaker's facial expressions should convey and clarify thoughts.
- The speaker's body movements should be appropriate and effective.
- The speaker's vocal delivery should enhance the speech with appropriate volume and rate, conversational quality, enthusiastic tone, clear enunciation, appropriate pauses, and appropriate vocal variety.

Language Choice

Language choice can enhance and clarify ideas considerably.

- Language choice should be appropriate to the assignment and audience.
- Word choice should be appropriate for the college level.
- Grammar should be appropriate and show college-level competence.
- Word pronunciations should be correct.

Speakers should always analyze their presentations. We are often called on to make reports or provide information in the workplace, in the groups of which we are members, and in classrooms. Because speaking is so prevalent, it is important for the speaker to step back and carefully and critically reflect on the speech, the situation, the audience, and the performance. If we hope to become effective communicators in public settings, we need to use reflective thinking to objectively analyze our performance and how successful we were. Figure 11.1 (earlier in this section) shows a sample speaker's self-evaluation form to facilitate this reflection process.

We spend much more time listening to speeches than we do making speeches, and though this section may seem to focus on making effective speeches, it is also important to be a critical consumer of speeches and other presentations. Figure 11.2 (earlier in this section) provides a sample listener's evaluation form for listeners to directly respond to the speaker in writing. It is useful for the speaker to obtain listeners' perspectives on a speech. Honest and tactful feedback can be invaluable. But it is also a good idea to self-evaluate presentations, even when you will not be passing your comments on to the speaker. Listeners are encouraged to use Figure 11.2 as a basis for creating their own evaluations and applying their own criteria to presentations.

The following informative speech outline provides full content. The speech was used earlier, in Chapter 9, to provide examples of the full sentence and presentational outlines.

A SAMPLE INFORMATIVE SPEECH WITH COMMENTARY

Sarah Johansen, University of Nebraska–Lincoln

TOPIC: Helen Keller International

TITLE: A Charity with Vision: Helen Keller International

GENERAL PURPOSE: To inform

SPECIFIC PURPOSE: To inform my audience about the charity organization Helen Keller International and raise awareness for its cause

THESIS: To inform my audience about the mission and history of Helen Keller International, how it acts to prevent blindness, and its actions to reduce malnutrition worldwide.

In her introduction, Sarah uses her listeners' senses to help them focus on what it would be like to lose one's sight and then makes the loss more relevant to them. This material helps to motivate and orient her listeners to the topic.

In each of her subpoints, Sarah reinforces Helen Keller's accomplishments, despite the loss of both sight and hearing.

Note how Sarah adds specific information to provide the listeners with more detail throughout her speech.

In the first main point of the body, Sarah talks about Keller's background and that of George Kessler, who helped establish the charity that became HKI.

Sarah expands on the historical information about HKI as well as the specific strategies they use to help the most vulnerable and disadvantaged people in the world.

Sarah's subpoints and sub-subpoints in her first main point provide a view of the organization and what it does to help people around the globe.

The second main point elaborates on the specific diseases and causes of vision loss and identifies ChildSight, the branch of HKI that works to help save the eyesight of underprivileged children.

Sarah provides information on the maladies treated and also shows how HKI trains medical teams and provides equipment and supplies to eradicate the problems.

The third main point describes what the organization does to reduce malnutrition and provide the needed vitamin and mineral supplements to save eyesight throughout the world. In this main point, Sarah shows us how HKI finds solutions to health problems that may be taken for granted in developed countries. HKI provides health-care answers that are beyond the means of people and even governments in these vulnerable populations.

INTRODUCTION

I. Close your eyes for just a moment. Without sight, you must depend on other senses to remain aware of everything going on around you. Now imagine losing your sense of hearing as well. How would you communicate with others and stay aware of your surroundings?

   A. Helen Keller was both blind and deaf and still managed to have an incredibly successful and inspirational life and was known for her intelligence and ambition.

   B. One of her many accomplishments was cofounding the organization Helen Keller International (HKI) in 1915 with George Kessler.

   C. The organization is a legacy Helen Keller left for us to continue, with her spirit and enthusiasm at its heart, in order to better the world.

BODY

II. Helen Keller International's Mission and History

   A. Helen Keller was blinded at the age of 2 after a terrible fever and soon after lost her sense of hearing.

   B. George Kessler was a New Yorker who survived the sinking of the *Lusitania* in 1915 and committed his life to helping soldiers who had lost vision in combat.

   C. George and his wife asked Helen Keller for her support and formed the Permanent Blind Relief War Fund for Soldiers & Sailors of the Allies in 1915, which helped blinded veterans learn how to read Braille, make chairs, and knit.

      1. The Fund expanded and incorporated civilians as well as veterans, and by 1970 the focus shifted to preventing blindness by distributing vitamin A capsules in Central America and in the Asia-Pacific region.

      2. The name Helen Keller International was adopted in 1977 and it serves not only the blind but also those who are underprivileged and at risk for blindness.

   D. According to www.hki.org, the mission statement is "to save the sight and lives of the most vulnerable and disadvantaged. We combat the causes and consequences of blindness and malnutrition by establishing programs based on evidence and research in vision, health and nutrition."

   E. HKI now serves in 22 countries across the globe in Africa, the Asia-Pacific region, and the Americas.

III. Helen Keller International and Preventing Blindness

   A. The number one treatable cause of blindness in the world is cataracts.

      1. According to the book *Principles of Human Anatomy,* a cataract is the loss of transparency of the lens of the eye, which has a number of causes, including age and sun exposure.

      2. HKI trains nurses and surgeons and provides medical equipment in underdeveloped countries so that cataract surgeries can be performed for as little as $12 a patient.

   B. Vitamin A deficiency is the leading cause of childhood blindness.

      1. According to *Africa News,* "an estimated 250,000 to 500,000 vitamin A-deficient children become blind every year, and half of them die within 12 months of losing their sight."

      2. HKI provides vitamin A supplementation to children twice a year in order to prevent blindness.

      3. Gary Heiting states that vitamin A helps keep the cornea of the eye healthy and helps prevent macular degeneration.

   C. In the United States, a program called ChildSight, a branch of HKI, has been established that screens the eyesight of, and delivers glasses to, underprivileged children.

IV. Helen Keller International and Reducing Malnutrition

   A. Vitamin A supplementation, according to www.hki.org, "not only can prevent a lifetime of darkness, but can also result in a 25% reduction in child mortality."

   B. HKI provides low-cost vitamin and mineral supplements to severely malnourished populations.

   C. The Homestead Food Production program created self-sufficient gardens in Cambodia, the Philippines, Bangladesh, and Nepal.

D. Food fortification program provides more nutritious foods for families and communities around the world.

CONCLUSION

V. Helen Keller International is an exceptional charity solely focused on the betterment of lives all around the world.

A. The treatment of blindness in both children and adults has improved the quality of life for many individuals in underprivileged countries.

B. Food production and sustainability provided by HKI will drastically affect the world's hunger and malnutrition problems.

C. Helen Keller's legacy lives on through this organization and will continue to help people all over the world.[9]

REFERENCES

Heiting, Gary. "Vitamin A and Beta Carotene: Eye Benefits." *All About Vision.* N.p., June 2011 (web). Retrieved May 19, 2012, from www.allaboutvision.com/nutrition/vitamin_a.htm.

Helen Keller International 2012 (web). Retrieved May 19, 2012, from www.hki.org.

"Nutrition; A Sweet Potato a Day." *Africa News,* Nov. 29, 2011. LexisNexis. (web). Retrieved May 19, 2012, from https://www.lexisnexis.com.

Tortora, Gerard J., and Mark T. Nielsen. *Principles of Human Anatomy*, 12th ed. New York: John Wiley & Sons, Inc., 2012. P. 728 (print).

In her conclusion, Sarah summarizes and synthesizes the main points of the speech and reinforces the remarkable work of the HKI charity.

Sarah makes her listeners aware of the beneficial effects of HKI's actions in areas of the world with high hunger, malnutrition, and mortality rates.

Sarah has references from a variety of sources. One has information about vitamins and the benefits for eyes and comes from a website. The HKI website provides unique insights into the organization and its work. One newspaper article came from *Africa News* and was accessed through LexisNexis, and the fourth source came from a textbook. The sources are varied and provide differing pieces of information for the speech.

Analysis and Evaluation

Sarah Johansen is a student at the University of Nebraska–Lincoln. The students' assignment was to give a 5-to-7-minute informative speech on a worthy charitable organization; it was presented in the fundamentals of communication class.

She uses her 20 to 30 seconds of introductory material to orient and motivate the listeners by getting them involved in the concept of vision loss. She asks them to close their eyes and rely on their other senses, and then asks what would happen if another sense was lost. Her rhetorical question further emphasizes the personal relevance of sensory losses and communication. She then discusses Helen Keller and how she and George Kessler founded Helen Keller International (HKI) in 1915 to help others deal with vision loss.

Sarah's first main point deals with the charity's mission and history by further elaborating on Keller's own sensory losses and the reason George Kessler committed his life to helping soldiers who had lost their vision in combat. She identifies their early work and what they did to help blinded veterans receive necessary food and vitamins as well as to raise their sense of self-worth. She elaborates on how the organization expanded to include civilians, as well as other steps they took to prevent blindness. She further identifies how the organization has grown and now serves 22 countries.

The second main point does a nice job of explaining three specific activities (cataract surgery, vitamin A supplementation, and ChildSight) undertaken by Helen Keller International to prevent and treat blindness; train medical staff; and provide medical equipment, glasses, and vitamin A all over the world. Sarah's supporting material indicates the extent to which large numbers of people benefit from the work of Helen Keller International.

Sarah's third main point centers on Helen Keller International's efforts to reduce malnutrition, a leading cause of blindness and death, around the globe. She specifies how vitamin A supplements can prevent blindness and reduce children's deaths by 25 percent. In many areas of the world, HKI provides vitamin and mineral supplements, helps create self-sufficient gardens, and supplies a food fortification program that offers more nutritious foods for families and communities.

The conclusion, while brief (30 seconds), accomplished what it was supposed to Sarah summarized and synthesized the work of a charity focused on the betterment o people around the globe. Her main purpose was to inform her listeners about the mis sion and history of Helen Keller International. She also raised awareness of the cause of blindness and some of the ways blindness can be treated and prevented, but als how the charity has done much to increase food production and sustainability so tha a hand-up, rather than a handout, is offered.

Now it's time for you to think about Sarah's speech: How would you evaluate th evidence Sarah provided? In much of her speech, she uses Helen Keller Internationa website facts and statistics. Does she provide enough oral footnotes to identify wher other information was gained? Are the sources reliable? Does she help you to conside this a viable charity? Does this speech make you think about the statement "the sky i the limit" when it comes to choices for the informative speech?

Summary

Information and Power

Objective 11.1 **Recognize** that information is powerful.

- Information has always been a powerful commodity.
- The ability to communicate information is essential.
- Public communicators should acknowledge the role of information in all areas and work to ensure that they present accurate and meaningful content in their communication efforts.

Distinctions Between Informative and Persuasive Speaking

Objective 11.2 **Explain** the distinctions between informative and persuasive speeches.

- We live in an information-oriented society in which the ability to present and receive informa- tion is vital. Now, as in the past, those people who possess information and communicate it effective- ly are the ones who possess power and command respect.
- Informative speeches are one of the most common we're asked or required to present. The goal of an informative speech is to increase understanding, while the goal of persuasive speaking is to change (alter) attitudes and/or behaviors. Information can be presented without attempting to persuade, but persuasion cannot be attempted without information.
- You must gain listeners' attention, motivate them to listen, and increase their understanding of the topic.

Topics for Informative Speeches

Objective 11.3 **Choose** appropriate topics for you informative speeches.

- Topics for informative speeches are almost limitless. Choose something interesting, about which you already have some knowledge, and that you can find additional information on through your research.
- Your topic should also be of interest and potentially useful for your listeners. Your specific purpose and the type of topic you choose will determine how you present the speech.

Preparing and Developing an Informative Speech

Objective 11.4 **Prepare and develop** an informative speech to meet your professor's specific criteria.

- Each instructor has specific criteria they want you to follow. Check your syllabus, with the instructor, if necessary, to determine all requirements, for both content and delivery.
- Your speech needs to gain and maintain attention.
- The more meaningful the topic and perspective, the more listeners pay attention to the speaker's message.
- Listeners want novel ideas and want to know "What's in it for me?"
- The audience will listen if you give them reasons to listen.
- The speech should be well organized so the listen- ers know where you're going and why.
- Your language should be clear, direct, and under- standable. It should give the listener a view of the topic at hand.
- Personalize the information to make it relevant, both for you and for your listeners.

Evaluate the Informative Speech

Objective 11.5 **Evaluate and assess** your own speeches prior to classroom presentation and apply evaluation criteria to the speeches of others.

- The sample evaluation criteria should make you aware of the characteristics of an effective informative speech and speaker.

- Competent communicators analyze their listeners so they know their choices will work. They find ample sources from a variety of references, and they work to show their listeners the importance of the topic.

Discussion Starters

1. What is the role of information in your life?
2. Explain the concept "information gives one power."
3. Provide 2 or 3 examples of a person who has the information and holds the power.
4. What advice would you give someone about selecting a topic for an informative speech?
5. Can you think of additional sources or places to find information?

6. Identify three topics that will work for an informative speech and explain how you can make them interesting and relevant for your audience.
7. Describe an effective informative speech and speaker.
8. Which of the criteria identified in the chapter mean the most to you as a listener?
9. In what ways has technology altered the way you find information?

Appendix 11

Informative Speech Topics

Here are some possible topics for informative speeches. The items listed are not titles of specific speeches and need to be narrowed to fit specific purposes, time limits, or other requirements set by your instructor. Almost any topic can be used to create informative or persuasive speeches. The key is in how you develop the ideas. If you're presenting information as information *only*, it becomes an informative speech. If you present an argument and evidence as supporting material, and you want your listeners to change something in some way, you're giving a persuasive speech.

The European experiment and its effect on the world's economy
The "sanitizing" of news
How Haiti has dealt with the aftermath of the earthquake
What does it mean when foods are labeled "organic"?
What it means to be a vegan
The high blood sugar epidemic
Eating disorders
Caffeine can harm your health
Caffeine can benefit you
The effects of energy drinks
World hunger
How "grandma's kitchen cures" can really help you
Learning financial literacy
Going green
Latest social media trends
The Green Movement
Mental health issues
Virtual schools
Social media have changed etiquette
Why are people divided by politics and religion?
ISIS and terrorist activities
Title IX and Sports
The Violence against Women Act
The watchdogs of student loans
Xenophobia and intercultural competence
Listening is linked to thinking
What are the areas of the brain?
Are the world's religions all that different?
Space exploration and private enterprise
How to safeguard yourself from identity theft
The appropriate way to use Skype in interview situations
Leadership skills and you
Have libraries become a thing of the past
Is ethical conduct an outdated practice?
Why do so many news anchors alter reality in their reporting?
Eating disorders are pervasive in our society
How to sponsor a child from developing countries
Why are pharmaceuticals so expensive?
What is autism?
How we can make the world a happier place for our animal friends?

Chapter 12
Persuasive Speaking

 ## Learning Objectives

Making Everyday Connections

In today's technological society, we often have to send emails prior to giving presentations in the workplace. We recently heard about Jason, a supervisor who asked Mark, one of his employees, how to create an email message and send it to inform all workers of an important upcoming meeting at which their input would be sought. The email itself had to be persuasive, and Jason was so caught up in how to even create and send an email, he forgot he needed to be persuasive. Luckily, Mark was email-savvy and also knew a great deal about persuasion. Jason asked for some speaking tips and then prepared for his meeting the following week.

The meeting began, and Jason started his speech. At first he was a little shaky, but when he saw the work crew listening carefully, he gained more confidence. The meeting went well. The crew asked questions and offered some other ways to view the issues, and every member was involved in the discussion. Jason thanked the employee who had first helped him, and asked if he'd be willing to help him out in a follow-up meeting. Mark was delighted because he felt that this meeting was the best they'd ever had—people listened, were involved, and were interacting as they never had before.

Mark's persuasive knowledge helped Jason create a more persuasive message. At the end of the meeting, workers' views had changed in a positive way toward Jason, the workplace, and the issues for which they had provided input.

Questions to Think About

1. How often do you think you are subjected to persuasion each day? How much do you try to persuade others each day?

2. Have you ever been in a work meeting at which true interaction on the part of supervisor and crew took place? Did the interaction help to get everyone talking, as it did in the example above?

3. Describe situations in your school, work, or personal life that involve persuasion.

4. Explain the strategies, words, or approaches that worked the last time you were able to persuade someone who initially resisted your request.

5. As a consumer of persuasion, what factors will make you say yes? Say no?

Persuasion is an everyday occurrence. If you aren't trying to persuade someone else, someone is trying to persuade you. Sometimes it's subtle; at other times it's not. When someone recommends a specific movie, book, or video; tweets a message of support for a fundraiser on Twitter; or asks you to vote for a specific candidate or donate to a certain cause, you are a consumer of persuasion.

Because persuasion is such a vital part of our everyday lives, it is important to understand how to deal with persuasive situations effectively. In this chapter, we'll discuss how to select a persuasive speech topic, how to enhance your credibility, and how to develop and prepare a persuasive message. In addition, we'll provide guidelines for persuading others and for being effective consumers of persuasion.

The Goal of Persuasive Speaking

12.1 **Identify** the goals of persuasion

persuasion

A communication process, involving both verbal and nonverbal messages, that attempts to reinforce or change listeners' attitudes, beliefs, values, or behavior.

Persuasion is a communication process, involving both verbal and nonverbal messages, that attempts to reinforce or change listeners' attitudes, beliefs, values, or behaviors. Communication scholar David Zarefsky says "persuasive strategies aim not only to provide information but also to affect audience members' attitudes and behavior. They ask for a greater degree of commitment from listeners than informative strategies do."[1] Is it possible to change people's attitudes, beliefs, or values without changing their behaviors? The answer is "yes." You might, for example, present your friend with reasons for attending one concert rather than another. Your friend might agree and still not buy a ticket. Were you persuasive? You might have been able to convince your friend that your ideas are valid but not able to alter her behavior. Which is more important?

The ultimate goal of all persuasion is action or change. Successful persuasion may accomplish one or more of the following: *reinforce* existing beliefs, attitudes, or behaviors; *change* existing beliefs, attitudes, or behaviors; or *lead to* new beliefs, attitudes, or behaviors. When you want to convince someone *not* to change, you try to reinforce the existing belief, attitude, or behavior. At other times, you may want a person to do something different. When a speaker's main goal is to achieve change or action, the speaker will pursue one of four subgoals: adoption, discontinuance, deterrence, or continuance of a particular behavior.[2]

Speakers whose topic is the environment face some stiff competition from listeners who believe the environment is a nonissue.

Persuasion is usually not a one-shot event; often, persuasion occurs over time, and the effect of a persuasive message on a listener is not apparent until some time after it has been received. In other words, the listener might think about the message for days or even weeks and, with additional experiences, messages, and information, decide a speaker was right. The listener might then decide to follow through on the speaker's request for action or change.

Adoption is an action subgoal asking listeners to demonstrate their acceptance of an attitude, belief, or value by performing the behavior suggested by the speaker. One of your classmates might give a speech on volunteering at the nearby nature reserve. If you had not previously even considered spending time at a nature reserve, or even know what is done in such a place, but decide to do so after the speech, you have displayed adoption. Your classmate persuaded you. This adoption of the persuasive message might be only temporary, and you might not stay with the program throughout your college career or after, but you have responded positively to your classmate's initial persuasive message: to adopt a behavior.

Discontinuance is the opposite of adoption. **Discontinuance** is an action subgoal that asks listeners to demonstrate their alteration of an attitude, belief, or value by *stopping* certain behaviors. If your action is discontinuance, you want your listeners to stop doing something—for instance, smoking, littering, eating too many sugary foods, or consuming wheat products. In these instances, you try to get your listeners to discontinue a negative behavior.

Deterrence is an action that asks listeners to demonstrate their acceptance of an attitude, belief, or value by avoiding certain behaviors. Sample deterrent messages are as follows: If you already eat a good breakfast, don't stop now; if you don't use illegal drugs, don't start now; if you are registered to vote, continue going to the polls. This action is similar to discontinuance in that you do not want a negative behavior to occur; but in deterrence, you are trying to *prevent* its occurrence rather than *end* its occurrence.

Continuance is an action asking listeners to demonstrate their acceptance of an attitude, belief, or value by continuing to perform the behavior suggested by the speaker. For example, if you eat breakfast, don't stop; continue to volunteer in the community; continue to purchase and consume more organic foods. This action is similar to adoption because you want a positive behavior to occur; but with continuance, you are trying to *keep* an existing behavior rather than *begin* a new behavior.

Note the first two actions, adoption and discontinuance, ask people to *change* their behavior, whereas the last two, deterrence and continuance, ask people *not to change* but to continue doing what they are already doing *or not change to something different.* Can you think of times when someone tried to persuade you to take action on one of these goals? They frequently occur in our interactions with others.

adoption

An action that asks listeners to demonstrate their acceptance of attitudes, beliefs, or values by performing the behavior suggested by the speaker.

discontinuance

An action that asks listeners to demonstrate their alteration of an attitude, belief, or value by stopping certain behaviors.

deterrence

An action that asks listeners to demonstrate their acceptance of an attitude, belief, or value by avoiding certain behavior.

continuance

An action goal that asks listeners to demonstrate their acceptance of an attitude, belief, or value by continuing to perform the behavior suggested by the speaker.

Getting others to change or not to change their behaviors is not always easy. A speaker might have to accept that a change in attitudes, beliefs, or values, such as adopting the idea of eating healthier foods, is part of the persuasive process and almost always occurs before a change in behavior can take place. Not all persuasive speaking leads to action, nor should persuasive speakers consider themselves failures if they do not obtain behavior change. Persuasion usually occurs over time; therefore, the speaker might not always be aware of whether the message was truly persuasive. Often, listeners are persuaded only after they have heard similar messages from a variety of people, over a period of time. Especially as a beginner at persuasive speaking, you should not always expect to obtain a change in attitude, action, or behavior, but you should be able to compel others to listen to what you have to say and to consider your point of view.

Topics for Persuasive Speeches

12.2 Choose a topic suitable for you, your listeners, and the assignment.

Some topics and themes lend themselves more readily to persuasive speaking than others. Current and controversial subjects are especially adaptable. The list of topics in the appendix at the end of this chapter illustrates the variety of possibilities. You will increase your likelihood of success if you follow these suggestions:

1. Whenever possible, select a topic in which you are interested, or about which you know something, want to speak, need to speak, or are personally concerned. Remember, it is not always possible to choose your own topic; sometimes someone else chooses it for you. For example, a nursing supervisor might tell one of the nurses that he has to speak to a group of visitors about the importance of using SPF 30 or higher sunblock to prevent skin cancer. Certainly, that might not be his first topic of choice, but he does meet some of the other criteria for speaking on the

Making Connections for Success

Everyday Acts of Persuasion

People often believe persuasion refers to situations only in which you change someone's mind and reverse a listener's beliefs. Actually, persuasion is broader. Our views have more substance than a simple, "Yes, I believe that," or "No, I disagree." Most of us have a range of commitment to any given idea. A persuasive speaker wants to move us one way or the other along a continuum. The economic problems leading to the recession of 2008-2009 were addressed by both Presidents George W. Bush and Barack Obama as well as Congress. Major economists believed that the only way to "save the nation" from greater problems and a bona fide depression was to provide a stimulus package to shore up financial institutions and automobile manufacturers. As soon as Obama stated he would increase the financial stimulus package, some journalists and members of the public began to complain that Obama was turning the United States into

a socialist state. Some newspapers touted the headline, "Obama's First 100 Days a Failure." Others praised his initiative as daring.

1. Identify one example in your own life of each of the above (strengthening, weakening, converting, or inducing an action). How did the speakers attempt to do so? What was the effect on you? Be prepared to talk about this effect.

2. What types of action subgoals have you experienced in the last day or two?

3. How did the persuader attempt to persuade you? How successfully?

4. Select an issue that is current but avoid one that is common knowledge or that has been discussed widely unless you plan to add a *new* perspective to it (see the persuasive speech appendix at the end of this chapter for a list of possible persuasive topics).

subject: knowledge of the topic, awareness of the need, and a personal and professional concern about the topic.

. Select a worthwhile subject of potential concern to your audience.

. Select a topic with a goal for influence or action. For example, the notion that exercise and eating well are good for your health might be a good persuasive theme, but if everyone in your audience is already healthy and physically in good shape, could you find a strong persuasive strategy?

Persuasive speeches often, but not always, deal with topics for which two or more opposing viewpoints exist and occur in situations in which the speaker's point of view differs from that of the audience. For example, the speaker might want the audience to support higher tuition because it will lead to higher quality instruction, but most of the audience may believe tuition is already too high. Especially when a speaker's goal is adoption or discontinuance, some difference must exist between the speaker's view and that of the audience, or persuasion is not needed. However, when the speaker's goal is deterrence or avoidance, the points of view of both speaker and audience might be more closely aligned. In such cases the speaker's goal is to *reinforce* beliefs, attitudes, or behaviors that are similar to those proposed in the speech.

Speakers may want their listeners to think about something from a new perspective and may try to influence the listeners to accept a specific point of view. The speaker's goal is to persuade the listeners that one viewpoint is sound, valid, or worthwhile, and the speaker wants to influence the listeners to accept that specific perspective. Such speeches typically address questions of fact, questions of value, questions of policy, or any combination of these three types of questions.

Questions of Fact

A question of fact asks what is true and what is false. Consider these questions: What is an advantage to being on LinkedIn? Who created Facebook? Where is the headquarters for Google? These questions can be answered with a fact that can be verified in reference books or on websites. Because they are so cut and dried, there can be little debate about them, thus making them weak topics for a persuasive speech.

question of fact
A question that asks what is true and what is false.

In contrast, persuasive speeches may be built on predictions of future events that will eventually become matters of fact. Consider these: Is the textbook a relic of the past? When will science find cures for the most deadly diseases of humankind? Will Americans elect a woman president? None of these questions can be answered with certainty, but a persuasive speaker could build an effective case predicting the answer to each.

Persuasive speeches can also be based on complicated answers to questions of fact or justifications for answers that are unclear. Why has wind energy not become more popular? Are the costs too great? Is it inefficient? Does the wind charger break down? Are hazards to the environment too great? Although no one answer covers the entire situation, a speaker could build a strong argument to show that one of these factors is the primary cause for decreased adoption of wind energy use.

Finally, some persuasive speeches may attempt to answer questions of fact that are not completely verifiable: Is Eastern medicine a rival to or superior to Western medicine? Does astrology provide us with real answers for our lives? Can acupuncture reduce pain more effectively than medicine? A speech on why we should reduce our consumption of sugar might be planned this way:

Specific Purpose

Thesis

SPECIFIC PURPOSE: To persuade my listeners that sugar is harmful to our health

THESIS: It is in our best interest to reduce consumption of sugar to lower the possibility of numerous health problems.

MAIN POINT

I. Seventy-nine million American adults have blood sugar levels that are too high.

SUBPOINTS

A. The normal range of blood sugar levels is …

B. High blood sugar levels are warning signs for further health problems.

MAIN POINT

II. Common ways we consume too much sugar

SUBPOINTS

A. Junk food

B. Carbonated beverages

C. Eating fast food because we're in a hurry

D. Grabbing a sugary treat because we need energy to make it through the day[3]

On the surface, questions of fact may appear more appropriate for an informative speech than for a persuasive one, but if you consider the difficulty of persuading an audience that college athletics are big business, that a major fire will destroy much of Southern California, or that the pyramids of Egypt were designed by an intelligence far superior to ours today, you can see that questions of fact offer rich possibilities for persuasion.

Questions of Value

question of value

A question that asks whether something is good or bad, desirable or undesirable.

A **question of value** asks whether something is good or bad, desirable or undesirable. Value is defined as a general, relatively long-lasting ideal that guides behavior. A value requires a more judgmental response than a fact. Here are some typical questions of value: Who is the most likeable celebrity in Australia? Who were the 10 best (or worst) U.S. presidents? Is a vegan diet really superior? The answers to these questions are not based solely on fact but on what each individual considers right or wrong, ethical or unethical, acceptable or unacceptable, or a good or a bad choice. People regularly make value-laden comments through social media. When was the last time you saw a Twitter follower weigh in with his or her opinion on the latest controversy playing out in the media?

The answers to questions of value may seem based solely on personal opinion and subjectivity, rather than on objective evidence, but this is not the case. Effective persuasive speakers use evidence to support their positions and are able to justify their opinions.

Values vary dramatically from one person to the next. Person *A* might think rap music is bad for society, and Person *B* might think it is good; Person *A* might think alcohol should be illegal on campus, and Person *B* might think it should be legal. When it comes to questions of value, one person's judgment is no better or worse than another's. People's values are usually complicated because they are rooted in emotion rather than reason. It is often extremely difficult to convince

eople to change their values. A speaker's position on a question of value might
e difficult to defend. You will need to gather a great deal of research and evidence
nd build a strong case to support one value over another—even though you know
our values are right—because your listeners also believe their values are right.

PECIFIC PURPOSE: To persuade my listeners that reducing clutter makes you more
roductive.

Specific Purpose

HESIS: Reducing clutter can make you more productive, mentally healthier, and save
ou time.

Thesis

AIN POINT

I. Unsolved emotional issues are often the cause of a cluttered lifestyle.

UBPOINTS

A. Clutter undermines real productivity.
B. The reality show *Hoarders* demonstrates the internal conflict about what is important in life.
C. "I know where everything is in that stack. Don't mess me up!" is a common refrain of those who clutter and hoard.

MAIN POINT

II. Organization experts and psychologists say that clutter is a sign that some portion of our lives is out of control.

SUBPOINTS

A. They say those who struggle with clutter are simply avoiding the need to make decisions about other things in life.
B. Anxiety, depression, and grief are some of the reasons we let clutter take over our lives.[4]

Questions of Policy

A **question of policy** goes beyond seeking a judgmental response to seeking a
course of action. Whereas a question of value asks whether something is right or
wrong, a question of policy asks whether something should or should not be done:
Should college health centers provide birth control to students? Should all plastic
water bottles be banned? Should Facebook allow pictures with graphic scenes, such
as violent assaults? Questions of policy involve both facts and values and are never
simple.

question of policy
A question that asks what actions
should be taken.

Persuasive speakers can defend an existing policy, suggest modifications of an
existing policy, and offer a new policy to replace an old one, or create a policy where
none exists. If you defend an existing policy, you must persuade your listeners that
what exists is best for the situation. If you want to modify or replace an existing policy,
you must persuade your listeners that the old policy does not work and that your new
one will. If you hope to create a new policy, you must persuade your audience a policy
is needed and yours is the right one for the situation.

When discussing questions of policy, persuasive speakers usually focus on three
considerations: need, plan, and suitability. If you believe things are not working as
some think, you must argue there is a *need* for change. When you advocate change,
you must provide a *plan,* or a solution. The plan tells the audience what you think
should be done. Finally, you must defend your plan by explaining its *suitability* for the
situation. Study the use of need, plan, and suitability in the following:

Specific Purpose	**SPECIFIC PURPOSE:** To persuade my listeners that each of us can make a difference in another's life
Thesis	**THESIS:** Each of us can have a tremendous impact on others, even people suffering from depression, by just taking a few moments to offer a kind comment or do something nice for them.
Need	I. One of every five young people and one of every four college students or adults suffer from some form of diagnosable mental illness.
	A. Suicide is the third leading cause of death among people ages 15–24, and the second leading cause of death in college students ages 20–24.
	B. About 19 percent of young people contemplate or attempt suicide each year.
	C. Forty-four percent of American college students reported feeling symptoms of depression.[5]
	II. Seventeen-year-old Graeme Carlson, a twelfth-grade student in Selkirk, Manitoba, created PingPongPositive.org to help others feel better about themselves and the world.
Plan	A. Graeme tells about a new friend who gave him a book to read because she thought he would really enjoy it.
	B. Graeme felt much better because of the act of friendship and the gift of the book.
	C. He decided to create ping-pong balls with uplifting messages and gave away 500 ping-pong balls after giving someone a compliment.
	1. He created a website to promote this unique way of paying it forward.
	2. Graeme also set up a Facebook page, a Twitter account, and YouTube clips.
	3. He received messages from all over Canada, the United States, Europe, and Asia.
	4. Canadian Broadcasting System (CBC) offices in Winnipeg ordered 250 specially designed ping-pong balls to help further the cause.
	III. Graeme says he feels good when he reads about what others have done with their ping-pong balls, and while he still suffers from depression, he knows that people really do care and that helps him feel better.
Suitability	A. You, too, can find a unique way to make others feel better, or you can add to the ping-pong balls going around the world.
	B. If each of us would compliment even one person and give him or her a ping-pong ball as a reminder of how much others mean to us, the world would be a healthier, happier place.[6]

Persuasive Claims

12.3 **Construct and support** a persuasive claim.

When attempting to answer questions of fact, value, and policy, we cannot always develop a formal logical answer that will irrefutably counter the objections of others. Formal rules of argument do not always determine who is right and who is wrong. Even when you supply compelling evidence to support your view, most evidence is not 100 percent clear-cut and may be interpreted in different ways. These factors make persuasive speaking especially challenging.

Aristotle, an ancient Greek philosopher, claimed that speakers had three modes of persuasion available to them: ethos, logos, and pathos. The speaker's actions and demeanor create each of these appeals during the speech. Aristotle believed one could appeal through **ethos**, or a speaker's ethical character. Speakers gain character or reputation through their ethical acts. Ethos is perceived in a speaker when the speaker identifies sources, is careful to give credit, does not offend the listeners, and generally establishes her- or himself as ethical. We often refer to the credibility of a speaker; perceived ethos leads to listeners' belief that a speaker is credible. **Logos** refers to the substance of the speech or the speaker's logical appeals. A speaker who is perceived

ethos
The speaker's character as perceived by the listeners.

logos
The substance of the speech or the logical appeals the speaker makes.

Making Connections for Success

Persuasive Speech Ideas on the Web

Have you ever thought about how famous people from the past sounded or how memorable speeches were constructed? Reading or listening to historically famous speeches or looking at lists of persuasive topics can be a motivation for your topic choices. Here are some ideas to help you find good examples as well as topics of interest.

1. Search "top 100 speeches" to access a list compiled by 137 of the leading scholars of American public address. Listen to one and try to determine why these scholars chose it as one of the most influential.

2. Search "speeches of influential women from around the world" and listen to or read one of them and evaluate the content.

3. Search "the top 10 greatest speeches of the 20th century" and listen to one to determine why it was included in such a prestigious list.

4. Are you interested in government, politics, or political debates? You can find the televised presidential debates on the web by searching "presidential debates." Choose one and see if you can determine why the ultimately successful candidate resonated with voters.

5. To get an idea about what other students have chosen for their persuasive topics, go to YouTube and search "persuasive speeches + topic (e.g., organ donation)." View two of the speeches. Do not copy these speeches but reflect on what each speaker did well and what he or she needed to improve.

6. A web search can help you find all kinds of persuasive topics. A number of communication professors include lists of possible topics (similar to the appendix of speech topics at the end of this chapter). Search "persuasive speech topics" and see what suggestions you find. Be prepared to share them with your instructor and classmates.

---

to have logos provides sensible reasons to support his or her arguments or to support substantial points made in the speech. **Pathos** is the emotional appeal that can have a powerful effect on an audience, but it must be carefully handled. Emotional appeals can get in the way, appear too artificial, or just simply obstruct the speaker's message. Thus, a speaker must carefully evoke appropriate emotions from listeners. All three of Aristotle's modes of persuasion are helpful in establishing oneself as a carefully prepared speaker creating a well-thought-out speech.

pathos

The speaker's evoking of appropriate emotion from the listeners.

Stephen Toulmin, a British philosopher, developed a model to help present everyday persuasive arguments.[7] Although not everyone uses Toulmin's model for understanding and presenting arguments, a brief discussion of the model may be helpful to both listeners and speakers as a means of evaluating arguments. Toulmin's approach to supporting a persuasive position or argument involves three basic parts: claim, data, and warrant. The *claim* is what the persuader wants or hopes will be believed, accepted, or done (or, in terms of what we discussed in the previous section, whether it is a fact, a value, or a policy). Claims, however, require evidence, or what Toulmin refers to as *data*. Data are the supporting materials or evidence that should influence the listener to accept the claim as stated. Unfortunately, a clear or irrefutable relationship between the claim and the data does not always exist. Thus, the persuader must explain the relationship between the claim and the data. Toulmin refers to this as the *warrant*. Here is a possible application of Toulmin's model:

CLAIM:	Despite the fact that wind energy is an achievable, totally safe, renewable form of energy and is good for the environment and the economy, the U.S. Congress seems to prefer to research and otherwise spend billions on oil rather than wind energy.
DATA:	Currently, the United States gives a production tax credit of 2.2-cents-per-kilowatt-hour benefit to encourage the use of wind-generated energy. That tax credit may soon end, and Congress is unlikely to renew it. Even though wind energy is beneficial, its use will slow down. "In the United States, the market this year is very, very busy …" Thomson Reuters quoted Vestas CEO Ditlev Engel, who spoke with a gathering of European ministers and senior officials, "But because of the potential lapse of the regulatory framework in the U.S., this market will probably go down 80 percent next year."[8]
WARRANT:	Wind is an inexpensive source of energy. Committing to a standard of 25 percent renewable electricity in the next 10 years would create much-needed new jobs, maintain current jobs, and substantially reduce our carbon footprint.

According to Toulmin's model, listeners can usually respond to the claims in three ways.

1. They can accept the claim at face value. This usually occurs when common knowledge holds that the claim is probably true. For example, a statement that U.S. educational programs need improvement is generally acceptable at face value.

2. They can reject the claim outright at face value. This usually happens when the claim is clearly false, such as the claim that U.S. lakes and streams have no pollution. It also occurs when listeners are biased against the claim or see no relationship between the claim and themselves. For example, if a claim that U.S. forests are not being depleted is made to a group trying to preserve the environment, it is unlikely they would accept this claim because of their biased views.

3. They can accept or reject the claim according to their evaluation of data and warrant. The person making the claim must provide evidence to support the claim or demonstrate that it is true.

Competent speakers must develop arguments strong enough to make the claim and supporting evidence stand on their own merits. They realize not everyone interprets the evidence in the same way they do, nor will everyone be convinced, even though the evidence they present may be, in their opinion, the best available. Because credibility is so important in the persuasive process, we'll discuss further how to establish it.

Establish Credibility (Ethos)

12.4 Explain how Aristotle's modes of presentation—ethos, logos, and pathos—increase your credibility

The most valuable tool you, as a persuasive speaker, can possess is credibility or believability based on the audience's evaluation of you as a person. Of course, you still need to have sound arguments and present them in such a way as to connect with the listeners, but unless you're perceived as credible, there's a chance your logic and appeal will not help you. Credibility is granted when you establish yourself as worthy of the listeners' attention from the beginning of your speech. At various points in this text, we have referred to ethos and to the speaker's credibility. Listeners assess your competence, knowledge, and experience; your charisma and energy; as well as your character. The audience is the ultimate judge of credibility, but you can do much to influence their opinion.

Actor Michael J. Fox has been public with his struggles against Parkinson's disease and shared personal experiences, which make him a credible and persuasive advocate for research to find a cure.

Competence

An audience judges your competence by the amount of knowledge, degree of involvement, and extent of experience you display. The more expertise you show in your subject, the more likely your audience will accept what you have to say. You can establish your expertise in several ways:

1. **Demonstrate involvement.** When Michael was a 16-year-old high school student, he spent a week on a mission trip to Guatemala. While there, the volunteers built 10 homes and helped provide food, clothing, and medical supplies to the villagers. Although his visit and subsequent volunteer efforts do not, in themselves, make him an expert on volunteerism, they establish his credibility as a speaker because of his firsthand involvement.

2. **Relate experience.** One young man volunteered at the Red Cross and talked about the ever-increasing need for blood donors because of illness and world calamities. He cited specific statistics about the amount of blood and supplies sent to Haiti, California, Japan, and Indonesia after the earthquakes. His own experience in helping get supplies ready to send made his listeners accept him as a knowledgeable person.

3. **Cite research.** Quoting information from written sources and interviews with experts can add weight and objectivity to your arguments. Mentioning respected sources adds to your credibility and indicates you are well read. Let's say you want to persuade your listeners they can overcome communication apprehension. The following research may enhance your credibility on this topic:

> According to James McCroskey, the communication professor who created the concept of communication apprehension, thousands of people in the United States alone suffer from some degree of communication apprehension. He has published hundreds of articles on the symptoms and effects of communication apprehension. McCroskey's website identifies him as the author, coauthor, or editor of 44 books and 200 journal articles. *The Quiet Ones: Communication Apprehension and Shyness* deals with communication apprehension.[9]

Character

An audience's judgment of your character is based on their perceptions of your trustworthiness and ethics. The best way to establish your character is to be honest and fair.

TRUSTWORTHINESS A speaker's **trustworthiness** is the audience's perception of the speaker's reliability and dependability. Others attribute trustworthiness on the basis of their past experiences with us. For example, instructors may judge our reliability according to whether we come to class every time it meets. Friends may evaluate our dependability according to how well we follow through on our promises. People who have had positive experiences with us are more apt to believe we are trustworthy.

trustworthiness
The audience's perception of a speaker's reliability and dependability.

ETHICS In Chapter 1, we defined *ethics* as an individual's system of moral principlesand stated that ethics play a key role in communication. Though this is certainly true in communication in general, it is especially so in persuasion. Persuasive speakers who are known to be unethical or dishonest are less likely to achieve their persuasive purpose than are people recognized as ethical and honest. You must earn your reputation as an ethical person through your actions. You can establish yourself as an ethical speaker when you:

1. **Cite sources when information is not your own and cite them accurately.** As you develop your speech, be sure you give credit to sources of information and to others' ideas. If you do not mention the sources of your information, you are guilty of plagiarism. Provide the audience with an **oral footnote**, such as "the following was taken from ..." or "this quotation is from... and cited in the *New York Times*." Be specific about from whom and from where your information came.

2. **Do not falsify or distort information to make your point.** Never make up information, attribute information to a source not responsible for it, take quotations out of context, or distort information to meet your purpose.

3. **Show respect for your audience.** When audience members perceive you are respectful, even though they may not agree with your point of view, they are more likely to listen. And when they listen, you at least have a chance of persuading them. Do not trick audience members into accepting your point of view or ridicule them if they disagree with you.

oral footnote
Providing, within the speech, the source that particular information comes from, such as, "According to Newsweek magazine of July 24, 2015...."

Charisma

As we stated earlier, other factors influence the way the audience perceives you. Among those is **charisma**, or the appeal or attractiveness the audience perceives in the speaker, contributing to the speaker's credibility. We often associate charisma with leaders who have special appeal for large numbers of people. Charismatic speakers seem to be sincerely interested in their listeners, speak with energy and enthusiasm, and generally seem attractive and likable. A credible speaker will take command of the speaking situation and engage the listeners so that they know the message is honest, well prepared, and relevant. Charismatic speakers are able to involve the audience in their messages.

charisma
The appeal or attractiveness that the audience perceives in the speaker, contributing to the speaker's credibility.

Making Connections for Success

Persuasive Speakers

Have you ever noticed how the particular situation makes some speakers effective at one time and neither effective nor credible at others? If you've ever watched the news, C-SPAN, *The O'Reilly Factor, Piers Morgan,* or *The Strombo Show,* or seen such public figures as Barack Obama, Scott Walker, Joni Ernst, or Hillary Rodham Clinton in more than one of those shows, you may notice different people: They may seem more credible, effective, and persuasive when they're communicating one-on-one rather than speaking on partisan issues. Well-known senators, for example, have been known to "rant and rave" when speaking in a Senate committee, but come across as much more mellow and contemplative when speaking with talk show hosts or to "regular" audiences. Think about public speakers (politicians, people in the news, media personalities, local officials, local celebrities) you've heard, either in the media or in person.

1. Who were the credible ones?
2. Were they persuasive? How so?
3. What characteristics made them effective?
4. What can you learn about persuasion from the effective speakers?

Your listener's evaluation of your credibility ultimately determines whether they accept or reject your persuasive goals. You should remember: Credibility is earned, it depends on others' perceptions, and it is not permanent. Credibility changes from topic to topic, from situation to situation, and from audience to audience; thus, you must establish your credibility each time you speak.

Becoming Effective Consumers of Persuasion

We spend a great deal of our lives listening to persuasive messages of one kind or another. It is important to think about what it means to be an effective consumer of those messages.

As listeners, we have both the right and the responsibility to take in accurate, reliable, and worthwhile information. Listen carefully to the message, and ask these questions:

> How knowledgeable is the speaker?
> What sources did the speaker use to gain additional information?
> Are these sources reliable and unbiased?
> Are there real advantages to accepting this position?
> Is the evidence presented in the argument worthwhile?
> Can I believe the evidence?
> Where can I get additional information?
> Does the argument seem logical?

It pays to closely analyze and evaluate the information presented, whether you are listening to an advertisement, a telemarketer, a political candidate, a religious leader, or a financial planner. Use questions like these to evaluate information:

> Is this *good* information?
> Is the information relevant to me?
> How can I learn more about this?
> What additional questions should I ask to make sure I obtain accurate and reliable information and sources?
> Does the information support the argument, or is it interesting but not essentially related?
> Is there sufficient support for the claims and arguments?
> Are there errors in the reasoning or the evidence?
> Does the message basically make sense? Why or why not?

Also pay attention to the person delivering the message:

> Is the speaker ethical and trustworthy? What is the evidence?
> Is the speaker competent and knowledgeable? What is the evidence?

Prepare and Develop a Persuasive Speech

12.5 Develop your persuasive speech by carefully researching your topic, organizing the content, providing appropriate supporting materials, and making strong, logical arguments.

In a classroom situation, you typically have only one opportunity to coax your audience to accept your persuasive purpose. Therefore, it is important to set realistic persuasive goals and to give some special thought to what is covered in previous chapters about researching, organizing, and gathering support for your speech.

Researching the Topic

Research for a persuasive speech must be especially thorough. You will need to gather as much information as possible about your topic because the more you know, the better equipped you will be to support your position. When doing your research, look primarily for evidence that supports and clarifies your views. If, in the process, you discover information that contradicts your stand, make note of it and look for material you can use to refute such information. Anticipating possible objections is especially helpful when your position is controversial and when your audience's opinions are likely to be split. If you know the arguments that could be used against you, you will be better able to support and defend your position.

Organizing the Speech

A persuasive speech requires making several special decisions that will affect its organization. Here are decisions especially related to persuasive speaking:

1. **Should you present one side or both sides of an issue?** The answer to this question depends on your audience. If your listeners basically support your position, then presenting one side may be sufficient. If their views are divided or opposed to your position, it may be more effective to present both sides. This decision also depends on your audience's knowledge of the topic and their evaluation of your credibility. If audience members are well informed and educated, presenting both sides of an argument helps minimize the effect counterarguments can have on your audience.

2. **When should you present your strongest arguments?** Presenting your strongest arguments at either the beginning or the end of your speech is more effective than presenting them in the middle. A good strategy is to state your strongest arguments early and then repeat them toward the end. Because audience attention is most likely to wander in the middle of a speech, this is a good time to present personal examples supporting your position.

3. **What is the best way to organize your persuasive speech?** The most effective sequence of presentation depends on your topic, specific purpose, and audience. Among the patterns of organization that work well for persuasive speeches are problem–solution, cause–effect, and Monroe's motivated sequence.

THE PROBLEM–SOLUTION PATTERN   A speech that follows the **problem–solution pattern** usually has two main points: the problem and the suggested solution. The problem is defined as a need, doubt, uncertainty, or difficulty, and the suggested solution remedies or eliminates the problem without creating other problems. A problem–solution approach could be used to address topics such as too few volunteers at the local food bank, the need for people to donate their time at a local museum, the increase in bullying, or an increase in the number of youth suicides because of bullying or cyber bullying.

problem–solution pattern
Order of presentation that first discusses a problem and then suggests solutions.

The problem–solution pattern, correctly used, should do more than state a problem and a solution; it should help the audience understand both the problem and the solution and why the solution will work. For example, a speech advocating legal consequences for bullying might follow this problem–solution pattern:

PROBLEM:
I. In recent months there has been a dramatic increase in the number of youth suicides.

SOLUTION:
II. Everyone, especially students, must learn the consequences of bullying people because of their sexuality, their abilities, their disabilities, or the mere fact they are different may lead to suicides, and ultimately may find the bully facing legal issues.

The problem–solution pattern usually includes three to five of the following:

1. A *definition and description* of the problem, including its symptoms and size
2. A *critical analysis of the problem,* including causes, current actions, and requirements for a solution
3. *Suggestions of possible solutions,* including a description of each solution's strengths and weaknesses
4. A *recommendation of the best solution,* including a thorough justification of its superiority over other proposed solutions
5. A *discussion of the best solution put into operation,* including a description of how the plan can be implemented

cause–effect pattern

An order of presentation in which the speaker first explains the causes of an event, problem, or issue and then discusses its consequences.

THE CAUSE–EFFECT PATTERN   In the **cause–effect pattern**, the speaker explains the causes of an event, problem, or issue and discusses its consequences. Causes and effects may be presented in two different sequences. A speaker may both describe certain forces or factors and then show the effects that follow from them or describe conditions or events and then point out the forces or factors that caused them.

Using the cause–effect pattern, a speaker might arrange a speech on the health risks of hunger in either of the following ways:

CAUSE:
I. Hunger is the world's number one health risk.

EFFECT:
II. Today alone, over 15,000 men, women, and children will die of hunger.

OR

EFFECT:
I. Hunger results in more deaths than tuberculosis, malaria, and AIDS combined.

CAUSE:
II. Hunger, malnutrition, and poverty cause senseless deaths.[10]

Because the cause–effect pattern can be used in a variety of ways, it is a useful format for either informative or persuasive speeches. As long as the cause can be directly related to the effect you are trying to prove, this pattern is an excellent choice for many different topics and a beneficial means of reaching your listeners.

Consider the following example of using the cause–effect pattern to discuss the effects of senseless deaths due to eating disorders. A speaker might begin by discussing eating disorders as having the highest mortality rate of all mental illnesses. Over eight million Americans experience eating disorders today. In fact, as many as two of every 100 students suffer from some type of eating disorder. Or, the speaker might reverse the process and first point out that many insurance firms don't offer coverage for treatment for these pervasive disorders, despite the fact that millions of affected men and women in the United States require intensive treatment.[11]

Regardless of the exact sequence, a speech organized by cause and effect has two main points: a description of the factors that are the *cause* and a prediction or identification of the subsequent *effect,* or vice versa. Topics such as eating disorders in young adults, television violence, gaining the "freshman 15," and new approaches to improving memory all lend themselves to the cause–effect pattern.

MONROE'S MOTIVATED SEQUENCE PATTERN   A widely used pattern of organization for the persuasive speech is the **motivated sequence**, developed by Professor Alan H. Monroe of Purdue University in the 1930s.[12] This pattern is specifically designed to help the speaker combine sound logic and practical psychology and is useful in persuasive speaking as well as in sales and marketing. The motivated sequence is particularly effective because it follows the human thinking process and motivates listeners to take action. The sequence has five steps: attention, need, satisfaction, visualization, and action.

Monroe's motivated sequence
A pattern of organization specifically developed for persuasive speaking that combines logic and practical psychology. Five steps are involved: attention, need, satisfaction, visualization, and action.

1. **Attention.** In the first step, the persuader attempts to create an interest in the topic so the audience wants to listen. This step takes place in the introduction and follows the guidelines for an effective presentation. The speaker is subtly saying, "Please pay attention. This is important to you."

2. **Need.** In the second step, the persuader focuses on the problem by analyzing the things that are wrong and relating them to the audience's interests, wants, or desires. At this point the speaker is saying, "This is wrong, and we must do something about it."

3. **Satisfaction.** In the third step, the persuader provides a solution or plan of action that will eliminate the problem and thus satisfy the audience's interests, wants, and desires. The speaker is saying, "What I have to offer is the way to solve the problem."

4. **Visualization.** In the fourth step, the persuader explains in detail how the solution will meet the audience's need. The speaker's message now becomes, "This is how my plan will work to solve the problem, and if you accept my solution, things will be much better."

5. **Action.** In the fifth and final step, the persuader asks the audience for a commitment to put the proposed solution to work. The speaker basically concludes by saying, "Take action!"

The following brief speech outline is used for the persuasive speech example later in the chapter. Michael Schwabe uses Monroe's motivated sequence to try to persuade his listeners to donate time and/or money to a specific mission.

SPECIFIC PURPOSE: To persuade my audience to donate time and/or money to missions in developing countries

Specific Purpose

INTRODUCTION Have you ever seen a disabled child abandoned by family because he or she couldn't work? I have. Have you ever seen a husband and father unable to provide for his family after losing both his arms in a work accident? I have. Have you ever heard the cries of help from a family living in a cardboard home with only three walls and half a roof? I have. Last week, you heard about how problems such as these are common among citizens of Guatemala. Last week, you heard about how a family of missionaries called Bethel Ministries is trying to help these citizens. What you *didn't* hear last week was *why this matters to you.* What you *didn't* hear was, "Why should I spend time or money to help these people?" Well, *today,* that's exactly what I'd like to tell you. I want to tell you why Bethel Ministries is worthy of your acknowledgment. To do this, I'd like to remind you of some of the problems facing Guatemalans, and explain how your time or money can directly solve many of these problems.

Attention

I. My experience when on a mission trip to Guatemala

(continued)

Need

BODY

II. Fifty-one percent of Guatemalans live below the international poverty line.
   A. Health care is extremely limited.
   B. There are only six hospital beds for every 10,000 citizens.
   C. Guatemalans are categorized as being at "high" risk of catching infectious diseases.
   D. The problems won't go away on their own.

Satisfaction

III. A small amount of money can work wonders for the citizens of Guatemala.
   A. Donations can directly benefit the people.
   B. Mission trips allow you to help with such things as wheelchair distribution, home construction, and medical care.

Visualization

IV. Imagine this scenario: A new house is built to protect families from the harsh weather, decreasing their exposure to the elements and illness; people are provided with medical care that allows them to work and support their families; and families can rebuild.

Action

CONCLUSION I encourage you, I implore you, I beg you—donate as much time or money to help missions in Guatemala as you can spare. If people like us don't or won't help, who will?[13]

The motivated sequence is most often used in persuasion. Advertisers also commonly use it because it sells ideas.

Supporting Materials

In persuasive speeches, speakers try to influence audience members through their impressive supporting materials. They choose these materials carefully to build the kind of appeal most likely to sway their listeners. On the basis of the topic and their audience analysis, persuasive speakers try to connect to their listeners' needs, to logic, or to emotions.

appeal to needs

An attempt to move people to action by calling on their physical and psychological requirements and desires.

APPEALS TO NEEDS An **appeal to needs** attempts to move people to action by calling on physical and psychological requirements and desires. Of course, different people have different needs, but most of us want to protect or enhance factors that affect our physical, safety, social, and self-esteem needs, according to psychologist Abraham Maslow. According to Maslow's hierarchy of individual needs, our lower-order needs must be satisfied before higher-order needs can be met.

Physical needs are our most basic physiological requirements, such as food, water, sleep, sex, and other physical comforts. *Safety needs* pertain to our desires for stability, order, and protection from violence; freedom from stress and disease; security; and structure. *Social needs* relate to our hopes to be loved and to belong and our needs for affection from family and friends, for membership in groups, and for the acceptance and approval of others. *Self-esteem needs* reflect our desires for recognition, respect from others, and self-respect.

Speakers can appeal to any of these needs to motivate listeners to take action. A speaker trying to sell individual retirement accounts would aim his appeal at our requirements for security and stability; a speaker who hoped to persuade us to lose weight would call on our needs for physical comfort, acceptance by others, and self-esteem. Our readiness to accept ideas or to take action depends heavily on the speaker's ability to relate a message to what we need.

logical appeal

An attempt to move people to action through the use of evidence and proof.

LOGICAL APPEALS (LOGOS) Attempts to move people to action through the use of evidence and proof are called **logical appeals**. When speakers lead their listeners to think, "Yes, that's logical" or "That makes sense," they are building a case by calling on their audience's ability to reason. To accomplish this, competent persuasive speakers use evidence such as statistics, examples, testimony, and any other supporting materials that will sway their listeners.

A logical appeal requires an ability to argue for your point of view. When you argue in persuasive speaking, you usually make a claim or state an argument or *proposition*, something you want your listeners to believe after you complete your speech. A claim or proposition usually assumes things can be done more than one way. For example, abortion should be illegal or it should be legal; the electoral process should or should not be changed. Speakers usually try to justify such a position with reason and evidence. The *justification*, or data, involves the use of all the supporting materials you can find to support your claim or proposition, including statistics, facts, examples, testimony, pictures, objects, and so on.

In presenting their evidence, persuasive speakers guide their listeners through a carefully planned sequence of thought that clearly leads to the desired conclusion. This train of logic may fall into one of four categories: deductive reasoning, inductive reasoning, causal reasoning, or reasoning by analogy.

Deductive reasoning is a sequence of thought that moves from general information to a specific conclusion. It presents a general premise (a generalization) and a minor premise (a specific instance) that lead to a precise deduction (a conclusion about the instance). One student set up his argument as follows:

GENERAL PREMISE:	People in developed countries consume too much sugar.
MINOR PREMISE:	Sugar causes health problems.
CONCLUSION:	Anyone who consumes too much sugar will have health problems.

deductive reasoning
A sequence of thought that moves from general information to a specific conclusion; it consists of a general premise, a minor premise, and a conclusion.

Great care must be taken to ensure that the premises are accurate because faulty premises can lead only to a faulty conclusion. For example:

FAULTY GENERAL PREMISE:	Democrats are radical in all their views.
MINOR PREMISE:	Harry Reid is a Democrat.
FAULTY CONCLUSION:	Harry Reid is radical in all his views.

The general premise must be both accurate and defensible before deductive reasoning can be used effectively as evidence to support a position.

Inductive reasoning is the opposite of deductive reasoning; it is a sequence of thought that moves from the specific to the general. An argument based on inductive reasoning usually progresses from a series of related facts or situations to a general conclusion. A student discussing the need to protect oneself from identity theft might lead her listeners through the following sequence of inductive reasoning:

inductive reasoning
A sequence of thought that moves from specific facts to a general conclusion.

FACTS:
1. Identity theft is a growing problem.
2. Identity theft can produce devastating results.
3. It's a hassle to get your identity and your good credit back.
4. Identity theft claims a new victim every 4.5 seconds.
5. You can protect yourself against identity theft.

CONCLUSION: You could be the next victim of identity theft unless you take steps to protect yourself.

When your facts can be verified, when the number of facts is sufficient, and when links between the facts and the conclusion are solid, inductive reasoning can be an excellent way to persuade an audience of the validity of your argument.

Inductive reasoning can also be misused. How often have you heard general statements such as the following: All college professors are radical liberals; all car salespeople are dishonest; religiously devout people of all kinds are ethical; all accounting majors are brilliant. Each of these generalizations is based on someone's past experience. The reality, however, is that limited past experience does not support the conclusion.

To avoid problems when using inductive reasoning, make sure your facts are accurate and that they support your conclusion. Furthermore, make sure your conclusion does not extend beyond the facts you have presented. You will undermine your own case if your conclusion is so general that someone can easily point out exceptions to it.

causal reasoning

A sequence of thought that links causes with effects; it either implies or explicitly states the word *because*.

reasoning by analogy

A sequence of thought that compares similar things or circumstances to draw a conclusion.

Causal reasoning is a sequence of thought that links causes with effects. Thus it always implies or includes the word *because*: Earth's temperature is rising *because* the ozone layer is thinning. As in any form of reasoning, it is necessary to support the conclusion with evidence. In the example in this paragraph, the speaker would go on to cite scientific evidence linking thinning ozone to rising temperatures. The more verifiable and valid the evidence, the more defensible is the conclusion about the cause-and-effect relationship between ozone and temperature. Even though other factors may also cause Earth's warming, the speaker's argument can be considered reasonable if it is based on scientific evidence that supports the speaker's point of view.

Reasoning by analogy is a sequence of thought that compares similar things or circumstances to draw a conclusion. It says, in effect, what holds true in one case will also hold true in a similar one. If you were to argue we should make every effort to use energy from renewable sources, you might use the following reasoning:

GENERAL PREMISE: The majority of energy used in the United States comes from nonrenewable sources, and our carbon footprint is harming the environment.

MINOR PREMISE: People in developing countries use energy from mostly renewable sources and do not have such a large carbon footprint.

CONCLUSION: U.S. citizens can use energy from renewable sources to reduce the carbon footprint of this nation.

Analogies are effective reasoning tools when used wisely and if there is appropriate support for the conclusion. The relationship in the analogy must be valid, and the conclusion should be based on the assumption that all other factors are equal. For instance, our example is based on the assumption that people in developing nations are careful with the use of energy—a positive action—and Americans would do well to emulate the conservation of a diminishing natural resource. If the argument implied that there were reasons for alternative energy other than that nonrenewable energy is a diminishing natural resource, the argument would fail. To avoid problems when using analogies, it is crucial to consider any dissimilarity that might refute your point.

You might wish to base your speech on a single form of reasoning, or you might prefer a combination of types of reasoning. Whatever your choice, remember: your argument is only as good as the evidence you use to support it.

EMOTIONAL APPEALS   Attempts to move people to action by playing on their feelings—for example, by making them feel guilty, unhappy, afraid, happy, proud, sympathetic, or nostalgic—are known as **emotional appeals**. Because emotions are extremely strong motivators, this form of appeal can be highly effective. Note how the following introduction to a persuasive speech appeals to the emotions:

emotional appeal

An attempt to move people to action by playing on their feelings.

My grandfather is a wonderful, caring person. He was always the person who would listen to me and lend me a shoulder to cry on. He is also one of the most intelligent people I've ever known. When I was growing up, Grandpa gave me suggestions to help me solve all kinds of problems, everything from completing my homework, to discussing why my friends were not friendly, to helping me find a summer job. Today, however, my grandfather doesn't know who I am, let alone my name, and he often doesn't even realize that I'm in the room with him. You see, Grandpa suffers from Alzheimer's disease. There is no cure, and we still don't know very much about it. What we do know, however, is that it takes the real person and his mind and leaves a hollow shell.

Emotional appeals can be so powerful that they sway people to do illogical things. When a student cheats on an exam, for example, there is no logical justification, but the student may believe she is justified from an emotional viewpoint because of parental pressure to get good grades. In fact, persuasive speakers often mix both logical and emotional appeals to achieve the strongest effect. Persuasive speakers need to be aware of the issue of ethics discussed throughout this text. A speaker must present valid, reliable information in a way that will appeal to listeners but will not violate their rights or responsibilities. The speaker should be fair, accurate in voicing views, careful in presenting information, and attentive to the strategies used. An ethical speaker uses emotional appeals carefully and truthfully.

Persuasive Strategies

Speakers need to use persuasive strategies to win over their listeners. First, the speaker needs to demonstrate *rhetorical sensitivity;* that is, the speaker needs to be aware of the audience, the situation, the time limits, and what listeners want and are willing to hear. The speaker is aware that listeners expect a strong, clear message to which the speaker is committed and in which the speaker believes. The speaker will also carefully adapt the message so listeners know it is relevant and important to them. The audience anticipates that the speaker will motivate them or make them want to hear the speech and learn more about the argument. The audience expects to understand the speaker's point. They expect the speaker to repeat and reinforce the message so that they are influenced to, at the very least, accept that the speaker has a point worth considering. All in all, the persuasive speaker will always keep the listener in mind while reinforcing the argument.

Fallacies in Argument Development

12.6 Recognize errors in your own thinking so you can correct them and present logical claims and evidence.

As both creators and consumers of persuasive messages, all of us must be able to analyze and evaluate others' as well as our own use of reasoning to support these messages. It is especially important to avoid presenting flawed arguments, thereby causing listeners to question your credibility. Arguments that are flawed because they do not follow the rules of logic—and, therefore, are not believable—are called **fallacies**. Flawed reasoning occurs all the time, and often people do not realize they used flawed arguments. As a critical thinker, however, you must understand what fallacies are, how to recognize them, and why you should not use them or let others use them in their communication.

fallacy
An argument that is flawed because it does not follow the rules of logic.

Many different types of fallacies are used in communication, but only the major errors are presented here. Let's look at basic fallacies in reasoning and evidence.

Fallacies of Reason

QUESTIONABLE CAUSE **Questionable cause** is a common fallacy and occurs when a speaker asserts something that does not relate to or produce the outcome claimed in the argument. It is a part of our nature to want to know what caused certain events to occur. If tuition increases, people want to know why; if the national deficit increases, we want to know why; if parking space on campus or at the shopping center is eliminated, we want answers! In a desire to know the cause of certain behaviors or events, we sometimes attribute what has happened to something unrelated to the situation. For example, if you claim attendance at home athletic events has increased because there's nothing else to do on campus you've used a questionable cause, especially if the number of activities on campus and in the community is the same as in previous years.

questionable cause
A fallacy that occurs when a speaker alleges something that does not relate to or produce the outcome claimed in the argument.

AD HOMINEM When someone attacks a person rather than the person's argument, he or she resorts to an **ad hominem** fallacy. This is also referred to as *name-calling*. If you call someone a jerk in response to an argument to diminish the relevance or significance of the argument, you are using name-calling as a refutation of the argument.

ad hominem
A fallacy that attacks a person rather than the argument itself. This is also referred to as *name-calling*.

This is merely a smoke screen; it shows an inability to provide good counterarguments or evidence to challenge what the other person claims. Name-calling, ridiculing, or personal attacks on another person can diffuse an argument, but it usually results in a bad argument and sidesteps the issue.

Fallacies of Evidence

FACT VERSUS OPINION   A major misuse of information involves the presentation of facts and opinions. Speakers who state opinions as if they are facts can mislead and may present a fallacious argument. For example, "our university's policy on drinking is too stringent" and "our university is short 250 parking spaces" are both statements of information. Which is fact, and which is opinion? The first statement is opinion, and the second is fact. How can you tell which is which? Facts can be verified; the lack of parking spaces can be verified, whereas the university's policy on drinking may or may not be stringent, which is a matter of opinion.

Giving opinions can be helpful in persuasive speeches or arguments, but to treat an opinion as though it were fact or a fact as though it were an opinion is an error in critical thinking. In either case, you will appear to claim too little or too much and raise questions about your competence and ethics.

red herring

A fallacy that uses irrelevant information to divert attention away from the real issue.

hasty generalization

A fallacy that occurs when a speaker does not have sufficient data and therefore argues or reasons from a specific example.

post hoc ergo propter hoc **fallacy**

A fallacy of reasoning in which one attributes something as a cause simply because it followed (came after) another incident.

either–or reasoning

A fallacy of reasoning in which only two options exist: There is black or white, right or wrong, but nothing in between.

To persuade the jury, an attorney in a courtroom must use facts and evidence, not opinions, and must avoid logical fallacies.

RED HERRING   Another misuse or avoidance of facts arise when one includes irrelevant information to divert attention from the real issue. This occurs when a speaker wishes to draw attention away from an issue being questioned or challenged. Have you ever questioned someone about something he or she did wrong, and the response didn't relate to the event to which you were referring? In fact, the person may change the subject or even attack your credibility to avoid a discussion of the issue. Irrelevant information used to divert attention from the real issue is referred to as a **red herring** fallacy.

HASTY GENERALIZATION   As a common critical thinking fallacy, the **hasty generalization** occurs when a speaker doesn't have sufficient data and therefore argues or reasons from a specific example. Conclusions are drawn from insufficient data or cases. It is not uncommon to find people make generalizations based on only one or a few examples. For instance, to argue male students think date rape is not a problem on their campus, a speaker might cite the opinions of two or three close friends. The speaker then states the following conclusion: "In surveying people I know, I've found most students do not believe date rape is a problem on our campus." The argument that date rape is not a problem might sound impressive, but the survey does not represent a large or representative sample of students; therefore, the claim is unjustified. The argument can be refuted as a hasty generalization.

POST HOC FALLACY   Another kind of faulty reasoning about what comes after something is the *post hoc ergo propter hoc* **fallacy**—from the Latin for "after that, therefore because of that." For example, you get an email message warning that if you delete the message and don't send to four or nine friends you will have bad luck; then, you get a flat tire on the way to work. Faulty reasoning may lead you to believe your failure to send the message caused the bad luck.

EITHER–OR REASONING   The kind of faulty reasoning found when someone claims that either something is right or it's wrong—there's no in-between—is called **either–or reasoning**. Former President George W. Bush claimed "people opposed to the war in Iraq are not patriotic—if you're not on our side, you're against us. If you don't support the war, you support terrorists."

Making Connections for Success

Recognizing Fallacies in Persuasion

We are constantly bombarded by attempts to persuade us to do something. Telemarketers ask us to take advantage of a credit card to solve our financial problems (and likely create new ones); four or five direct-mail advertisers send offers for better cable and Internet services; another set of calls and mailings wants us to donate to a worthy cause; a speaker pleads with us to donate blood to the local chapter of the Red Cross. Advertisers often use fallacious reasoning to make their products seem better. They relay on our need to know to get us to attend to their messages. They provide only enough data to pique curiosity, but then fail to give us enough information to make a judgment on the product. They give us

either–or situations and predict dire consequences if we don't buy their product or service.

Keep track of persuasive attempts for a two-day period. Identify and create a list of the number of times someone tries to persuade you and then analyze the content so you can share it with your class.

1. How many different persuasive attempts were made in that two-day period?
2. What kinds of reasoning did the persuaders use?
3. What strategies appealed to you? Which ones did not?
4. If any were successful, what made the persuasion a success?
5. Were the persuaders ethical? If so, how? If not, why?

When you develop or encounter reasoning or arguments that do not fit any of the fallacies described in the text but you doubt the argument's validity, put the argument to the following test: Can the argument be outlined? Do the data support the claim? Does a solid relationship exist between the data and the claim? It is not important to know the name of a specific type of fallacy, but rather to analyze how arguments are developed and used to determine whether they are valid.

Evaluate the Persuasive Speech

12.7 Evaluate and assess your own persuasive speeches and those of others

Here are some of the criteria used to evaluate the competence of speakers and the effectiveness of their persuasive speeches. Your instructor may consider these areas when assessing your speech. You should be aware of them while preparing a persuasive speech presentation.

Topic

The selection of a topic should meet the following criteria:

- The topic should merit the audience's attention.
- The audience should be able to see the relationship between the topic and speaker and between the topic and themselves.
- The topic should be able to receive adequate coverage in the time available. The topic should have been narrowed enough to be fully developed.

General Requirements

The following represent general requirements of most persuasive speech presentations:

- The purpose of the speech should clearly be to persuade and be stated as such.
- The speech should meet the time requirements set by the assignment.
- The speaker should cite sources of information that are not his or her own.

- The speech purpose should be relevant to the assignment and related to the audience.
- The speech should show evidence of careful preparation.

Audience Analysis

The speaker must shape the speech to suit the audience. As previously discussed, this often requires research into the listeners' past experiences, beliefs, attitudes, and values. The choices the speaker then makes regarding content and development of ideas should be tailored to the audience.

- The speech should reflect appropriate audience analysis.
- The speaker should relate to and refer to audience members to get them involved and interested in the topic.
- The speech should include a goal, that is, the audience should be asked to think something, believe something, or take action.
- The speech should show the audience why the topic is important and relevant to them.

Supporting Materials

Supporting materials supply documented evidence that the information conveyed in the speech is accurate and credible.

- Supporting materials help the audience to believe the information.
- Supporting materials should appeal to the audience's needs, logic, and emotions.
- Supporting materials should include a variety of factual statements, statistical data, personal experiences, analogies, contrasts, examples and illustrations, expert testimony, value appeals, and eyewitness accounts.
- Visual aids should be used where appropriate and helpful; they should follow guidelines established by the assignment.
- Supporting materials should be documented, cited correctly, and up to date.
- Supporting materials help the speaker establish and maintain credibility.

Organization

When judging organization, the evaluator looks for a carefully planned, well-developed persuasive speech and a unified approach to the material presented.

- The introduction should be properly developed.
  - It should orient the audience to the topic.
  - It should gain the audience's attention and arouse interest.
  - It should include a specific purpose and thesis statement.
  - It should define terms (if necessary).
  - It should motivate the audience to listen.
  - It should be relevant.
  - It should establish credibility.
- The organization of the body should be clear and easy to follow.
  - The main points should be clear and parallel in structure.
  - The main points should be related to the purpose of the speech.

- Transitions should provide appropriate links between ideas.
- The organizational pattern should be appropriate.
- The conclusion should be properly developed.
  - It should reinforce the purpose by reviewing the main points.
  - It should end with a memorable thought.
  - The audience should know what action is expected of them in response to the speech.

Figure 12.1 Speaker's Self-Reflection Evaluation Form

On completing your persuasive speech, take a few moments to reflect on what you presented. This form can help you organize your thinking about the speech. Put yourself in the place of your listeners and be specific in your comments on each aspect of the speech. Whenever there's a choice, circle the appropriate response and provide explanations. Always provide an explanation.

Name _____Title of Speech _____

Topic *I would stay with this topic because*

  OR, *I would change the perspective I present because* _____.

Research *How would you change the way you researched your speech?*
_____

Appropriateness *In what ways was this speech appropriate to you, the classroom, the situation, the audience, the time limits?*_____

Organization *My organization could be improved by*_____.

The introduction *What would you change and/or retain from the introduction you used?*_____

The body of the speech needed _____ to make it complete.

The conclusion was effective/ineffective in the following ways: _____.

I would change the conclusion as follows:

Explanation and clarity of ideas was effective/ineffective because _____.

The claims or arguments presented worked well/need change _____.

Analyze each of the following and provide a complete response *(at least one full sentence)*:

Support for ideas *(valid, worthwhile, ethical, sufficient number, clear?)*_____

Use of language _____

Visual delivery *(movement, gestures, eye contact, posture)*_____

Figure 12.1 Continued

Vocal delivery *(conversationality, sincerity, variety, ease of listening)*_____

The ways I adapted this speech to this audience: _____

If I were to give this speech again, I would change the following:

_____,

because _____.

What would you retain? Why? _____

What have you learned from this presentation? _____

Delivery

The delivery techniques provide evidence the speaker is aware of what the audience is interested in hearing, is involved in and enthusiastic about the topic, and is interested in sharing the material with the listeners.

- The speaker should be enthusiastic.
- The speaker should convey a persuasive attitude through focus, energy, and appropriate vocal variety.
- Nonverbal communication (gestures, movements, eye contact, posture, facial expression) should enhance and clarify the verbal delivery.
- The speaker should be aware of the audience's presence and reactions and should adjust her or his delivery accordingly.
- The speaker should be confident and poised.
- The speaker should convey a sense of the topic's relevance and importance.
- The speaker's vocal delivery should enhance the speech with appropriate volume, appropriate rate, conversational quality, enthusiastic tone, clear enunciation, appropriate pauses, and appropriate vocal variety.

Language Choice

Effective use of language is critical to communication. This is especially true when crafting a persuasive message. Clear, vivid, specific, and acceptable language enhances and clarifies ideas.

- Language choice should be appropriate to the assignment and audience.
- Language should be compelling.
- Word choice should be appropriate for the speaker, topic, situation, and audience.
- Grammar should be correct and show both competence and an awareness of the "formal" speaking situation.
- Word pronunciations should be accurate.

Speakers should evaluate their own speeches and those of others. The forms in Figures 12.1 and 12.2 can help you analyze and reflect on the speeches you give and those to which you listen.

Figure 12.2 Sample Listener Evaluation Form for Persuasive Speeches

Listeners are often called on to evaluate speakers. Some instructors have listeners complete an evaluation similar to this one. It provides the speaker with invaluable information. It is also a good critical thinking exercise for the listener.

Speaker _____ Topic _____ Date _____

1. How well did this speech meet the criteria for a persuasive speech? _____

2. What was the speaker's specific purpose? _____

3. What was the speaker's thesis? _____

4. Which arguments did you believe? _____

5. Which arguments did you have difficulty believing? _____

6. Were you convinced about the claim or argument the speaker presented?
   Why or why not? _____
   _____

7. What would it take to make you change your beliefs, attitudes, or behaviors about this topic?

8. How did this speaker and the stand taken in this speech influence you? _____
   _____

9. Did you hear any faulty reasoning in this speech? What kind? How could the reasoning be improved? _____
   _____

10. What types of evidence and support were provided for arguments, statements, and claims? _____
    _____

11. Was the speaker believable? Why or why not? What could the speaker do to be more believable? _____

12. Was the speaker ethical? Fair? Accurate? _____

13. What kinds of appeals were used? _____

14. Was the speaker easy to follow? Was the organization clear? _____
    _____

Guidelines

For Persuasive Speakers

1. **Establish yourself as an ethical communicator:** employ good research, oral footnotes, and careful use of language and information. This will increase your credibility as a speaker.

2. **Use repetition and restatement to help your listeners remember your speech.** This will significantly add to the clarity of your presentation.

3. **Use appropriate organizational patterns.** This will make your speech easy to follow.

4. **Select appropriate supporting materials.** This will bolster the arguments that you make in your speech.

5. **Use sound reasoning.** Think about Toulmin's model and make your claim, support your claim with evidence (data), and show how the claim and date connect (warrant). This will strengthen your argument.

A SAMPLE PERSUASIVE SPEECH WITH COMMENTARY

Michael Schwabe, University of Nebraska–Lincoln

SPECIFIC PURPOSE: To persuade my audience to donate their time and/or money to Bethel Ministries

THESIS: Bethel Ministries provides outstanding help for people in Guatemala and deserves to receive donations of your time and/or money to promote their work.

INTRODUCTION

Michael has a longer than usual introduction because he wants to make sure that he gets the listeners' attention and because he feels strongly (in fact, is quite passionate) about this particular charity. He orients the listeners to his topic, motivates them to pay attention, and establishes his own credibility because he has seen the situation in Guatemala and has helped the mission group bring about change.

Have you ever seen a disabled child abandoned by family because he or she couldn't work? I have. Have you ever seen a husband and father unable to provide for his family after losing both his arms in a work accident? I have. Have you ever heard the cries of help from a family living in a cardboard home with only three walls and half a roof? I have. Last week, you heard about how problems such as these are common among citizens of Guatemala. Last week, you heard about how a family of missionaries called Bethel Ministries is trying to help these citizens. What you *didn't* hear last week was *why this matters to you.* What you *didn't* hear was "Why should I spend time or money to help these people?" Well, *today,* that's exactly what I'd like to tell you. I want to tell you why Bethel Ministries is worthy of your acknowledgment. To do this, I'd like to tell you what I experienced when I worked with them, and then how you can benefit from assisting this family.

I. My experience

   A. When I was 16, I spent a week working in Guatemala.

      1. I went with Brookdale Church.

      2. This was our church's third trip with this mission family.

   B. I was a normal 16-year-old.

      1. I didn't expect to get much from this trip other than a cool vacation.

      2. However, I quickly found out this trip would have a much bigger impact on my life.

   C. When I went, we built over 10 houses in 5 days of work.

      1. Some of the most physically challenging work I've ever done (and I've worked on a horse farm most of my life)

      2. Incredibly rewarding experience

   D. Relationships

      1. On trips like these, the things I value most to this day are the relationships I built with the people on the mission team.

      2. I formed friendships not only with the Americans I came with but with the missionaries and the locals as well.

      3. I have memories and experiences that will bond me to these people for a lifetime.

   E. Lessons

      1. Other than relationships, the biggest thing I gained from this trip was a wealth of knowledge about myself.

      2. Seeing how people exist in such squalid conditions teaches you about your own life.

         a. What to be thankful for

         b. How to make the most out of what you have

         c. How to persevere when things are hard

         d. Strengths and weaknesses

         e. What's truly important to you

TRANSITION/BODY

In his first main point in the body of the speech, Michael follows the Monroe's motivated sequence pattern by creating the need. He provides statistics from World Bank, Rural Poverty Portal, and the CIA. He identifies problems with poverty and health care and reinforces the notion that these problems require outside assistance, as they will not go away on their own. His facts are compelling and make the listener stop to think about the situation in Guatemala, where 51 percent of the people live below the international poverty line, where children are malnourished, where hospitals are woefully inadequate, and where Guatemalans are at high risk for contracting contagious diseases.

II. Create need

   A. Poverty

      1. According to worldbank.com, accessed May 28, 2012, 51 percent of Guatemalans live below the international poverty line.

      2. According to ruralpovertyportal.org, as of 2006, over 70 percent of Guatemalans in rural areas live below the international poverty line.

B. Health care

    1. One-half of children below age 5 are chronically malnourished (CIA).

    2. There are only six hospital beds for every 10,000 citizens (CIA).

    3. CIA categorizes Guatemalans as being at "high" risk of catching infectious diseases.

C. These problems won't go away on their own—they require outside assistance.

III. Satisfy need

  A. Donations

    1. Donations to Bethel Ministries can directly benefit some of these situations.

    2. According to Bethel's website, water filters can be bought for only $50 and clean stoves for only $180.

    3. Two thousand dollars is all it takes to build an entirely new home for a family.

    4. Other donations go directly to the people of rural Guatemala—their education, medical treatment, nourishment, and many other needs.

  B. Missions trips

    1. Another amazing way to help the people of rural Guatemala is to actually *go* there yourself!

    2. Help with wheelchair distributions.

    3. Home construction

    4. Medical care

    5. Orphanage

  C. All of this assistance directly alleviates some of the issues plaguing the people in ways you can see for yourself.

IV. Visualization

  A. I know it may not seem as though building a house or providing a new stove will do much for a family, but imagine this scenario:

    1. A new house protects the family from harsh weather, decreasing their exposure to the elements and their sickness.

    2. This decrease in sickness reduces child mortality rates, leading to larger, healthier families.

    3. Cleaner stoves and safer water further reduce health risks to rural people.

    4. Without the need to pay for medicine, families can afford to send their children to school.

    5. These children can learn, possibly finding a way to send themselves to receive further education.

    6. With higher education, they are essentially raised from below the poverty line.

  B. Or, a scenario I've seen firsthand:

    1. Juan is electrocuted at work one day, and loses both arms as a result.

    2. He can't work.

    3. He can't provide for his family anymore.

    4. He can't afford a prosthesis on his own, or any real medical care for that matter.

    5. He sinks deeper and deeper into depression.

    6. One day, he meets Chris Mooney.

    7. Chris uses the donations of people like us to provide him with a new prosthetic arm.

    8. Juan can work again.

    9. Juan can provide for his family once more.

    10. His family can stop begging for food and money and begin to rebuild themselves.

    11. His children can go to school.

    12. They can laugh and play and have a normal childhood again.

In his second main point, Michael shows us how the money we donate to Bethel Ministries directly benefits these situations. He provides specific items and the amount needed to purchase each item. He makes the point that the money we give directly alleviate some of the major issues plaguing the country.

Michael does a good job of painting a word picture of the kinds of situations in which Bethel Missions has helped. He makes it clear that our money goes to support the work of helping the people, and what kinds of help they have already provided in Guatemala. He strengthens this appeal by reminding us that he's sharing things he's seen firsthand. His own obvious concern is evident. He makes it clear that donations are used to actually help those in need, even though he doesn't provide the percentage of what goes directly to the people, and what is used in administrative costs. It would have been helpful to have that breakdown. We don't know how much is spent in travel to Guatemala by Bethel Missions, but we do know that he has seen the good that has been done.

(continued)

While some of us may think that Michael is over the top in his language choice here, it is obvious that he is enthusiastic about his own experience on this mission trip and is passionate about the good work being done by this group. In his conclusion, he asks us to take action—donate time or money so that Bethel Ministries can help others. He makes the point that we can "see the evidence of [our] support in tangible things such as the houses built, the families saved, and the hope inspired." He makes us believe that our contributions are important and that Bethel Missions is worthy of our support.

CONCLUSION

V. Call to action

   A. Do you remember all those things I mentioned earlier that I've seen? Well here are a few other things I've seen.

      1. I've seen an abandoned child with cerebral palsy smile and feel safe and secure in a place where he or she is cared for and loved.

      2. I've seen a father with no arm receive a prosthesis funded completely by donations and who can now support his family again.

      3. I've seen grown men weep tears of joy because they now have a house that won't be washed away by heavy rain.

      4. I've seen former gang members turn their lives around.

      5. I've seen children being educated.

      6. I've seen people being inspired to better themselves.

      7. All of these things have been brought about by Bethel Ministries and the people who donate their money and time to their cause.

   B. There are many other worthy organizations you've heard about today, and will hear about again tomorrow.

      1. What sets Bethel Ministries apart is that you can see the evidence of your support.

         a. You can touch the houses you've built.

         b. You can meet the families you've saved.

         c. You can see the hope you've inspired.

      2. Henry Ford once said, "Time and money spent in helping people to do more for themselves is far better than mere giving."

         a. This is similar to the "giving a man a fish versus teaching him to fish" story.

         b. That's why this is important.

         c. You're not just providing a hot meal, or medical assistance, or a place to live. You're giving these people a chance to help themselves: to better their own lives and in turn better the lives of those around them. And, by doing this, you can reach far more than one family.

   C. Action: So I encourage you. I implore you. I beg you—donate as much time or money to Bethel Ministries as you can spare. If people like us won't help, who will?[14]

REFERENCES

Bethel Ministries website. See http://www.bethelministries.com/ for a vision statement, information about the founder and the work, and a list of items and their costs for helping people.

Central Intelligence Agency. The World Factbook: Central America and Caribbean-Guatemala. Accessed from https://www.cia.gov/library/publications/the-world-factbook/geos/gt.html, July 26, 2015.

Central Intelligence Agency. The World Factbook: Hospital Bed Density. Accessed from https://www.cia.gov/library/publications/the-world-factbook/fields/2227.html, July 26, 2015.

Rural Poverty Portal. Guatemala Statistics. Accessed from http://www.ruralpovertyportal.org/web/rural-poverty-portal/country/statistics/tags/guatemala, July 26, 2015.

The World Bank. Guatemala: An Assessment of Poverty, Poverty Reduction & Equity. Accessed from http://web.worldbank.org/WBSITE/EXTERNAL/TOPICS/EXTPOVERTY/EXTPA/0,,contentMDK:20207581~menuPK:443285~pagePK:148956~piPK:216618~theSitePK:430367,00.html, July 25, 2015.

Analysis and Evaluation

Michael Schwabe is a student at the University of Nebraska–Lincoln. He used his personal experiences with a charity, Bethel Ministries, to illustrate why we should donate time and/or money to this particular organization out of all the organizations who want our donations.

Michael's introduction is much longer than usual. He uses rhetorical questions to focus our attention on the dire situation in Guatemala, and repeats "I have" to illustrate how strongly he feels about the organization of which he was a volunteer. His personal experiences paint a word picture that allows the listener (reader) to see what kinds of situations the people in Guatemala face every day of their lives. While there's an obvious emotional appeal, Michael attempts to be as logical as possible by relating specific facts.

This speech is an example of Monroe's motivated sequence, and Michael does a good job of laying out all five steps: attention, need, satisfaction, visualization, and action. For each step, he provides evidence to support the concept. He paints a word picture of people in dire situations, facing a deep level of poverty, with little or no health care, and no way to solve the problem except through outside assistance. His picture shows us this charity works to provide a "hand-up," not a "handout," which differs from many other organizations who want our donations of time and money.

While emotional appeals are clearly presented, Michael also does a good job of being somewhat objective in his presentation. He identifies statistics and facts from the CIA and from the Rural Poverty Portal and the World Bank as evidence to support the ideas he presents about poverty and inadequate health care. His language helps to promote the organization, and it shows that he is passionate about the charity and its work. He makes it clear that he believes we will benefit as well by donating time and/or money to this worthy charity.

While he does not provide a specific breakdown of where our donated money goes, he does identify exact costs for the kinds of appliances and devices supplied to the Guatemalan people. The speech would have been stronger had he explained how much money actually goes to goods and services for the people served, and how much money is used in administrative, travel, and other costs. We also don't know if the volunteers paid their own way, or if they volunteered their time and the charity picked up their expenses. This would be good information to have if any of us were considering donations of time and/or money to Bethel Missions. His call for action (donating time or money) is clear from the outset of the speech, as Michael comments on that aspect several times. While his call that encourages, implores, and begs us to donate is a bit over the top, it does show how passionate he is about the charity, and passion for a topic sells the topic to an audience. It would be interesting to learn how many people made donations as the result of this speech.

And now it's your turn: How would you evaluate Michael's speech, using the criteria identified in this chapter? Did you find him to be passionate about the organization? Did he clearly identify all five steps in Monroe's motivated sequence? Did he make you think about donating time or money? What would you do to improve the speech? What would you add, change, or delete? What grade would you assign to Michael's speech?

Summary

The Goal of Persuasive Speaking

Objective 12.1 Identify the goals of persuasion.

- Persuasion is always about change—either in attitude or behaviors.
- The subgoals of persuasion (adoption, discontinuance, deterrence, or continuance) allow you to choose how you want the listeners to change.
- Be realistic in setting your persuasive goal and determining what you expect to achieve.

Topics for Persuasive Speeches

Objective 12.2 Choose a topic suitable for you, your listeners, and the assignment.

- Topics may begin with questions of fact, value, or policy.
- Your choice of one of these questions helps you determine what to include in the persuasive speech.
- While you start with yourself, you need to keep your listeners and their knowledge and interests in mind as you choose a topic.

Persuasive Claims

Objective 12.3 **Construct** your speech in ways to establish your credibility.

- Credibility is something the listeners attribute to you when you are seen as competent, with good character and a degree of charisma.
- Your speech should identify the sources of your information in oral footnotes and in the notes or bibliography section.

Establish Credibility (Ethos)

Objective 12.4 **Explain** how Aristotle's modes of presentation—ethos, logos, and pathos—increase your credibility.

- The speaker's actions and demeanor create each of these appeals during the speech.
- Ethos refers to the speaker's ethical character.
- Logos refers to the substance of the speech or the speaker's logical appeals.
- Pathos is the emotional appeal that can move an audience.
- Speakers must carefully use these modes to evoke appropriate behaviors and emotions in the listeners.

Prepare and Develop a Persuasive Speech

Objective 12.5 **Develop** your persuasive speech by carefully researching your topic, organizing the content, providing appropriate supporting materials, and making strong, logical arguments.

- **Present** a persuasive speech that demonstrates your ability to construct and support your persuasive goals.

- Careful research and organization will help you reach your listeners and help you meet the criteria for the assignment.
- Be sure to include enough supporting materials to provide sufficient evidence for the topic.
- Check your analysis to make sure you make strong, logical arguments.

Fallacies in Argument Development

Objective 12.6 **Recognize** errors in your own thinking so you can correct them and present logical claims and evidence.

- Fallacies in argument development should be avoided.
- Carefully analyze all your arguments to make sure they are logical and free of wrongful attribution and hasty generalizations.
- Criticize ideas, not the people who hold them.
- Don't mislead yourself or your listeners by reaching the wrong conclusion about your arguments.

Evaluating the Persuasive Speech

Objective 12.7 **Evaluate and assess** your own persuasive speeches and those of others.

- Look at the evaluation criteria provided by your instructor to make sure you have addressed and fulfilled those requirements.
- Apply evaluation criteria to your speech well before your class presentation so you can use those criteria to improve your speech.

Discussion Starters

1. In what instances have you seen persuasion work?
2. What factors influence your view of an effective persuasive message?
3. Why do we suggest that behavioral change is the ultimate goal of persuasion?
4. Identify three ways social media persuades.
5. What characteristics enhance your own evaluation of a speaker?
6. If speakers do not appear to be credible in your eyes, what can they do to gain or regain credibility?

7. What are the major differences between informative and persuasive speeches?
8. Are supporting materials used differently in a persuasive speech than in an informative speech? Explain your views.
9. How do you determine whether or not a speaker is effective?
10. What factors are essential in an effective persuasive speech?

Appendix 12

Persuasive Speech Topics

Here are some possible topics for persuasive speeches. The items listed are not necessarily titles of specific speeches and might need to be narrowed to fit specific purposes, time limits, or other requirements set by your instructor. Note that a wording change can move your topic from informative to persuasive. Almost any topic can be used to create informative or persuasive speeches. The key is in how you develop the ideas. If you present information as information *only*, it becomes an informative speech. If you present an argument and evidence as supporting material, and you want your listeners to change something in some way, you present a persuasive speech.

News in the United States is sanitized—how do we learn the truth?
Cyber bullying must be stopped
Facebook is a tool to eradicate social injustices
Twitter is more than just a way to link with others
The monitoring of Facebook helps control the masses
Sexting: crime or indiscretion?
The failure of the European experiment—or has it failed?
Reality shows are popular because …
Citizens are required to be socially responsible
How volunteerism can change both society and you
Society's views on same-sex marriage
The overmedication of people in developed countries
Children must be taught about money
There should be a tax on high-sugar drinks
Is marital infidelity a matter for the courts?
How we can reduce our blood sugar levels to achieve better health?
Nearly eight million children around the world are without life's necessities
Eating disorders are pervasive in our society
Virtual schools—necessary?
Why podcasts are better than broadcasts
The false-positive tests: screening for terrorists
Homeland security takes our freedoms away
Robo-readers and plagiarism
Robo-readers and scoring of written work
The controversy surrounding women's health
Why the Violence Against Women Act can help all of us
Student loans—the next financial debacle
Neighborhood watch—vigilantes in action?
Why arguments of politics and religion are best left inside the home
Ways we can personally help improve the economy
International adoptions should be promoted
How we can stop bullying?
Why has bullying become so prevalent?
Take the first step in going green
How do we solve the lingering problem with multitasking and air traffic control?
Are the airways really safer than highway traffic?
What should be done to improve public education?
How can we improve the barter system to take power away from Wall Street?
Caffeine: friend or foe?
Chinese medicine and acupuncture cure many diseases

How leadership skills can help groups communicate
Why you should not rely on energy drinks for the long term
Wind energy, bane or benefit?
Combating hunger, the world's number one health risk
World hunger and your contribution to solving the problem
E-books and learning: are the two mutually exclusive?

Chapter 13
Interpersonal Communication: A Theoretical Foundation

 ## Learning Objectives

This chapter will help you:

13.1 **Explain** what it means to connect with others through interpersonal communication.

13.2 **Compare and contrast** seven theories related to relationships and interpersonal communication.

13.3 **Outline** the roles of self-disclosure, privacy, gender, culture, and rhetorical sensitivity in interpersonal relationships.

CHAPTER OUTLINE

Connecting with Others via Interpersonal Communication

Theories of Interpersonal Communication

Self-Disclosure in Relationships

Making Everyday Connections

"Unplugged for 40 Days" is the headline of a newspaper article that speaks to how reliant on and, in some cases, addicted to social media we have become.[1] The article discusses Hillary Umland, a 31-year-old Catholic who decided to give up her 2- to 3-hour daily routine with Facebook, Twitter, and texting for Lent (a Christian period of 40 days of prayer, penance, fasting, and denial). According to the reporter, she had all of the withdrawal symptoms of any addiction, including "restlessness, feelings of alienation, insatiable longing." Umland says that days of staring aimlessly at her computer are over for at least a few more weeks. She admits that it's almost been a month now that she hasn't checked Facebook or Twitter and she said, "It sucks…. It really does kind of suck." Research indicates that 890 million people log on to Facebook daily, with 50 percent of 18- to 24-year-old users checking the site as soon as they wake up.[2] It is interesting that this is not the first time Umland has tried to give up social media—last year she says she lasted about two weeks, but claims this time she has more resolve.

When asked what she is doing since she is not glued to her computer and phone, she said, "I actually read now. I'm consecutively reading the same book, which I haven't done ever since … 2009."[3] Jim Jansen, a team leader and associate campus religious worker with the Office of Student Affairs at the University of Nebraska-Lincoln, says:

There's nothing wrong with Facebook, but if you talk to them (students), I think many of them will say it's kind of like a quick sugar high for relationships. Somewhere on that intuitive level, we can just feel the difference between the electronic connection and the real personal connection.[4]

Umland agrees with Jansen that reconnecting with the real world is a good idea and says she hopes the break from social media will help her renew relationships with living, breathing people. Unfortunately, according to Umland, that hasn't happened because the others in her life have not given up their media.

Questions to Think About

1. How can technology help or hurt personal relationships?

2. If all social media were turned off for a week, how would you react?

3. Which do you find more satisfying: communication via social media, including online and texting, or face-to-face communication? Why?

4. What are some of your most embarrassing social media gaffes and what did you do to explain them?

It is evident that more and more of our time is spent communicating with others using one form or another of social media, such as Facebook, Twitter, Pinterest, Instagram, YouTube, Vine, Snapchat, and LinkedIn. Facebook now has over 1.39 billion monthly active users. With an average time spent per Facebook visit around 20 minutes, in every 60 seconds, over 500 Facebook comments are posted, over 290,000 statuses are updated, and over 130,000 photos are uploaded.[5] The Pew Research Center found that 18- to 24-year-olds will, on average, send and receive approximately 4,000 text messages per month—or about 130 per day.[6] In May 2014, Snapchat users sent over 700 million photos and videos each day. The Pew Research Center's Internet & American Life Project survey of people 18 and older who use social networking sites (SNS) found that respondents tend to rate SNS as "very positive" in terms of personal rewards and overall satisfaction. Further, they found 61 percent of their sample of SNS users experienced feeling closer to another person, while 68 percent said they experienced feeling good about themselves.[7] There is no question that social media is changing how we meet, interact, and form relationships with others.

Whether in a coffee shop, workplace, library, student union, dorm, athletic event, or meeting, or on an airplane, train, website, or in any online or face-to-face setting where we interact verbally and nonverbally, the success or effectiveness of our interactions depends on our interpersonal communication skills. What does it mean to be a competent communicator in interpersonal situations? This chapter and the following chapters in this section provide answers to this question.

Connecting with Others via Interpersonal Communication

13.1 **Explain** what it means to connect with others through interpersonal communication.

Connecting with others and forming relationships are what interpersonal communication is all about. We often think of it as interaction that occurs only among those with whom we have close relationships. While it is true interpersonal communication is used in our close relationships, it also occurs in a variety of contexts and situations and can be impersonal and superficial or personal and intimate, private or public, and unstructured or highly structured. Our interpersonal competencies will likely differ not only from each other but also from situation to situation and from one person to another. Competent interpersonal communicators know how to adjust and communicate effectively with a variety of people from diverse backgrounds to establish short- or long-term relationships, whether in person or via social media.

Relationships

A **relationship** is an association between at least two people. It can be new or old, momentary or long lasting, superficial or involved, casual or intimate, friendly or unfriendly, relaxed or tense, hateful or loving, important or unimportant, good or bad, happy or unhappy, and so on. Relationships can also be described in terms of the level of intimacy or kinship—girlfriend, boyfriend, lover, partner, wife, husband, mother, father, child, uncle, cousin, stepparent, or stepchild. Sometimes relationships can be described on the basis of the roles people have in the relationship—roommates, Facebook friends, neighbors, boss and employee, coworkers, classmates, doctor and patient, ex-spouses, and so on.

Relationships can be described in terms of time spent together, such as, "I knew her in high school" or "They just met him the other day." Relationships may be based on shared activities or participation in events—"We play volleyball together," "We go to the same yoga classes," "He's in my class," "She works with me," or "We are from the same hometown."[8] Relationships are sometimes described in terms of situation or happenstance—"We met online," "We met on the plane," or "I sit behind you in our communication class." However we describe them, we all have relationships with others.

relationship

An association between at least two people, which may be described in terms of intimacy or kinship.

Interpersonal Communication

In Chapter 1, we defined interpersonal communication as creating and sharing meaning between persons who are in a relationship. This definition implies that

Making Connections for Success

Proper Email and Email Etiquette

To: professorsmith@gmail.com
From: partyallnightlong@gmail.com
Re: i have some questions about class

Hey, I am in your 2:30 class and I don't know what is expected of me on your next assignment—is it do on Tuesday or Thursday; your directions wasn't clear. I THINK THIS CLASS REQUIRES TOO MUCH WORK AND I DON'T HAVE THE TIME THIS WEEK TO GET IT DONE. I also need to be out of town next week so I am going to have to miss class. Will I miss anything when I am gone? I really enjoy having u as a techer.

1. How would you react if you were the professor receiving the email?
2. What email etiquette rules did Grant violate, if any? Explain.
3. Rewrite the email as you think it should be written.
4. Develop a set of etiquette guidelines you believe should be followed when sending email or text messages. Would your rules be the same for every audience?

More and more time is spent on social media rather than in face-to-face interactions. Which do you find more satisfying: social media and texting or face-to-face communication?

interpersonal communication occurs between two or more people, can be casual or formal, public or private, and some personal information is shared.

As noted above, interpersonal communication is often thought of as interaction only among those having close relationships. This, of course, is not always true; some individuals will disclose the most personal information about themselves or others to complete strangers via social media or to someone they are sitting next to on an airplane, but will not communicate the same information to a loved one they see every day. Thus, interpersonal communication occurs in a variety of contexts and situations and may be characterized in different ways. Our interpersonal competencies also differ from person to person, as well as from situation to situation. Those who are competent know how to tailor their interpersonal communication to suit people from diverse backgrounds and establish short- or long-term relationships.

Theories of Interpersonal Communication

13.2 **Compare and contrast** seven theories related to relationships and interpersonal communication.

Most of us want relationships to give our lives meaning and to fulfill a variety of social and psychological needs. Our motivations for staying in relationships are certainly varied and not always completely understood, as when people who have choices remain in abusive, codependent, or obsessive relationships. In this section, we discuss seven theories that help explain why we have such a strong desire to interact with and form and keep relationships with others: uncertainty reduction theory, uncertainty management theory, social information processing theory, social penetration theory, social exchange theory, interpersonal needs theory, and dialectical theory.

Uncertainty Reduction Theory

Our desire to know about others and to understand how and why they behave as they do can be partially explained by uncertainty reduction theory.[9] The core assumption of **uncertainty reduction theory**, developed by communication scholars Charles Berger and Richard Calabrese, is when people meet they seek to reduce the unknowns about each other. The more attracted they are to others, the stronger the desire to know more about them. A desire to reduce uncertainty about those individuals motivates us to have further communication with them.

The theory, according to Berger, suggests the drive to reduce uncertainty regarding those we meet is motivated by three prior conditions:

1. Anticipation of future contact: We will likely see them again.

2. Incentive value or reward: They can give us something we need.

3. Deviance: They act in a strange or unusual way.[10]

Berger believes these three factors are part of our natural curiosity because we really want to know more about the person. So, no matter how close we become to another, we always begin a relationship as strangers.

According to the theory, reducing uncertainty is necessary for a relationship to develop; as we increase our desire to enter a relationship with someone, we use more uncertainty reduction behavior. Berger describes three strategies used to learn about

uncertainty reduction theory
A theory suggesting that when we meet others, our need to know about them tends to make us draw inferences from observable physical data.

others. The first is referred to as "passive," when we unobtrusively observe others from a distance, or what some might refer to as "scoping out"; the second is referred to as "active," in which we ask a third party for information; and the third is referred to as "interactive," when we talk directly with the other person and request specific information by asking questions.[11]

To illustrate the three strategies, consider the following example: Olivia sees Sam across a crowded room at a party and is interested in meeting him. She observes that he is standing by himself and thus assumes he came to the party by himself, but she isn't sure (passive strategy). She knows nothing about Sam and doesn't know if he is dating anyone or if he is serious about someone, for that matter. Olivia's uncertainty is high, but so is her desire to find out more about him. She texts a friend who knows Sam and learns he is not dating anyone, but the friend doesn't know whether he came with anyone to the party (active strategy). Olivia's uncertainty has been somewhat reduced but certainly not eliminated. She decides that the only way to learn more about Sam is to be direct and talk with him (interactive strategy). She asks him if he is with anyone and finds out that he came by himself and that he is not dating anyone at the present time. The party ends; Olivia and Sam are still talking with each other and have enjoyed their time visiting, but now they must decide what will happen next with their relationship. After almost an hour of conversation, they decide to share cell numbers and email addresses with the idea they might continue the relationship. Sam texts Olivia about 10 minutes after they depart: "had a good time 2nite, c u soon 😊."

Of course at times our need to know about someone isn't a consideration or possible to pursue, because we have no interest in the person or he or she is not available to us.

Uncertainty Management Theory

Dale Brashers, a communication scholar who is interested in health communication, especially as it relates to those living with HIV or AIDS, developed uncertainty management theory to further refine uncertainty reduction theory. Brashers believes uncertainty is more complex than previously thought. His research found that patients with HIV sometimes preferred uncertainty to certainty.[12]

Uncertainty management theory takes into account the different ways people respond both psychologically and communicatively to uncertainty, especially in health decisions. The theory has three main features: (1) the interpretation and experience of uncertainty, (2) the effect of emotion related to uncertainty, and (3) the ways communication and emotion are managed when uncertainty exists.[13] While Brashers was specifically interested in health, this theory can be applied to many other situations. For example, a person going through a breakup after a long-term relationship suspects his or her spouse cheated, but stops short of confirming it because confirmation might be too painful. Uncertainty reduction theory suggests that seeking and gaining information is the best way to reduce uncertainty, but sometimes reduction is not the goal. Uncertainty management theory makes us aware that we can communicate in different ways, depending on whether our goal is to increase, decrease, or maintain uncertainty. In serious illness situations, for example, we will often seek out a second opinion that may offer a less certain outcome, because we hope the illness may not be as bad as first diagnosed.[14]

In addition to seeking or avoiding information, people use four other ways to manage their uncertainty, according to Brashers. First, those who live with lots of uncertainty learn to adapt to it. For example, Brashers and his colleagues found those with serious illness might focus on short-term diagnoses, which provide more certainty, rather than on the long-range

uncertainty management theory

A theory that takes into account different ways people react psychologically and communicatively to uncertainty.

As our desire to meet and learn about others increases, so does our desire to reduce our uncertainty about them. This motivates us to communicate with them.

outlook, which may be significantly more uncertain. The second way to manage uncertainty is to rely on the social support of others in order to cope. The positive or reassuring outlook of others can lead to feelings of hope or some relief from the uncertainty. The third way is to balance the need to know with the desire to *not* know. Finally, the fourth is learning to know which information to trust and which information to ignore.[15]

Social Information Processing Theory

social information processing theory

A theory suggesting that electronically mediated relationships grow only to the extent that people gain information about each other and use that information to form impressions.

Communication via social media is so prevalent it can no longer be ignored. With billions upon billions of online messages and opportunities to meet people online, we need to better understand how communication through social media affects our in-real-life relationships. **Social information processing theory**, developed by communication scholar Joe Walther, suggests that electronically mediated relationships grow only to the extent people gain information about each other and use it to form impressions.[16] In this regard, social information processing theory is consistent with uncertainty reduction theory. Social information processing theory, however, is limited to an attempt to explain the nature of online interactions and how those interactions can and do lead to real-life relationships.

Walther describes two features of electronic-mediated communication that provide a justification for social information processing theory:[17]

1. **Verbal cues.** When individuals are motivated to create impressions and develop relationships, they will use any verbal signs available to communicate. Thus, social media users create fully formed impressions of others based solely on the content of their digital messages.

2. **Extended time.** Social media used to exchange social information and form impressions of others is much slower than real-life interactions. Yet, given sufficient time, there is little reason to believe electronic-mediated relationships will be weaker than any other relationships.

As illustrated in the cartoon on the next page, social media allow people to become friends with others they have never met in real life, perhaps because the self-presentational aspects of Facebook, Twitter, Vine, and Snapchat differ from those in real life. Thus, it is likely that we have insufficient information to determine if this is someone with whom we wish to have an in-person relationship. According to Walther, people who meet online are able to make and sustain overwhelmingly positive impressions of each other. Walther goes on to say this is because they can present their most attractive traits, accomplishments, thoughts, and actions without much contradiction regarding their physical appearance or influence from third parties who may know of their dark side. Consider Melissa and David, who met at a party, and Brad and Lorraine who met online through Match.com. According to SIP theory, even though Brad and Lorraine met online, over time their relationship will possess the same qualities of closeness and connection as Melissa and David, who met face-to-face.

Hyperpersonal communication

Occurs when the communication and context affords message senders a host of communicative advantages over traditional face-to-face interactions.

Even though there are many benefits to online relationship development, those interactions come with a potential challenge. **Hyperpersonal communication** suggests that digital interactions can become exaggerated because the context affords message senders a host of communicative advantages over traditional face-to-face interactions.[18] Compared to ordinary face-to-face conversations, a hyperpersonal message sender has a greater ability to strategically develop and edit his presentation of self. If Andy seeks a romantic relationship through eHarmony.com, he may post personal pictures from a time when he was thinner and regularly working out at the gym. In other words, hyperpersonal users are able to select their messages for optimized presentation to others.

Communication through social media allows people to edit or sanitize their communication, thus creating an online image or persona, without worry of their nonverbal communication altering or contradicting their image or messages. For example, you view the Facebook profile of someone you met briefly at a community event. In her profile, the person describes herself as "quiet and reserved," lists her interests as "reading and working out," is a member of a group referred to as "volunteers to help the poor," and is active in her church. The few photos she has on her site show her with a few close friends and family members. Yet, you learn by observing some of her Facebook friends' sites that she loves to party and there are links to some pretty wild photos of her interacting at various gatherings. The messages are obviously contradictory; which version are you going to believe? The answer is what Walther labels as *warranting value of personal information*, or what he suggests is "the perceived validity of information presented online with respect to illuminating someone's offline characteristics."[19]

Perhaps the self-presentational aspects of Facebook differ in a number of respects from self-presentation in real life. In real life, friends for this fellow may be considerably harder to come by than they are on Facebook.

Our real-life observations of others exert less influence and do less to shape our communication behaviors because we use social media and the cues it provides to interpret and form impressions based on those cues.

Social Penetration Theory

Going beyond information gathering, **social penetration theory**, developed by social psychologists Irwin Altman and Dalmas Taylor, provides a view of how people connect with each other and how their communication moves from small talk to more intimate and self-revealing talk. Social penetration is the process of increasing disclosure and intimacy in a relationship.[20] Figure 13.1 illustrates the progression of our interactions as a relationship becomes more friendly or intimate.

According to the theory, as the relationship evolves, the interaction becomes more personal and intimate. The model resembles an onion or dartboard and looks at both the depth and the breadth of penetration. The **depth of penetration** is represented as penetration from external factual information (the outer ring) to inner feelings

social penetration theory
A theory suggesting that disclosures in a relationship become increasingly intimate as the relationship develops.

depth of penetration
The deepness or intimacy of the disclosure to others.

Figure 13.1 Social Penetration Model

Social penetration theory portrays relationship development as starting with factual information and small talk. As the relationship develops, conversations become more personal, including feelings about self and values.

From *Social Penetration: The Development of Interpersonal Relationships.* Copyright © 1973 by Irwin Altman and Dalmas Taylor.

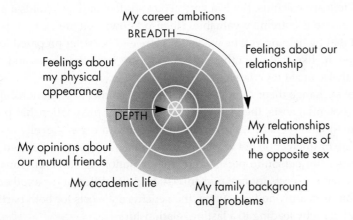

(the center of the circle or bull's-eye) revealing more private information about the self. The outer ring represents superficial communication, such as small talk, "Hi, I'm Joe from Clemson, South Carolina." The innermost circle, or bull's-eye, represents intimacy and close personal disclosures, such as "I love you with all my heart and soul." As the relationship becomes more intimate, it will involve more personal information and intimacy about one's self. **Breadth of penetration** is the range or spread of what an individual discloses to another about himself or herself. Thus, to have lasting relationships, what is disclosed must have both depth and breadth.

Social Exchange Theory

Social exchange theory is an interpersonal communication theory that explains why we form relationships. Have you ever entered a relationship and thought about the benefits that might be gained from it? Of course you have. For example, right after meeting someone, we are likely to sort out the pluses and minuses of forming a friendship. In other words, we try to determine whether the benefits of the relationship will outweigh the cost. Whether we do this subconsciously or consciously, we do it. Social psychologists John Thibaut and Harold Kelley originated **social exchange theory**, which is based on the assumption that people weigh the costs and benefits associated with entering a relationship and seek out relationships that benefit them while avoiding those that don't.[21]

Thibaut and Kelley believe that most of us are motivated to enter and maintain relationships in terms of the exchange of benefits and costs. A **benefit** is anything we perceive to improve our self-interest. It refers to things or relationships that bring us pleasure, satisfaction, or gratification. For example, outcomes such as good feelings, status, prestige, economic gain, or fulfillment of emotional needs are considered benefits of a relationship. **Costs** are negative things or behaviors we perceive to be not beneficial to our self-interest. For example, to enter or maintain a relationship takes time and physical and emotional energy, which are considered costs of the relationship.

The theory suggests that when we first meet someone, we mentally weigh the potential rewards and costs of creating a relationship with that person. For example, you are not very good at math but you are required to take calculus. You go to class and sit next to Jim. You briefly discuss the class and a little about the professor. You learn Jim has taken at least one other course from the professor and did exceptionally well. Because of this brief interaction, you perceive a number of potential benefits of becoming friends with Jim. You know he can help you with calculus, he is easy to talk with, and he appears to know his way around campus. Jim also weighs the benefits and costs of beginning a relationship with you. He thinks you are easy to talk with and likes your openness about seeking help from him.

Jim also knows there may be a potential downside to getting to know you better and creating a relationship. This is especially true if all you want from him is his time and help to learn calculus. Jim is a very active student and also holds a part-time job, so his free time is extremely valuable. He also knows you are an easy person to talk with and that by helping you he will learn more and be better prepared for the exams. In addition, he likes helping others. After factoring in all the pluses and minuses, Jim suggests that you get together to study for the first exam.

Social exchange theory implies if the benefits gained in a relationship are greater than any potential costs, then we likely would regard the relationship positively. But if the benefit gain (benefits minus costs) falls below a certain level, we might find a relationship or interaction not worth the potential cost. The ratio between benefits and costs varies from person to person and from situation to situation. Thus, a desirable ratio of benefits to costs for one person may be quite different for another person. If a relationship is healthy and satisfying, the benefits and costs for both parties are probably equal, thereby leading to a lasting relationship.

---

breadth of penetration

The range or spread of areas that are disclosed to others.

social exchange theory

A theory based on the assumption that people consciously and deliberately weigh the costs and rewards associated with a relationship or interaction.

benefit

Anything that is perceived to improve our self-interest.

costs

Negative things or behaviors that we perceive to be not beneficial to our self-interest.

Making Technology Connections

Online Relationships

Social media has indeed changed our ways of interacting and connecting with others. Lori and Jerome met for the first time through an online dating website. They viewed each other's posted pictures and information. They exchanged emails for a few days, regularly chatted on the phone and texted each other for about a week, and then agreed to meet for their first date. Everything just clicked between them. After six months of dating, Jerome proposed to Lori. Six months later, nearly one year after they first met online, Lori and Jerome got married. Lori and Jerome both agreed that they faced some challenges with meeting people online. Some people feed you exaggerations and lies and expect you to believe it. Many people think meeting someone online is odd, while others believe it paves the way for the future of dating.

You have read about uncertainty reduction theory, social information processing theory, and social exchange theory, all of which have given you insights into online relationships.

1. Which of the theories best describes your most recent interpersonal communication with others?
2. In what ways does social information processing help you to better understand relationship development?
3. What risks, if any, did Lori take in assuming that Jerome was honest in his communication?
4. What role does communication via social media have in your life and how do you see it differs from face-to-face interactions?

Interpersonal Needs Theory

Interpersonal communication literature consistently discusses the premise that each of us needs to include others in our activities and to be included in theirs, to exert control over others and have them control us, and to give affection to others as well as receive it from others. Will Schutz, a psychologist and one of the most respected leaders in the field of human relations, provides insight into our communication behaviors in his **interpersonal needs theory**. Schutz's theory consists of three needs: affection, inclusion, and control.[22] Although many other needs exist, according to Schutz, most interpersonal behavior and motivation can be directly related to the need for affection, inclusion, and control. Although needs differ from person to person, from situation to situation, and from culture to culture, knowing and understanding our interpersonal needs should help us see how they influence and motivate our interactions with others.

For most of us, our interpersonal needs do not remain static; desire and importance vary with circumstances. For instance, giving and receiving affection might be far more important in a relationship, especially as the relationship intensifies and moves toward bonding, whereas inclusion might be more significant when a relationship is coming apart. Awareness of personal needs and the needs of others also varies, depending on the depth of a relationship, the timing, the context, and so forth. Each need motivates us to interact with others in specific ways.

THE NEED FOR AFFECTION   The need for affection is the need to feel likable or lovable. The bottom line is that we need to belong and be loved. Every day we see people striving to fulfill this need; for example, people who join social groups or dating services are seeking to fulfill their need for belonging and love. According to Schutz's theory, a person who seems to be liked by many and therefore has adequately fulfilled this need is referred to as *personal*. Kory Floyd, a communication scholar, in his review of research related to communicating affection, found that people who give and receive affection are generally healthier and happier than those who receive or give little affection.[23]

THE NEED FOR INCLUSION   The interpersonal need for inclusion encompasses our needs to feel significant and worthwhile. Schutz describes individuals in terms of this need as *social, undersocial,* or *oversocial*. Undersocial people do not like being around other people; they find communicating with others threatening. They tend to be shy and find initiating conversations with others difficult.

interpersonal needs theory
A theory that provides insight into our motivation to communicate. This theory consists of three needs: affection, inclusion, and control.

Making Connections for Success

It's Me That Counts

Brad and Paige have been dating for more than six months. They agree that they have a very close relationship. After a romantic dinner at their favorite restaurant, Brad and Paige go back to Paige's apartment and are in the middle of some serious kissing when Paige says, "Brad, I want you to stop. I don't want to go any further." Brad says, "Are you kidding me? Don't you love me? I mean, it's not like we haven't been going out for six months." Paige does not respond immediately; she seems to have been caught off guard. Finally, she says, "Brad, I do know how you feel about me, and I trust you, but having sex right now just isn't right for me. I also don't want to end up having a kid before we are married." Brad quickly says, "But I thought you really cared about me. You know, Paige, I love you!" Paige replies, "I know, but I'm not ready for sex, and I really don't want to until I'm married—you have to understand that."

1. Is Brad's communication motivated more out of self-interest than interest in Paige? Explain.
2. How would you describe Brad and Paige's relationship based on their interaction with each other?
3. Describe the relationship in terms of social exchange theory.

Oversocial people cannot stop themselves from getting involved and communicating with others. They attempt to dominate conversations, often speak out of turn, and find it hard to keep quiet. They prefer situations in which they can take over relationships by dominating the flow of communication. The oversocial person fears being ignored by others. Perhaps you know people like this. How do you react to them?

Social people have satisfied their needs for inclusion. They are capable of handling situations with or without others, and few, if any, situations make them feel uncomfortable. They have confidence in themselves and are assertive enough to speak when they feel it is necessary to do so. The research suggests most of us feel mental and physical distress when our need for inclusion is not met, and thus we are motivated to engage others in order to belong.[24]

THE NEED FOR CONTROL   The third need is our motivation for power or influence in our relationships. As we mature, our need to have control or influence increases, which determines how a relationship will evolve. In relationships we find satisfying, control is shared, whereby each person has some say in what happens. These relationships foster mutual respect and shared responsibility. Relationships in which we have little or no say are generally much less satisfying and often are one sided.[25]

Of course, there are times when we wish to give up or relinquish control because we may not feel competent or we don't want to feel responsible for what happens. At times, too, we may feel overwhelmed by having too much control and responsibility, especially if we are not confident in our ability to make the right decisions.

The need for affection and inclusion for most of us is a motivator to interact with others. However, many isolate themselves from others for fear they will not be accepted or liked for who they are, or because they find interacting with others threatening.

Finally, most of us are happiest and most satisfied when we have moderate amounts of control.

Schutz's theory of needs clearly illustrates the reasons that motivate us to communicate with others. We develop relationships with others for many reasons. The social needs we've discussed explain a great deal about our motivation to form relationships, but relationships are developed for other reasons: to avoid or lessen feelings of loneliness, to learn more about ourselves, and to share our lives with others.

Dialectical Theory

Dialectical theory suggests relationships, as well as individuals, confront many tensions that push and pull in many different directions at the same time. For example, you might want to be out with your friends for the evening, but you have an important paper due in a few days you haven't started. Thus, you have to decide between being with your friends or beginning your paper. Or, you might want your best friend to spend more time with you; then, when your friend does, you decide you want more time to yourself. This might lead to your friend saying, "I thought you wanted to spend more time together, and now that we can, you're never around. So what do you want?" These examples illustrate the contradictory impulses or tensions resulting from the push and pull in different directions. Each person has opposing yet intersecting desires, which tug at the relationship in various ways. Three dialectical tensions are commonly identified in the research: connected–autonomy, openness–closedness, and novelty–predictability.[26]

dialectical theory

An interpersonal communication theory that suggests that contradictory impulses push and pull us in conflicting directions with others.

CONNECTION–AUTONOMY Relationships require both the desire to connect to another person and the desire to retain autonomy as an individual. We want to connect to others, such as partners, friends, parents, siblings, or coworkers, but we also want to retain some control and independence or autonomy over our lives. We desire our close relationships to be defined as "us," but this does not mean we want to sacrifice our individuality or control over who we are.

When connection or integration is overly emphasized in a relationship, it can lead to the feeling of being smothered or consumed by a partner, friend, parent, or coworker, so we feel entrapped and controlled by the relationship, thus leaving us with no life of our own. Intimacy at its highest level requires a bonding that connects us with another person emotionally, intellectually, and physically, but it does not mean or require a complete loss of self. In healthy relationships, a reasonable balance of being connected and maintaining autonomy is sustained. Relationships that move too far in one direction or the other in terms of control versus autonomy are usually extremely unstable and potentially destructive.

OPENNESS–CLOSEDNESS The second dialectic tension is the desire to be open and expressive on the one hand and closed and private on the other. But even at the beginning of new relationships, when we seek as much information as we can about the other person, a counterforce cautions against revealing too much too soon about ourselves. This tension between self-disclosing and keeping our privacy continues throughout the various stages of relationship development. We know that open expression is a necessary prerequisite for us to reach intimacy and bond with another person. We also know that when we reveal ourselves to another individual, both we and our relationship are more vulnerable. All of us therefore face the dilemma of how much self-disclosure or honesty we should allow with friends, relatives, and romantic partners and how much will be too much. Too much self-disclosure, as you will read later in this chapter, can lead to strains on a relationship and is a sign of not being a competent or, at the very least, not a thoughtful communicator. Relationships grow on the strength of the trust established between partners. When the trust between partners is violated by revealing private information or by telling a partner something he or she is not prepared to hear, the relationship is at risk for deterioration or termination.

NOVELTY–PREDICTABILITY   To develop and build healthy relationships, a certain amount of predictability is needed. Without some stability or constancy, the potential for uncertainty and ambivalence is too great for a long-term relationship to survive. Therefore, we need relationships that accommodate a certain amount of predictability. Families are a central stabilizing force in most people's lives and provide an anchor for security in a very unpredictable world. Predictability is a comfort to most of us because we know what to expect. Too much predictability in some aspects of a relationship, however, may make the relationship routine and boring, thus requiring a call for something unique or different. The dialectical tension created by the desire for predictability and consistency versus novelty and uncertainty in a relationship requires communication competence to relieve the tension and to prevent destructive conflict from occurring. For example, your roommate wants to stay in and rent a movie, but you want to go out dancing with friends. You could solve the problem by telling your roommate that you would like her to join you and that you would be more than happy to rent a movie tomorrow night instead. Pushes and pulls, or dialectic tensions, will always be part of every relationship, and how we communicate will likely determine whether the relationship grows, stagnates, or terminates.

MANAGING RELATIONAL TENSIONS   How we deal with the tensions in our lives creates some interesting communication challenges. It is also important to understand that relationships have both private and public dimensions and do not exist in a vacuum. Many tensions or pushes and pulls from outside a relationship, as well as inside, can directly or indirectly affect how the parties in a relationship deal with or manage their dialectical tensions. Communication scholars Leslie Baxter and Barbara Montgomery suggest a number of approaches for managing dialectical tensions.[27] The least helpful in dealing with tensions is *denial* that tension exists. How many times have you heard someone who faces stress or tension say, "Everything is fine—there's no problem." The denial strategy is avoidance or cover-up, which often leads to lying or deception, if not to you, then most certainly to others. The dialectical tension does not disappear by denying its existence; it must be dealt with through open communication. If a friend is really struggling with school and seems down, you must continue to talk with him or her to uncover the problem. You might start out by saying, "I know you're having a tough time with your classes. How can I help you?" You hope the friend will open up and talk about the issue. You need to listen and be supportive.

Baxter suggests most people use a variety of strategies to manage their dialectical tension.[28] The most often chosen are selection, segmentation, reframing, moderation, and reaffirmation. The strategy of *selection* is a strategy in which one end of the dialectical tension is chosen over the other. For example, a married couple wants to be by themselves over the Thanksgiving holiday find themselves in a dilemma with their in-laws, who want to spend the holiday with them. They might choose to go along with the in-laws to avoid tension.

The strategy of *segmentation* is a tactic in which a couple compartmentalizes different aspects of their relationship. For example, a couple might manage the tension between being open and being closed with each other by deciding to share information about their mutual friends but not to discuss their past romantic encounters because that might be too hurtful or too insensitive. Thus, by agreement, some things are open for discussion and others are closed.

Reframing is a strategy that allows tensions to be redefined so that tension is diluted, is made less obvious, or is even made to disappear. Couples who have long-distance relationships might say being apart has brought more intimacy and closeness to their relationship. Even though the relationship has a great deal of stress due to their physical separation, the couple have reframed it by suggesting that distance allows for greater intimacy and closeness.

Making Connections for Success

Networking on the Internet: Motivation and Need to Form Relationships

In a July 3, 2006, *Time* magazine article entitled "You Gotta Have Friends," author Robert Putnam writes that "Americans are more socially isolated today then we were barely two decades ago." People search for relationships and connections with others and in the process turn to the Internet, which itself may be more of the problem than the solution. The information you provide about yourself through social media can and has been used in investigations by universities, local police, employers, and other agencies. For example, students have been expelled or reprimanded for hate speech, for posting indecent pictures, and for criticizing a teacher. Employers search social media for information on potential hires as well. Here are some questions you should think about and others you might want to discuss in class before placing any information about yourself on social media:

1. What techniques do you use to make a good first impression on others? Do they work?
2. Why do you think so many people are willing to reveal exceptionally personal information through social media?
3. Which of the theories described in this chapter illustrates best why people use social media?
4. What are some of the risks you face by placing personal information online?

The strategy of *moderation* is characterized by compromises in which deals are struck to help reduce tensions. For example, a parent wants to know everything about your private life and constantly asks questions about personal things you really do not want to share. You choose to answer some of the less private questions but ignore the most personal ones, thus reducing some of the tension created by the questions.

Reaffirmation is the strategy in which individuals recognize that dialectical tensions will always be present, and therefore you should accept them and even embrace the challenges they produce. For example, you know a good friend has extremely liberal views on social issues that are totally contrary to your views. You know you will never agree on whether to use and/or legalize marijuana, but you might have some interesting discussions about the subject and perhaps even educate each other. You should not ignore your friend's opinion or deny dialectical tension, but should consider it part of being human. Relationships always experience pushes and pulls, and to grow a lasting relationship, the parties must manage and control the tensions through communication. The result of not managing and controlling tensions will likely be conflict.

Self-Disclosure in Relationships

13.3 **Outline** the roles of self-disclosure, privacy, gender, culture, and rhetorical sensitivity in interpersonal relationships.

Relationships are built on interaction. The more sincere, honest, and open the interactions, the stronger and more lasting the relationship is likely to be. Much of our interpersonal communication, however, is small talk. Such light conversation might not provide a means for us to learn who we are, to fulfill our interpersonal needs, or to grow in our relationships. Nonetheless, it does maintain an important opening to further interaction. Self-disclosure is one type of interaction that changes as a relationship becomes closer.

To reduce uncertainty, as suggested by uncertainty reduction theory, and to meet our physical and emotional needs, we must communicate who we are; we must disclose information about ourselves, as suggested by social penetration theory. **Self-disclosure**, or the voluntary sharing of information about ourselves that another person is not likely to know, can be as simple and nonthreatening as telling our name or as complex and threatening as revealing deep feelings.

self-disclosure

Voluntary sharing of information about the self that another person is not likely to know.

Making Connections for Success

The Importance of Small Talk

The ability to connect with others through small talk can lead to big things, according to Debra Fine, author of *The Fine Art of Small Talk*.[29] A former engineer, Fine recalls being so uncomfortable at networking events she would hide in the restroom. Now a professional speaker, Fine says the ability to connect with people through small talk is an acquired skill. Successful people know how to use small talk effectively and know its importance in entering and maintaining relationships.

1. Do you find making small talk easy or difficult? Why?
2. Develop a set of tips for general social icebreakers and business or professional icebreakers that might improve your small talk and share them with others in your class.
3. Do you think communication via social media affects small talk? In what ways? Is communicating on Facebook or Twitter a form of small talk? Why or why not?
4. What are some different ways you would use to move beyond small talk?
5. When is it appropriate to move beyond small talk?

When self-disclosure occurs in caring relationships, it usually results in greater self-understanding and self-improvement. In addition, our self-disclosure to others encourages them to reciprocate and creates an atmosphere that fosters interpersonal communication and meaningful relationships.

Why Do We Self-Disclose?

Many abilities differentiate human beings from other animals, one of which is to keep and share information about ourselves. We self-disclose for a variety of reasons: for others to better understand who we are, to gain sympathy, to see what others think, to gain trust, or to connect with others and establish relationships. Self-disclosure is essential if we are to form and maintain relationships. Here we will discuss three reasons why we self-disclose: self-presentation, relationship building, and catharsis.

self-presentation

An intentional self-disclosure tactic used to reveal certain aspects about ourselves for specific reasons.

To reduce uncertainty and to meet our physical and emotional needs, we must communicate who we are; we must disclose information about ourselves. When self-disclosure occurs in caring relationships, it usually results in greater self-understanding and self-improvement.

SELF-PRESENTATION Self-presentation is an intentional self-disclosure tactic used to reveal certain aspects about ourselves for specific reasons. When asked in an employment interview, for example, to talk about yourself, you are often requested to discuss your background, experiences, and accomplishments. When you disclose information about yourself that may not be known to the interviewer, you are engaged in self-presentation. The purpose of providing information about yourself is to emphasize that you are the person best suited for the job. For example, you tell the interviewer you are a highly organized person with excellent communication skills or that you are a team player and you enjoy meeting and working with people from a variety of backgrounds. You might disclose, for example, you come from a relatively poor background and you have worked to help pay your tuition—you imply by your statements you are self-sufficient in the hope the interviewer will judge you positively.

Thus, when appealing to others, we tend to describe ourselves in more favorable terms (more favorable than we really deserve) to impress others with whom we want to have a relationship. In short, we

sometimes bend the truth to enhance our own appeal to establish relationships. Many good examples of this can be found in online dating services (Match.com and the like). The self-descriptions some of us give are, to say the least, not very accurate. In fact, some of us describe ourselves in very flattering terms because we realize this is a good way to gain more contacts and establish relationships. So, clearly impression management now occurs both online and in face-to-face meetings.

RELATIONSHIP BUILDING   We self-disclose to start or maintain relationships. Self-disclosure via small talk or social conversation is one way we enter into relationships with others. The level of self-disclosure at some point can move to more intimate and self-revealing talk as the relationship develops. There are, of course, exceptions to this progression, and the depth and number of interactions can vary dramatically from one relationship to another. In addition, moving from light social talk to more intimate and revealing talk does not necessarily imply the relationship will automatically be a quality relationship.[30]

A relationship's location on the continuum between casual acquaintance and intimate confidant is determined by how people interact with each other and by their specific communication behaviors. The way we communicate with another person reflects the nature and type of relationship.

CATHARSIS   Self-disclosing communication can be a form of communicative release or catharsis. This is especially true when we want to rid ourselves of information causing tension, guilt, or sadness.[31] It is a way of getting something off our mind to reduce stress. For you as a student, examples include telling your parents you are in debt because you've been gambling or that you aren't doing as well in school as they think because you've been oversleeping. The benefit of this type of disclosure is that it rids us of dealing with an issue or problem by ourselves and invites sympathy or help.

The rapid development of social media has led to new ways to help others cope with the loss of a dear friend or loved one. Increasingly, one or more family members may honor their loved one by preparing a commemorative Facebook page that memorializes the life of the deceased. These pages have become a "place" where mourners can "visit" with their departed loved one and connect with other mourners, leave messages of condolence, share stories about the deceased, and leave messages directed to the deceased. These cathartic messages function as part of **transcorporeal communication**— a process through which a living person sends a digital message to a deceased person through a website or social networking site. "Trans" indicates that communication occurs beyond the state of human life, and "corporeal" indicates a relationship to a physical material body.[32] Deceased individuals no longer maintain a physical presence. Therefore, we direct our digital messages toward a person who is in a different state of being physically present. Communicating in this manner, which is often exhibited in Facebook memorial walls and groups, reconnects the living with the deceased and helps us make cathartic sense of our lives without our friends and loved ones.

transcorporeal communication
A process through which a living person sends a digital message to a deceased person through a website or social networking site.

When Shouldn't We Self-Disclose Too Much?

Although full disclosure can be cleansing, it can also be harmful, risky, unwise, or insensitive, as well as detrimental to a relationship. At one time or another, most of us have chosen not to say what was on our minds or not to tell others something about ourselves, themselves, or others because it might be hurtful. There are many reasons for withholding information, but it is usually to protect others, to avoid a potentially negative reaction, or to avoid hurting others or ourselves. Self-disclosure, therefore, is not always wise or appropriate.

The open and honest sharing of our feelings, thoughts, concerns, and secrets with others is at the heart of self-disclosure. This openness and honesty would be ideal, but it is not always practical or wise. Ultimately, self-disclosure must be based on personal judgment rather than rigid rules. The key should always be concern for both self and others.

Self-Disclosure and Privacy

privacy

The claim of individuals, groups, or institutions to determine for themselves when, how, and to what extent information about themselves is communicated to others.

How much is too much self-disclosure and when does it begin to invade or affect our privacy? **Privacy** is "the claim of individuals, groups, or institutions to determine for themselves when, how, and to what extent information about themselves is communicated to others."[33] These are not easy questions to answer because what might be appropriate for one situation may not be for another. Thus, an important task for people in relationships is the negotiation of privacy boundaries.[34] Privacy boundaries work in a way very similar to personal space boundaries. Just as we control and protect access to our physical self—for example, how close we allow others to come to us—in the same way we control and protect our privacy boundaries. Sandra Petronio, a communication scholar and expert in the area of privacy and how we manage our privacy boundaries, states:

> Revealing private information is risky because there is a potential vulnerability when revealing aspects of the self. Receiving private information from another may also result in the need for protecting oneself. In order to manage disclosing and receiving privacy information, individuals erect a metaphoric boundary to reduce the possibility of losing face and as a means of protection. Also, people use a set of rules or criteria to control the boundary and regulate the flow of private information to and from others.[35]

The process of sharing more and more personal information about one's self with another person encourages further intrusion into one's privacy, whether wanted or unwanted. Privacy boundaries would seem to be common sense, but they are not always clear to either party in a relationship. For example, a man and a woman have been dating for several years and have been sexually intimate, but are not married. The couple might try to control the privacy of their relationship because revealing past relational secrets could be embarrassing, or they could be fully open about their relationships with others. The determination of what should be kept private from each other and what should be kept private from others is usually negotiated by the mutual consent of the parties involved in the relationship.

When or if the boundaries of a relationship are violated or crossed, tensions may result, creating an imbalance. Thus, negotiations between relationship partners often involve what can and should be shared and what is or should be off limits. Boundaries are erected to protect, control the flow of information, and regulate vulnerability. When one partner violates the privacy of the other, for example, attempts are made to reconstruct the privacy boundary by changing the topic or by avoiding the situation.

Self-Disclosure and Gender

Using the terms *women* and *men* as identifiers to describe or distinguish communication between the sexes is troublesome. The terms imply sameness across all women and all men that might or might not be true. For example, to say, "Women disclose their feelings more often than men do" is probably true, but it may not be true for all women or all men. Some men disclose more feelings than some women do, and vice versa. Thus, we must be careful to avoid stereotyping solely based on biological sex differences.[36]

Making Connections for Success

The Dark Side of Technology: Freedom and Temptation

Facebook, Twitter, Vine, Snapchat, texting—all offer myriad communication possibilities to help us stay connected, broaden our social networks, and communicate more frequently and efficiently with friends, family, or work colleagues. But there is a dark side to these communication options and the freedom to share whatever personal information, opinions, or photos one chooses. With new and emerging communication tools come increased risks and temptations—from the mildly irritating tendency to waste time to potentially harmful and dangerous behaviors, such as cyber bullying or sexting, which is "sending, receiving, or forwarding" inappropriate photos via a cell phone.[37]

A recent survey found that one in five teens had sent or posted a naked picture of herself or himself, and a third had received a picture or video of this type via text message or email.[38] The criminal justice system is now involved, and teens are being prosecuted and labeled as sex offenders. Although these teens may evade the law, the online trail is harder to escape. The labels and youthful indiscretions may follow them for years, creating problems when applying to college or for a job or running for public office.

1. What cautions can be applied to other forms of online communication?
2. What responsibilities come with the freedom to communicate via social media?
3. Do you think sexting should be considered a felony, or is it simply bad judgment? Should the law be involved in regulating online behavior? If so, what types of behavior?
4. Teens and technology can be a volatile combination. Why do you think this is so?
5. With access to the Internet and other technology occurring at increasingly younger ages, what safeguards, if any, can or should be put in place?

Some research and some authors support the idea that men and women do communicate using different sets of rules and meanings. Deborah Tannen, in her book *You Just Don't Understand: Women and Men in Conversation,* reviewed many research studies and takes the position that women's verbal and nonverbal behaviors are different from men's. For example, she found that men talk less personally or inclusively when compared to women, and that women tend to make more validating and confirming statements than men do.[39]

Women are more likely to talk about their relationships and disclose a deeper level of intimacy, but men often do not center their talk on relational closeness.[40] Concerning relationships, many men take the attitude "If it ain't broke, why fix it?" Women may be more likely to express the attitude "If it's going well, how can we make it go better?" Women tend to send and receive more email than men, and they use it in a richer and more engaging way. Women are more likely than men to use email to write their friends and family, sharing news and worries; to plan events; and to forward jokes and funny stories. While both men and women appreciate email for its efficiencies and convenience, women are more likely to gain satisfaction from emails, especially when it comes to nurturing their relationships.[41]

Women seem to disclose more to those with whom they are close, whereas men seem to disclose more to those whom they trust. It also appears that men and women differ in the defensive and protective strategies used to reduce embarrassment and maintain privacy boundaries. Men's defensive strategies include blaming the incident on something else, laughing at their own behavior, or retreating from the situation, whereas women's defensive strategies often include blaming others and criticizing themselves. No matter how privacy is defined or explained, the means by which people regulate the release of private information is through disclosure.[42]

All of us should have someone with whom we can share our feelings and thoughts because it is generally good for our well being and personal satisfaction. Self-disclosure is the most sensitive and beautiful form of communication we can engage in, but it must be done with care.

Self-Disclosure and Culture

In general, people from different cultural backgrounds tend to follow similar patterns of self-disclosure. For example, people from various cultures are likely to begin relationships with small talk and progress to more intimate levels of interaction as the relationship continues. Of course, differences do exist, especially in the initial contact stage, in some cultures; but, in general, as people become friends, those differences seem to diminish.

Think about some of the characteristics that describe your cultural background, however, and how they might or might not influence your communication. Do you see yourself simply as an American, or identify with some other ethnic or racial group: African American, Filipino American, Latino, Vietnamese, Korean, German, or white? Do others view you the same way? How does your ethnicity affect your communication and with whom you choose to communicate? Do you use certain expressions understood only by members of your ethnic group? When you interact with people from a different ethnic group, how difficult is it for you to communicate? The answers to these questions will help you understand cultural differences and why interacting with people from diverse backgrounds is much more complex than simply exchanging information. It requires thought, recognition of differences, and some adjustments for communication to be meaningful to both parties. Not everyone thinks and communicates in exactly the same way. This may be especially important to remember when we interact with people from cultures different from our own. Disclosure is culturally regulated by norms of appropriateness, so we must understand cultural differences.

Self-Disclosure and Rhetorical Sensitivity

rhetorical sensitivity

A cautious approach to self-disclosure in which the situation and factors about the other person are considered before communication begins.

According to communication scholars Roderick Hart and Don Burks, **rhetorical sensitivity** is an alternative form of communication that can be applied to situations in which wide-open self-disclosure could be harmful. For example, you want to tell your friend to stop eating junk food because she is really putting on weight. Instead of telling her what you really think, you say, "Eating all that junk food can't be good for you," in the hope your friend will get the message. It represents a cautious approach to exchanging information while developing a relationship.[43] Rhetorically sensitive people can balance their self-interest with the interests of others. They can adjust their communication to take into account the beliefs, values, and mood of the other person. Considering the other person's views or feelings does not mean changing your own, but it does mean finding an effective way to communicate your thoughts without offending or hurting the other person.

Honest self-disclosure can be harmful if it is stated in a way that damages the relationship. Rhetorically sensitive individuals generally display the following attributes:

- They accept personal complexity; they understand that every person is made up of many selves. For example, one person may be a mother, a daughter, a Republican, an Asian American, an abuse victim, a student, and a consumer.

- They are flexible and avoid rigidity in communicating with others.

- They do not change their own values, but can communicate them in a variety of ways to avoid offending others.

- They sense when it is appropriate to communicate something and when it is not.[44] Rhetorically sensitive people understand self-disclosure and know how to adapt their messages to a particular audience and situation.

- They are aware of the language they choose, such as gender-inclusive nonsexist language; they do not use homophobic or racist language or inappropriate jokes that offend others.

Guidelines

Suggestions for Appropriate Self-Disclosure

There are no hard and fast rules when it comes to self-disclosure, but self-disclosing to others should be based on common sense and good judgment. Here are some suggestions that might help you use self-disclosure appropriately and competently:

1. **Use reasoned self-disclosure.** Although open and honest relationships are desirable, it is important to recognize situational constraints. For example, as a youngster, you might have been caught shoplifting from a local store. You shoplifted only that one time and were required to do some community service. However, you are now running for public office, and you must decide whether to disclose the fact that you stole from a local store. To do so would more than likely hurt your chances of winning the election. However, if you know that something you did is going to come out, mentioning it before it does come out illustrates that you are not hiding anything.

2. **Make self-disclosure a two-way process.** One-sided self-disclosure generally leads to relationships that are not very enduring, meaningful, or healthy. For example, once a mutual give-and-take is established, if one person self-discloses, the other person will usually follow suit. As trust increases between individuals, self-disclosure will likely expand, and with continued self-disclosure, relationships will become stronger.

3. **Make self-disclosure appropriate to the situation and the person.** When we disclose personal information about ourselves, we run the risk of being hurt or rejected. We can somewhat minimize the risk if we carefully match the disclosure to the person and the situation. Self-disclosure should be a slow process; rushing it, as some have done on the Internet, can unnecessarily increase vulnerability.

4. **Consider diversity.** The appropriateness and the level of self-disclosure vary by culture, group, and individual. The Japanese culture, for example, does not foster self-expression in the same way that U.S. or Korean cultures do. Even within the United States culture differences can be found among groups, such as between men and women. Consider these differences as you decide how much, to whom, and when to disclose personal information.

5. **Be open and honest.** The goal of self-disclosing is to match the amount and kind of self-disclosure to the situation. Thus, open and honest sharing of our feelings, concerns, and secrets with others is at the heart of self-disclosure. This does not mean, however, that we must disclose everything or that we cannot withhold information if it is likely to hurt us or someone else.

6. **Base self-disclosure on personal judgment.** Ultimately, self-disclosure must be based on personal judgment rather than rigid rules. Self-disclosure should, if used properly, be the most sensitive and meaningful form of communication we engage in as we enter and maintain relationships. For many reasons, we sometimes find it difficult to disclose to others. However, when relationships are based on mutual feelings and genuine communication, they cannot help but grow and mature.

Summary

Connecting with Others via Interpersonal Communication

Objective 13.1 Explain what it means to connect with others through interpersonal communication.

- Connecting with others and forming relationships are what interpersonal communication is all about.
- Interpersonal communication is creating and sharing meaning between persons who are in a relationship.
- Interpersonal communication allows relationships to become established and to grow, satisfying our social needs.

Theories of Interpersonal Communication

Objective 13.2 Compare and contrast seven theories related to relationships and interpersonal communication.

- Uncertainty reduction theory asserts that when people meet, they often seek to reduce uncertainty about each other.
- Uncertainty management theory takes into account the different ways people respond both psychologically and communicatively to uncertainty.
- Social information processing theory suggests that electronically mediated relationships grow only to

the extent that people gain information about each other and use the information to form impressions.

- Social penetration theory provides a view of how people connect with each other and how their communication moves from small talk to more intimate and self-revealing talk.
- Social exchange theory suggests that if the benefits gained in a relationship are greater than any potential costs, then we likely would regard the relationship positively.
- Interpersonal needs theory consists of three needs: affection, inclusion, and control.
- Dialectical theory suggests that relationships, as well as individuals, confront many tensions that push and pull them in many different directions at the same time.

Self-Disclosure in Relationships

Objective 13.3 **Outline** the roles of self-disclosure, privacy, gender, culture, and rhetorical sensitivity in interpersonal relationships.

- Relationships are built on interaction. The more sincere, honest, and open the interactions, the stronger and more lasting the relationship is likely to be.

- We self-disclose for a variety of different reasons for others to better understand who we are, to gain sympathy, to see what others think, to gain trust or to connect with others and establish relationships.
- There are many reasons for withholding information, but it is usually to protect others, to avoid a potentially negative reaction, or to avoid hurting others or ourselves.
- Just as we control and protect access to our physical self—for example, how close we allow others to come to us—in the same way we control and protect our privacy boundaries.
- Women are more likely to talk about their relationships and disclose a deeper level of intimacy, but men often do not center their talk on relational closeness.
- In general, people from any cultural background tend to follow similar patterns of self-disclosure.
- Rhetorical sensitivity is an alternative form of communication that can be applied to situations in which wide-open self-disclosure could be harmful.

Discussion Starters

1. Describe the behaviors of a person who is interpersonally competent.
2. Discuss the seven interpersonal communication theories and decide which best explains our need to know others and to form relationships.
3. What are some inappropriate communicative behaviors you have observed in interpersonal situations? Why do you think these behaviors occur? Why did these behaviors bother you?
4. Describe rules or guidelines for proper or polite communication you wish others practiced.

5. Explain the difference between being rhetorically sensitive and being honest in self-disclosure.
6. Is honesty always the best policy when self-disclosing Explain.
7. Why is small talk so difficult for some of us and why do we often dread it?
8. Develop a set of rules you think should be applied when self-disclosing personal information to others through social media.

Chapter 14

Developing and Maintaining Relationships: From Formation to Dissolution

 ## Learning Objectives

This chapter will help you:

14.1 **Characterize** the importance of interpersonal communication competence.

14.2 **Identify** the stages of rel̶a̶t̶i̶o̶n̶opment and growth.

14.3 **Identify** the ̶ration and dissolution.

14.4 **Explain** wha̶ wnat causes it, and why it can be benefi̶ ̶strategies to manage and resolve it.

14.5 **Apply** effective interpersonal communication skills and competencies in personal and professional relationships.

Making Everyday Connections

Taylor likes getting things done as painlessly and efficiently as possible. When she leaves her part-time job at the local neighborhood restaurant to go to her apartment, she walks as fast as she can with her head down. She seldom, if ever, stops to talk with anyone because she doesn't know many others and doesn't want to draw attention to herself. At her apartment building, she enters the elevator for her ride to the ninth floor. Because she is somewhat shy, she stands in the corner of the elevator and hardly looks at anyone. One other person is on the elevator with her, but nothing is said. It is an awkward silence. As the door opens on the third floor, the guy who has been riding with Taylor begins to walk out, turns, looks at Taylor, and says, "Hi, I'm Zack." As he holds the door open, he says, "You work at the restaurant down the street, right?" With a smile, she nods and mumbles her name. Zack says, "I didn't know you lived here." Taylor responds, "Yeah, I am somewhat new here and really don't know too many people." Zack replies, "I've only been here about six months and just started my first year at 'the U' Taylor. If you give me your number, maybe we could get together sometime." Taylor smiles and quickly rattles off her cell phone number, and Zack enters it into his cell.

A few days later, Zack texts Taylor to see if she would like to meet. She texts back, "Sure, what did you have in mind?" Taylor decides to see if Zack has a Facebook page—so she can learn more about him.[*]

Questions to Think About

1. What effect do emotions and mindset have on the early stages of a relationship?

2. Describe in your own words what happens to communication during the various stages of relationship development, moving from a first encounter to being a friend or intimate friend.

3. What type of communication occurs when a relationship is in its early stages? When it is in trouble?

4. Describe the ways social media can affect relationship development.

5. How have you used social media to create a relationship? How did the relationship develop?

[*]The above scenario was originally created by Stephanie Whitlow, an honor student at Wayne State College in Wayne, Nebraska. With her permission, it was revised and edited by one of the authors.

It is a human tendency to evaluate almost everything and everyone and form attitudes about the people, objects, and events in our lives. As we encounter other individuals at school, at work, or in our neighborhoods, we develop attitudes and feelings about each. These interpersonal evaluations fall along a dimension ranging from liking to disliking and also help determine the type of relationship that may be formed—for example, friend, close acquaintance, superficial acquaintance, or annoying acquaintance.

In Chapter 13, we noted that relationships have the potential to form anytime two people make contact, whether face-to-face or online. Most contacts are made accidentally, depending on factors such as those described in the chapter's opening scenario. Contacts can also occur based on seating arrangements in classes or the physical arrangements of a workplace, both of which increase the odds you will come into repeated contact with certain people, while at the same time decreasing the odds such contact will occur with others. As a result, although this might not seem all that surprising, physical proximity, meeting online, and timing are often how people meet and begin relationships.

In this chapter, we discuss interpersonal communication competence as the overriding factor that determines and affects the type and depth of relationships formed and the length of time they last. The chapter also explores why some people are interpersonally attracted to others and explains the stages most relationships go through; these stages are best exemplified by the theory of relationship stages.

This chapter also covers relationship dissolution, when relationships are in trouble, the theory of dissolution stages, interpersonal conflict, conflict management, and finally how to improve interpersonal communication competence in relationships.

Interpersonal Communication Competence

14.1 **Characterize** the importance of interpersonal communication competence.

Whether we get to know others might have little or nothing to do with their specific characteristics or ours. Usually, the likelihood two people will become acquainted has to do with contact through physical proximity and a positive rather than a negative experience at the time of the face-to-face or social media contact. After you encounter a person several times and easily recognize him or her, you will likely become comfortable interacting with the person or at least making casual conversation. The relationship development and your reception often depend on how well you and the other person interact. Of course, we know that sometimes we interact better than at other times.

Competent communicators recognize it is unlikely they will always communicate perfectly, but they usually continue to try to do so. Competence implies appropriateness. What this means is that competent communicators can adapt to particular situations and individuals. They know how to use language appropriately no matter the situation, whether a friend's wedding, an intimate moment, or a job interview.

So, what are the skills associated with competence in interpersonal communication situations? According to communication scholars, five skills lead to competence in interpersonal communication.[1] They are as follows:

1. The ability to adapt and know how to communicate in specific situations, for example, when to be empathic and comforting or when to talk and when to listen.

2. The ability to adapt and appropriately communicate in specific interactions, for example, know when to speak out aggressively and when to be reserved and more deferential.

3. The ability to understand your own and the other person's values, beliefs, attitudes, or feelings. In other words, how does the other person view himself or herself or what does he or she think about various people, issues, or events?

4. The ability to self-monitor. Self-monitoring is the ability to regulate your communication both before and during an interaction. It is a form of rhetorical sensitivity (see discussion in Chapter 13 on rhetorical sensitivity). In other words, a person who self-monitors can attend to the feedback of others and recognize the impact of what they say.

5. The ability to be fair and ethical. This means treating people as unique human beings. It is a commitment to self-respect and respect for others as well. An interpersonally competent communicator is sensitive to all ideas and perspectives discussed. They know everyone sees the world differently; thus they are considerate of those who disagree with them.

The Guidelines box below offers concrete ways these competencies can result in more satisfying interpersonal relationships.

We are influenced by first impressions on a daily basis, whether observing people in a store or coffee shop, or meeting people for the first time, such as new roommates, study partners, classmates, or friends of someone you know.

Guidelines

Suggestions for Effective Interpersonal Interactions

Conversation with others is a two-way responsibility; you can't rely on the other person to carry the conversation for you—a monologue is not a conversation. To become effective at interacting, you must be fully connected and work to ensure that the other person feels connected and comfortable. Here are some suggestions:

1. **Use the other person's name as much as possible as you talk with him or her.** Some ways you can remember are: Say the name at least three times when first interacting with someone you just met. Have the person restate it or spell it for you if necessary. Knowing and recalling a person's name creates the impression that the person matters to you and helps make small talk a bit more comfortable.

2. **Look at the other person, but strive for balance and comfort in eye contact.** When you look at the other person, you indicate you are paying attention and are interested in him or her. It also shows you are confident in yourself.

3. **Be careful in your use of eye contact with people from cultural or ethnic backgrounds different than your own.** For example, Hispanic and Japanese cultures believe staring at someone or looking into someone's eyes is disrespectful. When communicating with people from these cultures, you might focus on the face in general, but not directly on their eyes.

4. **Encourage the other person to talk about himself or herself.** People generally like to talk about themselves. It can be a strong motivator for continuing the conversation. Listen carefully and ask questions such as, "What are you planning to do after graduation?" "What did you like most about ____ (the play, the movie, the book, the game, and so on)?" "What does your work involve?" "What do you like to do in your spare time?" "What do you enjoy most about your work?" and "Tell me about yourself." Use follow-up questions to keep the person talking, if necessary.

5. **Keep the conversation casual, light, and positive.** Moving too quickly to disclose personal information can be threatening and a real conversation stopper. In addition, no one likes negative people or whiners. If you come across as one, your likelihood of future interaction is dramatically reduced.

6. **Be confident and listen carefully to what is being said.** It is critical to have confidence to make small talk. Confidence doesn't mean arrogance; it does mean you are not afraid to enter into conversation with others. It is likely the other person may have similar reservations about chatting with you as you might have about them. Your interest, will also motivate the others to continue the conversation rather than end it abruptly.

7. **Keep abreast of current events.** Know what is going on around you: Watch the news; use the Internet; read current magazines and newspapers (or web news) on a regular basis. This knowledge can help because current events are often the topics of small talk. Your awareness of current events makes small talk easier; plus, it shows others you are concerned about what is going on around you.

8. **Use casual talk to help reduce the uncertainty between your and others.** This will increase your chances of initiating and developing a more lasting relationship.

9. **Know when and how to end the conversation.** It is important to know when the conversation should end. Initial conversations are not usually intended to last very long. If they run too long you run the risk of boredom and discomfort. Even if the conversation is going well and you both are enjoying yourselves, you might end it before it becomes uncomfortable. Ending a conversation can be awkward or difficult, but your best strategy is to have a few well-rehearsed exit lines. Make sure you use the person's name when exiting—for example, "Debra, I'd better move on to other guests. I enjoyed visiting with you" or "Jim, I would like to get some food before it's gone."

Relationship Formation

14.2 Identify the stages of relationship development and growth.

Whether or not two specific individuals ever come in contact with each other may depend on circumstance and situation. We are influenced daily by others we meet and by their first impressions. How and why a relationship develops may depend on interpersonal attraction and how the relationship manages the stages of coming together or growth.

Interpersonal Attraction

Most of us develop relationships quite routinely, although the process is easier for some people than for others. **Interpersonal attraction** is the desire to interact with

interpersonal attraction

The desire to interact with someone based on a variety of factors, including physical attractiveness, personality, rewards, proximity, or similarities.

someone based on a variety of factors, including physical attractiveness, personality, rewards, proximity, or similarities. Although these are perhaps obvious referents, interpersonal attraction is a complex phenomenon. Communication scholars James McCroskey and Thomas McCain identified three types of attraction: (1) social attraction ("He would fit into my circle of friends."), (2) physical attraction ("I think she's or he's hot."), and (3) task attraction ("My confidence in her ability to get the job done makes me want to work with her.").[2] In other words, interpersonal attraction has a lot to do with evaluating others.

Any given person (including you) is liked by some people, disliked by some, and seen as neutral by many others. Why? This question is not easily answered, but, to some extent, differences in attraction depend on the person making the evaluation. Attraction also depends, in part, on the similarities and differences between the evaluator and the person being evaluated. As acquaintances evolve from first encounters to more engaged relationships, two additional factors come into play: the need to associate with someone and reactions to observable physical attributes.

What leads to attraction and eventual friendship? More than seven billion people inhabit our planet, and several thousand of them could conceivably become your friends. That is exceedingly unlikely to happen, however. Any one of us is likely to become aware of, interact with, and personally know only a small fraction of these individuals. However, social media now allow us to have hundreds of acquaintances all over the world. Most online acquaintances remain online acquaintances or friends with whom we may share personal information, but they seldom become intimate friends.

When two people come into contact and experience a relatively positive effect, either in person or online, they begin a transition to the initiating stages of a possible relationship. They may simply remain superficial acquaintances who exchange friendly greetings whenever they happen to encounter one another but never interact otherwise. Or they may begin to talk in person or text each other, learn each other's names, and exchange bits and pieces of personal information. At this point, they might be described as close acquaintances or online friends. Which of these two outcomes depends on the extent to which each person is motivated by the need to associate or the need for inclusion (discussed in Chapter 13) and the way each person reacts to the observable attributes of the other or the perceived attributes based on the messages they exchange online.

"Love at first sight," or being wowed, is a phenomenon expressed in various ways by different cultures. No matter the expression, the underlying idea is the same: that sometimes seeing someone for the first time can bring a powerful feeling of attraction toward that person. We all have heard the phrase, "Beauty is only skin deep." It is a warning about giving too much weight to outward appearance. But research seems to indicate that even if we want to follow this advice, we can't, because physical appearance is such a powerful factor in our attraction to others.[3] So, even when we want to, it is difficult to ignore or avoid physical attraction as a motivator to establish a relationship.

PHYSICAL ATTRIBUTES   When we like—or dislike—some people at first sight, it is an indication we have observed something about them that provides positive or negative information. For example, if a stranger reminds you of someone you know and like, association extends your response to the person.[4]

You tend to like the stranger simply on the basis of a superficial resemblance to someone else. In other instances, the cue might not be related to a specific person in your past but to a subgroup of people to whom you respond positively—the stranger has a Wisconsin accent and you have a fondness for people from your home state. In a similar way, resemblance to a specific person you dislike or to a subgroup of people you dislike can cause you to instantly dislike or avoid a stranger. As we discussed in

Chapters 2 and 5, stereotypes are poor predictors of behavior; nevertheless, we find we do react to other people on the basis of superficial characteristics.

Most of us know that reacting to stereotypes on the basis of appearance is meaningless. However, people do, in fact, respond positively to those who are extremely attractive and negatively to those who are very unattractive.[5] This is especially true in the early stages of interpersonal contact with strangers. We commonly accept or reject people on the basis of observable characteristics, such as skin color, sexual orientation, height, weight, accent, and hair color. Physical attractiveness is a very powerful message and influences many types of interpersonal evaluations.

COMMUNICATION AND ATTRACTION   How does attractiveness affect relationships and interpersonal communication? Most people, according to one study, fear rejection by those who are more attractive than they are. Many people tend to reject others who are far less attractive than they believe themselves to be; in other words, they say, "I can do better than that." In general, most of us move toward those who are similar to us in attractiveness.

The idea that "opposites attract" is as old as the adage "birds of a feather flock together" and appears to have little truth to it. In plays, movies, and television series, a familiar story line is one where two quite different people are attracted to each other, in part because they are so different. Think, for example, of Marge and Homer Simpson or a movie such as *Shrek*. In contrast, such real-life pairings are relatively rare.[6]

Why do these exceptions occur, and what explains them? If one person in a relationship is more attractive than another, for example, people tend to infer that the less attractive person in the relationship has an attribute that "balances" the mismatch, such as wealth, power, intelligence, sex appeal, or fame. For example, in the classic 1991 animated movie *Beauty and the Beast,* the beast's appearance is unattractive, but his kindness, gentleness, and bravery make Belle (who was extremely beautiful) fall in love with him and make it believable. However, the overall conclusion of most research is that similarity is a much stronger basis for attraction than are differences.[7]

CHEMISTRY OR PHYSICAL ATTRACTION   Whether we wish to accept it or not, physical appearance does play a role in determining relationships. Although this attractiveness might not always predict the outcome of a relationship, research suggests that physical attractiveness is important as an attention getter.[8] Most of us are

Making Connections for Success

Soul Mate Online—Finding the Right One

Go online and type in any of the following search terms— "finding a date," "finding a relationship," or "finding a mate"— and you will discover over a million different sites. Here are some of their slogans:

> "When you are ready to find the love of your life."
> "A marriage a day, a match every 17 minutes."
> "Genuine People, Real Love."
> "Over 100,000 current members searching for meaningful relationships."
> "Ever wish there was an easy way to find the person you were meant to be with?"
> "To create a deep and meaningful connection."

Internet sites such as eHarmony.com, Match.com, and hundreds more offer ways to meet others, find a date, get married, be friends, or to connect.

1. Why do you think websites such as those listed above are so popular?
2. How would you describe the perfect mate?
3. How can you be sure you have found the perfect mate?
4. If you were to go online to look for a relationship, what criteria would you use to determine whether you would make a face-to-face connection with someone?
5. What, if any, problems might you encounter with these types of services? What problems do you see if you provide personal online information for others to read?

aware that sometimes our first impressions and reasons for being attracted to another are not completely rational. Sudden lust, love at first sight, or the intense dislike of someone with whom we have had no previous contact can seem inexplicable. Many social psychologists suggest relationship development has a lot to do with the "chemistry" between the individuals in the relationship. Either the chemistry is right and the relationship develops, or it's a mismatch and the relationship never seems to move beyond the initial stages. The chemistry explanation probably holds some truth, but many other variables influence the development of a relationship.

We are most often attracted to individuals who support us and have similar interests, attitudes, likes, and dislikes. In fact, when asked to characterize the ideal friend, people often describe someone who is similar to their perceptions of themselves. Those who are religious tend to seek other religious people; those who like sports, other sports fans; and those who like children, others who like children. Opposites do sometimes attract, as described above, but relationships in which important attitudes or behaviors differ significantly are often strained and more likely to deteriorate than are those where there are no major disparities.

Usually, opposites don't attract, but when they do, underlying similarities are present because similarity is usually a much better predictor of attraction. When seemingly opposite people are attracted to each other, they typically find they have a great deal in common—though this similarity may not be visible to casual, outside observers.

MEETING ONLINE In Chapter 13, we discussed how initial interactions online could result in relationships, as well as the limitations in the growth of those relationships. According to communication scholars Malcolm Parks and Kory Floyd, conflicting theories on interpersonal communication and relationship development exist. Because online interaction is limited by fewer social cues (i.e., nonverbal communication) and potential feedback delays can lead to uncertainty (and difficulty in reducing uncertainty about the other person), the development of personal relationships might be prevented, or at least restrained.[9]

Online interactions are generally assumed to lack many typical characteristics of face-to-face discussions that can aid in relationship development. An important question researchers ask is, "Are the conditions that exist in face-to-face interactions necessary for a relationship to develop into something that is ongoing or lasting?" Although the interactions between people who communicate through social media rather than face-to-face communication indicate what people want in a lasting relationship, evidence is not conclusive that their mediated communication will lead to one. In research studies of personal online ads placed by heterosexual and homosexual men and women, several trends emerged: (1) Heterosexual men wanted what heterosexual women offered—physical attractiveness; (2) heterosexual women sought what heterosexual men offered—financial security; (3) homosexual men emphasized physical attractiveness in their ads even more than did heterosexual men; and (4) homosexual women tended to play down the importance of physical attractiveness.[10] Online ads placed by people ages 50 or above tend to place much less emphasis on physical appearance and instead focus on less sexual relational goals.[11] Of course, with our ability to use Skype and FaceTime, the differences between face-to-face and online interactions are dramatically reduced. Although these encounters can be very similar, they also can be more carefully controlled and choreographed than face-to-face interactions.

Parks and Floyd, found women are more likely to form online relationships than men and also found age and marital status were not related to the likelihood of developing a personal online relationship. People who were married and divorced, according to their survey results, were equally likely to form personal relationships over the Internet. In fact, of the 176 people Parks and Floyd surveyed, about 30 percent developed personal relationships. The more in-depth and personal an online relationship becomes, the more likely it is that communication will move beyond the computer or social media device to more private and direct channels, such as the telephone, letters, or face-to-face communication.[12] As with all relationships, online relationships go through stages of initiation, maintenance, and sometimes deterioration and termination.

Relationships: Initiation or Coming Together

Communication scholars such as Mark Knapp and Anita Vangelisti believe that for relationships to move beyond a brief encounter, they must go through various stages of growth and patterns of communication.[13] Although the relationship stages in Knapp and Vangelisti's model are generally romantic in nature, they do not suggest that only romantic relationships or mixed-gender relationships are included. In fact, Knapp and Vangelisti suggest any and all kinds of relationships can reach the highest level of commitment. David McWhirter and Andrew Mattison, research psychologists, found that when same-sex intimate relationships form, the same patterns or stages of development occur as with mixed-sex pairs.[14]

Knapp and Vangelisti strongly emphasize that the model simplifies a complex process. For example, in their model they show each stage adjacent to the next, seeming to suggest that when a communicating couple left one stage they entered the next. This is not their intention. Each stage actually contains behaviors from other stages, so stage identification is a matter of emphasis.[15]

Knapp and Vangelisti further explain that not all relationships go through the stages at the same rate, in the same way, or necessarily sequentially, and many relationships move in and out of the stages as they progress or regress. They note we should resist the temptation to perceive stages of coming together as only "good" and those of coming apart as only "bad." In fact, sometimes the termination of a relationship may be a good thing or, conversely, becoming more intimate with someone may not necessarily be a good thing. The coming-together sequence, however, often progresses from initiating to experimenting, intensifying, integrating, and ultimately, bonding.[16]

INITIATING   Initiating is the stage during which individuals meet and interact for the first time. The initial interaction might consist of a brief exchange of words, either online or in person. If conversation does not begin, the initiating stage may end, and the potential relationship might not progress any further. Whether the interaction continues depends on various assessments the individuals make—for example, whether the other person is attractive or unattractive, approachable or unapproachable. A connection must be made to motivate one or both of the individuals to continue the interaction if a relationship is to develop.

During the initiating stage, we mentally process many impressions that lead to a key decision: "Yes, I do want to meet you" or "No, I am not interested in you." It might take less than 15 seconds to determine whether a relationship will progress. At this stage, most of us feel extremely vulnerable and cautious. Social media plays a larger and larger role in how people from all over the world meet and interact and, ironically, seems to encourage less caution despite the potential dangers of getting to know someone online and the need to assess whether the information others share is truthful and accurate.

EXPERIMENTING   Experimenting is the stage of coming together that requires risk taking because little is known about the other person. You attempt to answer the question, "Who is this person?" This stage can be extremely awkward, consisting mainly of small talk: "What's your name?" "Where are you from?" "What's your major?" "Do you know so-and-so?" Such conversation serves several important functions in the development of a relationship: (1) It uncovers similarities and interests that might lead to deeper conversation; (2) it serves as an audition for the potential friend; (3) it lets the other person know who you are and provides clues to how he or she can get to know you better; and (4) it establishes the common ground you share with the other person.

Relationships in the experimenting stage are "generally pleasant, relaxed, overtly uncritical, and casual."[17] Most relationships, according to Knapp and Vangelisti, do not progress very far beyond the experimenting stage. However, relationships that remain at the experimental level can become satisfying friendships or acquaintances.

INTENSIFYING The intensifying stage marks an increase in the participants' commitment and involvement in the relationship. Simply put, the two people become close friends. The commitment is typified by an increased sharing of more personal and private information, or self-disclosure (see Chapter 13), about self and family. At this stage it would not be unusual to share confidences such as "My mother and father are affectionate people," "I love you," "I am a sensitive person," "I once cheated on an exam," "My father is having another relationship," "I was promoted," "I drink too heavily," and "I don't use drugs."

Although the relationship deepens at this stage, there is still a sense of caution and testing to gain approval before continuing. In typical romantic relationships, we see much testing of commitment—sitting close, for instance, may occur before holding hands, hugging, or kissing. As the relationship matures, the participants become more sensitive to each other's needs. During this phase, verbal communication changes, depending on how the individuals interact with each other. For example:

1. Forms of address become informal—a first name, nickname, or a term of endearment is used.

2. Use of the first-person plural becomes more common—"We should do this," or "Let's do this."

3. Private symbols begin to develop—special slang, nicknames, or jargon or conventional language forms with mutually understood, private meanings.

4. Verbal shortcuts occur because of familiarity with each other—for example, washing dishes might become "dishes," or "let's go to sleep" might become "bedtime."

5. More direct expressions of commitment may appear—"We really have a good thing going" or "I don't know who I'd talk to if you weren't around." Sometimes such expressions receive an echo—"I really like you a lot" or "I really like you, too, Taylor."

6. Each partner acts increasingly as a helper in the other's daily process of understanding what he or she is all about—"In other words, you mean you're …" or "But yesterday you said you were…."[18]

INTEGRATING When integrating occurs, the relationship has a sense of togetherness. Others expect to see the individuals together, and when they do not, they often ask about the other person. The two people have established a deep commitment, and the relationship has become extremely important to them. Many assumptions take place between the individuals. For example, sharing is expected, and borrowing from the other person usually needs no formal request because it is assumed to be all right.

Although a strong mutual commitment characterizes this stage of a relationship, it does not mean a total giving of oneself to the other. The verbal and nonverbal expressions of the integrating stage take many forms. For example, some individuals believe their relationship is something special or unique. Some share rings, pins, pictures, and other artifacts to illustrate to themselves and others their commitment to each other. The two may begin to behave in similar ways. Still others indicate their sense of togetherness through word choice—*our* account, *our* apartment, *our* car.

BONDING The final stage in a relationship's development and growth is bonding, the public announcement of the commitment—as when a couple announces that they are engaged or getting married. Bonding involves the understanding that the commitment has progressed from private knowledge to public knowledge, thus making a breakup of the relationship more difficult.

The integrating stage of relationship development conveys a sense of togetherness. The two people have established a deep commitment, and the relationship has become extremely important to them.

The relationship at this stage is contractual in nature, even though a formal contract, such as a marriage license, is not required. Both parties must understand, however, that a relationship exists, which entails explicit and implicit agreements to hold it together. The commitment implies the relationship is "for better or for worse" and is defined according to established norms, policies, or laws of the culture and society in which it exists.

It takes time and energy to maintain a relationship. Most people in relationships, no matter how good they are, know and accept that some conflict is inevitable. They also know that conflict, if handled appropriately, can lead to a stronger and lasting relationship.

Relationship Maintenance Strategies

In Chapter 13 we explained, through the various interpersonal communication theories, why we seek relationships and their importance to our well-being as humans. Our focus, for the most part, was on creating relationships and positive interactions; however, we also believe that at times maintaining healthy relationships includes some unpleasant interactions and conflicts.

Relational maintenance behaviors help us understand how we sustain a relationship so it continues to grow and thrive. In Chapter 13 we discussed social exchange theory in terms of cost and benefits. Let's say you recently met someone with whom you have become friends. Both you and your new friend are satisfied with the costs and benefits of the relationship. Laura Stafford and Dan Canary, two communication researchers, determined five primary relational maintenance behaviors couples can use to build and maintain relationships. They are positivity, openness, assurances, blending social networks, and sharing tasks.[20]

Making Connections for Success

Getting to Know Others: How Relationships Begin

The following is taken from an essay titled "The Donut Shop Experiment," written by Jonathan Butler, a high school history teacher in Riverside, California. According to Mr. Butler, he and a group of his friends and relatives wanted to do something crazy on a Saturday night. They were tired of board games and television. So about 10 of them, some under 30 and some over—brothers, a sister, a friend, in-laws, and parents—struck on an idea that the group of them would infiltrate a little café in twos and threes, at differing times, until all were seated around the counter. They would arrange themselves as couples chatting, an old man sitting alone, or three friends in a row. Their plan was to interrelate—"get acquainted"—as total strangers appearing to get to know one another. Their plan was to see how the others in the café would react.

They chose a doughnut shop with a truck-stop atmosphere that lacked promise socially. Then one of them asked the cashier, "Say, do you use bleached flour in these donuts?" From that one question, conversation flowed and relationships began to form.

Butler writes, "The conversation ranged from food to politics to music to how strangers never talk in strange places like a café." The people in the café, according to Butler, reflected on what they were doing and laughed, realizing that an improbable conglomerate of people had formed some kind of community.

The group of 10 left the café and arrived back at Butler's home, dazed by the experience. Butler ends the story with these words: "How thin the walls that divide us from one another at ballparks and grocery stores and restaurants. How paper-thin."[19]

1. What do you think Butler means by his last statement?
2. Why is it so easy to communicate with those we don't know via social media but not as easy when we are in face-to-face situations?
3. What does Butler's café experiment tell us about communication and relationships?
4. What does it mean to have "people skills"?
5. How would you explain the above story using Knapp and Vangelisti's stages of coming together?

POSITIVITY Communicative behaviors make others feel good or comfortable around us. For example, communicative behaviors include acting friendly or cheerful; being patient and forgiving; being optimistic, courteous, cooperative, complementary, and polite; and avoiding criticism. Individuals who typically communicate in this way are fun and pleasant to be around. Couple partners who engage in these types of behaviors often show affection for each other, seldom complain, and keep their relationship strong.

OPENNESS Openness occurs when a person is willing to interact with a friend or relational partner about their relationship. Those who use this relational maintenance strategy are willing to self-disclose their thoughts and feelings, and ask how the other person feels about the relationship. People who use the openness strategy like to have talks about how the relationship is going and like to share their needs and wants in regard to the relationship.

ASSURANCES Assurances, according to Stafford and Canary, are the verbal and nonverbal behaviors one or both partners in a relationship use to demonstrate their commitment or faithfulness to the other. When someone expresses assurances, he or she shows commitment to the relationship and implies it has a future.

BLENDING SOCIAL NETWORKS This is similar to what is often referred to as the "social network" that includes common friends, coworkers, and family relationships. For example, close friends are likely to know each other's families and share social friends and other associates. Common friends help a couple bond the relationship.

SHARING TASKS Each person in the relationship does his or her fair share of the work that needs to be done and takes equal responsibility for what faces them. For example, if a friend lets you borrow her computer when yours is not working, you might let her use your car to run an errand. If your partner cooks a meal, then you might offer to clean up afterward. Sharing tasks requires effort and energy to make the relationship work. Thus, both individuals contribute to the relationship, which makes it more stable. At times, however, a couple struggles to keep the relationship together and signs arise that it is in trouble.

Relationship Dissolution

14.3 Identify the stages of relationship deterioration and dissolution.

Not every relationship is destined to last. The way both parties handle a relationship's dissolution can affect the well-being of both.

Signs That Show a Relationship Is in Trouble

Before we concede a relationship is over, certain warning signs, as well as some possible repair strategies, might help to prevent its breakup. At least three signs point to problems: aggressive behavior, lies, and betrayal.

AGGRESSIVE BEHAVIOR A preliminary warning sign a relationship is heading toward trouble occurs when one of the parties becomes a little too aggressive by aiming hurtful communication at the other. At some time we all say something we wished we hadn't said to someone about whom we care. However, whether intentional or not, when people communicate hurtful statements to one another with increasing frequency, it is a sign that their relationship may be in trouble.

LIES Another warning sign of trouble in a relationship is when one deceives another with lies. Whether the lie is significant or trivial, it weakens the relationship's foundation, which is trust. Recent research findings indicate when people find themselves on the receiving end of lies, they react with mistrust of, and dislike toward, the liar.[21]

"In my ad, I lied about my age."

As the young woman in this cartoon discovers, lies occur in many different contexts and are told for many different reasons.

SOURCE: © The New Yorker Collection 2003 Lee Lorenz from cartoonbank.com. All rights reserved.

We are all more or less adept at the art of deception. As you already know, online dating is extremely popular for creating relationships, but as the cartoon suggests, not everyone provides completely truthful information. Researchers report that online dating profiles are full of misinformation and deception. A survey of users of online dating services report that 86 percent of those participating believed that others misrepresented their physical appearance.[22]

The research objective was to compare online profile information with actual observed characteristics. They found that when describing height, weight, and age online as part of a personal profile, 48 percent lied about their height, 60 percent lied about their weight, and 19 percent lied about their age. It was also found that males lied slightly more than females regarding height and weight, but when it came to age women lied more than men.[23] According to the researchers, men tended to overestimate their height, while women mainly underestimated their weight.

Another study by the same researchers found several patterns in those who used deception that were missing from those who were more truthful. For example, those who were more likely to be less than truthful would not use "I" to reference themselves; they would also use indirect adjectives, such as "not boring" instead of "exciting," as well as provide shorter descriptions of themselves.[24]

Given the fact most of us engage in deception at some time, how can it be recognized? The answer seems to involve careful attention to both verbal and nonverbal cues. In addition to nonverbal cues, such as blinking more when a lie is being told or exaggerated facial expressions, other signs of lying sometimes are present in the tone of voice or in the words chosen.[25] When people lie, their pitch often rises, especially if they are highly motivated to lie. Another sign is taking longer than expected to answer a question or describe events. Detection of lying is far from certain; some people are very skillful liars.

BETRAYAL Another warning sign of a relationship in trouble is betrayal. For example, if you tell a friend a personal secret and especially ask for complete confidentiality, and the friend then spreads the story to others, you have been betrayed. Some common examples of betrayal include extramarital affairs, gossip, and harmful criticism behind someone's back. Deception and betrayal are similar; in fact, they are almost synonymous. The difference is that betrayal violates a confidence and an agreed-on expectation.

Making Connections for Success

Deception in a Relationship

I (Darin) have always been a little concerned about Olivia—she is such a charmer. She told me she was through with Aaron, her old boyfriend. We began sleeping together, spending a couple of nights plus weekends together at each other's places. Then a friend of mine told me that she saw Olivia with her "ex," and it didn't look as if they had parted ways. My friend also said that Olivia and her "ex" appeared to be intensely involved with each other. I saw Olivia today, and she didn't act differently. In fact, she acted as if everything was the same.

1. What would you do in this situation?
2. What would you tell Darin to do?
3. What does a situation like this do to a relationship?
4. Is there anything that Olivia can do to explain her behavior to Darin?
5. Are there any considerations that Darin should take into account before he jumps to conclusions?

Making Connections for Success

When It Might Be OK to Lie

Zach knows that Steph would be terribly hurt if she knew Zach had seen his former girlfriend the other evening. So Zach told Steph that he had a late-night meeting with his professor to go over an assignment. He knew even though his meeting with his former girlfriend was completely innocent that it would have opened an old wound that has never completely healed for Steph, who feels jealous and a bit insecure about his past relationship. Zach claims that the "truth," if discovered, would end or certainly make his relationship with Steph very difficult.

1. Knowing that the truth might have ended his relationship with Steph, whom he loves and doesn't want to lose, what do you think Zach should have done?
2. Assuming that deception is an all-too-common aspect of social life, what are its effects?
3. Is omission, or leaving out information, the same as lying? Why or why not?
4. Why is it easier to lie online than in person?

Relationships injured by deception and betrayals are often not repairable because of the amount of hurt caused by such breaches of trust. However, situations such as out of hand arguments or simple misunderstandings can often be corrected or resolved. In these cases, competent communication can repair and possibly save the relationship.

Relationships: Coming Apart or Breaking Up

Most people in relationships at one time or another have their differences or declines as a result of disclosures, lies, or betrayal. Couples can use relationship maintenance behaviors to help them deal with these issues. How partners in the relationship interact with each other during periods of disagreement will lead to a strengthening or deterioration of the relationship. There are no guarantees that a commitment to have a relationship at one point in time will result in a lasting relationship at another point in time. When a relationship stops growing and differences begin to emerge, the coming-apart process begins. Some relationships go through some or all of the stages in this process and emerge stronger than before, but when the forces that pull a relationship apart are stronger than the forces that hold it together, the relationship will end.

As they did for the coming-together process, Knapp and Vangelisti described the stages a relationship goes through when it is coming apart. Similar to the coming-together stages, those of coming apart, according to Knapp and Vangelisti, do not flow necessarily in a sequential order, and it is likely that relationships often move into and out of the different stages. The coming-apart process has five stages: differentiating, circumscribing, stagnating, avoiding, and terminating.[26]

DIFFERENTIATING   In differentiating, the first stage of coming apart, the differences between the individuals are highlighted and become forces that slow or limit the growth of the relationship. The pair's communication tends to focus on how each differs from the other, and tolerance of these differences decreases. Indeed, differences that were once overlooked or negotiated now become the center of attention, putting stress on the relationship and its existence. Typically, things once described as "ours" now become "mine:" "This is my apartment," "These are my books," and "They are my friends."

Conversations often move from mild disagreement to heated anger: "Do I have to do all the work around here? You don't do a thing." "Why is it that your so-called friends never clean up after themselves?" "I pay the water bill, but you're the one who takes long showers." Conflict

When one or both partners become aggressive and/or use hurtful messages, it is a warning sign the relationship is in trouble. As the frequency of hurtful messages increases, it becomes less likely the relationship can be repaired.

begins to overshadow the more positive aspects of the relationship and might lead to abuse of one or both parties in the relationship.

CIRCUMSCRIBING   In the circumscribing stage, information exchange is reduced, and some areas of difference are completely avoided because conversation would only lead to a deepening of the conflict. Comments during this stage might include the following: "I don't want to talk about it." "Can't you see I'm busy?" "Why do you keep bringing up the past?" "Let's just be friends and forget it." Communication loses some of its personal qualities, is less spontaneous, and becomes increasingly superficial as the relationship becomes more strained. Interactions, in their amount and depth of disclosure, resemble those of the initiating and experimenting stages of coming together: "Have you eaten?" "Did I get any calls today?" "I saw Joe, and he said to say hi."

People in the circumscribing stage often conceal their faltering relationship in public. A couple might sit in cold silence and stare stonily into space on their drive to a party. But once they arrive at their destination, they put on their party personalities—they smile, tell jokes, and do not disagree with one another. When they return to the privacy of their car, they resume their cold behavior.

STAGNATING   The relationship reaches a standstill at the stagnating stage. The participants avoid interaction and take care to sidestep controversy. Some people believe this is the "boring" stage of a relationship, but they don't do anything about it. Little hope remains for the relationship once it has deteriorated to this stage, yet one of the participants might still want it to be revived.

During stagnation, both verbal and nonverbal communication tend to be thoroughly thought out, and the partners plan what to say, the interactions are stylized and cold. Both parties are apt to reflect unhappiness and act as if each is a stranger to the other.

Often the stagnation stage is relatively brief, but sometimes it is extended because of complications. For example, some people are seriously distressed by the loss of their relationship, even though they know a split is the right decision. Children or others may count on the survival of the relationship, thus the breakup is more difficult.

Making Connections for Success

The Dark Side of Interpersonal Relationships

Most of what we have discussed to this point about entering and maintaining relationships has been more or less positive. Our goal is to discuss the positive aspects of relationships and how to be a successful communicator in interpersonal situations. However, we all know that relationships can at times have a painful and negative side. Consider this scenario:

Elissa and Josh met in a history course. He was athletic, good looking, and sensitive, and had a great personality. They began dating and appeared to be the perfect couple. Elissa began spending more and more time with Josh and less and less time with her college girlfriends. Elissa felt that was a lot easier than responding to Josh's endless questions about her whereabouts and what she was doing every moment of the day. Elissa's friends noticed a dramatic change in her personality. She seemed to lose interest

in the things she loved to do before she met Josh. She became distant and moody—just not herself. Elissa doesn't understand Josh's behavior because she has asked him a thousand times if he loves her and trusts her and he always answers, "Of course I do."

1. What do you think is going on?
2. What do you think happens to communication in an abusive relationship?
3. What are the warning signs someone is in an abusive relationship?
4. Provide examples of verbal abuse.
5. Why is the phrase "If you loved me, you would …" a red flag and sign of potential abuse?
6. How has technology increased the opportunities for abuse in relationships?
7. What can you do if you find yourself in an abusive relationship?

Others may prolong the situation out of fear of additional pain and in hope of getting the relationship back on track, or even in an attempt to punish the other person.

AVOIDING   Up to this point, participants in the relationship still see each other or share the same living quarters. But physical or emotional distancing and eventual separation mark the fourth stage, the avoiding stage. The basic message is, "I'm not interested in being with you anymore." As far as the participants are concerned, the relationship is over, and they have no interest in reestablishing it.

At times, the interaction in this stage is brief, direct, unfriendly, and even antagonistic: "I really don't care to see you." "Don't call me—we have nothing to discuss." "I'm busy tonight. For that matter, I'm going to be busy for quite some time."

TERMINATING   The last stage in the breaking up of a relationship occurs when the individuals take the necessary steps to end it. Termination can be early—that is, when the relationship has barely begun—or it can occur after many years. For relationships that break up in the early stages of development, such as initiating or experimenting, the feelings of parting are usually not complex or lasting.

The interaction during this stage is self-centered and seeks to justify the termination: "I need to do something for myself—I've always put more into the relationship than I've gotten out of it." "We just have too many differences that I didn't know existed until now." "I found out we just weren't meant for each other." When both individuals know the relationship is ending, they say good-bye to each other in three ways: in a summary statement, in behaviors signaling the termination or limited contact, and in comments about what the relationship will be like in the future, if there is to be any relationship at all.[27]

Summary statements review the relationship and provide a rationale for its termination: "Although our love used to be very special, we both have changed over the years. We are not the same couple we were when we first met." Ending behaviors reflect new rules of contact: "It would be good for both of us not to see so much of each other." "I wish you would stop coming over all the time." Finally, when the relationship is over, the participants state their preferences for dealing with each other in the future: "I don't want to see you anymore." "We can get together once in a while, but I only want us to be friends and nothing more."

The stages of coming together and coming apart are complex and continuous as we move into, through, and out of relationships. Knapp and Vangelisti acknowledge that not all relationships move through each of the escalating and deescalating stages at the same pace or always in sequential order, but they state most relationships go through the interaction stages systematically and sequentially. They also suggest it is possible for people to skip steps during both the growth process and the deterioration of a relationship. You might have had or heard of relationships that go from the initiating stage—"Hi, my name is …"—to "Let's go to your place so that we can get to know each other better." These relationships move from the initiating step right to the intensifying step. Termination may also occur suddenly and without warning in this situation, thus violating or skipping all the steps of coming apart. For example, in *Runaway Bride*, a popular movie in the late 1990s, Julia Roberts portrays a character who falls in love with several different men, but in each case, she leaves them standing at the altar because she does not believe the relationship is right.

Duck's Phases of Dissolution

Communication scholar Steve Duck offers an alternate theory to that of Knapp and Vangelisti about how relationships dissolve. He theorizes that dissolving relationships go through a rather complex decision-making process and don't always follow a specific order of stages. According to Duck, relationship breakups often occur sporadically, inconsistently, and with uncertainty over a period of time, but in deciding what to do about a potential breakup, a person proceeds through the following four phases: intrapyschic, dyadic, social, and grave-dressing. The termination of the relationship is strongly affected by the partners' social networks, and the influence of others outside the relationship is often reflected in any or all of the phases of a breakup. The uncertainty, or "on again, off again" approach, some relationships take as they dissolve defines the phases of Duck's approach.[28]

THE INTRAPSYCHIC PHASE During the intrapsychic phase, people begin to internally assess their dissatisfaction with each other. This phase involves perception, assessments, and decision making about the relationship. In this phase, communication may actually decrease at times, and each of the partners might seek comfort from others outside the relationship. The intrapsychic phase is similar in some respects to the differentiating stage, in which differences between the individuals in the relationship become noticeable to at least one of them. Communication may decrease or become more self-centered and thus lead to more conflict and argument rather than negotiation.

THE DYADIC PHASE In the dyadic phase, those in a relationship discuss the status of their relationship. The interactions vary from cooperative to uncooperative in discussing the partners' unsatisfying traits or behaviors and whether to address the problem or to separate. Much negotiation, persuasion, and argument take place during this phase; each person tries to get the other person to comply or change in some fashion. Sometimes the dyadic phase ends with an agreement to repair the relationship, but if it doesn't, the relationship may eventually move on to the next phase. The dyadic phase would be consistent with what may occur as a relationship moves through Knapp and Vangelisti's differentiating stage to the circumscribing stage. This phase is likely to be characterized by more conflict and less negotiation; the partners might also avoid topics or issues that may inflame the interaction. Thus, when interaction occurs during this phase, it moves toward more impersonal or formalized conversations, as illustrated in the circumscribing stage.

THE SOCIAL PHASE In the social phase, the relationship difficulties become more public within the context of family, friends, coworkers, or other acquaintances. Most relationships that break up, except possibly secret love affairs, do not stand completely alone and usually have an impact on others outside the dissolving relationship. For example, the children are usually affected if parents separate. During this phase, the opinions and feelings of others often have an impact on what a couple eventually does. The children of a married couple might influence the couple to stay together in spite of their differences. The concern might become, "What, if any, kind of relationship should be continued? How should it be presented to others?" Other issues include where to place blame, how to save face, how to explain what has happened, and who should be sought out for support or approval for the decision.

The social phase includes most aspects of the remaining three stages of Knapp and Vangelisti's coming-apart process: stagnating, avoiding, and termination. It is clear the relationship has reached what appears to be an impasse, and therefore it is most unlikely to continue. However, the major difference between the two approaches is that Duck emphasizes the impact of the relationship breakup on others as well as the influence of others on the relationship. Knapp and Vangelisti's stages do not address this issue directly. According to Duck, the individuals seek out the approval of others, whereas Knapp and Vangelisti are more concerned with how individuals justify the breakup to themselves.

THE GRAVE-DRESSING PHASE Duck names the final phase *grave-dressing* because after the breakup, each partner gives an account of why the relationship ended. This phase includes some similarities to the termination stage, because it is in this stage, according to Knapp and Vangelisti, that individuals begin to justify to others why the relationship had to end. These explanations aid in the healing process, in coping, and in recovery from the breakup itself. It is not unusual for one or both individuals in the relationship to explain to others why the relationship dissolved. For example, if the relationship ended on friendly terms, you might hear statements such as, "It just didn't work—we were too different" or "We needed time to grow, so we decided not to see each other for a while." If the relationship ended on unfriendly terms, however, you might hear explanations such as, "He always wanted things for himself—he was selfish" or "She never seemed to be satisfied with what I'd do for her." Men and women handle relationship failures differently. Women tend to confide in their friends, whereas men tend to start a new relationship as quickly as possible.[29]

Not all relationships, however, end with mutual agreement the relationship should be terminated. You are probably aware of situations where one partner did not want to lose the other, but the person ending the relationship simply saw no reason to continue it. In such a case, the grave-dressing phase is usually one sided; the person ending the relationship might say, "It just wasn't working," or "I have found someone new." Meanwhile, the person who does not want the relationship to end looks for a way to keep it going and cannot face the fact it is over. The person tries to justify to themselves and others the termination is only temporary and the other person will come to his or her senses and return.

Each phase poses certain communication challenges. Duck refers to the challenges as "social management problems." In the intrapsychic phase, one must have the ability to discuss the perceived differences with one's partner. In the social phase, one must be able to discuss the breakup with others outside the relationship. Clearly, as relationships move into and out of various phases, communication plays a significant role.

Simply put, relationships can be messy at times. This is true for even the best and most stable relationships because of the tensions that arise in all relationships from time to time. In fact, most romantic partners converse with each other less than a few hours a day, rarely self-disclose, often fight, on occasion become verbally and even physically violent, are rude to each other, and are more concerned with themselves than with sharing intimacies.[30] It is therefore not unusual that relationships don't measure up to the ideal because most relationships—whether romantic, family, close friendship, or work related—encounter daily challenges. The conflicts that emerge from these challenges are discussed in the following section.

Interpersonal Conflict

14.4 **Explain** what interpersonal conflict is, what causes it, why it can be beneficial, and strategies to manage and resolve it.

Conflict, like dialectic tensions in relationships, occur for a variety of reasons, most are actions to block or interfere with others' interests because of incompatibility perceptions.

Conflict, according to communication scholars William Wilmot and Joyce Hocker, "is an expressed struggle between at least two interdependent parties who perceive incompatible goals, scarce resources, and interference from others in achieving their goals."[31] The key terms in the definition are *expressed struggle, interdependent parties, incompatible goals, scarce resources,* and *interference from others.* Suppose you want to go to a dance on Friday evening with several of your friends, but your best friend wants to go to a movie. Both of you explain what you want to do (expressed struggle): you want to go to the dance, neither of you wants to go out without including the other on Friday evening (interdependent parties), you cannot go to both the dance and the movie in the same evening (incompatible goals), neither of you can afford to do both because of time and money (scarce resources), and your other friends will not

conflict

An expressed struggle between at least two interdependent parties who perceive incompatible goals, scarce resources, and interference from others in achieving their goals.

consider going to the movie (interference). You have incompatible goals, and it seems one person must lose for the other to win.

The word *conflict* almost automatically brings to mind such things as fight, abuse, aggressiveness, violence, mistreatment, argument, disagreement, quarrel, clash, and differences. None of these words has a positive tone or gives us any reason to believe anything good can come from conflict. Wilmot and Hocker suggest words such as exciting, strengthening, helpful, clarifying, growth producing, creative, courageous, enriching, intimate, opportune, and energizing could also be associated with conflict.[32]

We often exert much energy to avoid conflict, when in fact disagreements and differences of opinion can ultimately lead to compromise and far better solutions for everyone. Conflict plays such a major role in our lives that we need to understand its causes, why it is often destructive, and how we can better manage it or at least control it.

What Causes Conflict?

Conflict occurs on many different levels, in all aspects of our lives, whether in our classes, our university, our communities, our organizations, or our country. Conflict is a natural and normal part of any relationship. Suppose you asked a large number of people to describe the major factor that contributes to conflict in interpersonal relationships. How do you think they would answer? The number one answer you would likely receive is poor or inadequate communication. However, if you asked the same people for the best way to resolve or eliminate conflict, they would more than likely also say communication. Isn't it interesting that communication is cited as both a cause and a solution for resolving conflict? We often attribute the causes for and the resolution of conflict to "communication" and not to us. In other words, we don't take responsibility for conflict but rather blame it on our communication. If we use communication effectively and carefully, we can reduce or at least manage conflict more readily.

Faulty communication is a social factor that can lead to conflict. Individuals communicate in ways that anger or annoy others, even though it might not be the communicator's intention to do so. Have you ever been harshly criticized in a way you believed was unjustified, insensitive, unfair, and not the least bit helpful? If you have, you know this type of perceived criticism leaves you feeling upset, angry, and ready to attack, thus setting the stage for conflict, even though the criticism might not have been a result of incompatible goals.

A faulty attribution, such as errors concerning the causes of others' behaviors, is another social factor that may lead to conflict.[33] When individuals believe their goals or interests have been thwarted, they generally try to determine reasons. Was it poor planning on their part? Was it simply a case of bad luck? Was it a lack of the appropriate resources to reach the goal? Or was it because of someone's intentional interference? If it is concluded that the last-mentioned is the reason, the seeds for conflict may be planted, even if the other person actually had nothing to do with the situation.

Another cause of conflict is faulty perceptions and our tendency to perceive our own views as objective and reflective of reality but to perceive others' views as biased or not based in reality. As a result, stereotyping or prejudices create conflicting views by magnifying differences between our views and those of others, especially others whom we believe are different from us. Differences may be magnified for many of us when we confront cultures different from our own. For example, some Americans believe all Muslims are terrorists and refuse to accept that most Muslims are peace-loving people.

Finally, personality traits or characteristics can lead to conflict. This is especially true of type A individuals: those who are highly competitive, like to win,

Making Connections for Success

Conflict Online

Conflict can occur just as easily online as it does in face-to-face communication. Some people believe there is a tendency to communicate more forcefully and directly online than in face-to-face interactions. For example, a colleague emails you a political cartoon that belittles your preferred candidate in an election. Your colleague tells you your candidate is an idiot. You send back a political cartoon poking fun at his or her political candidate. Thus, rather than resolving conflicts or differences, the conflicts tend to escalate more readily online.

1. Why does online conflict occur so easily?
2. What can you do to reduce online conflicts?
3. Create a guide for improving online communication etiquette. What advice would you give others to reduce or prevent online conflicts?

For help, search the Internet, using the keywords "online etiquette."

are always in a hurry, and are relatively irritable when others interfere with attaining goals. Type A individuals, because of their nature, are more likely to get into conflicts than type B individuals, who are calmer and less irritable about events around them.

So, what causes conflict? Conflict does not stem solely from incompatible goals. On the contrary, conflict often results from social factors such as long-standing grudges or resentment, the desire for revenge, inaccurate social perceptions, ineffective communication, and similar factors. Although the major cause of conflict may be incompatible goals, the social causes of conflict are also factors to consider.

Does Conflict Have to Be Destructive?

Conflict does *not* have to be destructive. It becomes so when the involved parties are unwilling to negotiate their differences and instead engage in harmful and hurtful tactics—a win-at-any-cost approach. Here are some ways in which conflict can or may be destructive:

- When the resolution of a conflict ends with a winner and a loser
- When individuals act too aggressively, when they withdraw from each other, when they withhold their feelings from each other, or when they accuse each other of causing their problems
- When it prevents us from doing our work or feeling good about ourselves
- When it forces us to do things that we do not want to do
- When the outcome is more important than the relationship
- When conflict is a form of bullying and there is a power difference between parties— "the winner takes all"[34]

Of course, not all relationship breakups result from conflict, nor are they all necessarily destructive or harmful. However, when conflict results in the termination of relationships and leaves one or both of the parties feeling foolish, inadequate, or angry, it is usually destructive and hurtful.

When Is Conflict Beneficial?

Doubtless, most of us see more disadvantages than benefits in conflict. However, not all conflict is destructive. For example, it is fine to have conflicts over ideas, but it is not acceptable or appropriate to attack someone personally for his or her ideas. It can be beneficial to have disagreements or conflicting views about ideas because of the potential to exchange valuable information or to gain a better understanding of an issue.

Here are other potential benefits of conflict:

- It can bring out problems that need to be solved.
- It can bring people together to clarify their goals and look for new ways to do things.
- It can eliminate resentments and help people understand each other.
- It can bring out creativity in solving our differences.
- It can produce acceptable solutions that allow people to live more in harmony with each other.
- It can help people pay attention to other points of view.
- It can bring new life into a relationship and strengthen it.

Constructive conflict is characterized by a we-orientation, cooperation, and flexibility.[35] If possible, it is good to reach a solution agreeable to all. This does not mean we have to feel warm and fuzzy while the differences are worked out, but it does mean that conflicting parties must be willing to negotiate, respect the other party's differences, and cooperate to resolve differences.

Constructive conflict can be frustrating and difficult as well as contentious; it requires competent communicators who are knowledgeable, skillful, sensitive, committed, and ethical in resolving their differences. Many people believe the more they discuss their differences, the more likely they will be to resolve them. Of course, that is possible, but most of the time more communication leads to further difference and disagreements. If, however, the parties who try to resolve differences understand and use conflict management strategies in their communication, rather than just more of the same communication, they are more likely to reach some agreement and resolution.

What Are Useful Strategies for Conflict Management or Resolution in Interpersonal Relationships?

Because most interpersonal conflicts can be costly in terms of time, stress, energy, and other resources, people experiencing conflict generally choose to resolve their differences as quickly as possible if they can. Of course, in some situations conflicts are not confronted, and sometimes conflicts go on for an indefinite time; but, generally speaking, these conflicts are not beneficial to a relationship's growth. We need to learn how to deal with conflict in beneficial ways. How we deal with disagreements or conflict can either strengthen a relationship or split it apart. In other words, conflict can be managed well, or it can be managed poorly.

The research literature refers mainly to five options to resolve conflict: withdrawing, accommodating, forcing, negotiating, and collaboration.[36] Each strategy involves a different outcome, which can be positive, negative, or both in its effect on relationships involved in conflict.

WITHDRAWING When we choose to avoid further conflict by either psychologically or physically removing ourselves from the situation, we are withdrawing. This can be done by changing the topic, cracking jokes, ignoring, or leaving the situation altogether. Usually, when a withdrawal strategy is used, the conflict is temporarily avoided, but it really doesn't go away. Withdrawal is a temporary escape from the conflict, but both parties know it has not been resolved.

Stonewalling is a powerful form of avoiding conflict.[37] When people exhibit stony silence, refuse to discuss problems, or physically remove themselves from another person who is complaining, disagreeing, or attacking, they are said to be stonewalling. Consider the following discussion between a mother and daughter:

MELISSA: We need to discuss your unwillingness to set a budget. Your use of the credit card is going to bankrupt your father and me.

TIFF: It isn't a problem, and there is nothing to talk about.

MELISSA: We have to talk about it because you're ruining our credit.

TIFF: Get a life; I am not ruining anything. I'll pay you back. [leaves the house]

Tiff is stonewalling by withdrawing from the conflict and claims she has everything under control. She believes discussing her use of the credit card will only intensify the conflict between her and her mother. Her mother is likely becoming frustrated with Tiff's stonewalling, which can also communicate Tiff's disapproval, self-righteousness, indifference, and defensiveness toward her mother.

Research indicates avoidance is frequently used to manage conflict.[38] Many of us want to avoid conflict whenever we can. One research study found that 50 percent of the time, college students used avoiding or withdrawing strategies to keep conflict from escalating.[39] Other research studies found that men use stonewalling more often than women do because of their fear they won't be able to control themselves.[40]

An advantage to withdrawal is that it gives time for one or both of the involved individuals to think about it and to calm down before again trying to deal with the conflict. The disadvantage is that it can create more hostility and ultimately make dealing with the conflict more difficult in the long run. So withdrawal can be a useful strategy, but it is also limited in its ability to truly resolve the conflict.

ACCOMMODATING   A person who uses accommodating as a means for managing or resolving conflicts does not assert his or her own needs but rather prefers to go along to get along. This form of conflict management requires one person to yield or give in to another person's needs and desires.[41] The accommodator sets aside his or her concerns in favor of pleasing the other person because holding the relationship together is more important than continuing the conflict. In some situations, when someone accommodates another to resolve a conflict, the accommodating person gives up because the conflict just isn't worth the stress and destruction of the relationship, so in a sense it is a win–win situation. Of course, if one person always accommodates another in a committed relationship, there is winning and losing, and that imbalance can eventually lead to future conflicts.

Accommodation tactics, according to communication scholars Alan Sillars and Bill Wilmot, include giving up or giving in, disengagement, denial of needs, or a desire to get along.[42] When a person *gives up or gives in* to the other person, he or she basically says, "Have it your way," "I don't want to fight about this," or "Whatever." If the person *disengages,* he or she says, "I don't care," "I don't want any part of it," or "I don't have the time to fight about this." If the person *denies* his or her own needs, the person says, "I am OK; you go without me" or "I can take care of it, even if I have to stay longer." Finally, if the person is motivated by *desire to get along,* he or she says, "It's more important to work together than it is for me to get what I want" or "I am unhappy and miserable when we fight. Let's let this go and start over again. I don't even know why we are fighting."

FORCING   Forcing is a strategy where one person has power and dominance over another. It can result in aggression and could include threats, criticisms, hostile remarks, jokes, ridicule, sarcasm, intimidation, fault finding, coercion, or manipulation. Extreme cases of forcing include date rape, child abuse, battering, bullying,[43] and sexual harassment. This is a lose–lose situation. The person with the power claims victory, and the other person loses. However, in this situation, the competition is unfair because one individual has more control and power over the other, which ensures a victory regardless of the virtue of the other person's position.

Of course, on occasion the dominance of one person could serve the relationship, as in an emergency situation when a decision must be quickly made. However, the essence of force is to pressure others to agree with something so we get what we want. The more force we use to get others to do what we want or to agree with us, the more likely it is that resentment will increase, leading to more destructive types of conflicts.

NEGOTIATING   Negotiating usually involves a give-and-take process and leads to each party having some satisfaction and some dissatisfaction with the outcome. In other words, "Give a little and get a little." Some people interpret this to be a lose–lose style of conflict management. Compromise only truly works if there is shared power because if one of the parties is perceived as powerless, there is no compelling need to compromise.[44]

Many of us are led to believe compromise or negotiation is a good way for both parties in a conflict to resolve their differences. We are told it is fair because it means both parties win something and both lose something. Thus compromise appears on the surface to be a reasonable approach to conflict, although it has potential problems. The most obvious problem is that the quality of the solution might be reduced. This is especially true if one of the parties in the conflict actually had a better solution that had to be compromised to reach agreement. Compromise can become an easy way out and might prevent creative new solutions from emerging. In addition, the compromise approach is often not the first choice in personal relationships because it frequently requires one or both parties to give in or give up on what they want.

Despite the negative aspects of negotiating or compromising, it might be the only possible way to approach a conflict. This is most likely true when the parties involved have equal power, if no other alternative is available, if the outcome is not critical, if essential values are not undermined, or if the settlement is only temporary until a better one can be found.

COLLABORATION   Collaboration is a strategy of conflict management that requires cooperation and mutual respect. It usually involves a problem-solving approach and addresses all concerns of both parties to arrive at a mutually satisfying solution. It is a "we" rather than a "me" approach to negotiation. It might require extra effort by both parties because more resources and considerations of new options that meet the approval of both parties might be needed.

For collaboration to work as a strategy, both parties must recognize a conflict exists, and they must want to find creative ways to resolve their differences. When both parties recognize a conflict, they usually engage in some sort of confrontation, which is the opposite of avoidance. Degrees of confrontation range from the very violent (often depicted in the media) to the respectful. For collaboration to be successful, both parties must be willing to resolve their differences, treat each other as equals, be honest and open in their differences, be empathetic toward each other, and be willing to listen to each other's points of view.

The collaboration strategy is usually considered a win–win situation for both sides in the conflict. Both sides believe they have accomplished or gained something from the solution because of their willingness to listen to each other concerning the issues. In addition, when both parties believe they have the opportunity to voice their opinions and they have agreed in good faith to settle the dispute, it truly is a win–win situation. The collaboration strategy to manage conflict is the best strategy for a relationship, because it shows that each party cares about the other's wellbeing and interests. According to Wilmot and Hocker, collaborating, as a conflict management style, produces consistently positive outcomes that leave the participants satisfied with their decisions, the process, and the growth in their interpersonal relationship.[45]

Many scholars agree conflict is inevitable in all relationships and it need not be destructive. It often produces stronger and more durable relationships. Conflict in itself should be considered neither negative nor destructive, but a natural part of any relationship.

Relational Repair Strategies

For situations when both parties want to preserve the relationship, Steve Duck, a communication scholar we read about earlier in our discussion of dissolution phases, suggests the following tactics for repairing a damaged relationship between couples:

- Engage in more open and honest communication and exhibit a willingness to listen to the other person with an open mind.
- Be willing to bring out the other person's positive side.
- Evaluate the potential rewards and costs for keeping the relationship together versus the rewards and costs for changing or ending it.
- Seek out the support of others to help keep the relationship together.
- Both parties must be willing to focus on the positive aspects of their relationship.
- Both parties must be willing to reinterpret the other's behaviors as positive and well intentioned.
- Both parties have to be willing to reduce negativity and keep a balanced perspective.[46]

Repairing relationships requires cooperation and mutual agreement; both parties must want to preserve the relationship. Relationship repair also requires effective interpersonal communication.

Improving Communication Competence in Relationships

14.5 **Apply** effective interpersonal communication skills and competencies in personal and professional relationships.

The goal of this text is to encourage readers to become competent communicators who can connect with others and develop relationships, whether personal or professional. Communication scholars Brant Burleson and Wendy Samter consider the following interpersonal skills important in developing and maintaining relationships: *conversational skill* (the ability to initiate, maintain, and terminate enjoyable casual conversations), *referential skill* (the ability to convey information clearly and unambiguously), *ego supportive skill* (the ability to make another person feel good about himself or herself), *comforting skill* (the ability to make others feel better when depressed, sad, or upset), *persuasive skill* (the ability to sway people to modify their thoughts and behaviors), *narrative skill* (the ability to entertain through jokes, gossip, stories, and the like), and *regulations* (the ability to help someone who has violated a social custom to fix the mistake effectively).[47] How would you rate yourself on each of the above communication skills? Most of us would likely rate ourselves as fairly good at most with room for improvement in each of them.

In the remainder of this chapter, we will provide suggestions to help you become a more competent communicator, one who possesses the following characteristics:

1. Effective communicators address issues clearly and try to avoid ambiguous or abstract statements.
2. Effective communicators are likely to treat others with respect and therefore would not deliberately yell abuses or throw temper tantrums.
3. Effective communicators know that praise, making the other person feel special, and telling that person what he or she wants to hear will most likely produce desired responses.[48]

At first glance, these statements make a lot of sense. However, they are characterized by shades of gray. Each of us can probably think of times when being a little abstract or ambiguous was better than being too clear or direct in our communication. In certain situations, getting angry or throwing a tantrum might be appropriate to get across a point. You can probably also think of situations in which too much praise or too much agreement can lead to mistrust. Interpersonal situations often require a variety of communication strategies, some of which may violate expected norms.

Although we do not endorse unethical behaviors, disrespect, or rudeness, some situations demand unusual strategies.

The following section offers a variety of behaviors and actions to improve interpersonal communication.

Establish Supportive and Caring Relationships

Establishing supportive and caring relationships is important to our well-being, and this process is generally easier when communication is both positive and supportive.[49] Eric Simon and Leslie Baxter, communication scholars, describe the following positive strategies for romantic exchanges:

1. **Act** cheerful and positive when talking to the other.
2. **Do** favors for the other or help with tasks.
3. **Initiate** celebrations of special events from your shared past, such as the first time you met.
4. **Do** things to surprise the other person.
5. **Suggest** that you go out to eat together at a favorite or special restaurant.
6. **Create** a romantic environment, perhaps with candlelight and flowers.
7. **Give** the other person items of sentimental value, such as gifts or cards.
8. **Suggest** ways to spend time doing things together.[50]

Assurances include the following verbal and nonverbal actions:

1. **Physically** display affection through kisses and hugs.
2. **Express** aloud to the other person what it would be like without him or her.
3. **Reminisce** aloud with the other about good times you had together in the past.
4. **Say** "I love you."
5. **Express** long-term commitment to the relationship.
6. **Act** playfully toward the other person.[51]

The research findings suggest that engaging in behaviors such as these increases relationship commitment and satisfaction. However, Simon and Baxter found females were more likely than males to report use of assurance and romance strategies, which suggests that females tend to undertake more relationship maintenance activity than do their male partners.[52]

Nurture a Supportive Environment

Positive and supportive communication occurs in caring, open, flexible, warm, animated, and receptive environments. In such environments, communication is constructive and centers on the individuals and their relationship. Following are some descriptions of how people feel when constructive communication is at the center of the relationship.[53] One of the most effective and constructive means of demonstrating care and support for someone is to invite more communication.

Positive and supportive communication environments are caring, open, flexible, warm, animated, and receptive.

Invite More Communication

Many of us listen to others express their feelings and then immediately express our own. This gives the impression we don't even acknowledge the other's existence, let alone what he or she has said. In contrast, skilled and caring communicators do not usually respond immediately with ideas, judgments, or feelings or express their own views. Instead, they invite others to express more of their thoughts by responding with noncommittal responses such as these:

Interesting.

Uh-huh.

You did, huh?

I see.

Oh.

Really?

Or they might be more direct in asking the other person to continue, saying, for example,

That's interesting. Go on.

Tell me about it.

Let's discuss it.

Tell me everything.

I understand. What else happened?

Such invitations to talk can contribute much to the development of a meaningful relationship. The willingness to listen and reserve judgment creates a positive and supportive environment that, in effect, tells people they are valuable, they are loved, and they have control over their own behavior.

Summary

Interpersonal Communication Competence

Objective 14.1 **Characterize** the importance of interpersonal communication competence.

Competent communicators recognize they will not always communicate perfectly in every situation; adapt and know when to be empathic and comforting; know when to speak out aggressively and when to be reserved and more deferential; understand values, beliefs, attitudes, and feelings; know how to self-monitor; and recognize it is a two-way responsibility for effective interactions.

Relationship Formation

Objective 14.2 **Identify** the stages of relationship development and growth.

How and why a relationship develops may depend on interpersonal attraction and how the people manage the stages of coming together or growth of the relationship.

- Interpersonal relationships depend on interpersonal attraction.
- Interpersonal attraction is the desire to interact with someone and is based on physical attraction, personality, rewards, proximity, or similarities.

- Coming together includes the following stages: initiating, experimenting, intensifying, integrating, and bonding.
- Relational maintenance behaviors or strategies help to sustain relationships so they grow and thrive. These include positivity, openness, assurances, blending social networks, and sharing tasks.

Relationship Dissolution

Objective 14.3 **Identify** the stages of relationship deterioration and dissolution.

Not every relationship is destined to last a lifetime. The way both parties handle a relationship's dissolution can affect the well-being of both.

- Warning signs a relationship is in trouble include aggressive behavior, lies, and betrayal.
- The coming-apart process has five stages—differentiating, circumscribing, stagnating, avoiding, and terminating—according to Mark Knapp and Anita Vangelisti.
- Duck's phases of dissolution include the intrapsychic, dyadic, social, and grave-dressing phases.

Interpersonal Conflict

Objective 14.4 Explain what interpersonal conflict is, what causes it, why it can be beneficial, and strategies to manage and resolve it.

Conflict is an expressed struggle between at least two interdependent parties who perceive incompatible goals, scarce resources, and interference from others. Conflict can occur on many different levels in a variety of situations and contexts.

- The number one cause of most conflicts is inadequate communication.
- Conflict does not have to be destructive.
- Conflict can be beneficial and lead to stronger and better relationships.
- Each conflict resolution strategy involves different outcomes, which can be either positive or negative in their effects on relationships. In the withdrawal strategy, we choose to avoid further conflict. In the accommodating strategy, we do not assert our own needs but prefer to go along. In the forcing strategy, one person has power and dominance over another person. Negotiating is a give-and-take process and can lead to each party's having some satisfaction and some dissatisfaction with the outcome. Collaboration requires cooperation and mutual respect.
- To help restore or possibly save a relationship, competent communicators know how to use repair strategies and effective interpersonal communication.

Improving Communication Competence in Relationships

Objective 14.5 Apply effective interpersonal communication skills and competencies in personal and professional relationships.

Interpersonal skills are important in developing and maintaining relationships: *conversational skill* (the ability to initiate, maintain, and terminate enjoyable casual conversations), *referential skill* (the ability to convey information clearly and unambiguously), *ego supportive skill* (the ability to make another person feel good about himself or herself), *comforting skill* (the ability to make others feel better when depressed, sad, or upset), *persuasive skill* (the ability to sway people to modify their thoughts and behaviors), *narrative skill* (the ability to entertain through jokes, gossip, stories, and the like), and *regulations* (the ability to help someone who has violated a social custom to fix the mistake effectively).

- A supportive and caring relationship is important to our well-being; the process is generally easier when communication is both positive and supportive.
- In a supportive environment, communication between individuals usually reflects caring, openness, flexibility, warmth, animation, and receptivity.
- The best way to develop and maintain relationships is to invite more effective communication.

Discussion Starters

1. In your opinion, what communication behaviors play the strongest role in the development of relationships? Explain.
2. What did you agree with and disagree with in the explanation of the stages of relationship development?
3. Compare and contrast Knapp and Vangelisti's coming-apart stages with Duck's dissolution stages. What stages best describe these stages for you?
4. Describe what you think it takes to have a lasting relationship.
5. In relationship breakups you have had, were there coming-apart stages similar to what either Knapp and

Vangelisti or Duck presented? How were they similar and how were they different?

6. Describe a conflict of which you were a part that resulted in a positive outcome.
7. How has online communication affected your relationships–the quality of communication messages, and conflict?
8. What advice would you give someone who wanted to improve his or her interpersonal communication?
9. Do you know any competent interpersonal communicators? What attributes make them competent?

Chapter 15
Group and Team Communication

 ## Learning Objectives

This chapter will help you:

15.1 Understand the differences among a group, team, or project or work team and their roles in our everyday lives.

15.2 Explain how and why groups are formed, and how culture influences group formation.

15.3 Describe the characteristics of small groups.

15.4 Explain how a group's culture, size, and norms affect group communication.

15.5 Distinguish among different types of groups—both face-to-face and social media.

15.6 Describe the role of ethics in small-group communication.

15.7 Explain the advantages and disadvantages of participating in groups and how to overcome the disadvantages.

Making Everyday Connections

Amy and her classmates Mark, Sally, and Bethany are spending an evening in the library, working on a group project for their management class. Another group member, Susan, commutes to campus and has a young child at home. Since the group is meeting late at night, Susan joins the group meeting via Skype. Amy prepared an agenda and attempts to keep the group focused. Bethany is drifting in and out of paying attention, checking her texts with her boyfriend. About 10 minutes into the meeting, since she is joining the group via Skype, Susan begins to have trouble hearing what the other group members are saying. Whenever Susan tries to say something, only half of what she says comes through clearly. Mark becomes very frustrated because he has to repeat himself. Annoyed, Sally opens her Facebook page and begins instant messaging with a few friends about other topics. Amy struggles to keep the group on task. Frustrated with the Skype troubles, Amy tells Susan because of the problems with Skype she will fill her in on what the group has accomplished in class. Amy continues the meeting. She asks specific questions of Bethany and Sally to gauge their opinions and pull them into the conversation. Bethany puts her phone away and Sally closes her Facebook page. The group works together for the next hour. After they finish, Amy, Bethany, Mark, and Sally head toward home but decide to stop for a late-night snack. They really enjoy each other's

company and find that they have a lot of things in common with each other.

When Amy returns to her dorm room, she quickly checks her email, scans Facebook, and sees that group member Bethany has texted to ask if anything is due for class tomorrow. Amy briefly replies, puts her iPhone on her nightstand, and tries to fall asleep. Just as she is about to drift into dreamland, she receives another text message. It's Susan, apologizing for the Skype problems and asking what time the group is meeting tomorrow. Amy replies and exchanges a few more texts. Exhausted, Amy tweets, "Long day ... gnite all!"

Questions to Think About

1. How would you characterize the relationships of this group?

2. What are some of Amy's strengths and weaknesses as leader?

3. Based on your experiences, describe the benefits and consequences of using social media while doing a group project.

4. Aside from the obvious problems with Skype detailed above, what other challenges might social media pose as a group tries to accomplish its task?

5. Describe your experiences working in groups.

Employment and hiring data clearly indicate that teamwork and working in groups are hiring prerequisites and necessary abilities for a successful career with most organizations. Many variables contribute to a group's success or failure. Prior success cannot guarantee a group will produce similarly successful results. Nonetheless, understanding key principles and factors, along with improving your competencies as a group member or group leader, can increase the chances for achieving personal satisfaction and group success.

This chapter explains how group members communicate, what a small group is and its defining characteristics, the purposes groups can serve, the applicable social media and their effects on group interaction, the importance of ethical behavior in groups, and the advantages and disadvantages of groups. Chapter 16 explores leadership, member participation, problem solving and decision making, conflict management, and group performance evaluation.

Small-Group Communication: Making the Connection to Our Everyday Lives

15.1 **Understand** the differences among a group, team, or project or work team and their roles in our everyday lives.

Small-group communication requires a variety of communication competencies, including the ability to ask effective questions, listen, deal with interpersonal relationships, resolve conflicts, and to present ideas clearly. In addition, constructive group

Making Connections for Success

Group Members

Think about two or three groups you recently observed or were a member.

1. Create a list of the communicative characteristics or behaviors of the ideal group member.

2. Create a list of the communicative characteristics or behaviors of those who have deviated from the ideal group member.

3. Do the same for the group leader.

4. In what ways do your communicative characteristics or behaviors reflect or deviate from those of the ideal member?

communication requires that group members respect one another, provide credible information, support each other, foster a positive climate, challenge each other's ideas and positions, persuade each other, and hold high ethical standards.

If you were to list the times you have participated in groups during the past month, you would have evidence of how common group participation is in your life. The family is probably the predominant small group. However, if you are like most, you have participated in many groups, some small and some large, such as completing a class assignment or project or discussing a dorm, team, social, family, campus, or community issue.

What a Group or Team Is

For our purposes, we define a **group** as a collection of individuals who influence one another, have a common purpose, take on roles, are interdependent, and interact. If any element is missing, what exists is a collection of independent people, not a group. A group of students standing at a corner waiting for a bus, for example, meet only some criteria of a group. They have a common purpose (transportation), they may interact, and they may make an impression on one another. But they do not constitute a group according to our definition because they are not interdependent and they do not take on roles. They do share certain basic goals, such as getting to a destination safely. They don't expect to interact in the future, however, and usually don't perceive themselves as part of a group—unless some type of emergency occurs, which will change their status radically.

So what determines whether, and to what extent, we perceive several persons as forming a group? Coherent groups—ones high in connectivity or belonging—show the following characteristics: (1) Members interact with one another often, (2) the group is important to its members, (3) members share common goals and outcomes, and (4) the members are similar to one another in important ways. The more a group shares these characteristics, the more it is seen by its members as a coherent entity—a *group* to which they choose to belong.[1]

Small-group communication involves the exchange of information among a relatively small number of people, ideally five to seven, who have a common purpose, such as solving a problem, making a decision, or sharing information. Effective group communication requires an honest, flexible, assertive, enthusiastic, and tolerant communication style. Effective group members recognize the importance of all group members' input and ensure the opportunity for everyone to participate. They are willing not only to listen to others but also to discuss ideas and issues, whether they agree or disagree with them.

group

A collection of individuals who influence one another, have a common purpose, take on roles, are interdependent, and interact together.

Project or Work Teams

Because groups known as project teams or work teams are so common in our society and in the classroom, we focus on them here. Many scholars who study groups believe a distinction exists between group involvement and team involvement.[2]

The photo on the left shows a collection of people who happen to be in the same place at the same time; they do not make up a group. The photo on the right shows a group in which the members interact with one another and share common goals and outcomes. Moreover, they feel they are, in fact, part of a group (team).

team

A special form of group that is characterized by a close-knit relationship among people with different and complementary abilities and by a strong sense of identity.

A **team** is a special form of group, characterized by close-knit relationships among people with different and complementary abilities and by a strong sense of identity. Similar to groups, teams involve interaction, interdependence, common goals, personality, commitment, cohesiveness, and rules. Teams do differ from groups, however, in three ways:

1. Teams are more likely to consist of people with diverse abilities. For example, a surgical team might include several surgeons, an anesthetist, and a number of nurses, each contributing a different skill or perspective to the operation. Both a group and a team consist of several people, each working toward the common goal of the group, whereas teams also have individuals with a specialization in, or a different perspective on, a common situation. For example, players on a football team usually have specific specialties or roles that help contribute to the team's overall effectiveness.

2. Teams usually develop more interdependence. A sports team, for example, usually cannot succeed unless all the players believe they are part of a unit, whereas in a problem-solving group, members might work independently, only coming together to present and discuss each other's solutions. They might eventually see themselves as a unit, or not, depending on the group's communication and cohesiveness, but this wouldn't be necessary to the group's overall success.

3. Members of teams have a high degree of group identity and are more likely to identify themselves as team members than as individuals who happen to be on a team.[3]

Thus, all teams consist of groups, but not all groups are teams.

Project or work teams have existed for years in almost every type of organization. Typically, project or work teams consist of a variety of individuals who get together to solve problems or make decisions. In a **project team**, the individuals are usually specialists assigned to coordinate the successful completion of an assigned task; for example, the creation of a university's web page might require a web designer, a web programmer, a graphic designer, a marketing specialist, a university administrator, an information technology (IT) specialist, and a legal advisor. Project teams in general work quickly to determine what needs to be done. They often possess little history, usually work under a deadline, and may have difficulty establishing mutually agreed-on relationships.

A **work team** is a group of people responsible for an entire work process or segment of the process that delivers a product or service to an internal or external customer. Work teams usually are subdivisions of a larger group, such as small

project team

Individuals representing different specialties who are assigned to coordinate the successful completion of an assigned task.

work team

A group of people responsible for an entire work process or a segment of the process that delivers a product or service to an internal or external customer.

groups handling different projects within the larger class of students, and can exist for an indefinite time or until a specific project is completed. Work teams can also serve many purposes, including solving problems, making decisions, socializing, and learning. A group of four or five students assigned to a class service project with a community agency could be considered a work team. They are a team if the assignment has clear, well-defined goals; if each member of the group has precisely explained duties and responsibilities; if rules and expectations of members' behaviors have been established; and if team members collaborate to accomplish their goal or goals.

The work team is ideally suited for solving workplace problems. Each person brings his or her own special expertise to the table and coordinates efforts with others on a common solution.

Although some distinctions can be made between groups and teams, they are not dramatic. They actually exist on a continuum; some collections of individuals will have more characteristics of a group, whereas others will more closely constitute a team. At the same time, it is important to note that *all* work teams are also groups, whether large or small, and they must use the same principles and practices of effective group communication if they are to succeed.

Formation and Development of Groups

15.2 **Explain** how and why groups are formed, and how culture influences group formation.

The best known theory or model of group development and process is Tuckman's classic model, which illustrates five stages groups pass through from beginning to end.

- *Forming* is the first stage and occurs when members of the group first meet. The members form initial impressions of each other and start to deal with the task as they focus on getting along with each other. The group, according to Tuckman, avoids conflict, controversy, as well as initial tensions that may arise during initial interactions.

- The second stage, *storming*, occurs when members begin to take on important issues and when differences and emotions about the issues start to surface. It is the stage when individuals argue or defend their position or point of view.

- *Norming* is the third stage. The group has worked through most of its differences and determined the rules and norms for how they will continue to work together. Recognition is given to individual members for their knowledge, skills, or abilities, and the members feel as though they are now part of a group.

- The fourth stage is what Tuckman refers to as *performing*. It is in this stage that members work together as a group. They show high identification with the group and recognize their interdependency. Unfortunately, not every group reaches this stage of development for a number of reasons, the least of which is an inability of the group to work together or failure of members to fully engage in the group's goals.

- The final stage is *adjourning*, in which the group essentially completes its task and is ready to move on to other tasks or to disband.[4]

Of course, many factors influence how a group moves through the various stages and the order in which they occur, or even how long a group remains in a specific stage. Although the model may appear simplistic and not fitting for every group situation, it does illustrate the typical experiences of most who have participated in small groups.

Cultural Influences on Group Formation

Cultural factors, such as an individualistic or collectivistic orientation, can have a profound effect on how people perceive groups and group activities. All cultures vary in the degree to which they emphasize individualism and collectivism. If you have an individualistic orientation, you tend to stress self or personal goals and achievements over group goals and achievements.[5] For example, most North Americans value self-help, self-sufficiency, self-actualization, and personal achievements. According to communication scholars Carolyn Calloway-Thomas, Pamela Cooper, and Cecil Blake, the United States, Canada, Australia, the Netherlands, and New Zealand are nations that tend to foster and celebrate individual accomplishments.[6] Generally, people who have individualistic perspectives find working in groups challenging and often frustrating because they have trouble putting their own goals after those of the group.

If you hold a collectivistic orientation, which is more predominant in Asian and Latin American countries such as Japan, China, Taiwan, Pakistan, Colombia, Guatemala, and Panama, you are likely to put aside your individual goals for the well being of the group.[7] Collectivistic cultures have a "we" consciousness and a tendency to focus on group or team accomplishments. They also have a propensity toward working in groups and find such work to be rewarding and satisfying. For example, American companies often are financially oriented and value individual leadership and autonomy. Employees have clearly defined roles, and are responsible for meeting specific goals. Each employee makes decisions in his or her realm of authority or expertise, and the company defines who can make which decisions and about what. In contrast, Japanese companies tend to take a more intuitive approach to management. Employees' roles are not as precisely defined, and members are expected to work as teams to meet group goals. Decision-making is a group process, with large numbers of people involved in each decision. No culture, however, is entirely individualistic or collectivistic. All cultures constitute a mix of individualism and collectivism, but usually one or the other dominates.[8]

How you contribute to a group may depend on whether you have an individualistic or collectivistic orientation. These two perspectives have implications for group formation and collaboration. See Table 15.1 for a comparison of individualistic and collectivistic approaches to joining and working in groups or teams.

Another force that brings people together to form groups is a *common goal*. Examples of common goals include protesting a change in dormitory visitation rules, fighting a road expansion into a neighborhood, lobbying for a safer community,

Table 15.1 Individualistic and Collectivistic Orientations: A Comparison of Small Groups

Individualistic Assumptions	Collectivistic Assumptions
Individuals make better decisions than groups do.	The group's decision should supersede individual decisions.
Leaders and not the group members should do the planning.	The group should do the planning.
Individuals should be rewarded for their performance.	Reward and recognition should be shared among group members.
Competition among individual group members is good.	Teamwork is more important than competition.
The best way to get things done is to work with individuals as opposed to an entire group.	The group is the best way to accomplish goals.
Groups or teams are often perceived as a waste of time.	The commitment to the group is strongest when the group reaches consensus.

Adapted from S. A. Beebe and J. M. Masterson, *Communicating in Small Groups*, 10th ed. (Boston: Allyn and Bacon, 2015), 18; and J. Mole, *Mind Your Manners: Managing Business Cultures in Europe* (London: Nicholas Brealey Publishing Limited, 1995).

supporting a charity, or working for equal campus access for physically impaired students. The goal itself draws people into a group, even though their approaches to the goal may differ.

Characteristics of Small Groups

15.3 Describe the characteristics of small groups.

Small-group characteristics include interdependence, commitment, cohesiveness, and the gender makeup that give each group its uniqueness. These characteristics also help to determine who will join a group, how well the group functions and achieves its goals, and how members interact.

Interdependence

Probably the most essential characteristic of a small group is **interdependence**—the fact that group members are mutually dependent. Interdependence is reflected in all the other group characteristics; without it there would be no group. Interdependence is built on each member's willingness to subordinate his or her individual desires and goals to accomplish the group's goal.

    Groups function best and are most satisfying for their members when each individual recognizes and respects the crucial role interdependence plays in group processes. A group's success is indeed based on each member's cooperation, accountability, and willingness to work toward a common goal.

interdependence
Mutual dependence of group members on one another.

Commitment

Another important characteristic of a group is commitment—to the task, to the group, and to the other individuals in the group. **Commitment** is the desire of group members to work together to complete their task to the satisfaction of the entire group. Members' commitment often stems from interpersonal attraction, they are drawn to others who seem to have similar interests; commonality of attitudes, beliefs, and values; the fulfillment of interpersonal needs; and the rewards the group can offer. A massive study by the Gallup Organization of over 1.4 million workers in 66 countries found that "trusting that one's coworkers share a commitment to quality is a key to great ... performance."[9] Commitment is essential to group success. It is also essential because without it groups perform as individuals, but with it they become a powerful unit of collective performance.[10]

    Commitment is important to a group's effectiveness and ultimate success. How often have you been involved with other students doing a group assignment in which one or two members did most, if not all, of the work and the others did little or nothing? Those who do little or nothing not only lack commitment, they also make group work frustrating for those who are committed to doing the work. For a group to be truly effective, all members must be committed to each other and to the successful completion of the assigned task.

commitment
The desire of group members to work together to complete a task to the satisfaction of the entire group.

Cohesiveness

As an extension of commitment, **cohesiveness** refers to the attraction group members feel for one another and their willingness to stick together. Consider two groups. In the first, members truly like one another, strongly desire the goals the group seeks, and believe they could not find another better, more satisfactory group. In the second, the opposite is true: Members don't care for one another, they do not share common goals, and actively seek other, more rewarding groups. Which group would exert a stronger pull on its members? The answer should be obvious: the first. The rewards

cohesiveness
The attraction that group members feel for each other and their willingness to stick together; a form of loyalty.

Making Connections for Success

The Challenge: Building Cohesiveness and Trust in Online Groups

Building cohesiveness and trust in online groups may be a bit more difficult than in face-to-face interactions. It requires special effort to ensure that group members get to know each other and know the rules they must follow to be successful and cohesive.

1. Why is group cohesiveness likely to be more difficult in an online group than a face-to-face group?
2. What do you think could be done to ensure cohesiveness within an online group?
3. How could you create a "social space" and encourage its use to obtain cohesion within an online group?
4. In what ways might social media be used to influence individual group members' feelings of cohesion and commitment?

for being in the first group outweigh those of leaving the group. Cohesiveness is based on each member's need to remain in the group and the group's ability to provide members with rewards, making it worthwhile to give time and energy to the group. In a sense, cohesiveness is a form of loyalty or commitment.

However, cohesiveness in a group does not automatically ensure success, and when loyalty is too strong, it can create problems. It can lead to conformity or unwillingness to change an unsuccessful decision or policy. Cohesiveness is a positive force when it attracts members of the group toward one another and increases effective group interaction, but it becomes a negative influence if group members "go along simply to get along" or lose the ability to question group decisions. For example, you may be a member of a club, sorority, fraternity, or team where some members cheated or used illegal drugs, but no one calls them out because of loyalty to the organization, even though these members' actions could ultimately destroy the organization's reputation.

Gender Makeup

The differences between the way individuals display masculine behaviors and feminine behaviors in groups are not always clear, and the results of research are not always accurate or fair to one gender or the other. Much of the research examining feminine and masculine traits is done by comparing averages. Thus, specific individual behaviors are usually not accounted for, leaving only averages for our consideration.

Research related to biological sex shows that groups consisting of both males and females are more likely to be dominated by males talking than by females talking. Males on average tend to demonstrate more task-related behavior than do females; that is, males tend to be more goal oriented than most females and can be more impatient about moving on to the next issue or problem. Females tend to offer positive responses to others' comments and, in general, express their personal opinions more readily than males. Males are more likely to have greater objectivity in their comments than are females.[11]

Because of stereotypical beliefs, females are sometimes perceived as less competent than males in solving problems or making decisions. However, little, if any, difference between the problem-solving abilities of males and females has been found by researchers. The research does suggest that men appear to be better than women at certain kinds of problem-solving tasks, such as technical or mechanical issues, but that difference is reduced or eliminated when males and females work together and when all are highly motivated to solve the problem.[12]

Making Connections for Success

Gender and Groups

Do males and females really live in two separate worlds? John Gray has popularized gender differences in his two books *Men Are from Mars, Women Are from Venus* and *Why Mars and Venus Collide.* Gray's popular books claim that males and females differ not only in what they think but also in how they communicate. In mixed-sex groups, males' speech is mainly task oriented or instrumental, such as giving information, opinions, and suggestions. They tend to talk more, tell more jokes, and offer more solutions. Conversely, females are generally more supportive and facilitative in their communication, including agreeing, expressing interest in what others say, and encouraging others' participation. Females share feelings, display interest in other group members, and listen intently to them.

1. On the basis of your experiences in groups, do you find the above to be an accurate description of how males and females communicate in groups? Explain.

2. How would you characterize Gray's analysis of males and females participating in groups as too simplistic?

3. Can you think of ways that males and females can adjust their communication styles to be more effective within groups?

4. If you were to make recommendations to both males and females about communicating in groups, what would you tell them?

When groups compete, it appears that, on average, females are more coopera-tive with their opponents than males are. Females are more likely to share resources with their opponents and are interested in fairness more than in winning. Males, on average, are more willing than females to engage in aggressive behavior and gain advantage through deception and deceit. In addition, males are more likely to be antisocial, using revenge and verbal aggression, whereas females tend to choose socially acceptable behavior, such as reasoning and understanding, to solve conflict.[13]

When groups are small, females prefer to work with other females, whereas most males don't seem to have a preference. When comparing the research on males and females based on gender rather than biological sex, we are beginning to find that dif-ferences are based less on biological sex than on masculine and feminine traits. That is, individuals who have masculine traits, whether they are male or female, are more likely to be competitive and attempt to dominate and control interactions. While these traits lead to obtaining the group's goal, they can also lead to dissatisfaction among group members and reduce the amount of interaction by some members who are intimidated by the controlling members. Feminine individuals—of either sex—are less likely to display those behaviors of their masculine counterparts, and may be seen as weak, lacking in control, and trying to satisfy everyone while accomplishing little.[14] It is important that both masculine and feminine traits be balanced in order to reach the group's objectives, and to do so while maintaining a cohesive group. The research reviewed helps to explain some of the differences in how males and females interact in groups and teams. We must emphasize again, however, that much of the research reflects generalizations rather than specifics, thus not all males and females exhibit these behaviors.

Establishing a Group Culture

15.4 **Explain** how a group's culture, size, and norms affect group communication.

group culture

The pattern of values, beliefs, norms, and behaviors that is shared by group members and that shapes a group's individual "personality".

Just like societies, organizations, and other large groups, small groups develop unique cultures. **Group culture** "is the pattern of values, beliefs, norms, and behav-iors shared by group members that shape a group's individual 'personality.'"[15]

Group culture is created by many factors, including the interaction patterns of group members, the roles members are assigned, the purpose for the group, the mixture of people included in the group, members' behaviors, and norms and rules followed by the group.

The group's culture underlies all of its actions and behaviors. Group culture is not static; it constantly changes and develops as it adapts to each new situation or event it confronts as well as to the needs of the group and its members. A group's culture is expressed in behaviors such as how its members organize, who begins the interactions, how much interaction is allowed by any one member, who interacts with whom, how formally or informally people behave, how much or how little conflict is permitted, how much or how little socializing takes place, and how much or how little tolerance for ambiguity the group allows.

Group Size

Group size refers to the number of participants and has important ramifications for the group's effectiveness. Although a group has no perfect number of members, groups of certain sizes seem appropriate for certain kinds of tasks. For example, five-member groups are the most effective for dealing with intellectual tasks; coordinating, analyzing, and evaluating information; and making administrative decisions. Many small-group experts recommend that groups have no fewer than three and no more than nine members. They also advise an odd number of participants (five, seven or nine) for some decision-making and problem-solving groups, helps to ensure fewer stalemates, and thus a lower likelihood that voting will end in a tie.

A group that is too small can limit the information and ideas generated, whereas a group that is too large can limit the contribution each person can make. When deciding on the most effective size for a group, consider the following points:

1. Large groups reduce the time and amount of individual interaction.
2. Large groups provide a greater opportunity for aggressive members to assert their dominance. As a result, less assertive members might feel isolated and might withdraw from the group altogether.
3. Large groups make it difficult to follow a set agenda. It is easy for someone in a large group to switch topics or introduce subjects that are not related to the group's original priorities.

norms

Expected and shared ways in which group members behave.

Group culture is created by many factors, including the interaction patterns of the group's members, the roles members are assigned, the group's purpose, the mixture of people included in the group, members' behaviors, and norms and rules followed by the group.

Group Norms

The expected and shared ways group members behave are called **norms**. Both informal and formal guidelines determine which behaviors are acceptable and which are not. In most group situations, the norms are informal and unwritten. In some social groups, such as a book club or cooking group, certain behaviors are expected. At a minimum, it is assumed members will respect each other, show up on time for meetings, attend the majority of gatherings, allow others time to communicate, and support other members' contributions and opinions.

For a group to function effectively, its members must agree on how things are to be done. Therefore, no matter what their size or task, groups establish norms. This is done for a variety of reasons; the strongest one is that shared ways of behaving enable members to attain group goals and to satisfy interpersonal needs. Without guidelines for behavior, most groups would be ineffective and disorganized.

In formal situations, to increase efficiency and order, many groups use pre-established rules to guide their interaction.

Robert's Rules of Order is the most widely used authority on conducting social, business, and government meetings.[16] Such formal rules specify the roles of members, how meetings are conducted, and how topics for discussion are introduced, discussed, and accepted or rejected by the group's members. When it is important to maintain formal order, a group may appoint a parliamentarian to ensure the rules are correctly interpreted and followed.

Norms also develop in online groups. For example, group members develop ways of communicating with each other both formally and informally and devise their own ways of communicating via email, Skype, or other online means.[17] Groups tend to use emails to chat and coordinate meeting times or use doodle.com, a meeting planning website, to schedule times and to communicate with those who were not present or available to meet. As online groups mature over time, so does conformity to the norms of the group.

Purposes and Types of Groups

15.5 **Distinguish** among different types of groups—both face-to-face and social media.

So far, you have read about what a group is and is not, how a group is formed, and the role culture plays in groups. It is also important to understand the types of groups and why they are formed. Small groups fall into one of two major categories: *primary* and *secondary*. Each serves different human needs, but characteristics of each are found in almost every group in which we participate.

Primary Groups

Primary groups focus on social or interpersonal relationships among members and exist primarily to satisfy what are labeled primary needs, such as those we discussed in terms of interpersonal communication: the need for inclusion (belonging) and affection (esteem, likeability, love). Primary groups are usually long term and include family; roommates; friends who meet to socialize; coworkers sharing time off together; and other groups of friends who might share vacations, card games, and so on. The groups might at times make decisions, solve problems, or take on a particular task, but their main purpose is to socialize, support one another, chat about a variety of topics, let off steam, and enjoy each other's company.

Primary groups are at the heart of interpersonal communication, and are important to understanding small-group communication in general.[18] The main purposes of the primary group are member enjoyment and companionship and support among members. Primary groups are not the main focus of this and the next chapter; typically, primary groups are studied in sociology, psychology, and interpersonal communication courses.

primary group
A group that focuses on social and interpersonal relationships.

Secondary Groups

Secondary groups, are the main focus of this and the next chapter, and exist to accomplish tasks or achieve goals. They are formed for the purpose of doing work, such as completing a class assignment, solving a problem, or making a decision. Members join together to exert power over their situation and others. The main reason for secondary groups is to get something done, but they can also help members achieve their primary needs for socialization and affection. Secondary groups include a variety of types of groups: decision-making, problem solving, committees, learning and information sharing, and therapy or personal growth.[19]

secondary group
A group that exists to accomplish tasks or achieve goals.

People come together in groups to *make decisions* on issues such as deciding what to do for homecoming decorations, where to hold a dance, which play to stage, or which computer is the most practical for a department's needs. It is not unusual for groups to vote on such issues to determine the decision. Voting is done especially when no clear agreement is reached about which is the most acceptable option. When voting, groups usually accept the majority's position. Discussing alternatives with others helps people decide which choice is the best not only for them but for the group as a whole. In addition, when everyone in the group participates in the decision-making process, all are more likely to accept the final outcome and help carry it out. Most of us resent being told what to do; we are more tolerant of a decision if we help to shape it.

Small groups can also excel at *solving problems*. People form problem-solving groups in almost every imaginable context: in the workplace, in government, in school, and sometimes at home. The problems they attempt to solve include how to improve health care, how to make a better product, how to perform a task more effectively or efficiently, how to stop violence, how to resolve the crime problem on campus, how to improve the image of fraternities on campus, and how to share computer time with your siblings.

As you can see, groups serve a variety of purposes and often multiple purposes at the same time. For example, a group can solve problems while simultaneously functioning as a learning, social, cathartic, or therapeutic outlet for its members. It was customary in the early and middle years of the 20th century for most people to work relatively independently of one another. Even in large organizations, people had individual responsibilities and coordinated with others only when necessary. Recently, the value of having people work in groups has been recognized, and a group approach has been implemented in many settings, including the workplace and the classroom.

Committees are groups that are either appointed or elected and have been assigned a specific task by a larger group or person with authority, such as a teacher, supervisor, or leader. Committees are usually formed to solve problems, make decisions, or gather information for another group or a larger group so it can make decisions or solve problems. Committee work is often seen as time consuming, and many people react negatively to it. This is unfortunate and is likely due to the people who are members of the committee or the lack of defined goals assigned to the committee. If properly led, with clearly identified goals, committees can investigate and report findings; recommend a course of action; formulate policies, principles, or guidelines for carrying out actions; and derive satisfaction from working together.

The most common reason people join small groups is to *share information and to learn from one another*. The sharing of information occurs in all kinds of group settings; the most familiar ones are corporations, schools, religious organizations, families, and service or social clubs. The underlying purpose of learning or information-sharing groups is to educate, inform, or improve understanding related to specific issues or areas of concern.

Therapeutic group sessions primarily help people alter their attitudes, feelings, or behaviors about some aspect of their personal life. For example, a therapeutic group might include people who have drinking, drug, or other problems, such as coping with the loss of a loved one. Usually, the therapeutic group is led by a professional who is trained in group psychotherapy or counseling.

As with most communication contexts, groups are not purely primary or secondary. Small groups you will be involved in are likely to include elements of all the groups described: social, task, decision-making, problem solving, personal growth, and learning.

Social Media Groups

Social media are changing the way we share information and work in groups, so face-to-face interactions are not always necessary. With the introduction of Skype, FaceTime and a variety of other social media, it is possible to carry on group communication as if you were face-to-face with others who may be in a variety of different locations. As you know, both text and voice communication can take place online in groups. Such methods or approaches can be effective when something has to be decided quickly and it is not possible to gather everyone together at the same time. This form of communication is referred to as asynchronous communication, which means that message responses have slight or prolonged time delays and participants must alternate sending and receiving messages. Another drawback is that nonverbal communication, such as facial and body expressions—and, in the case of texting, vocal expression—is limited.

The number of nonverbal and verbal cues allowed by a medium determines its richness. For example, face-to-face interactions would be the richest because they provide for a wide range of both verbal and nonverbal cues to convey meaning and make interpretation of the received messages easier. This does not mean that online group interactions will necessarily lead to misunderstandings, but it does mean that misunderstandings are more likely to occur during online texting interactions than during teleconferencing, videoconferencing, or face-to-face interactions.

Synchronous communication occurs when the interaction is face-to-face or when the interaction is in real time, and messages are sent and received at once. Even though some online interactions, such as Skype and FaceTime, are close to real time, they may contain some delay, and participants may take turns being sender and receiver.

While asynchronous online interaction can be beneficial, it can also create some distinct challenges, especially when instant messaging is used. One study found that instant messages can provide social support similar to that of face-to-face or phone interactions, but the feeling of disconnect from each other seems more predominant.[20] The disconnected feeling, according to the researchers, isn't so much the lack of nonverbal communication, but rather the result of multitasking. That is, those who are interacting are also doing a variety of other activities, such as having multiple instant messaging windows open or browsing the Internet.

As technologies continue to improve, the notion that face-to-face interaction is the richest in terms of quality and influence may not hold true. Research that compares various forms of interaction finds "face-to-face conversations may not always be the rich, deep, and inherently superior means of communication."[21]

Whenever technology is used, it increases the chances for misunderstanding; thus, we need to carefully consider the messages we craft and carefully interpret the ones we receive to keep misunderstandings to a minimum. Several factors must be considered when comparing online communication to other forms of group interaction. Each form has its distinct advantages and disadvantages; no one form is necessarily better than any other. Many differences in online versus face-to-face communication are attributed to the comfort level of those who use it. Those who have grown up with social media are generally more able to adapt to online communication than are those who haven't.[22]

Ultimately, the success of any technology for group interaction depends on two factors: accessibility and use. We use technology to communicate within groups if the technology is readily available and if all members know how to use it effectively.

Today more and more group interaction occurs via social media, where a group in one location can easily interact with other groups in multiple locations throughout the world.

Making Connections for Success

Entering and Participating in an Online Group

It's your turn to either join or create your own online group, if you haven't already done so. Those of you who already participate in an international online group may skip the following and proceed to the questions listed. For those of you who aren't in an online group, go to www.groups.yahoo.com. Groups can be found for almost everything and anything, or you can create your own group. You will need to participate in an online group to answer the questions below. It is easy to connect with people who share your interests to discuss sports, health, relationships, school, and news and to communicate with a variety of individuals.

1. How do interactions differ when communicating online versus communicating in face-to-face groups?
2. How many and in what types of online groups do you participate?
3. What are the interesting and exciting aspects of the online group? How are they more interesting and exciting than face-to-face groups?
4. How can group members help to establish and uphold online group rules?
5. What are some problems you have encountered in online groups, and how have you dealt with them?

In addition, if the technologies are to be empowering and helpful, group members must agree on mutual expectations and rules to guide the use of each technology. If an individual fails to check messages regularly, comes poorly prepared to a web conference, or is not included in the exchanges of the other group members, the group will likely not be very successful. Groups who use technology to communicate are aware that different types of technologies affect the richness and speed of their communication. Clearly, training and experience in the appropriate application of electronic communication technologies are critical to success in today's interactive world.

Ethical Behavior in Group Communication

15.6 Describe the role of ethics in small-group communication.

For groups to perform effectively, leaders and members must be ethical. All people in civilized societies are expected to follow certain behavioral assumptions—laws, rules, standards, or agreed-on norms. It is important to realize that groups, by their very nature, take on a collectivistic orientation in that the successful group must be more important than the individual. This perspective can raise ethical considerations about the commitment one has toward other group members and the group goal. This does not mean individuals should condone unethical behaviors, such as intentionally deceiving one another or manufacturing information or evidence to persuade others in the group to accept a particular point of view.

The expectations that people will be respectful of each other's opinions apply especially to behaviors within groups and raise some special ethical concerns all groups and group members should consider when participating in group-related activities. The bottom line is that every group member, as well as the group as a whole, must be ethical, honest, respectful, fair, flexible, and responsible in actions and communication.

Guidelines

Ethical Group Behavior

1. **All group members should have the right to state an opinion or a unique perspective.** No one should be prevented from speaking openly, even when expressing unpopular views. Of course, group members must also be sensitive and responsible in making sure their honest statements do not violate someone else's civil rights. Similarly, it is inappropriate to ridicule or belittle members of the group in private or public because they may disagree with a certain point of view. Disagreeing with another person's ideas is in no way wrong; it is wrong, however, to attack the person instead of the idea.

2. **Group members should be willing to share all legitimate information that might benefit the group in reaching its goal.** Deliberately withholding information that might benefit the group is a violation of the group's trust and is unethical. Times might arise when withholding information to protect the group or specific group members may be appropriate. For example, not divulging something a group member says about another member avoids creating bad or hurt feelings. If a group member or members have a vested interest outside the group that results in introducing false, faulty, or misleading information or in withholding information, however, it is the obligation of the member or members to notify the group or excuse themselves from the group.

3. **All group members should conduct themselves with honesty and integrity.** Members of a group should not deliberately deceive or present false or untruthful information. It is unacceptable to present inaccurate information in an attempt to persuade others to accept a particular viewpoint. The same principle holds for the group itself: It is wrong for the group to present results based on misrepresentation of facts. It is deceitful to persuade others to accept conclusions supported by misinformation.

4. **Confidential information shared in the group should remain confidential.** It is extremely unethical to share private information outside the group.

5. **Group members must use information ethically.** Members should give credit to the source of the information, should not falsify data or information, and should present all relevant information and all points of view to prevent bias. Ethical use of information helps produce effective, sound results, whatever the task.[23]

Working in Groups or Teams: Advantages and Disadvantages

15.7 **Explain** the advantages and disadvantages of participating in groups and how to overcome the disadvantages.

As you know, with many activities you have participated in, whether it be in academics, athletics, recreation, or your personal life, there are advantages and disadvantages. Knowledge of the advantages and potential disadvantages of working in groups, helps you set more realistic expectations and capitalize on the values of the groups while minimizing the potential downsides.

Advantages

Take a moment to think about all the groups to which you belong: student organizations, clubs, religious groups, social groups, work groups, and informal groups of friends. Why did you join them in the first place? It doesn't take a scholar to tell you that people join groups for many reasons, and your reasons are probably similar to those that motivate others to join groups. Paul Paulus, a social psychologist, suggests people join groups for at least five common reasons:

1. *Groups help satisfy important psychological and social needs,* such as the need for attention and affection or the need to belong. Imagine what it would be like to be absolutely alone, in total isolation from others. Very few of us find such a prospect appealing.

2. *Group membership helps people achieve goals that otherwise might not be accomplished.* Groups make it easier to perform certain tasks, solve difficult problems, and make complex decisions that might overwhelm one individual.

3. *Group membership provides multiple sources of information and knowledge that might not be available to one individual.*

4. *Groups help meet the need for security.* The old saying that there is safety in numbers rings true in many situations; belonging to groups can provide protection and security against common enemies. For example, people join neighborhood watch groups to protect themselves from criminal activity.

5. *Group membership also contributes to an individual's positive social identity*—it becomes part of a person's self-concept. Of course, the more prestigious and restrictive the groups to which a person is admitted, the more that person's self-concept is bolstered.[24]

Other advantages to participating in groups or teams include innovation and creativity, as supported by the maxim "two heads are better than one," especially when it comes to working on difficult tasks or solving complex problems.[25] You are more likely remember what you discussed because you actively engaged in a discussion with others rather than passively thought about it. According to Beebe and Masterson, working in groups and teams helps to improve learning and comprehension; for example if you are scheduled to take an exam, they indicate studying by yourself doesn't allow for the asking and answering of questions. Beebe and Masterson also suggest discussion helps you learn and comprehend more of what you learn better than if you did it by yourself.[26]

The Disadvantages of Working in Small Groups

Most of what we have said so far about groups has been positive, and it is true that groups have many advantages over individuals working alone. But limitations related to groups can also lead to less effective and less satisfying outcomes.

GOING ALONG TO GET ALONG   Too much cohesiveness can lead to conformity and blind loyalty to a group even when it is not in the individual group member's best interest to conform. Groups can become too cohesive or committed, resulting in **groupthink**—a dysfunction in which group members see the harmony of the group as more important than considering new ideas, critically examining their own assumptions, changing their own flawed decisions, or allowing new members to participate.[27] The following situation illustrates groupthink. Students are asked to choose one of three solutions to a certain social problem and join with other students who selected the same solution. Usually, all three solutions are chosen and each group's task is to defend its solution and to persuade the instructor that its solution is the best of the three. As an incentive for preparing a sound argument, students are told the instructor will accept only one group solution as the best.

As the groups begin to work, their members make a modest effort to pull together and define their argument. Each group selects a representative to present its argument. After hearing each representative, the instructor announces he or she is undecided regarding which group offered the best solution. Therefore, all groups have one more chance to develop their arguments. The instructor also announces that students who did not like their group's solution are welcome to join another group. No one switches groups, even though some are tempted to do so after hearing presentations by other group representatives.

groupthink

A dysfunction in which group members value the harmony of the group more than new ideas, fail to critically examine ideas, hesitate to change flawed decisions, or lack willingness to allow new members to participate.

To raise the stakes, the instructor states the groups with the second- and third-best solutions will be assigned a homework project over the weekend, whereas the winning group will be exempt. In response, the intensity within each group builds. Members pull their chairs closer together and talk more forcefully about their solution. They support one another's views more openly. The common objective has become clear and compelling: To avoid the research project, the students are motivated to persuade their instructor. Oddly enough, this particular type of motivation can be hazardous. Groupthink is more likely to occur when a group's cohesiveness and commitment are too high and when the group is under pressure to achieve consensus at the expense of doing the best possible work. Once this collective state of mind develops, it seems groups become unwilling and perhaps unable to change a decision, even if they realize it is a poor one.

Research on groupthink indicates it is a real and pervasive phenomenon and explains some of the disastrous group decisions.[28] According to Irving Janis, a specialist in organizational behavior, eight symptoms lead to groupthink. They fall into three categories:

1. **Overestimation of the group's power and morality**
   - An illusion the group is invulnerable creates excessive optimism and encourages taking extreme risks
   - A belief the group will not be judged on the basis of the ethical or moral consequences of its decisions

2. **Closed-mindedness**
   - A tendency to rationalize or discount negative information that might lead members to reconsider their assumptions before making a decision
   - Stereotypical views of other groups as too weak and stupid to warrant genuine attempts to negotiate differences

3. **Pressures toward uniformity**
   - Individual self-censorship of differences that deviate from the group (that is, members are inclined to minimize their uniqueness and doubt the importance of their individual contributions)
   - A shared illusion of unanimity that pushes members to conform to the majority view as a result of self-censorship and the assumption that silence means consent
   - Pressure on group members who express arguments that differ from the majority to conform by making it clear dissent is contrary to what is expected of all loyal members
   - The setting of "mindguards" against threatening information to protect the group members from adverse information that might shatter their shared complacency regarding their decisions[29]

Procedures can be used to minimize the possibility of groupthink. Here are some examples:

- Assign one group member to be a "devil's advocate" who intentionally questions and criticizes the group's actions.
- Encourage members to "kick the problem around."
- Ensure that every group member has an opportunity to voice an opinion.
- Encourage individuals to express disagreement without being chastised by the group for doing so.

- Set a guideline that prevents leaders from stating their conclusion or opinions first.
- Invite outside experts to participate in the group or review conclusions to ensure all views have been considered.[30]

TIME-CONSUMING NATURE OF GROUP WORK A second disadvantage of groups is that the decision-making or problem-solving process can be time consuming. It almost always takes longer to accomplish something when a group does it. The more members in a group, the more time it takes to achieve the group's objectives. Individuals can almost always complete a task in a shorter amount of time than a group. For example, if you were to take a math problem-solving test, you would probably read each problem silently to yourself, write notes to yourself on scratch paper, and then attempt to solve the problems. If you were in a group, you would first have to discuss each problem, decide how the problem should be solved, and then work out the solution to the problem. In other words, group work is different from individual work because interaction must take place between and among the members. How can you ensure that groups use their time wisely and effectively?

VARYING INTERACTION A third disadvantage is unequal contribution by all group members. One reason for this is time, but it also happens because each member has a different communication style and comfort level with the group. Some members might dominate and overwhelm conversations, whereas other members might not contribute at all. Furthermore, the most verbally aggressive and dominant person in the group might not have the best ideas. What can be done to ensure that everyone has an equal opportunity to participate in and contribute to the group?

UNFAIR WORKLOADS A fourth disadvantage of groups is that members believe the workload is unfair. The most frequent complaint we hear from students about working on group projects is they believe some group members lack motivation and do not do their fair share of the work. This is referred to as social loafing. **Social loafing** is the tendency for individuals to lower their work effort after they join a group.[31] For example, suppose you and several other majors are forming a communication club. Your first task is to develop bylaws and gain approval of the university to have the club on campus. Everyone in the group knows the task and agrees to help. A meeting is scheduled to discuss these matters. Will all the group members put forth equal effort? Probably not. Some will do as much as they can, whereas others will simply do little or nothing; they may show up with a few ideas but do not take the task seriously because they were too busy doing other things. Social loafers can also be irresponsible by not showing up on time or not showing up at all because they believe others will do the work for them. Lack of motivation seems to be the central reason for social loafing. Although there is no magical list of procedures or behaviors to reduce social loafing, here are a few suggestions: Make outputs individually identifiable, increase commitment to the task and the sense of task importance, make sure each person's contribution is unique—not identical—to those of others, and build group cohesiveness. If these suggestions do not work, and if it is possible or reasonable, eliminate non-contributors from the group.

social loafing

Tendency for individuals to lower their work effort after they join a group.

A disadvantage of groups is that not all members are committed to do their fair share of the work.

Making Connections for Success

Effective Groups

Imagine you are part of a campus group the dean of student affairs has assigned to determine ways to make your campus greener. The group is made up of a variety of students all selected by the dean. Everything seems perfect except for one member who recently had a personal crisis and is very distracted and constantly looks at his text messages. His behavior affects the group's ability to focus on the problem at hand.

1. How would you deal with the situation?
2. What would you say to the group member who is going through the crisis?
3. What would you say to other group members?

PRESSURE TO FAIL   A fifth disadvantage is that the weaker group members control the outcome and therefore require others who might want to excel to do only the minimum necessary to get the job done and no more. In fact, members who do not cooperate and do excel beyond other group members might find themselves teased, chastised, or worse for breaking the group's norm. For example, Sam has 2 weeks of school left before she is to graduate and begin her new job as sales representative for a national distributor. In her organizational behavior class, she was assigned a major group project. She knows no matter what she does on the group project she will pass and therefore doesn't need to do very much. Thus, when meeting with her group, she says, "Hey guys, we don't have to take this assignment so seriously. All we have to do is to get done." By encouraging the group to do the minimum, Sam pressures the group to fail.

GROUPHATE PHENOMENON A final disadvantage results from negative experiences some have had in previous groups in which members lacked effective communication skills or disliked group work. This dislike for groups has been termed the **grouphate phenomenon**.[32] For some people, group work is so distasteful they avoid group situations whenever possible. In our experience, those who hate participating in groups the most are those who have little or no skill or lack training in how to communicate in groups.

grouphate phenomenon
Dislike for groups.

Summary

Small-Group Communication: Making the Connection to Our Everyday Lives

Objective 15.1 **Understand** the differences among a group, team, or project or work team and their roles in our everyday lives.

- Small-group communication involves the exchange of information among a relatively small number of people, ideally five to seven.
- In small-group communication, a small number of people share a common purpose, influence one another, take on roles, are interdependent, and interact with one another.

Formation and Development of Groups

Objective 15.2 **Explain** how and why groups are formed, and how culture influences group formation.

- Tuckman's model describes five stages of group formation, process, and development.
- Cultural factors, such as an individualistic or a collectivistic orientation, affects how people from different cultures perceive groups and group activities.

Characteristics of Small Groups

Objective 15.3 **Describe** the characteristics of small groups.
- The most essential characteristic of a group is its interdependence, or the mutual dependence among members.
- The members' commitment to the group is key to the group's success.
- Cohesiveness, the attraction among the group members, is important, but when it becomes too strong, it can interfere with good decision-making.
- The differences between the way men and women communicate in groups are not clear, and the results of research are not always accurate or fair to one gender or the other.

Establishing a Group Culture

Objective 15.4 **Explain** how a group's culture, size, and norms affect group communication
- Group culture is the pattern of values, beliefs, norms, and behaviors shared by group members that shape a group's individual personality. The following factors may influence the group's culture:
- The group size has important ramifications for a group's effectiveness; a group that is too small can limit information and ideas; a group that is too large can limit individual contributions.
- Group norms, the informal and formal guidelines or rules of expected behaviors that are established by group members, guide the group's interaction.

Purposes and Types of Groups

Objective 15.5 **Distinguish** among different types of groups—both face-to-face and social media.
- Primary groups focus on social or interpersonal relationships and include family, close friends, Facebook friends, coworkers, and neighbors.
- Secondary groups, which exist to accomplish tasks or achieve goals, include decision-making, problem-solving, committee, learning, and therapy groups.
- Project groups or work teams are responsible for an entire work process or a segment of the process that delivers a product or service to an internal or external customer.
- Social media change how and when groups can meet and enable groups with members in different locations to make decisions quickly if necessary.

Ethical Behavior in Group Communication

Objective 15.6 **Describe** the role of ethics in small-group communication.
- For groups to perform at a high level, both leaders and members must be ethical. Group members should have a right to speak openly, share information with the group, be honest and act with integrity, keep shared information confidential if asked to do so, and use information ethically.

Working in Groups or Teams: Advantages and Disadvantages

Objective 15.7 **Explain** advantages and disadvantages of participating in groups and how to overcome them.
- Group membership helps satisfy psychological and social needs, achieve goals that otherwise might not be accomplished, provide multiple sources of information, meet the need for security, and contribute to an individual's social identity.
- Members can become too cohesive or committed, groupthink may result, groups are time consuming, not all members contribute equally, the social loafer can affect the outcome, pressure to fail, and grouphate can occur.

Discussion Starters

1. Describe why it is important to know how to work in a group or on a team.
2. Suggest behaviors that would make group work more efficient.
3. Which group characteristic (interdependence, commitment, cohesiveness, group size, or group culture) do you think is the most important for a group to succeed? Why?
4. Discuss two norms in your class that could be applied to a group.
5. Describe a recent event in which groupthink occurred and why it occurred.
6. Explain what you think are the differences, if any, that females and males brought to a group discussion in which you have participated.
7. In what ways has social media changed the way we enter and work in groups?
8. Describe what it means to be an ethical group member.
9. From your experiences, how can a "social loafer" affect a group's climate, motivation, and productivity?
10. Describe three behaviors that should help you become a better group member.

Chapter 16
Participating in Groups and Teams

Learning Objectives

CHAPTER OUTLINE

This chapter will help you:

16.1 Understand how effective groups and teams establish goals and assign roles.

Group and Team Building

16.2 Understand the difference between leadership and leaders and the various leadership styles and behaviors they exhibit.

Leadership

16.3 Differentiate among the roles of group members and explain their various contributions.

Member Participation

16.4 Describe conflict, its impacts, and the conflict management strategies that can manage it.

Managing Group Conflict

16.5 Explain the reflective thinking process and functional communication theory.

Problem Solving and Decision Making

16.6 Describe the role of evaluation in small-group performance.

Evaluating Small-Group Performance

Making Everyday Connections

When she was a student, Dana hated meetings because she always found them to be such a waste of time. She now works as an account executive for the IPG Corporation in Omaha, a large international advertising and marketing company. A typical day for her begins at 7:30 a.m. taking her two boys to school and then arriving at work around 8:00 a.m. Most days for Dana start with a web conference with her counterparts in Tokyo, Milan, New York, and Chicago to discuss the implementation and development of a survey for a major international client. At 9:30 a.m. she meets with her team to discuss the design of the survey; at 11:00 she is off to meet with the production staff of a local client to discuss the results of another survey; at noon she has a luncheon meeting with members of the Omaha Community Foundation to plan a fund-raiser for a new soccer field for kids. After dinner, at 7:30 p.m., she will join the neighborhood association, which is meeting to discuss the neighborhood summer picnic. Meetings, meetings, meetings …

Questions To Think About

1. What is the message or take away from what you just read?
2. Describe the number and the types of meeting you participated in during the past two weeks.
3. Describe the outcomes, whether positive or negative, of at least one of the meetings that you listed in your previous response. What contributed to its outcome?

Meetings have been the butt of many jokes and often have led to frustration, but working in groups can be a good experience and can lead to outcomes that are far better than those achieved by individuals. If you are like most people, you have been in meetings in which meaningful interaction took place, time was used wisely, good progress was made toward a particular goal, lots of ideas were shared, respect for each person's contributions was shown even though disagreement and conflict sometimes occurred, differences were resolved by open discussion, and decisions were supported by everyone. People leave such meetings with a real sense of accomplishment.

This chapter explores seven crucial aspects of small-group communication that can facilitate an effective meeting: team building, leadership, member participation, methods of group problem solving and decision making, conflict management, and evaluation. All of these skills are necessary for a successful career.

Group and Team Building

16.1 Understand how effective groups and teams establish goals and assign roles.

Not all groups will become teams or work as teams, but it is important to understand that the more a group acts like or becomes a team, the more likely it will be successful. A team tends to be more successful or effective because when people know they are part of a team, they usually cooperate more fully; they form a close-knit relationship and a strong sense of identity. For groups to establish a team approach, they must first set very clear and specific goals, as well as determine roles.

Setting Goals

It is unusual, when participating in a group, to find that all members participate with the same amount of enthusiasm or motivation. One way to avoid this problem is for the group to establish goals that are not only clear and specific but also challenging and worthwhile for each group member.[1] If group members believe the goals are trivial and unimportant, they will likely not participate; or, if they do, it will be with little or no motivation. If the group members understand their work effort and decisions will result in rewards, be appreciated, and be considered worthwhile, however, they are more likely to take ownership of their actions and behaviors as well as be motivated to accomplish their goals.

How can a group effectively determine whether its goals are clear and specific? If a group's goal is vaguely stated, the group will likely find it more difficult to organize its **agenda** or strategy and to know when it has arrived at a solution or conclusion. For example, a topic such as "campus crime is on the rise" provides little or no direction for what needs to be done. However, if the topic is restated as, "What specific actions should be taken by the university to help reduce the crime rate on campus by the end of the year?" this tells the group exactly what it needs to accomplish: identify specific actions for reducing crime this year. If the group also believes that the proposed specific actions could be used to reduce crime, this could be an incentive for the group to accomplish its goal. It would also give them a reason to take ownership of the solutions they generate.

Determining Roles

Once the group has established and understands its goal, it must determine the roles of its members. Everyone in the group should be responsible for something. For example, a football team requires a head coach (a leader), assistant coaches (a subgroup within the larger group), players who have the talent and desire to fill the positions necessary to play the game, public relations people to promote the team, and so on. Everyone on the team has roles and assigned duties. Football players cannot function as a team if no structure is in place or if the coaches and players are uncertain of the roles they are supposed to fulfill. The same is true of any group or team; if the members are uncertain of their roles and there is no structure, the group or team will not be able to function effectively.

Members of a team have a strong sense of identity with the group, and they cooperate fully because each has a specific role to play. This is a very effective group form.

agenda

A list of all topics to be discussed during a meeting.

Leadership

16.2 **Understand** the difference between leadership and leaders and the various leadership styles and behaviors they exhibit.

Try the following with your friends. Ask them to rate themselves on a ten-point scale ranging from 1 (very low) to 10 (very high) on their leadership potential. Unless they are unusual, here's what you'll likely find: Most will rate themselves as average

Making Connections for Success

Team Building a YouTube Video

Whether you are a group of students or a group of employees, team building and teams are going to be part of your life. Teams can be built in many ways, but what we do know is that to have a successful team, *everyone* on the team must have a role and participate and the team must have some structure to function effectively.

Your instructor assigned groups of five to seven students to make a creative and innovative YouTube video about a communication concept of each group's choice. The task of the group is to create a video that illustrates the concept in an innovative and creative way. It is important for everyone in the group to participate both in the creation of the video and its presentation to the class.

1. What was the initial reaction of the group to this assignment?
2. How did the group organize itself as to how it was going complete the assigned task?
3. What skills do you think will be needed for the group to successfully complete the assigned task?
4. What creative solutions were suggested and how were they received by group members?
5. What would an outside observer have seen as the strengths and weaknesses of the group?
6. What roles were determined and how were individuals assigned to those roles?
7. Did the group become a team and, if so, what made it a team rather than a group?

or above average.[2] This indicates they view themselves and leadership potential favorably. So, what is leadership? In a sense it is a lot like love: easy to recognize but hard to define. **Leadership** is *an influence process* that includes any behavior that helps to clarify a group's purpose or guide a group to achieve its goals. A **leader** is a person who is assigned, selected, or emerges to take the leadership role of a group or team. In most cases, only one person has the title of leader, although at times the assigned or appointed leader, should there be one, does not show leadership. It is also possible that when no leader is appointed or assigned, someone emerges as the leader or two or more people emerge and share the leader responsibilities via their leadership behaviors. In other words, a leader is a role or title held in a group, whereas leadership is the behavior that influences or facilitates group members to achieve the group's goal or goals.

Leading a Group or Team

A leader is the person usually at the center of a group's attention or the person to whom the group members address their messages. A leader can be identified by his or her position or title, such as police chief, mayor, council president, chairperson of a committee, boss, teacher, coach, captain, father, mother, and so on. But this method of identification requires caution. Even though a title signifies a person is the stated leader, it does not mean the person has leadership skills.

Another way to identify a leader is by the behaviors he or she displays in guiding a group or team. If a person communicates a direction and the group members follow that direction to reach a goal, that person is demonstrating leadership as well as the power and ability to get others to accomplish the goal.

In most cases, a leader's ability to lead determines the success or failure of a group or team. Granted, not all successes or failures can be directly traced to the person in charge because the participants, the nature of the task to be accomplished, and the information available for completing the task also contribute to the outcome. The role of the leader in a small-group project is to ensure that the task is done. To do this, the leader must be objective enough to determine how the group is functioning and whether it is progressing toward its goal. This requires, at times, the ability to "step back" and examine the group objectively.

Leaders must help address at least two sets of needs found in all groups. **Task needs** are related to the content of the task and all behaviors that lead to the completion of the task, including defining and assessing the task, gathering information, studying the problem, and solving the problem. **Maintenance needs** are related to organizing and developing a group so that members realize personal satisfaction from working together. Maintenance needs pertain to intangibles such as atmosphere, structure, role responsibility, praise, and social–emotional control. To meet both task and maintenance needs, leaders in small groups must perform a number of functions:

Initiating—preparing members for discussion
Organizing—keeping members on track
Maintaining effective interaction—encouraging participation
Ensuring member satisfaction—promoting interpersonal relationships
Facilitating understanding—encouraging effective listening
Stimulating creativity and critical thinking—encouraging evaluation and improvement

Leadership Styles and Behavior

All leaders are not alike. They may share certain characteristics or qualities to a degree, but more than likely they differ in personal, behavioral, or leadership style. Research has identified two useful dimensions by which to classify leaders: as task-oriented or relationship-oriented leaders or by the amount of power they yield to group members.

---

leadership

An influence process that includes any behavior that helps clarify a group's purpose or guides the group to achieve its goals.

leader

A person who is assigned, selected or emerges to take the leadership role of a group or team.

task needs

Needs related to the content of the task to be done and all behaviors that lead to the completion of it.

maintenance needs

Needs related to organizing and developing a group so that members can realize personal satisfaction from working together.

Figure 16.1 Leadership Styles: Task and Relationship Orientation

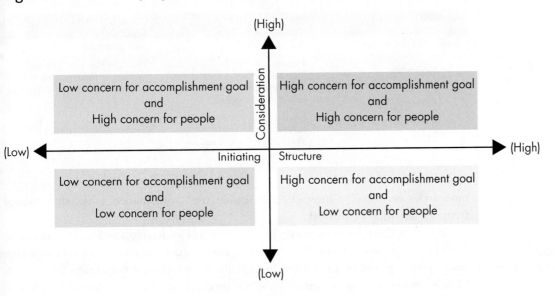

LEADERSHIP AND TASK OR RELATIONSHIP ORIENTATION Although there are as many different leadership styles as leaders, research on leader behavior suggests that most leaders can be described as **initiating structure** (or task-oriented) leaders or **consideration** (or relationship-oriented) leaders.[3] Leaders who initiate structure tend to focus on getting the job done. They engage in actions such as organizing work, making sure rules are followed, setting goals, and ensuring that everyone knows who is in charge. For example, the vice president at Google in charge of finding talented workers thrives in her position by being extremely particular in hiring, a fanatical user of social networking, and apolitical when critiquing new ideas.[4] You may have experienced leaders like this, and in some group situations, this style can get the job done or the problem solved, but leaders who adopt this style tend to sacrifice relationship development unless it will help get the task done more quickly.

Leaders who lead by consideration tend to focus on interpersonal relationships and being liked by group members. They engage in such actions as doing favors for group members, taking time to explain things to them, and watching out for their well-being. Leaders who do not focus on consideration usually don't care about the group members or whether the group members like them or not. (See Figure 16.1 for an overview of the two styles.)

Is either of these styles superior? Probably not. Both offer a mix of advantages and disadvantages. Leaders who show concern for others generally foster stronger morale, but such leaders often avoid telling others what to do or offering critical feedback to improve the contribution of group members. This could result in inefficiency and failure to accomplish tasks in a timely manner. In contrast, when leaders focus solely on attaining goals, efficiency may be good, but group members feel no commitment to the outcome or to the leader. It appears that leaders who are able to use a blend of both styles are likely to have groups that are highly productive and committed and enjoy working together to get the task done. In other words, leaders who can balance the two styles are often considered superior leaders.

LEADERSHIP AND POWER DISTRIBUTION Leadership may also be classified according to how much or how little power the leader assigns to group members. Researchers have identified three primary styles of leadership: autocratic, democratic, and laissez-faire,[5] each having a distinctive approach to group communication (see Table 16.1). However, many leaders cannot be easily classified as having one of the

initiating structure
A dimension of leadership that focuses on getting the job done.

consideration
A dimension of leadership that focuses on establishing good interpersonal relationships and on being liked by group members.

Table 16.1 Leadership Styles: A Comparison

Autocratic	Democratic	Laissez-Faire
Keeps complete control	Shares control	Gives up control
Sets policy and makes all decisions for the group	Involves members in setting policy and making decisions; does not make any decisions without consulting group members	Gives total freedom to group members to make policies and decisions; gets involved only when called on
Defines tasks and assigns them to members	May guide task assignment to be sure work is accomplished, but allows members to divide work	Completely avoids participation

autocratic leader

A leader who has control and makes decisions with little or no consultation with others.

democratic leader

A leader who shares control and makes decisions in consultation with others.

laissez-faire leader

A leader who gives up control, is passive, and usually requires that others take over if the group is to succeed.

three styles exclusively. Often, effective leaders use a combination, which may change from one situation to the next.

In theory, the differences among the three styles of leadership are clear. The **autocratic leader** has complete control, the **democratic leader** shares control, and the **laissez-faire leader** gives up control. In practice, though, the three styles are not always so clear-cut. Most leaders do not use the same style all the time but vary their style to match each situation. Certain circumstances, group members, or group purposes call for direct control, whereas others require little or no control. For example, a military leader in combat and a doctor in a medical emergency will undoubtedly be autocratic leaders. Such situations require immediate action, and putting decisions to a vote could create problems. Autocratic leaders can have a negative impact on a group—for example, a jury foreman who imposes her opinion or rushes the decision so that other jurists agree with her.

The democratic leadership style is most often used when a leader is elected. For example, the president of the student government and the chair of a committee would probably use a democratic style. This style is most common when the leader is both a representative and a member of the group. Laissez-faire leadership is often used when a leader does not want to impose a rigid structure because the group members are sufficiently competent and mature to accomplish their goal without much, if any, influence from the leader. An example would be a group conducting a study session. If such a group decided it needed a leader, it would take appropriate action, but in most cases, the group neither desires nor requires any assistance, and so it remains leaderless.

Leaders are not always free to follow the leadership style they prefer. For example, people who would rather be democratic or laissez-faire leaders might discover that pressures from others, the need to get things done in a certain way, or the desire to save time and energy requires them to be more autocratic than they would like to be. On other occasions, when it is important for members to agree with a decision, leaders are more likely to use a democratic style. No single leadership style is perfect in all situations.

Making Connections for Success

What Makes a Leader?

Imagine two different groups of college students that meet to discuss how they would implement the new regulations for their dorm's common room. In one of the groups, you are the only member who comes to the meeting prepared. None of the other members know the rules or are prepared to discuss them and their implementation. In the second group, all of the group members have knowledge of the rules and are fully prepared to focus on implementation.

1. If you were asked to lead the two groups, what leadership style do you think you would use in each, and why?
2. What problems might you encounter in each of the two groups, if any?
3. Explain the characteristics or skills needed to be an effective leader in each of the two groups.
4. Of the qualities or skills you have identified, which do you think is the most important for each of the two groups and why?

Researchers have concluded skilled leaders have the ability to understand a situation and adapt their behaviors to meet its particular constraints.[6] Leadership entails the capacity to determine the most appropriate style and behaviors for given situations.

Research, although not conclusive, suggests the democratic leadership style is superior to the autocratic style in getting a task done and at the same time satisfies group members.[7] Autocratic leaders are likely to get more done, but member satisfaction is considerably lower. Probably the most significant research finding is that autocratic leaders generate more hostility and aggression among group members, whereas democratic leaders produce more originality, individuality, and independence.[8]

Leadership and Gender Differences

Women have made great strides in assuming leadership roles in elected offices (e.g., governors, mayors, and legislators). They have also been appointed to the Supreme Court and cabinet positions, hold high rank in the military, and head major corporations. Women are also the leaders in creating and building a culture of creativity in organizations. They are the ones stimulating people's minds by constantly pushing and creating new trends and ideas.[9] Eighteen women took the reins of Fortune 500 companies in 2011, bringing the total to about 3.6 percent.[10] Thus, while there has been improvement, the gender gap between men and women still exists not only in leadership positions but in equal pay as well.

Early research on small-group leadership found that men usually emerged as leaders; but today it seems that biological sex is irrelevant, although psychological gender is not. It now appears that task-oriented women emerge as leaders as often as men who are task oriented. A study of groups of women found that those who emerged as leaders combined intelligence with masculinity or androgyny (exhibiting both masculine and feminine characteristics).[11] A study examining groups consisting of both males and females found that, regardless of sex, masculine and androgynous members stood out as leaders more often than feminine members.[12] It appears that leaders today are chosen not on the basis of biological sex, but rather on performance. The research related to gender and leadership shows that men and women lead equally well, and group members are equally satisfied with both.[13] It is clear that women have made great strides in recent years and have proven to be effective leaders in a variety of settings and situations.

Do male leaders and female leaders differ in their style or approach to leadership? What do you think? This debate has gone on for well over 30 years. Marilyn Loden, in her book *Feminine Leadership or How to Succeed in Business without Being One of the Boys*, contends that the sexes do indeed differ in terms of leadership style.[14] Loden believes female leaders often adopt a style that emphasizes cooperation and indirect means of management, whereas males tend to exhibit an "I'm in charge" directive strategy. However, recent research on male and female leadership done by social scientists has generally found no consistent or significant difference between the sexes in terms of leadership style. In fact, if you want to find differences between leadership styles in men and women, you would have to first ask, "Which woman and which man?"[15] The question is, "Who is right?"

Because of the complexity of the subject, finding the answer to this question is not simple. In a review of 150 research studies, Alice Eagly and Blair Johnson found potential differences

Leadership style can be classified by how much or how little power the leader assigns to group members. Democratic leaders, for example, guide and direct the group, and though committed to being open to all points of view, they represent only a majority or plurality of points of view of the group.

Every group member must be willing to contribute to, and take responsibility for, the success of the group. Successful group outcomes depend on group members' assuming various roles that are productive and beneficial to the group's outcome.

Making Connections for Success

Are Women Better Leaders?

According to a special report "As Leaders, Women Rule,"[17] more women are taking on leadership roles in government and business. The report stated that gender differences in leadership abilities were often small but that women, when rated by their peers, underlings, and bosses, scored higher than their male counterparts on a wide variety of measures—from producing high-quality work to goal-setting to mentoring employees. Using elaborate performance evaluations of women executives, researchers found that women overall received higher ratings than men on almost every leadership skill measured.

1. On the basis of what this report suggests—that women are better leaders—why don't women hold more leadership positions?

2. Defend or refute the report's contention that women are better leaders.

3. When considering the traits we generally associate with leadership, are those traits likely to be more masculine or feminine? Explain.

4. Who do you think is an effective female leader? An effective male leader? What do they have in common? What, if any, are their differences?

between male and female leadership styles on two dimensions: (1) task accomplishment versus maintenance of interpersonal relationships and (2) participative (democratic) versus directive (autocratic) leadership style.[16]

Sex-role stereotypes suggest female leaders might show more concern for interpersonal relations and tend to be more democratic in their leadership style than male leaders are. Results of Eagly and Johnson's study, however, did not support these stereotypes. Their results suggest that no evidence supports any substantial difference between men and women regarding the first dimension (task accomplishment versus maintenance of interpersonal relationships). There is, however, a significant difference between males and females regarding the second dimension (participative versus directive leadership style). Eagly and Johnson found women were more democratic, or participative, in style than men were. What do you think accounts for this difference?

The difference in leadership style might exist because, as evidence suggests, women generally possess better interpersonal skills than men do. In addition to the remaining hurdles for women, emerging evidence suggests gender stereotyping in the workplace is weakening. In a 2006 report, the inconsistency between the stereotype of women and that of leaders in terms of specific traits has steadily decreased, particularly among women.[18] However, this cause-and-effect connection is only speculative. Thus, generalizing about male and female leadership behaviors can be misleading for a variety of reasons. It is when men and woman are treated as if socialized in different cultures that we tend to stereotype—for example, that men are task oriented and powerful, while woman are emotional and powerless.[19] Unfortunately, when women violate expectations of being warm and nurturing and act in more masculine ways, they are more likely to be treated with hostility and rejection.[20] Further research must be done before a definitive conclusion can be drawn about gender differences in leadership style and whether (and in what situations) those differences might be to a leader's advantage or disadvantage.[21]

Member Participation

16.3 **Differentiate among the roles of group members and explain their various contributions.**

A group's success requires actively involved and committed members. Just like leaders, members of groups have certain responsibilities and roles.

Making Connections for Success

Choosing a Leadership Style

Kristen was recently hired by IPG, an international marketing firm, because of her excellent interpersonal skills and tech savvy. She was asked by her boss to lead a web conference for a diverse group of marketing personnel in several different countries.

1. What should Kristen do to prepare for the conference?

2. Do you have any recommendations for what leadership style Kristen should take given that the conference is web based?

3. Does a leader require a different set of skills when conducting an international web conference? If so, what should they be?

4. What, if any, considerations should Kristen take into account, given that she is female and some of the participants live in other countries in which very few or no women hold leadership roles?

Roles of Group Members

Group scholars Kenneth Benne and Paul Sheats developed a comprehensive list of roles that group members can assume.[22] Benne and Sheats classified the roles into three categories: group task, group building and maintenance, and self-centered roles. The most successful groups include members who fill the task and building/maintenance roles, and who avoid the self-centered roles.

Group task roles help the group accomplish its task or objective. They include behaviors that provide direction, propose ideas, and make suggestions to solve problems—these roles are referred to as *initiators* or *contributors*. Group members may also take on *information seeker* or *information giver* roles. The information seeker looks for more information or clarification of ideas, while the information giver provides information that includes facts and examples. Furthermore, members may become an *evaluator/critic,* who evaluates the information and conclusions regarding their usefulness and accuracy; an *energizer,* a motivator who keeps the group moving toward its goal; an *orienter,* who periodically summarizes what has been discussed; or a *coordinator,* who clarifies and shows relationships among ideas, viewpoints, and suggestions.

Group building and maintenance roles help define a group's social atmosphere. The *encouragers* offer praise and recognize the contributions of others. *Harmonizers* are the mediators for disagreements and always try to ensure a positive climate. *Compromisers* attempt to avoid and solve conflicts and find acceptable solutions. *Gatekeepers* manage the flow of interaction in the group. *Standard setters* remind the group of its goals. *Followers* cooperate to work together with other group members. Finally, *feeling expressers* articulate the group's feelings and attitudes.

Guidelines

Planning and Managing a Meeting

1. Identify a purpose, plan an agenda, and distribute the agenda in advance.

2. Invite only people who need to be there (*not* everyone who might have an opinion on the topic).

3. Establish start, break, and stop times, and stick to them.

4. Assign a leader to keep the discussion on track.

5. Decide what follow-up actions are needed after the meeting and set deadlines for their completion.

6. Avoid holding unnecessary meetings.

7. Don't let people drone on, dominate, or avoid participation during discussions.

8. Don't allow conversations to wander off the subject.

9. Follow up to make sure that members act on decisions made at the meeting.

From Harrison Conference Services, Business Schools at the University of Georgia and Georgia State University.

Some individuals may adopt *self-centered roles,* which are generally counterproductive or destructive to a group and tend to hinder group progress. Among them are the *aggressors,* who deflate others to make themselves look better. *Blockers* resist others' ideas and in general disagree with everything. The *recognition seekers* are similar to aggressors in that they want to be the center of the group's attention. Jokers or people who engage in horseplay are referred to as *buffoons. Dominators* are autocrats, who want to be in charge. *Help seekers* are in the group only to satisfy their own needs. Finally, *withdrawers* just don't say or do anything.

In most groups, members are eager to make constructive contributions. From time to time, however, you will encounter individuals whose attitudes are not so positive. For the good of the group, it is important to recognize such people and learn how to cope with them.

Contributions of Group Members

Both the leader and all group members must recognize and handle counterproductive contributions. Sometimes the best approach to these situations is to discuss them openly: "John, you've been quiet about this problem. What do you think?" "Sally, your jokes seem to indicate that you don't believe the issue is very serious. Why?" Sometimes conflict needs to be resolved with a vote by the group. This lets members know the position of the majority so that discussion can continue.

Each group participant should study the agenda in advance in order to be ready to discuss. Probably one of the biggest weaknesses of beginning group participants is being unprepared to discuss; thus valuable time, effort, and input are lost. Successful group outcomes depend on open-mindedness, a positive attitude, the ability to listen, a willingness to contribute, and preparation.

Reaching Group Members' Consensus

The goal of most groups is to arrive at decisions or solutions that are agreed on and acceptable to at least most, if not all, of the group members. The process of reaching consensus assumes that all group members have been able to express how they feel and think about the alternatives and have been given equitable opportunities to influence the outcome. However, it is important that consensus not come too quickly; if it does, the group may be a victim of groupthink, as introduced in Chapter 15. Consensus on controversial issues usually is not arrived at easily. It requires a certain amount of patience and a willingness to look for areas of agreement. This process, of course, can be very time consuming.

Is the time taken to reach consensus worth the effort? It has been proven again and again that groups using effective group discussion methods, such as open communication, come prepared to discuss, are willing to challenge ideas and evidence, and almost always arrive at better-quality decisions than individuals alone.[23] It has also been shown that groups reaching agreement, regardless of the time it takes, are more likely to take ownership of their decisions and maintain their agreement longer.[24]

Communication scholars Steven Beebe and John Masterson provide three recommendations for reaching consensus in groups:

1. Groups have a tendency to change topics and to get off track, so members should try to keep themselves oriented toward the group's goal. Groups often don't reach consensus because they engage in discussing issues irrelevant to their goal.

2. Members should be other oriented and sensitive to all ideas. Listen and do not constantly interrupt one another. Make a good faith effort to set aside your views and seek to understand others.

3. Promote group member interaction and dialogue. It is important that everyone feels that his or her voice is heard and that no one withholds his or her views, even when those views are contrary to those held by others.[25]

Managing Group Conflict

16.4 Describe conflict, its impacts, and the conflict management strategies that can manage it.

When you hear the word *conflict*, what comes to mind? For most people, it conjures up terms such as *argument, dislike, fight, stress, hate, competition, disagreement, hostility, discord, friction, disunity*, and so on. All of these words do relate to conflict. However, they illustrate only the negative side of the concept. After all, in U.S. society, most people value and stress the importance of agreement and getting along with others. However, our society also loves competition. Sayings such as "All's fair in love and war" or "Stick to your guns" are often cited as representative of the American way. But the desire to get along with others and yet to best them in competition contradict each other. The idea that if one person wins, another must lose is implanted in almost every American's mind early in life.

On the one hand, we would like to avoid conflict and preserve unity. On the other hand, we cannot experience the thrill of winning unless we enter into conflict. Is there any middle ground between these two polarities? Can conflict be resolved only by forcing someone to lose? Must conflict always hurt someone?

Whenever people come together to communicate, conflict is nearly inevitable. But conflict does not always have to be harmful. In fact, it can be productive and, if properly managed, it can result in better decisions and solutions to problems.

Conflict and Group Communication

Communication scholars William Wilmot and Joyce Hocker assert that communication and conflict are related in the following ways: Communication behavior often *creates* conflict, communication behavior *reflects* conflict, and communication is the *vehicle* for the productive or destructive management of conflict.[26] *Conflict* was defined in Chapter 14 defined as "an expressed struggle between at least two interdependent parties who perceive incompatible goals, scarce resources, and interference from others in achieving their goals."[27]

Effective group decision making and problem solving often depend on conflict and open disagreement. The benefits of group conflict, when it is understood and controlled, include a deeper understanding of group members and issues, greater involvement and increased motivation, better decisions, and enhanced group cohesiveness. These benefits are more likely when groups accept collaboration and compromise.

Of course, too much conflict can create unmanageable tension and heighten disagreement, resulting in personal attacks on individual group members. If personal attacks come to dominate meetings, they produce no benefits and usually lead to hurt feelings, withdrawal, and eventually the disbanding of the group.

In collaboration, negotiating and problem solving are used to find a solution that fully meets the needs of all parties involved in a group conflict. In other words, each party achieves its desired results. **Principled negotiation** is a procedure that helps group members negotiate consensus by collaboration through the expression of each different need and a search for alternatives to meet those needs. For example, suppose you are serving on a committee to select the commencement speaker, and some committee members want to bring in a controversial speaker. Some of the more radical members want to select Bill Ayers (an elementary education theorist who was a 1960s antiwar activist; who cofounded the violent left wing organization the Weather

principled negotiation

A procedure that helps group members negotiate consensus by collaboration through the expression of each differing need and a search for alternatives to meet those needs.

A committee consisting of management and labor discusses a benefit issue in a conference setting. To gain consensus, members who are not in agreement negotiate until agreement is reached. They do this by identifying different needs and searching for alternatives to meet those needs.

Underground, which conducted a campaign to bomb public buildings during the 1960s and 1970; and who now is a retired professor in the College of Education at the University of Illinois at Chicago, where he held the titles of Distinguished Professor of Education and Senior University Scholar). Other members are recommending Ann Coulter (an American social and political commentator who is well known for her conservative political opinions and the controversial way she defends them), Bill Maher (a former stand-up comedian and host of *Politically Incorrect*, and now host of *Real Time* on HBO, in which he uses a lot of profane language and has been extremely controversial regarding conservative women), or Rick Warren (an American evangelical minister and author—who holds traditional evangelical views on social issues such as same-sex marriage and stem cell research). Much discussion ensues, but both sides eventually see the benefits of each view and agree that a controversial speaker would be good, but not one as controversial as Ayers, Coulter, Maher, or Warren. Ultimately, they decide to invite Timothy Donald "Tim" Cook, an American business executive, and the CEO of Apple Inc. Cook joined Apple in March 1998 as Senior Vice President of Worldwide Operations—he also served as Executive Vice President of Worldwide Sales and Operations—and was Chief Operating Officer until he was named the CEO of Apple on August 24, 2011, when he succeeded Steve Jobs. The collaboration between the committee members generated by the initial conflict has resulted in a speaker they could all agree on. The result is an ideal solution in which both sides win.

The positive outcomes of conflict, according to Gloria Galanes and Katherine Adams, are as follows:

1. Conflict can produce better understanding of both issues and people.
2. Conflict can increase member motivation.
3. Conflict can produce better decisions.
4. Conflict can produce greater cohesiveness among group members.[28]

Conflict Online

Groups, whether they are face-to-face or online, can experience conflict. Online group interaction certainly has its benefits in that it has been regarded as a way to eliminate status disparities and to increase individual participation. The research on conflict seems to indicate inconsistencies between online and face-to-face conflict regarding which is better or worse.[29] As you might suspect, it is easier for those using web-based discussions to be a bit bolder in their use of inflammatory or negative comments than it is in face-to-face interactions.

Research concludes that online group interactions are more likely to display relational and task conflict over procedures than face-to-face group interactions. The conflict is often over the use of the technology itself because often group members become frustrated with it or simply do not know how to use it effectively.[30] It is recommended that groups using web-based group discussions become familiar with the technology and that they spend time creating social and procedural norms to ensure that each group member fully accepts and understands them.[31]

Ethical Behavior and Conflict

Adam and Galanes assert that using ethical behaviors during a conflict situation creates a better understanding of the issues and increases cohesiveness while minimizing destructive outcomes, such as hurt feelings and personal attacks.[32] They list a number of suggestions to help individuals behave ethically during conflicts:

1. Express disagreements openly and honestly. It is important to put disagreements on the table for discussion.

2. Stick to the issues. Be direct and get to the point.

3. Use rhetorical sensitivity when presenting your disagreements. Don't simply put down others' ideas or views.

4. Criticize the idea and not the person.

5. Base disagreements on solid evidence and good reasoning, not on rumor, emotions, or unsubstantiated information.

6. Be receptive to disagreements. Don't become defensive simply because someone disagrees with you. Keep an open mind and listen carefully.

7. Always remain calm even if someone attacks you. Take a reasoned approach and do not take the attack personally.

8. Look for ways to integrate ideas and to negotiate differences whenever possible.

Problem Solving and Decision Making

16.5 **Explain** the reflective thinking process and functional communication theory.

Although the goal of most classroom discussions is to share information, the goal of most other discussions is to solve problems and make decisions—for example, How can we raise more money for new computers? How can we prevent date rape? What can be done to eliminate unethical behavior in our organization?

When solving problems and making decisions, groups must consider the alternatives and arrive at a consensus for the solution. To do this most effectively, they must first take an organized and thorough approach to determining the exact nature of the problem.

Determining and Stating the Problem

Unless an instructor or situation determines a topic to be discussed, the initial step of a classroom group is to select a topic. This is not always easy; after all, the topic has to be both important and interesting to everyone in the group to ensure a good discussion. A starting place might be areas that need improvement on your campus: What should be the role of athletics on the campus? Should better protection be provided for students who attend evening classes? The surrounding community is also a source for discussion topics: What can be done about public parking in the downtown area? What can the business community do to help college students get better jobs? State, regional, and national issues can provide a broader base for topics: Can the state provide sufficient funding to the university? What should be the role of the federal government in providing loans to students? Selecting from thousands of topics and problems takes time. However, if the group does its homework, picking a topic that is agreeable to all members should not be difficult.

After a topic or problem is selected or provided, it should be stated in the form of a question. When phrasing discussion questions, whether for a classroom learning experience or another context, keep the following in mind:[33]

1. The wording should reflect the discussion purpose or task at hand; for example, what should be done to make our campus a green campus?

2. The wording should focus attention on the real problem; for example, what can be done to establish a recycling program on campus?

3. The wording should specify whose behavior is subject to change; for example, how can we encourage students to recycle?

Discuss the Problem and Its Solution

In group situations, whether in the classroom or another context, it is important to determine a plan or procedure for discussing and solving a problem.

DEWEY'S REFLECTIVE THINKING John Dewey, a philosopher during the 1900s, described the mental steps taken by individuals when solving problems. The steps developed by Dewey are referred to as "reflective thinking" steps because they provide a logical, rational way of generating solutions to a problem and deciding on a solution.[34] The Dewey reflective thinking steps are often used by groups as an effective and efficient way to solve problems and make decisions. Here are Dewey's five steps to help solve problems and make decisions:

1. **Clearly identify or define the problem you are trying to solve.** The discussion of a topic can be a good exercise, but if the discussion is not clearly focused or goals are not clearly defined, as suggested earlier in the chapter, the discussion might wander without direction. For example, a group that decides to discuss the quality of public education but does not define its purpose for discussing the topic will likely not come to any conclusion. The group should focus on a clearly identified issue or problem, such as, "How can public education be improved with limited resources?" Thus, the discussion should center on the symptoms of the problem, how big or important is the problem, and why does it need solving.

2. **Analysis of the problem, what are its causes, or the conditions underlying the problem.** Do not start suggesting solutions until the problem has been fully analyzed. Most group scholars generally agree that problems should be thoroughly researched and undestood to arrive at the best solutions. This step will help you not to think of solutions prematurely or before you have a complete understanding of the causes, effects, and symptoms of the problem under discussion. Thus, this step requires that you analyze the causes, what if anything is being done now to solve the problem, why the current approach, if any, isn't working, and how the problem should be approached.

3. **Suggestions of possible solutions.** Describe and list possible solutions to the problem and then discuss each proposed solution's strengths and weaknesses.

4. **Select the best solution then discuss why it is the best and how it will solve the problem.** This step requires an open and free discussion that allows for different points of view but also compromise to arrive at the best possible solution.

5. **Once the best solution is decided upon the group now must decide how it will be put into operation.** Are there any major barriers to putting the solution into action and what is the best way to get the solution into action? Although the reflective thinking steps were designed sequentially and should be followed as such, it is not unusual for groups to deviate from the order when necessary. Thus, it is a good idea to assign some members to monitor the procedures to ensure that the group does not deviate too far from its structure.[35]

GOURAN'S AND HIROKAWA'S FUNCTIONAL THEORY Dewey's classic work focuses on the group problem-solving and decision-making process. Communication researchers Dennis Gouran and Randy Hirokawa built on Dewey's work with their functional theory, which describes how communication can help or hinder group problem solving and decision making.[36] Functional theory assumes that groups want to make good decisions and focuses on ways to improve a group's functional communication. It also assumes the group has all the necessary information and resources needed, as well as the communicative and thinking ability to do the best job. Further,

Gouran and Hirokawa indicate that if those conditions are present, group success depends on three additional factors.

1. **The first factor pertains to the task.** Functional theory asserts that five task requirements must be met for a group to successfully complete its goal:
   - Members fully understand the problem or issue being discussed.
   - They know the minimum criteria for a successful solution.
   - They identify all reasonable solutions from which to choose.
   - They evaluate the advantages and disadvantages of all the reasonable solutions against the agreed-upon criteria for selecting the best solution.
   - They select the best solution.

2. **The second factor pertains to how group members use communication to overcome any obstacles they may confront.** A group's success may face many obstacles. For example:
   - A group may fail to find all of the pertinent information or to share all of the relevant information with one another.
   - Instead of making determination of the best solution the first priority, some group members may put relationships first in order to avoid disagreements or to pressure others to conform and get along.
   - Some group members may be more interested in their own interests instead of what is best for the group.

   As suggested earlier in this chapter, it is important for group members and leaders to deal with members who directly affect the quality of a group's decision.

3. **The third factor pertains to the participants' willingness to review and reconsider their decisions.** The issue is one of commitment to their decision.
   - If any potential flaws arise, the group must be willing to take a second look even it means starting over. The group should review the process and decision to ensure the best possible choice is being made.

In solving problems and making decisions, it is always wise to incorporate a process that follows a plan such as the one suggested by Dewey or by Gouran and Hirokawa. The reflective thinking steps should be used as a guide to decision making, not as an exact formula in approaching every problem. Organization and direction are important in group problem-solving interaction, but inflexible, lockstep organizations can stifle or reduce a group's ability to arrive at the best solutions. According to researchers and group scholars, group members prefer to have direction and a process to follow during group work. Having a plan helps groups generate ideas and come to better decisions and essentially saves time and energy as well as reducing frustrations.[37]

Brainstorming

Sometimes groups find themselves unable to formulate new ideas or be creative in solving a particular aspect of a problem. In such cases, they may find brainstorming helpful. Brainstorming, a technique used to generate as many ideas as possible within a limited amount of time, can be used during any phase of the group discussion process to produce topics, information, or solutions. During the brainstorming session, group members suggest as many topic-related ideas as they can think of, no matter how far-fetched they might seem. One person records the ideas for later analysis. The leader lets the comments flow freely and may prompt the group by suggesting extensions of new ideas that have been voiced.

The leader of a brainstorming group should create an open atmosphere that encourages creativity and spontaneity. Therefore, it is important that the leader be a person of high energy who responds enthusiastically to new ideas. The leader should provide reinforcement and support to all members and encourage the members to

Groups are usually formed because a task must be accomplished or a problem must be solved. The problem illustrated in this photo is obvious, but how to address it requires the group to find a solution.

contribute even if they hit a dry spell. For example, the leader can use prompts such as these: "Let's generate at least two more ideas." "We've done great up to now—let's try one more time to generate some really innovative ideas."

Group members, as well as the leader, must not express disapproval (communicated by comments or looks) of any items until all ideas have been generated. Once the group has run out of ideas or time, the results should be evaluated. During this stage, members should work together to appraise each and every idea. The goal is to determine which idea or ideas merit more attention. It is appropriate to discard unfeasible or weak ideas, to improve undeveloped ideas, to consolidate related ideas, and to discuss further the most promising ones.

Brainstorming via Technology

Groups can share new information and ideas via electronic brainstorming. For example, group members can generate ideas, solutions, or strategies and input those thoughts online. This approach adopts the same principles face-to-face brainstorming uses, except all the ideas are input online. Advantages of this method include the speed of recording, the ability for group members to send their ideas simultaneously, and the ability for a group to work together even if they are physically separated.

Another advantage, according to the research, is that electronic brainstorming generates more ideas than traditional brainstorming.[38] It has been speculated that the increase in ideas and contributions by group members results from the anonymity of the person generating the idea.[39] Group members feel less pressure and less embarrassment about ideas that are later rejected. The ideas that are generated are considered not on the basis of who suggested them but solely on their merit and quality. Like traditional brainstorming, electronic brainstorming encourages group interaction by allowing individual group members to build on the ideas of others.

Evaluating Small-Group Performance

16.6 Describe the role of evaluation in small-group performance

It is important for groups and group members to understand they are responsible for their successes and failures. It is the responsibility of the group to fix its own problems or at least attempt to do so. Of course, when a group cannot resolve a problem, or if a split occurs in the group, sometimes an outside negotiator is necessary, but that should occur only after all other efforts have failed.

To ensure success, every group must periodically evaluate its effectiveness. The evaluation can take place at any time but especially at the end of one task and before another begins.

Evaluation is also important in classroom exercises. As students learn about group communication, they need their instructor's feedback and evaluate themselves. Such self-evaluation should consider the following questions:

1. Are we using our time efficiently? If not, why not?
2. Does everyone have an opportunity to participate?
3. Do some people dominate the discussion?
4. Do people listen to what others are saying?

5. Does each person bring adequate information and research to the discussion?

6. Is the atmosphere free from personal conflict?

7. Does the group communication stay within the agenda?

8. Are members happy with the direction of the discussion? If not, why not?

9. Do we set realistic goals for our meetings?

10. Do we get things accomplished? If not, why not?

For an evaluation to produce results, its findings must be made known to all members of the group. A crucial requirement for such sharing is a nonthreatening atmosphere. The leader and all members must be willing to examine the situation without becoming defensive. If the group is not getting its job done, or if its members are unhappy, corrective steps must be taken.

Summary

Group and Team Building

Objective 16.1 **Understand** how effective groups and teams establish goals and assign roles.

A team is generally more effective than a group because each participant knows that he or she is part of the team and tends to cooperate more fully, establish closeness, and show a strong sense of identity.

- For a group to take a team approach, it must set clear and specific goals.
- For the team to function effectively, each team member must have a clear understanding of the roles he or she plays.

Leadership

Objective 16.2 **Understand** the difference between leadership and leaders and the various leadership styles and behaviors they exhibit.

Leadership is an influence process that includes specific behaviors while a leader is assigned or emerges from the group.

- Leadership is a behavior that helps clarify a group's purpose or guides a group to achieve its goals.
- Leadership style can be measured in two ways: by orientation to either task (concern for accomplishment) and relationship (concern for people) or by the amount of power the leader yields to the members (autocratic, democratic, or laissez-faire styles).
- Sex-role stereotypes suggest that female leaders show more concern for interpersonal relations and tend to be more democratic in their leadership style than male leaders.

Member Participation

Objective 16.3 **Differentiate** among the roles of group members and explain their various contributions.

Successful groups depend on group members' performing a variety of roles, such as group task and building and maintenance roles. Self-centered roles also come into play, which can be counterproductive and destructive.

- Group task roles help accomplish the group's task or objective; group building and maintenance roles define the social atmosphere of the group.
- Self-centered group contributions are generally counterproductive and destructive to the group; the best approach to handling counterproductive and destructive behaviors is to discuss them openly.

Managing Group Conflict

Objective 16.4 **Describe** conflict, its impacts, and the conflict management strategies that can control it.

Groups can experience conflicts, as is true anytime two or more people come together. However, competently trained groups know how to use principled negotiation, a procedure that helps group members negotiate consensus by collaborating to find alternatives to meet differing needs.

- Effective group decision making and problem solving often depend on conflict and open disagreement.
- Online interactions may be more likely to display relational and task conflict than face-to-face interactions.
- Principled negotiation, a procedure that helps groups negotiate consensus, takes into account the other party's views.

- Ethical behavior can help groups increase their understanding of issues and enhance group cohesiveness while minimizing destructive outcomes.

Problem Solving and Decision Making

Objective 16.5 Explain the problem solving and the decision making process.

The goal of most small-group communication is to solve problems or make decisions.

- To do this effectively, groups must be able to state the problem clearly.
- Reflective thinking focuses on the decision-making process and includes becoming aware of the problem, defining and describing it, arriving at possible solutions, evaluating advantages and disadvantages, and then choosing the best solution. Functional theory focuses on the communication process and assumes groups make the best decisions when they have all of the information and resources available to them.

- Groups sometimes find themselves unable to generate new ideas or come up with decisions; thus, brainstorming can be the answer.
- Brainstorming by technology can result in superior results.
- The goal of most groups is to arrive at consensus in their decisions.

Evaluating Small-Group Performance

Objective 16.6 Describe the role of evaluation in small-group performance.

To ensure continuous success and progress, groups should periodically undertake a self-analysis and look for areas in which to improve.

Discussion Starters

1. Describe a competent leader of a group or team.
2. Based on what you read in the chapter do you think men or women make better leaders? Explain.
3. In groups you have participated in, what roles do most participants take?
4. How would you get withdrawn group members back into a discussion without embarrassing them?
5. Set up your organizational strategy for solving the following problem: What should be the role and responsibility of the university in monitoring cultural discrimination?
6. Describe a situation in which brainstorming would be appropriate.
7. Determine the criteria that you think would effectively evaluate a group.

Appendix

Career Development: Preparing for Your Future

Learning Objectives	Outline
This chapter will help you:	
A.1 Describe the qualities employers seek in applicants.	Understanding Qualities Employers Seek
A.2 Explain how to conduct an effective job search.	Conducting the Job Search
A.3 Explain the steps in preparing for a job interview.	Preparing for an Interview
A.4 Describe yourself to potential employers in an effective and competent way to give them information and reasons to hire you.	The Interview
A.5 Explain why employers may accept or reject an applicant.	Getting the Job Offer

It is never too early to prepare for your future, whether you are a first-year student or a senior who is about to graduate. The important part of preparation is getting started, and those who do this early will likely be the best prepared. In this appendix, we examine what you should do to prepare for the internship and employment search—and what you can expect to encounter and how you can make the best impression in the interview.[1]

Understanding Qualities Employers Seek

A.1 Describe the qualities employers seek in applicants.

The National Association of Colleges and Employers (NACE) surveyed 260 (25 percent of its members) employers between August and October 2014 regarding the skills and qualities they look for when hiring new employees. The results of the survey are summarized in Table A.1. The bottom line is that employers are looking for talented people who are flexible and able to adapt to all kinds of situations.

Dr. Kelli Smith, former Assistant Director of Career Services at the University of Nebraska–Lincoln, suggests that students get as much experience in team building and working in teams as possible.[2] According to Smith, companies are looking for individuals who can work with others. One company recruiter asks students the following question: "When you work as a part of a team, what unique role do you play?" Smith said, "Hiring people who are team players is important to many organizations

Table A.1 Skills and Qualities Employers Seek

Skill/Quality	Average Weighted Rating
Ability to make decisions and solve problems	4.70
Ability to verbally communicate with persons inside and outside the organization	4.60
Ability to obtain and process information	4.60
Ability to plan, organize, and prioritize work	4.05
Ability to analyze quantitative data	4.04
Technical knowledge related to the job	4.20
Proficiency with computer software programs	4.01
Ability to create and/or edit written reports	3.70
Ability to sell or influence others	3.60

Skills are rated on a 5-point scale, with 5 = extremely important, 4 = very important, 3 = somewhat important, 2 = not very important, and 1 = not important.
Source: *Job Outlook 2014, National Association of Colleges and Employers.* The report is available to NACE members at http://www.naceweb.org/about-us/press/skills-employers-value-in-new-hires.aspx. Last reviewed on February 21, 2015.,

that have downsized and have fewer management positions because they are much more team-oriented." What is your role when working with others? Is it leading, organizing, brainstorming, or something else?

Internships are also important. Smith suggests that students get involved in internships related to the jobs they will seek after graduation. She says students who have had internships can say they have done the job or similar work, thus giving them a better chance at getting a job than those with no experience. "Such experiences are also key for networking and helping students decide whether or not a certain career is the right fit for them," Smith said.

Almost every career requires skills such as writing, speaking, reading, listening, decision-making, researching, reasoning, creativity, persuasion, leadership, interpersonal communication, and organization. In addition, a number of characteristics may be important for specific jobs: achievement, ambition, assertiveness, competitiveness, dependability, initiative, listening, motivation, oral communication, people orientation, responsibility, and responsiveness.[3] The way you acquire these skills and behaviors is, to a great extent, up to you. Without them, no matter how bright and knowledgeable you might be, landing a job will be extremely difficult, if not impossible.

Employers also look for creativity. Is the applicant spontaneous? Some recruiters will ask "off the wall" questions just to see if this "throws" an applicant. How does an applicant respond in these tough situations? Can the applicant be creative

Making Connections for Success

Thinking about Your Future

Think about what each person must be able to demonstrate in order to land a job. Skills! That one word means a lot to your future. The recurring theme among the experts we surveyed is an emphasis on skills and competencies, rather than on completing specific studies.

1. What do you think are the most important skills employers are looking for, and how would you prove you have them?

2. What advice about your preparation for career interviews do you seek at this time?

Some exceptional sources you might consider to help you answer the above questions and prepare for your job interview are the following: P. Klaus, *Brag: The Art of Tooting Your Own Horn without Blowing It* (New York: Warner Books, 2004); D. Bolles, *What Color Is Your Parachute?* (Berkeley, CA: Ten Speed Press, 2010) (Bolles also has a website you should consider: www.jobhuntersbible.com); M. Carole, *Perfect Phrases for the Perfect Interview* (New York: McGraw-Hill, 2005); J. E. Wall, *Jobseekers Online Goldmine* (Indianapolis, IN: JIST Works, 2006); and M. Yates, *Knock'Em Dead: The Ultimate Job Seekers Guide* (Cincinnati, OH: Adam Media Corp, 2006). Annually, *U.S. News & World Report* describes "best careers." This can be a helpful resource for college students.

with the answers? This is very important to most employers because in business situations with customers, employees often have to respond to sudden changes and unfamiliar problems. What employers look for most in applicants are personal qualities such as assertiveness, self-motivation, ambition, and a competitive instinct. Employers say they can usually learn whether applicants have these qualities by how they present themselves and by the types of activities or jobs they have held while in school.

Conducting the Job Search

A.2 **Explain** how to conduct an effective job search.

In today's economic times, even an applicant with superb qualifications faces tremendous competition for the best jobs. According to placement service data, the average applicant should spend 15 to 25 hours per week searching for employment, but the person who is highly motivated will treat the search as if it were a job itself. The more time a person spends searching, the sooner and more likely he or she will be hired.[4]

Networking

Newspaper and online ads, professional magazines, placement services, former teachers, and people working in jobs you are interested in can all be good sources of job leads. However, the most productive approach to locating jobs is networking. Networking is the systematic contacting of people who can provide information about available jobs or who can offer jobs. Relatives, friends, classmates, colleagues, and people at social and professional gatherings are all potential sources of information. If one of your contacts does not personally know of any job openings, ask if he or she knows of anyone who might. Then contact that person. In this way, your network expands from one person to another, and you gain information from each new contact. Many social networking sites such as Facebook, LinkedIn, or Twitter can be helpful when seeking job opportunities. LinkedIn, the best-known site to connect those with jobs to those looking for work, has over 332 million users and continues to grow.[5] It is not unusual for employers to search networks to find new candidates. LinkedIn allows the user to list past experiences, awards, and skills as well as links to presentations, portfolios, and other documents. But LinkedIn should not be a passive resource where one hopes an organization finds the profile and reaches out for employment opportunities. Users should use LinkedIn to research industries, employers, and key people at organizations of interest. Connecting to professional groups or alumni associations expands the potential number of contacts.

Making Connections for Success

Networking via Social Media

Many online networks will help you with your job search and with preparing you for the job interview. LinkedIn is one professional network many professionals are turning to; it provides a variety of support for professionals and potential employees. It currently has more than 150 million registered users in over 200 countries. It offers an excellent way to connect with others via social media, and it's not uncommon to have professional contacts on Facebook and Twitter as well.

1. Go to LinkedIn and determine how it can help you in your search and preparation for a job.

2. Visit the LinkedIn Learning Center online for information and specific resources available. Take time to review Learning Webinars to learn about developing an online presence and engaging with your network. Plan to complete your profile fully, including a professional summary, work history, and education.

Career Fairs

Most college campuses hold career fairs, which are useful for networking as well as for making contacts with organizations for internships or jobs. Contact the career services office at your college or university and ask when the next career fair will take place in your area. You should attend as many career fairs as time permits. You don't have to wait until your senior year to attend a career fair. By making contact with an organization early in your education, you can establish a relationship with that company as well as be in the best position for getting an internship or a job after graduation.

Some career centers, private employment organizations, or even employers may host "virtual" career fairs where job seekers connect via some form of chat (email, video, phone) during set online meeting times. These types of events usually include job postings and an opportunity for job seekers to post a résumé.

The Internet

One of the most valuable tools available in preparing for the employment interview is the Internet. For example, you can learn how to prepare for the interview, write a résumé, research organizations, find job opportunities, find out what questions are commonly asked in interviews, and even get advice on what to wear to an interview. Most colleges and universities have a career services office you can visit in person or contact through a home page. The career services' home page can be an extremely valuable source of information. The University of Nebraska's (UNL) Career Services, for example, provides information pertaining to almost every aspect of careers and the employment interview. For example, the "job search preparation" area leads to information on *networking*, job search strategies, résumé tips and a sample résumé, how to write cover letters and sample cover letters, whom to give as references, and interviewing tips.

Here are two sample websites for job searches and career information. Conduct an Internet search to find additional sources:

- *Hotjobs.com* (search by job category and advanced search allows geographical limiters).
- *CareerBuilder.com* (search by job type, industry, or field of interest).

In addition, consult targeted websites appropriate to your needs. Such websites may have a geographic focus to learn about opportunities in the community in which you want to work; industry focus such as government, nonprofit, or education; or types of positions such as internship listing sites.

It is increasingly common for job applicants to connect with potential employers electronically. If you fill out an online application, here are some suggestions:

- Proof your information as carefully and as thoroughly as you can—ask someone who is competent in editing to read it to ensure it is error free.
- Follow instructions on the website. You should, however, be careful when providing personal information such as Social Security number. Unless the site is secure, it is recommended that you not provide your Social Security number.
- Look at the entire application site before filling out anything to plan what and how you will respond. Make sure you understand how the "submit" options work so that your application information is received.
- Submit separate applications for each individual position in which you have an interest. Update or change your profile as appropriate to fit each position.

- Cover letters may not be requested or allowed on the site, but often there are open text boxes where parts of your cover letter could be included, if appropriate.

- Contact the employer directly about specific openings after submitting electronically to ensure your materials were received.[6]

Here are some additional suggestions for applying via email:

- Make sure your email account name will add to your credibility.

- Use a meaningful and short subject line and include your name (for example, "Application from Mary Smith regarding your sales representative position").

- Use the format the employer requests and include your résumé in the text or as an attachment. Write it as a formal business letter, using an appropriate greeting.

- If you attach your résumé and cover letter via email, use a standard font such as Times New Roman or Arial. You may want to save your documents in PDF form so they may be easily viewed on a variety of email and web browsers. [7]

Preparing for an Interview

A.3 **Explain** the steps in preparing for a job interview.

Preparing for a job interview takes planning and some thought about what will be expected of you as an applicant. Initial job interviews typically average only 20 to 30 minutes—a short time in comparison to the time you spend earning a college degree. *Yet these are probably the most important minutes you will spend in determining your future.* You would be surprised to learn how many applicants fail to plan adequately. Instead, they enter the interview saying essentially, "Here I am, now what?" This gives the impression they are indifferent, an impression that is seldom dispelled in the course of the interview. It's up to you to ensure you do not leave an impression of indifference and that you present a positive picture of yourself.

Writing a Résumé

A résumé is a written document that briefly and accurately describes an individual's personal, educational, and professional qualifications and experiences. A well-written résumé increases a person's chances of making a good impression. A poorly written résumé can seriously jeopardize a person's chances, even though he or she may be well qualified.

Examples of chronological résumés listing experience from most recent to least recent (see Figure A.1), a chronological résumé and letter of application (see Figure A.2), a chronological résumé with relevant experience and letter of application (see Figure A.3), and, an internship résumé and cover letter of inquiry (see Figure A.4) are shown on pages 386–389.

A résumé is an extremely powerful form of communication. Because it represents an applicant, it must be accurate, complete, and neat. The contents and layouts of résumés vary as widely as the number of individuals who apply for jobs. A general rule, and the safest, is to keep it simple; limit it to one or two pages; and list items within each section, beginning with the most current one. Employers are busy and do not have time to read lengthy, overly involved reports.

Most résumés include the following sections: introductory information, career objective, educational training, work experiences, extracurricular activities, and references (which is an optional section). The introductory information section should include the applicant's name, address, phone number, and email address. As an

Figure A.1 Self-Prepared Résumé and Cover Letter, Emphasizing Key Words from Job Description

This figure illustrates a résumé and cover letter format many students use. The résumé layout is fairly standard, but it may vary depending on the work experiences of the individual.

Chronological Resume

The chronological resume format lists experiences in reverse chronological order (most recent to least recent). This is the style most commonly used by recent graduates.

TIP: Use quantities in your experience descriptions to communicate results and your level of responsibility.

Lauren Adamson
ladamson@hotmail.com

Current Address
479 Oak Street
Lincoln, NE 68508
402-555-3223

Permanent Address:
1054 Plum Avenue
Ashland, NE 68888
314-555-6389

OBJECTIVE

A position in agribusiness with special emphasis on customer interaction and product marketing

EDUCATION

University of Nebraska–Lincoln
Bachelor of Science, December 2014
Majors: Agribusiness and Agricultural Economics, GPA: 3.59

Study Abroad: New Zealand Study Tour/Lincoln University
Christ Church, New Zealand, Spring 2013

EXPERIENCE

Student Ambassador, August 2012 - present
College of Agricultural Sciences and Natural Resources (CASNR), Lincoln, NE
- Coordinate and participate in college outreach and recruitment activities
- Generate public and student awareness of CASNR programs
- Conduct campus tours and answer questions for prospective students

Owner/Operator, March 2011 - present
Adamson Farms, Ashland, NE
- Develop, manage and financially operate a 75 sow farrow-to-finishing hog operation
- Monitor animal health, market product, process records, and operate and maintain equipment

Agricultural Youth Coordinator, September 2012 - October 2013
Nebraska Department of Agriculture, Lincoln, NE
- Planned and coordinated the 21st annual Nebraska Agricultural Youth Institute (NAYI), a 7-day conference for 180 high school juniors and seniors
- Administered an $80,000 budget and dispersed funds to youth educational programs
- Coordinated activities of 20 college-age ambassadors responsible for conducting NAYI

ACTIVITIES & HONORS

Agribusiness Advisory Council
Ag Economics/Agribusiness Club President (2014) and Membership Chair (2013)
Nebraska Agricultural Youth Council
College of Agricultural Sciences & Natural Resources Advisory Board
Gamma Sigma Delta, Agricultural Honorary

Caleb Richards
2222 Wilcox Street
Lincoln, NE 68500
crichards@hotmail.com
314-555-6389

OBJECTIVE

To obtain a chemist position utilizing laboratory, organization and analytical skills

EDUCATION

Bachelor of Science (May 2015)
University of Nebraska-Lincoln
Major: Chemistry   Minor: Mathematics   GPA: 3.6/4.0

EXPERIENCE

Undergraduate Research Assistant, August 2013- Present
UNL Chemistry Department, Lincoln, NE
- Develop procedure for making Ti02 nanotubes of designated lengths
- Obtain results and revise procedures based on designated parameters
- Perform hydrothermal method and analyze nanotubes

Lab Technician, May 2012-August 2013
GeneSeek, Inc., Lincoln, NE
- Prepared polyacrylamide slab gels
- Oversaw cleaning and maintenance of instruments

SKILLS

Instrumentation and Technology
- Spectroscopic Technology - NMR, UV-Vis, HPLC, GC/MS, IR, Brillouin, XRPD, DSC
- Molecular modeling programs including ChemSketch

Laboratory Procedures and Techniques
- Multistep Reactions, Workup, Analysis, Acid Hydrolysis
- Titrations, distillations, crystallizations, recrystallizations, polymerizations, and chromatography
- Basic and advanced wet-bench techniques
- Preparation of stock solutions and reagents

HONORS AND AWARDS

- Dean's List, 4 years
- American Chemical Society
- Mortar Board
- Ed & Susan StettlerAcademic Scholarship

TIP: In academic and career areas requiring technical skills, incorporate a Skills section describing experience with processes, instrumentation or equipment.

Resume and cover letter reviews by Career Services
225 Nebraska Union
Weekdays, Walk-ins 10 a.m.-4p.m.
By appointment via MyPlan (Blackboard) or 402.472.3145

Figure A.2 Self-Prepared Functional or Combination Résumé

This functional résumé emphasizes a person's skills. The résumé layout is fairly standard, but it may vary, depending on the work experiences and skills of the individual. It might be most useful by those making a career change. The combination résumé merges elements of both chronological and functional styles. A summary of qualifications or strengths is emphasized in this example.

Chronological Resume

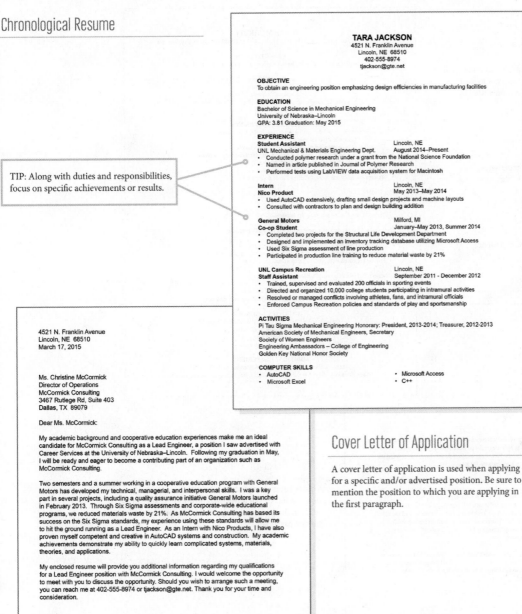

TIP: Along with duties and responsibilities, focus on specific achievements or results.

TARA JACKSON
4521 N. Franklin Avenue
Lincoln, NE 68510
402-555-8974
tjackson@gte.net

OBJECTIVE
To obtain an engineering position emphasizing design efficiencies in manufacturing facilities

EDUCATION
Bachelor of Science in Mechanical Engineering
University of Nebraska–Lincoln
GPA: 3.81 Graduation: May 2015

EXPERIENCE
Student Assistant — Lincoln, NE
UNL Mechanical & Materials Engineering Dept. — August 2014–Present
- Conducted polymer research under a grant from the National Science Foundation
- Named in article published in Journal of Polymer Research
- Performed tests using LabVIEW data acquisition system for Macintosh

Intern — Lincoln, NE
Nico Product — May 2013–May 2014
- Used AutoCAD extensively, drafting small design projects and machine layouts
- Consulted with contractors to plan and design building addition

General Motors — Milford, MI
Co-op Student — January–May 2013, Summer 2014
- Completed two projects for the Structural Life Development Department
- Designed and implemented an inventory tracking database utilizing Microsoft Access
- Used Six Sigma assessment of line production
- Participated in production line training to reduce material waste by 21%

UNL Campus Recreation — Lincoln, NE
Staff Assistant — September 2011 - December 2012
- Trained, supervised and evaluated 200 officials in sporting events
- Directed and organized 10,000 college students participating in intramural activities
- Resolved or managed conflicts involving athletes, fans, and intramural officials
- Enforced Campus Recreation policies and standards of play and sportsmanship

ACTIVITIES
Pi Tau Sigma Mechanical Engineering Honorary: President, 2013-2014; Treasurer, 2012-2013
American Society of Mechanical Engineers, Secretary
Society of Women Engineers
Engineering Ambassadors – College of Engineering
Golden Key National Honor Society

COMPUTER SKILLS
- AutoCAD
- Microsoft Excel
- Microsoft Access
- C++

4521 N. Franklin Avenue
Lincoln, NE 68510
March 17, 2015

Ms. Christine McCormick
Director of Operations
McCormick Consulting
3467 Rutlege Rd, Suite 403
Dallas, TX 89079

Dear Ms. McCormick:

My academic background and cooperative education experiences make me an ideal candidate for McCormick Consulting as a Lead Engineer, a position I saw advertised with Career Services at the University of Nebraska–Lincoln. Following my graduation in May, I will be ready and eager to become a contributing part of an organization such as McCormick Consulting.

Two semesters and a summer working in a cooperative education program with General Motors has developed my technical, managerial, and interpersonal skills. I was a key part in several projects, including a quality assurance initiative General Motors launched in February 2013. Through Six Sigma assessments and corporate-wide educational programs, we reduced materials waste by 21%. As McCormick Consulting has based its success on the Six Sigma standards, my experience using these standards will allow me to hit the ground running as a Lead Engineer. As an Intern with Nico Products, I have also proven myself competent and creative in AutoCAD systems and construction. My academic achievements demonstrate my ability to quickly learn complicated systems, materials, theories, and applications.

My enclosed resume will provide you additional information regarding my qualifications for a Lead Engineer position with McCormick Consulting. I would welcome the opportunity to meet with you to discuss the opportunity. Should you wish to arrange such a meeting, you can reach me at 402-555-8974 or tjackson@gte.net. Thank you for your time and consideration.

Sincerely,

Tara Jackson

Tara Jackson

Enclosure

Cover Letter of Application

A cover letter of application is used when applying for a specific and/or advertised position. Be sure to mention the position to which you are applying in the first paragraph.

7

Figure A.3 Self-Prepared Transition or Academic Résumé

The transition résumé is helpful when converting a high school résumé to a college résumé. The academic résumé is useful when applying for academic scholarships, awards, honors, or graduate or professional school.

Chronological Resume With Relevant Experience

The chronological resume format lists experiences in reverse chronological order (most recent to least recent). This is the style most commonly used by recent graduates.

TIP: Emphasize significant experience, paid or unpaid, by creating a "Relevant Experience" section.

TIP: Additional, non-related experience may be listed simply to show ability to manage time, handle money or work with the public, etc.

DAVID MORETTI
56 Valley View Road | Lincoln, NE 68510 | 402-555-5487 | dmoretti@yahoo.com

OBJECTIVE
To obtain a position in the human services field working with at-risk youth.

EDUCATION
Bachelor of Arts
University of Nebraska-Lincoln
Majors: Psychology and Sociology, GPA: 3.2, Major GPA: 3.5
May 2015

RELEVANT EXPERIENCE
Psychiatric Technician, Adolescent Services, Lincoln Regional Center
Lincoln, NE September 2014–Present
- Observe and document resident behaviors for 12-18 year old clients.
- Participate in treatment team meetings and provide input on treatment plans.
- Implement Individualized Treatment Plans for over 25 clients.
- Provide positive reinforcement for appropriate behavior.
- Enforce residence unit rules, and discipline as necessary.

Big Brother, YMCA
Lincoln, NE, December 2012–December 2014
- Provided support and mentoring for 2 adolescents.
- Trained 7 other volunteers to be Big Brothers.

Recreation Therapy Intern, Lancaster County Health Department
Lincoln, NE, September 2013–August 2014
- Planned and coordinated social and recreational outings.
- Accompanied individuals and small groups on recreational community trips.
- Provided residents with opportunity to interact with peers.

Volunteer, Nebraska Center for Children and Youth
Omaha, NE, Summer 2013
- Served as Volleyball Coach for 3 teams of 10 players each.
- Assisted Activities Director with programming, equipment, and marketing.

ACTIVITIES & HONORS
Undergraduate Psychology Association (Active President)
Psi Chi Psychology Honorary
Dean's List
A.J. Lacey Scholarship

ADDITIONAL EXPERIENCE
Team Member, Target, Lincoln, NE, September 2011–May 2013
Shop Attendant, Highlands Golf Course, Omaha, NE, January 2010–August 2011

---

56 Valley View Rd.
Lincoln, NE 68510
January 20, 2015

Pat Trebor
Program Director
New Beginnings
340 South 21st St.
Phoenix, AZ 99701

Dear Pat Trebor:

Upon my graduation from the University of Nebraska–Lincoln in May 2015, I hope to become a part of a program such as New Beginnings, working with at-risk youth. I was happy to see the Program Leader on the New Beginnings web site. I have completed the online application and am submitting my resume for the position.

Having begun my college career as a pre-med student, I have a solid background in Chemistry as well as Physiology. My academic move to Psychology built upon this base, and, in combination with my volunteer, intern, and work experiences, has brought me to a place from which I can make a positive difference and significant contribution to the mission of New Beginnings. As a Psychiatric Technician, I have demonstrated the ability to think and act quickly and effectively. Moreover, I have proven myself disciplined in time management and resourceful by managing full-time coursework, part-time employment, and campus involvement.

Thank you for your consideration of my qualifications for the Program Leader position with New Beginnings. I would be happy to visit with you about the opportunity in more detail at your convenience. If you wish to arrange such a meeting, please contact me 402-555-5487 or dmoretti@yahoo.com.

Sincerely,

David Moretti

David Moretti

Enclosure

Cover Letter of Application

A cover letter of application is used when applying for a specific and/or advertised position. Be sure to mention the position to which you are applying in the first paragraph.

Resume and cover letter reviews by Career Services
225 Nebraska Union
Weekdays, Walk-ins 10 a.m.-4p.m.
By appointment via MyPlan (Blackboard) or 402.472.3145

FIGURE A.4 Internship and Cover Letter of Inquiry

Internship résumé highlights course work and areas of internship to potential employers and the cover letter of inquiry is used when uncertain about what jobs or positions are available with a particular employer.

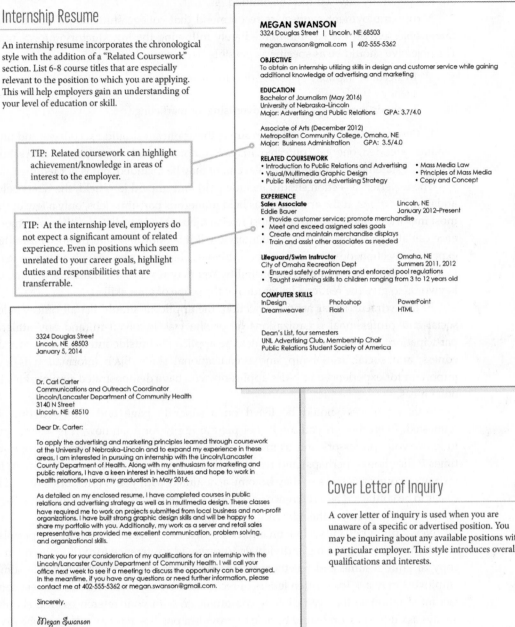

Internship Resume

An internship resume incorporates the chronological style with the addition of a "Related Coursework" section. List 6-8 course titles that are especially relevant to the position to which you are applying. This will help employers gain an understanding of your level of education or skill.

TIP: Related coursework can highlight achievement/knowledge in areas of interest to the employer.

TIP: At the internship level, employers do not expect a significant amount of related experience. Even in positions which seem unrelated to your career goals, highlight duties and responsibilities that are transferrable.

MEGAN SWANSON
3324 Douglas Street | Lincoln, NE 68503

megan.swanson@gmail.com | 402-555-5362

OBJECTIVE
To obtain an internship utilizing skills in design and customer service while gaining additional knowledge of advertising and marketing

EDUCATION
Bachelor of Journalism (May 2016)
University of Nebraska–Lincoln
Major: Advertising and Public Relations   GPA: 3.7/4.0

Associate of Arts (December 2012)
Metropolitan Community College, Omaha, NE
Major: Business Administration   GPA: 3.5/4.0

RELATED COURSEWORK
- Introduction to Public Relations and Advertising
- Visual/Multimedia Graphic Design
- Public Relations and Advertising Strategy
- Mass Media Law
- Principles of Mass Media
- Copy and Concept

EXPERIENCE
Sales Associate   Lincoln, NE
Eddie Bauer   January 2012–Present
- Provide customer service; promote merchandise
- Meet and exceed assigned sales goals
- Create and maintain merchandise displays
- Train and assist other associates as needed

Lifeguard/Swim Instructor   Omaha, NE
City of Omaha Recreation Dept   Summers 2011, 2012
- Ensured safety of swimmers and enforced pool regulations
- Taught swimming skills to children ranging from 3 to 12 years old

COMPUTER SKILLS
InDesign   Photoshop   PowerPoint
Dreamweaver   Flash   HTML

Dean's List, four semesters
UNL Advertising Club, Membership Chair
Public Relations Student Society of America

3324 Douglas Street
Lincoln, NE 68503
January 5, 2014

Dr. Carl Carter
Communications and Outreach Coordinator
Lincoln/Lancaster Department of Community Health
3140 N Street
Lincoln, NE 68510

Dear Dr. Carter:

To apply the advertising and marketing principles learned through coursework at the University of Nebraska–Lincoln and to expand my experience in these areas, I am interested in pursuing an internship with the Lincoln/Lancaster County Department of Health. Along with my enthusiasm for marketing and public relations, I have a keen interest in health issues and hope to work in health promotion upon my graduation in May 2016.

As detailed on my enclosed resume, I have completed courses in public relations and advertising strategy as well as in multimedia design. These classes have required me to work on projects submitted from local business and non-profit organizations. I have built strong graphic design skills and will be happy to share my portfolio with you. Additionally, my work as a server and retail sales representative has provided me excellent communication, problem solving, and organizational skills.

Thank you for your consideration of my qualifications for an internship with the Lincoln/Lancaster County Department of Community Health. I will call your office next week to see if a meeting to discuss the opportunity can be arranged. In the meantime, if you have any questions or need further information, please contact me at 402-555-5362 or megan.swanson@gmail.com.

Sincerely,

Megan Swanson

Megan Swanson

Attachment

Cover Letter of Inquiry

A cover letter of inquiry is used when you are unaware of a specific or advertised position. You may be inquiring about any available positions with a particular employer. This style introduces overall qualifications and interests.

applicant, you are not required to provide information that might be used in a discriminatory way. This includes your age, sex, marital status, race, religion, and other data as set forth by the Title VII Equal Employment Opportunity Act of 1972 and other affirmative action laws. The inclusion of such facts in a résumé is up to the applicant, but it is generally advised they be omitted.

Many employment counselors recommend that college students include a brief career objective on the résumé immediately following the introductory information. The objective should be as specific as possible. Two examples:

> To become a public relations director in either a major corporation or an agency.
> To obtain experience in sales, advertising, or marketing.

In the educational section of the résumé, the applicant should list colleges and universities attended, degrees conferred, majors, minors, special major subjects, and scholarships. A statement about grade achievement may be included, but is not required.

The experience section should include paid and unpaid jobs held, the dates held, and their locations. If the applicant has held numerous part-time jobs, only a few of the most important, most recent, and most relevant jobs should be listed. Other job experience can always be discussed at the interview if it is appropriate to do so. Within this experience section, describe your responsibilities. Start each phrase with an action verb followed by details about the responsibility. You may want to use numbers, dollars, or keywords to give the reader a better idea of the scope of your skills.

In the extracurricular activities section, the applicant should list all offices held, social and professional organizations he or she was involved in, and any athletic participation. This section demonstrates the applicant's outside interests; well roundedness; and social, leadership, and organizational skills. Such information is less important for experienced or older applicants who have demonstrated similar skills in other areas.

Your references should be listed on a separate page and provided only if requested. Even though you might not plan to apply for a job now, it is wise to get to know your professors and to make sure they get to know you. Find appropriate times (office hours, perhaps) and reasons (discussion of a paper or an assignment) to visit with your professors so they become acquainted with you. Professors will find it easier to be contacted as a reference or write a letter of recommendation for you if they know who you are, and the reference will be more personal and believable.

Never put a person's name on a reference list unless you have his or her permission to do so. When asking individuals to serve as a reference for you, give them a copy of your résumé and tell them what kind of job you are seeking. While some employers may ask for written letters of recommendation, most will just request contact information so they can directly communicate with your references. You should always ask if the person would be able to provide a positive reference. If he or she says no or seems hesitant, then move on to someone else.

After you write your résumé, proofread it carefully for errors and omissions. Then ask a counselor or career advisor in the career services office or a professor to suggest improvements. If you follow these steps, your completed résumé should be acceptable.

Creating Your Website or Blog

Many of today's job applicants successfully use social media or create websites as a way to get their résumé or portfolio out to others. By doing this, you create another avenue and effective means of selling yourself and what you have to offer, if you do it carefully and follow the guidelines already suggested in this appendix. You should develop these sites with professionalism to showcase your creative, design, technical, and writing skills.

Making Connections for Success

The Dark Side of the Web

Some employers now require applicants to provide passwords for their social media sites along with their résumés and references. Companies not asking for passwords have taken other steps—asking potential employees to friend their HR managers or to log on to a company computer while interviewing. Other employers ask hired employees to sign no disparagement agreements that essentially prevent the employee from saying or writing anything negative about an employer on social media.[8]

1. How will you respond to such requests should you be asked?

2. What can you do to avoid having your social media pages become a negative influence on whether or not you are hired?

Researching the Organization via the Web

Before arriving for an interview, you should know the full name of the company and background information on the company's history; where its headquarters, plants, offices, or stores are located; what products or services it offers; and what its economic growth has been as well as its future prospects. Such knowledge demonstrates your initiative and interest to the interviewer and can serve as a springboard for discussion. This also shows you have an interest in the company, rather than giving the impression you're settling for whatever job you can find.

Begin your search by conducting an online search for the organization. Pursue the sites fully; often there is an "about" or "organization information" tap that describes the organization—its history, locations, services, products, subsidiaries, and so on. You will likely find additional sites that provide information about organizations in the news, competitive information, and other tidbits that will clearly indicate you have been thorough in doing your homework and are truly interested in the organization. You can also visit your campus or career service's library if you are unable to find the desired information online.

Developing Questions to Ask the Interviewer

In preparation for the interview, make a list of possible questions to ask the interviewer. Sometimes an interviewer might choose to say little or to stop talking altogether, in which case it becomes your responsibility to carry the conversation by asking questions and continuing to emphasize your qualifications for the job. How you ask the question is important; for example, if you know some travel is involved, and you want to travel, instead of asking, "How much traveling is involved in the job?" you might ask, "What kinds of opportunities for travel are there?" The latter question conveys more enthusiasm than the former. Sample questions you might ask include: "Are there training programs for new employees?" "What's the next step up from the starting position?" "Will I be able to continue my education?" "Why do you work for the organization or company?" "What do you like most about working for the organization or company?"

The Mock Interview

It is highly recommended you prepare by participating in several mock interviews prior to interviewing with potential employers. Most university and college career services offer mock interviews. These are done to help prepare you for the questions you are likely to be asked and to give you advice on how to present yourself more effectively. These mock interviews may also be video recorded so you can see just how you appear in the interview and what you might need to do to create a better impression.

If the career services center doesn't offer mock interviews, ask an advisor, a friend, or a classmate to rehearse with you. The mock interview should be as realistic as possible so you experience what the actual interview may be like.

How to Dress for an Interview

Your primary goal in dressing for an interview is to feel great about the way you look while projecting an image that matches the requirements of the job and the company. Go for perfection. Wear professionally pressed clothing in natural fabrics. Although casual clothing in many workplace settings is acceptable today, it is still wise to be conservative in what you wear to an interview. A good guide for interview clothing is to dress "one step above" what you would wear on the job. You want to be remembered as a professional with skills, not for inappropriate attire.

The Interview

A.4 **Describe** yourself to potential employers in an effective and competent way to give them information and reasons to hire you.

Research suggests most interviewers develop a strong opinion about a job applicant within the first 30 seconds. If you do poorly at the opening, your chances of getting the job are slim, no matter how brilliantly you handle the rest of the interview. It might seem unfair or superficial, but people do judge others on the basis of first impressions, and such impressions can be long lasting.

Creating a Favorable First Impression

Think of the employment interview for what it is—a sale. You must sell yourself, and the best way to do that is to know yourself thoroughly, both your strengths and your weaknesses. If you create a positive first impression with recruiters, they will more likely show a positive regard toward you, provide you with more detailed information about the job, sell their organization to you, and ultimately spend less time asking questions.[9]

As a job applicant, show good judgment and common sense about appearance, assertiveness, being on time, and being at the right place. Always maintain eye contact with the interviewer; it shows that you are confident. Most interviewers greet the applicant with a handshake. Make sure your clasp is firm.

Before leaving, try to find out exactly what action will follow the interview and when it will happen. Shake hands as you say goodbye and thank the interviewer for spending time with you. If you plan ahead and follow these simple suggestions, you should be able to avoid any serious problems.

Frequently Asked Questions

Successful applicants listen carefully to the entire question and think before responding. They are honest and, while rehearsed and prepared, do not give canned answers. They are enthusiastic, speak positively about themselves and their experiences, and ask questions of the interviewer. Here are some common questions interviewers ask and some possible responses to them.

1. **"What can you tell me about yourself?"** This is not an invitation to give your life history. The interviewer is looking for clues about your character, qualifications, ambitions, and motivations. The following is a good example of a positive

response. "In high school, I was involved in competitive sports, and I always tried to improve in each sport in which I participated. As a college student, I worked in a clothing store part time and found that I could sell things easily. The sale was important, but for me, it was even more important to make sure the customer was satisfied. It wasn't long before customers came back to the store and specifically asked for me to help them. I'm very competitive, and it means a lot to me to be the best."

2. **"Why do you want to work for us?"** This is an obvious question, and if you have done research on the company, you should be able to give a good answer. Organize your reasons into several short sentences that clearly spell out your interest. "You are a leader in the field of electronics. Your company is a Fortune 500 company. Your management is very progressive."

3. **"Why should I hire you?"** Once again, you should not be long winded, but you should provide a summary of your qualifications. Be positive and show that you are capable of doing the job. "Based on the internships I have participated in and the related part-time experiences I have had, I can do the job."

4. **"How do you feel about your progress to date?"** Never apologize for what you have done. "I think I did well in school. In fact, in a number of courses I received the highest exam scores in the class." "As an intern for the X Company, I received some of the highest evaluations given in years." "Considering that I played on the university's volleyball team and worked part time, I think you'll agree that I accomplished quite a bit during my four years in school."

5. **"What would you like to be doing five years from now?"** Know what you can realistically accomplish. You can find out by talking to others about what they accomplished in their first five years with a particular company. "I hope to be the best I can be at my job, and because many in this line of work are promoted to area manager, I am planning on that also."

6. **"What is your greatest weakness?"** You cannot avoid this question by saying that you do not have any; everyone has weaknesses. The best approach is to admit your weakness but show that you are working on it and have a plan to overcome it. If possible, cite a weakness that will work to the company's advantage. "I'm not very good at detail work, but I have been working on it, and I've improved dramatically over the past several years." "I'm such a perfectionist that I won't stop until a report is written just right."

7. **"What is your greatest strength?"** Do not brag or become too egotistical, but let the employer know that you believe in yourself and that you know your strengths. "I believe my strongest asset is my ability to persist in getting things done. I feel a real sense of accomplishment when I finish a job and it turns out just as I'd planned. I've set some high goals for myself. For example, I want to graduate with highest distinction. And even though I had a slow start in my first year, I made up for it by doing an honors thesis."

8. **"What goals have you set, and how did you meet them?"** This question examines your ability to plan ahead and meet your plan with specific actions. "Last year, during a magazine drive to raise money for our band trip, I set my goal at raising 20 percent more than I had the year before. I asked each of my customers from last year to give me the name of one or two new people who might also buy a magazine. I not only met my goal, but was the top salesperson on the drive."

Here are a few other questions commonly asked in the employment interview:

What is your dream job?
What type of supervisors do you do your best work for?

What kind of legacy did you leave in college?

What are the differences between a leader and a manager?

What motivates you to get up in the morning?

Do you consider yourself a risk taker?

What was the last risk you took?

What five characteristics would make you a great salesperson?

No matter what question you are asked, answer it honestly and succinctly. Most interviewers are looking for positive statements, well-expressed ideas, persuasiveness, and clear thinking under pressure.

If you are asked a question that violates the affirmative action laws, you can decline to answer. You might say, "Can you explain how that question is relevant to the position being offered?" You might simply ask the interviewer why he or she is asking you that question. Make sure that you are tactful, but be firm in letting the interviewer know he or she is doing something illegal.

Many employers use a behavioral interviewing style. Rather than ask if you have a specific skill or trait, the employer asks you to provide a specific example of a time when you demonstrated the skill or trait. For these questions, tell a brief but descriptive story with a clear:

- Beginning (the situation or challenge being faced)
- Middle (the action that you specifically took)
- End (the results)

If you do not have the direct experience requested, provide examples of similar situations. Use stories with positive outcomes whenever possible, but if not, add what you learned from the experience.

Interviewing and Technology

Approximately 150 million employment interviews are conducted in the United States each year, resulting in hundreds of thousands of jobs filled. Surveys have indicated that 82 percent of all companies are using or will be using videoconference technology such as Skype to conduct recruiting interviews.[10] Although the technology allows the mediated interview to be comparable to face-to-face interviews, there are significant differences. Some find it more difficult to interact freely and naturally while on screen. Because visual cues are limited by seeing only the upper body or faces of participants, nonverbal cues are fewer. One study found employers had trouble "reading nonverbal behaviors such as facial expression, eye contact, and fidgeting" and determining "whether a pause was due to the technology, or the applicant being stumped."[11] If you are asked to interview via video, make sure you test the technology prior to the interview. Maintain an uncluttered, professional background and dress professionally. Look at the camera rather than the screen or keyboard to maintain eye contact.

Many employers use telephone interviews as a way to identify and recruit candidates for employment. Phone interviews are often used to screen candidates and narrow the pool of applicants who will be invited for in-person interviews. They are also used as a way to minimize the expenses involved in interviewing out-of-town candidates. With the increase in cell phone usage, the phone interview has its own challenges. Make sure the phone is fully charged and you have a strong signal. You may want to purchase a headset to increase the sound quality as well as keep your hands free during the interview.

Writing a Thank You Note

You should always follow up every interview with a brief but professional note, thanking the interviewer for his or her time. The thank-you note should follow as soon as possible, but promptness is not as important as what you say. A thank-you note should be sent regardless of whether or not you think you will get an offer. If you can send a hand-written note, it is a very personal way of saying thank you and likely will make a good impression on the interviewer. If much of the correspondence with the employer was conducted via email, a formal thank-you may be sent through email, which also helps provide a more timely response to the employer.

Getting the Job Offer

A.5 **Explain** why employers may accept or reject an applicant.

You have worked hard to prepare yourself to launch your career. Some final considerations may help you present yourself in the best possible light.

Factors Leading to Job Offers

A well-rounded applicant with good grades, some relevant work experience, a variety of extracurricular activities, an all-around pleasant personality, and effective written and oral communication skills is more likely to get job offers than are those who do not possess these qualities, according to Jason Meyers of *Collegiate Employment Institute Newsletter*.[12] Meyers says, "Sounds too good to be true? Perhaps it is, but a candidate who strives to attain these qualities and who comes across as a hard-working, mature individual should have a promising career outlook."[13]

A research study cited by Meyers in his article asked recruiters to describe what they believed to be the qualities of a well-rounded individual. They listed maturity, ability to be part of a team, good work ethic, good decision-making skills, superior work habits, and good judgment. Another study cited by Meyers found the most popular characteristics recruiters sought in job applicants fit two categories: (1) quantifiable characteristics, such as grade point average, education, and work experience; and (2) interpersonal characteristics, such as communication skills, personality, and career and management skills. The study suggests that a balance of the quantifiable characteristics and interpersonal characteristics is what makes an ideal job candidate.[14]

It seems that those who are well prepared; have effective communication skills; are mature, motivated, hard-working, team players; and can make good decisions will always be in demand. You must ask yourself how you match up to these qualities now and try to improve in those areas in which you are not as strong. You must also be able to demonstrate that you actually possess these qualities through the actions you have taken.

Factors Leading to Rejection

Employers from numerous companies were asked, "What negative factors most often lead to the rejection of an applicant?" Here are their responses:

1. Negative personality or poor impression; more specifically, lack of motivation, ambition, maturity, aggressiveness, or enthusiasm, or lack of respect—not knowing the interviewer's name or using his or her first name shows disrespect

2. Inability to communicate; poor communication skills

3. Lack of competence; inadequate training

4. Over exaggerated skills and experience on the résumé

5. Lack of specific goals

6. Failure to clean social media sites; digital junk—pictures that might be either good or bad or seem scandalous

7. Lack of interest in type of work, showing a bad attitude, or exhibiting a slight arrogance during the interview

8. Unwillingness to travel or relocate

9. Poor preparation for the interview and/or showing up late

10. Lack of experience

11. Demonstrating emotional distress[15]

You must realize that a rejection or not receiving a job offer has a lot to do with the number of people seeking jobs and the number of jobs available. You can, of course, enhance your chances of getting job offers by being prepared and presenting yourself in a positive and energetic way.

Glossary

A

abstract word   The symbol for an idea, quality, or relationship.

ad hominem   A fallacy that attacks a person rather than the argument itself. This is also referred to as *name-calling*.

adoption   An action that asks listeners to demonstrate their acceptance of attitudes, beliefs, or values by performing the behavior suggested by the speaker.

advance organizer   A statement that warns the listener significant information is coming.

agenda   A list of all topics to be discussed during a meeting.

analogy   A comparison of two things that are similar in certain essential characteristics.

androgynous   Having both male and female traits.

Androgyny   A socially constructed concept related to having both masculine and feminine traits.

antonym   A word, phrase, or concept that is opposite in meaning to another word, phrase, or concept.

appeal to needs   An attempt to move people to action by calling on their physical and psychological requirements and desires.

artifact   A personal ornament or possession that communicates information about a person.

asynchronous   Channels of communication that allow participants to take turns serving as sender and receiver.

attitude   An evaluative feeling, or way of thinking about oneself, others, events, ideas, or objects.

attribution   The complex process through which we attempt to understand the reasons behind others' behaviors.

audience   The collection of individuals who have come together to watch or listen to someone or something, such as to listen to a speech.

audience analysis   The collection and interpretation of data about characteristics, attitudes, values, and beliefs of an audience.

autocratic leader   A leader who has control and makes decisions with little or no consultation with others.

B

belief   A conviction or confidence in the truth of something that is not based on absolute proof.

benefit   Anything that is perceived to improve our self-interest.

body   The main content of a speech that develops the speaker's general and specific purposes.

brainstorming   A technique used to generate as many ideas as possible within a limited amount of time, which can be used to produce topics, information, or solutions to problems.

breadth of penetration   The range or spread of areas that are disclosed to others.

brief example   A specific instance used to introduce a topic, drive home a point, or create a desired response.

bypassing   A misunderstanding that occurs between a sender and a receiver because of the symbolic nature of language.

C

captive participant   A person who is required to hear a particular speech.

causal reasoning   A sequence of thought that links causes with effects; it either implies or explicitly states the word *because*.

cause–effect pattern   An order of presentation in which the speaker first explains the causes of an event, problem, or issue and then discusses its consequences.

channel   The means by which messages flow between sources and receivers.

charisma   The appeal or attractiveness the audience perceives in the speaker, contributing to the speaker's credibility.

chronemics   The study of how people perceive, structure, and use time as communication.

closure   Filling in of details so that a partially perceived entity appears to be complete.

cognitive complexity   A measure of our ability to process and store simple to complicated information.

cohesiveness   The attraction that group members feel for each other and their willingness to stick together; a form of loyalty.

collectivistic orientation   Tendency to put aside individual goals for the well-being of the group.

commitment   The desire of group members to work together to complete a task to the satisfaction of the entire group.

communication   The simultaneous sharing and creating of meaning through human symbolic interaction.

communication apprehension   The most severe form of speech anxiety; an anxiety syndrome associated with either real or anticipated communication with another person or persons.

communication via social media   Any communication transmitted through digital devices or platforms (iPhones, text messaging, Facebook, Twitter, Vine, Snapchat, etc.).

communications   Generally used to denote the delivery systems for mediated and mass communication.

complementing   The use of nonverbal cues to complete, describe, or accent verbal cues.

conclusion   Closing statements that focus the audience's thoughts on the specific purpose of a speech and bring the most important points together in a condensed and uniform way.

concrete word   A symbol for a specific thing that can be pointed to or physically experienced.

conflict   An expressed struggle between at least two interdependent parties who perceive incompatible goals, scarce resources, and interference from others in achieving their goals.

connotation   The subjective meaning of a word; what a word suggests because of feelings or associations it evokes.

consideration   A dimension of leadership that focuses on establishing good interpersonal relationships and on being liked by group members.

context   The broad circumstances or situation in which communication occurs.

continuance   An action goal that asks listeners to demonstrate their acceptance of an attitude, belief, or value by continuing to perform the behavior suggested by the speaker.

contrast definition   A definition that shows or emphasizes differences.

convenience The ease with which people connect with others through social media.

coordination Suggests that ideas with the same level of importance use the same kind of numbers (Roman and Arabic) and letters (capitalized and noncapitalized) to visually indicate the relationships between ideas.

costs Negative things or behaviors we perceive to be not beneficial to our self-interest.

credibility A speaker's believability, based on the audience's evaluation of the speaker's competence, experience, character, and charisma.

critical listening Listening that judges the accuracy of the information presented, determines the reasonableness of its conclusions, and evaluates its presenter.

critical thinking The ability to analyze and assess information.

culture A set of interpretations about beliefs, values, norms, and social practices that affect behaviors of a relatively large group of people.

D

dating A form of indexing that sorts people, events, ideas, and objects according to time.

deceiving Purposely misleading others by using nonverbal cues to create false impressions or to convey incorrect information.

decoding The process of translating a message into the thoughts or feelings that were communicated.

deductive reasoning A sequence of thought that moves from general information to a specific conclusion; it consists of a general premise, a minor premise, and a conclusion.

definition by example Clarifying a term, not by describing it or giving its meaning but by mentioning or showing an example of it.

democratic leader A leader who shares control and makes decisions in consultation with others.

demographic analysis The collection and interpretation of characteristics (age, gender, religion, occupation, and so on) of individuals, excluding values, attitudes, and beliefs.

denotation The objective meaning of a word; the standard dictionary definition.

depth of penetration The deepness or intimacy of the disclosure to others.

descriptive feedback Describing to the sender what you perceived the message to mean.

descriptors Words used to describe something.

deterrence An action that asks listeners to demonstrate their acceptance of an attitude, belief, or value by avoiding a certain behavior.

dialectical theory An interpersonal communication theory that suggests that contradictory impulses push and pull us in conflicting directions with others.

digital literacy The set of attitudes, understanding, and skills needed to handle and communicate information and knowledge effectively, in a variety of media and formats.

discontinuance An action that asks listeners to demonstrate their alteration of an attitude, belief, or value by stopping certain behaviors.

doublespeak The deliberate misuse of language to distort meaning.

dyadic communication An exchange of information between two people.

E

either–or reasoning A fallacy of reasoning in which only two options exist: There is black or white, right or wrong, but nothing in between.

emotional appeal An attempt to move people to action by playing on their feelings.

empathic listening Listening to understand what another person is thinking and feeling.

empathy The intellectual identification with or vicarious experiencing of the feelings, thoughts, or attitudes of another.

entertainment speech A speech that provides enjoyment and amusement.

environment The psychological and physical surroundings in which communication occurs.

ethnocentrism A learned belief that our own culture is superior to all others.

ethos The speaker's character as perceived by the listeners.

etymology A form of definition that traces the origin and development of a word.

euphemism The use of an inoffensive or mild expression in place of one that might offend, cause embarrassment, or suggest something unpleasant.

evaluate To analyze, assess or judge information.

evaluating The listener analyzes evidence, sorts fact from opinion, determines the intent of the speaker, judges the accuracy of the speaker's statements and conclusions, and judges the accuracy of his or her own decisions.

evaluative listening Listening to judge or analyze information.

example A simple, representative incident or model that clarifies a point.

expert opinion Ideas, testimony, conclusions, or judgments of witnesses or recognized authorities.

extemporaneous delivery A delivery style in which the speaker carefully prepares the speech in advance but delivers it using only a few notes and with a high degree of spontaneity.

eye behavior A category of kinesics and a subcategory of facial expressions that includes any movement or behavior of the eyes.

eye contact The extent to which a speaker looks directly at audience members.

F

facework A term used to describe the verbal and nonverbal ways we act to maintain our own presenting image.

facial expressions Configuration of the face that can reflect, augment, contradict, or be unrelated to a speaker's vocal delivery.

facial management techniques Control of facial muscles to conceal inappropriate or unacceptable responses.

factual illustration A report of something that exists or actually happened.

fallacy An argument that is flawed because it does not follow the rules of logic.

feedback The response to a message that a receiver sends back to a source.

figurative analogy A comparison of things in different categories.

force The intensity and volume level of the voice.

full-sentence outline An outline that expands on the ideas you have decided to include in your speech. It identifies the main points and subpoints you will cover, written as full sentences.

functional approach Using more than one nonverbal message at a time to look for meaning.

Fundamental attribution error Perceiving others as acting as they do because they are "that kind of person" rather than because of any external factors that may have influenced their behavior.

G

gender   A socially constructed concept related to learned masculine and feminine behaviors.

gender-inclusive language   Language that does not discriminate against males or females.

general purpose   The overall goal of a speech, usually one of three overlapping functions: to inform, to persuade, or to entertain.

gesture   A movement of the head, arms, or hands that helps to illustrate, emphasize, or clarify an idea.

"go viral"   A phrase used to describe a message that reaches enormous audiences by "infecting" viewers and users with the message.

grammar   Rules that govern how words are put together to form phrases and sentences.

group   A collection of individuals who influence one another, have a common purpose, take on roles, are interdependent, and interact together.

group culture   The pattern of values, beliefs, norms, and behaviors that is shared by group members and that shapes a group's individual personality.

grouphate phenomenon   Dislike for groups.

groupthink   A dysfunction in which group members value the harmony of the group more than new ideas, fail to critically examine ideas, hesitate to change flawed decisions, or lack willingness to allow new members to participate.

H

haptics   Tactile, or touch, communication; one of the most basic forms of communication.

hasty generalization   A fallacy that occurs when a speaker does not have sufficient data and therefore argues or reasons from a specific example.

hearing   The passive physiological process in which sound is received by the ear.

high-context culture   A culture in which the meaning of the communication act is inferred from the situation or location.

hyperpersonal communication   Occurs when the communication and context affords message senders a host of communicative advantages over traditional face-to-face interactions.

hypothetical illustration   A report of something that could happen, given a specific set of circumstances.

I

idioms   Words whose meanings cannot be understood according to ordinary usage.

illustration   An extended example, narrative, case history, or anecdote that is striking and memorable.

impression management   Creating a positive image of oneself to influence the perceptions of others.

impromptu delivery   A delivery style in which a speaker delivers a speech with little or no planning or preparation.

indexing   A technique to reduce indiscrimination by identifying the specific persons, ideas, events, or objects a statement refers to.

indiscrimination   The neglect of individual differences and overemphasis of similarities.

individualistic orientation   Tendency to stress self or personal goals and achievements over group goals and achievements.

inductive reasoning   A sequence of thought that moves from specific facts to a general conclusion.

information   **1.** Knowledge communicated or received concerning a particular fact or circumstance; news. **2.** Knowledge gained through study, communication, research, instruction, etc.; factual data.

information processing   Assigning meaning to the stimuli that have been selected and attended to.

information relevance   Making information relevant to an audience to give them a reason to listen.

informative speech   A speech that enhances an audience's knowledge and understanding by explaining what something means, how something works, or how something is done.

initiating structure   A dimension of leadership that focuses on getting the job done.

intelligibility   Speaker's vocal volume, distinctiveness of sound, clarity of pronunciation, articulation, and stress placed on syllables, words, and phrases.

intentional communication   A message that is purposely sent to a specific receiver.

interactivity   Refers to the ability of a communication tool to facilitate social interaction between groups or individuals.

interference   Anything that changes the meaning of an intended message.

interdependence   Mutual dependence of group members on one another.

internal preview   Short statements that give advance warning, or a preview, of the point(s) to be covered.

internal summary   A short review statement given at the end of a main point.

interpersonal attraction   The desire to interact with someone based on a variety of factors, including physical attractiveness, personality, rewards, proximity, or similarities.

interpersonal communication   The creating and sharing of meaning between people who are in a relationship.

interpersonal needs theory   A theory that provides insight into our motivation to communicate. This theory consists of three needs: affection, inclusion, and control.

interpret   Explaining the meaning of information.

interpretation   Assigning of meaning to stimuli.

interpreting   The process of understanding the meaning of the message from the speaker's point of view and letting the speaker know that you understand.

interview   A carefully planned and executed question-and-answer session designed to exchange desired information between two parties.

intrapersonal communication   The process of understanding information within oneself.

introduction   Opening statements that orient the audience to the subject and motivate them to listen.

J

jargon   Language used by certain groups or specific disciplines that may be technical or too specialized to be understood by the general population.

K

kinesics   Sometimes referred to as "body language"; any movement of the face or body that communicates a message.

L

laissez-faire leader   A leader who gives up control, is passive, and usually requires that others take over if the group is to succeed.

language   A structured system of signs, sounds, gestures, or marks that is used and understood to express ideas and feelings among people within a community, nation, geographic area, or cultural tradition.

leader   A person who is assigned or selected to take the leadership role of a group or team.

leadership An influence process that includes any behavior that helps clarify a group's purpose or guides the group to achieve its goals.

listening A cognitive activity that is defined as the active process of receiving, constructing meaning from, and responding to spoken or nonverbal messages.

listening for enjoyment Listening for pleasure, personal satisfaction, or appreciation.

listening for information Listening to gain comprehension.

literal analogy A comparison of members of the same category.

logical appeal An attempt to move people to action through the use of evidence and proof.

logical definition A definition consisting of a term's dictionary definition and the characteristics that distinguish the term from other members of the same category.

logos The substance of the speech or the logical appeals the speaker makes.

low-context culture A culture in which the meaning of the communication act is inferred from the messages being sent and not the location where the communication occurs.

M

main points The principal subdivisions of a speech.

maintenance needs Needs related to organizing and developing a group so that members can realize personal satisfaction from working together.

manuscript delivery A delivery style in which a speaker writes the speech in its entirety and then reads it word for word.

mass communication Occurs when professionals communicate with or to a large number of people via radio, television, newspapers, magazines, books, or movies.

memorized delivery A delivery style in which a speaker memorizes a speech in its entirety from a word-for-word script.

message The communication produced by the source.

metaphor A figure of speech that associates two things or ideas, not commonly linked, as a means of description.

mind mapping A visual organizational strategy that uses words or symbols to identify the concepts and their connections to each other.

miscommunication The understanding that social media may naturally inhibit the clarity of communication.

Monroe's motivated sequence A pattern of organization specifically developed for persuasive speaking that combines logic and practical psychology. Five steps are involved: attention, need, satisfaction, visualization, and action.

muted group theory Suggests that underrepresented groups (women, poor, people with disabilities, seniors, gays, blacks, Hispanics, etc.) often are not as free or as able to say what they mean, when and where they wish.

N

narrative or storytelling An organizational strategy using a reporting of ideas and situations, as in a "story," but without the traditional components of a story.

nonverbal communication Behaviors, symbols, attributes, or objects—whether intended or not—that communicate messages with social meaning.

norms Expected and shared ways in which group members behave.

O

observation A method of collecting information about an audience in which the speaker watches audience members and notes their behaviors and characteristics.

oculesics Study of eye movement or eye behavior.

online communication apprehension Anxiety and nervousness associated with communicating through social media.

online communication attitude Attitudes that shape how we interact with other people and how we present ourselves through social media.

online self-disclosure The degree to which an individual self-regulates what they reveal about themselves using social media.

online social connection The belief that online communication enables social contact.

operational definition A definition that explains how an object or concept works or lists the steps that make up a process.

oral footnote Providing, within the speech, the source that particular information comes from, such as, "According to *Newsweek* magazine of July 24, 2015...."

organizing Arranging ideas and elements into a systematic and meaningful whole.

outlining Arranging materials in a logical sequence, often referred to as the blueprint or skeleton of a speech, and writing out that sequence in a standardized form.

P

paralanguage The way we vocalize, or say, the words we speak.

parallelism Style in which all ideas, main points, subpoints, and sub-subpoints use similar grammatical forms and language patterns.

pathos The speaker's evoking of appropriate emotion from the listeners.

pause A brief stop in speaking to gain attention, add emphasis, separate, or otherwise punctuate ideas.

pendulum effect Escalating conflict between two individuals or groups that results from their use of polar terms to describe and defend their perceptions of reality.

perception The process of selecting, organizing, and interpreting information to give personal meaning to the communication we receive.

perception checking Asking questions in order to see if your interpretation is correct.

perceptual set A fixed, previously determined view of events, objects, or people.

personal-social identity continuum The two ways the self can be categorized: at a personal level, in which the uniqueness of the individualis emphasized; and at the social identity level, in which the self is thought of as a member of a group.

persuasion A communication process, involving both verbal and nonverbal messages, that attempts to reinforce or change listeners' attitudes, beliefs, values, or behavior.

persuasive speech A speech that attempts to change listeners' attitudes or behaviors by advocating or trying to gain acceptance of the speaker's point of view.

pitch How low or high the voice is on a tonal scale.

planned repetition The deliberate restating of a thought to increase the likelihood that the audience will understand and remember it.

polarization The tendency to view things in terms of extremes.

post hoc ergo propter hoc **fallacy** A fallacy of reasoning in which one attributes something as a cause simply because it followed (came after) another incident.

preliminary outline A list of all the points that may be used in a speech.

presentational aids Materials and equipment, such as diagrams, models, real objects, photographs, tables, charts, and graphs, that speakers may use to enhance the speech's content and delivery.

presentational outline A concise, condensed outline with notations, usually a combination of full sentences and key words and phrases.

primary group A group that focuses on social and interpersonal relationships.

principled negotiation A procedure that helps group members negotiate consensus by collaboration through the expression of each differing need and a search for alternatives to meet those needs.

privacy The claim of individuals, groups, or institutions to determine for themselves when, how, and to what extent information about themselves is communicated to others.

problem–solution pattern Order of presentation that first discusses a problem and then suggests solutions.

process A series of actions that has no beginning or end and is constantly changing.

project team Individuals representing different specialties who are assigned to coordinate the successful completion of an assigned task.

proxemics The study of the use of space and of distance between individuals when they are communicating.

proximity The grouping of two or more stimuli that are close to one another.

psychological analysis The collection and interpretation of data about audience members' values, attitudes, and beliefs.

public communication Transmission of a message from one person who speaks to a number of individuals who listen.

public speaking The art of effective oral communication with an audience.

Q

question of fact A question that asks what is true and what is false.

question of policy A question that asks what actions should be taken.

question of value A question that asks whether something is good or bad, desirable or undesirable.

questionable cause A fallacy that occurs when a speaker alleges something that does not relate to or produce the outcome claimed in the argument.

questionnaire A set of written questions that is distributed to respondents to gather desired information.

R

rate Speed at which a speaker speaks, normally between 120 and 175 words per minute.

reasoning by analogy A sequence of thought that compares similar things or circumstances to draw a conclusion.

receiver The individual who analyzes and interprets the message.

red herring A fallacy that uses irrelevant information to divert attention away from the real issue.

regulating The use of nonverbal cues to control the flow of communication.

relationship An association between at least two people, which may be described in terms of intimacy or kinship.

remembering Recalling something from stored memory; thinking of something again.

repeating The use of nonverbal cues to convey the same meaning as the verbal message.

repertoire Wide range of communication behaviors from which effective communicators make choices.

replicability When communication occurs in an environment that makes it easy to record and redistribute past messages.

responding Overt verbal and nonverbal behavior by the listener, indicating to the speaker what has and has not been received.

reviewing the current media A technique for developing a list of possible topics by looking at current publications, television, movies, and other forms of public communication.

rhetorical sensitivity A cautious approach to self-disclosure in which the situation and factors about the other person are considered before communication begins.

S

secondary group A group that exists to accomplish tasks or achieve goals.

selection Sorting of one stimulus from another.

selective attention Focusing on a specific message while ignoring or downplaying other stimuli.

selective exposure The deliberate choices we make to experience or to avoid particular stimuli.

selective retention The processing, storing, and retrieving of information that we have already selected, organized, and interpreted.

self-concept A person's perceived self, which consists of an organized collection of beliefs and attitudes about self.

self-disclosure Voluntary sharing of information about the self that another person is not likely to know.

self-esteem A person's feelings and attitudes toward him- or herself.

self-fulfilling prophecy Expectations we have of ourselves or that others have of us that help to create the conditions that lead us to act in predictable ways.

self-image A person's mental picture of him- or herself.

self-inventory A list of subjects that you know about and find interesting.

self-monitoring The willingness to change behavior to fit situations, the awareness of effects on others, and the ability to regulate nonverbal cues and other factors to influence others' impressions.

self-presentation An intentional self-disclosure tactic used to reveal certain aspects about ourselves for specific reasons.

semantics The study of meaning, or the association of words with ideas, feelings, and contexts.

sex The anatomical and physiological differences between males and females that are genetically determined.

sexist language Language that creates sexual stereotypes or implies that one gender is superior to another.

signpost A word, phrase, or short statement that indicates to an audience the direction a speaker will take next.

silence An extended period of time without sound.

similarity The grouping of stimuli that resemble one another in size, shape, color, or other traits.

slang Language used by groups to keep the meaning of the communication within the group. Slang words change frequently and are specific to specific regions or groups.

small-group communication An exchange of information among a relatively small number of people, ideally five to seven, who share a common purpose, such as completing a task, solving a problem, making a decision, or sharing information.

social cues The verbal and nonverbal features of a message that offer more information about the context, the meaning, and the identities of the involved parties.

social exchange theory A theory based on the assumption that people consciously and deliberately weigh the costs and rewards associated with a relationship or interaction.

social information processing theory A theory suggesting that electronically mediated relationships grow only to the extent that people gain information about each other and use that information to form impressions.

social loafing Tendency for individuals to lower their work effort after they join a group.

social media Highly accessible technologies that facilitate communication, interaction, and connection with others.

social network A group of individuals who are connected by friendship, family, common interests, beliefs, or knowledge.

social penetration theory A theory suggesting that disclosures in a relationship become increasingly intimate as the relationship develops.

source The creator of the message.

spatial pattern An order of presentation in which the content of a speech is organized according to relationships in space.

specific purpose A single phrase that defines precisely what is to be accomplished in a speech.

speech anxiety Fear of speaking before an audience.

statistics Numerical data that show relationships or summarize or interpret many instances.

stereotyping The categorizing of events, objects, and people without regard to unique individual characteristics and qualities.

style-switch A term that identifies when people from co-cultures speak the language of their own culture but switch to that of the dominant culture when needed and appropriate.

subordination Clearly identifies the hierarchy of ideas: The most important points are main points and are supported by subpoints (that is, they are subordinate to the main points); the outline uses specific rules for format.

substituting The use of nonverbal cues in place of oral messages when speaking is impossible, undesirable, or inappropriate.

survey interview A carefully planned and executed person-to-person question-and-answer session during which the speaker tries to discover specific information that will help in the preparation of a speech.

synchronous Channels of communication that allow participants to simultaneously serve as sender and receiver.

synonym A word, term, or concept that is the same or nearly the same in meaning as another word, term, or concept.

system Combination of parts interdependently acting to form a whole.

systematic desensitization A relaxation technique designed to reduce the tenseness associated with anxiety.

T

task needs Needs related to the content of the job to be done and all behaviors that lead to the completion of it.

team A special form of group that is characterized by a close-knit relationship among people with different and complementary abilities and by a strong sense of identity.

temporal structure Refers to the time it takes to send and receive messages.

territoriality The need to identify certain areas of space as one's own.

testimony Opinions or conclusions of witnesses or recognized authorities.

thesis A sentence that states specifically what is going to be discussed in a speech.

time-sequence (or chronological) pattern An order of presentation that begins at a particular point in time and continues either forward or backward.

topical pattern An order of presentation in which the main topic is divided into a series of related subtopics.

transactional Exchange of communication in which the communicators act simultaneously; that is, encoding and decoding occur at the same time.

transcorporeal communication A process through which a living person sends a digital message to a deceased person through a website or social networking site.

transition A phrase or word used to link ideas.

trustworthiness The audience's perception of a speaker's reliability and dependability.

U

uncertainty management theory A theory that takes into account different ways people react psychologically and communicatively to uncertainty.

uncertainty reduction theory A theory suggesting that when we meet others, our need to know about them tends to make us draw inferences from observable physical data.

unintentional communication A message that is not intended to be sent or was not intended for the individual who received it.

V

value A person's perceived self, which consists of an organized collection of beliefs and attitudes about self.

verbal immediacy Identifies and projects the speaker's feelings and makes the message more relevant to the listener.

vividness Active, direct, and fresh language that brings a sense of excitement, urgency, and forcefulness to a message.

vocal pause A hesitation, usually short in duration.

vocal quality The overall impression a speaker's voice makes on his or her listeners.

vocal variety Variations in rate, force, and pitch.

vocalics See *paralanguage*

voluntary participant A person who chooses to listen to a particular speech.

W

word A symbol that stands for the object or concept that it names.

work team A group of people responsible for an entire work process or a segment of the process that delivers a product or service to an internal or external customer.

Endnotes

Chapter 1

1. "Tinder Rape Suspect Had Prior Arrest," *The Daily Reveille*, July 29, 2014.
2. "Pope Francis Urges Young People Not to Waste Time on Internet," *NBC News*, August 5, 2014.
3. Facebook Newsroom, retrieved November 3, 2014, from http://newsroom.fb.com/.
4. International Association for the Wireless Telecommunications Industry, retrieved November 3, 2014, from www.ctia.org/advocacy/research/index.cfm/aid/10323.
5. "18-24-Year-Old Smartphone Owners Send and Receive Almost 4K Texts per Month," retrieved November 3, 2014, from http://www.marketingcharts.com/online/18-24-year-old-smartphone-owners-send-and-receive-almost-4k-texts-per-month-27993/.
6. C. Smith, "By the Numbers: 26 Amazing Snapchat Statistics," retrieved November 3, 2014, from http://expandedramblings.com/index.php/snapchat-statistics/3/.
7. L. A. Samovar and R. E. Porter, *Communication between Cultures*, 6th ed. (Belmont, CA: Wadsworth Publishing Co., 2007).
8. "The Twitter Revolution," *The Wall Street Journal*, Saturday/Sunday, April 18–19, 2009.
9. National Association of Colleges and Employers, *Job Outlook 2015—Student Version*, retrieved March 1, 2015, from www.jobweb.com/studentarticles.aspx?id=2121; Partnership for 21st Century Skills, www.21stcenturyskills.org/; 21st Century Workforce Commission, *A Nation of Opportunity: Strategies for Building Tomorrow's 21st Century Workforce* (Washington, DC: U.S. Department of Labor, 2000); *Spanning the Chasm: A Blueprint for Action* (Washington, DC: American Council of Education, 1999).
10. Personal conversations with business executives, personnel managers, and recruiters, March 2015.
11. J. Walther, "Interpersonal Effects in Computer-Mediated Interaction: A Relational Perspective," *Communication Research* 19 (1992): 52–90.
12. N. Postman, *Technopoly: The Surrender of Culture to Technology* (New York: Vintage Books, 1992).
13. Aristotle, *The Rhetoric and Poetics of Aristotle*, trans. W. R. Roberts and I. Bywater (New York: The Modern Library, 1954), 24–25.
14. W. M. Smail, *Quintilian on Education*, Book XII, Chapter 1 (Oxford, U.K.: Clarendon Press, 1938), 108.
15. U.S. Census Bureau, "Overview of Race and Hispanic Origin: 2010," released March 2011, retrieved March 21, 2012, from http://2010.census.gov/2010census/.
16. D. K. Berlo, *The Process of Communication* (New York: Holt, Rinehart, & Winston, 1960), 23.
17. L. Forsdale, *Perspectives on Communication* (Reading, MA: Addison-Wesley, 1981).
18. H. J. Leavitt and R. Mueller, "Some Effects of Feedback on Communication," *Human Relations* 4 (1951): 401–10.
19. N. K. Baym, *Personal Connections in the Digital Age* (Malden, MA: Polity Press, 2010), 6–12.
20. P. B. O'Sullivan, S. Hunt, and L. Lippert, "Mediated Immediacy: A Language of Affiliation in a Technological Age," *Journal of Language and Social Psychology* 23 (2004): 464–90.
21. N. S. Baron, "Letters by Phone or Speech by Other Means: The Linguistics of Email," *Language and Communication* 18 (1998): 133–70.
22. R. L. Daft and R. H. Lengel, "Information Richness: A New Approach to Managerial Behaviour and Organizational Design," *Research in Organizational Behaviour* 6 (1984): 191–233.
23. "The ALS Association Announces Initial Commitment of $21.7 Million from Ice Bucket Challenge Donations to Expedite Search for Treatments and a Cure for ALS," ALS Association, October 2, 2014, retrieved November 4, 2014, from http://www.alsa.org/news/media/press-releases/ibc-initial-commitment.html.
24. B. S. Wood, ed., Development of Functional Communication Competencies: Grades 7–12 (Urbana, IL: ERIC Clearinghouse on Reading and Communication Skills and Speech Communication Association, 1977), 5.

Chapter 2

1. R. L. Scott, "On Viewing Rhetoric as Epistemic: Ten Years Later," *The Central States Speech Journal* (Winter 1976): 261.
2. T. Harnden, "Caroline Kennedy Repeats 'You Know' 142 Times in Interview," Telegraph.co.uk, January 25, 2009, 1.
3. W. V. Haney, *Communication and Organizational Behavior: Text and Cases*, 3rd ed. (Homewood, IL: Irwin, 1973), 289–408. The term *perceptual set* is similar to what W. V. Haney refers to as "programming" or "frozen evaluation" in his book *Communication and Interpersonal Relations: Text and Cases*, 5th ed. (Homewood, IL: Irwin, 1986), 205–06, 408–38.
4. M. Piattelli-Palmarini, *Inevitable Illusions: How Mistakes of Reason Rule Our Minds* (New York: Wiley, 1994), 17.
5. Ibid., 18–19.
6. http://thinkexist.com/quotation/it_ain-t_so_much_the_things_we_don-t_know_that/345904.html.
7. C. Stewart and W. Cash Jr., *Interviewing: Principles and Practices*, 13th ed. (New York: McGraw-Hill, 2011), 32.
8. S. Kassin, *Psychology* (Upper Saddle River, NJ: Prentice Hall, 1998); D. T. Gilbert and P. S. Malone, "The Correspondence Bias," *Psychological Bulletin* 117 (1995): 21–28; F. Van Overwalle, "Dispositional Attributions Require the Joint Application of the Methods of Difference and Agreement," *Personality and Social Psychology Bulletin* 23 (1997): 974–80; E. E. Jones, "The Rocky Road from Acts to Dispositions," *American Psychologist* 34 (1979): 107–17; and R. A. Baron and N. R. Branscombe, *Social Psychology*, 13th ed. (Boston: Pearson, 2012), 86.
9. H. M. Cheverton and D. Byrne, "Development and Validation of the Primary Choice Clothing Questionnaire." Presented at the meeting of the Eastern Psychological Association, Boston, February 1998, 9-1-9-2; D. Mack and D. Rainey, "Female Applicants, Grooming and Personnel Selection," *Journal of Social Behavior and Personality*

5 (1990): 399–407; and B. P. Meier, M. D. Robinson, and G. L. Clore, "Why Good Guys Wear White: Automatic Inferences about Stimulus Valance Based on Brightness," *Psychological Science* 15 (2004): 82–87.

10. C. S. Fichten and R. Amsel, "Trait Attribution about College Students with a Physical Disability: Circumplex Analysis and Methodological Issues," *Journal of Applied Social Psychology* 16 (1986): 410–27; S. J. McKelvie, "Stereotyping in Perception of Attractiveness, Age, and Gender in Schematic Faces," *Social Behavior and Personality* 9 (1994): 753–60; and M. L. Shannon and C. P. Stark, "The Influence of Physical Appearance on Personnel Selection," *Social Behavior and Personality* 31 (2003): 613–24.

11. The definition is based on work found in J. N. Martin and T. K. Nakayama, *Intercultural Communication in Contexts,* 5th ed. (New York: McGraw Hill, 2010), 84–93; L. A. Samovar and R. E. Porter, *Communication between Cultures,* 7th ed. (Belmont, CA: Wadsworth, 2010), 19–33; E. R. McDaniel, L. A. Samovar, and R. E. Porter, "Understanding Intercultural Communication: An Overview," in *Intercultural Communication: A Reader*, 13th ed., eds. L. A. Samovar, R. E. Porter, and E. R. McDaniel (Boston: Wadsworth, 2012), 10–13; D. W. Klopf and J. C. McCroskey, *Intercultural Communication Encounters* (Boston: Allyn and Bacon, 2007), 6–7.

12. N. L. Gage and D. C. Berliner, *Educational Psychology,* 6th ed. (Boston: Houghton Mifflin, 1998), 152–53.

13. McDaniel, Samovar, and Porter, 13–16.

14. N. Dresser, *Multicultural Manners* (New York: Wiley, 1996), 89–90.

15. Martin and Nakayama, 5; and McDaniel, Samovar, and Porter, 13.

16. L. P. Stewart, P. J. Cooper, A. D. Stewart, and S. A. Friedley, *Communication and Gender,* 4th ed. (Boston: Allyn and Bacon, 2003), 44–45.

17. J. T. Wood, *Gendered Lives,* 7th ed. (Boston: Wadsworth, 2011), 40–45.

18. K. L. Floyd and G. B. Ray, "Mapping the Affectionate Voice: Vocalic Predictors of Perceived Affection in Initial Interactions," *Western Journal of Communication* 67 (Winter 2003): 56–73.

19. Ibid., 68.

20. D. Tannen, *You Just Don't Understand: Women and Men in Conversation* (New York: Morrow, 1990); D. Tannen, *Talking from 9 to 5: How Women's and Men's Conversational Styles Affect Who Gets Heard, Who Gets Credit, and What Gets Done at Work* (New York: Morrow, 1994); J. T. Woods, *Gendered Lives: Communication, Gender, and Culture* (Boston: Cengage, 2013).

21. J. T. Wood, *Interpersonal Communication: Everyday Encounter,* 7th ed. (Boston: Wadsworth, 2013), 79.

Chapter 3

1. B. Corcoran, "My Favorite Mistake," *Newsweek,* January 23, 2012: 60.

2. A. Gerike, *Old Is Not a Four-Letter Word: A Midlife Guide* (Watsonville, CA: Papier Mâchè Press, 1997).

3. D. J. Bem, "Self-Perception Theory," in *Advances in Experimental Social Psychology*, vol. 6, ed. L. Berkowitz (New York: Academic Press, 1972).

4. J. W. Kinch, "A Formalized Theory of Self-Concept," *American Journal of Sociology* 68 (January 1963): 481–86.

5. Ibid., 481.

6. Ibid., 482–83.

7. H. Tajfel and J. C. Turner, "The Social Identity Theory of Intergroup Behavior," in *The Social Psychology of Intergroup Relations*, 2nd ed., eds. S. Worchel and W. G. Austin (Monterey, CA: Brooks-Cole, 1986), 7–24.

8. K. J. Reynolds, J. C. Turner, N. R. Branscombe, K. I. Mavor, B. Bizumic, and E. Subasic, "Interactionism in Personality and Social Psychology: An Integrated Approach to Understanding the Mind of Behavior," *European Journal of Personality* 24 (2010); 458–82.

9. K. Neff, "Don't Fall into the Self-Esteem Trap Try a Little Self-Kindness," *New Yorker Magazine* (December 2014): 75–80.

10. P. J. Oaks and K. J. Reynolds, "Asking the Accuracy Question: Is Measurement the Answer?," in *The Social Psychology of Stereotyping and Group Life*, eds. R. Spears, P. J. Oaks, N. Ellemers, and S. A. Haslam (Oxford: Blackwell, 1997), 51–71.

11. A. M. Ledbetter, "Measuring Online Communication Attitude: Instrument Development and Validation," *Communication Monographs* 76 (2014): 463–86.

12. Ibid., 463–86.

13. S. Lau and L. K. Kwok, "Relationships of Family Environment to Adolescent's Depression and Self-Concept," *Social Behavior and Personality* 27 (2000): 41–50.

14. Ibid., 41–50.

15. H. Giles, S. Davis, J. Gasiork, and J. Giles, *Successful Aging: A Communication Guide to Empowerment* (Barcelona: Aresta, 2013), 22.

16. Ibid., 25–36.

17. D. T. Miller, "The Norm of Self-Interest," *American Psychologist* 54 (1999): 1053–60.

18. C. Kanagawa, S. E. Cross, and H. R. Markus, "Who Am I? The Cultural Psychology of the Conceptual Self," *Journal of Personality and Social Psychology Bulletin* 27 (2001): 90–103.

19. Ibid., 90–103.

20. S. A. Ribeau, J. R. Baldwin, and M. L. Hecht, "An African-American Communication Perspective," in *Intercultural Communication: A Reader*, eds. L. A. Samovar and R. E. Porter (Belmont, CA: Wadsworth, 1994), 143; J. R. Baldwin and M. Hecht, "Unpacking Group-Based Intolerance: A Holographic Look at Identity and Intolerance," in *Intercultural Communication: A Reader*, 10th ed., eds. L. A. Samovar and R. E. Porter (Belmont, CA: Wadsworth, 2003), 358.

21. J. B. Beckwith, "Terminology and Social Relevance in Psychological Research on Gender," *Social Behavior and Personality* 22 (1994): 329–36; J. T. Wood, *Gendered Lives: Communication, Gender and Culture*, 11th ed. (Belmont, CA: Wadsworth, 2013), 19.

22. J. T. Wood, *Gender Lives: Communication, Gender, and Culture*, 9th ed. (Belmont, CA, Thomson Wadsworth, 2012), 40–41.

23. Ibid., 44–45.

24. Ibid., 44–45.

25. N. Grieve, "Beyond Sexual Stereotypes. Androgyny: A Model or an Ideal?" in *Australian Women: Feminist Perspectives*, eds. N. Grieve and P. Grimshaw (Melbourne, Australia: Oxford University Press, 1980), 247–57.

26. J. T. Wood, 127–40.

27. D. A. Vogel, M. A. Lake, S. Evans, and K. H. Karraker, "Children's and Adults Sex-Stereotyped Perceptions of Infants," *Sex Roles* 24 (1991): 601–16.

28. M. E. Heilman, R. F. Martell, and M. C. Simon, "The Vagaries of Sex Bias: Conditions Regulating the

Underevaluation, Equivaluation, and Overevaluation of Female Job Applicants," *Organizational Behavior and Human Decision Processes* 41 (1988): 98–110.

29. M. Chen and J. A. Bargh, "Nonconscious Behavioral Confirmation Processes: The Self-Fulfilling Consequences of Automatic Stereotype Activation," *Journal of Experimental Psychology* 33 (1997): 541–60; T. Claire and S. T. Fiske, "A Systematic View of Behavioral Confirmation: Counterpoint to the Individualist View," in *Intergroup Cognition and Intergroup Behavior*, eds. C. Sedikides, J. Schopler, and C. A. Insko (Mahwah, NJ: Erlbaum, 1998), 205–31.

30. B. A. Bettencourt and N. Miller, "Gender Differences in Aggression as a Function of Provocation: A Meta-Analysis," *Psychological Bulletin* 119 (1996): 422–47.

31. D. Tannen, *You Just Don't Understand: Women and Men in Conversation* (New York: Morrow, 1990), 24–25.

32. C. E. Epstein, *Deceptive Distinctions: Sex, Gender, and the Social Order* (New Haven, CT: Yale University Press, 1988), 25.

33. M. R. Gunnar-Von Gnechten, "Changing a Frightening Toy into a Pleasant Toy by Allowing the Infant to Control Its Actions," *Developmental Psychology* 14 (1978): 157–62; J. H. Block, "Differential Premises Arising from Differential Socialization of the Sexes: Some Conjectures," *Child Development* 54 (1983): 1335–54; J. T. Spence and R. L. Helmreich, *Masculinity and Femininity: Their Psychological Dimension and Antecedents* (Austin: University of Texas Press, 1978).

34. Women in the Labor Force: A Databook and Highlights of Women's Earnings, retrieved 2014, from http://www.dol.gov/wb/stats/recentfacts.htm#rates.

35. Bureau of Labor Statistics, U.S. Department of Labor, Current Population Survey, retrieved January 12, 2015, from http://bls.gov/cps/cpsaat03.htm.

36. U.S. Department of Labor, "Population and Labor Force Participation, by Sex," retrieved January 12, 2015, from http://www.dol.gov/wb/stats/population_LF_13.htm.

37. U.S. Department of Labor, "Quick Stats 2010," retrieved January 12, 2015, from www.dol.gov/wb/factsheets/QS-womenwork2010.htm.

38. R. Rosenthal and L. Jacobson, *Pygmalion in the Classroom: Teacher Expectation and Pupils' Intellectual Development* (New York: Holt, Rinehart, & Winston, 1968), vii; T. Good and J. Brophy, *Looking in Classrooms*, 4th ed. (New York: Harper & Row, 1987).

39. C. S. Carver, L. A. Kus, and M. F. Scheier, "Effects of Good versus Bad Mood and Optimistic versus Pessimistic Outlook on Social Acceptance versus Rejection," *Journal of Social and Clinical Psychology* 13 (1994): 138–51.

40. M. D. Alicke, D. S. Vredenburg, M. Hiatt, and O. Govorun, "The Better Than Myself Effect," *Motivation and Emotion* 25 (2001): 7–22; Y. Klar, "Way beyond Compare: The Nonselective Superiority and Inferiority Bias in Judging Randomly Assigned Group Members Relative to Their Peers," *Journal of Experimental Social Psychology* 38 (2002): 331–51.

41. R. B. Sanitioso and R. Wlodarski, "In Search of Information That Confirms a Desired Self-Perception: Motivation Processing of Social Feedback and Choice of Interactions," *Personality and Social Psychology Bulletin* 30 (2004): 412–22.

42. B. R. Schlenker, M. F. Weigold, and J. R. Hallam, "Self-Serving Attribution in Social Context," *Journal of Personality and Social Psychology* 58 (1990): 855–63.

43. M. H. Bond, "Chinese Values," in *The Handbook of Chinese Psychology*, ed. M. H. Bond (Oxford, UK: Oxford University Press, 1996), 208–26.

44. R. Kurzban and J. Weeden, "Hurry Date: Mate Preferences in Action," *Evolution and Human Behavior* 26 (2005): 227–44.

45. C. M. Shaw and R. Edwards, "Self-Concepts and Self-Presentations of Males and Females: Similarities and Differences," *Communication Reports* 10 (1997): 55–62.

46. Ibid., 55–62.

47. A. L. Gonzales and J. T. Hancock, "Mirror, Mirror on my Facebook Wall: Effects of Exposure to Facebook on Self-Esteem," *Cyberpsychology, Behavior and Social Networks* 14 (2011): 79–83.

48. Ibid., 79–80.

49. Ibid., 79.

50. E. Goffman, *The Presentation of Self in Everyday Life* (Garden City, NY: Doubleday, 1959).

51. M. R. Barrick, J. A. Shaffer, and S. W. DeGrassi, "What You See May Not Be What You Get: Relationships among Self-Presentation Tactics and Ratings of Interview and Job Performance," *Journal of Applied Psychology* 94 (2009): 1394–411.

52. S. J. Wayne, R. C. Liden, I. K. Graft, and G. R. Ferris, "The Role of Upward Influence Tactics in Human Resource Decisions," *Personnel Psychology* 50 (1997): 979–1006; L. A. Witt and G. B. Ferris, "Social Skill as Moderator of the Conscientiousness-Performance Relationship: Convergent Results across Four Studies," *Journal of Applied Psychology* 84 (2003): 808–20; R. Vonk, "The Slime Effect: Suspicion and Dislike of Likeable Behavior toward Superiors," *Journal of Personality and Social Psychology* 74 (1998): 849–64; and R. A. Baron, "Self-Presentation in Job Interviews: When There Can Be 'Too Much of a Good Thing,'" *Journal of Applied Social Psychology* 16 (1986): 16–28.

Chapter 4

1. Huffington Post, March 3, 2012, originally cited at http://www.huffingtonpost.com/2012/03/03/rush-limbaugh-apologizes-to-sandra-fluke_n_1318718.html. (Newer post retrieved June 25, 2015 from http://www.huffingtonpost.com/2013/03/21/rush-limbaugh-sandra-fluke-advertisers_n_2923643.html.)

2. Huffington Post, March 5, 2012, http://www.huffingtonpost.com/2012/03/02/rush-limbaugh-sandra-fluke-sex-slut_n_1316625.html.

3. Leslie Salzillo, "Time Magazine Affirms—Rush Limbaugh Is in Trouble," DailyKos, February 19, 2015, http://www.dailykos.com/story/2015/02/19/1365413=5/-Time-Magazine-J…a-Groups-Are-Pushing-Rush-Limbaugh-Off-Public-Radio?detail-email#. Accessed February 20, 2015.

4. D. R. Harfield, CLP, personal communication, March 25, 2015.

5. Ibid.

6. The Power of Words, YouTube, www.youtube.com/watch?v=Hzgzim5m7oU. Accessed March 1, 2012.

7. P. H. Collins, *Fighting Words: Black Women and the Search for Justice,* synopsis on University of Minnesota Press website, retrieved May 10, 2012, from www.upress.umn.edu/book-division/books/fighting-words.

8. C. Kramerae, *Women and Men Speaking* (Rowley, MA: Newbury, 1981).

9. M. Houston, "Multiple Perspectives: African American Women Conceive Their Talk," *Women and Language* 23 (2002): 11–23.

10. L. A. Samovar and R. E. Porter, eds., *Intercultural Communication: A Reader* (Belmont, CA: Wadsworth, 2003), 358.

11. Helpful African Proverbs, compiled by Kane Mathis, retrieved January 29, 2012, from www.kairarecords.com/kane/proverbs.htm.

12. G. A. Miller, *The Psychology of Communication* (Baltimore: Penguin, 1967).

13. L. Carroll, *Alice's Adventures in Wonderland, Through the Looking Glass, and The Hunting of the Snark* (New York: Modern Library, 1925), 246–47.

14. A. Korzybski, *Science and Sanity: An Introduction to Non-Aristotelian Systems and General Semantics* (Lancaster, PA: Science Press Printing, 1933).

15. P. Dickson, *Slang!* (New York: Pocket Books, 1990).

16. Ibid.

17. W. Lutz, *Doublespeak: From "Revenue Enhancement" to "Terminal Living": How Government, Business, Advertisers, and Others Use Language to Deceive You* (New York: Harper & Row, 1987), 3–4.

18. Ibid.

19. K. Cushner, A. McClelland, and P. Safford, *Human Diversity in Education: An Integrative Approach*, 3rd ed. (New York: McGraw-Hill, 2010).

20. Adapted from W. V. Haney, *Communication and Organizational Behavior*, 3rd ed. (Homewood, IL: Irwin, 1973), 211–330; and *Communication and Interpersonal Relations*, 5th ed. (Homewood, IL: Irwin, 1986), 213–405.

21. News bulletins from W. R. Espy, "Say When," *This Week*, July 13, 1952, quoted in W. V. Haney, *Communication and Organizational Behavior*, 396.

22. D. Tannen, *You Just Don't Understand* (New York: Morrow, 1990).

23. C. Miller and K. Swift, *The Handbook on Nonsexist Writing*, 2nd ed. (New York: Harper & Row, 1988).

24. Guidelines may be found in a variety of places. One interesting website is the Coe College, Cedar Rapids, IA, speaking center and writing center, found at www.public.coe.edu/~wcenter/handouts_nonsexist.php. Another source is B. D. Sorrels, *Nonsexist Communicator: Solving the Problem of Gender and Awkwardness in Modern English* (Englewood Cliffs, NJ: Prentice Hall, 1983).

25. E. T. Hall, *The Hidden Dimension* (Garden City, NY: Doubleday, 1966).

26. S. Trenholm, *Thinking through Communication*, 4th ed. (Boston: Allyn and Bacon, 2005), 72.

27. G. Deutscher, "Does Your Language Shape How You Think?" *New York Times* online, August 26, 2010, retrieved January 14, 2015, from www.nytimes.com/2010/08/29/magazine/29language-t.html?_r=0&page wanted=print.

28. Ibid.

29. Ibid.

30. Ibid.

31. Hall, 1966.

32. N. Postman, *Technopoly* (New York: Alfred A. Knopf, 1992), 4.

33. Ibid.

34. S. T. Fiske and S. E. Taylor, *Social Cognition* (Reading, MA: Addison-Wesley, 1984), 190–94.

35. J. J. Bradac, J. W. Bowers, and J. A. Courtright, "Three Language Variables in Communication Research: Intensity, Immediacy, and Diversity," *Human Communication Research* 5 (1979): 257–69.

36. Lord Chesterfield, Philip Stanhope quotations, retrieved January 25, 2015, from http://www.brainyquote.com/quotes/authors/p/philip_stanhope.html#J6eWL2lQdOoJx95H.99.

Chapter 5

1. M. L. Knapp and J. Hall, *Nonverbal Communication in Human Interaction*, 7th ed. (Belmont, CA: Wadsworth/Cengage Learning, 2010), 5.

2. Ibid., 12–21.

3. M. Argyle, F. Alkema, and R. Gilmour, "The Communication of Friendly and Hostile Attitudes by Verbal and Nonverbal Signals," *European Journal of Social Psychology* 1 (1971): 385–402.

4. B. M. DePaulo, J. J. Lindsay, B. E. Malone, L. Muhlenbruck, K. Chandler, and H. Cooper, "Cues to Deception," *Psychological Bulletin* 129 (2003): 74–118.

5. D. Matsumoto, B. Franklin, J. Choi, D. Rogers, and H. Tatani. "Cultural Influences on the Expression and Perception of Emotion," in W. Gudykunst and B. Mody, eds., *The Handbook of International and Intercultural Communication* (Thousand Oaks, CA: Sage, 2002), 107–26; and M. S. Remland, *Nonverbal Communication in Everyday Life*, 3rd ed. (Boston: Pearson, 2009), 152.

6. T. Novinger, *Intercultural Communication: A Practical Guide* (Austin: University of Texas Press, 2001), 64.

7. M. S. Remland, 211.

8. D. Matsumoto et al., 107–206.

9. B. Mesquita and J. Leu, "The Cultural Psychology of Emotion," in S. Kitayama and D. Cohen, eds., *Handbook of Cultural Psychology* (New York: Guildford Press, 2007), 734–59.

10. D. E. Madell and S. J. Muncer, "Control over Social Interactions: An Important Reason for Young People's Use of the Internet and Mobile Phones for Communication?" *Cyber Psychology and Behavior* 10 (2007): 137–40.

11. J. Kruger, N. Epley, J. Parker, and Z. W. Ng, "Egocentrism over Email: Can We Communicate as Well as We Think?" *Journal of Personality and Social Psychology* 89 (2005): 925–36.

12. B. M. DePaul and D. A. Kashy, "Everyday Lies in Close and Casual Relationship," *Journal of Personality and Social Psychology* 74 (1998): 63–79.

13. P. Eckman, *Telling Lies: Clues to Deceit in the Marketplace, Politics, and Marriage*, 3rd ed. (New York: Norton, 2001); and B. E. Malone and B. M. DePaulo, "Measuring Sensitivity to Deception," in J. A. Hall and F. Bernieri, eds., *Interpersonal Sensitivity: Theory, Measurement, and Application* (Mahwah, NJ: Erlbaum, 2001): 103–24.

14. N. L. Etcoff, P. Ekman, J. J. Magee, and M. G. Frank, "Lie Detection and Language Comprehension, *Nature* 40 (2000): 139.

15. M. O'Sullivan, "The Fundamental Attribution Error in Detecting Deception: The Boy-Who-Cried-Wolf Effect," *Personality and Social Psychology Bulletin* 29 (2003): 1316–27.

16. T. H. Feeley and M. A. Turck, "The Behavioral Correlates of Sanctioned and Unsanctioned Deceptive Communication," *Journal of Nonverbal Behavior* 22 (1998): 189–204; and A. Vrij, L. Akehurst, and P. Morris, "Individual Differences in Hand Movements during Deception," *Journal of Nonverbal Behavior* 21 (1997): 87–102.

17. L. Anolli and R. Ciceri, "The Voice of Deception: Vocal Strategies of Naïve and Able Liars," *Journal of Nonverbal Behavior* 21 (1997): 259–85.

18. J. M. Tyler, R. S. Feldman, and A. Reichert, "The Price of Deceptive Behavior: Disliking and Lying to People Who Lie to Us," *Journal of Experimental Social Psychology* 42 (2006): 69–77.

19. Ibid., 69–77.

20. J. A. Hall and D. Matsumoto, "Gender Differences in Judgments of Multiple Emotions from Facial Expressions," *Emotion* 3 (2004): 201–06.

21. C. Mayo and N. M. Henley, eds., *Gender and Nonverbal Behavior* (Secaucus, NJ: Springer-Verlag, 1981).

22. R. Rosenthal and B. M. DePaul, "Sex Differences in Accommodation in *Nonverbal Communication*," in R. Rosenthal, ed., *Skill in Nonverbal Communication* (Cambridge, MA: Oelgeschlager, Gunn & Hain, 1979): 68–103.

23. S. W. Janik, A. R. Wellens, J. L. Goldberg, and L. F. Dell'osso, "Eyes as the Center of Focus in the Visual Examination of Human Faces," *Perceptual and Motor Skills* 4 (1978): 857–08.

24. D. Leathers, *Successful Nonverbal Communication: Principles and Applications* (New York: Macmillan, 1986).

25. P. Andersen, *Nonverbal Communication: Forms and Functions* (Long Grove, IL: Waveland Press, 2008).

26. C. L. Kleinke, "Gaze and Eye Contact: A Research Review," *Psychological Review* 100 (1986): 78–100.

27. P. G. Zimbardo, *Shyness: What It Is, What to Do about It* (Reading, MA: Addison-Wesley, 1977).

28. P. Greenbaum and H. W. Rosenfield, "Patterns of Avoidance in Responses to Interpersonal Staring and Proximity: Effects of Bystanders on Drivers at a Traffic Intersection," *Journal of Personality and Social Psychology* 36 (1978): 575–87.

29. P. C. Ellsworth and J. M. Carlsmith, "Eye Contact and Gaze Aversion in Aggressive Encounter," *Journal of Personality and Social Psychology* 33 (1973): 117–22.

30. Ibid.

31. C. Izard, *The Psychology of Emotions* (New York: Plenum, 1991); and P. Rozin, L. Lowery, and R. Ebert, "Varieties of Disgust Faces and the Structure of Disgust," *Journal of Personality and Social Psychology* 66 (1994): 870–81.

32. P. Ekman and K. Heider, "The Universality of a Contempt Expression: A Replication," *Motivation and Emotion* 12 (1988): 303–08; and P. Ekman, "Are There Basic Emotions?" *Psychology Review* 99 (1992): 550–53.

33. B. Knutson, "Facial Expression of Emotions Influence Interpersonal Trait Inferences," *Journal of Nonverbal Behavior* 20 (1996): 165–82.

34. H. Aguinis, M. Simonsen, and C. Pierce, "Effects of Nonverbal Behavior on Perceptions of Power Bases," *Journal of Social Psychology* 138 (1998): 455–70.

35. M. T. Motley, "Facial Affect and Verbal Context in Conversation: Facial Expression as Interjection," *Human Communication Research* 20 (1993): 3–40.

36. M. Zukerman, D. T. Larrance, N. H. Spiegel, and R. Klorman, "Controlling Nonverbal Displays: Facial Expressions and Tone of Voice," *Journal of Experimental Social Psychology* 17 (1981): 506–24.

37. P. Ekman, W. V. Friesen, and P. Ellsworth, "Methodological Decisions," in P. Ekman, ed., *Emotion in the Human Face*, 2nd ed. (Cambridge, UK: Cambridge University Press, 1982), 7–21.

38. P. Ekman and W. V. Friesen, "The Repertoire of Nonverbal Behavior: Categories, Origins, Usage, and Coding," *Semiotica* 1 (1969): 49–98.

39. D. S. Berry and L. Zebrowitz-McArthur, "Perceiving Character in Faces: The Impact of Age-Related Craniofacial Changes on Social Perception," *Psychological Bulletin* 100 (1986): 3–18.

40. J. M. Montepare and L. Zebrowitz-McArthur, "Impressions of People Created by Age-Related Qualities of Their Gaits," *Journal of Personality and Social Psychology* 54 (1988): 547–56.

41. W. Wells and B. Siegel, "Stereotyped Somatypes," *Psychological Reports* 8 (1961): 77–78.

42. M. A. Collins and L. A. Zebrowitz, "The Contribution of Appearance to Occupational Outcomes in Civilian and Military Settings," *Journal of Applied Social Psychology* 71 (1995): 129–63.

43. B. Gillen, "Physical Attractiveness: A Determinant of Two Types of Goodness," *Personality and Social Psychology Bulletin* 7 (1981): 277–81.

44. J. Levav and J. J. Argo, "Physical Contact and Financial Risk Taking," *Psychological Science* 21 (2010): 804–10.

45. R. Heslin and T. Alper, "Touch: A Bonding Gesture," in J. M. Wiemann and R. P. Harrison, eds., *Nonverbal Interaction* (Beverly Hills, CA: Sage, 1983), 47–75.

46. S. M. Jourard, *Disclosing Man to Himself* (Princeton, NJ: Van No strand, 1968).

47. Levav and Argo, 2010.

48. L. M. Kneidinger, T. L. Maple, and S. A. Tross, "Touching Behavior in Sport: Functional Components, Analysis of Sex Differences and Ethological Considerations," *Journal of Nonverbal Behavior* 25 (2001): 43–62.

49. E. T. Hall, *The Silent Language* (Greenwich, CT: Fawcett, 1959) and *The Hidden Dimension* (Garden City, NY: Doubleday, 1969).

50. J. K. Burgoon, D. B. Buller, and W. G. Woodall, *Nonverbal Communication: The Unspoken Dialogue*, 2nd ed. (New York: Harper & Row, 1996), 122.

51. K. Nishiyama, *Doing Business in Japan: Successful Strategies for Intercultural Communication* (Honolulu: University of Hawaii Press, 2000), 28.

52. M. L. Knapp, *Essentials of Nonverbal Communication* (New York: Holt, Rinehart and Winston, 1980), 7; M. L. Knapp and J. Hall, *Nonverbal Communication in Human Interaction*, 7th ed. (Belmont, CA: Wadsworth Cengage Learning, 2010).

53. S. E. Quasha and F. Tsukada, "International Marriages in Japan: Cultural Conflict and Harmony," in L. A. Samovar, R. E. Porter, and E. R. McDaniel, eds., *Intercultural Communication: A Reader*, 13th ed. (Boston: Wadsworth Cengage Learning, 2012), 129.

54. Ibid., 129.

55. Ibid., 129.

56. "You Are What You Drive: A Silver SUV Broadcasts a Very Different Message from a Green Sedan," *USA Weekend Magazine*, October 20, 2002, 20–21.

Chapter 6

1. D. R. Harfield, CLP, Unpublished manuscript based on International Listening Association Convention, March 2011, Johnson City, TN; W. Gallagher, *Rapt Attention and the Focus of Life* (New York: The Penguin Press, 2009); and, N. Herrmann, *The Creative Brain.* (Lake Lure, NC: The Ned Herrmann Group, 1993).

2. Harfield.

3. Harfield.; J. Brownell, *Listening: Attitudes, Principles, and Skills,* 4th ed. (Boston: Allyn and Bacon, 2010); L. A. Janusik and D. Wolvin, "24 Hours in a Day: A Listening Update to the Time Studies," paper presented at the meeting of the International Listening Association, Salem, OR, 2006; A. Wolvin and C. Coakley, *Listening,* 5th ed. (Dubuque, IA: William C. Brown Co., 1998).

4. J. Brownell, 14.

5. L. A. Janusik and A. D. Wolvin, "24 Hours in a Day. A Listening Update to the Time Studies," paper presented at the meeting of the International Listening Association, Salem, OR, 2006; also, R. Bohlken, "Substantiating the Fact That Listening Is Proportionally Most Used Language Skill," *The Listening Post* 70 (1999): 5.

6. S. Baker, "Identifying Communication Skills Necessary to Succeed in the Ever Changing and Competitive Workplace," unpublished master's thesis, University of Northern Iowa, 2009.

7. National Association of Colleges & Employers, Job Outlook 2015: The Candidate Skills/Qualities Employers Want, retrieved March 1, 2015, from www.naceweb.org/s10262014/candidate_skills_employer_qualities/.

8. L. A. Janusik, "Teaching Listening. What Do We Know? What Should We Know?" *International Journal of Listening* 16 (2002): 5–39; and C. Coakley and A. Wolvin, "Listening in the Educational Environment," in M. Purdy and D. Borisoff, eds., *Listening in Everyday Life: A Personal and Professional Approach,* 2nd ed. (Lanham, MD: University Press of America, 1997), 179–212.

9. L. A. Janusik, "Teaching Listening. What Do We Know? What Should We Know?" *International Journal of Listening* 16 (2002): 5–39; and L. A. Janusik and A. D. Wolvin, "Listening Treatment in the Basic Communication Course Text," in D. Sellnow, ed., *Basic Communication Course Annual* (Boston: American Press, 2002).

10. L. A. Janusik and A. D. Wolvin, "24 Hours in a Day. A Listening Update to the Time Studies," paper presented at the meeting of the International Listening Association, Salem, OR, 2006.

11. M. Imhof and T. Weinhard, "What Did You Listen to in School Today?" paper presented at the 25th Annual Convention of the International Listening Association, Fort Myers, FL, April 2004.

12. Priorities of Listening Research: Four Interrelated Initiatives: A White Paper Sponsored by the Research Committee of the International Listening Association, 2008.

13. "Did You Know? 2015," retrieved March 7, 2015, from https://www.youtube.com/watch?v=PcZg51Il9no.

14. "Google Search Statistics," internet live stats, retrieved July 4, 2015, from http://www.internetlivestats.com/google-search-statistics/.

15. A. D. Wolvin, *Listening in the Quality Organization.* (Ithaca, NY: Finger Lakes Press, 1999).

16. J. Brownell, 14.

17. D. R. Harfield, personal phone conversation, January 29, 2015.

18. D. R. Harfield, personal phone conversation, January 29, 2015.

19. L. A. Janusik, "Researching Listening from the Inside Out: The Relationship between Conversational Listening Span and Perceived Communication Competence," UMI Proquest: Digital Dissertations, 2005, www.lib.uni.com/dissertations.

20. D. R. Harfield, personal correspondence, March 7, 2015.

21. Herrmann, *The Creative Brain.*

22. Herrmann, *The Creative Brain.*

23. W. Gallagher, *Rapt Attention and the Focus of Life* (New York: The Penguin Press, 2009).

24. J. Brownell, *Listening,* 15.

25. A. Wolvin, ed., *Listening and Human Communication: 21st Century Perspectives* (Boston: Blackwell Publishing, 2009).

26. "Empathy," Dictionary.com, retrieved March 13, 2012, from dictionary.reference.com/browse/empathy.

27. C. L. Simonds and P. J. Hoel, *Communication for the Classroom Teacher* (Boston: Allyn and Bacon, 2010).

28. R. Nichols, "Factors Accounting for Differences in Comprehension of Material Presented Orally in the Classroom," doctoral dissertation, University of Iowa, 1948.

29. Self Perceptions and Personal Bias, Public Speaking: The ACA Open Knowledge Online Guide, retrieved March 12, 2012, from http://textcommons.org/node/122.

30. D. Harfield, personal communication, March 12, 2012.

31. D'Angelo, *The Teaching of Critical Thinking* (Amsterdam, The Netherlands: B. R. Gruner, 1971), 7; R. H. Ennis, "A Taxonomy of Critical Thinking Dispositions and Abilities," in J. Baron and R. Sternberg, eds., *Teaching Thinking Skills: Theory and Practice* (New York: Freeman, 1987).

32. C. Angove, "The Rise of Social Media in Organizations: How to Turn the Internet into Interactive Dialogue," unpublished master's degree research project, University of Northern Iowa, May 2012.

33. P. E. Emmert and V. Emmert, unpublished ILA Convention papers, 1997, 1998; M. L. Beall, unpublished ILA Convention papers, 1997, 1998, 2001, 2004, 2006, 2007, 2008.

34. D. Baer, "Here's Why Writing Things out by Hand Makes You Smarter," *Business Insider,* December 16, 2014, retrieved January 5, 2015 from http://www.businessinsider.com/handwriting-helps-you-learn-2014-12.

35. Key in "Death by PowerPoint" in your search engine. You may be surprised to get more than 2 million hits. Check further by checking amazon.com, and you'll find six or more books on the subject. If you learn to make effective presentations, you'll be able to enhance your speech and not bore your listeners to death.

36. D. Bawden, Digital Literacy, SciTopics, December 29, 2008, retrieved March 12, 2012, from www.scitopics.com/Digital_Literacy.html.

37. A. Adhikari, "Digital Literacy Training," retrieved from www.guardian.co.uk/higher-education-network/higher-education-network-blog/2011/oct/10/digital-literacy-collaboration.

38. P. Gilster, *Digital Literacy* (Hoboken, NJ: John Wiley & Sons, 1998).

39. G. M. Chen and W. J. Starosta, *Foundations of Intercultural Communication* (Lanham, MD: University Press of America, 2005), 93.

40. M. L. Beall, "Asian Perspectives on Intercultural Listening," unpublished paper presented at the World Communication Association Summer Conference, Lincoln, NE, August 2002.

41. M. L. Beall, "Perspectives on Intercultural Listening," in A. Wolvin, ed., *Listening and Human Communication: 21st Century Perspectives* (Boston: Blackwell Publishing, 2009); M. L. Beall, "Intercultural and Intergenerational Listening," presentation at the Western States Communication Association, Monterey, CA, February 2011.

Chapter 7

1. Upper Rio Grande Workforce Development Board, "What Skills Do Employers Want" retrieved February 24, 2015, from http://www.urgjobs.com/pdf/Skills.pdf.

2. S. Adams, "The 10 Skills Employers Most Want in 2015 Graduates," retrieved February 25, 2015, from

http://www.forbes.com/sites/susanadams/2014/11/12/the-10-skills-employers-most-want-in-2015-graduates/.

3. J. Swan, University of Northern Iowa, personal conversations, February 2015.

4. "Public speaking," Merriam-Webster Online Dictionary, retrieved February 14, 2015, from http://www.merriam-webster.com/dictionary/public%20speaking.

5. "Social media," Merriam-Webster Online Dictionary, retrieved February 14, 2015, from www.merriam-webster.com/dictionary/social%20media.

6. Students may wish to surf the web to find topics. Keying in "Topics for Speeches" on Google netted nearly 55 million hits in 0.30 second on March 7, 2015. Another site that also offers topics and help for choosing topics is www.faculty.cincinnatistate.edu/gesellsc/publicspeaking/topics.html. YouTube is a source for useful video clips, and Hulu provides TV episodes. Many college and university speech communication departments put lists up on their own websites. Web searches, Facebook, and LinkedIn may give you information about people and how to contact them. Pinterest provides a wealth of information on a variety of topics of personal interest.

7. "Writing Guide: Informative Speaking," Colorado State University, retrieved February 27, 2015, from http://writing.colostate.edu/guides/guide.cfm?guideid=52. (Many colleges have similar web pages with similar information.)

8. S. J. Lind, "Teaching Digital Oratory: Public Speaking 2.0," *Communication Teacher 26*, 3 (2012): 163–69.

Chapter 8

1. "Did you Know 2014?" retrieved February 25, 2015, from https://www.youtube.com/watch?v=XrJjfDUzD7M.

2. Ibid.

3. Ibid.

4. Ibid.

5. G. Couros, "Why Social Media Can and Is Changing Education," *Connected Principals*, March 21, 2011, retrieved February 25, 2015, from http://georgecouros.ca/blog/archives/1860.

6. Abdullah Al-Asmari, "My Saudi Arabia." This University of Northern Iowa Graduate Student shared insights about Saudi Arabia with the intercultural communication class. His presentation was about two and a half hours, and these remarks are adapted from that lecture.

7. Abdullah's remarks were in the form of a lecture presentation to the class, so additional information supplemented the information he provided. The primary source was: "Middle East: Saudi Arabia," *The World Factbook,* Central Intelligence Agency, retrieved June 18, 2012, from https://www.cia.gov/library/publications/the-world-factbook/geos/sa.html.

8. Adapted from remarks made in an oral defense of an unpublished master's thesis by Anna Levina, titled "Recent Jewish Immigrants' Communication in Postville, Iowa: A Case Study," University of Northern Iowa, June 3, 2003.

9. E. Griffin, "Axiology," in *A First Look at Communication Theory*, 8th ed. (Boston: McGraw-Hill, 2011).

10. Mission One Million, "Needs," retrieved March 3, 2015, from http://www.mission1m.org/about_the_need.html.

11. Ibid.

12. Ibid.

13. Ibid.

14. Ibid.

15. Mission One Million, "History of the Organization," http://www.mission1m.org/about_overview.htm.

16. "Orphans," UNICEF press center, retrieved March 3, 2015, from www.unicef.org/media/media_45279.html.

17. "Africa's Orphaned Generations," UNICEF, 2011, retrieved March 3, 2015, from www.unicef.org/sowc06/pdfs/africas_orphans.pdf.

18. Ibid.

19. C. J. Loomis, "Warren Buffett Gives Away His Fortune," CNN Money, June 25, 2006, retrieved March 3, 2015, from http://money.cnn.com/2006/06/25/magazines/fortune/charity1.fortune/.

20. "Africa's Orphaned Generations," Part 2, UNICEF, 2011.

Chapter 9

1. Fast Facts: Hunger, World Vision Blog, June 3, 2011, retrieved March 15, 2015, from http://blog.worldvision.org/causes/fast-facts-hunger/.

2. B. Senauer, "Ending Global Hunger in the 21st Century: Projections of the Number of Food Insecure People," *Applied Economic Perspectives and Policy* 23 (1) (2012): 68–81, retrieved March 15, 2015, from http://aepp.oxfordjournals.org/content/23/1/68.short.

3. Smithsonian Institute and Museums, http://www.si.edu/, retrieved March 15, 2015.

4. Earth Day; The History of a Movement, retrieved March 15, 2015, from http://www.earthday.org/earth-day-history-movement?gclid=CMvWp9THyMYCFQYJaQodD4QMzw.

5. T. Buzan, *Mind Maps at Work: How to Be the Best at Work and Still Have Time to Play* (New York: HarperCollins, 2004). Also, "How to Make a Mind Map in 8 Steps," retrieved March 15, 2015, from https://www.google.com/search?q=%E2%80%9CHow+to+Make+a+Mind+Map+in+8+Steps.%E2%80%9D&espv=2&biw=1292&bih=690&site=webhp&tbm=isch&tbo=u&source=univ&sa=X&ei=_5s9VfGGPMijyATI4YH4AQ&ved=0CCQQsAQ.

6. Ibid.

7. "Eating Disorder Statistics," South Carolina Department of Mental Health, retrieved March 15, 2015, from http://www.state.sc.us/dmh/anorexia/statistics.htm.

8. "Worldwide Orphan Facts, Figures and Statistics," SOS Children's Villages, retrieved March 15, 2015, from http://www.sos-usa.org/our-impact/childrens-statistics.

9. J. Robinson, "Silent Assassin: The Ticking Time Bomb of Stress," HuffPost Healthy Living retrieved March 15, 2015, from http://www.huffingtonpost.com/joe-robinson/stress-screenings_b_3347483.html.

10. "Laughter Is the Best Medicine: Health Benefits of Humor and Laughter," HELPGUIDE.ORG, retrieved March 15, 2015, from http://www.helpguide.org/articles/emotional-health/laughter-is-the-best-medicine.htm.

11. Ibid.

12. Lee Iacocca, cited in Glenn Van Ekeren, *Speaker's Sourcebook II* (Englewood Cliffs, NJ: Prentice Hall, 1994), 73.

13. "Laughter Is the Best Medicine," op. cit.

14. Ibid.

15. "Choosing to Adopt," retrieved March 15, 2015, from http://adoption.about.com/od/adopting/bb/befrdecideadopt.htm.

16. D. Zarefsky, *Public Speaking Strategies for Success*, 5th ed. (Boston: Allyn and Bacon, 2008), 222.
17. "What Are Sleep Deprivation and Deficiency?" National Heart, Lung, and Blood Institute, retrieved March 15, 2015, from http://www.nhlbi.nih.gov/health/health-topics/topics/sdd/.
18. "Eating Disorders," National Institutes of Mental Health, retrieved March 15, 2015, from http://www.nimh.nih.gov/health/publications/eating-disorders-new-trifold/index.shtml.
19. J. Rifkin, "The Bio Tech Century," delivered May 1998, City Club of Cleveland, OH, retrieved March 15, 2015, from http://www.americanrhetoric.com/.

Chapter 10

1. Graham D. Bodie, "A Racing Heart, Rattling Knees, and Ruminative Thoughts: Defining, Explaining, and Treating Public Speaking Anxiety," *Communication Education* 59(1) (Jan. 2010): 70–105.
2. J. C. McCroskey, "The Communication Apprehension Perspective," in J. A. Daly and J. C. McCroskey, eds., *Avoiding Communication: Shyness, Reticence, and Communication Apprehension* (Beverly Hills, CA: Sage, 1984), 13.
3. Many sources identify "glossophobia," or "fear of public speaking," as one of our greatest fears. *The New Book of Lists* (2006) by David Walleechinsky, Amy Wallace, Ira Basen, and Jane Farrow says that 73 percent of Americans identify "fear of speaking" ahead of fear of spiders, snakes, and death.
4. X. Liao, "Effective Communication in Multicultural Classrooms: An Exploratory Study," unpublished master of arts thesis, University of Northern Iowa, May 2003.
5. Hugh Jackman, Pre-Oscars (2009) interview as seen on YouTube. Retrieved on April 15, 2012, from http://www.youtube.com/watch?v=eRjPaTUD3N4
6. K. K. Dwyer, *Conquer Your Speech-Fright: Learn How to Overcome the Nervousness of Public Speaking* (Belmont, CA: Wadsworth Publishing, 1997), 73–83.
7. Merriam Webster online dictionary, retrieved April 1, 2015, from http://www.merriam-webster.com/dictionary/meditation.
8. M. Ricard, A. Luts, and R. J. Davidson, "The Mind of the Meditator," *Scientific American*, November 2014, 39–45.
9. S. Chaiken, "Communicator Physical Attractiveness and Persuasion," *Journal of Personality and Social Psychology* 37 (1979): 1387–97. Many other current studies identify physical attractiveness as a factor in attending to another's speech. This article provides a more complete foundation for current work.
10. W. J. Seiler, "The Effects of Visual Materials on Attitude, Credibility, and Retention," *Speech Monographs* 38 (Nov. 1971): 331–34; W. J. Seiler, "The Conjunctive Influence of Source Credibility and the Use of Visual Materials on Communicative Effectiveness," *Southern Speech Communication Journal* 37 (Winter 1971): 174–85; and P. Brett, "A Comparative Study of the Effects of the Use of Multimedia on Listening Comprehension, *System* 25 (Mar. 1997): 39–53.
11. Ibid.
12. *Presentations That Persuade and Motivate* (The Results-Driven Manager Series), Harvard Business School Press, June 11, 2004.

13. William Germano, "The Scholarly Lecture: How to Stand and Deliver," *The Chronicle of Higher Education* 50(14, B15) (Nov. 28, 2003).
14. Personal conversation with Dr. Victoria DeFrancisco, University of Northern Iowa, January 20, 2012.

Chapter 11

1. "Information," Dictionary.com. Retrieved February 19, 2015, from http://dictionary.reference.com/browse/information?s=t.
2. American Diabetes Association, "National Diabetes Statistics Report, 2014," retrieved February 19, 2015, from http://www.diabetes.org/diabetes-basics/statistics/.
3. R. Alexander, "Does a Child Die of Hunger Every 10 Seconds? *BBC News*, June 17, 2013.
4. S. J. Crow, C. B. Peterson, S. A. Swanson, N. C. Raymond, S. Specker, E. D. Eckert, and J. E. Mitchell, "Increased Mortality in Bulimia Nervosa and Other Eating Disorders," *American Journal of Psychiatry* 166: 1342–46.
5. "Milestones," *Time*, May 28, 2012, 21; D. Martin, "Evelyn B. Johnson, Pilot and Instructor, Dies at 102," *New York Times*, May 12, 2012.
6. "'Smart Bomb' Drug Targets Breast Cancer," *NewsmaxMedia*, June 3, 2012, retrieved June 3, 2012, from http://www.newsmaxhealth.com/health_stories/herceptin_breast_cancer/2012/06/03/454338.html?s=al&promo_code=F185-1.
7. Mayo Clinic, "Eating Disorders: Symptoms," retrieved June 28, 2012, from http://www.mayoclinic.com/health/eating-disorders/ds00294/dsection=symptoms; also, "Eating Disorder Statistics," South Carolina Department of Mental Health, retrieved May 28, 2012, from http://www.state.sc.us/dmh/anorexia/statistics.htm.
8. Eligible Receiver, *Frontline*, PBS, retrieved February 19, 2015, from http://www.pbs.org/wgbh/pages/frontline/shows/cyberwar/warnings/.

Chapter 12

1. D. Zarefsky, *Public Speaking: Strategies for Success,* 5th ed. (Boston: Allyn and Bacon, 2008), 412.
2. Adapted from W. Fotheringham, *Perspectives on Persuasion* (Boston: Allyn and Bacon, 1966), 33.
3. Dr. D. Brownstein, "The Country's #1 Health Crisis," *News - max Health,* May 30, 2015.
4. C. Cudworth, "Sometimes It's the Junk in Your Head That Needs Cleaning Out," Takeaways, retrieved June 4, 2012, from http://fengshui.about.com/od/thebasics/qt/clearclutter.htm.
5. "Statistics about Depression," retrieved June 4, 2015, from http://psychcentral.com/blog/archives/2010/09/02/statistics-about-college-depression/.
6. G. Carlson, interviewed by Canadian Broadcasting Corporation staff at FM 89.3 Radio, Winnipeg, Manitoba, June 11, 2015; http://podcast.cbc.ca/mp3/podcasts/mbinforadio_20120611_71114.mp3.
7. S. Toulmin, *The Uses of Argument* (Cambridge, UK: Cambridge University Press, 1969), 94–145.
8. H. Clancy, "Exec Predicts Dead Calm for U.S. Wind Energy Production," GreenTech Pastures, retrieved June 11, 2015, from http://www.zdnet.com/blog/green/exec-predicts-dead-calm-for-us-wind-energy-generation/21394.

9. J. McCroskey, retrieved June 4, 2015, from www.jamescmccroskey.com.

10. L. Talerico_Hedred, managing editor, World Vision Blog, "Fast Facts: Hunger," retrieved June 11, 2015, from http://blog.worldvision.org/causes/fast-facts-hunger/.

11. South Carolina Department of Mental Health, "Eating Disorder Statistics," retrieved May 31, 2015, from http://www.state.sc.us/dmh/anorexia/statistics.htm.

12. K. German, B. E. Gronbeck, D. Ehninger, and A. H. Monroe, *Principles and Types of Speech Communication*, 17th ed. (Boston: Allyn and Bacon, 2010), 185–205.

13. M. Schwabe, "Volunteering with Bethel Missions in Guatemala." Persuasive speech given at the University of Nebraska–Lincoln, used with permission.

14. Ibid.

Chapter 13

1. L. Stinson, "Unplugged for 40 Days," *Journal Star*, April 2, 2011, D1, D3.

2. The top 20 valuable Facebook statistics, February 2015, retrieved from https://zephoria.com/social-media/top-15-valuable-facebook-statistics/.

3. L. Stinson, "Unplugged for 40 Days," *Journal Star*, April 2, 2011, D1, D3.

4. Ibid., D3.

5. The top 20 valuable Facebook statistics, February 2015, retrieved from https://zephoria.com/social-media/top-15-valuable-facebook-statistics/.

6. "18-24-Year-Old Smartphone Owners Send and Receive Almost 4K Texts per Month," retrieved November 3, 2014, from http://www.marketingcharts.com/online/18-24-year-old-smartphone-owners-send-and-receive-almost-4k-texts-per-month-27993/.

7. L. Raine, A. Lenhart, and A. Smith, "The Tone of Life on Social Networking Sites, *Pew Internet Reports*, February 9, 2012, retrieved February 16, 2012, from http://www.pewinternet.org/Reports/2012/Social-networking-climate.aspx.

8. M. L. Knapp and A. L. Vangelisti, *Interpersonal Communication and Human Relationships*, 6th ed. (Boston: Allyn and Bacon, 2009).

9. C. R. Berger and R. J. Calabrese, "Some Explorations in Initial Interactions and Beyond: Toward a Developmental Theory of Interpersonal Communication," *Human Communication Research* 1 (1975): 98–112; and C. R. Berger, "Response–Uncertain Outcome Values in Predicted Relationships: Uncertainty Reduction Theory Then and Now," *Human Communication Research* 13 (1986): 34–38.

10. C. R. Berger, "Beyond Initial Interaction: Uncertainty, Understanding, and Development of Interpersonal Relationships," in H. Giles and R. St. Clair, eds., *Language and Social Psychology* (Oxford, UK: Blackwell, 1979), 122–44.

11. E. Griffin, *A First Look at Communication Theory*, 8th ed. (New York: McGraw-Hill, 2012).

12. D. E. Brashers, J. L. Neidig, S. M. Haas, L.W. Cardillo, and J. A. Russel, "'In an Important Way, I Did Die,'" Uncertainty and Revival among Persons Living with HIV or AIDS," *AIDS Care* 11 (1999): 201–19; D.E. Brashers, "Communication and Uncertainty Management," *Journal of Communication* 51 (2001): 477–97.

13. D. E. Brashers, "A Theory of Communication and Uncertainty Management," in B. Whaley and W. Samter, eds., *Explaining Communication Theory* (Mahwah, NJ: Lawrence Erlbaum, 2007): 210–18.

14. Brashers, 2001, 477–97.

15. Ibid., 477–97.

16. J. B. Walther, "Interpersonal Effects in Computer-Mediated Interaction: A Relational Perspective," *Communication Research* 19 (1992): 52–90.

17. Ibid., 52–53.

18. J. B. Walther, Computer-Mediated Communication: Impersonal, Interpersonal, and Hyperpersonal Interaction, *Communication Research* 23 (1996): 3–43.

19. J. B. Walther, "Social Information Processing Theory: Impressions and Relationship Development Online," in L. A. Baxter and D. O. Braithwaite, eds., *Engaging Theories in Interpersonal Communication* (Newbury Park, CA: Sage, 2008), 391–404.

20. I. Altman and D. Taylor, *Social Penetration: The Development of Interpersonal Relationships* (New York: Holt, Rinehart & Winston, 1973); and Knapp and Vangelisti, 13–19.

21. W. Thibaut and H. H. Kelley, *The Social Psychology of Groups*, 2nd ed. (New Brunswick, NJ: Transaction Books, 1986), 9–30; and E. Griffin, *A First Look at Communication Theory*, 6th ed. (New York: McGraw-Hill, 2006), 122–25.

22. W. C. Schutz, *The Interpersonal Underworld* (Palo Alto, CA: Science and Behavior Books, 1966), 13–20.

23. K. Floyd, *Communicating Affection: Interpersonal Behavior and Social Context* (Cambridge, UK: Cambridge University Press, 2006).

24. R. F. Baumeister and M. R. Leary, "The Need to Belong: Desire for Interpersonal Attachments as a Fundamental Human Motivation," *Psychological Bulletin* 117 (1995): 497–529.

25. R. G. Kuijer, B. P. Buunk, J. F. Ybema, and T. Wobbes, "The Relation between Perceived Inequity, Marital Satisfaction and Emotions among Couples Facing Cancer," *British Journal of Social Psychology* 41 (2002): 39–56.

26. J. T. Wood, "Dialectical Theory," in *Making Connections: Readings in Relational Communication*, 2nd ed., eds. K. M. Galvin and P. J. Cooper (Los Angeles, CA: Roxbury, 2000), 132–38; L. A. Baxter, "Dialectical Contradictions in Relationship Development," *Journal of Social and Personal Relationships* 7 (1990): 69–88; and L. A. Baxter, "Thinking Dialogically about Communication in Interpersonal Relationships," in *Structure in Human Communication*, ed. R. Conville (Westport, CT: Greenwood, 1994).

27. L. A. Baxter and B. Montgomery, *Relation: Dialogues and Dialect* (New York: Guilford, 1996), 185–206.

28. L. A. Baxter, "Dialectical Contradictions in Relationship Development," *Journal of Social and Personal Relationships* 7 (1990): 69–88.

29. D. Fine, *The Fine Art of Small Talk* (New York: Hyperion, 2005).

30. A. L. Sillars and M. D. Scott, "Interpersonal Perception between Intimates: An Integrative Review," *Human Communication Research* 10 (1983): 153–76.

31. J. M. DeGroot, *Reconnecting with the Dead via Facebook: Examining Transcorporeal Communication as a Way to Maintain Relationships* (Doctoral dissertation, Ohio University, 2009). ProQuest Digital Dissertations, AAT 3371475.

32. J. W. Pennebaker, *Opening Up: The Healing Power of Expressing Emotions* (New York: Guilford, 1990).

33. V. J. Derlega, S. Metts, S. Petronio, and S. T. Margulis, *Self-Disclosure* (Newbury Park, CA: Sage, 1993), 74.

34. S. Petronio, "The Boundaries of Privacy: Praxis of Every-day Life," in S. Petronio, ed., *Balancing the Secrets of Private Disclosures* (Hillsdale, NJ: Erlbaum, 2000), 9–15.

35. S. Petronio, "Communication Boundary Management: A Theoretical Model of Managing Disclosure of Private Information between Marital Couples," *Communication Theory* 1 (1991): 311; and S. Petronio and J. P. Caughlin, "Communication Privacy Management Theory: Understanding Families," in D. O. Braithwaite and L. A. Baxter, eds., *Engaging Theories in Family Communication: Multiple Perspectives* (Thousand Oaks, CA: Sage, 2006), 35–49.

36. D. Lithwick, "Teens, Nude Photos and the Law," *Newsweek*, February 23, 2009, 18.

37. N. Gibbs, "Second Thoughts about Kids and Cell-Phones," *Time*, March 5, 2009, 56.

38. J. T. Wood, *Gendered Lives: Communication, Gender, and Culture*, 8th ed. (Belmont, CA: Wadsworth, 2009), 123–24.

39. D. Tannen, *You Just Don't Understand: Women and Men in Conversation* (New York: Quill, 2001).

40. C. K. Riessman, *Divorce Talk: Women and Men Make Sense of Personal Relationships* (New Brunswick, NJ: Rutgers University Press, 1990).

41. The Pew Internet & American Life Project report is based on the findings of a variety of tracking surveys on Americans' use of the Internet between March 2000 and September 2005. Retrieved July 10, 2009, from www.pewinternet.org/pdfs/PIP_Women_and_Men_online.pdf.

42. S. Petronio, "Communication Strategies to Reduce Embarrassment Differences between Men and Women," *The Western Journal of Speech Communication* 48 (1984): 28–38.

43. R. P. Hart and D. M. Burks, "Rhetorical Sensitivity and Social Interaction," *Speech Monographs* 39 (1972): 75–91.

44. S. W. Littlejohn and K. Foss, *Theories of Human Communication*, 9th ed. (Belmont, CA: Wadsworth, 2008).

Chapter 14

1. B. H. Spitzberg, "What Is Good Communication?" *Journal of the Association for Communication Administration* 29 (2000): 103–19; J. T. Woods, *Interpersonal Communication Everyday Encounters*, 7th ed. (Boston: Wadsworth Cengage, 2013), 30–33; K. Floyd, *Interpersonal Communication*, 7th ed. (New York: McGraw-Hill, 2011), 28–30.

2. J. C. McCroskey and T. A. McCain, "The Measurement of Interpersonal Attraction," *Speech Monographs* 41 (1974): 261–66.

3. M. A. Collins and L. A. Zebrowitz, "The Contributions of Appearance to Occupational Outcomes in Civilian and Military Settings," *Journal of Applied Social Psychology* 25 (1995): 129–63; and I. Van Straaten, R. G. Engels, C. Finkenauer, and R. W. Holland, "Meeting Your Match: How Attractiveness Similarity Affects Approach Behavior in Mixed-Sex Dyads," *Personality and Social Psychology Bulletin* 35 (2009): 685–97.

4. S. M. Andersen and A. Baum, "Transference in Interpersonal Relations: Influences and Affect Based on Significant Representations," *Journal of Personality* 62 (1994): 459–97.

5. M. A. Collins and L. A. Zebrowitz, 129–63.

6. N. Angier, "Opposites Attract? Not in Real Life," *The New York Times*, July 8, 2003, F1, F6; and P. M. Buston and S. T. Emlen, "Cognitive Processes Underlying Human Mate Choice: The Relationship between Self-Perception and Mate Preferences in Western Society," *The Proceedings of the National Academy of Sciences* 100 (2003): 8805–10.

7. I. Van Straaten, R. G. Engels, C. Finkenauer, and R. W. Holland, "Meeting Your Match: How Attractiveness Similarity Affects Approach Behavior in Mixed-Sex Dyads," *Personality and Social Psychology* 35 (2009): 685–97.

8. W. M. Bernstein, B. O. Stephenson, M. L. Snyder, and R. A. Wicklund, "Causal Ambiguity and Heterosexual Affiliation," *Journal of Experimental Social Psychology* 19 (1983): 78–92; K. H. Price and S. G. Vandenberg, "Matching for Physical Attractiveness in Married Couples," *Personality and Social Psychology* 5 (1979): 398–400; and M. Lea, "Factors Underlying Friendship: An Analysis of Responses on the Acquaintance Description Form in Relation to Wright's Friendship Model," *Journal of Social and Personal Relationships* 6 (1989): 275–92.

9. M. R. Parks and K. Floyd, "Making Friends in Cyberspace," *Journal of Communication* 45 (1996): 84; and J. B. Walther and M. R. Parks, "Cues Filtered Out, Cues Filtered In: Computer-Mediated Communication and Relationships," in *Handbook of Interpersonal Communication*, 3rd ed., eds. M. L. Knapp and J. A. Daly (Thousand Oaks, CA: Sage, 2002), 529–63.

10. A. Feingold, "Gender Differences in Effects of Physical Attractiveness on Romantic Attraction: A Comparison across Five Research Paradigms," *Journal of Personality and Social Psychology* 59 (1990): 981–93; and S. A. Meyers, "'Your Mother Would Like Me': Self-Presentation in the Personals Ads of Heterosexual and Homosexual Men and Women," *Personality and Social Psychology Bulletin* 19 (1993): 131–42.

11. J. Coupland, "Past the 'Perfect Kind of Ague'? Styling Selves and Relationships in Over-50 Dating Advertisements," *Journal of Communication* 50 (2000): 9–30.

12. Parks and Floyd, 85.

13. M. Knapp, *Social Intercourse: From Greeting to Good-Bye* (Boston: Allyn and Bacon, 1978), 3–28; and M. L. Knapp and A. L. Vangelisti, *Interpersonal Communication and Human Relationship*, 6th ed. (Boston: Allyn and Bacon, 2009), 33–37.

14. D. P. McWhirter and A. M. Mattison, *The Male Couple* (Englewood Cliffs, NJ: Prentice-Hall, 1998).

15. Knapp and Vangelisti, 33.

16. Ibid., 37–42.

17. Ibid., 39.

18. Ibid., 40.

19. Adapted from an article written by Jonathan Butler titled "The Donut Shop Experiment," in *The Front Porch Where People Share Life*, published by The Front Porch, LLC, © 2002.

20. L. Stafford and D. Canary, "Maintenance Strategies and Romantic Relationships: Type, Gender, and Relational Characteristics," *Journal of Social and Personal Relationships* 8 (1991): 217–42.

21. J. M. Tyler, R. S. Feldman, and A. Reichert, "The Price of Deceptive Behavior: Disliking and Lying to People Who Lie to Us," *Journal of Experimental Social Psychology* 42 (2006): 69–77.

22. J. T. Hancock, C. Toma, and N. Ellison, "The Truth about Lying in Online Dating Profiles," *Proceedings of ACM ChI 2007 Conference on Human Factors in Computing Systems* (2007): 449–52.

23. Ibid., 451.

24. C. L. Toma and J. T. Hancock, "Reading between the Lines: Linguistic Cues to Deception in Online Dating Profiles," *Proceedings of ACM CSCW10 Conference on Computer-Support Cooperative Work* (2010): 5–8.

25. B. M. DePaul, J. J. Lindsay, B. E. Malone, L. Muhlenbruck, K. Chandler, and H. Cooper, "Cues to Deception," *Psychological Bulletin* 129 (2003): 74–118.

26. Knapp and Vangelisti, 43–47.

27. M. L. Knapp, R. P. Hart, G. W. Friedrich, and G. M. Shulman, "The Rhetoric of Goodbye: Verbal and Nonverbal Correlates of Human Leave-Taking," *Speech Monographs* 40 (1973): 182–98.

28. S. W. Duck, ed., *Personal Relationships 4: Dissolving Personal Relationships* (London: Academic Press, 1982); L. A. Baxter, "Accomplishing Relationship Disengagement," in *Understanding Personal Relationships: An Interdisciplinary Approach*, eds. S. W. Duck and D. Perlman (Beverly Hills, CA: Sage, 1985), 243–66; S. W. Duck, *Human Relationships: An Introduction to Social Psychology* (Beverly Hills, CA: Sage, 1986); and S. Duck, "A Topography of Relationships: Disengagement and Dissolution," in *Personal Relationships*, ed. S. W. Duck, (London: Academic Press, 1982), 1–30.

29. K. A. Sorenson, S. M. Russel, D. J. Harkness, and J. H. Harvey, "Account-Making, Confiding, and Coping with the Ending of a Close Relationship," *Journal of Social Behavior and Personality* 8 (1993): 73–86.

30. L. A. Baxter and B. Montgomery, *Relation: Dialogues and Dialect* (New York: Guilford, 1996).

31. W. Wilmot and J. Hocker, *Interpersonal Conflict*, 8th ed. (New York: McGraw-Hill, 2011), 11.

32. Ibid., 33, 37.

33. R. A. Baron, "Attributions and Organizational Conflict," in *Attribution Theory: Applications to Achievement, Mental Health, and Interpersonal Conflict*, eds. S. Graha and V. Folkes (Hillsdale, NJ: Erlbaum, 1990), 185–204; and R. Cropanzano, ed., *Justice in the Workplace* (Hillsdale, NJ: Erlbaum, 1993), 79–103.

34. Wilmot and Hocker, 47.

35. Wilmot and Hocker, 101.

36. Knapp and Vangelisti (2009), 384; K. Floyd, *Interpersonal Communication*, 2nd ed. (New York: McGraw-Hill, 2011), 375; A. C. Filley, *Interpersonal Conflict Resolution* (Glenview, IL: Scott, Foresman, 1975); D. D. Cahn, "Intimate in Conflict: A Research Review," in *Intimates in Conflict: A Communication Perspective*, ed. D. D. Cahn (Hillsdale, NJ: Erlbaum, 1990), 1–24; W. W. Cupach and D. J. Canary, *Competence in Interpersonal Conflict* (New York: McGraw-Hill, 1997); and R. Blake and J. Mouton, *The Managerial Grid* (Houston: Gulf Publishing, 1964).

37. A. L. Sillars, S. G. Coletti, D. Parry, and M. A. Rogers, "Coding Verbal Conflict Tactics: Nonverbal and Perceptual Correlates of the Avoidance–Distributive–Integrative Distinction," *Human Communication Research* 9 (1982): 83–95; and Wilmot and Hocker, 152.

38. Q. Wang, E. L. Fink, and D. A. Cai, "The Effect of Conflict Goals on Avoidance Strategies: What Does Not Communicating Communicate," *Human Communication Research* 38 (2012): 222–52.

39. J. Gottman and S. Carrere, "Why Can't Men and Women Get Along? Developmental Notes and Marital Inequities," in *Communication Relational Maintenance*, eds. D. Canary and L. Stafford (New York: Academic Press, 1994).

40. J. Gottman, *Why Marriages Succeed and Fail: And How You Can Make Yours Last* (New York: Simon and Schuster, 1994); and J. Gottman, *The Marriage Clinic: A Scientifically Based Marital Therapy* (New York: Norton, 1999).

41. K. Neff and S. Harter, "The Authenticity of Conflict Resolutions among Adult Couples: Does Women's Other-Oriented Behavior Reflect Their True Selves," *Sex Roles: A Journal of Research* (2002): 403–21.

42. A. L. Sillars and W. W. Wilmot, "Communication Strategies in Conflict and Mediation," in *Communicating Strategically: Strategies in Interpersonal Communication*, eds. J. Wiemann and J. A. Daly (Hillsdale, NJ: Erlbaum, 1994), 163–90.

43. J. S. Neuman and B. A. Baron, "Social Antecedents of Bullying," in *Workplace Bullying: Development in Theory, Research*, 2nd ed., eds. S. Einarsen, H. Hoel, D. Zapf, and C. L. Cooper (London: CRC Press, 2010): 201–27.

44. Wilmot and Hocker, 163.

45. Ibid., 168–74.

46. S. W. Duck, "A Perspective on the Repair of Personal Relationships: Repair of What, When?" in *Personal Relationships 5: Repairing Personal Relationships*, ed. S. W. Duck (New York: Macmillan, 1984).

47. B. R. Burleson and W. Samter, "Effects of Cognitive Complexity on the Perceived Importance of Communication Skills in Friends," *Communication Research* 17 (1990): 165–82; W. Samter and B. R. Burleson, "Evaluations of Communication Skills as Predictors of Peer Acceptance in a Group Living Situation," *Communication Studies* 41 (1990): 311–26; B. R. Burleson, J. G. Delia, and J. L. Applegate, "The Socialization of Person-Centered Communication: Parent's Contributions to Their Children's Social-Cognitive and Communication Skills," in *Explaining Family Interactions*, eds. M. A. Fitzpatrick and A. L. Vangelisti (Thousand Oaks, CA: Sage, 1995), 34–76.

48. Knapp and Vangelisti, 403.

49. J. M. Reisman, "Friendliness and Its Correlates," *Journal of Social and Clinical Psychology* 2 (1984): 143–55.

50. E. P. Simon and L. A. Baxter, "Attachment-Style Differences in Relationship Maintenance Strategies," *Western Journal of Communication* 57 (Fall 1993): 423.

51. Ibid., 423.

52. Ibid., 428.

53. Ideas for this section are derived from a Parent Effectiveness Training workshop and from T. Gordon, *Parent Effectiveness Training* (New York: Wyden, 1970).

Chapter 15

1. B. Lickel, D. L. Hamilton, G. Wieczorkowski, A. Lewis, S. J. Sherman, and A. N. Uhles, "Varieties of Groups and the Perception of Group Inactivity," *Journal of Personality and Social Psychology* 78 (2000): 223–46.

2. S. A. Beebe and J. T. Masterson, *Communicating in Small Groups: Principles and Practices*, 11th ed. (Boston: Allyn and Bacon, 2015), 6–12.

3. G. Lumsden, D. Lumsden, and C. Wetthoff, *Communicating in Groups and Teams: Sharing Leadership*, 5th ed. (Belmont, CA: Wadsworth, 2010).

4. B. Tuckman, "Developmental Sequence in Small Groups," *Psychological Bulletin* 63 (1965): 384–99; B. Tuckman and M. A. Jensen, "Stages of Small-Group Development Revisited," *Group and Organization Studies* 2 (1977): 419–27.

5. B. B. Haslett and J. Ruebus, "What Differences Do Individual Differences in Groups Make?" in *The Handbook of Group Theory and Research*, 2nd ed., eds. L. R. Frey, D. S. Gouran, and M. S. Poole (Thousand Oaks, CA: Sage, 1999), 115–38; and C. H. Hui and H. C. Triandis, "Individualism–Collectivism: A Study of Cross-Cultural Research," *Journal of Cross-Cultural Psychology* 17 (1986): 225–48.

6. C. Calloway-Thomas, P. J. Cooper, and C. Blake, *Intercultural Communication Roots and Routes* (Boston: Allyn and Bacon, 1999), 113–14.

7. Ibid., 114.

8. H. C. Triandis, "Cross-Cultural Studies of Individualism and Collectiveness," in *Cross-Cultural Perspective*, ed. J. Berman (Lincoln: University of Nebraska Press, 1990); and G. Hofstede, *Cultures and Organizations: Software of the Mind* (New York: McGraw-Hill, 1991).

9. M. Buckingham and C. Coffman, "Item 9: Doing Quality Work," *Gallup Management Journal* [online], Spring 2002, retrieved on July 7, 2011, from www.gallupjournal.com/q12Center/articles/19990517.asp.

10. J. R. Katzenbach and D. K. Smith, "The Discipline of Teams," *Harvard Business Review* (March–April 1993): 111–20.

11. L. P. Stewart, P. J. Cooper, A. D. Stewart, and S. H. Friedley, *Communication and Gender*, 4th ed. (Boston: Allyn and Bacon, 2003), 44–50; D. N. Maltz and R. A. Borker, "A Cultural Approach to Male–Female Miscommunication," in *Language and Social Identity*, ed. J. J. Gumperz (Cambridge, U.K.: Cambridge University Press, 1982), 195–216; and E. Baird, "Sex Differences in Group Communication: A Review of Relevant Research," *Quarterly Journal of Speech* 62 (1976): 179–92.

12. B. F. Meeker and P. A. Weitzel-O'Neil, "Sex Roles and Interpersonal Behavior in Task-Oriented Groups," *American Sociological Review* 42 (1977): 91–105; R. L. Hoffman and N. K. V. Maier, "Quality and Acceptance of Problem Solutions by Members of Homogeneous and Heterogeneous Groups," *Journal of Abnormal and Social Psychology* 62 (1961): 401–07.

13. J. D. Rothwell, *In Mixed Company: Communicating in Small Groups and Teams* (Boston: Wadsworth, 2013), 32–35; J. C. McCroskey, V. P. Richmond, and R. A. Stewart, *One on One: The Foundations of Interpersonal Communication* (Englewood Cliffs, NJ: Prentice-Hall, 1986), 244–47; M. E. Roloff, "The Impact of Socialization on Sex Differences in Conflict Resolution" (paper presented at the annual convention of the International Communication Association, Acapulco, Mexico, May 1980); E. A. Mabry, "Some Theoretical Implications of Female and Male Interaction in Unstructured Small Groups," *Small Group Behavior* 20 (1989): 536–50; and W. E. Jurma and B. C. Wright, "Follower Reactions to Male and Female Leaders Who Maintain or Lose Reward Power," *Small Group Research* 21 (1990): 97–112.

14. J. Bond and W. Vinacke, "Coalition in Mixed Sex Triads," *Sociometry* 24 (1961): 61–65; B. A. Fisher, "Differential Effects of Sexual Composition Interaction Patterns in Dyads," *Human Communication Research* 9 (1983): 225–38; Jurma and Wright, "Follower Reactions," 97–112; and D. J. Canary and B. H. Spitzberg, "Appropriateness and Effectiveness Perceptions of Conflict Strategies," *Human Communication Research* 14 (1987): 93–118.

15. G. J. Galanes and K. Adams, *Effective Group Discussion*, 14th ed. (New York: McGraw-Hill, 2013), 147.

16. The Official Robert's Rules of Order Website, retrieved on July 7, 2011, from www.robertsrules.com.

17. T. Postmes, R. Spears, and M. Lea, "The Formation of Group Norms in Computer-Mediated Communication," *Human Communication Research* 26 (July 2000): 341–70.

18. K. Adams and G. J. Galanes, *Communicating in Groups Applications and Skills*, 9th ed. (New York: McGraw-Hill, 2015), 10.

19. Ibid., 10–11.

20. B. S. Boneva, A. Quinn, R. Kraut, S. Kiesler, and I. Shklovski, "Teenage Communication in the Instant Messaging Era," in *Computers, Phones and the Internet: Domesticating Information Technology*, eds. R. Kraut, M. Brynin, and S. Kiesler (New York: Oxford University, 2006): 201–18; J. B. Walther, T. Loh, and L. Granka, "Let Me Count the Ways: The Interchange of Verbal and Nonverbal Cues in Computer-Mediated and Face-to-Face Affinity," *Journal of Language and Social Psychology* 24 (2005): 36–65.

21. N. K. Baym, Y. B. Zhang, and M-C. Lin, "Social Interactions across Media: Interpersonal Communication on the Internet, Face-to-Face, and the Telephone," *New Media & Society* 6 (2004); 299–318.

22. J. Peter and P. M. Valenburg, "Research Note: Individual Differences in Perceptions of Internet Communication," *European Journal of Communication* 21 (2006): 213–26.

23. Galanes and Adams, 15–17.

24. P. B. Paulus, ed., *Psychology of Group Influence*, 2nd ed. (Hillsdale, NJ: Erlbaum, 1989).

25. R. A. Cooke and J. A. Kernaghan, "Estimating the Difference between Group versus Individual Performance on Problem-Solving Tasks," *Group & Organizational Studies* 12 (September 1987): 319–42.

26. Beebe and Masterson, 14.

27. I. L. Janis, *Groupthink: Psychological Studies of Policy Decisions and Fiascoes*, 2nd ed. (Boston: Houghton Mifflin, 1983); and J. D. Rothwell, 247–55.

28. P. E. Tetlock, R. S. Peterson, C. McGuire, S. Change, and P. Feld, "Assessing Political Group Dynamics: A Test of the Groupthink Model," *Journal of Personality and Social Psychology* 63 (1992): 403–25.

29. Janis, *Groupthink*.

30. Adams and Galanes, 188–190.

31. S. J. Karau and K. D. Williams, "Social Loafing: A Meta-Analytic Review and Theoretical Integration," *Journal of Personality and Social Psychology* 65 (1993): 681–706; B. K. Latané and S. Harkins, "Many Hands Make Light the Work: The Causes and Consequences of Social-Loafing," *Journal of Personality and Social Psychology* 37 (1979): 822–32; B. G. Schultz, "Improving Group Communication Performance," in *The Handbook of Group Communication Theory and Research*, eds. L. R. Frey, D. S. Gouran, and M. S. Poole (Thousand Oaks, CA: Sage, 1999), 371–94; and Beebe and Masterson, 82–83.

32. S. Sorensen, "Grouphate" (paper presented at the International Communication Association, Minneapolis, Minn., May 1981).

Chapter 16

1. F. LaFasto and C. Larson, *When Teams Work Best: 6,000 Team Members and Leaders Tell What It Takes to Succeed* (Thousand Oaks, CA: Sage, 2001), xii–xiii; and C. Larson and M. LaFasto, *Teamwork: What Must Go Right, What Can Go Wrong* (Newbury Park, CA: Sage, 1989).

2. R. A. Baron and N. R. Branscomber, *Social Psychology*, 13th ed. (Boston: Pearson, 2012), 392.

3. F. E. Fiedler, *A Theory of Leadership Effectiveness* (New York: McGraw-Hill, 1967); and P. Weissenberg and M. H. Kavanagh, "The Independence of Initiating Structure and Consideration: A Review of the Evidence," *Personnel Psychology* 25 (1972): 119–30.

4. M. Conlin, "Champions of Innovation," *Business Week*, June 2006, 19–26.

5. R. K. White and R. Lippitt, *Autocracy and Democracy: An Experimental Inquiry* (New York: Harper & Row, 1960), 26–27; and K. Adams and G. J. Galanes, *Communicating in Groups: Applications and Skills,* 9th ed. (New York: McGraw-Hill, 2015), 260.

6. L. G. Bolman and T. E. Deal, *Reframing Organizations: Artistry, Choice, and Leadership*, 2nd ed. (San Francisco: Jossey-Bass, 1997); and G. Morgan, *Images of Organizations*, 2nd ed. (Thousand Oaks, CA: Sage, 1997).

7. Adams and Galanes, 261; R. K. White and R. Lippitt, "Leader Behavior and Member Reaction in Three 'Social Climates,'" in *Group Dynamics: Research and Theory*, 2nd ed., eds. D. Cartwright and A. Zander (New York: Harper & Row, 1960), 527–53.

8. Adams and Galanes, 259.

9. M. Conlin, "Champions of Innovation," 20.

10. Petrecca, "Number of Female Fortune 500 CEOs at Record High," *USA Today*, October 26, 2011, retrieved April 20, 2012, from USA Today.com

11. A. B. Gershenoff and R. J. Foti, "Leader Emergence and Gender Roles in All-Female Groups: A Critical Examination," *Small Group Research* 34 (April 2003): 170–96.

12. J. A. Kolb, "Are We Still Stereotyping Leadership? A Look at Gender and Other Predictors of Leader Emergence," *Small Group Research* 28 (August 1997), 370–93.

13. S. B. Shimanoff and M. M. Jenkins, "Leadership and Gender: Challenging Assumptions and Recognizing Resources," in *Small Group Communication: Theory and Practice*, 8th ed., eds. R. Y. Hirokawa, R. S. Cathcart, L. A. Samovar, and L. Henman (Los Angeles: Roxbury, 2003), 184–98.

14. M. Loden, *Feminine Leadership or How to Succeed in Business without Being One of the Boys* (New York: Times Books, 1985).

15. S. C. Koch, "Evaluative Affect Display toward Male and Female Leaders of Task-Oriented Groups," *Small Group Research* 36 (2005): 678–703.

16. A. H. Eagly and B. T. Johnson, "Gender and Leadership Style: A Meta-Analysis," *Psychological Bulletin* 108 (1990): 233–56.

17. E. E. Duehr and J. E. Bono, "Men, Women, and Managers: Are Stereotypes Finally Changing?" *Personnel Psychology* 59 (2006): 459–71; A. H.Eagly and S. Sczesny, "Stereotypes About Women, Men, and Leaders: Have Times Changed?" In M. Barreto, M. K. Ryan, and M. T. Schmitt, eds., *The Glass Ceiling in the 21st Century* (Washington, D.C.: American Pscyhological Association, 2009): 21–47, and "Business Women Differ from Business Men in Style, Not Skill," 2008, retrieved on July 13, 2009, from www.coaching-for-new-women-managers.com/business-women.html.

18. L. M. Grob, R. A. Meyers, and R. Schuh, "Powerful/Powerless Language Use in Group Interactions: Sex Differences or Similarities?" *Communication Quarterly* 45 (Summer 1997): 282–303.

19. Eagly and Sczesny, 2009: 21–47.

20. D. Forsyth, M. Heiney, and S. Wright, "Biases in Appraisal of Women Leaders," *Group Dynamics: Theory, Research, and Practices* 1 (1997): 98–103; S. Shackelford, W. Wood, and S. Worchel, "Behavioral Styles and the Influence of Women in Mixed-Sex Groups," *Social Psychology* 59 (1996): 284–93; and A. Eagly, S. Karau, and M. Makhijani, "Gender and the Effectiveness of Leaders: A Meta-Analysis," *Journal of Personality and Social Psychology* 117 (1995): 125–45.

21. R. Sharpe, "As Leaders, Women Rule: New Studies Find That Female Managers Outshine Their Male Counterparts in Almost Every Measure," *Business Week* 2000–2009, retrieved July 14, 2009, from www.businessweek.com.

22. K. D. Benne and P. Sheats, "Functional Roles of Group Members," *Journal of Social Issues* 4 (1948): 41–49.

23. R. Y. Hirokawa, "Consensus Group Decision-Making, Quality of Decision and Group Satisfaction: An Attempt to Sort 'Fact' from 'Fiction,'" *Central States Speech Journal* 33 (1982): 407–15.

24. R. S. DeStephen and R. Y. Hirokawa, "Small Group Consensus: Stability of Group Support of the Decision, Task Process, and Group Relationships," *Small Group Behavior* 19 (1988): 227–39.

25. S. A. Beebe and J. T. Masterson, *Communicating in Small Groups*, 11th ed. (Boston: Pearson, 2015), 206–207.

26. W. Wilmot and J. Hocker, *Interpersonal Conflict*, 9th ed. (New York: McGraw-Hill, 2014), 13.

27. Ibid., 11.

28. Adams and Galanes, 229.

29. E. Hobman, P. Bordia, B. Irmer, and A. Chang, "The Expression of Conflict in Computer-Mediated and Face-to-Face Groups," *Small Group Research* 33 (2002): 439–65.

30. Ibid.

31. Adams and Galanes, 234.

32. Adams and Galanes, 242–44.

33. R. V. Harnack, T. B. Fest, and B. S. Jones, *Group Discussion: Theory and Technique*, 2nd ed. (Englewood Cliffs, NJ: Prentice-Hall, 1997): 153–54.

34. J. Dewey, *How We Think* (Lexington, MA: Heath, 1910).

35. S. A. Beebe and J. T. Masterson, *Communicating in Small Groups*, 11th ed. (Boston: Pearson, 2015), 271.

36. D. S. Gouran and R. Y. Hirokawa, "Effective Decision Making and Problem Solving in Groups," in *Small Group Communication*, 8th ed., eds. R. Y. Hirokawa, R. S. Cathcart, L. A. Samovar, and L. D. Henman (Los Angeles: Roxbury, 2003): 27–38.

37. B. J. Broome and L. Fulbright, "A Multistage Influence Model of Barriers to Group Problem Solving: A Participant-Generated Agenda for Small Group Research," *Small Group Research* 26 (February 1995): 25–55.

38. M. C. Roy, S. Gauvin, and M. Limayem, "Electronic Group Brainstorming: The Role of Feedback on Productivity," *Small Group Research* 27 (1996): 215–47; and C. Andriopoulos and P. M. B. Dawson, *Managing Change, Creativity, and Innovation* (Thousand Oaks, CA: Sage Publications, 2009).

39. J. J. Sosik, B. J. Avolio, and S. S. Kahai, "Inspiring Group Creativity: Comparing Anonymous and Identified Electronic Brainstorming," *Small Group Research* 29 (1998): 3–31; W. H. Cooper, R. B. Gallupe, S. Pollard, and J. Cadsby, "Some Liberating Effects of Anonymous Electronic Brainstorming," *Small Group Research* 29 (1998): 147–77; and "Electronic Brainstorming Has Been Found to Be an Effective Means of Generating Many Good-Quality Ideas," *News-Medical.Net*, August 9, 2004, retrieved July 7, 2009, from www.news-medical.net.

Appendix

1. K. B. Barbour, F. B. Berg, M. Eannace, J. Greene, M. Hessig, M. Papworth, C. Radin, E. Rezny, and J. Suarez, *The Quest: A Guide to the Job Interview* (Dubuque, IA: Kendall/Hunt, 1991), 47.

2. Interview with Dr. Kelli Smith, former Assistant Director of Career Services, University of Nebraska, Lincoln, May 5, 2012.

3. C. J. Stewart and W. B. Cash Jr., *Interviewing Principles and Practices*, 14th ed. (New York: McGraw-Hill, 2014), 189.

4. Career Connections. http://www.careerconnections-ct.com/index.asp?Type=B_BASIC&SEC=%7B0997C37D-5A8F-4283-807C-4C94E01BAE34%7D, retrieved February 21, 2015.

5. LinkedIn, http://www.statista.com/statistics/274050/quarterly-numbers-of-linkedin-members, retrieved February 21, 2015.

6. Ibid., 14.

7. *Preparing for the Job Search,* a booklet prepared by the University of Nebraska Career Services, 2014: 15.

8. M. Valdes and S. McFarland, "Resume, References and Passwords, Please," *Lincoln Journal Star,* Sunday, March 25, 2012: B8.

9. T. W. Dougherty, D. B. Turban, and J. C. Callender, "Confirming First Impressions in the Employment Interview: A Field Study of Interviewer Behavior, *Journal of Applied Psychology* 79 (1994): 659–65.

10. D. S. Chapman and P. M. Rowe, "The Impact of Videoconference Technology, Interview Structure, and Interviewer Gender on Interviewer Evaluations in the Employment Interview: A Field Experiment," *Journal of Occupational and Organizational Psychology* (2001): 279; C. J. Stewart and W. B. Cash Jr., *Interviewing Principles and Practices,* 14th ed. (New York: McGraw-Hill, 2014): 9, 127–28.

11. Chapman and Rowe, 279–298; Stewart and Cash, 9.

12. J. Meyers, "The Ideal Job Candidate," *Collegiate Employment Institute Newsletter,* July 15, 1989: 6.

13. Ibid., 6 résumé.

14. Ibid., 6.

15. *The Endicott Report: Trends in the Employment of College and University Graduates in Business and Industry* (Evanston, IL: The Placement Center, Northwestern University, 1980), 8. In the May 2012 interview, Dr. Smith said that the rejection reasons companies give today are not different from what they were in 1980, and Tina V., "Job Rejections: Reasons from an HR Point of View," tina-v.hubpages.com, retrieved September 20, 2012.

Index

Credits

Photo Credits

Cover, Rawpixel/Fotolia; pages 1, Radharc Images/Alamy; 6, Morphart/Fotolia (printing press); 6, David Grossman/Alamy (photo); 7, Oleksiy Mark/Fotolia (www graphic); 7, Avantgarde/Fotolia (telegraph); 7, Adrio/Fotolia (vintage telephone); 7, YouTube (icon); 7, Facebook (icon); 7, Twitter (icon); 8, Ambrophoto/Shutterstock; 24, Kablonk Micro/Fotolia; 25 (left), Columbus Dispatch/Doral Chenoweth III/AP Images; 25 (right), Richard Drew/AP Images (right); 27, Wavebreakmedia/Shutterstock; 30, Tomas Del Amo/Alamy; 32, Michael Zito/Zumapress/Newscom; 35, Optometric Extension Program Foundation; 42, J.Paul Guilloteau/Express-Rea/Redux; 45 (left), Jabin Botsford/The Washington Post/Getty Images; 45 (right), Chip Somodevilla/Getty Images News/Getty Images; 52, Anton Gvozdikov/Shutterstock; 56, Image Source/Getty Images; 63, William casey/Shutterstock; 66, David Gray/Reuters/Corbis; 67, C.M. Wiggins/AB5 Wenn Photos/Newscom; 69, Peter Steiner/The New Yorker Collection/The Cartoon Bank; 73, Pablo Martinez Monsivais/AP Images; 75, Lithian/Fotolia; 78, Highwaystarz/Fotolia; 81, Diego Cervo/Shutterstock; 86, Sue Cunningham Photographic/Alamy; 92, Sean Motola/123RF; 96, Medioimages/Photodisc/Getty Images; 98 (left), Val Lawless/Shutterstock; page 98 (right), Sigrid Olsson/PhotoAlto Agency RF Collections/Getty Images; 103, Haraz N. Ghanbari/AP Images; 107 (left), Gerry Broome/AP Images; 107 (right), Mark Humphrey/AP Images; 110, Age Fotostock/Alamy; 113, Monika Graff/The Image Works; 119, Oshvintsev Alexander/Shutterstock; 122, Flying Colours Ltd/Photodisc/Getty Images Text Credits; 124, Monkey Business Images/Shutterstock; 127, C.W. McKeen/Syracuse Newspapers/The Image Works; 131, Stockphoto mania/Fotolia, 139, Radius Images/Alamy, 143, Monkey Business/Fotolia; 146, Barbara Stitzer/PhotoEdit, Inc; 153, Digital Vision./Getty Images; 154, Simon Potter/Getty Images; 157, Manuel Balce Ceneta/AP Images; 161, Wavebreakmedia/Shutterstock; 167, PhotoInc/Getty Images; 170, Robert Kneschke/Fotolia; 179, Nancy Kaszerman/Zumapress/Newscom; 180, zumaamericasseven/Newscom; 183, Emmanuel Dunand/AFP/Getty Images; 187, Andres Rodriguez/Fotolia; 193, Annie Pickert Fuller. Pearson Education; 197, Mariela Lombard/Zumapress/Alamy; 198, Lisa O'Connor/Zuma Press/Alamy; 202, File/AP Images; 212, Simone van den Berg/Shutterstock; 217, David Gray/Reuters/Landov; 220, Cleve Bryant/PhotoEdit; 224, Monkey Business Images/Shutterstock; 226, Yuri_Arcurs/Getty Images; 235, Lightpoet/Shutterstock; 236 (slide 1), Melissa Beall; 236 (slide 2), Melissa Beall; 237 (slide 3), Melissa Beall; 237 (slide 4), Melissa Beall; 237 (slide 5), Melissa Beall; 237 (slide 6), Melissa Beall; 242, Fuse/Getty Images; 245, Racorn/Shutterstock; 248, Action Press/Zuma Press/Newscom; 250, Anthony Bolante/Reuters/Landov; 255, Eye35/Alamy; 265, Golden Pixels LLC/Shutterstock; 267, Junfu Han/AP Images; 274, Rick Mackler/Globe Photos/Zumapress/Alamy; 284, Bikeriderlondon/Shutterstock; 297, Alex Mares-Manton/Asia Images/Getty Images; 300, Antoine Arraou/PhotoAlto/Alamy; 301, Oliveromg/Shutterstock; 303, Cardiw/Cagle Cartoons; 306, Stephen Oliver/Alamy; 310, Denkou Nature/Alamy, 317, Westerso Getty Images; 319, Bokan/Fotolia; 323, Gareth Boden/Pears Education; 326, Sergey Ryzhov/Shutterstoc; 328, Lee Loren The Cartoon Bank; 329, Monkey Business Images/ Shutt stock; 340, Blend Images/Shutterstock; 343, Robert Kneschk Fotolia; 346 (left), RosaIreneBetancourt 8/Alamy; 346 (righ Dreamstime; 347, Auremar/Fotolia; 352, Michael Ventur Alamy; 355, Ariel Skelley/Getty Images; 360, Xixinxin Shutterstock; 363, William Perugini/123RF; 365, Monk Business Images/Shutterstock; 369 (top), Andres Rodrigue Fotolia; 369 (bottom), Auremar/Shutterstock; 374, Ste Skjold/PhotoEdit; 378, Matauw/Fotolia

Text Credits

Chapter 1, page 2, quotation, "Pope Francis Urges Young Pe ple Not to Waste Time on Internet," NBC News, August 5, 20 Chapter 1, page 3, quotation, L. A. Samovar and R. E. Port Communication between Cultures, 6th ed. (Belmont, C Wadsworth Publishing Co., 2007). Chapter 1, page 4, quotatic Ronald Reagan: "Farewell Address to the Nation," January 1989. Chapter 1, pages 5–6, quotation, Sohaib Athar, tweeted May 2, 2011. Chapter 1, page 9, quotation, W. M. Smail, Quint ian on Education, Book XII, Chapter 1 (Oxford, U.K.: Clare don Press, 1938), 108. Chapter 1, page 10, table, U.S. Cens Bureau. Chapter 2, page 31, quotation, R. L. Scott, "On Viewi Rhetoric as Epistemic: Ten Years Later," The Central Sta Speech Journal (Winter 1976): 261. Chapter 2, page 38, quo tion, T. Harnden, "Caroline Kennedy Repeats 'You Know' 1 Times in Interview," Telegraph.co.uk, January 25, 2009, p. Chapter 2, page 39, quotation, M. Piattelli-Palmarini, Inevitab Illusions: How Mistakes of Reason Rule Our Minds (New Yor Wiley, 1994), 17. Chapter 2, page 39, quotation from Artem Ward, http://thinkexist.com/quotation/it_ain-t_so_much_th things_we_don-t_know_that/345904.html. Chapter 2, page 4 quotation, C. Stewart and W. Cash Jr., Interviewing: Principl and Practices, 13th ed. (New York: McGraw-Hill, 2011), 3 Chapter 2, page 41, quotation, The definition is based on wo found in J.N. Martin and T.K. Nakayama, Intercultural Cor munication in Contexts, 5th ed. (New York: McGraw Hi 2010), 84–93; L.A. Samovar and R. E. Porter, Communicatic between Cultures, 7th ed. (Belmont, CA: Wadsworth, 201 19–33; E.R. McDaniel, L. A. Samovar, and R. E. Port "Understanding Intercultural Communication: an Overvie in Intercultural Communication: A Reader, 13th ed., eds. L. Samovar, R. E. Porter, and E. R. McDaniel (Boston: Wadswort 2012, 10–13; D. W. Klopf and J. C. McCroskey, Intercultur Communication Encounters (Boston: Allyn and Bacon, 200 6–7. Chapter 2, page 45, quotation, Nick Wing, "When Th Media Treats White Suspects And Killers Better Than Black Vi tims", The Huffington Post, 8/14/2014. Chapter 3, page 5 quotation, Corcoran, "My Favorite Mistake," Newswee January 23, 2012: 60. Chapter 3, page 58, figure, J. Kinch, " Formalized Theory of the Self-Concept," American Journal Sociology 68 (January 1963): 481–486. University of Chicag ess. Chapter 3, page 63, quotation, Based on S. A. Ribeau, R. Baldwin, and M. L. Hecht, "An African-American Communication Perspective," in Intercultural Communication: A Reader, ed. L. A. Samovar and R. E. Porter (Belmont, CA: Wadsorth, 1994), 143; J. R. Baldwin and M. Hecht, "Unpacking roup-Based Intolerance: A Holographic Look at Identity and tolerance," in Intercultural Communication: A Reader, 10th l., eds. L. A. Samovar and R. E. Porter (Belmont, CA: Wadsorth, 2003), 358. Chapter 3, page 65, quotation, D. Tannen, ou Just Don't Understand: Women and Men in Conversation Jew York: Morrow, 1990), 24–25. Chapter 3, page 66, quota-n, C. E. Epstein, Deceptive Distinctions: Sex, Gender, and the cial Order (New Haven, CT: Yale University Press, 1988), 25. hapter 3, page 69, A. L. Gonzales and J. T. Hancock, "Mirror, irror on my Facebook Wall: Effects of Exposure to Facebook Self-Esteem," Cyberpsychology, Behavior and Social Net-orks 14 (2011): 79–83. Chapter 4, page 74, quotation, Huffing-n Post, March 3, 2012, http://www.huffingtonpost.com/ 12/03/03/rush-limbaugh-apologizes-to-sandra-fluke_n 318718.html. Chapter 4, page 74, quotation, Huffington Post, arch 5, 2012, http://www.huffingtonpost.com/2012/03/02/ sh-limbaugh-sandra-fluke-sex-slut_n_1316625.html. Chapter 4, age 75, quotation from YouTube Video, The Power of Words, uTube, www.youtube.com/watch?v=Hzgzim5m7oU. Acces-d March 1, 2012. Chapter 4, page 75, quotation from poem, ck Prelutsky, "New Kid on the Block." Chapter 4, page 77, x, Based on D. R. Harfield, CLP, personal communication, nuary 12, 2012. Chapter 4, quotation from Samovar and rter, L. A. Samovar and R. E. Porter, eds., Intercultural Com-unication: A Reader. (Belmont, CA: Wadsworth, 2003), 358. hapter 4, page 77, quotation from African proverb, Helpful frican Proverbs, compiled by Kane Mathis. Retrieved on nuary 29, 2012, from: www.kairarecords.com/kane/prov-bs.htm. Chapter 4, page 78–79, quotation, L. Carroll, Alice's dventures in Wonderland, Through the Looking Glass, and he Hunting of the Smark (New York: Modern Library, 1925), 6–47. Chapter 4, page 83, quotation, K. Cushner, A. McClelland, d P. Safford, Human Diversity in Education: An Integrative pproach, 3rd ed. (New York: McGraw-Hill, 2010). Chapter 4, age 84, quotation, Based on News bulletins from W. R. Espy, ay When," This Week, July 13, 1952, quoted in W. V. Haney, ommunication and Organizational Behavior, 396. Chapter 4, age 85, D. Tannen, You Just Don't Understand (New York: lorrow, 1990). Chapter 4, page 88, box, Based on E. T. Hall, The lidden Dimension (Garden City, NY: Doubleday, 1966). hapter 4, page 88, quotation, S. Trenholm, Thinking through ommunication, 4th ed. (Boston: Allyn and Bacon, 2005), 72. hapter 4, page 89, block quotation, E. T. Hall, *The Hidden imension* (Garden City, NY: Doubleday, 1966). Chapter 4, page , quotation from Neil Postman, N. Postman, *Technopoly* (New ork: Alfred A. Knopf, 1992), 4. Chapter Chapter 4, page 90, uotation from Neil Postman, S. T. Fiske and S. E. Taylor, *Social ognition* (Reading, MA: Addison-Wesley, 1984), 190–94. Chapter 4, age 92, President Franklin D. Roosevelt message. Chapter 4, age 93, quotation, President Barack Obama. Chapter 4, page 4, quotation, N. Postman, *Technopoly* (New York: Alfred A. nopf, 1992), 4. Chapter 5, page 97, quotation, M. L. Knapp nd J. Hall, *Nonverbal Communication in Human Interaction*, th ed. (Belmont, CA: Wadsworth/Cengage Learning, 2010), 5. hapter 5, page 106, quotation, Cicero, as quoted in Jan H. Blits, Spirit, Soul, and City". Lexington Books, 2006. Chapter 5, age 114, quotation, S. E. Quasha and F. Tsukada, "Interna-onal Marriages in Japan: Cultural Conflict and Harmony," in

L. A. Samovar, R. E. Porter, and E. R. McDaniel eds., *Intercultural Communication: A Reader*, 13th ed (Boston: Wadsworth Cengage Learning, 2012), 129. Chapter 6, page 123, quotation, A. D. Wolvin, Listening in the Quality Organization. (Ithaca, NY: Finger Lakes Press, 1999. Chapter 6, page 125, figure 6.2, Depicted by Dwight R. Harfield, and used with permission. Chapter 6, page 126, figure 6.3, Depicted by Dwight R. Harfield, and used with permission. Chapter 6, page 127, quotation, J. Brownell, Listening: Attitudes, Principles, and Skills, 4th ed. (Boston: Allyn and Bacon, 2010). Chapter 6, page 129, quotation, Based on Judi Brownell, Listening: Attitudes, Principles, and Skills, 4e. Published by Allyn and Bacon, Boston, MA, pp. 151–52. Copyright © 2010 by Pearson Education. Chapter 6, page 130, box, Adapted from Judi Brownell, Listening: Attitudes, Principles, and Skills, 4e. Published by Allyn and Bacon, Boston, MA, pp. 151–52. Chapter 6, page 135, quotation, D. Harfield, personal communication, March 12, 2012. Chapter 6, page 138, box, Based on C. Angove, "The Rise of Social Media in Organizations: How to Turn the Internet into Interactive Dialogue," unpublished master's degree research project, University of Northern Iowa, May, 2012. Chapter 6, page 138, D. Baer, "Here's Why Writing Things Out By Hand Makes You Smarter." Business Insider, December 16, 2014. Retrieved from http://www.businessinsider.com/ handwriting-helps-you-learn-2014–12 on January 5, 2015. Chapter 6, page 139, quotation, Gilster, Digital Literacy (Hoboken, NJ: John Wiley & Sons, 1998). Chapter 6, page 140, page 140, G. M. Chen and W. J. Starosta, (2005). Foundations of Intercultural Communication. Lanham, MD: University Press of America, 93. Chapter 7, page 144, J. Swan, University of Northern Iowa, personal conversations, February 2015. Chapter 7, page 152, quotation, "Writing Guide: Informative Speaking," Colorado State University. Retrieved February 27, 2015, from http://writing.colostate.edu/guides/guide.cfm? guideid=52. Chapter 7, page 165, quotation, S. J. Lind, "Teaching Digital Oratory: Public Speaking 2.0." Communication Teacher, 26, 3, 163–169 2012. Chapter 8, page 172, quotation, G. Couros, "Why Social Media Can and Is Changing Education," Connected Principals, March 21, 2011. Retrieved February 25, 2015 from http://georgecouros.ca/blog/archives/1860. Chapter 8, page 172–173, quotation from Abdullah, Based on "Middle East: Saudi Arabia," The World Factbook, Central Intelligence Agency. Retrieved June 18, 2012, from https:// www.cia.gov/library/publications/the-world-factbook/ geos/sa.html. Chapter 8, page 179, quotation, John F. Kennedy, presidential inaugural address, 1961. Chapter 8, page 182, axiology definition, E. Griffin, "Axiology," in A First Look at Communication Theory, 8th ed. (Boston: McGraw-Hill, 2011). Chapter 8, page 182, quotation, Mission One Million, "Needs." Retrieved March 3, 2015, from http://www.mission1m.org/ about_the_need.html. Chapter 8, page 183, quotation, Mission One Million, "Needs." Retrieved March 3, 2015, from http:// www.mission1m.org/about_the_need.html. Chapter 8, page 184, "Africa's Orphaned Generations," UNICEF, 2011. Retrieved March 30, 2012, from www.unicef.org/sowc06/ pdfs/africas_orphans.pdf. Chapter 8, page 185, figure, Based on Africa's Orphaned Generations, Ch2, UNICEF, http:// www.unicef.org/sowc06/pdfs/africas_orphans.pdf, retrieved March 31, 2012. Chapter 9, page 196, quotation, "Eating Disorder Statistics," South Carolina Department of Mental Health Retrieved March 15, 2015 from http://www.state.sc.us/dmh/ anorexia/statistics.htm. Chapter 9, page 196, "Worldwide Orphan Facts, Figures and Statistics," SOS Children's Villages.

Retrieved July 28, 2012, from http://www.sos-usa.org/about-sos/what-we-do/orphan-statistics/pages/global-orphan-statistics.aspx. Chapter 9, page 198, "Laughter Is the Best Medicine: Health Bene?ts of Humor and Laughter," HELPGUIDE.ORG. Retrieved May 20, 2012, from http://www.helpguide.org/life/humor_laughter_health.htm. Chapter 9, page 198, quotation, B. McEwen and G. Chrousos, "Stress: The Time Bomb in Your Body," Health report. Retrieved May 20, 2012, from Stress.Newsmax.com. Chapter 9, page 198, Lee Iacocca, cited in Glenn Van Ekeren, Speaker's Sourcebook II (Englewood Cliffs, NJ: Prentice Hall, 1994), 73. Chapter 9, page 199, quotation, "Laughter Is the Best Medicine: Health Benefits of Humor and Laughter," HELPGUIDE.ORG. Retrieved March 15, 2015, from http://www.helpguide.org/articles/emotional-health/laughter-is-the-best-medicine.htm. Chapter 9, page 199, quotation, Based on "Laughter Is the Best Medicine: Health Benefits of Humor and Laughter," HELPGUIDE.ORG. Retrieved March 15, 2015, from http://www.helpguide.org/articles/emotional-health/laughter-is-the-best-medicine.htm. Chapter 9, page 200, quotation, "Adoption Facts." Retrieved May 28, 2012, from http://adoption.about.com/od/adopting/bb/befrdecideadopt.htm. Chapter 9, page 200, quotation, Zarefsky, Public Speaking Strategies for Success, 5th ed. (Boston: Allyn and Bacon, 2008), 222. Chapter 9, page 202, quotation, Rifkin, "The BioTech Century," delivered May 1998, City Club of Cleveland, OH. Retrieved March 15, 2015, from http://www.americanrhetoric.com/. Chapter 9, page 202, quotation, Based on "What Are Sleep Deprivation and Deficiency?" National Heart, Lung, and Blood Institute. Retrieved March 15, 2015, from http://www.nhlbi.nih.gov/health/health-topics/topics/sdd/. Chapter 9, page 202, President John F. Kennedy, inaugural address, January 20, 1961. Chapter 9, page 202, quotation, President Barack Obama, inaugural address, January 21, 2013. Chapter 9, page 202–203, quotation, Based on "Eating Disorders," National Institutes of Mental Health. Retrieved March 28, 2015, from http://www.nimh.nih.gov/health/publications/eating-disorders-new-trifold/index.shtml. Chapter 9, page 203, quotation, Zarefsky, Public Speaking Strategies for Success, 5th ed. (Boston: Allyn and Bacon, 2008), 222. Chapter 9, page 206–208, "Helen Keller International," informative speech by Sarah Johansen, Fundamentals of Communica-tion student, University of Nebraska–Lincoln, used with permission. Chapter 10, page 215, X. Liao, "Effective Communication in Multicultural Classrooms: An Exploratory Study," unpublished master of arts thesis, University of Northern Iowa, May 2003. Chapter 9, page 207, Mission, Goals and Values of Helen Keller International. Chapter 9, page 207, "Nutrition; A Sweet Potato a Day." Africa News, Nov. 29, 2011. LexisNexis. (web). Retrieved May 19, 2012, from https://www.lexisnexis.com. Chapter 10, page 237, quotation, William Germano, "The Scholarly Lecture: How to Stand and Deliver," The Chronicle of Higher Education 50 (14, B15) (November 28, 2003). Chapter 10, page 238, quotation, President Abraham Lincoln, The Gettysburg Address, November 19, 1863. Chapter 10, page 239, quotation Personal conversation with Dr. Victoria DeFrancisco, University of Northern Iowa, January 20, 2012. Chapter 11, page 251, quotation, Based on "Milestones," Time, May 28, 2012: 21; D. Martin, "Evelyn B. Johnson, Pilot and Instructor, Dies at 102," New York Times, May 12, 2012. Chapter 11, page 252, Based on "'Smart Bomb' Drug Targets Breast Cancer," Newsmax Media, June 3, 2012. Retrieved June 3, 2012, from http://www.newsmaxhealth.com/health_stories/herceptin_breast_cancer/2012/06/03/454338.html?s=al&promo_code=F185-

Chapter 11, Based on Mayo Clinic, "Eating Disorders: Symtoms." Retrieved June 28, 2012, from http://www.mayoclin com/health/eating-disorders/ds00294/dsection=sympton also, "Eating Disorder Statistics," South Carolina Departme of Mental Health. Retrieved May 28, 2012, from http://ww .state.sc.us/dmh/anorexia/statistics.htm. Chapter 11, pa 253, Based on Eligible Receiver, Frontline, PBS. Retrieve February 19, 2015, from http://www.pbs.org/wgbh/page frontline/shows/cyberwar/warnings/. Chapter 12, page 26 D. Zarefsky, Public Speaking: Strategies for Success, 5th e (Boston: Allyn and Bacon, 2008), 412. Chapter 12, page 27 H. Clancy, "Exec predicts dead calm for U.S. wind energy pr duction," GreenTech Pastures. Retrieved June 11, 2015, fro http://www.zdnet.com/blog/green/exec-predicts-dea calm-for-us-wind-energy-generation/21394. Chapter 12, page 27 Based on J. McCroskey. Retrieved June 4, 2015, from ww .jamescmccroskey.com. Chapter 12, page 278, Lindsey Taleric Hedren, managing editor, World Vision Blog, "Fast facts: Hunge Retrieved June 11, 2012, from http://blog.worldvisic .org/causes/fast-facts-hunger/. Chapter 12, page 279–28 M. Schwabe, "Volunteering with Bethel Missions in Gua mala." Persuasive speech given at the University of Nebrask. Lincoln, used with permission. Chapter 12, page 284, quotatic President George W. Bush. Chapter 12, page 290–292, N Schwabe, "Volunteering with Bethel Missions in Guatemal. Persuasive speech given at the University of Nebraska–Lincol used with permission. Chapter 13, page 298, L. Stinso "Unplugged for 40 Days," Journal Star, April 2, 2011: D1, D Chapter 13, page 299, M. L. Knapp and A. L. Vangelis Interpersonal Communication and Human Relationship 6th ed. (Boston: Allyn and Bacon, 2009). Chapter 13, page 3C C. R. Berger, "Beyond Initial Interaction: Uncertainty, Unde standing, and Development of Interpersonal relationships," H. Giles and R. St. Clair, eds., Language and Social Psycholog (Oxford, UK: Blackwell, 1979), 122–44. Chapter 13, page 30 D.E. Brashers, "A Theory of Communication and Uncertain Management," in B. Whaley and W. Samter, eds., Explainir Communication Theory (Mahwah, NJ: Lawrence Erlbau 2007): 210–18. Chapter 13, page 302, J. B. Walther, "Interpe sonal Effects in Computer-Mediated Interaction: A Relation Perspective," Communication Research 19 (1992): 52–9 Chapter 13, page 303, J. B. Walther, "Social Information Pr cessing Theory: Impressions and Relationship Developme: Online," in L. A. Baxter and D. O. Braithwaite, eds., Engagir Theories in Interpersonal Communication (Newbury Park, C. Sage, 2008), 391–404. Chapter 13, page 303, figure, From Soci Penetration: The Development of Interpersonal Relationship Copyright © 1973 by Irwin Altman and Dalmas Taylor. Chapter 1 page 309, Robert Putnam, "You Gotta Have Friends,". Tin magazine, July 3, 2006. Chapter 13, page 312, J. W. Pennebake Opening Up: The Healing Power of Expressing Emotions (Ne York: Guilford, 199. Chapter 13, page 312, S. Petronio, "Th Boundaries of Privacy: Praxis of Everyday Life," in S. Petroni ed., Balancing the Secrets of Private Disclosures (Hillsdale, N Erlbaum, 2000), 9–15. Chapter 14, page 319, Stephanie Whitlo an honor student at Wayne State College in Wayne, Nebrask with her permission. Chapter 14, page 319, Based o B. H. Spitzberg, "What is Good Communication?" Journal the Association for Communication Administration, 29 (200) 103–19; J. T. Woods, Interpersonal Communication Everyda Encounters, 7th ed. (Boston: Wadsworth Cengage, 2013), 30–3.

Floyd, Interpersonal Communication, 7th ed. (New York: cGraw-Hill, 2011), 28–30. Chapter 14, page 320, J. S. Caputo, C. Hazel, and C. McMahon, Interpersonal Communication: ompetency through Critical Thinking (Boston: Allyn and con, 1994), 98–99. Chapter 14, page 323, Based on A. Fein-ld, "Gender Differences in Effects of Physical Attractiveness Romantic Attraction: A Comparison across Five Research radigms," Journal of Personality and Social Psychology 59 990): 981–93; and S. A. Meyers, "'Your Mother Would Like e': Self-Presentation in the Personals Ads of Heterosexual d Homosexual Men and Women," Personality and Social ychology Bulletin 19 (1993): 131–42. Chapter 14, page 325, . L. Knapp and A. L. Vangelisti, Interpersonal Communica-on and Human Relationships, 6th ed. (Boston: Allyn and con, 2009). 33. Chapter 14, page 325, M. L. Knapp and A. L. ngelisti, Interpersonal Communication and Human Rela-onships, 6th ed. (Boston: Allyn and Bacon, 2009). 40. Chapter , page 326, Based on an article written by Jonathan Butler led "The Donut Shop Experiment," in The Front Porch Where ople Share Life, published by The Front Porch, LLC, © 2002. hapter 14, page 333, Wilmot and J. Hocker, Interpersonal Con-ct, 8th ed. (New York: McGraw-Hill, 2011), 11. Chapter 14, age 335, W. Wilmot and J. Hocker, Interpersonal Conflict, 8th l. (New York: McGraw-Hill, 2011), 11. Chapter 14, page 339, S. . Duck, "A Perspective on the Repair of Personal Relation-ips: Repair of What, When?" in Personal Relationships 5: epairing Personal Relationships, ed. S. W. Duck (New York: lacmillan, 1984). Chapter 14, page 339, M. L. Knapp and A. L. angelisti, Interpersonal Communication and Human elationship, 6th ed. (Boston: Allyn and Bacon, 2009), 33–37. hapter 14, page 340, Based on E. P. Simon and L. A. Baxter, Attachment-Style Differences in Relationship Maintenance rategies," Western Journal of Communication 57 (Fall 1993): 23. Chapter 15, page 346, Based on G. Lumsden, D. Lumsden, nd C. Wetthoff, Communicating in Groups and Teams: Sharing eadership, 5th ed. (Belmont, CA: Wadsworth, 2010). Chapter 15, age 347, Based on B. Tuckman, "Developmental Sequence in mall Groups," Psychological Bulletin 63 (1965): 384–99; . Tuckman and M. A. Jensen, "Stages of Small-Group Devel-opment Revisited," Group and Organization Studies 2 977):419–27. Chatper 15, page 348, table, Adapted from . A. Beebe and J. M. Masterson, Communicating in Small roups, 10th ed. (Boston: Allyn and Bacon, 2015),18; and J. Iole, Mind Your Manners: Managing Business Cultures in urope (London: Nicholas Brealey Publishing Limited, 1995). hatper 15, page 349, M. Buckingham and C. Coffman, "Item 9: 'oing Quality Work," Gallup Management Journal [online], pring 2002. Retrieved on July 7, 2011, from www.gallupjour-al.com/q12Center/articles/19990517.asp. Chapter 15, page 51, G. J. Galanes and K. Adams, Effective Group Discussion, 4th ed. (New York: McGraw-Hill, 2013), 147. Chapter 15, page 55, N. K. Baym, Y. B. Zhang, and M-C. Lin, "Social Interactions cross Media: Interpersonal Communication on the Internet, ace-to-Face, and the Telephone," New Media & Society 6 2004); 299–318. Chapter 15, page 357, Based on K. Adams and . J. Galanes, Communicating in Groups Applications and kills, 9th ed. (New York: McGraw-Hill, 2015), 10. Chapter 15,

page 357–358, Based on P. B. Paulus, ed., Psychology of Group Influence, 2nd ed. (Hillsdale, NJ: Erlbaum, 1989). Chapter 15, page 359, Based on G. J. Galanes and K. Adams, Effective Group Discussion, 14th ed. (New York: McGraw-Hill, 2013), 188–190. Chapter 15, pages 359–360, Adams and Galanes, Communicating in Groups Applications and Skill, 187–9. Chapter 16, page 367, figure, Michael Seiler. Chapter 16, page 369, S. C. Koch, "Evaluative Affect Display toward Male and Female Leaders of Task-Oriented Groups," Small Group Research 36 (2005): 678–703. Chapter 16, page 370, A. H. Eagly and B. T. Johnson, "Gender and Leadership Style: A Meta-Analysis," Psychological Bulletin 108 (1990): 233–56). Chapter 16, page 371, From Harrison Conference Services, Business Schools at the University of Georgia and Georgia State Univer-sity. Chapter 16, page 372–373, Based on S. A. Beebe and J. T. Masterson, Communicating in Small Groups, 11th ed. (Boston: Pearson, 2015), 206–207. Chapter 16, page 373, W. Wilmot and J. Hocker, Interpersonal Conflict, 9th ed. (New York: McGraw-Hill, 2014), 13. Chapter 16, page 374, G. J. Galanes and K. Adams, Effective Group Discussion, 14th ed. (New York: McGraw-Hill, 2013), 147. Chapter 16, page 375, Based on G. J. Galanes and K. Adams, Effective Group Discussion, 14th ed. (New York: McGraw-Hill, 2013), 147. Chapter 16, pages 375–376, Based on R. V. Harnack, T. B. Fest, and B. S. Jones, Group Discussion: Theory and Technique, 2nd ed. (Englewood Cliffs, NJ: Prentice-Hall, 1997): 153–54. Chapter 16, page 376, S. A. Beebe and J. T. Masterson, Communicating in Small Groups, 10th ed. (Boston: Pearson, 2012): 248–49. Appendix, page, 382, table, Job Outlook 2014, National Association of Colleges and Employers. The report is available to NACE members at http://www.naceweb.org/about-us/press/skills-employers-value-in-new-hires.aspx. Last reviewed on February 21, 2015. Appendix, pages 384–385, D. LaGesse, "Turning Social Net-working into a Job Offer: Believe It or Not, It's Often the Weak Connections That Help You Land an Interview," U.S. News & World Report, May 2009, 44–45. Appendix, pages 385, Prepar-ing for the Job Search, a booklet prepared by the University of Nebraska Career Services, 2011: 14. Appendix, page 388, Used by permission of the University of Nebraska-Lincoln Career Services. Appendix, page 391, M. Valdes and S. McFarland, "Resume, References and Passwords, Please," Lincoln Journal Star, Sunday, March 25, 2012: B8. Appendix, page 394, D. S. Chapman and P. M. Rowe, "The Impact of Videoconference Technology, Interview Structure, and Interviewer Gender on Interviewer Evaluations in the Employment Interview: A Field Experiment," Journal of Occupational and Organizational Psychology (2001): 279. Appendix, page 395, J. Meyers, "The Ideal Job Candidate," Collegiate Employment Institute News-letter, July 15, 1989: 6. Appendix, pages 395–396, Based on The Endicott Report: Trends in the Employment of College and University Graduates in Business and Industry (Evanston, IL: The Placement Center, Northwestern University, 1980), 8. In the May, 2012, interview, Dr. Smith said that the rejection rea-sons companies give today are not different from what they were in 1980, and Tina V., "Job Rejections: Reasons from an HR Point of View" tina-v.hubpages.com. Last retrieved September 20, 2012.